# International Business

This is the third edition of the widely respected text *International Business*, which offers a comprehensive yet critical overview of the phenomenon of globalisation and its impacts on key aspects of the business environment as it fundamentally alters corporate strategy.

This updated edition covers the core international business topics and themes, including multinationals, internationalisation, and international market entry, as well as a new focus on risk, business models, and hyperglobalisation. With dedicated chapters on the role of non-market actors in international business, the book provides a multi-disciplinary worldview for readers.

Featuring a wealth of case studies and pedagogy, the new edition examines the rise of India and China as well as growing levels of risk within the global system. The book looks at those developed economies which have been the core drivers behind the trend towards hyperglobalisation. The author explores and guides students through what this means for the study of international business.

A comprehensive and engaging text, supplemented by online resources, this book is the ideal accompaniment to international and global business learning.

**Colin Turner** is Senior Lecturer in Management at Heriot-Watt University, UK

T0383068

# International Business

## Themes and Issues in the Modern Global Economy

THIRD EDITION

Colin Turner

Routledge
Taylor & Francis Group

LONDON AND NEW YORK

Designed cover image: shaunl

Third edition published 2024
by Routledge
4 Park Square, Milton Park, Abingdon, Oxon, OX14 4RN

and by Routledge
605 Third Avenue, New York, NY 10158

*Routledge is an imprint of the Taylor & Francis Group, an informa business*

© 2024 Colin Turner

First edition published by Routledge 2003
Second edition published by Routledge 2010

*British Library Cataloguing-in-Publication Data*
A catalogue record for this book is available from the British Library

ISBN: 978-1-138-73568-2 (hbk)
ISBN: 978-1-138-73882-9 (pbk)
ISBN: 978-1-315-18450-0 (ebk)

DOI: 10.4324/9781315184500

Typeset in Berling-Roman
by Deanta Global Publishing Services, Chennai, India

Access the Support Material: www.routledge.com/9781138738829

# CONTENTS

# CASE STUDIES

# BOXES

# FIGURES

# TABLES

# PREFACE

In the protected period (almost 12 years) between the completion of the second edition and the writing of the third edition, there have been substantial changes within the field of international business. As we were writing the second edition, we were still trying very hard to understand the legacy of the global financial crisis. In the period since then, the legacy has become clearer with regard to the deglobalisation movements that have fed off the global financial crisis. Moreover, this global scepticism has been cemented by the COVID-19 pandemic, which not only severely restricted the operation of the global system but was, in many ways, directly caused by it. The certainty provided by an ongoing and deepening globalisation process has been shaken. However, among all these events, the process of international engagement and interaction continued and was enhanced. Indeed, over the past decade, we have seen China further emerge as a global economic power and have seen international connectivity through the global flows of data become intensified. This globalisation is not so much going backwards or stopping; it is simply evolving. As it has always done. If there is a continuity that has emerged from this change, then it is that the complexity of operations that is the hallmark of international business has been brought into sharper relief.

In this third edition, although, as shown below, we have given greater emphasis to some factors, the approach remains essentially the same as in previous editions. As with all authors, our slant on international business is deeply rooted in our own specific academic background and preferences. Although there are certain core aspects of the international business curriculum (such as the emphasis on the multinational firm), there is also a great variation in the range of the curriculum and how the subject is dealt with in international business texts. Some of these texts are re-badged economics books; some are purely descriptive and neglect theory; others are essentially strategy books, whereas others adopt a regional or functional approach. We have deliberately done none of these.

Many books also reflect their own particular cultural context in terms of content, presentation, or both. Although conscious of the fact that we are all creatures of our own cultures, we have tried to be as culturally neutral as possible and to avoid an overly Eurocentric approach. For example, we have attempted to use examples and case studies from across the world. However, we acknowledge that we cannot totally escape our European roots.

Our approach is also rooted in the fundamental belief that business students need an education that, as well as enabling them to develop functional knowledge, skills, and understanding, also broadens their outlook in terms of understanding the political, economic, and social context of business. In the contemporary world, their horizons need to broaden to take international issues into account. All too often, the business curriculum is only internationalised in a desultory way, perhaps by the addition of a couple of 'international' sessions at the end of a finance or marketing module. In our view, this is not enough.

We wanted to develop an integrated text in which, although individual chapters can stand alone, there is a common theme underpinning the text, namely globalisation. This has remained the overarching theme of all editions of the text, as it remains the core environmental driver of the processes examined. Although there are opposing views about the degree to which globalisation exists or whether the world is globalising or internationalising, there is at least some consensus that there has been an increase in the degree of economic interdependence during recent decades. This is a useful starting point for debate and study. It is the extent and implications of such interdependence for business that permeate each of the chapters. Moreover, the financial and economic crises have invited speculation about the future of globalisation. In addition to globalisation, other themes recur throughout the volume. These include issues surrounding development and business; the role of emerging economies; the use of information and knowledge as a key business resource; and corporate responsibility and pressure for an expanded policy agenda for international institutions.

Our intention is that individual chapters should, as far as possible, provide a mix of theory and practice. Theory is important to give students a framework and context for applications and practice and can deepen their understanding of issues. The body of theory chosen is relevant to the subject matter of each chapter but, where appropriate, is linked back to the core concepts of globalisation and international integration.

In order to achieve our objective of drawing out the impact of globalising or internationally integrating forces on economic governance and business and to highlight common themes and linkages, the book itself has been subdivided into five distinct sections dealing with environmental, markets, enterprise, civil society, and resource issues. Each chapter, bar the conclusion, is included in a section. Unlike the second edition, we wanted to include the analysis of globalisation in an analysis of the shifting international business environment, which, as such, would have looked out of place as a standalone chapter. What is new within the third edition is a renewed focus on civil society issues, reflecting that in business there is a need to look at the broader set of stakeholders involved in and impacted by the globalisation process.

*** 

Part I deals with trends and developments in the international economy that shape the business environment and, thus, the development of corporate strategies and operations. Chapter 1 explores the major trends, drivers, and patterns in the international economy and highlights those factors that have led commentators to talk about globalisation. In the process, it highlights the main questions posed by globalisation and tentatively identifies indicators of globalisation and ways in which international economic integration affects business. These themes are dealt with more fully in Chapter 2, where some formative analysis of business adaptation to globalisation is addressed. Chapter 3 then moves on to examine how states strategise in global environments, especially with regard to the issue of international competitiveness. Chapter 4 examines the architecture and role of international institutions, the actions of which have a profound effect on the business environment and whose role is profoundly affected by globalisation. The chapter also throws the spotlight on frequently heard criticisms of international institutions. Chapter 5 deals with regional integration, the rise of which parallels the rise of globalisation and which many commentators argue has become a major consideration in the choice of business location. Key themes, like whether regional integration is complementary to globalisation or is liable to fragment international markets, are discussed.

Part II is a new section of the book and looks at developments within the major types of markets in the global system, namely developed, emerging, and developing economies. In Chapter 6, developed economies are addressed with a focus on how risks are increasingly within them. Chapter 7 has shifted away from a focus on the so-called BRIC economies towards a focus on the two real emerging economies, namely China and India. So much is written about emerging economies, we decided that separate treatment of them was warranted in order to distinguish what makes them 'special' and also to highlight areas in which change is still required. Emerging economies also make an appearance in other chapters in this volume. The final chapter in this part, Chapter 8, looks at the thorny problem of development and globalisation and at differential regional development patterns, identifying those regions that have managed to integrate themselves into world production and trading systems and those that appear marginalised. In the process, it sets out different theoretical explanations of the development process and links development to the growing integration of production networks.

Part III focuses on the multinational enterprise within the international context. Chapter 9 builds upon the previous chapters by looking at issues of market selection and entry. This is further enhanced in Chapter 10, where the form and nature of the MNC are explored, offering a mix of theory and practice within the analysis. Chapter 11 is about the internationalisation of small- and medium-sized enterprises, particularly from the perspective of international entrepreneurship. Chapter 12 is also new and discusses individual business functions with a view to determining how internationalisation affects them. The enterprise chapter, Chapter 12, covers the cultural issues that have to be confronted when conducting business across borders.

Part IV is based on the premise that as firms become more global or international (depending on one's view of the growing interdependence that is underway), they will increasingly source their needs from more diverse international factor markets. These create a new range of issues via engagement with civil society issues. Chapters 13, 14, and 15 deal with a range of issues, from the ethical (labour and the exploitation of natural resources) to concerns about the possibility of 'races to the bottom' (labour and the environment again). A common theme in each chapter is how these factors of production are feeding into growing pressure for regulation above the level of the nation state and how some of the issues surrounding these factors are contributing to the reconsideration of the configuration of firms' production systems and value chains.

Part V looks beyond civil society issues and examines the human and naturally occurring resources that facilitate the development of international business but are also impacted by these globalising forces. Chapter 16 looks at the international monetary system and how this remains a force for instability within the system. Chapter 17 is a new chapter and reflects the author's interest in understanding how infrastructure enables the global system across three sets of infrastructures, namely transport, energy, and information. Chapter 18 is also a new chapter that looks at how the data economy is changing international business. Chapter 19 – the final themed chapter – looks at the challenge of natural resources for the global economy through the lens of the food-water-energy nexus.

The final chapter, Chapter 20, briefly draws together recurrent themes and how they relate to international business.

The reader is the best judge of the extent to which we have achieved our objectives. The project turned out to be more ambitious than anticipated, but it also confirmed how important it is to encourage the development of an international perspective and to discourage parochialism in business graduates. While it is certainly true that not all business graduates will end up working for multinationals, we do believe that virtually all businesses and their employees these days are affected by international developments, whether it is international regulations or the entry of foreign actors into their domestic market. An international perspective enables businesses, including those with a primary or sole focus on the domestic market, to anticipate such developments and thus respond to them more effectively.

Colin Turner,
Hull and Edinburgh, June 2023

# ABBREVIATIONS

| | |
|---|---|
| ACP | African Caribbean Pacific |
| ACLU | American Civil Liberties Union |
| AFTA | Asian Free Trade Area |
| AGOA | Africa Growth and Opportunity Act |
| AIIB | Asian Infrastructure Investment Bank |
| APEC | Asia Pacific Economic Cooperation |
| ASEAN | Association of Southeast Asian Nations |
| BAT | Baidu, Alibaba, and Tencent |
| BCM | Billion cubic metres |
| B/D | Barrels per day |
| BGS | Born Globals |
| BIS | Bank for International Settlements |
| BOO | Build-own-operate |
| BOOT | Build-own-operate-transfer |
| BOT | Build-operate-transfer |
| BRIC | Brazil, Russia, India and China |
| BRI | Belt and Road Initiative |
| CARICOM | Caribbean Community and Common Market |
| CBD | Convention on Biological Diversity |
| CEO | Chief Executive Officer |
| CET | Common External Tariff |
| CIA | Central Intelligence Agency |
| CITES | Convention on International Trade in Endangered Species |
| COMESA | Common Market for Eastern and Southern Africa |
| COVID-19 | Coronavirus disease 2019 |
| CPEC | China-Pakistan economic corridor |
| CPI | Corruption Perceptions Index |
| CRTA | Committee on Regional Trade Agreements |
| CSR | Corporate Social Responsibility |
| CTE | Committee on Trade and Environment |
| DDA | Doha Development Agenda |
| DPW | Dubai Ports World |
| DSU | Dispute Settlement Understanding |

| | |
|---|---|
| ECB | European Central Bank |
| ECOWAS | Economic Community of West African States |
| EEC | European Economic Community |
| EFTA | European Free Trade Area |
| EICC | Electronic Industry Code of Conduct |
| EKC | Environmental Kuznets Curve |
| EMIT | Group on Environmental Measures and International Trade |
| EMU | Economic and Monetary Union |
| EPA | Economic Partnership Agreement |
| EPZ | Export processing zone |
| ESG | Environmental, social, and corporate governance |
| EU | European Union |
| FAO | Food and Agricultural Organisation |
| FCPA | Foreign and Corrupt Practices Act |
| FDI | Foreign Direct Investment |
| FII | Foreign Indirect Investment |
| FSA | Firm specific advantage |
| FTA | Free trade area |
| FEW | Food Energy Water |
| G8 | Group of Eight leading industrialised states |
| G20 | Group of Twenty leading industrialised states |
| GATS | General Agreement on Trade in Services |
| GATT | General Agreement on Tariffs and Trade |
| GDP | Gross Domestic Product |
| GFC | Global Financial Crisis |
| GIS | Global Information System |
| GLOBE | Global Leadership and Organisational Behaviour Effectiveness |
| GM | General Motors |
| GNP | Gross National Product |
| GSP | Generalised System of Preferences |
| GVC | Global Value Chain |
| HIPC | Heavily Indebted Poor Countries |
| HQ | Headquarters |
| HRM | Human Resource Management |
| IAEA | International Atomic Energy Authority |
| IBRD | International Bank for Reconstruction and Development |
| ICSID | International Centre for the Settlement of Investment Disputes |
| ICT | Information and communication technology |
| IDA | International Development Agency |
| IEA | International Energy Agency |
| IGAD | Inter-Governmental Authority on Development |
| IHRM | International Human Resource Management |
| ILO | International Labour Organization |
| IMF | International Monetary Fund |
| IMO | International Maritime Organisation |

| | |
|---|---|
| IMAS | International Market Selection |
| IMS | International Monetary System |
| IP | Innovation Process |
| IPR | Intellectual Property Right |
| IRA | Inflation Reduction Act |
| ISO | International Organisation for Standardisation |
| ITO | International Trade Organisation |
| LGBT | Lesbian, Gay, Bisexual and transgender |
| LNG | Liquefied natural gas |
| LSE | Large-sized enterprise |
| MEA | Multilateral environmental agreement |
| MFN | Most favoured nation |
| MIGA | Multilateral Investment Guarantee Agency |
| MNE | Multinational enterprise |
| MSR | Maritime Silk Route |
| NAALC | North American Agreement on Labour Co-operation |
| NAFTA | North American Free Trade Area |
| NATO | North Atlantic Treaty Organization |
| NGO | Non-governmental organisation |
| NICS | Newly industrialised countries |
| NTB | Non-tariff barrier |
| NYSE | New York Stock Exchange |
| OBM | Original brand manufacturing |
| OECD | Organisation for Economic Cooperation and Development |
| OEM | Original equipment manufacturing |
| OPEC | Organisation of Petroleum Exporting Countries |
| PAG | Premier Automotive Group |
| PPP | Polluter pays principle |
| PR | Public Relations |
| PTA | Preferential trade agreement |
| R&D | Research and development |
| RCEP | The Regional Comprehensive Economic Partnership |
| RMB | Renminbi |
| RTA | Regional trade agreement |
| SAA | Stability and Association Agreements |
| SADC | South African Development Community |
| SAR | Saudi Arabian Riyal |
| SBU | Strategic Business Unit |
| SE | Samsung Electronics |
| SEA | Single European Act |
| SEM | Single European Market |
| SME | Small and medium-sized enterprise |
| SOE | State Owned Enterprise |
| SPS | Sanitary and Phytosanitary measures |
| SREB | Silk Road Economic Belt |

| | |
|---|---|
| SWF | Sovereign wealth fund |
| TBRS | Trust Beneficiary Rights |
| TBT | Technical Barriers to Trade |
| TPP | Trans-Pacific Partnership |
| TRIPS | Trade-related Intellectual Property |
| UDHR | Universal Declaration of Human Rights |
| UAE | United Arab Emirates |
| UBI | Universal Basic Income |
| UK | United Kingdom |
| UKIP | United Kingdom Independence Party |
| UN | United Nations |
| UNCTAD | United Nations Conference for Trade and Development |
| UNDP | United Nations Development Programme |
| UNEP | United Nations Environmental Programme |
| UNFCCC | United Nations Framework Convention on Climate Change |
| US | United States |
| USMCA | The United States-Mexico-Canada Agreement |
| USSR | Union of Soviet Socialist Republics |
| WAEMU | West African Economic and Monetary Union |
| WEF | World Economic Forum |
| WTO | World Trade Organisation |

# PART I

# THE STRATEGIC CONTEXT OF THE SHIFTING INTERNATIONAL BUSINESS ENVIRONMENT

The last decade has seen a substantial change in the international business environment. The consensus that formed around the notion that globalisation was an inevitable process of change that offered unequivocal gains to all parts of the global system has been increasingly challenged. A number of events, from the global financial crisis to the COVID-19 pandemic, have served to underline how global interconnectivity can work against the interests of a state and its citizens. Moreover, there has been an increasingly hostile approach by populations to what globalisation means for their economic well-being. This places an adaptive tension upon businesses that see the benefits of globality, but which face markets that appear less amenable to the process. The four chapters within this part of the book seek to draw attention to these processes whilst outlining the perspectives which drove the system towards globality.

The first chapter explores the form and nature of globality, looking at the core indicators of the globalisation process and those arguments which also stressed that the process was always overstated. Nonetheless, globalisation has met with increased scepticism from parts of the population, and the chapter looks at the core explainers as to why these drivers have been curtailed. These themes are built upon by the second chapter, which looks at business strategy in a global context, looking at how businesses in both a passive and active sense are impacted by these processes of change. The third chapter reflects how international strategy is not simply a corporate phenomenon but is also reflected in how states seek to position themselves within the global systems. This draws on themes reflected within Chapters 4 and 5, where states seek to ensure their strategic interests are secured through international governance systems and in the trend towards regionalism.

DOI: 10.4324/9781315184500-1

# CHAPTER 1

# GLOBALISATION AND THE CHANGING BUSINESS ENVIRONMENT

## OBJECTIVES

This chapter will help you to:

- Understand what is meant by the term 'globalisation'.
- Identify and appraise the main drivers behind globalisation.
- Describe the extent of and limits to globalisation, including whether a turn away from globalisation is occurring.
- Assess the controversies surrounding globalisation.
- Identify how the interaction between business and globalisation works (you will have a much fuller view of this by the time you have worked your way through this book).

In the final quarter of the 20th century, it became apparent that fundamental changes were afoot in the world economy that profoundly affected business, politics, society, citizens, and the ways in which various stakeholders interacted with each other. This process became known as 'globalisation' – a frequently overused and contested term that came to mean all that was good or bad in the world economy, depending upon one's viewpoint. For those who welcomed the supremacy of markets and economic liberalism, globalisation offered the possibility of boundless growth and prosperity, not only for developed countries but also for those developing countries brave enough and able to embrace rather than resist globalisation in all its manifestations. For others, globalisation threatened rising inequality, economic anarchy, and a surrender of political control. In developed countries, job losses and the unravelling of social progress were anticipated as a result of greater competition from low-cost countries, whereas developing countries feared that their former colonial subjugation had been replaced by the dominance of market forces and their agents in the form of multinational enterprises. During the formative decades of the 21st century, anti-globalisation forces are coming more to the

DOI: 10.4324/9781315184500-2

fore, although the long-term impact on the international business environment remains far from clear.

The focus of this volume is on the implications of globalisation for the international business environment and, thus, for international business. The primary purpose of this chapter is to establish a context and platform for subsequent chapters. It begins with an exploration of the concept of globalisation and a discussion of key drivers in the process. The analysis then highlights the main debates surrounding globalisation, before attempting to measure key indicators of globalisation with a view to linking the theoretical debate about globalisation with what is actually happening in the world economy and the international business environment. It concludes with preliminary thoughts about how globalisation has changed the way business operates before assessing contemporary challenges to globalisation processes.

## WHAT IS GLOBALISATION?

Globalisation is a complex phenomenon, contested in terms of its definition, extent, and implications and, therefore, in terms of the most appropriate response to it. Economists, political scientists, sociologists, anthropologists, and lawyers, among others, have all debated the meaning of the term within the context of their respective academic disciplines.

Definitions of globalisation vary and highlight different aspects of the globalisation process. Some highlight the compression of space and time resulting from enhanced information and communications technologies. Others speak of the homogenisation of markets and cultures or of increased interconnectivity and integration into a single economic unit free from barriers to trade. Others focus on the firm, speaking of enterprises that operate on a global scale with manufacturing taking place in several countries or, more precisely, of firms demonstrating a high degree of functional integration across internationally dispersed economic activities. In short, globalisation is a multi-dimensional phenomenon, making it difficult to reach a commonly agreed-upon definition with consensus around the weighting that should be given to specific factors. A useful starting point in the context of international business is a definition which appeared in the IMF's World Economic Outlook in the mid-1990s, which defined globalisation as:

> The growing interdependence of countries world-wide through the increasing volume and variety of cross-border transactions in goods and services and of international capital flows, and also through the more rapid and widespread diffusion of technology.

This definition is a useful starting point for understanding globalisation, highlighting interdependence, the increasing number and range of cross-border transactions in terms of trade and investment, and the important role played by technology. In order to understand globalisation in terms of its deeper meaning and significance (or at least in terms of its implications for economic governance and business), it is essential to analyse the key, closely linked drivers behind the globalisation process in an attempt to understand how this interdependence has arisen.

## Globalisation driver one: the changing economic paradigm – from demand management to neo-liberalism

The growing interdependence of economies referred to in the above definition of globalisation has only taken place because of the growing acceptance of economic liberalism as the preferred method of 'managing economies'. Indeed, the idea of managing economies is a contradiction in terms in the context of neo-liberalism, an approach based on limiting the role of government to the provision of an environment in which businesses can flourish and which relies heavily on unleashing the forces of competition.

Liberal economic ideas initially took root in external economic policy. The philosophy of the General Agreement on Tariff and Trade (GATT), set up in the aftermath of the Second World War, was essentially liberal. GATT's objective was the progressive reduction of tariff barriers, a reaction to the damaging protectionist spiral that had occurred in the 1930s. GATT met with some success: in 1950, the weighted average tariffs in Germany, the UK, and the US, for example, were 26 per cent, 23 per cent and 18 per cent respectively. Following the Uruguay Round, the last completed round of multilateral trade talks, the weighted average tariff in advanced industrialised countries was less than four per cent. As tariff removal gained ground, the removal of non-tariff barriers to trade became increasingly important within GATT and its successor organisation, the WTO.

Composed solely of developed countries upon its formation, the membership of the GATT/WTO subsequently expanded to include many countries to which GATT's philosophy had previously been alien. For example, during the 1990s, many former Communist countries acknowledged the benefits of free trade by applying for membership. In December 2001, the landmark accession of Communist China to this arch-neo-liberal international economic organisation took place. Ukraine followed suit in May 2008. In 2012, after long and difficult negotiations, Russia finally became a WTO member.

By the end of the 1970s, liberal economic ideas, hitherto more dominant in the external economic environment, began to permeate thinking about domestic economic policy management. During the 1950s and 1960s, the prevailing orthodoxy was based on Keynesian economics, particularly the belief that by managing demand, governments could exercise significant control over their economies. However, the international economic troubles of the 1970s challenged many basic assumptions about economic policy. Not surprisingly, the shift in policy occurred first in the United States, where the idea of competitive capitalism was strongest. Its main proponent was President Ronald Reagan, whose primary domestic mission was to roll back the frontiers of the state. Indeed, the term 'Reaganomics' was invented to describe his programme of free market economics. Closely allied to this thinking and practice was the UK government of Margaret Thatcher, which came into office in 1979. Thatcherism swept away many economic sacred cows to such an extent that the Labour government elected in 1997 took as given many of the reforms that had been introduced so controversially in the 1980s. Although liberal economic thinking caught on most quickly and extensively in the US and the UK, it also started to influence economic policy in the rest of the developed world, albeit adapted to the specific political and cultural context of individual countries. By the mid-1980s, for example, liberalism had become so pervasive that it formed the basis of the European Union's (EU) transformational single market programme.

Acceptance of free market ideology, albeit often adapted to specific political and cultural circumstances, quickly spread beyond the advanced industrialised world. Countries like Hong Kong, Taiwan, Singapore, and South Korea had long accepted the benefits of openness in external economic policy and had followed a development path of export promotion that took advantage of engagement with the global economy. However, this development also tended to be accompanied by extensive state direction and guidance of their economies – a grip that began to loosen somewhat towards the end of the 20th century. Ideas about free trade and the introduction of liberal economic policies in the form of deregulation, privatisation, and a generally reduced role for the state began to be introduced, to varying degrees, in Latin America, parts of Africa, and other parts of Asia. Economic liberalism rapidly replaced communism following the fall of the Berlin Wall in 1989 and the disintegration of the Soviet Union in 1991. Most noteworthy of all has been the phased introduction of the market into China, the hitherto 'sleeping economic giant' of Asia. This process began in the early 1980s and occurred without the dismantling of the state and party apparatus that occurred in the former Soviet Union. Since the early 1990s, India, too, has embarked upon the path of reducing the role of the state and liberalising markets.

The extension of competitive liberalism into domestic economic policy has increased the complexity of interdependence and deepened the globalisation that has taken place, with significant implications for corporate strategies and behaviour. At one level, changing regulations and attitudes create additional and more secure investment opportunities, not only through traditional market entry modes like mergers and acquisitions and joint ventures but also increasingly through participation in privatisation programmes in developed countries, newly industrialised economies, transitional economies, and in many developing countries. At a deeper level, the greater openness arising from the spread of liberal ideas and policies encourages the emergence of a mindset and a strategy that operates beyond traditional national market boundaries.

Cracks have begun to appear in the loose consensus around the alleged benefits of neo-liberalism and the market. The most obvious example of this stems from the 2016 election of Donald Trump as US president. This resulted initially in rhetoric about how the US economy had been taken advantage of in its trade relations and how he would put 'America first' and then in concrete action in the form of withdrawal from the Transpacific Partnership (TPP) negotiations and the imposition of hefty tariffs on US steel imports, which raised the spectre of a retaliatory spiral of rising tariffs and increased protectionism. Trump's victory resulted in the irony of the world's most heralded capitalist economy rejecting international competition (competition which the President, at least, claimed was unfair) and leaving China, still communist politically, if not economically, flying the flag of free trade.

Trump's election win was also part of a rising tide of populism in a number of places, a trend which represents a turning away from an outward-looking agenda towards a more inward-looking, nationalistic one. The result of the 2016 UK referendum to leave the EU was clearly influenced by populist feeling. Those campaigning for the UK's departure deny that the decision represents a rejection of internationalism, claiming that the UK has gained greater freedom to trade with the rest of the world on its own terms whereas those who campaigned for the UK to remain in the EU view the decision as isolating the UK in a world in which influence comes from membership of a larger grouping. Populist movements are apparent in other European countries, although he extent to which they have gained or will gain influence and their potential impact on the open trade and investment policies of recent decades is still far from clear.

## Globalisation driver two: the spread of international governance and regulation

As legal barriers to trade and investment fell in line with growing economic liberalism, it became progressively easier and more attractive for companies to trade and invest across borders, leading to questions about the most appropriate location of policies to regulate the business environment. These questions were levelled not only at conventional matters of external commercial policy, such as trade, but also at topics like investment, technical standards, competition policy, and labour standards – issues traditionally regarded as matters of domestic policy. From the perspective of MNEs wishing to operate seamlessly across borders, it is time-consuming and costly to adapt their products and processes to different national regulations and much more efficient to comply with one set of rules agreed upon at a supranational level – whether regionally or globally.

The shift from what Prakash and Hart (2000) term 'shallow' integration (trade-led integration brought about by tariff reductions) to deep integration (harmonisation or, at least, approximation of domestic regulations) has not progressed as far at the international as it has at the regional level. In the case of the EU, which has experienced the deepest integration of all regional organisations, much of what is perceived as domestic policy, at least in market regulation terms, has already shifted from the nation state to the regional level by way of the Single European Market (SEM). As Chapter 5 demonstrates, the pressures for deeper regional integration are also present in several geographical regions. However, challenges to this trend have grown, not only in Europe (Brexit and the emergence of political movements deeply critical of the EU in several European countries) but also in North America, where President Trump made plain his dislike of the North American Free Trade Area (NAFTA) and led to its replacement with a new agreement (see Chapter 5).

In part, this upward policy shift is a manifestation of the globalisation trend and originated with the progressive reduction of tariff barriers among GATT contracting partners and later among WTO members. As integration through trade developed, other barriers to integration were thrown into the regulatory spotlight, resulting in the emergence of a trade agenda with both a broader (for example, the Uruguay Round incorporated agriculture and services trade) and a deeper scope. Technological developments, particularly developments in ICT and the emergence of e-commerce, have also posed new challenges to traditional governance structures.

Moreover, the spectre of a shift to a higher level of governance on a number of erstwhile domestic issues has strengthened the argument that integrative trends are blurring national boundaries and eroding the sovereignty of nation states. Perspectives on desirable or likely outcomes vary, resulting in a number of complex questions. The answers to these questions are of utmost importance to business, given that governance structures scope out the regulatory framework in which businesses operate and hence shape their operating environment and the strategic options available to them. Such questions include

- Is there a case, particularly given the emerging international regulatory gap, for greater global self-regulation?
- Is the world moving towards a system of multi-level governance in which national, regional, and international interests work together to perform tasks traditionally performed by nation states?
- Does the tendency to shift part of the public policy agenda to an international level represent the death knell of national sovereignty or a redefinition of sovereignty that will enable greater regulation of the activities of MNEs?
- Is the demise of the nation state exaggerated given that the emerging multilateral international governance system is not supranational and is based on the nation state?
- Does the apparently growing resistance to deeper integration, both at the regional and international level (as suggested by the failure to conclude the Doha round of multilateral trade talks at the WTO), together with the erosion of support for economic neo-liberalism, represent a fundamental backlash to the globalisation process, or are they simply part of the inevitable to and from of political discourse?

## Globalisation driver three: finance and capital spread

The additional trade and investment generated by globalisation requires parallel movements of capital and finance (see Chapter 16). Deregulation, liberalisation, and technological change have combined in recent decades to transform the finance sector to support the growing number of transnational transactions. Finance was traditionally always a heavily regulated, and hence fragmented, activity geographically, but with the emergence of the Eurodollar markets in the 1960s (markets in dollars held outside the US banking system and control), this began to change. US reforms in the 1970s made it easier for US banks to operate abroad and for foreign banks to gain access to the US banking market and opened up securities markets and other financial services to varying degrees. In the UK, the 'Big Bang' of 1986 ended the demarcation between banks and securities houses and allowed foreign firms entry to the stock exchange. Other European exchanges have undergone similar reforms. Within the broader context of the SEM, it became much easier for banks and other financial institutions to operate throughout the EU. A key component of the SEM was the removal of the remaining controls on capital movements within the EU. Without such a measure, the additional trade, investment, and industrial restructuring resulting from the creation of the SEM would not have been possible.

On a multilateral level, negotiations on the liberalisation of financial services continued after the end of the Uruguay Round, resulting in the 1997 Financial Services Agreement, according to which binding commitments were made to provide non-discriminatory national treatment and market access in financial services to firms from other WTO members. Work continues to liberalise trade in financial services further on a multilateral basis. Multilateral organisations like the International Monetary Fund (IMF) have also played a part in dealing with and facilitating co-operation in relation to a range of international financial crises (see Chapter 16), such as the 1997 Asian financial crisis, the 2008 credit crunch, and the problems that have beset individual countries within the eurozone, which could have spread financial instability on a much wider scale without co-ordinated action.

These developments have also increased both the complexity and volatility of international financial markets (see Chapter 16). A range of new financial instruments, many of which are inherently volatile, such as derivatives, have emerged to serve a broader marketplace. Although more mobile capital is clearly needed to support a more integrated international economic system and all parts of the production chain within multinationals, this mobility also brings with it more volatility. Individuals and institutions, for example, are able to transfer vast amounts rapidly around the globe to arbitrage between exchange and interest rates. Such movements can intensify crises and transmit crises from country to country, or even from region to region. The 1997 Asian financial crisis, and more latterly, the 2007–09 global financial crisis were prime examples of contagion in an interdependent world.

The combination of more open markets with the adoption of new information and communications technologies (ICTs) has transformed international capital movements. In principle, capital can now be transferred around the world in an instant. In practice, although significantly reduced, regulatory barriers continue to prevent the full collapse of time and space for financial transactions. However, the potential for instantaneous financial transactions spanning the globe remains and is moving nearer to realisation.

A further consequence of these trends is a weakening of the link between currencies and their traditional locations – the nation state – and the multiplication of the forms of money. The former trend is particularly marked for the US dollar, which has become the currency of choice in a number of Latin American countries and elsewhere. Indeed, there are as many dollars in circulation outside as inside the United States. The birth of the euro also reflected a movement away from the strong identification of currency with national territory and heralded the demise of such prominent currencies as the German mark, the French franc, the Italian lira, and the Spanish peseta. The possibility of further regional currencies, albeit unlikely in the short term, cannot be ruled out.

The link between national territories and means of payment has also been further weakened by the growth of cryptocurrencies. These are digital assets, the first of which was bitcoin, established in 2009, and of which there are now several thousand, which act as a medium of exchange but bypass traditional central banking systems and regulations. Although daily transactions in such currencies reached hundreds of millions of dollars by early 2022, they remain minuscule compared to trading in traditional currencies. However, their growth has been rapid and has given rise to concern about their potential for money laundering and other forms of legal activity; lack of protection for users; the danger of creating a bubble, the bursting of which could spread economic damage across the globe; and the possibility of losses through technical malfunction or malware.

In short, globalisation requires financial mobility and flexibility to yield the full mutual and potential benefits of increased connectivity. However, this carries with it the dangers of volatility and instability and the possibility of spreading negative as well as positive impacts. This is possible in all fields, but examples have been particularly marked in the financial sector, as the aforementioned examples of the 1997 Asian financial crisis and the 2008 credit crunch showed. In the former case, fears over debt resulted in a rush away from the baht, Thailand's currency, resulting in contagion and setting off a similar chain of events in other countries both inside and outside the region. In the case of the latter, given the greater international interdependence of financial markets, problems arising from unsafe loans in the US sub-prime mortgage market quickly spread beyond the US, causing problems for European banks, and even leading to the collapse of Iceland's banking system. The knock-on effect of this crisis was a more general global economic slowdown, which had impacts of varying severity throughout the world.

## Globalisation driver four: the diffusion of information and communication technology

Technological innovation and its diffusion have clearly played a significant role in the redefinition and reorganisation of commercial and economic space known as 'globalisation' by facilitating restructuring of the manufacturing system, transforming the configuration of value chains, and lowering the cost of and speeding up transportation and communication. Indeed, for companies in many sectors, the development of new technology and/or its exploitation makes the difference between success and failure. This is increasingly the case not only in explicitly technological sectors but also, with the advent of e-commerce, for example, in traditionally less technologically sensitive sectors such as retailing.

However, technology's precise significance in the globalisation process is a subject of some controversy. Technological determinists such as Kevin Kelly (1999) have argued that technology is the prime mover of change and that it makes globalisation inevitable and irreversible. A more eclectic approach maintains that technological developments, although central to the transformation of intra- and inter-state and enterprise relationships, are not sufficient to bring about such change on their own account. Other social, political, and economic factors, such as the spread of neo-liberal economic philosophy with its themes of liberalisation, deregulation, and open markets, are also needed to maximise the impact of globalisation. Indeed, technology interacts with the other drivers of globalisation to achieve the above transformational effects. In other words, technology is an important facilitator of change rather than its primary mover.

Even without the more extravagant claims for technology, it is possible to identify the far-reaching effects of its diffusion. Transportation and telecommunications technologies have transformed space-time distances, reducing the effective economic distance between nations and organisations. Transportation technologies are concerned with the carriage of goods and people and, through progress from horsepower, sail, and steam to the internal combustion engine and the jet engine, have significantly reduced the time taken to travel large distances. From 1500 to the mid-19th century, average travel times using horse-drawn carriages and sailing ships were about ten mph. In the mid-19th century, steam trains and steamships operated at an average of 65 mph and 35 mph, respectively. The advent of jet aircraft in the 1960s meant that the transport of people and high-value, low-volume goods at 500–700 mph became possible. These faster transportation times have lowered a significant barrier to trade and have helped reduce the lead time between placing an order and the delivery of the goods ordered. This is particularly important in relation to just-in-time management and trade in goods which are reactive to changes in fashion and consumer tastes and have contributed to trade growth.

Given the fall in tariffs since the formation of the WTO, aggregate transport costs can be several times higher than tariffs. Reductions in transport costs are therefore good for trade. In the second half of the 20th century, the trend for transport costs in all modes was downward, reinforcing the globalisation trend, a trend which can be undermined by rising fuel costs.

Communications technology, increasingly converging with computer technologies into ICTs, has resulted in the virtually instantaneous transfer of data and information throughout the world. Such technology has resulted in lower transaction and operational costs. In 1930, the cost of a three-minute telephone call between New York and London at 1990 prices was almost $250. By 1990, the equivalent cost was 75 cents. Innovations such as e-mails and Skype have reduced communication costs further. The value of telecommunications has also risen as a result of the increase in the size of the network. Greater diffusion of network services and increasing access to these networks enhances their value and contribution to business, an argument which also applies to the internet and the technology associated with e-commerce. This relatively new form of business organisation is potentially a prime agent of de-territorialisation. However, cross-border payments, taxation, and consumer protection issues, among others, require resolution before e-commerce fulfils its potential.

There are also pushbacks from states with regard to the capability of the system to allow free and easy flow of data across borders. The long-advanced notion of the internet as a seamless global entity has long since passed. Indeed, the borders that exist in the physical world are now increasingly common in the on-line environment. These are themes that are addressed more completely in Chapter 18. In addition to these barriers to the free flow of data, there are increased international barriers to the free movement of high technology across borders, especially where such technologies can be used for military and/or security purposes or where their utilisation brings them into direct competitive conflict with firms from the exporting state.

## Globalisation driver five: social and cultural convergence

A consequence of greater liberalisation and the spread of global communications technology is a degree of social and cultural convergence, in itself a pre-condition for globalisation. This does not imply that a global culture has replaced or is replacing the diversity of local and national cultures in the world, a fear expressed by many anti-globalists. The range and deep-rootedness of beliefs, values, experiences, and symbols are too extensive for that. However, helped by the global consolidation of mass media, especially in broadcasting, and by the power of the Internet, there is growing recognition of common symbols and experiences. Such commonality does not need to be deeply embedded, or even much more than superficial, before it becomes useful for the development of a global mindset and hence global marketing. Social and cultural convergence across boundaries is only possible when there is no clash with more profoundly held cultural beliefs specific to a particular place or grouping, such as religion.

The emergence of a global consumer, or at least consumers with common preferences across a significant part of the globe, creates opportunities for the creation of global products – that is, homogeneous products that can be sold throughout the world on the basis of global marketing and advertising campaigns. Truly global products are relatively few and far between, but where their existence is possible, they increase the viability and desirability of developing international production systems and value chains, with all the potential gains in terms of scale economies and utilisation of different comparative advantages.

However, these processes of convergence have suffered substantive pushbacks, especially where national and even regional cultures have proved resilient to global pressures. Indeed, it can be argued that these processes of reasserting national cultures are a direct by-product of globalisation, where it seems a logistical resistance to the power of the social superpower that is able to assert its influence through mainstream and increasingly social media. A desire to preserve this cultural diversity in the face of such power has led to the emergence of nationally focussed media channels and local content rules to ensure a level playing field for national cultures and related products and services.

---

### Box 1.1: The butterfly defect

The notion of the 'butterfly defect' was developed by economists Ian Goldin and Mike Mariathasan and reflected that there is an inherent defect within the global economic system born of the high and rising degree of interconnectivity within political, economic, social, technological, and environmental systems. The central argument is that as the global system – through hyperglobality – has grown more complex through rising interconnectivity between the aforementioned systems, so the global system becomes more unpredictable and difficult to manage. This perception was born of the author's experience of the global financial crisis and reaffirmed by the spread of the COVID-19 pandemic. They argue that the virtual and physical links between these systems have allowed the system to develop in a haphazard and unplanned fashion. It has become impossible to fully understand the legacy of any single agent's impact upon the global system.

This process is borne of the universal reach of globalisation, which creates a lot of formal and informal interconnections that can often be implicit within everyday human economic and social activity. These links create a situation where there is a divorce between the responsibility of an event occurring and the cause of that event occurring. This is created by the fact that there are often only very indirect links between the event and its causes. This breakdown limits the ability of any agent to take mediating action to mitigate against any event occurring, as decisions cannot be linked to outcomes. The resultant systemic risk is created through three main channels:

1. A cascading shock is created when a tipping point within the system is reached, creating a system-wide impact.

2. Where a shock is created through risk sharing and/or contagion.

3. A common shock created by an indirect process acting upon a system.

The authors argue that these common systemic forms of risk have been compounded as a result of globalisation, creating two new geographic types of risk. These are vector and density risks. Vector risks are created where there is an increased density of users, which creates both proximity and connectivity, which allows for the rapid spread of malign forces (such as diseases). Density risk is created where economically salient activities become concentrated in a few locations globally. Thus, when one of these concentrations of activity is damaged or impacted, its effects quickly ripple throughout the rest of the system. For example, a disruption to a major logistics or air passenger hub can easily disrupt flows in international logistics and global passenger traffic. These were also evident in the impact of the 2011 floods in Thailand (see case study).

The legacy of these processes is that as much as globalisation can be seen as a positive force within the global system, it can also be an incredibly disruptive force. This has been evidenced not simply through the GFC but also in the more recent COVID-19 pandemic and also in the Russia-Ukraine conflict. This, the authors argue, can be countered by resilient globalisation where economic activity is more dispersed, which allows for systems to adapt quicker to any disruption. This means a more inclusive global system with more activity focussed upon developing states to remove vector and density risks.

## DIVERGENT VIEWS OF GLOBALISATION

The debate about globalisation is highly significant as it frames the business environment, both domestically and internationally, and shapes corporate strategies. However, globalisation has proved to be a highly controversial process. The controversy arises from differing interpretations of the strength and significance of changes in the world economy and their impact on different stakeholders. The most fundamental question concerns whether the economy is becoming truly global or simply more inter-national. A pure global economy implies a borderless economic space in which the integration of operations and markets takes place according to economic and market imperatives, as opposed to the fragmentation of production and markets that has traditionally occurred because of continuing barriers between countries. An international economy implies no fundamental shift in the underlying principles of economic organisation but simply more cross-border transactions. Globalisation brings fundamental implications for governance and political organisation, whereas internationalisation, although posing governance challenges at national and international levels, can be absorbed within existing governance frameworks.

Are the changes to the world economy discussed so far in this chapter to be welcomed or resisted? A different answer would be forthcoming, depending on who you asked! Another salient issue is whether globalisation is inevitable and irreversible. If this is the case, the best path for those concerned about the consequences of globalisation is to work within the existing framework but to push for incremental improvements in the international business environment. Just how global is the global economy anyway? Hirst, Thompson, and Bromley (2009) argue that the world economy was more global before the First World War (1914–18) – if this theory is correct, then continuing contemporary international integration might not be inevitable.

Degrees of international economic integration can be located on a globalisation/fragmentation continuum (see Figure 1.1). At the globalisation end sits what Kenichi Ohmae (1994) calls the 'borderless world', that is, a world in which all obstacles to the movement of the factors of production have been removed. At the other end is a world of individual nation states that continue to be divided by barriers to trade and commerce. Reality lies somewhere in between: as barriers disappear and the economy becomes more internationalised, the world moves towards the globalisation end of the continuum, whereas the construction of barriers marks a shift towards fragmentation and reduced internationalisation. The characterisation of 'ideal types', although removed from reality, provides a useful benchmark against which to judge the implications of different outcomes.

A borderless world is truly global in the sense that, as a result of policy changes and the rapid development of transport and communications technology, national borders have become increasingly irrelevant. This process is facilitated by the emergence of a single, homogenised world culture as the result of the globalisation of the media, particularly via satellite broadcasting. Divergent policy outcomes are possible in this scenario.

A pure market forces view would argue that greater uncertainty and volatility is a price worth paying for giving free rein to unregulated market forces – the best guarantee of wealth generation through enterprise. From the corporate standpoint, competition is intensified within domestic and export markets, requiring increasingly rapid adjustments to changes in the business environment. More profoundly, a borderless world encourages the growth of genuinely stateless enterprises that plan according to the dictates of the market and regard national borders as an irrelevance. This requires a global conception of markets and a striving for critical mass as both a defensive and offensive response to intensified competition. It also undermines the role of the nation state in the organisation of economic and political activity.

Not everyone regards market forces, or Adam Smith's 'invisible hand', so positively. In order to overcome the consequences of market failure, others argue not for a retreat within national boundaries but for a strengthening of international governance. By developing governance structures that correspond with the scope and scale of modern international business, civil society can regain some control over key economic actors. The challenge of achieving this is immense and requires a greater willingness to reconcile conflicting interests and reach compromises than has hitherto been the case.

**FIGURE 1.1** The globalisation/fragmentation continuum

To a degree, this characterisation of the 'borderless world' is a straw man that can easily be knocked over by numerous examples of the persistence of nation state power and of strong cultural differences between nations. However, this does not exclude the possibility that the world is moving in the direction of fewer borders. The important question is how far it has moved along the continuum.

Somewhere in between these two extremes lies the scenario outlined by Hirst and Thompson (Hirst, Thompson, and Bromley 2015). They do not deny that there is greater interconnectedness among the world's economies and markets. However, they are of the view that much of the case for globalisation and the ungovernability of world markets is overstated. They claim that the existence of genuine stateless MNEs is almost unknown and that most firms are transnational, based in one state while trading and operating in a variety of countries and maintaining strong links with the home country. Alan Rugman has elaborated on this view by arguing that most multinationals have strong regional rather than global presences.

The world economy itself is also far from global: capital flows, trade, and investment are concentrated in the advanced economies, with developing countries marginalised, although evidence suggests that this trend is becoming less pronounced (see below). The advanced economies, particularly if they engage in policy co-ordination, so the argument goes, have the capability to exert strong governance pressures over the world economy and retain strong powers to influence economic events. Again, contrary to the views of many critics of globalisation, the advanced economies are not finding it easy to have their own way. The failure hitherto of the WTO to reach an agreement on the Doha Round is, in part, a consequence of developing states asserting themselves. These states may not yet be able to achieve policy outcomes that they perceive to be in their interests, but they have managed to block initiatives which they regard as being against their interests.

Rather than describe the growing economic interdependence as globalisation, Hirst and Thompson refer to a shift towards a more 'inter-national' economy. In doing so, they stress the original meaning of the word 'international' – that is, 'between nations'. Through the use of the concept of inter-nationalism, Hirst and Thompson acknowledge the growing interconnection between national economies. Despite these tighter links, Hirst and Thompson argue that domestic and international frameworks remain separate for economic policy-making purposes. They also maintain that international events do not necessarily directly penetrate the national economy but have an indirect effect through national policy and processes or work 'automatically' through market forces. This has very different implications for business: greater interdependence still intensifies competition, and companies continue to seek entry into new markets via a variety of modes, but the strategy is developed to take into account regional and national differences.

Underpinning much of the debate about globalisation is the belief that MNEs are significant economic entities in their own right and yield greater economic power than many nation states. Table 1.1 compares the 2021 GDP (gross domestic product) of a number of nation states with the market capitalisation of some of the world's biggest companies in the same year. The figures in Table 1.1 demonstrate the power of technology companies in the contemporary global system. These companies now have market capitalisations that rival the GDP of large states. While they do represent different

**TABLE 1.1** Ranking of countries and companies by GDP and market capitalisation ($ bn)

| State | GDP/market capitalisation |
| --- | --- |
| United States | 21,433 |
| China | 14,343 |
| Japan | 5,082 |
| Germany | 3,861 |
| India | 2,861 |
| UK | 2,829 |
| France | 2,716 |
| **Apple** | **2,125** |
| Italy | 2,024 |
| **Microsoft** | **1,942** |
| **Aramco** | **1,888** |
| Brazil | 1,840 |
| Canada | 1,736 |
| Russia | 1700 |
| **Amazon** | **1,688** |
| **Alphabet** | **1656** |
| South Korea | 1647 |
| Australia | 1397 |
| Spain | 1393 |
| Mexico | 1269 |
| Indonesia | 1119 |
| **Facebook** | **939** |
| The Netherlands | 907 |
| Saudi Arabia | 793 |
| Turkey | 761 |
| **Tencent** | **736** |
| Switzerland | 703 |
| Poland | 596 |

things (GDP is a measure of the goods and services produced within an economy, and market capitalisation is a value created by the share price multiplied by the number of shares), the largest companies have a value that is equivalent to a large, developed industrial economy.

Although the observations arising from Table 1.1 do not, in themselves, reveal anything about the economic and indeed political power yielded by individual companies nor are direct comparisons between market capitalisation and GDP entirely justified, they do act as a useful rule of thumb that show that, when considered as economic units, the world's biggest companies are of a similar size to all but the world's largest economies. In other words, MNEs are important economic entities in their own right. In addition, MNEs are often criticised for their role in developing countries. The above analysis indicates that when it comes to dealing with MNEs, all but the biggest developing countries are dealing with better-resourced organisations with potentially more economic and political clout than themselves. Concentration of economic power in the hands of private organisations is not new, as witnessed by the history of the East India Company and the Hudson Bay Company, for example, in previous centuries. The number, range, and diverse origins of large MNEs in the contemporary world, however, are unprecedented.

## Box 1.2: The deglobalisation imperative

For a long period of time, globalisation was always seen as a one-way process, even though history does indicate that it has ebbed and flowed over time. In the early 21st century, there has been a marked trend towards deglobalisation. This trend is not so much a rejection of globalisation per se or of a return to autarky and isolationism, but more a growing push back against the forces of hyperglobality where there was a rapid expansion in speed, scale, and intensity of globalisation. In this sense, deglobalisation is about a more managed, 'less chaotic process'. This process of deglobalisation is being driven by a number of interlinked processes, the most notable of which are below.

- The rise of localisation. The increased emphasis upon sustainability within the global system emphasises the need to minimise the carbon footprint of global processes such as transport. Thus, there is an increased desire to lower carbon footprints through sourcing goods and services locally.
- The localised cost of globality. This has been an ongoing issue, but the legacy of globalisation has been a live political issue as awareness of its cost in terms of employment, social cohesion, and economic wellbeing becomes a more salient political issue.
- Geopolitical tension. There is evidence that rising geopolitical tension is leading to a decoupling process between the western and eastern systems, creating a more fragmented and, over the longer term, bipolar global system. This will be enforced by higher degrees of regionalism and localism.
- National populism. This is a political movement that tends to use the term 'globalist' as an insult. Globality is seen as an elite preoccupation which – according to populists – is designed to impoverish and disenfranchise local communities in developed states.

- Technological fragmentation. Technology is meant to be a core enabler of the process of globalisation but is increasingly being controlled to limit its impact. For reasons of domestic and international security, the spread of technology is being curtailed through export bans or simply through limiting and filtering data flows across borders.
- Self-sufficiency. The belief was that globality would deliver security of supply. A number of shocks across a number of sectors have turned this on its head, and states are pushing for secure domestic supplies of goods such as energy, semiconductor chips, etc.

While the list is not exhaustive, it nonetheless suggests lower degrees of interconnectivity between countries due to a mix of security, cohesion, economic, and sustainability reasons. However, globalisation has matured to such an extent that a full-scale decoupling would be very difficult and counterproductive. What is emerging is a new model for the global system that stresses proximity as a source of security and an emergence of globalisation as a source of vulnerability. History does suggest that this is not historically unique and that globality does return as political sentiment changes.

## MEASUREMENT OF GLOBALISATION

This section attempts to measure globalisation trends. The objective is not to develop precise indicators but to provide evidence to help investigate some of the claims about globalisation, such as whether it is inclusive or not. firms. The indicators presented below attempt to address the following dimensions of interdependence:

- *Scope*: that is, the extent to which international economic integration is truly global rather than confined to the 'triad' of North America, Europe, and Japan/East Asia.
- *Intensity*: the depth, embeddedness, and extensiveness of the integration that has taken place, both between countries and within firms.
- *Sensitivity*: the degree to which events in one part of the global system transmit themselves to other parts of the system. The more integrated the system, the more rapid and complete the transmission of the effects of economic developments and crises throughout the system.

### Scope

Given that world economic activity is dominated by advanced industrial economies and, increasingly, by China, the term 'globalisation' has been criticised as a misnomer. In other words, the relative and actual position of developing countries has not noticeably improved as a result of globalisation, and their weak integration into the world economy has effectively excluded them from any of the benefits claimed by globalisation.

## Growth

The view that globalisation is not really global and that it favours the already rich, advanced, and industrialised economies is borne out to a degree. Certainly, as Table 1.2 shows, world income is heavily concentrated in the advanced economies of North America, Europe, and Japan. In 2022, despite containing only 14 per cent of the world's population, the world's most advanced economies accounted for over 40 per cent of world GDP. Conversely, emerging and developing countries, which include 86 per cent of the world's population, account for around 60 per cent of world GDP.

**TABLE 1.2** Share of world GDP, exports of goods and services, and population in 2023 (%)

|  | GDP | Exports | Population |
|---|---|---|---|
| **Advanced economies** | **41.17** | **61** | **14** |
| US | 15.2 | 13 | 4.3 |
| Japan | 3.7 | 3 | 1.6 |
| EU | 14.6 | 29 | 5.7 |
| Other advanced economies | 7.7 | 16 | 2.4 |
| **Emerging and Developing Economies** | | | |
| **Africa & Middle East** | | | |
| Middle East & North Africa | 5.9 | 4 | 3 |
| Sub-Saharan Africa (SSA) | 3.2 | 2 | 15 |
| SSA (excl. S Africa & Nigeria) | 1.9 | 1 | 11 |
| **Emerging and Developing Asia** | 33.7 | 19 | 48 |
| China | 18.9 | 10 | 18 |
| India | 7.5 | 3 | 18 |
| Excluding China and India | 7.3 | 6 | 12 |
| **Latin America and the Caribbean** | 7.3 | 6 | 8 |
| Brazil | 2.3 | 1 | 2.8 |
| Mexico | 1.8 | 2 | 1.7 |
| Emerging and Developing Europe | 7.1 | 6 | 4 |
| Central Asia and the Caucuses | 3 | 2 | 2 |
| Russia | 2.7 | >1 | 2 |

Source: Derived from IMF (2023) *World economic outlook*, April 2023

Although a direct correlation between the share of the world's population and the world's GDP is not necessarily a realistic aspiration, the above figures do indicate that world economic activity is dominated by relatively few economies. Over time, if the proponents of the market are correct, greater integration should result in a more even spread of economic activity. To a certain extent, this has already occurred, given that in 2007, the share of the advanced industrial economies in world GDP was 56 per cent. Further analysis shows that emerging and developing Asia has been the region which has increased its share of world GDP at the expense of the advanced economies, from 20 per cent in 2007 to around 38 per cent in 2022, a remarkable increase in a relatively short time. Over half of Asia's increased share was accounted for by China, but India and other emerging Asian nations also experienced significant growth in their shares. Conversely, the rest of the world saw only marginal improvements in its share of world GDP; the share of sub-Saharan Africa, for example, only grew from 2.3 to 3.2 per cent during the period in question at a time when its share of the world's population grew from 11.6 per cent to 15 per cent. In other words, the distribution of world GDP remains skewed, but less so than it was. Moreover, these bare figures say little about changing wealth distribution within countries or regions or about the causation underpinning the shifting shares.

## Goods and services exports

Table 1.3 traces the changing regional composition of merchandise trade exports since 1948, the year the GATT officially came into existence. The relative shares of the main trading regions have fluctuated over time. Developed countries continue to dominate world exports, but less so than in the past. During the early post-war period, economic reconstruction in Europe and Japan in particular contributed to the developed nations increasing their share of world exports from 66 per cent in 1948 to almost 73 per cent in 1963, peaking at 76.3 per cent in 1973. Since then, the trend has been mostly downward, falling to 56 per cent in 2022. North America's share of world trade has declined steadily and consistently over several decades; the share of the US in world trade has fallen to less than half its level at the time of the formation of the GATT. During this period, Japan's share of world trade grew inexorably, before peaking in the early 1990s, after which it fell back following its loss of economic momentum and competitiveness. Although Europe's share of world trade has been in decline since the early 1970s, when it peaked at over 50 per cent before falling to 37 per cent in 2022, it remains the world's foremost trading region. However, Europe's supremacy is coming under increasing pressure from Asia, led by China.

The declining share of world trade by developed countries does not represent a fall in the value of their exports, which have continued to grow rapidly since the end of the Second World War, but is indicative of even faster export growth in the rest of the world. The share of developing countries in world exports declined steadily in the quarter century following the end of the war. However, since 1993, the share of world trade in developing countries has increased impressively, from around a quarter to 44 per cent in 2022. Rising commodity prices and the impressive export growth of the large emerging economies, particularly China, whose share of world exports grew from 2.5

**TABLE 1.3** Changing regional composition of merchandise trade exports (%), 1948–2017

| | 1948 | 1953 | 1963 | 1973 | 1983 | 1993 | 2003 | 2007 | 2016 | 2022 |
|---|---|---|---|---|---|---|---|---|---|---|
| North America | 28.1 | 24.8 | 19.9 | 17.3 | 16.8 | 18.0 | 15.8 | 13.7 | 14.3 | 10 |
| US | 21.7 | 18.8 | 14.9 | 12.3 | 11.2 | 12.6 | 9.8 | 8.6 | 9.4 | 7.9 |
| South & Central America | 11.3 | 9.7 | 6.4 | 4.3 | 4.4 | 3.0 | 3.0 | 3.7 | 3.3 | 5.4 |
| Europe | 35.1 | 39.4 | 47.8 | 50.9 | 43.5 | 45.4 | 46.0 | 42.5 | 38.4 | 37 |
| Africa | 7.3 | 6.5 | 5.7 | 4.8 | 4.5 | 2.5 | 2.4 | 3.1 | 2.2 | 2.5 |
| Middle East | 2.0 | 2.7 | 3.2 | 4.1 | 6.8 | 3.5 | 4.1 | 5.3 | 5.0 | 6 |
| Asia | 14.0 | 13.4 | 12.6 | 15.2 | 19.1 | 26.1 | 26.1 | 28.0 | 34.0 | 43 |
| Japan | 0.4 | 1.5 | 3.5 | 6.4 | 8.0 | 9.9 | 6.4 | 5.3 | 4.2 | 3.4 |
| China | 0.9 | 1.2 | 1.3 | 1.0 | 1.2 | 2.5 | 5.9 | 9.0 | 13.6 | 15 |
| India | 2.2 | 1.3 | 1.0 | 0.5 | 0.5 | 0.6 | 0.8 | 1.1 | 1.7 | 1.5 |
| Developing countries | 31.4 | 28.3 | 22.6 | 20.2 | 26.8 | 25.2 | 30.3 | 36.6 | 42.4 | 44 |
| Developed countries | 66.4 | 68.2 | 72.9 | 76.3 | 68.2 | 73.3 | 67.1 | 59.7 | 54.9 | 56 |

Source: UNCTAD (2023)

per cent in 1993 to almost 15 per cent in 2007, underpin this major and ongoing shift in the structure of world trade. Not all developing regions have fared so well. Africa and Central and South America's share of world trade has contracted significantly over the decades, whereas the Middle East's share rises and falls in line with the fluctuations in energy prices.

Trade in services (which includes transport; travel; construction; insurance and pension services; financial services; telecommunications, computer, and information services; maintenance and other repair services; personal, cultural, and recreational services; and government services) have become increasingly important international transactions. In 1980, the value of world commercial services trade was equal to 18 per cent of the value of world merchandise exports, rising to almost 23 per cent in 2022. This growing role for service trade reflects a long-run faster growth rate for services than for goods exports, a continuing structural shift in many economies away from agriculture and industry towards services, and the growth of digital and knowledge-based services.

As with merchandise trade, the developing countries' share of world commercial service exports lags behind that of developed countries. Europe is the world's dominant service exporter; the UK, Germany, France, and the Netherlands are major contributors to the 51 per cent of world commercial service exports from Europe. However, Europe's dominance has been declining, largely as a result of an upsurge in services exports from the emerging markets of Asia, whose share of world services exports has increased from less than 14 per cent in 1980 to almost 29 per cent in 2022 (see Table 1.4). Elsewhere, the share of emerging and developing country services exports in world services exports has not shown any growth since 1980; if anything, there has been a slight decline in their share.

## FDI

The growing complexity of world economic integration means that it is no longer sufficient to use trade in goods and services as measures of interdependence. Foreign direct

**TABLE 1.4** Changing regional composition of commercial services exports (%), 1980–2022

|  | 1980 | 1990 | 2000 | 2007 | 2013 | 2020 |
|---|---|---|---|---|---|---|
| North America | 12.4 | 19.3 | 22.2 | 16.3 | 16.4 | 15 |
| South and Central America | 4.8 | 3.8 | 3.2 | 2.8 | 3.1 | 3 |
| Europe[1] | 58.1 | 53.1 | 48.5 | 51.0 | 47.2 | 51 |
| Africa | 3.5 | 2.4 | 2.1 | 2.6 | 1.9 | 2 |
| Asia | 13.7 | 16.8 | 20.7 | 22.9 | 26.2 | 29 |

Source: UNCTAD (2023)

[1] Figures for Europe for 1980 and 1990 are for Western Europe only. From 2000 onwards, they include Central and Eastern Europe.

investment (FDI) has grown even more rapidly than trade in goods and services since 1980. For decades, the world's stock of FDI has been growing significantly faster than the growth of trade in goods and services, which, in turn, has grown several times faster than world GDP. However, the value of world FDI remains far below the value of world trade: in 2022, world FDI inflows totalled $1.6 trillion, compared to $26.9 trillion for world merchandise trade. Nevertheless, FDI is highly significant because of its interaction with trade and its contribution to the intensity of interdependence.

Over the very long term, there have been some significant shifts in the composition of world FDI. According to Dicken, in 1938, two-thirds of world FDI was located in developing countries. Most FDI at the time was composed of investments by colonial powers in their overseas possessions. Subsequently, FDI became a phenomenon that primarily took place in developed countries. As Table 1.5 shows, by 1980, developed countries accounted for 86 per cent of FDI inflows and 94 per cent of outflows. Developed-country dominance continues, but since 2000, developing countries have been attracting a greater share of FDI. By 2022, the developed countries' share of FDI had fallen to 47 per cent of FDI inflows from 81 per cent in 2000, with the share of developing countries rising to 53 per cent from 18 per cent during the same period.

Although the share of developing countries in FDI inflows has generally been on an upward trend in recent decades, much of this increased share is concentrated in specific regions (see Table 1.6). For example, 60 per cent of FDI flowing into developing countries in 2022 ended up in East Asia, particularly in China and Hong Kong, which together accounted for 39 per cent of developing country FDI inflows. Within Latin America, over 60 per cent of FDI inflows are directed towards the larger, more advanced, and more populous economies of Mexico and Brazil. Containing 18 per cent of the world's population, Africa accounted for just 5 per cent of global FDI in 2022. Within Africa, the distribution of FDI is heavily concentrated in resource-rich countries, such as Angola and Nigeria. The least developed African countries receive very little FDI.

Developing countries have gradually taken a bigger role in FDI outflows in the last 50 years. In 1970, almost 100 per cent of FDI outflows originated from developed countries; by 2022, this figure had fallen to 74 per cent with the developing world's share growing from less than one per cent in 1970 to over 26 per cent in 2022. Once more, this increased developing world participation is mostly due to Asia, where the emerging economies have sought to gain a foothold in developed markets and, in the case of China, in particular, have been investing heavily in developing countries, especially in Africa and increasingly in South America.

## Intensity

The intensity of international economic integration relates to the depth and embeddedness of the integration that has taken place between countries and within firms. The deeper the cross-border corporate linkages and the greater the density of network interconnections, the more difficult it will be to disentangle the integration of recent years. Keohane and Nye (1999) usefully distinguish between 'thin' and 'thick' globalisation. They describe the original 'Silk Road' as an example of thin globalisation: although an

**TABLE 1.5** FDI by type of economy, 1970–2021

| 1. Inflows | 1970 | | 1980 | | 1990 | | 2000 | | 2010 | | 2016 | | 2021 | |
|---|---|---|---|---|---|---|---|---|---|---|---|---|---|---|
| | $ bn | % total | $ bn | % total | $ bn | % total | $ bn | % total | $ bn | % total | $ bn | % total | $bn | % of total |
| Developed | 9.6 | 71.3 | 47.6 | 86.1 | 165.6 | 82.2 | 1146.2 | 81.2 | 700 | 50.4 | 1032 | 59.1 | 745.7 | 47 |
| Developing | 3.9 | 28.7 | 7.7 | 13.9 | 37 | 17.8 | 256.1 | 18.2 | 690 | 49.6 | 714 | 40.9 | 836.6 | 53 |
| World | 13.4 | 100 | 55.3 | 100 | 202.6 | 100 | 1411.4 | 100 | 1390 | 100 | 1746 | 100 | 1582.3 | 100 |
| | | | | | | | | | | | | | | |
| 2. Outflows | | | | | | | | | | | | | | |
| Developed | 14.1 | 99.7 | 50.7 | 94.1 | 217.6 | 94.8 | 1102.7 | 89.0 | 983 | 70.6 | 1044 | 71.9 | 1269.2 | 74 |
| Developing | 0.5. | 0.3 | 3.1 | 5.9 | 11.9 | 5.2 | 133.3 | 11.0 | 358 | 25.7 | 383 | 26.4 | 438.4 | 26 |
| World | 14.2 | 100 | 53.8 | 100 | 229.60 | 100 | 1239.2 | 100 | 1392 | 100 | 14525 | 100 | 1707.6 | 100 |

Source: Derived from UNCTAD, *World investment reports*

**TABLE 1.6** Distribution of FDI inflows among developing countries, 2022

| | $bn | % of developing country FDI |
|---|---|---|
| **Africa** | **82990.5** | **9.9** |
| • North Africa | 9335.2 | 1.1 |
| • West Africa | 13848.6 | 1.7 |
| • Central Africa | 9408.9 | 1.1 |
| • East Africa | 8178.7 | 1 |
| • Southern Africa | 42219.2 | 5 |
| **Latin America & the Caribbean** | **134547.8** | **16** |
| • South America | 88148.9 | 11 |
| • Central America | 42494.7 | 5 |
| • Caribbean | 3814.2 | 0.5 |
| **Asia** | **618983.4** | **74** |
| • East Asia | 328918 | 39 |
| • South-East Asia | 175313.9 | 21 |
| • South Asia | 52416.8 | 6.3 |
| • West Asia | 55334.3 | 6.6 |
| **Oceania** | **138.9** | **0.1** |
| **Total developing countries** | **836,570** | |

Source: UNCTAD, *World investment report*, 2023

important economic and cultural link between Europe and Asia, the trade itself involved only a small group of traders, and the goods reached only a relatively small elite of consumers. Thick globalisation encompasses links that are both extensive and intensive. In the modern world, these links involve flows of capital, goods, information, knowledge, people, and resources.

Thickening links represent more than simply an increase in the number of links but also a qualitative transformation of these connections. For MNEs, this means greater complexity in their cross-border operations, including the international integration of production systems and marketing arrangements. In particular, this implies the growth of intra-industry and intra-firm trade. Intra-industry trade refers to transactions in similar but differentiated goods within the same sector, whereas intra-firm trade consists of trade between a parent company and its affiliates abroad or between affiliates of the same country. The growth of both intra-industry and intra-firm trade reflects the increasing internationalisation of production and a greater intensity of cross-border links.

The changing role and modus operandi of MNEs have caused some speculation that, although the world has previously been as open to trade as it is today, the current intensification of networks signifies a major break with the past. The key to this argument is the changing relationship between trade and investment. As the previous section shows, the scope of globalisation can be measured by looking at the geographical breakdown of trade and investment. Such indicators are useful, traditional measures of economic interdependence, but they do not tell the whole story, nor do they reflect the complex inter-relationship between the two indicators.

The 'steps' view of internationalisation (see Chapter 11) posits that companies initially trade before investing, enabling them to test the market. Furthermore, exporting can involve small or large quantities, whereas overseas production requires a minimum size for it to be worthwhile. Exporting is also easier and less risky than FDI. FDI requires the long-term, direct commitment of assets to a foreign environment and greater knowledge, managerial expertise and experience, and organisational restructuring. Even in this relatively straightforward view of the world, FDI is more complex than the simple displacement of exports by investment. In the initial stages of FDI, an overseas affiliate creates a demand for capital goods or intermediate goods and services; this demand may be satisfied by the parent company or by other companies. Complex manufacturing operations like car producers, for example, often act as magnets that pull their domestic suppliers abroad. Even in this simple case, therefore, FDI both replaces and creates trade and changes its composition.

The advent of globalisation encourages and seeks to maximise gains from the integration of international production systems and value chains across borders. This change resulted from the continuing liberalisation of trade and trade-related activity through the GATT-WTO framework, regional liberalisation measures such as the SEM, and the unilateral freeing up of FDI rules throughout the world. This process has also been driven along by technological developments, especially in the realm of ICTs that have enabled firms to process more information at drastically reduced costs and given them greater ability to manage complex organisational structures, including extended and dispersed production and value chains.

The upshot of these changes is that access to foreign markets and factors of production have improved tremendously, creating more choices about how to serve those markets and organise production. As barriers have fallen, the markets themselves have also grown, resulting in both greater opportunities and greater competitive pressures, requiring firms to constantly assess their strategies to keep ahead of their competitors. In short, the traditional rationale for FDI (the need to gain access to specific markets) has declined, whereas factors such as cost differences between locations, the quality of infrastructure and the labour force, and the ease of conducting business across borders have increased in importance. This results in integrated international production and distribution systems on a global scale and greater intra-firm trade.

Figures on the growth of intra-firm trade are not easy to obtain, but those that do exist confirm the increasing complexity of corporate integration in this changed international environment and the intensification of cross-border links. UNCTAD has estimated that about one-third of world trade has been internalised within MNE systems and that a further one-third involves exports of MNEs outside their own corporate networks.

The distinction between traditional multi-domestic FDI and the more complex, integrated efficiency-seeking variety can be blurred, as the example of the EU shows. When the SEM was first mooted in the mid-1980s, Europe's trading partners were concerned about the potential for a 'fortress Europe' in which internal integration was combined with higher barriers to the rest of the world. Therefore, US, Japanese, and other Asian companies with eyes on the large and lucrative European market increased their FDI in Europe so that they would be firmly established there once the barriers went up. Fortress Europe never happened. Indeed, the SEM increased the access of foreign companies to the European market, and the foreign investors quickly appreciated that the SEM offered them opportunities to take advantage of scale economies and to specialise within the framework of a regional strategy. In other words, the initial defensive FDI to Europe was not wasted as firms sought to exploit their comparative advantage within the European market and embarked upon cross-border production within Europe to take advantage of new opportunities.

The implications of the intensification of networks within firms are far-reaching. According to traditional economic and trade theory, resource allocation, the core of economics, is undertaken by the market or the state. This function appears to be increasingly taking place within corporate systems, thereby becoming less transparent and more difficult to regulate, and supports the writings of transaction cost and internalisation theorists. The increased intensity of cross-border linkages discussed above not only reflects a difference in the number of links but also represents a different and more complex relationship between a parent company and its foreign affiliates.

## Sensitivity

Interdependence and connectivity lie at the heart of globalisation, with the result that the effects of economic trends and developments in one part of the global system transmit themselves more rapidly and completely to other parts of the system. This has both positive and negative effects. Reduced barriers between nations have the potential to facilitate trade and investment, thereby boosting positive effects on growth and employment, intensifying competition, and encouraging greater efficiency. Indeed, the more integrated the system, the more rapid and complete this transmission will be.

However, negative as well as positive factors are spread more readily in a more interconnected world, giving rise to greater volatility and uncertainty at certain times and providing ammunition to those urging a retreat from globalisation. The main consideration regarding this volatility is whether the positives outweigh the undoubted negatives arising from this greater sensitivity to distant events. As later chapters on emerging and developing economies (see Chapters 7 and 8) show, those countries which have engaged more with the rest of the world have fared much better in the long term than those that have not.

The transmission of effects throughout the world economic system is not new, as there has always been a degree of interconnectedness in the world economy. The globalisation argument is that the greater interconnectedness of recent years results in a greater sensitivity to what happens elsewhere. For example, in both 1973 and 1980, the oil price shock, which occurred before the emergence of the concept of globalisation, stimulated world-wide inflation and the onset of international recession. However, deregulation, greater market access, and assistance from ICTs have subsequently extended the range of channels and items that can be the source of almost instant transmission of changes in fortune. In 2000, for example, after a period of intense hype in world stock markets about the vast profits to be made from technology stocks, particularly the so-called 'dot com' companies, the bubble burst and the value of technology shares plummeted on the world's markets. The early 21st century economic crisis in Argentina, coupled with devaluations in Brazil, its major trading partner, also precipitated a banking and economic crisis in neighbouring Uruguay. Financial crises are the most obvious manifestation of contagion, examples of which follow.

1. The 1992 and 1993 crises in the Exchange Rate Mechanism (ERM): as a result of intolerable strains with the European Monetary System (EMS), the pound sterling and the Italian lira left the EMS, and the bands around which member currencies were allowed to fluctuate were extended from ± 2.25 per cent to ± 15 per cent.

2. The 1994 'tequila' crisis: Mexico devalued the peso against the dollar by 14 per cent. Panic selling of pesos resulted in the floating of the currency and speculative attacks against other Latin American currencies, especially those of Argentina, Brazil, Peru, and Venezuela. Brief speculative attacks also occurred against the currencies of Thailand, Hong Kong, the Philippines, and Hungary.

3. The 1997 Asian crisis: this crisis began in Thailand following concerns about foreign debt, a trade deficit, and a weak banking system. It began with a sudden movement away from the domestic currency to the US dollar. These concerns spread quickly to other East Asian countries and also infected economies in Latin America and eastern Europe.

4. The 2008 credit crunch: problems in the US sub-prime mortgage market rapidly spread throughout the financial system in the US and Europe, bringing down some well-known financial institutions. This financial crisis rapidly became a more general economic crisis with ramifications on growth throughout the world, albeit to varying degrees.

The sensitivity of markets to events outside national boundaries in an interdependent world is not confined to the financial sector. Case study 1.1 demonstrates how the perfectly rational response to globalisation in the form of integrated supply chains and production networks brings with it not only benefits in terms of cost savings and enhanced competitiveness but also the potential for lost production and revenue when events conspire to create a break in that supply chain.

## CASE STUDY 1.1: THE US INFLATION REDUCTION ACT: AN EMERGING US-EU TRADE DISPUTE?

In August 2022, the US Senate approved President Biden's Inflation Reduction Act (IRA), whose focal aim is the rejuvenation of US manufacturing through the prioritisation of green technology. This is what the US government seeks to achieve via the offering of substantial subsidies (at least $370 billion over a decade, though, in practice, it is expected to be much more). These direct subsidies (via tax credits to manufacturers of green technology) are also supported via a series of tax incentives offered to US consumers to buy US-made green technology goods, as well as procurement rules that favour US producers. These are embedded with local content rules, which mean that to be eligible for such support, a minimum share of any product has to be manufactured in the US. The motives for the targeting of green technology are not simply to push back against climate change and stimulate US manufacturing; it is also a desire to challenge the lead that China has been able to establish in the manufacture of these technologies. In total, it is expected that the IRA will stimulate somewhere in the region of $1.2 trillion in investment.

The sheer size of these subsidies is likely to have disruptive effects upon the global trading system. Such subsidies and other levels of support are clearly highly discriminatory in favour of US business and FDI and are of such a size that many of the US' rivals in the development of green technology are complaining with regard to the unlevelling of the global playing field in these technologies. For the US, these subsidies are merely a countermeasure to the level of subsidies offered by the Chinese government to its own manufacturers. It is expected that the US IRA will divert investment flows from other states into the US to take advantage of these levels of support, which few other states can match. The ultimate risk of the IRA is that it could stimulate a trade war, further erode the agreed rules for state support within the WTO agreements, and create a 'race to the bottom for state subsidies'.

The EU has been especially vocal, arguing that the IRA is a direct contravention of WTO rules on subsidies. There is the possibility that Europe could respond to the IRA by seeking to take the US to the WTO. However, this takes time and tends to have limited effect. For example, the US-EU dispute over aircraft subsidies took over 17 years to solve, and even then, there was no clear winner. Moreover, there is increased concern as to whether the WTO has the capacity to deal with such a large case anymore. In addition, there is the risk that should the EU win the case at the WTO, it risks a trade war with the US – something that neither wants but which their economic rivals would relish. The EU could also respond with its own subsidies – something the USA is comfortable with – but the capacity to offer such support is very asymmetric across the EU (as this is a state-based capability), and this would pose a direct threat to the integrity of the Single Market. Moreover, much of the IRA's support occurs through the tax system – something that is also a state-based competence. Alternatively, this could be done by the EU, as it did with the recovery funds allocated to promote the recovery from COVID-19. However, there is a large gap between states as to the desire to engage with such fiscal stimulation. For many liberals, the best way to match the US is through economic reform and deregulation, not more money.

**QUESTIONS**

1) How do you believe the EU should respond to the stimulus provided by the IRA?
2) Does the IRA underline the obsolescence of the WTO?

## WHAT DOES GLOBALISATION MEAN FOR BUSINESS?

Globalisation and its associated drivers shape the environment in which business operates. The speed of change within this environment and the greater intensity of competition resulting from lower barriers to cross-border transactions and greater interdependence between countries and markets require firms to constantly monitor their external environment and adjust accordingly.

In broad terms, it is useful to distinguish between two forms of globalisation in the business context: globalisation of production and globalisation of markets. Globalisation of production involves decisions about where production is most efficiently carried out. Lower barriers to trade and investment mean that production locations that may not previously have been considered may become feasible, enabling firms to take advantage of particular locational advantages, whether it be land, labour, resources, or something else. Globalisation of production may take the form of concentration of production in one location, enabling firms to benefit from scale economies, or it may result in extended value chains across several borders, with each production stage occurring in the most competitive location. Offshoring and outsourcing are examples of the latter phenomenon, which is also partially responsible for the growth of intra-firm trade discussed above. Globalisation of markets involves a decision about where to sell products. This requires an analysis of whether standards and tastes have converged sufficiently to enable the same product to be sold in several markets or even globally (rare), and whether one or several marketing strategies need to be developed.

Many factors need to be taken into account by firms (see Figure 1.2) when assessing how to respond to the external environment. In broad terms, globalisation lowers trade and cross-border investment barriers, which in turn intensifies competition in both domestic and foreign markets, with clear implications for prices, costs, innovation, and efficiency. Globalisation reduces the fragmentation of markets and encourages the emergence of a global, or at least multinational, perspective on products and markets.

There is no definitive response in an increasingly connected world to the complex interplay of forces facing firms, which vary across industries, regions, and time and are open to differing interpretations. Pure globalists would argue that the globalisation drivers encourage the growth of the truly stateless enterprise that plans according to the dictates of the market and considers national borders an increasing irrelevance.

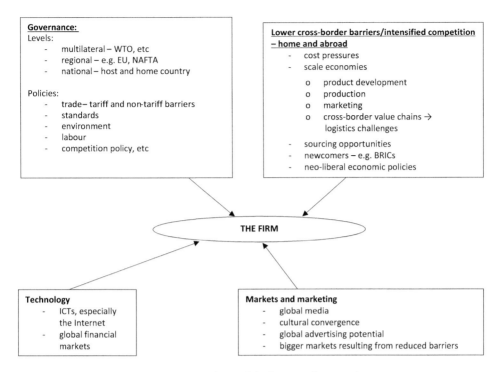

**Governance:**
Levels:
- multilateral – WTO, etc
- regional – e.g. EU, NAFTA
- national – host and home country

Policies:
- trade – tariff and non-tariff barriers
- standards
- environment
- labour
- competition policy, etc

**Lower cross-border barriers/intensified competition – home and abroad**
- cost pressures
- scale economies
  - o product development
  - o production
  - o marketing
  - o cross-border value chains →
    logistics challenges
- sourcing opportunities
- newcomers – e.g. BRICs
- neo-liberal economic policies

**THE FIRM**

**Technology**
- ICTs, especially the Internet
- global financial markets

**Markets and marketing**
- global media
- cultural convergence
- global advertising potential
- bigger markets resulting from reduced barriers

**FIGURE 1.2** Pressures and opportunities from globalisation shaping the operating environment of the firm

Characteristics of such strategies include a global conception of markets and a striving for critical mass as both a defensive and offensive response to intensified competition in domestic and foreign markets with all the associated pressures on prices, costs, efficiency, and the need to innovate. Such developments, so the argument goes, will ultimately spill over into the transfer of dominant cultures, facilitating the emergence of global products. In this world, market forces come to dominate not only economic but also political life as national governments find it increasingly difficult to exercise any real control over what happens within their borders. Others acknowledge increased interdependence and the accompanying intensification of competition but argue that nation states and markets retain their importance, albeit perhaps in a slightly different way. They may argue for a consolidation of operations within a region but continue to see significant differentiation with other regions.

## THE FUTURE?

It is easy to be carried away by the rhetoric of globalisation. Undoubtedly, there has been a big increase in economic integration and interdependence in recent decades. However, are there trends underway which could undermine this interdependence in the long run?

While the technological progress that has underpinned globalisation continues, difficulties within institutions that have hitherto supported greater international integration and signs of economic nationalism in key countries give cause to wonder whether globalisation is slowing or even coming to an end. The Doha Round of multilateral trade talks under the auspices of the WTO has floundered (see Chapter 4) as divisions between members appear to be hardening at the expense of the multilateral system. One consequence has been a rapid rise in the number of bilateral and regional trade agreements (see Chapter 5), although the renegotiation of NAFTA and the UK's decision to leave the European Union casts doubts over the future of regionalism. A movement away from collaboration with other countries has the potential to be exclusive and discriminatory, resulting in new trade and investment barriers. The development of the EU, a regional organisation, in any case, had stalled as a result of its preoccupation with constitutional affairs.

As economic conditions became tougher following the 2008 crisis, protectionist sentiment and economic nationalism became more common. Concerns about the impact of Chinese exports and a massive US trade deficit, along with security fears, culminated in the election of Donald Trump as US President, elected on the basis of 'America First', an early, but by no means isolated, manifestation of which was the imposition of 25 per cent tariffs on steel and aluminium imports, which quickly resulted in retaliatory measures from US trading partners and could spill over into an all-out trade war.

Geopolitical factors also potentially serve to fragment the world once more. The destruction of the World Trade Centre in New York in 2001 sowed division across the world, and the civil war in Syria has resulted in a proxy war between Western nations and Russia and its allies along the lines of the Cold War. The assertive nationalism of Russia, which culminated in the 2014 annexation of Crimea and the 2022 Ukraine conflict, has contributed to this tension. Meanwhile, China's growing economic power is reflected in its increasing world role and the possibility that its version of capitalism (that is, state capitalism or economic freedom accompanied by strong state control) will become the dominant model of development.

The above economic and political factors, plus the greater heterogeneity resulting from the assertion of their place in the world by the emerging economies (as demonstrated by their leading role in the WTO talks) and conflicts over the movement of people, all potentially serve to increase conflict and increase the tension and distance between nations. Harvest of the benign impacts of globalisation all depend upon a consensus around its benefits and a recognition of a core, at least, of common interests from the opening of world markets and borders. The above factors do not necessarily mark an end to globalisation as we know it, but they do endanger it or, at the very least, will require some adjustments to the business environment.

## CASE STUDY 1.2: THE 2011 FLOODS IN THAILAND AND THE IMPACT ON GLOBAL SUPPLY CHAINS.

Globalisation has two faces. It provides opportunities for the development of global production networks through clustering and agglomeration effects, which offer economies of scale and cost efficiencies. These opportunities arise from reduced barriers to international commerce resulting from regulation and transport and communication innovations. Multinational enterprises have taken advantage of these trends by outsourcing tasks which were previously carried out at greater cost in-house and by trading in parts and components. These parts can either be supplied by overseas factories of the MNE itself or by purchasing from other firms located overseas. Such developments have been particularly pronounced in Asia, where the more relatively advanced economies of Japan, South Korea, Taiwan, and Singapore experienced a weakening of their competitiveness, in part from rising labour costs, and transferred some stages of their supply chains to cheaper locations elsewhere in the region. Accompanying this trend was a reliance on just-in-time management and a tendency to concentrate on fewer, or even single, suppliers, which necessitates efficient infrastructure and reliability of suppliers and contractors.

Thailand was a major beneficiary of this system. However, Thai companies and overseas investors in Thailand have also experienced the possible negative impacts of such interdependence. In 2011, following months of unprecedented rain, Thailand experienced devasting floods across 65 of its 77 provinces, resulting in the loss of over 800 lives, thousands made homeless, and an economic cost estimated at over $45 billion by the World Bank.

Many industrial facilities were flooded, and production was halted for varying periods of time. Particularly affected were the automotive and high technology sectors, such as communications equipment, electrical machinery, and office and computing equipment. Given the aforementioned reliance on lean global supply chains and just-in-time manufacturing, the impact of the floods was felt outside Thailand. Honda, for example, suffered from an immediate shortage of parts and components following the flood-induced shutdown of its plant in Ayutthaya, resulting in temporary production cuts in its facilities around the world. Indeed, all of Japan's major vehicle manufacturers, already suffering from the aftermath of the Fukushima earthquake and tsunami earlier in 2011, suffered production losses as a result of the floods in Thailand. Indeed, Toyota, Nissan, and Honda's car production experienced collective losses of over 400,000 units. This experience encouraged a reconsideration of the industry's strategy of relying on limited, or even single, suppliers in favour of a wider range of suppliers and the holding of bigger inventories.

Those sectors with a significant involvement in production networks exhibit both a relatively high presence of MNEs and a high export intensity. This has been particularly marked in the electronics industry in Thailand, which has become the world's primary force for hard disc production, accounting for almost 43 per cent of the world's hard drives. The Thai floods had a major impact on Western Digital (the producer of one-third of the world's hard discs), Seagate, Samsung, and Toshiba, among others. The impact arose from both the direct loss of production by these MNEs and from the disruption of deliveries from their main suppliers, many of whom were also concentrated in the flood-affected regions. Restoration of production occurred in stages and largely returned to previous levels within 4-5 months. In the meantime, the shortage of hard discs affected PC manufacturers, especially those with limited stocks of hard discs, resulting in higher prices for hard disc drives, thereby helping the manufacturers offset some of the costs of recovery from the floods.

In short, although most companies were able to return to previous production levels within a relatively short space of time following the 2011 Thai floods, from a business perspective, there were significant costs in terms of lost production and jobs and disruption way beyond the flood-affected areas. These costs were accentuated by the emergence of lean supply chains and the reliance on just-in-time production, which has played a major part in Thailand's development. Disruptions arising from natural and other events are far from unknown, although the episode in Thailand was particularly damaging and highlighted the need for companies to develop strategies to minimise the risks of global supply chains and production networks. Suggested actions have included the holding of larger inventories, employing a larger number of suppliers, and a reduced emphasis on agglomeration and clustering. Adoption of such measures would represent a shift away from a just-in-time to a just-in-case strategy and would imply that firms do not necessarily attempt to maximise their cost and efficiency gains from vertical specialisation and economies of scale. However, it does not imply a rejection of international production networks but rather a focus on better management of the associated risks.

## QUESTIONS

1. Consider the potential benefits and vulnerabilities of global supply chains.
2. What does the example of the 2011 floods in Thailand reveal about the risks of the greater interdependence generated by globalisation?
3. What can be done to reduce the risks to international business arising from natural disasters and other disruptions?
4. Identify other examples of events in which the ramifications have spread across borders.

## KEY POINTS

- There is a general consensus that international economies and markets have become more interdependent, with fundamental implications for global governance and corporate behaviour. However, controversy reigns about the precise nature of these implications.
- The growth of neo-liberalism and global governance, financial and capital market liberalisation, the diffusion of ICTs, and a degree of social and cultural convergence have underpinned the move to greater international economic interdependence and globalisation.

- The largest multinationals are significant economic entities in their own right, similar in size to medium-sized economies.
- The developing country's share of world trade in goods and services and of investment has increased in recent years, but much of this is down to the performance of China.
- FDI growth has changed the nature of interdependence, resulting in complex, cross-border networks that allocate resources. This has contributed to high levels of intra-firm and intra-industry trade.
- Globalisation and greater integration of markets result in the rapid transmission of the impact of events, both good and bad, from one country to another.
- Globalisation helps shape the business environment, resulting in greater risks and new opportunities.
- Two decades into the 21st century, there is growing speculation that globalisation may have peaked.

## DISCUSSION QUESTIONS

1. It is often argued that globalisation undermines the role of the nation state. Do you agree, and if this assertion is true, what are its implications?

2. Taking into account indicators of scope, intensity, and sensitivity (and any other evidence you deem relevant), assess the extent to which we live in a globalised world.

3. 'Globalisation is a fact of life. But I believe we have underestimated its fragility.' – Kofi Annan, former UN General Secretary. Explain this statement and identify and assess factors that could support it.

4. 'It has been said that arguing against globalisation is like arguing against the laws of gravity.' – Kofi Annan, former UN General Secretary. Explain and assess this statement.

5. Identify and assess how globalisation influences the competitive environment of international business. How have these influences changed business behaviour?

6. 'Globalisation will make our societies more creative and prosperous, but also more vulnerable' – Lord Robertson (British politician). Explain and assess this statement.

7. 'Economic globalisation has brought prosperity and development to many countries, but also financial crises … and increasing poverty and marginalisation' – Anna Lindh, former Swedish Foreign Minister.

8. Explain the thinking behind the above statement and the extent to which the statement is justified.

9. Is the world turning away from globalisation? Consider the evidence on both sides of the argument.

## ACTIVITIES

1. Research an anti-globalisation group and critically assess its arguments.
2. Choose two or three of the largest multinational enterprises and determine whether they are truly global in scope and strategy or have a more regional dimension to their activities.
3. 'Globalisation is good'. Hold a whole-class debate on this topic. It is likely to be a heated and not necessarily conclusive occasion.
4. There is speculation that globalisation is running out of steam. Identify and scrutinise arguments in support of this view and consider whether they do indeed undermine the globalisation process.

## SUGGESTED FURTHER READINGS

The literature on globalisation is vast and growing. The following books and articles give a representative flavour of what is available.

Bhagwati, J. (2007). *In defence of globalization: A new afterword*, Oxford: Oxford University Press.
Dicken, P. (2014). *Global shift*, 7th ed, London: Sage Publishing.
Eriksen, T. (2014). *Globalization: The key concepts*, 2nd ed, London: Bloomsbury.
Ferguson, Y., & Mansbach, R. (2008). *Globalization: The return of borders to a borderless world*, Abingdon, Oxon: Routledge.
Friedman, T. (2005). *The world is flat: A brief history of the globalized world in the 21st century*, London: Penguin.
Hart, J., & Prakash, A. (Eds.). (2018). *Coping with globalisation*, London: Routledge, pbk edn.
Held, D., Barnett, A., & Henderson, C. (Eds.). (2005). *Debating globalization*, Cambridge: Polity.
Hirst, P., Thompson, G., & Bromley, S. (2009). *Globalisation in question*, 3rd ed, Cambridge: Polity Press.
Hirst, P., Thompson, G., & Bromley, S. (2015). *Globalization in question*. Chichester: John Wiley & Sons.
IMF. (2023) IMF data. https://www.imf.org/en/Data
Kelly, P. F. (1999). The geographies and politics of globalization. *Progress in Human Geography, 23*(3), 379–400.
Keohane, R. O., & Nye, J. S. (1999). Governance in a globalizing world. In *Power and governance in a partially globalized world* (pp. 193–218). Routledge.
King, S. (2017). *Grave new world: The end of globalization, the return of history*, New Haven & London: Yale University Press.
Lechner, F., & Boli, J. (Eds.). (2014). *The globalization reader*, 5th ed, Chichester: Wiley.
Prakash, A., & Hart, J. A. (Eds.). (2000). *Coping with globalization*. London: Routledge.

Scholte, J. (2005). *Globalization: A critical introduction,* 2nd ed, Basingstoke: Palgrave.

Steger, M. (2017). *Globalization: A very short introduction,* Oxford: Oxford University Press.

Stiglitz, J. (2006). *Making globalization work,* New York: W.W. Norton and Co.

Stiglitz, J. (2017). *Globalization and its discontents revisited: Anti-globalization in the age of Trump,* London: Penguin.

UNCTAD. (2023). UNCTADStat. https://unctadstat.unctad.org/EN/

# CHAPTER 2

# INTERNATIONAL CORPORATE STRATEGY IN GLOBAL MARKETS

## OBJECTIVES

This chapter will help you to:

- Understand the key dimensions of business models.
- Comprehend how the global process alters the process of value creation/destruction.
- Identify the major dimensions of international strategy.
- Comprehend the core internal and external drivers underpinning international strategy.

The shift from a purely domestic focus to one with a higher degree of internationalisation poses many challenges for firms. These arise from two sources. First, the firm can be a passive recipient of such changes. For firms of all sizes and across all industries, it is increasingly difficult to remain isolated from the impact of globalisation on their business environment. Secondly, the firm can be active in seeking out international markets. The latter is very much the focus of this book and is based on the recognition that international strategy is different from purely domestic actions. The move towards a more spatially diverse business configuration increases the complexity of operations and exposes the firm to a new set of challenges. The aim of this chapter is to set the context for the rest of this volume by outlining the core tenets of international strategy. While the main focus is on market-based strategies, the chapter begins with an examination of globality within enterprise business models as a means of understanding the motivations for such strategies and concludes with a consideration of non-market actions, which operate as a flanking function in developing international actions.

## GLOBALITY AND THE BUSINESS MODEL

When understood at the international level, globality is conventionally understood as the end state of the process of globalisation. However, understanding that globalisation

DOI: 10.4324/9781315184500-3

is a dynamic process of change that ebbs and flows over time (from Chapter 1) suggests that globality as a meta-level phenomenon is likely to be elusive. When addressed at the corporate level, globality refers to a state where the firm's ability to create value rests upon its participation in global/international product/factor markets. When viewed in this context, it is useful to view the impact of globality upon the corporate entity through the lens of the business model.

The business model is a simple explanation of how a business works (Mahgretta 2002), how it becomes financially sustainable, and how it creates value. In its simplest form, it reflects the interaction and interdependence between the operational and the marketing side of a business to create a credible value proposition that seeks to enable the commercial sustainability of the entity.

The implicit themes of globality within the business model are that these questions are driven, at least in part, by the firm's passive or proactive engagement with the global system. That is, it adapts to global conditions by altering operations, its value proposition, or marketing actions, or otherwise goes and seeks sourcing and/or marketing opportunities overseas. As firms are embedded within the global economic system, they are subject either directly (through their activities) or indirectly (through the operation of global markets) to such adaptive tensions.

While there are a multitude of definitions for business models (notably in terms of their components), most business models can be simplified to three basic components, namely:

- The concept of the business with regard to those opportunities and strategies that underpin its existence.
- Business capabilities with regard to the resources to enable the execution of operations and strategies.
- The value proposition, which defines how the business seeks to offer benefits to all relevant stakeholders.

Expressed in these terms, globality (as a proactive measure) occurs within business models because firms perceive that there is value in doing so. This value is not simply value for shareholders through lowering costs or increasing revenues (i.e., simple financial sustainability), but value can also be shaped by broader stakeholder issues in the process (such as local communities).

In terms of operations and sourcing, globality implies (as suggested in Table 2.1) that new opportunities open up for either better quality and/or cheaper inputs via the operation of transnational production networks. This often means that the global business model not only has to operate across multiple territories but also has to deal with multiple firms within them. The resultant complexity for the business in its operations can also create new risks for the business, as these processes can lead to a degree of opaqueness within the firm's extended commercial system. It is evident that with the opening of low-cost manufacturing in the Far East, the opportunities for extended supply chains have opened up, but this has also meant businesses have faced new risks, as underscored by Apple's experience with Foxconn (see Box case study 2.1). The trend towards extending (spatially) supply chains has been a core trend in business as they seek to reconfigure

**TABLE 2.1** Corporate value and the global economy

| Global value creation | Global value destruction |
|---|---|
| • Novel value propositions | • Oveextended value networks |
| • Capture value from new locations | • Supply chain risk driven by complexity |
| • Generate extra revenue from new market opportunities | • Economic risk |
| • Cost efficiencies from new sourcing | • Political risk |
| • Reach new customers | • Logistical disruption |
| • Re-monetise existing resources and competencies | |
| • Expanded innovation | |

business models to aid sustainability without placing unnecessary risks upon the system. It also underlines how sensitive (despite its internal focus) the business model is to changes in the external operating environment.

On the marketing side, firms configuring across markets will understand that demand can differ markedly across spaces. This is arguably one of the biggest sources of turbulence across space, as the value attached by customers to products can vary widely due to cultural, technological, economic, and even political factors. Such sources of turbulence can be structural and/or cyclical. It can also mean, as explored below, that value propositions may have to vary across geographic markets. Business models need to reflect this demand heterogeneity in the production networks to ensure inventories are not excessive and that what is produced is demanded.

Globality within business models is expressed through a number of criteria to the extent that the global forces can proactively or reactively shaped business value creation process through:

- Adapting value propositions to multi-market operations.
- Adapting to multi-territoriality public policy considerations.
- Shaping and reconfiguring enteral partners/value networks to underpin value proposition.
- Allowing access to resources and/or markets.
- Opening up innovation processes to multi-national processes of knowledge creation.
- Adapting marketing processes to maximise resource transfer.

As stressed within the initial chapter, and as indicated by works such as Goldin and Mariathasan (2014), the maturity of globalisation is such that all firms can be considered to be embedded within a global system. As such, all business models are, at the very least, going to be passive recipients of global forces. The firms with a general pacificity towards globality will be those that may have a solely domestic focus but will be impacted by a number of processes, such as how global markets determine the processing of core inputs (like raw materials). There is also the issue that the complexity of global supply chains may also render purely domestic firms vulnerable, despite their lack of explicit strategy to engage in such activities. It suggests that second-tier suppliers or customers that lie overseas can have a direct bearing on the value-creating capabilities of the firm.

This leads us to offer the notion that four main types of business models can be identified. This list is by no means definitive nor exhaustive but offers a set categorisation.

1) *The passive internationaliser*: this is a firm with an overwhelmingly nationally focused model but has to adapt elements of the model due to changes in its external environment. This could be the result of shifting global market processes, new supply chain knowledge, innovation, or changes in customer actions. In short, this firm has a model that is more global by default than by design, and as a means of enabling long-term financial sustainability, the firm taps into global processes and change.

2) *The micro-national*: these are small or medium-sized firms (discussed in more depth in Chapter 11) that proactively seek international opportunities. This is either by means of generating extra sales and/or from sourcing efficiencies. These are frequently niche businesses that will seek to occupy niches across multiple territories, especially where home-based niches are mature or of limited size. Importantly, these firms are rapid internationalisers whose existence breaks the convention that the intensity of internationalisation is correlated directly with scale.

3) *The meta-national:* this is a type of multi-national business that seeks to configure its business model to tap into global networks of innovation. Instead of following the convention of building a business model based solely on the 'internationalisation' of home country advantages, it seeks to operate global scale, tapping into the fact that relevant knowledge is globally dispersed and contextually embedded, and using this to add value through its concentration.

4) *The multi-national*: these are businesses that build a business model upon owning assets and operating the production of goods and services across more than one state in addition to those in their home state, this will be discussed in more detail in Chapter 10. This implies complex value chains and differential marketing strategies, as well as geographically cognate value propositions (see below).

## CASE STUDY 2.1: SWISS CHOCOLATE

For many, chocolate and Switzerland are synonymous. The rise of Swiss chocolatiers to global prominence was due to a mix of perceived quality of products and ceaseless innovation. Chocolate initially reached Switzerland in the 18th century, largely as a spillover from trade in the commodity in Northern Italy. However, by the 20th century, the aforementioned innovation and quality had rendered Switzerland the leading chocolate-producing nation. The early Swiss pioneers created the basis for industrial-scale manufacture of chocolate while allowing for substantial product innovation, with up to 16 different sorts of chocolate being developed by the mid-19th century based on varying types of ingredients. In this period, a cluster of chocolate manufacturers grew in the canton of Vaud (in the west of the country) and had 32 manual chocolate-making businesses by the mid-1830s. As tourism to Switzerland rose through the mid-19th century, the reputation of Swiss chocolate spread throughout the rest of Europe. This was largely aided by the innovation of milk (rising from the surplus milk generated by its cows) and nut chocolate and of conching (a mixing technique that improved flavour) by these Swiss producers. The innovation of milk chocolate was especially important in allowing the major Swiss chocolate firms (such as Nestlé, Suchard, and Lindt) to emerge and develop a global presence. In the 1840s, chocolate production spread to other German-speaking cantons. From this area, the firm Lindt emerged based on innovative techniques that allowed for the rise of self-melting chocolate. Also emerging from this area was Tobler, which produced the most famous of all Swiss chocolate, the Toblerone.

In practice, the heyday of Swiss chocolate was between 1890 and 1920, as its international reputation grew rapidly due to a mix of tourism and the adoption of the region by Europe's aristocracy of Switzerland as a favoured destination. This latter group was seen as an especially important ambassador for the international expansion of Swiss chocolate. For example, Lindt aimed its marketing at elite girls finishing schools in western Switzerland, where Europe's elite educated their daughters. This propelled very high growth rates as the number of Swiss chocolate manufacturers rose from 13 to 23 between 1888 and 1910. Moreover, the number of people employed in the industry rose tenfold, and production rose from 13 to 40,000 tonnes (two-thirds of which were exported). By 1918, Switzerland had 55 per cent of the global market and was, to all intents and purposes, a chocolate superpower. While these figures fell away with the downturn of the 1920s and 1930s, the post-World War II era saw its position recover, with sales recovering to 26,000 tonnes by the 1950s compared to 160,000 tonnes in the early 21st century. Throughout the latter half of the 20th century, international competition forced the Swiss chocolate industry to streamline but still keep strong to its traditions. This adherence to traditions remains a core source of competition differential for Swiss chocolate manufacturers.

By the beginning of the 21st century, the industry was facing further challenges due to a mix of factors, namely:

- Customer preferences away from sugary foods towards more health-conscious products.
- Steeper rises in the price of cocoa beans.
- Competition on the high street, eroding margins.
- Low rates of economic growth.
- Customer trend towards small, local 'craft' manufacturers.

This shift in tastes is especially problematic as the 'war on sugar' (notably in the US, UK, and other advanced economies) takes effect and as businesses need to rethink their business models. Moreover, other potentially mass markets (such as China) are not exhibiting the growth to take up the resultant slack. The effect upon Swiss manufacturers was to reposition them at the premium end of the market and away from the mass market. These trends are fairly ubiquitous across the sector, raising questions as to whether this core aspect of Swiss branding has a long-term future. There is a close link between the sector and the chocolate sector. This importance is reflected in the subsidies offered to local input producers under the so-called 'Chocolate Law', which offers agricultural subsidies to enable Swiss producers to compete against imports. However, under pressure from the WTO, these are being phased out.

The focus on quality seems to be working for high-end manufacturers like Lindt (a major niche provider), which positions its products as indulgences rather than products for regular consumption. There is also a trend towards dark chocolate, which has a lower sugar content. Despite this repositioning, competition remains intense, especially within the US, where there are large businesses with strong brands which are working towards introducing more specialised niche chocolates. Nestlé (the other major Swiss chocolate company) has sought to sustain its position in the mass market and has suffered accordingly. However, it has attempted to solve this problem by expanding its brands, especially those with a strong local identity, and by seeking to segment core brands with premium variations. A final problem for the big companies is that the rise of 'craft' chocolatiers has also nibbled away at the market shares of both Nestlé and Lindt. The response by the major firms is to expand their retail presence.

## QUESTIONS

1. To what extent does the obesity epidemic pose a challenge for operators?
2. How should they respond to this challenge?

## THE GLOBAL BUSINESS MODEL AND INTERNATIONAL STRATEGY

In some parts of the literature (notably, Porter 2008), there is a tendency to use the terms 'business model' and 'strategy' interchangeably. In truth, they are distinct. The business model is how the firm seeks to create value in the marketplace. In this context, strategy (though part of the value constellation of the business model) is about how the firm seeks to position itself to maximise its longer-term sustainability. As such, the business model describes how the firm adds value, whereas strategy seeks to identify how the value-creating capability and consequent firm sustainability will evolve through its market positioning. As the firm seeks to define its position, it may redefine its business model, or it may choose its position according to where it perceives it adds the greatest value. The link between the two defines the state of the business model alongside the evolution of the long-term strategy. In short, the business model and strategy must be contiguous.

In terms of international strategy and the business model, the theme is how the firm, by shifting into new markets or reconfiguring its value chain across multiple states, can add value and thereby aid corporate sustainability. Moving into international markets (proactively) suggests either that domestic resource generation may be limited or that new markets offer greater resource generating potential. There is also the question that the shift in the business model towards a greater degree of internationality may be more passive/reactive as the firm – to sustain its value proposition – feels compelled to move into international markets. This may be shaped by a shift in the firm's value network or where new innovations or knowledge led the firm to move overseas to exploit.

The essence of the strategy lies in the sense of creating a sense of a competitive differential – something that has a direct alignment with the centrality of the firm's stated value proposition. In doing so, it defines how all parts of the company fit together to create a competitive differential. This again finds a parallel with the logic of the business model of aligning the operating and customer-facing sides of the business. The difference between the two lies in the temporal dimension, in that the business model is in effect the day-to-day, short-term 'story' of the business and how it seeks to create value and strategy is how that model will seek to evolve over time to secure a chosen position within the competitive landscape. One of the major differences between strategy and the business model is that the former describes competition, whereas the latter does not, as it focuses on operating a commercial system.

As will be stressed below within the integration-responsiveness framework, there is a clear alignment with business model themes on the operational and marketing sides. However, these reflect purely cost pressures and market opportunities with regard to the external environment. In terms of the business model, the international strategy reflects a process whereby the firm begins to shift its business model as its competitive environment changes, where the firm seeks to move into new markets or find new sourcing/operational opportunities as either market changes threaten its value proposition or where that value proposition can be reinforced by these external processes.

## THE FORM AND NATURE OF INTERNATIONAL STRATEGY

Reflecting themes from the business model literature, international strategy emerges as a proactive set of actions based on a firm undertaking and dealing with the consequences of international diversity. This is driven by:

- The globalisation of markets.
- Firms following customers overseas.
- The desire to overcome the limitations of the home market.
- Exploitation of differences between countries and regions based on culture, regulation, and specific economic factors.

International strategies can also be based on the firm exploiting its strategic capabilities (see below), the internationalisation of its value chains, and the enhancement of its knowledge base.

The most evident expression of international strategy is the expansion of the spatial dimension of the firm. This comprises three core elements:

1. The extension of the geographic reach of the business.
2. The increasing penetration of the MNE in current host economies.
3. The integration of the international activities of the firm.

The first element involves extending the geographic boundaries of the firm, thereby giving rise to the need for an international strategy as the firm has to deal with a more diverse spread of competitive conditions than it has encountered previously. This does not merely involve competitive strategy but can also include all aspects of the firm's value chain. As later chapters indicate, there is a thriving academic debate on the form and nature of this geographic spread (see Chapters 9 and 10). The inference is that over time, the firm will gradually extend its geographic reach to as many countries as feasible given commercial constraints (see below).

The second aspect, market penetration, alludes to the tendency towards greater involvement in states where the firm has already entered or established a presence. This could involve an increase in the number of value-adding activities undertaken within a location or an expansion of the number of segments in which the firm is seeking to establish a presence.

The third element of international strategy is based on the integration and coordination of the firm's overseas activities to enhance its competitive position. As later chapters highlight (see Chapter 9), this can occur through exploiting location-bound factors or through ensuring that knowledge generated locally is transferred throughout the rest of the organisation for the mutual benefit of its constituent parts.

Overall, thinking about the development of international business characterises international strategy from three different but overlapping perspectives.

## Standardisation-adaptation

From this perspective, strategies are differentiated according to the degree of standardisation (or adaptation) pursued by the firm. Frequently, the degree of standardisation is based on one or more of the mixes of marketing elements (price, place, product, promotion). Thus, a standardisation strategy is characterised by uniformity across locations of the marketing mix, whereas adaptation reflects a higher degree of adjustment to local conditions. This perspective focuses on the market-offering aspect of international strategy.

## Concentration-dispersion

Linked to Porter's notion of international competition (see Porter 2008), this perspective is concerned with the spatial design of the firm. The core idea is that the firm needs to achieve the optimal spread of activities as a means of achieving competitive advantage. The objective is to achieve synergies across locations and/or exploit local competitive advantages for the benefit of the firm. As a result, strategies are differentiated according to the degree of concentration or dispersion of activities across the global economy. This perspective focuses on the structural/organisational aspects of international strategy.

## Integration-interdependence

This is concerned with the organisation and orchestration of the activities of the firm. The central concern is the extent to which subsidiaries are treated as separate profit centres with a high degree of discretion for local managers. At the other end of the spectrum, there is potential for the centre to regard units as part of a broader, overarching strategic objective. Thus, strategies are differentiated according to the degree to which integration takes place across multiple locations. This perspective focuses on the competitive aspect of international strategy (see below).

These differing perspectives on the form and nature of international strategy have been used as the basis for the categorisation of different strategy types. At the core of the issues underpinning these different categorisations of the form and nature of international strategy is the global-local dilemma, which reflects the degree to which products, processes, and strategies can be standardised across – or need to be adapted to – local markets. Resolving this dilemma has led to the emergence of a common typology of MNE strategy, which is reflected in the integration/responsiveness framework (see Figure 2.1).

The pressure towards global integration highlights the need for – or the desirability of – standardisation of the processes and activities across space, an integrated approach towards strategy, and the concentration of activities to support the objectives of the operation. National responsiveness reflects adaptable marketing strategies as well as the need for sufficient discretion to be given to local managers to achieve these objectives. Thus, the integration-responsiveness framework is entirely consistent with the objectives of the trio of approaches to the international strategy outlined above, which differ across a number of dimensions (see Figure 2.1).

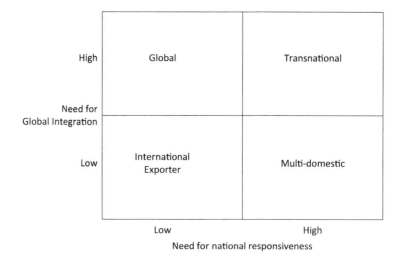

**FIGURE 2.1** Integration-responsiveness framework

## The international exporter

Of all the types of strategy and structure, this is mentioned the least, probably because it represents a minimalist international strategy. Indeed, the company may not even think of itself as an international company, as its structure and configuration may be entirely national. Often, the firm will export opportunistically, while its domestic customers represent its core market. However, this form of business may be purely transitional; it may move to other forms and structures as it matures and as opportunities for overseas sales and production increase (see Chapter 10).

## The global company

The global company produces standardised products and a uniform value proposition across multiple markets. This standardisation is normally extended to other elements of the marketing mix. Ensuring such uniformity means that these companies are also characterised by integrated structures with only limited discretion afforded to local managers. As a result, most decision-making is centralised with strict levels of operational control from the centre. These strategies and structures are common in sectors where economies of scale are available and central to securing competitive positioning. The strategic configuration of the global company is centralised, often upon the home country of the firm.

## The multi-domestic company

This type of structure/strategy formation is characterised by a series of independent subsidiaries within which local managers are given a high degree of discretion over the marketing mix. As a result, strategy is characterised by a high degree of adaptation, with operations being country-centred and value propositions determined locally. As a consequence, there is little coordination between strategic business units (SBUs), as there is little overlap between them due to the idiosyncratic nature of the strategy followed within each locality. As a result, most, if not all, value-adding activities are undertaken within the host economy. This strategy depends on the firm being able to differentiate the product offering sufficiently on a bespoke basis with few opportunities for economies of scale. This differentiation has to be a sufficient source of competitive advantage to overcome the lack of economies of scale in the production process.

## The transnational company

The transnational company adopts a form of structure/strategy based on the firm operating as a loose network of businesses. In this approach, the firm moves beyond the conventional trade-off in terms of integration and responsiveness by being locally responsive while allowing for sufficient coordination between SBUs to realise economies of scale and scope. In short, this represents a hybrid strategy between multi-domestic and global strategies. Thus, by capturing knowledge from all parts of the organisational network, the transnational company can ensure that it benefits from the experience of others, even if value propositions are not uniform. As a result, the transnational must integrate flows of parts, components, finished goods, funds, skills, intelligence, ideas, knowledge, and other scarce resources. These are shared around the company for the benefit of all subsidiaries.

\* \* \*

Much of the literature on international strategy and structure has focused on the extremes of global and multi-domestic strategies. Early advocates of global strategy argued that it would become the dominant form of strategy as globalisation created uniformity across markets (see Levitt 1983) and that localised firms would be vulnerable to firms that competed on a global basis. Such views were based on the assumption that the market was characterised by the globalisation of consumer preferences and that scale economies were available from production processes. Yip (1989) has argued that there are four major benefits from adopting a global strategy:

1. Economies of scale and replication: these apply not merely to products (which have diminished as a source of advantage over time) but also to the ability to replicate knowledge across units.

2. Economies from international production: these efficiencies are created by integrating operations across space to exploit local competitive advantages that feed into efficiencies in the value chain.

3. Economies of learning: due to the integrated nature of the firm, learning and innovation in one market are transferable to another.

4. Competing strategically: the firm can use its scale to compete more effectively in targeted national markets through, for example, cross-subsidisation.

However, pressures still remain for local adaptation, especially as the conditions under which pure globality occurs are rare. Adaptation pressures are created not only by the sustenance of national differences in customer preferences but also by national laws and regulations, location-specific distribution channels, and different levels of economic development.

## CASE STUDY 2.2: APPLE, FOXCONN, AND MANUFACTURING STRATEGY

Foxconn is a leading Taiwanese contract ICT manufacturer with an estimated 1 million employees in China based across nearly 30 locations. One of Foxconn's main customers was Apple in 2011, which used the company for low-value, labour-intensive aspects of the production of its products based mainly in factories in Shenzhen, Chengdu, and Zhengzhou. Foxconn mainly employed unskilled, migrant labour to undertake these tasks based upon the utilisation of very long production lines with very little automation. What automation that does exist tends to be used to compensate for unskilled/inexperienced workers. However, it is rarely used to replace labour per se.

Apple's manufacturing strategy is based on three considerations (in order of importance): flexibility, quality, and cost. For Apple, the attractiveness of Foxconn lay in its flexibility in terms of new products, design changes, and volume produced. This flexibility is something that Foxconn became legendary for within the industry. The modular design of the production system allows for speedy rearrangement of lines (by adjusting staffing, reconfiguring tasks, etc.) to adapt to the changing needs of the client. This reflected that, for Apple, there was no trade-off between scale and quality within the Foxconn production process.

Despite Foxconn and Apple being perceived as partners, the relationship between them is very unequal. Apple's extensive use of sub-contractors belies a belief that value creation within the business lies within corporate leadership, innovation, design, and marketing. Apple uses its power to pressure manufacturers to offer sharp discounts on supplies. This put pressure on Foxconn to lower production costs and seek efficiencies to maintain profitability. In 2009, Foxconn did this by squeezing wages and lowering benefits. These were seen as a direct result of the pressure applied to Foxconn by Apple to lower its component and manufacturing costs. While Apple's profits soared over the period 2009–2012, Foxconn's have declined. Of Apple products, it was estimated that 58.5 per cent of the value of an iPhone (as measured by the retail price) was captured by Apple; only 1.8 per cent was captured by Chinese labour.

However, by 2010, this high-pressure strategy started to affect the workforce. Indeed, workers were unable to take a day off, and the sick were compelled to work. In 2010, pressure groups were drawing attention to the high suicide rates in Foxconn's Chinese factories. In 2010, there were at least 18 attempts, with 14 dying and four surviving. Many of these workers were young (between 17 and 25 years old). Apple's immediate response was to begin to shift work away from these factories due to them being seen as too great a risk to the business and its reputation. It was evident in the investigation that fingers began to point not just at Foxconn but also at Apple for the trading conditions that it set within the partnership. It was felt that Apple's pressure, not just in terms of cost but also through its secretive culture and short delivery cycles (to enable flexibility and create surprise products), was a key factor in the pressure exerted. For example, Apple was very keen on last-minute alterations to its products, which placed pressure on the business to undertake short-notice adaptations of production lines. This competition against time led to increased work schedules and excessive overtime so as to meet sales quotas within a set period. Foxconn's failure to attain this would blow its strategy, so it inevitably applies pressure on workers to offer more hours.

The response of workers to these conditions was to engage in disruptive action, notably in 2012. Recognising that tight production systems between Foxconn locations in China would lead to collective strength, the workers began protesting the conditions. This led to some damage to the factories, and Foxconn used force to put these disruptions down. For Apple, the legacy was increased concerns over delays to the iPhone 5 as these factories were disrupted. Moreover, those phones that were delivered were increasingly seen as being of inferior quality as quality inspections were flagging. Foxconn felt that these quality lapses were caused by a poor attitude, causing further plant disruption.

Eventually, both Foxconn and Apple were on the PR drive, with Terry Gou (Foxconn's founder) apologising, though they did attribute the suicides to personal problems rather than work issues. The result was to improve conditions with wage increases, a workers' hotline, control over overtime, and psychological testing for new workers. However, there are concerns as to the extent to which these measures are empty promises and just PR. Apple defined its partners but eventually placed pressure on them to adapt, as the negative image of its Western customers was extremely negative.

### QUESTION

What do you believe the experience of Apple in this case offers as an exemplar of the problems of global sourcing?

## THE ENVIRONMENTAL CONTEXT OF INTERNATIONAL BUSINESS

An assessment of the operating environment of an international business is core to developing an international strategy. Many of the chapters within this text assess assorted aspects of the political, economic, social, and legal considerations that need to be addressed in the development of international strategy. As chapters on the MNE and internationalisation indicate, the information sensing undertaken by the MNE to add to its knowledge of markets is central to strategy development. Thus, the starting point for the formation of an international strategy is information gathering to improve the firm's knowledge of the international marketplace (this is explored further in Chapter 10).

Turning information gathering into knowledge and a strategy depends upon an assessment of the material gathered. Perhaps the most common framework for analysing such information is Porter's 'Five Forces' framework, which facilitates the assessment of the competitive environment facing the firm in terms of the following forces:

- The bargaining power of buyers: the firm will need to know how powerful customers are within any market, as this will determine the most appropriate strategy to be followed and will even influence whether entry is desirable. In a global marketplace, buyers have increased choice from an increasingly diverse set of suppliers, thereby eroding further any market power of the enterprise.
- Bargaining power of suppliers: the influence of suppliers will be pivotal, as it will influence not merely the operations of the business but also the extent to which the

firm will be able to seek cost advantages from these firms. As suggested above, the power of existing suppliers can be expected to diminish as firms are able to procure from an expanded (and increasingly transparent) supplier base.

- The threat of new entrants: the ability of the targeted segment to attract new entrants is also important, as this will influence the long-term sustainability of the chosen position and influence strategy. This reflects that potential competition can influence market positioning and strategy in recognition that the firms' actions could generate a reach within the niche.
- Threat of substitutes: strategy will clearly be influenced by the ability of users to switch between products. In an increasingly transparent global marketplace, it is supposed that consumers have greater awareness of the alternatives to existing offerings and be able to substitute products to minimise customer sacrifice.
- Rivalry: a central tenet of Porterian analysis is that nothing is better for compet- itiveness than competition itself, though it is evident that entry strategy will be influenced by the intensity of the rivalry within the chosen segment. Again, this stresses that internationalisation will increase the population of firms within any given niche, causing adaptation by incumbents in terms of products, pricing, and promotion.

While the use of the 'Five Forces' is an inexact science, it does highlight the strategic concerns that influence a firm's decision to enter a market and how the firm will try to compete once it is in the market. However, the plethora of concerns that shape the international environment are only indirectly referred to within this framework. For example, political and legal issues often have a direct influence on these forces as they shape the background against which these firms operate. Internationalisation increases the rivalry between firms by:

1. Lowering seller concentration.
2. Increasing the diversity of competition.
3. Increasing excess capacity.
4. Increasing the bargaining power of suppliers.

The above implies that firms need an initial competitive advantage (see Chapter 10) if they are to mitigate these competitive forces when seeking to enter new locations. Generally, competitive advantages are easier to find in less developed markets, where the forces tend to be less intense than in developed states. However, a core weakness of the five forces framework when developing international strategy is that it does not directly address cross-border issues.

## THE INTERNAL CONTEXT OF STRATEGY

The internal environment for the development of international strategy is shaped by two linked considerations. The first concerns the core tangible and intangible resources that are used to carry out the strategic plan, and the second relates to how the international business configures and coordinates the value chain to ensure the effective operation of the firm across borders. To establish a competitive advantage, resources must be scarce and relevant. To sustain a competitive advantage, resources must be characterised by:

- Durability.
- Lack of transferability.
- Lack of replicability.

The simple fact is that physical resources such as capital and finance conform to none of these. As a result, the longer-lived source of competitive advantage is based more on intangible, especially human, resources. Intangible resources such as technology, reputation, and branding can all deliver a competitive advantage and create and sustain a position in the medium to long term. However, each of these is subject to erosion through assorted processes, such as the replication of technology or the erosion of brands. A longer-lasting source of advantage is intangible human resources such as embedded skills and know-how.

Organisational capabilities, based on the ability of a firm to undertake a particular activity, support resources. These may consist of combining the aforementioned resources to create a source of competitive advantage. In order to sustain an advantage, the firm has to possess a distinctive competence that differentiates it from the rest of the marketplace. These core competencies make a disproportionate contribution to customer value and operate as the basis for entering new markets. Like resources, these core capabilities are difficult to imitate and are durable sources of advantage for the business.

Many theories of international business (see Chapters 10 and 11) underline the importance of the internal environment of the firm to yield distinctive resources and competencies that enable it to overcome the difficult problem of the liability of foreignness. For many international businesses, the ability to leverage core resources and key capabilities from one market to another forms the basis of international strategy. Thus, great importance is attached to the ability to replicate key capabilities internally in order to make the firm successful within and across host markets.

It is these resources and capabilities and the ability to apply them across multiple markets that are central to a firm creating a competitive advantage across international markets. In this context, international markets allow firms to earn a greater return from these resources than would be available if they were limited to the domestic market. However, this element of exploitation of existing resources and capabilities is compounded by the increased capability of the firm to access and develop new resources and capabilities through the market entry process.

## Box 2.1: The future of the Airbus A380

The Airbus A380 is the world's largest passenger airline, costing over $25 billion to develop. The A380 is so big that those airports that wished to have it operating from facilities had to upgrade terminals and other infrastructure with the demands placed on such structures by its sheer size. The plane can hold up to 853 passengers in an all-economy class configuration, though in the normal three-class format (i.e., first, business, and economy), the number is 525. In strategic terms, the plane was a move by Airbus to challenge the dominance of Boeing over the large aircraft market. The A380, after making its initial flight in 2005, formally entered service in 2007, with Singapore Airlines making the first commercial flight. As of September 2019, Airbus had delivered 216 aircraft based on an order book of 317. While 19 airlines have ordered A380s, the single largest customer was Emirates – the Dubai-based carrier – which has ordered 142, with 98 having been delivered. Of those that are outstanding, Emirates has deferred 12 due to a lack of space at the Dubai airport and will not take any more before 2019–2020 at the earliest.

However, the A380 has had to face a long history of criticism with regard to its prospects. This is not helped by its seeming dependence on a single major customer – Emirates. The aircraft is built for hub and spoke air routes (based on traffic from a diverse set of locations being concentrated within a hub). However, this model of network design is falling out of favour as point-to-point systems (based on flights between two locations) gain popularity on the back of the rise of low-cost carriers. This erodes the perceived main benefit of the A380, which is the ability to generate a lower cost per passenger. As such, the aircraft was only ever seen as suitable for a few routes which generate high traffic flows (for example, between congested hub airports). However, underlying all of this is the anticipation for what the demand for such large aircraft will be; Boeing sees it as 700 over the next 20 years, while Airbus sees it as double that. The point is that if passengers want frequent hub departures from hubs and more direct links to smaller airports, then the market for mid-sized planes will grow, not for the very large ones. Moreover, many of these smaller aircraft can now fly longer distances. As such, many see the A380 as a niche product.

However, its size rendered it attractive to the Gulf super connectors (Emirates, Etihad, and Qatar Airways) who are seeking to link Europe and Asia via their hubs. The major European carriers have limited demand for such capacity as they will fly them from already busy hubs on a few routes (mainly trans-Atlantic) where departure times are restricted by the need to arrive at a reasonable hour. Emirates has been especially proactive, not merely because of its parent's group hub strategy but also because it may seek to influence the future development of the A380 to align it with its strategy for route expansion.

By 2016, it was becoming evident that the future for the A380 was not as rosy as planned. The first sign was when Singapore Airlines – the first carrier to fly the plane – decided not to renew the lease of five of its nine A380s when their lease expired in 2017. This is compounded by the fact that Air France has opted against buying a further two A380s and that Malaysia Airlines is trying to dispose of its A380s. The fate of the other four was uncertain at the time of writing. This confirms the trend noted above that carriers are losing interest in big planes. In 2014, Boeing did not sell a single jumbo jet, with just 18 being produced in 2016. Airbus itself has decided to cut production of the A380 by 50 per cent to 12 per cent from 2018 (even though the production infrastructure is geared to supply 48 a year). This has not been aided by the fact that its main customer, Emirates, has hit commercial difficulties as the uncertain geopolitics of the Middle East and low oil revenues for these locations have hit passenger numbers. This means future large orders are unlikely. As a result, Airbus has been seeking to increase sales in Asia, notably in China and Japan. These areas have fast-growing passenger numbers and congested infrastructure, and, as such, should seem like potentially lucrative markets. However, by 2017, Chinese airlines had only bought five with the state's aviation regulator being sceptic of the value of such large planes. However, by July 2017, Airbus had not won a single order for the aircraft in over two years. As a result, the company scaled back production even further, from the planned reduction of 12 per cent in 2018 to 8 per cent in 2019. This was likely to be sustained into the 2020s.

**QUESTION**

To what extent do you believe the Airbus A380 is simply an unnecessary product in a shifting marketplace?

## THE GLOBALISATION OF THE VALUE CHAIN

The value chain has been central to assessing the impact of globalisation on both industries and firms. The value chain (see Porter 1996) conceptualised the development of products as passing through a chain of activities, with each stage increasing the value of the product. Importantly, the accumulation of these sequential activities adds more value to the product than the sum of the added value of the actions. The use of the value chain framework is complementary to the assessment of the internal environment and is based on analysing the operations of the business according to the nine generic primary and supporting activities outlined below.

As suggested, these activities are interdependent. The manner in which one activity is conducted can impact the cost and/or effectiveness of another. Thus, for example, higher costs in one part of the value chain may lead to cost reductions elsewhere in the operations of the business as the firm seeks to mitigate such effects through increased efficiency. These linkages are not merely internal to the firm but include connections with third-party suppliers and buyers. This reflects the fact that the firm's value chain is part of a larger value system. Porter (1996) argues that the nature of the value chain reflects the chosen competitive scope of the firm, which is based on:

- The number of segments served.
- The range of industries served.
- The vertical scope of the firm.
- The geographical scope.

The above are important as they shape the configuration of the value chain, including how and where each activity is performed and how and where different units undertake these activities.

Porter (1986) stressed that a core component of international strategy is how the firm decides to spread activities within the value chain across all locations. Generally, downstream activities (i.e., those that are more related to the end-user) are normally focused on the locality where the buyer is located. Upstream activities, as well as support activities, can usually be divorced from this perceived necessity. Such differentiation between activities is important as it implies that downstream activities create and rely upon competitive advantages that are normally country-specific whereas upstream activities tend to take place in the entire range of states where the firm competes. Furthermore, multidomesticity will tend to be more common where downstream activities are central to competitive advantage. If upstream activities are more important, then global strategy is more common. Consequently, Porter (1986) identifies two dimensions of international competition:

- Configuration: that is, where a firm locates particular value-adding activities across the global economy.
- Coordination: that is, how geographically dispersed activities are coordinated with each other.

Across both primary (i.e., the main operational aspects of the business) and secondary (i.e., those activities that facilitate the primary actions) activities, the impact of globalisation through coordination can be affected in many ways (see below).

## Primary activities

Inbound logistics: depending on the dispersal of inputs and where the main operations are undertaken, inbound logistics becomes ever more important. With a more dispersed network of suppliers, coordination is needed to ensure that logistics delivers the appropriate inventory at the right price. The quality of transnational infrastructure and competition in the supply of logistics services also become important determinants of how this activity can shape competitive advantage.

Operations: in a global economy, firms face decisions regarding where to locate production and may shift operations according to the competitive advantage of states. For example, where labour is an important input, the firm may transfer its location to areas where this resource is abundant. The firm may also segment the operations of the business to exploit local advantages. This creates a need for effective coordination within a network of plants.

Outbound logistics: the need for partially completed products to be transferred to other plants, as well as the need for completed products to reach increasingly transnational buyers, requires an effective and timely logistical system which needs to reach all markets and ensure that the inventory of all parts of the firm's operations is met.

Marketing and sales: the firm must choose what products to sell and where. This requires an assessment of the degree of coordination needed in terms of branding, accounts, and pricing.

Service: decisions have to be taken as to where and how customers are serviced. Should they be serviced locally, or can the process be centralised? There has been a trend (via outsourcing) to disperse aspects of the service operation to locations such as India. This has been facilitated by new technology.

## Supporting activities

Firm infrastructure: with the aid of new technology, activities such as accounting, legal management, etc. have become increasingly dispersed throughout the global economy. For example, data inputting has been outsourced to remote locations, and the advent of video conferencing allows all managers to undertake coordinated management roles.

Human resource management: the pool of resources upon which the enterprise draws to undertake its activities is broadened by the process of globalisation. This refers not merely to activities at the local level but to the expansion of the pool of potential top managers. This shift in configuration created a need for coordination of these labour resources to ensure they are complementary to the firm's objectives.

Technology development: the process of research and development becomes more dispersed as the firm seeks to develop a number of centres to undertake this activity to exploit local advantages. This new configuration requires the coordination of such efforts to avoid overlap and ensure ideas are exchanged between different subsidiary units.

Procurement: a major impact of the globalisation process has been the widening of the choice of where to source inputs. As a result, the location of the purchasing function is diversified. This requires the coordination of purchases common to all units and to ensure that different suppliers in different locations are managed effectively.

\* \* \*

The above underlines that competitive advantage can be sourced from the manner in which activities are configured and coordinated across locations. The firm faces a choice of whether to centralise or localise these activities as a means of creating a competitive advantage. As already mentioned, such choices reflect the activity and whether it is upstream or downstream. The more dispersed the firm becomes and the more sourcing opportunities become available, the greater the opportunity for cross-border activity. Porter (1986) argues that the interaction between coordination and configuration creates the opportunity for the firm to develop its preferred type of strategy (see Figure 2.2). Thus, as mentioned above, global strategy is only possible when a specific set of conditions are in place. In other cases, different degrees of adaptation to local conditions will occur.

## NON-MARKET STRATEGIES

The existence of non-market strategies reflects the need for firms to engage with non-market components in the international business environment. The non-market environment comprises the social, political, and legal structures that shape interactions both within and outside markets. As such, non-market transactions cover those interactions that the firm undertakes with:

- Individuals.
- Interest groups.
- Government entities.

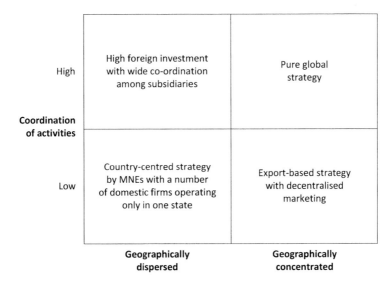

FIGURE 2.2 The configuration/coordination matrix

These actions are guided not by the market but by public and private institutions. Strategy reflects the reality that markets exist within a political and legal context that the firm seeks to influence as a means of supporting and enhancing its competitive positioning.

Non-market strategies can be voluntary or involuntary. Throughout this text, there are numerous references to codes of conduct and regulations with which firms work when establishing their broad strategic direction. A clear implication of the internationalisation of business is that the non-market environment has grown increasingly complex as the number of host economies within which an MNE operates grows. As later chapters highlight, the non-market environment of international business has not been unaffected by the process of globalisation. This is highlighted by the emergence of transnational governance structures and national and non-governmental bodies that reflect the broad range of issues affected by this process.

According to Barron (2006), the non-market environment is characterised by the following:

- Issues: these are the basis of non-market strategies and tend to be industry-specific (such as environmental regulations, etc.). Issues are specific occurrences that have the potential to impact the performance of the business and can operate as a constraint upon managerial discretion and their ability to adapt to shifts in their environment.
- Interests: these are all the parties that have a stake in or a preference for the issue. This includes not merely the firm (and other commercial entities affected by the issue) but also activists, pressure groups, and the public.
- Institutions: these exist as the forum within which the issue will be addressed. Typically, this will include governmental and non-governmental entities.
- Information: this relates to what interested parties know or believe about the issues and forces affecting their development.

Across all industries, these components interact to shape the non-market environment. The nature of the interaction between these components varies from issue to issue. In the modern global economy, interaction, interdependence, and integration between national economies often create overlap between policy domains (as highlighted most evidently by the environmental debate).

The salience of non-market factors to MNEs has been highlighted by the emergence of issues such as environmental protection, labour policy, trade policy, competition policy, human rights, and corporate and social responsibility. This non-exhaustive list highlights issues that are of sufficient importance that their management and control can have important consequences for managerial discretion and MNE performance. They create a desire for firms to influence the development of such issues to ensure they are compatible with management objectives. The response to particular issues will be proportionate to the effect of the issue upon the firm. This underlines the interrelatedness between market and non-market strategies. Indeed, the existence of externalities indicates that an MNE's market activities can generate non-market issues and change within the non-market environment. This can stimulate a reaction from non-market forces to which the MNEs have to react and/or adapt.

Clearly, there exist channels of mutual influence between market and non-market environments. As a result, just like its market equivalent, the non-market is characterised by competition. This competition is characterised by interaction between political entities seeking influence to ensure that their perspective on an issue prevails. Such competition is overseen and managed by public and private institutions such as legislatures, courts, regulatory agencies, and public opinion. Thus, the non-market environment is responsive to the strategies of firms and other stakeholders.

Shifts within the non-market environment arise from both internal and external sources. Barron (1995) identifies five sources for such changes:

- Scientific discovery and technological advancement: this can produce fundamental changes within both market and non-market environments. In the latter, awareness of new technologies can spawn legislation and new controls upon business activities. As new technologies evolve, a series of non-market issues often emerge. For example, globalisation has spawned a series of moral and ethical issues (many of which are highlighted within Chapter 13).
- New understandings: increased public understanding of new issues can result in pressure for change in the corporate sector. For example, pressure for US firms to disinvest in Sudan came from concerted pressure group activity.
- Institutional change: legal decisions, shifts in government policy, regulation, or market pressures can also affect the non-market environment. For example, court decisions regarding promotion or product safety can shape actions undertaken by the firm.
- Interest group activity: interest groups are involved in lobbying political and public bodies to draw attention either to their members' interests or to specific issues. The effectiveness of such actions is judged in terms of increasing awareness amongst the public or generating change in legislation.
- Moral concerns: public opinion over specific issues (such as privacy or the use of child labour) can generate a moral climate whereby specific corporate actions can be deemed inappropriate or even outlawed.

Given the many and diverse interests inherent within the dynamics of the non-market environment, there is a significant incentive for firms to make this aspect of their activities more predictable. This requires a proactive non-market strategy whereby the firm attempts to manage issues. For some businesses, maintaining a full-time proactive strategy can be prohibitive, and reactive strategies may have to be followed.

The more market opportunities are created by the government, the more salient non-market strategies become. In a global economy of nation states, host governments can exert some degree of control over their own market environment. Though, as mentioned, this action has an increased transnational dimension. However, these trends mean that governments can create market opportunities for MNEs. Such opportunities can also be created by private politics and moral concerns (see Chapter 13). This underlines the integrated nature of international strategy and the need for market-driven actions to be complemented and supported by a series of non-market actions.

In terms of the frameworks offered for the market-based international strategy identified above, it is apparent that the market environment can be influenced by the non-market environment. Porter's five forces can all be directly and indirectly influenced by the non-market environment via pressure from consumers, suppliers, rivals, substitutes, and barriers to entry, as can the value of resources. In addition, the ability to configure and co-ordinate across borders is also influenced by non-market issues. Indeed, Baron (2006) maintains that non-market strategies can also be delineated along the same lines identified by Bartlett and Ghoshal (1989):

- Global non-market strategies: these involve issues where the firm applies universal principles across all locations, including trade and ethical stances.
- International non-market strategies: this is where parent company experience is transferred and adapted across markets.
- Multi-domestic non-market strategies: this is based on issue-specific actions that are tailored to individual states.

## THE INTEGRATED NATURE OF INTERNATIONAL STRATEGY

International strategy reflects a need for market and non-market aspects to be mutually supportive. While an effective market strategy is necessary for successful performance, a non-market strategy is rarely sufficient on its own. As much as market strategies respond to opportunities, non-market strategies are needed to monitor and influence the political processes through which such opportunities emerge. Thus, performance depends on the mutually supportive nature of market and non-market strategies, given the evident synergies between these two sets of actions as both are geared towards improving enterprise performance.

Exploiting the synergies between the twin planks of strategy means including both in the process of strategy formation. Thus, when entering host economies, the interaction between market and non-market actions needs to be accounted for in the positioning of the business. This requires a firm to take both market and non-market positions. The latter reflects a deliberate choice of specific issues that influence performance within and across host market economies. Such actions are geared not merely to sustain market position but also to sustain the legitimacy of the MNE within those locations within which it operates. As such, they determine the nature of the relationships that the firm will forge with non-market actors within these locations.

As highlighted in later chapters, non-market positioning can have a direct bearing on market strategies through, for example, an MNE's position on issues such as the environment relating to its corporate social responsibility, which will impact its mission statement. Differentiation extends into non-market environments and can even be leveraged back in some cases to underpin market positioning. For example, as the environment has become of greater public concern, so many MNEs have placed this issue at the heart of their strategy. A very obvious example of this is General Electric, which is seeking to become the market leader in environmental technology.

As with the resource-based view of international strategy, non-market strategy also reflects the skills and competencies possessed by the firm and its ability to secure positioning. Effective non-market strategy depends upon the firm possessing inimitable and difficult-to-replicate skills in areas of non-market interaction. This can include several classes of action, namely:

• Expertise in dealing with the media, the public, the government, and interest and activist groups.
• Knowledge of the processes and procedures of the institutions where issues are resolved.
• A reputation for responsible actions.

Where these skills are absent, the firm can outsource this aspect of the work to other parties, such as lobbyists. In addition, the MNE may use networks (such as trade bodies) to combine competencies to create a more effective and influential non-market body.


## CONCLUSION

The internationalisation of firms has generated both adaptive and reactive behaviour. The most evident impact has been upon the intensity of competition faced by firms. However, all elements of the value chain have been affected by these broad environmental changes. For firms, this means they have to reconsider the form and nature of their strategic position as well as the sources of competitive advantage and attain a new fit with the shifting environment within which they operate. This involves both an assessment of the external environment and of those internal drivers that form and shape competitive advantage. There is an increasing sense that, in a more complex environment made up of a multitude of political institutions, there is a need to consider the non-market determinants of corporate strategy. This implies that non-market actions need to be integrated into market-based activities to create an integrated, holistic international strategy.

## KEY POINTS:

- Globalisation creates new value-creating opportunities for businesses, but it also exposes the business to new risks.
- Business model globality reflects the passive and active forces shaping this value-creating process.
- International strategy reflects decisions by MNEs regarding the degree of global integration versus national responsiveness.
- The choice of strategy reflects the internal and external drivers faced by the MNE.
- MNEs need to integrate non-market activities into their international strategies.

## DISCUSSION QUESTIONS

1. What do you understand by value in a business context? How does globalisation shape this understanding?
2. Explore the major debates surrounding the decision by MNEs to geographically disperse their value chains.
3. Assess the extent to which a global strategy is truly global.

## GROUP EXERCISE

1. Identify a global business. Seek to identify the core facets of its business model.

## SUGGESTED FURTHER READINGS

Baron, D. P. (1995). Integrated strategy: Market and nonmarket components. *California Management Review*, 37(2), 47–65.

Baron, D. (2006). *Business and its environment*, 5th ed, London: Pearson.

Ghoshal, S., & Bartlett, C. A. (1989). The multinational corporation as an interorganizational network. *Academy of Management Review*, 15(4), 603–626.

Goldin, I., & Mariathasan, M. (2014). *The butterfly defect: How globalization creates systemic risks, and what to do about it*, Princeton: Princeton University Press.

Leavitt, T. (1983). The globalization of markets. *Harvard Business Reviews*, 61, 92–102.

Magretta, J. (2002). Why business models matter. *Harvard Business Review, 80*(5), 86–92.

Porter, M. E. (1986). Changing patterns of international competition. *California Management Review, 28*(2), 9–40.

Porter, M. E. (1996). What is strategy? *Harvard Business Review,74*(6), Nov-Dec, 61–78.

Porter, M. E. (2008). *On competition*, Boston: Harvard Business Press.

Tallman, S., & Cuervo-Cazurra, A. (2021). Global strategy. In I. Duhaime, M. Hitt, & M. Lyles (Eds.), *Strategic management: State of the field and its future*, Oxford: Oxford University Press.

Tallman, S., & Pedersen, T. (2015). What is international strategy research and what is not? *Global Strategy Journal, 5*(4), 273–277.

Yip, G. S. (1989). Global strategy… in a world of nations. *Sloan Management Review, 31*(1), 29–41.

Zott, C., Amit, R., & Massa, L. (2011). The business model: Recent developments and future research. *Journal of Management, 37*(4), 1019–1042.

# STATE STRATEGY AND COMPETITIVENESS

## OBJECTIVES

At the end of this chapter, the student will be able to:

- Understand the importance of the state in international business.
- Comprehend the nature of the competition state.
- Demonstrate an awareness of competitiveness.
- Understand core indicators of competitiveness.

## INTRODUCTION

A core building block of the international business system is the state. International business is, by its very nature, trade between states based on commercial entities located within and operating between them. As suggested in Chapter 1, there was an opinion forming that globalisation would render states obsolete. However, there is an increasingly strong body of work that suggests that states (far from being rendered irrelevant as a consequence of the process of globalisation) are increasingly prominent in it. This is not merely in terms of creating the conditions in which international business can prosper (and, by doing so, allowing the state to prosper), but also in terms of how states adapt to and even push back the globalisation process. Initially, this chapter will seek to develop an awareness of the role of states in the international system. This will focus on two core themes: competition and competitiveness. The former will focus on debates surrounding the competition, and the latter will focus on those actions that shape its ability to be attractive to international businesses. However, before we engage in these debates, it is necessary to understand the form and function of the state and its role in international business.

DOI: 10.4324/9781315184500-4

# THE ROLE OF THE STATE IN INTERNATIONAL BUSINESS

As of 2017, there are 195 states in the world. These states are the means through which the global economic and political system is divided to create a patchwork of territories. In the context of the study of international business, the state represents the macro-level of analysis of business. These are basic factors that are external to the business and are seen as uncontrollable, but which still influence organisational behaviour, thinking, and decision-making. These, in turn, can be expected to affect its performance and strategies. These factors will include economic growth, development, policy, demographics, legal, political, and social issues. On top of this are other issues, such as technological change and natural forces. These factors reflect that the dominant form of state in the post-war era is the nation state. The nation state is a territorial state based around representing the interests of a defined community (i.e., the nation) that differentiates itself by history, ethnicity, language, and/or religion. As different nations gained their own states (especially after the end of colonialism), the political map grew more complex. This was compounded by states adapting and adopting rules to reflect their own nations' priorities. In this context, states are seen as a means through which the transaction costs of engaging in international business are seen to rise as a result of state preferences and jurisdictional discontinuities created by different currencies, laws, and regulatory systems.

In a world of global systems, the political fragmentation of space into discrete territories leads to the compartmentalisation of international business into a state-based narrative. This has its most evident expression in areas like trade and investment (key benchmarks and indicators of the global economy) expressed in terms of state narratives. What this means for business is that the work it faces is complex, comprising a multitude of divergent economic, political, social, legal, and technological environments. This can muddy market selection (see Chapter 9) to the extent that many states have sought to rationalise this process through regional integration (see Chapter 5).

There are widely accepted to be five dimensions to the state:

1) Population: the state is a community of people; without people, there is no state. Across the global economy, the population of states can vary widely, with two states (China and India) comprising almost 40 per cent of the total global population. The population of the state are citizens of the state (which gives them specific rights and obligations) over which the state exercises control via government. What the right size population is for a state reflects the size of the territory, available resources, standard of living, expected production of goods and services, and security needs.

2) Territory: the state is a defined territorial unit which is demarcated with borders that are recognised by other states. The state exercises sovereignty over the territory, to which all entities operating and located within it are subject. This jurisdiction not only includes land but also maritime waters (as agreed by the UN) and those water courses and bodies flowing across or existing within the territory and air space (to a limit) above the state.

3)  Government: this is the method and agencies through which the state formally exercises sovereign control and normally comprises three elements (the legislature, judiciary, and executive). The relationship between these three elements is defined by the form of government. These forms can be, for example, monarchy, aristocracy, dictatorship, or democracy. It can also be presidential, parliamentary, unitary, federal, or a mixture of these.

4)  Sovereignty: as suggested above, this is the element that is seen to be most exclusive to the state (though, as themes within Chapter 1 suggest, this has been challenged by globalisation). However, without sovereignty, the state cannot exist, as it needs to exercise supreme power over its population and territory. Sovereignty has two dimensions: internal sovereignty, which refers to its supreme power within the borders of its territory, and external sovereignty, which means the state operates free from external influence or control. However, sovereignty is not absolute, as any state has to engage with states and therefore respects international laws, treaties, and actions of organisations such as the UN.

5)  International recognition: this is a more recent addition to the core features of the state, but as the number of states has grown (especially since the end of the Second World War and the end of colonialism), this has grown in importance as any state's sovereignty has to be recognised by other states. This is important in cases like Taiwan, where its recognition is controversial, as is also evident in the case of Palestine.

The function of the state is linked directly to the need to generate economic growth, which generates the tax base that in turn supports the activities of the state. Through these revenues, the state offers public goods, namely the provision of internal and external security (through the provision of an army, etc.) and the offering of infrastructure (both economic and social) to support wealth creation. This latter theme positions the state as an entity within the international capital system, where it engages with the system to generate the maximum revenue. This has led to policy and strategy informed by the logic of what has come to be known as the competition state.

## CASE STUDY 3.1: DUBAI WORLD AND THE US PORTS

In 2005, DP World, a state-owned business located in the UAE, agreed to acquire the UK-based operator P&O, which, among other things, ran port operations in six US ports. As part of the process, the firms had to request a review of this process under US law to ensure that this overseas investment did not impact the interests of the host. The initial results of this review by the US Congress' Committee on Foreign Investment in the US (which comprises representatives of 12 US agencies and departments) which focused on port security felt that there were no grounds to resist this acquisition. However, this decision was resisted by a number of members of Congress who felt that there were direct security concerns as a result of the acquisition.

The resistance to the acquisition was largely based upon the security threat posed by the fact that Dubai World hailed from a state that had, in their opinion, a history of being an operational and financial base for terrorism. This resistance was set against a post-9/11 environment where there was an increased security threat from Middle Eastern states. This was also evidenced, in the minds of Congress, by the fact that the UAE was the alleged base for the 9/11 hijackers. Thus, despite the UAE having a strong, pro-US government, the fear of radical Islam led to a fear that this critical port infrastructure could be rendered vulnerable due to its ownership by a UAE-based business. This was in spite of the US government seeking to reassure Congress that the acquisition only involved six ports and that DP World would not own any ports nor manage their operations. Such negativity led to DP World selling these port assets to a US-based business.

The notion of national security in the case of DP World reflected a novel set of circumstances. The post-9/11 environment was one where a siege mentality was common, with the US becoming more insular and even suspicious of outside influence, especially those from the Middle East. To many elected officials, the notion of a Middle Eastern government running US ports was abhorrence. To many, this would have woven the foreign company into the fabric of critical infrastructure. The public pressure that drove this hostility was inevitable in the post-9/11 environment, despite the assurance of the operator. In this case, the threat of terrorism became a legitimate concern in the process of reviewing foreign investment. The notion of protecting the homeland and ensuring homeland security became a legitimate tool of government in the foreign investment process. This exposes decisions to value-laden, not subjective, criteria. National security raises strong emotions that can be captured by extreme, populist viewpoints. The dangers of this are the risk of backlash: beneficial investment could be deterred or blocked and undermine cooperation with foreign governments in the name of national security.

### QUESTION

To what extent is internal security a legitimate reason for protectionism?

## THE COMPETITION STATE

The rise of the competition state is seen as a direct parallel to the decline of the welfare state. In the latter case, the role of the state was to promote the welfare of citizens through insulation from market forces. This was done largely through the provision of strong welfare states and aspects of protectionism that limited the exposure of key sectors to internal and/or external competition. The rise of the competition state turned this upon its head, where states increasingly strategised to promote the marketisation of economic activity to enable those activities located within the borders of the state to be competitive in terms of the global marketplace. In the face of globalisation, states are seen to be in competition with each other to attract footloose capital. It is through the attraction of footloose global capital that the state will best secure improvements in the welfare of its citizens.

As such, the primary motivation for states is to establish a demarcated space that is internationally competitive through creating a pro-business environment. This strategy is reflected in domestic governance and policy, and notably a shift by states towards the following characteristics:

- A shift from macro-economic to micro-economic forms of intervention (i.e., deregulation etc.).
- A shift from the creation of 'national champions' and of strategic industries and self-sufficiency towards a flexible response to shifting competitive conditions in global markets
- An emphasis upon the control of inflation (over full employment) to generate the goal of non-inflationary growth.
- The promotion of fiscal restraint over fiscal expansion due to the logic of crowding out the private sector.
- The indirect promotion of welfare through the trickle-down effects of enterprise, innovation, and profitability.

The result of these shifts is that the state is formed to act more like a market player that sets policy to steer market forces to maximise the returns for its territory. This makes its citizens more dependent upon market forces. In practice, it can be argued that the state is compelled, within this context, to become a strategist that develops a strategy that can deliver economic growth and rising living standards through managing competitive conditions. This reflects themes explored within the first chapter with regard to the state not being sovereign over or subservient to still exist; it does so as a complement (not in opposition to) global forces. This could be, for example, in aiding adaptability or in compensating for or allowing the adjustment of globalisation's losers to the process of change. The importance of the logic of the competition state is that it demonstrates both how the state has had its power eroded by global forces and how it still remains a central actor in the global system.

The logic of the competition state is underpinned by three propositions, namely

1) That the global economy forces states to compete for global capital.
2) That supply-side policies are the only response to inter-state competition.
3) That the welfare state will irrevocably decline.

Each of these propositions can be contested. First, a key contention has been that the structural constraints offered by global forces are in effect not that strong, with no real evidence of external determinism in national policies. In addition, as highlighted by the compensation hypothesis, welfare states have been sustained as an institutional foundation for engaging with international competition as it is used to compensate losers from the process of globalisation and therefore legitimise the process.

Genschel and Seelkopf (2015) argue that the rise of the competition state can be seen as an adaptive response to a series of (frequently overlapping) changes, namely

- Globalisation: which, it is argued, has undermined the welfare state by exposing it to international competition. Through this process, the state can no longer impose high taxes or costly regulations on footloose businesses.
- Government overload: as the welfare state has grown, states have become unable to cope with the demands placed upon them, notably as fiscal deficits expand, creating pressure for reform.
- The crisis in 'Fordism': Fordism is a system based on the mutual reinforcing of mass consumption and production. As demand became saturated and fell, unemployment rose alongside falling profit levels and lower economic growth. This in turn increased government spending as expectations for state action to solve these problems rose, resulting in government overload and public deficits.
- The spread of neo-liberalism: this aided the shift to competition state by focusing on competitiveness and leading to policy frameworks that secured this objective. Moreover, this integrates the focus on competitiveness within domestic economic policy.

A closer examination of the theory suggests that all of its predictions do not match up. First, the evidence that firms actually compete with each other via tax rates, etc., is patchy, with there being – in practice – a multitude of factors that drive this process. For example, while tax rates vary with state size (as expected by the theory), competition is not the only factor creating this tension, as this pressure will increase with the size of the state, and there is little impact on labour taxation. Second, with regard to convergence between states on key policy strategies, there is clear convergence on those policy variables that are most exposed to international competition, namely corporate tax rates. Where the policy measure is more sheltered, this policy convergence tends to be less obvious. Third, with regard to the impact on the welfare state, there is no evidence of what has been termed the 'compensation thesis' (that globalisation increases welfare spending as those who lose demand compensation as a result). This suggests that the impact of globalisation upon the welfare state is not straightforward, with this tending to be bolstered in smaller states but challenging in large states.

The logical endpoint of narratives shaped by the competition state is a perception that seeks direct parallels with business. Under this narrative, the point of the state is to seek to maximise the welfare of its citizens through direct commercial imperatives. In crude terms, this would be measured by a simple trade surplus as an indicator of the success or otherwise of the economy to generate sales (via the overseas performance of its businesses) and of its ability to attract mobile capital into its economic base. This is a simple restatement of mercantilism, which saw trade between states as a zero-sum game and that a state's power relative to other states was a direct legacy of their ability to have a positive trade balance. However, such arguments have been largely discredited by the complexities of the modern commercial system with a multi-national production system and the belief that trade is mutually beneficial. This also reflects a deeper resistance to positioning the state as a business, as the state has to undertake functions that have higher levels of social value, which are by their nature unprofitable. In addition, the state has undertaken economic activities that only deliver benefits over the long term and would, therefore, be underprovided by market-based agents. This includes socio-economic goods such as education and infrastructure. In addition, positioning the state as a business ignores the fact that the laws of comparative advantage state that a state will be competitive in some industries and uncompetitive in others. Finally, the parallel of using trade balance as a proxy for profit ignores that that balance has as much to do with the balance of domestic savings and investment as with the innate competencies and capabilities of the businesses located within the territory of the state.

Nonetheless, there can be little doubt that the progressive onset of globalisation has led to many states seeking to develop strategies that seek to position them as a means of competing in the global economy. Palan, Abott, and Deans (1999) identify seven types of strategies deployed by states.

1) *Large markets*

These are states that use the incentive of scale to create an advantage. This reflects a logic that smaller states have a competitive disadvantage driven by size, as economies of scale and ancillary benefits linked to trade and investment are unavailable to them. The most evident expression of this shift towards large markets can be seen in the pursuit of regional integration between many small and mid-size states to counter the economic power of large states. However, to simply make a link between scale and competitiveness is not straightforward, as it assumes price factors drive market share and ignores the role of non-price factors in international markets.

2) *The capitalist development state*

In East Asia, this has been an important model where the state has played an important role in engineering growth and development. This strategy has fused the public and private sectors to enable the former to direct and attain development goals. The state steered business towards the creation of national champions who would compete in global markets. For these states, it has been a successful strategy as it has enabled them to attain rapid rates of growth while reducing social and economic inequity. These states also moved up the product cycle from producing low-value to high-value goods, as well as rapid advancements in infrastructure and education. Though there have been costs in terms of some restrictions (initially at least) on personal freedoms and environmental degradation.

3) *The 'shielders' strategy'*

This is a process of selective integration wherein in some sectors the state is open to the full intensity of global competition, whereas in others the state constructs an assortment of protectionist devices to protect strategic interests such as security, culture, or some other facet of national life. This strategy is common among some European states (notably the Nordic and continental European states), where a generous welfare system is sustained as a means of offering productivity improvements and promoting innovation. Moreover, these states seem to be especially good at identifying and occupying distinct market niches; this is often based on higher rates of innovation. This also reflects an industrial strategy deployed by these states that seeks to facilitate and enable their adaptation to global markets.

4)  *Hegemonic strategy*

These are powerful states within the system that seek to use their powerful political position within the global economy to gain a competitive advantage. This will be achieved by being able to gain preferential access to otherwise scarce and/or valuable resources and/or by seeking to shape international rules to its advantage. This highlights that the hegemon can use its power in a positive fashion (to foster inter-state cooperation along agreed rules), negatively (through seeking to shape rules to its own advantage), and structurally (the hegemon gains advantages from being at the centre of the global system). Convention dictates that there can only be one hegemon, but if examined on a regional level, then the scope for more than one emerges. Moreover, there seems to be little long-term advantage from the process, as the dominant global hegemon has not remained stable and unchallenged as the identity of the global hegemon has shifted over time.

5)  *Low-cost leader*

These are strategies deployed by states (especially those that are less developed) that seek to gain market share and/or attract investment by producing low-cost or low-value products. These aim to attract investment from developed states by being low-cost locations, though cost will only be one factor shaping this location decision. These stress the MNE as a motor for the development of less developed states. However, for many, the role of the MNE in the process of economic development has been a mixed blessing. However, in recent times, the strategy has reinforced its salience with the rise of China, which used low-cost manufacturing to gain market share at the expense of developed states and then sought to move to higher-value activities.

6)  *Parasitical niche*

These are states (many of them small) that use their sovereignty to develop laws that are aimed at attracting business from other states (many of them frequently neighbours). The most evident form of parasitical strategy is the tax haven, where firms offer either reduced regulation or corporate tax to create a competitive advantage. However, the subject is a very vulnerable one, as larger states seek to clamp down on this process as they seek to act against tax avoidance, denial of revenues, and the opportunistic behaviour of these states. This, coupled with the relative lack of power of these states, suggests that this might – over the long term – not be a sustainable strategy.

7)  *'Not in the game'*

These are states – often logistically peripheral to the global economy – that are disengaged from the global economy. While these states may sell natural resources to the global economy, they do not, in effect, offer a coherent market position. The source of this can often lie in the conditions of state failure, where the political and economic system is unstable and – as such – cannot offer a safe and low-risk environment for business. These further limit long-term investment, which further erodes their potential capability to participate within the global economy. The absence of stability within many of these states means that international competitiveness is not a major domestic political or economic priority for these states.

\*\*\*

This typology underscores how states are adapting to the challenge of globalisation. For all states in all categories (bar the last), the objective is gaining and sustaining competitiveness. This follows on from the theme that states are adapting to globalisation through the development of strategies that can improve the welfare of their citizens. The pervasiveness of such debates underscores how preeminent these themes, driven by the rise of the competition state, have become in the development of state strategy in international markets. There is no incentive for states to opt out of the system of competitiveness between states. On that basis, a fuller examination of what competitiveness actually is and how it is shaped and developed needs to be examined.

## CASE STUDY 3.2: SAUDI ARABIA AND THE SAUDI VISION 2030

Saudi Vision 2030 (hereafter termed Vision 2030) represents a long-term plan by the Saudi Arabian government to reduce the Kingdom's dependence upon oil (while only 30–40 per cent of its GDP, oil generates 85 per cent of export earnings and the vast majority of government revenue). In doing so, the aim of the strategy is to alter the state's economic model to rely more completely upon the private sector as the primary driver of employment, development, and growth generation. Currently, the public sector accounts for some two-thirds of GDP, with the private sector very dependent upon public sector contracts. The strategy of the diversification is in many ways a simple restatement of what has been a long-held desire of the Saudi Authorities to make it less dependent on what can be unstable commodity prices of oil and gas. However, these past successes have been very limited in terms of their ability to shift the economy away from the dominance asserted by the oil and gas sector. This became especially evident with the oil price collapse between 2014 and 2016 when the Saudi state saw revenues collapse and economic austerity measures imposed. There was also a distinct political component to the process, as the Saudi authorities had to be seen to increase economic freedom in the aftermath of the Arab Spring and to head off any popular resentment that could emerge from the absence of opportunities for its young population, which is expected to expand by nearly 5 million by 2030. In the years 2003–2014, oil prices were rising continuously, which allowed for a big expansion in state spending on education and infrastructure. However, this spending failed to solve the issues of youth unemployment, economic inequality, and the persistent strain upon public services.

The Vision 2030 document encompasses a number of themes, of which the main ones are:

- Sovereign fund: the aim is to expand this fund, enhance investment opportunities regionally, and expand its finance from SAR 600 billion to more than SAR 7 trillion.
- Freedom from oil: the plan aims to increase non-oil revenues by 600 per cent by 2030 (from SAR 163 billion to SAR 1 trillion) and increase non-oil exports to 50 per cent (from 16 per cent in 2016) of the total to become a top-15 economy

(it is currently 19th). Integral to this is the target to increase the private sector's contribution from 40 per cent to 65 per cent of GDP, increase foreign direct investment from 3.8 per cent to the international level of 5.7 of GDP, localise over 50 per cent of military equipment spending by 2030, and increase Saudi-isation (local content) in the oil and gas sectors from 40 per cent to 75 per cent.

- Aramco Initial Public Offering: the government will offer less than 5 per cent of the giant state-owned oil company in a public offering, with the funds generated being directed towards the above Sovereign Fund.
- Green Card: this aims to make it easier for non-Saudis (especially other Arabs and migrants from other Muslim-majority states) to find employment within the state. It will also seek to open up the state to tourism in all states.
- 30 million pilgrims: in line with the above, the government is seeking to increase the number of pilgrims to 80 million by 2030 (it is currently 8 million). This will involve a heavy investment in infrastructure in and around key religious sites.

In short, the strategy aims to diversify both the sources of revenue for the state and the means through which those revenues are generated. Arguably the biggest change is the intention to sell a portion of Saudi Aramco. The creation of Aramco (in the 1970s) was at the forefront of energy nationalism in the region, as it was created by nationalising four US oil companies with long-standing interests in the Kingdom. Its partial sell-off represents at least a partial pullback from entrenched 'resource nationalism'. As previous attempts at diversification have met with institutional resistance inside the government, the plan also involves a degree of streamlining of decision-making. This meets long-term scepticism by outside investors as to the ability of the reform to be truly implemented as envisaged, as internal resistance to such strategies has a long history. Indeed, scepticism towards the plan is shaped not just by internal resistance but also by the belief that it should have been promoted when the oil price was high, and the Saudi authorities had more fiscal flexibility. For Saudi Arabia to move beyond being a 'rentier state' (where the state buys loyalty and social/political harmony by distributing unearned wealth) is a big change, forcing many Saudis to find jobs in sectors that they otherwise would not have considered.

Part of the controversy surrounding the Vision 2030 programme is the extent to which it will alter the social contract between the state (i.e., the ruling al Saud family) and the various other constituencies – with the rest of the royal family, religious clerics, business elites, tribal leaders, and different social groups. For example, it is feared that the opening up of the system could be proactively resisted by the strong clerical establishment, which many fear for a higher degree of female participation in the workforce, but also that the programme seeks to modernise the economy, which could find it in direct conflict with the traditional themes stressed by the strong degree of religiosity. This could also be evident in the push for more tourism for the economy. This does reflect that there is a risk of backlash to the programme, especially where their strategy is seen as excessively pro-western by conservative sections of Saudi Society. The plan is likely to be attractive to younger segments of Saudi society.

Overall, many have criticised the plan as being little more than a marketing ploy by the Saudi movement to head off dissent. It has also been criticised by many for what is seen as its unrealistic financial expectations. Indeed, if the oil price stays low and government spending stays high, then there is a very real risk that the state could run out of money. If this leads to a cutback in programmes, then social order problems could result. Indeed, by 2017, a dose of reality seemed to be impacting the plan as many of the goals were set to be attained over a longer period.

## QUESTION

To what extent do you agree that the Vision 2030 is an excessively optimistic strategy?

# STATE COMPETITIVENESS: INDICATORS AND DETERMINANTS

The narratives offered by the competition states lead to a focus in public policy upon competitiveness. Competitiveness is a matter of some conjecture. However, the fundamental outcomes are widely accepted, namely that a competitive state means that the citizens within the state are able to enjoy rising welfare as indicated through a high and rising standard of living and rising prosperity. It is widely accepted that – for most states – the standard of living (and therefore competitiveness) is determined in no small part by productivity, where productivity is the efficiency and effectiveness with which a state's resources are used. Such efficiency and effectiveness are usually indicated by measures such as output per unit, labour, and/or capital employed. As such, progressive improvements in the standard of living of citizens can only be sustained by advances in productivity. This will happen through innovation within existing businesses or through new entry into high-productivity sectors. Moreover, these processes will enable these businesses to use the advances in national productivity to allow businesses located within them to enjoy rising market shares within chosen market segments or through an ability to attract foreign direct investment.

This focus on productivity is evident in what is arguably the most widely acknowledged classification currently offered, namely the definition offered by the World Economic Forum (WEF). The WEF defines it as '

> the set of institutions, policies and factors that determine the level of output in a country per unit of labour' (WEF 2017)

At the micro level, competitiveness matters as it starts to have a big influence on the ability of the state's firms to compete internationally. This means not just the ability to sustain market share within their chosen segments but also through the ability of these businesses to adapt to changing global trends (including increased domestic competition from overseas entrants) and to also spot and take advantage of new commercial opportunities. This is seen especially in smaller states that are unable to exploit scale economies in market positioning (and lack the advantages of large home markets). This is evident, for example, in the case of Switzerland, which regularly tops the WEF rankings (see Table 3.2). Importantly, the focus on competitiveness is not merely about those sectors of the economy exposed to international competition; it is also important for the non-traded sector. Any inefficiencies within this segment of the national economy can have a direct and tangible impact upon the traded sector. This is evident in the criteria identified by the WEF as the main drivers of competitiveness (see below).

Importantly, the notion of a state's competitiveness is not driven solely by cost factors. Simply arguing that low costs render a state competitive is to misunderstand the concept that low wages may simply mask poor productivity. Moreover, the goal of the state should be high productivity that supports higher wages and a higher standard of living. Low wages can hinder a state's long-term competitiveness if they inhibit innovation and deter the development of and investment in higher skills. Moreover, measures like devaluations to render a state's output competitive can at best be short-term. Thus, breaking the link between low cost and competitiveness underscores the eclectic approach offered by WEF as to the main measurements of competitiveness. These are based on 12 areas that are subdivided into three sub-indices:

- *Basic requirements*: these are the core issues that states at the early stages of development tackle first.
- *Efficiency enhancers*: this deals with the efficiency of markets and other factors that suggest the adaptability of the state to global forces, especially with regard to higher-value activities.
- *Innovation and sophistication*: this assesses the extent to which a state can utilise high-quality business processes and research as well as innovative public and private sector practices.

These are reflected in Table 3.1.

Examining Table 3.2, it is evident that there is a developed/developing country split in the degree of competitiveness exhibited by states. Of the top 10, six are

**TABLE 3.1** WEF pillars of competitiveness

| Basic requirements | Efficiency enhancers | Innovation and sophistication |
| --- | --- | --- |
| • Institutions<br>• Infrastructure<br>• Macro-economic environment<br>• Health and primary education | • Goods market efficiency<br>• Labour market efficiency<br>• Financial market development<br>• Higher education and training<br>• Technological readiness | • Business sophistication<br>• Innovation |

Source WEF (2017)

**TABLE 3.2:** The top/bottom 10 most and least competitive states (2019) (rank out of 141)

| Most competitive (rank) | Least competitive (rank) |
| --- | --- |
| 1. Singapore | 141. Chad |
| 2. United States | 140. Yemen |
| 3. Hong Kong SAR | 139. Congo Democratic Republic |
| 4. The Netherlands | 138. Haiti |
| 5. Switzerland | 137. Mozambique |
| 6. Japan | 136. Angola |
| 7. Germany | 135. Burundi |
| 8. Sweden | 134. Mauritania |
| 9. United Kingdom | 133. Venezuela |
| 10. Denmark | 132. Madagascar |

Source: WEF (2017)

Western European. It is also evident that three of these states (notably Switzerland and Singapore) are relatively small states; the Swiss economy is only the 19th largest globally, while Singapore is the 40th. In both of these small states, each has learned to survive and prosper by becoming very open and exposed economies. Interestingly, China does not feature in the top 10, despite being arguably the world's most successful trading nation. Indeed, China only comes in at 26 in the rankings. This is due to factors such as a low level of technological readiness and its uneven development. On the flip side, those states that are deemed the least competitive are mainly in Africa and suffer from low levels of economic development, with many of the basic requirements being absent (see Chapter 8). The non-African states are those that can be broadly deemed failing (see below) and/or that are undergoing substantive political, economic, and/or social turmoil.

The narrative offered by the WEF reflects clear continuities on the issues engendered within what has become the conventional framework for understanding the determinants of state competitiveness, namely Porter's 'Diamond'. These parallel frameworks are bound by their prognosis that competitiveness is based on competition and creating the conditions for competition both within and external to the state. In short, the diagnosis is that there is nothing better for competitiveness than competition itself. This diagnosis has its ultimate expression within the concept of clusters. These are groups of businesses within identical product groups in which intense competitive pressure is generated. It is this pressure that forces firms within the cluster to increase productivity, foster innovation, and push for increased returns. Moreover, the intensity of competition enables these firms to adapt easily to the challenges of international competition and operating within overseas markets. It is Porter's contention that firms working under such conditions operate according to the criteria outlined within the Diamond model. This model suggests that getting the conditions right within the home market

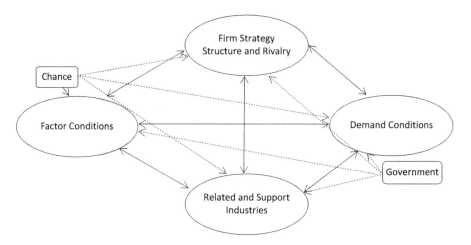

**FIGURE 3.1** Porter's Diamond
Source: Porter (1990)

can translate into an international advantage (again underlining the parallels with the WEF framework). The core components are highlighted in Figure 3.1.

Looking at each of these determinants in turn allows for a fuller understanding of the conditions which allow clusters to drive the international competitiveness of states.

1) Factor conditions: this is related to the factors of production, notably their availability, quality, and efficiency of usage. These issues, such as infrastructure and knowledge, become important due to such factors, which in turn suggest the importance of education and health care. Included in this treatment are not just labour resources but also natural and financial resources.

2) Related and supporting industries: this stresses that the success of business in international markets is also shaped by the existence of suppliers and/or customers who enable the firm to adapt to shifting commercial conditions. These businesses can offer access to know-how at all points in the firm's value chain and can either share or offer complementary resources.

3) Home demand conditions: this reflects that there is a direct relationship between the firm's ability to generate economies of scale and lower transaction costs and the size of the home market. It is believed that if these are available to the firm, then others will also take advantage of these conditions, creating the basis of a cluster within that single location.

4) Strategy, structure, and rivalry: this reflects firm-specific capabilities, notably with regard to its management and organisation and its ability to adapt to rivalry. This in turn can be a direct derivative, especially with regard to business culture, the intensity of rivalry within this locality, and the need for firms to continually adjust for competitive conditions.

These core four determinants were later complemented by two others:

5) Government: these can play an important role in stimulating the development of industries and companies by not just merely creating the conditions in which such businesses can evolve and flourish (through support for education and training, for example), but also through their ability to finance infrastructure and healthcare and even support risky innovations and investment.

6) Chance: in most markets' serendipity can be an important factor as it can reveal opportunities for innovation and for new businesses to start up and exploit new opportunities.

## Competitiveness issues

There can be little doubt that debates about competitiveness have become dominant policy narratives. However, there is by no means a consensus that competitiveness should be the major focus of government strategy or that it is the best way to drive improvement in the welfare of a state's citizens. It is evident that competitiveness is an issue that has been shaped by debates formed in Western economies to solve Western problems that were historically specific (i.e., low growth, emerging competition, etc.). Given this heritage, can it be universally accepted as a legitimate strategy for all states, irrespective of their heritage, level of development, etc.? Moreover, debates about competitiveness are about firms rather than states (given the presumption that states do not compete), and framing the provision of social goods (such as health care, education, and infrastructure) merely in terms of commercial enablement seems rather short-sighted. Ultimately, the salience of debates on competitiveness reflects the success of neo-liberal thinking in permeating public policy and how this logic is at the crux of contemporary state governance.

This latter point forms the crux of Fougner's (2008) critique of the WEF's criteria for the determinants of competitiveness. The WEF is formed with the notion that MNEs are homeless and that states in effect compete for their 'business'. As such, states are merely assessed in terms of their attractiveness for the footloose entrepreneur and their 'aggressiveness' in terms of their ability to transform resources into value-added goods and services. In addition, the WEF criteria should also be seen as actions designed intentionally to shape state strategy through the provisions of key benchmarks to which states are expected to adhere if they are to be competitive and drive welfare improvements for their citizens. States are therefore encouraged by this process to study the best businesses and follow their example. It has to be remembered that this benchmarking is done by representatives of the world's top 1,000 companies and therefore follows their agenda and interests; states have no say as to whether they are included or not. There is, of course, the notion to be explored as to whether such benchmarks are always and everywhere relevant.

By default, many of the criticisms of the WEF can be extended to Porter's Diamond model, notably its neo-liberal bias. However, the Diamond has attracted many outright criticisms. The first is that it is opaque as to where competitive advantage is created. Is it by the state or the MNE? In this context, the model shows a poor understanding of

MNE operations. Second, the model seems to dismiss the notion that foreign-owned subsidiaries can actively contribute to the competitive advantage of nations, as the model focuses on the creation of domestically sourced advantages. Third, the relevance of the model to small open economies can be questioned, as the notion of clustering seems to imply a scale that can only apply to large states. As such, for small states, clustering may occur on a supranational level. Fourth, the Diamond Model seems to discount the role that national culture can play in the determination of the factors that drive competitiveness. Any model cannot discuss national environments without understanding how national culture shapes this context. Fifth, there are methodological problems with the work related to the selection of industries, its generalisability, comparability of results, and its ultimate predictive power. Sixth, there is a lack of attention to macro variables within the model. For example, Porter plays down the importance of wage rates and exchange rates as determinants of international competitiveness. Seventh, the model seems to lack dynamism. In seeking to explain clusters, it offers no real explanation as to how to create new industries. Eighth, there is a criticism that Porter's work is simply not rigorous and specific enough, notably in terms of the lack of specificity in terms of definitions and the relationships between core variables. While there is a certain validity to such criticisms, it has to be remembered that the model is exactly that and that it offers new explanations for competitiveness but merely offers a framework in which it can be assessed.

## STATE FAILURE

As shaped by the themes of competitiveness and competition states, there is an expectation upon states to deliver progressive welfare improvements for their citizens by proactively engaging with the global economy. In the terms stressed here, this stresses the path where markets encourage business. However, the role of the state in driving benefits for their citizens extends beyond these simplistic notions, as we expect a state to have control of its territory, have secure borders, and deliver key public goods to socially, politically, and economically integrate their respective territories. However, many states fail to attain either of these. Debates on state failure have come from two directions: relative state failure and absolute state failure.

### Relative failure

This stream of work is focused on relative economic performance and why some states fail to achieve the rates of growth of other states. This is based on the work of Acemoglu and Robinson (2012), who seek to explain the income disparity between states. Their explanation for differences in relative growth is that those states that are lagging tend to be characterised by what they term 'extractive' institutions. These are institutions where political and economic power is concentrated in the hands of dictators or elites. In short, those in power do not offer sufficient incentives for their citizens to create wealth. The argument is that democracy, through spreading power, also spreads economic power, allowing for incentives for hard work and innovation based on the rule of law and free markets; these are 'inclusive' institutions. This suggests that explanations based on climate, culture, or ignorance fail to offer an adequate explanation. What is core, according to the authors, are protection of intellectual property, plural political structures, government accountability, and a strong (but not overpowering) central government.

While many may agree that 'vested' interests can stall innovation, what Acemoglu and Robinson offer tends to be a very ethnocentric view of the world, suggesting that the Western system is best. The authors suggest that the most successful states are those that bear the strongest similarities to the US Constitution. The inference of their analysis is that the West will continue to innovate, and China will decline without reform. The authors are sceptical of the positive role of a strong state in the economic system. This can be treated with scepticism, as not only are Western institutions also subject to hijacking by special interests (through patents, for example), but also China's 'extractive' institutions (despite reform to remove corruption) seem to be delivering growth. Second, does a plural system lead to open economic institutions? The example of India arguably suggests not. In this case, universal suffrage and democracy have not always delivered open economic institutions. The example of the rise of populism across Western systems also suggests that in a democratic system, electorates can feel disconnected from elites, which has rendered them exposed to extreme views.

## Absolute failure

This is where a state fails to fulfil its core duties to its citizens due to its inability to provide basic public goods, notably security. As such, these states are characterised by internal violence to the extent that the government lose legitimacy in the perception of its citizens. In short, its power to assert its territoriality within a demarcated space is contested by at least one faction. These can reflect deep-seated cleavage within the territory based on factors such as religion, culture, or ethnicity. In addition, many failed states cannot control their borders with power limited to specific zones (such as the capital city), tend to have high and rising levels of criminal violence, flawed institutions (such as an absence of accountability), destroyed or failing infrastructure, public services are neglected and underfunded, and income inequality grows due to corruption and prejudice.

The likelihood of failure of a state tends to occur when a set of three conditions is exhibited by the state. The first of these is when a state favours a closed economic system (i.e., its openness to trade is low or non-existent); the second is when the infant mortality rate is high (which serves as a proxy for the quality of life); and finally, when a state is undemocratic (this is seen to feed on itself as creating an ever-closed system). Though, as suggested above, the link between each of these can be disputed. The fact that research tends to focus on African states tends to steer towards these indicators. There are three signals that a state is likely to fail: economic (caused by rapid falls in real incomes and living standards that create a spiral of decline); political (where subversion of democracy by a closed elite leads to factionalism); and deaths in combat (if these are rising very quickly, then the state can be seen to be failing). There is no single benchmark that suggests a strong state is becoming weak, as tipping points can be difficult to recognise. What can be concluded is that it is essentially man-made based on leadership errors made for personal gain that create the conditions for failure.

## CASE STUDY 3.3: DJIBOUTI – TAKING ADVANTAGE OF STRATEGIC POSITION

Djibouti is a small state located on the Horn of Africa which formally gained independence from France in 1977. It has a population of nearly a million and covers an area of a little over 23,000 km². Like many small states, it struggles to create an effective competitive positioning in a global economy dominated by Europe, China, and the US. It is a state that, by and large, has its room for manoeuvre tightly contained by external economic events and processes. Indeed, Djibouti is a relatively barren country, with its port proving to be the cornerstone of its economy. Djibouti's position on the Bab el-Mandeb Strait (which is a key entry and exit point to the Suez Canal) has given it a high degree of strategic importance for many leading industrialised and industrialising states. Djibouti has proved to be an area of stability in what is an unstable region of the global economy. This has led to large investments by a number of superpowers in the port facilities of the state, notably France, the US, China, and Japan, among others.

The strategic outlook for the state has been driven by an accumulation of four factors, namely:

- The Ethiopian-Eritrean war of 1998–2000.
- The rapid economic transformation in Ethiopia.
- Shifts in US strategy in Africa and the Arabian Peninsula since 9/11.
- The upsurge in piracy along the Gulf of Aden and Somali coasts.

Djibouti's weight within the global economy is enhanced by its membership in the Inter-Governmental Authority on Development (IGAD), a regional economic grouping which consists of the Horn of Africa States and indeed hosts its headquarters. The importance of Djibouti as a port was historically driven by its function as the railhead for Ethiopia. This was expanded after independence, with Ethiopia remaining the port's biggest customer. This trade increased not only in the aftermath of the Ethiopian-Eritrean war but also as a result of Ethiopia's increased rate of development in the post-war environment. Though there is a fear that Djibouti could become dependent on Ethiopia, this has led the state to resist attempts by Ethiopia to take an equity holding in the port. This has been compounded by the increased importance that the US placed upon the port in the post-9/11 security environment, with Djibouti operating as the core logistics hub (including a launch pad for drone activity) for East Africa and the Arabian Peninsula. Here, the US acts in concert with its allies, notably the French, who have a long-standing military presence in the state. This has been compounded by the rise of multilateral anti-piracy measures in the Gulf of Aden and Indian Ocean. For these reasons, Djibouti has become a core hub for North Atlantic Treaty Organization (NATO) and European Union (EU) forces. It is also host to military infrastructure from Asian states, notably Japan (which had its first overseas military base since 1945) and China, which has built cooperation agreements in the region.

All others give Djibouti an outsised geo-strategic importance that belies its small size. It has located commercial investment in its port facilities from Dubai World, which has used the port as a stepping stone for its expansion into the rest of Africa. This has allowed it to emerge as a regional energy hub for Northeast African states but also for the military forces located within its borders. This positioning and geo-strategic importance bring in significant revenues for the state. Over the longer term, there is talk about Djibouti being at the head of a regional corridor for transport and energy. This, at the moment, seems some way off. However, the state is likely to face increased competition as the region starts to settle down as piracy subsides. Already, ports in Eritrea and Somalia are looking to attract some of their traffic, though Djibouti's regional primacy is unlikely to be challenged for some significant time. Indeed, FDI into Djibouti since 2012 seems to reinforce that many of the major leading industrial and military powers see the state's position as a regional hub as being sustained. This is also true for many of the regional exporters who also persist in using Djibouti as their port of choice.

## QUESTION

What are the main risks to Djibouti from its positioning as a strategic maritime hub?

## CONCLUSIONS

Despite the progressive onset of globalisation, the state remains a prominent force within the global economic system. However, the state is adapting to the pressures of the global economy, and this has its most evident expression with the rise of the competition state. As a consequence of this, states are seeking to position themselves to deliver a set of commercial conditions that attract footloose businesses and/or facilitate the emergence of innovative, high-value businesses. This creates a focus on competitiveness among states, which is determined by a diverse set of factors. However, as much as the debate has focused on competitiveness, there is also a need to consider the possibility and actuality of absolute and relative state failure.

## KEY POINTS

- The state is at the cornerstone of the global system.
- The state determines the rule of engagement for international business.
- State strategies attract investment and promote its development.
- More states are hostile to hyperglobalisation.

## QUESTIONS FOR DISCUSSION

1) To what extent are there parallels between state strategy and corporate strategy? What are the main differences?

2) Why does national competitiveness matter?

3) Why is state failure so rare?

## ACTIVITIES

Using the WEF competitiveness framework, choose a state and assess its main strengths and weaknesses with regard to its international competitiveness.

## SUGGESTED FURTHER READINGS

Acemoglu, D., & Robinson, J. A. (2012). *Why nations fail: The origins of power, prosperity and poverty*. New York: Crown.

Acemoglu, D., & Robinson, J. A. (2013). *Why nations fail: The origins of power, prosperity, and poverty*, New York: Crown Business.

Fougner, T. (2006). The state, international competitiveness and neoliberal globalisation: Is there a future beyond 'the competition state'? *Review of international studies*, *32*(1), 165–185.

Fougner, T. (2008). Neoliberal governance of states: The role of competitiveness indexing and country benchmarking. *Millennium*, *37*(2), 303–326.

Genschel, P., & Seelkopf, L. (2015). The competition state. In Leibfried (ed.) *The Oxford handbook of transformations of the state*, 234–249.

Palan, R., & Abbot, J. with Phil Deans. (1999). *State strategies in the global political economy*, London: Pinter.

Porter, M. E. (1990). The competitive advantage of nations. *Competitive intelligence review, 1*(1), 14.

Rodrik, D. (2012). Who needs the nation state? Centre for economic policy research working paper, no. 1040. www.cepr.org.

World Economic Forum (WEF) (2017). Global competitiveness report. www.wef.org.

# CHAPTER 4

# GOVERNANCE ISSUES IN AN INTEGRATING WORLD ECONOMY

## OBJECTIVES

This chapter will help you to:

- Understand the link between globalisation and the changing role of international institutions.
- Describe the functions of the main international institutions;
- Identify and assess the arguments of critics of international institutions;
- Assess the crisis in the WTO;
- Describe how international institutions can have a direct impact on international business.

Increasing international economic integration and the emergence of cross-border, and even globally, integrated networks of production and distribution raise the need for regulation that spreads across the customary regulatory (that is, state) boundaries and beyond the reach of traditional regulatory authorities. This increased difficulty in regulating business is welcomed by arch neo-liberalists: the placing of the activities of the private sector beyond the reach of the state fulfils a basic tenet of neo-liberal philosophy – that is, the removal of the state from as much economic life as possible. For others, globalisation, through its bypassing of the state, undermines democracy and excludes non-elite groups, whether they be labour interests in the developed world or developing countries, from decisions that have a significant impact on their well-being.

Assuming that it is not possible to put the globalisation genie back into the bottle, the focus of regulatory attention must shift from the national to the supranational level. The majority of international institutions were established immediately after World War II to deal with the problems facing the post-war world. They have since evolved to take account of subsequent international political and economic changes, encountering scathing criticism

DOI: 10.4324/9781315184500-5

along the way. According to some, the globalisation imperative has superseded the nation state and undermined national sovereignty and democracy. Some critics go further and assert that international institutions have been captured by big business and have driven the globalisation agenda to the detriment of the rest of society. Other critics acknowledge the enlargement of market boundaries and the need for regulation to correspond to the world, as it is not the world as it was. Their remedy is not to dismantle international institutions, as urged by some, but to reform existing institutions or establish new international institutions and/or instruments of governance. George Monbiot, a strident critic of globalisation, is one example of this: his solution to the problems of globalisation as he sees them is not to destroy international institutions, seen by many anti-globalisation campaigners as the tools of globalisation, but to reform them so they become more democratic.

The purpose of this chapter is to examine contemporary international institutions that have an impact on the world economy and on business and to address key questions about their role in a more integrated international economy. The chapter begins by briefly tracing the evolution of contemporary institutions and establishing their scope in relation to business and the challenges facing them. It then outlines the characteristics and functions of the main institutions and considers the criticisms commonly directed at them. In order to pursue these points in more detail, particular emphasis is placed on the case of the WTO.

## LIBERAL INTERNATIONALISM AND THE GLOBAL GOVERNANCE SYSTEM

The established institutional architecture reflects the prevalence of the dominant paradigm of liberal internationalism throughout the 20th century. This is based upon states creating cooperative intergovernmental agreements to promote a rules-based system to promote the spread of liberal democracy and the spread of economic and social liberalism. This means, in practice, the spread of liberal economics based upon the spread of economic reform, lower levels of state intervention, and sustainable public finances. The underlying logic – in economic terms – is to promote market-led reform based on seeking to create uniform rules of interstate interaction. It is believed that this will promote – through solving common problems through cooperation and the promotion of market-led growth – systemic stability. This process of multilateral cooperative action was legitimised through the progression of globalisation and the interdependence that emerged as a consequence.

In the mid-to-late 20th century as well as the formative decades of the 21st century, the advance of liberal internationalism was led by the US and its allies. In this context, the emergence of the global governance architecture is to enable all states to cooperate to agree on the basics of a market-led system. The logic is that through the development of multilateral organisations, any systemic instability could emerge from the asymmetric distribution of power within the global system. The logic of the multilateral governance system is that all states are treated equally and cooperatively. This promotion of systemic stability was linked to creating agreements for the basics of international economic engagement through agreed trading rules through the GATT and, more latterly, the WTO. The system also gives order to the global financial system (through the IMF) and promotes market-led economic development through the World Bank. Each of these sought – in their respective domains – to promote market-driven stability.

The logic is that multilateralism replaces the potential destabilising forces of unilateral action. In economic terms, this process has its most high-profile expression in the Washington Consensus, which stressed that if a state wanted support from the global financial system, then it had to adopt pro-market reforms such as privatisation, economic reform, and liberalisation, lower government spending and debt, and remove barriers to trade and investment, among others. The logic was not merely doctrinal but also to limit the potential contagion effects throughout the rest of the global system. While these policy descriptions have proved controversial, they do have any underlying consistency with liberal internationalism. However, these economic measures and a consensus upon economic liberalism have been undermined by the 2008 Global Financial Crisis and the rise of populism, where 'globalists' and 'globalism' have been stigmatised as an elite preoccupation. The argument is that the preoccupation with the global ignores the impact of such policies upon the 'local'. As we shall see as this chapter progresses, the increased disillusionment with liberal internationalism (in this case with regard to its economic implications) has impacted the efficacy of the institutions to operate as promoters of a liberal economic system.

## CASE STUDY 4.1: CHINA AND MARKET ECONOMY STATUS

When China acceded to the WTO in 2001, it joined with non-market economy status. This meant that, at the point of joining, China allowed other states to judge the prices of Chinese goods differently from other states due to the high degree of government intervention within the economy. This support often came in more covert ways through favourable terms for credit, energy, and raw materials that were often offered to Chinese manufacturers at subsidised prices. This support made it difficult for other states to assess the true domestic (i.e., Chinese) prices of goods and services being traded and the margins that were attached to such goods. Thus, it became difficult to assess whether China was dumping goods or simply exploiting a natural cost-based advantage. As a result, both the EU and the US placed anti-dumping duties upon Chinese goods. This they did by using the 'third country' method, where Chinese prices were compared to those in another similar state.

For China, this non-market economy designation was a transitory status that was to be removed after 15 years. However, when this deadline was reached and then lapsed and there was no rescinding of the non-market economy status by either the US or the EU, the Chinese raised the issue with the WTO. China felt that it had made sufficient progress on the reform of prices that it should be judged the same as every other state (that is, dumping occurs when the price of exports is lower than local prices). For other states, there was still a lot of remaining ambiguity over the true value of Chinese prices and the extent to which they were being suppressed by the tacit mechanisms noted above. China could not definitively prove that it was operating as a market. For the US, countries could still use their discretion on such issues even if China was no longer automatically considered a non-market economy. For China, this gave countries a free rein to continue to discriminate – unfairly in its opinion. Thus, it was considering retaliatory tariffs for those states that continued to apply these anti-dumping duties.

At the core of the issue are the core differentials between Western and Chinese interpretations of how capitalist systems function. In the case of China, where there is a strong degree of state-based – as opposed to market-based – capitalism, there is the convention and expectation of a high degree of state intervention to steer and direct the economy to support the state's territorial and geostrategic objectives. This runs in contrast to the liberal notions of market economy that underpin the Western notion of capitalism. This strong role for Chinese state-owned and state-influenced businesses runs to the core of how states choose to manage their economies. Nonetheless, in June 2019, China withdrew its claim when the WTO found that it was to continue to accept anti-dumping levies. The pulling of the case was done before the case was finally published, so as to allow China to save face. However, the issue of how the WTO can function with two rival forms of capitalism remains unresolved.

## QUESTIONS

1) What do you understand by 'dumping'?
2) How do you reconcile strong state intervention with a liberal trading system?

## THE EVOLUTION AND SCOPE OF CONTEMPORARY INTERNATIONAL INSTITUTIONS

The major contemporary international organisations were established not to deal with globalisation but to contribute to the formation of the architecture of the post-1945 world and to prevent a repetition of global conflict. The United Nations (UN) was primarily concerned with the preservation of peace and security, although as it has evolved, it has taken on a number of economic and business-related functions. In the economic sphere, the victorious allied powers were of the opinion that a totally new system of trade and finance relationships should be established to avoid the currency volatility and trade conflicts that contributed to the pre-war economic instability. Accordingly, the International Monetary Fund (IMF) and the World Bank were created at the 1944 Bretton Woods Conference; the IMF was originally designed to oversee international financial markets and the World Bank to assist with reconstruction. The third leg of the Bretton Woods system was to be the International Trade Organisation (ITO). The Havana Charter setting up the ITO was never ratified, partly because of US concerns about the erosion of sovereignty. Instead, the GATT, never intended to be more than a transitional device preceding the ITO, became the primary, and very successful, instrument of progressive trade liberalisation. It was not until the WTO came into being in 1995, 47 years after the GATT came into effect, that the construction of the Bretton Woods institutions was complete.

All the major institutions set up in the aftermath of World War II have subsequently undergone significant change as unenvisaged political and economic changes have brought about a coordinated international response. The IMF's role, for example, has changed; the first challenge to it was the collapse of the Bretton Woods system of fixed exchange rates in the early 1970s. Moreover, with the expansion of its membership, the IMF's reach has become global, and, as well as shouldering the responsibility of international financial stability, the IMF has become a key player in development finance.

## The United Nations (UN)

Well known for its role in maintaining international peace and security, the 193-member UN also plays a significant role in fostering international cooperation in international economic, social, cultural, and humanitarian problems and in promoting respect for human rights and freedoms. As such, UN activities have significant implications for international business, both in terms of helping to create a safe, stable, and favourable environment for business and development and more directly in terms of specific initiatives like the United Nations Environment Programme (UNEP) (see Chapter 15) and the Global Compact, which commits signatories to operate along the line of corporate social responsibility in the areas of human rights, the environment, labour, and corruption.

The UN has six main organs: the General Assembly, the Security Council, the Economic and Social Council, the Trusteeship Council, the International Court of Justice, and the Secretariat. Most of the economic work of the UN is the responsibility of the Economic and Social Council. This body oversees many of the UN's programmes and funds, including the United Nations Conference for Trade and Development (UNCTAD), UNEP, and the United Nations Development Programme (UNDP); consults with NGOs; and is the vehicle by which the UN's specialised agencies work with the UN. There are 15 specialised agencies, or autonomous organisations, that work with the UN and each other through the coordinating mechanism of the Economic and Social Council.

## The International Monetary Fund (IMF)

Established as part of the Bretton Woods institutions in 1944 with 45 members, the IMF was a central part of the framework for economic cooperation that was intended to avoid some of the economic policies that had contributed to the 1930s Depression. The IMF's main objectives are the promotion of international monetary cooperation, the facilitation of the balanced growth of international trade, the promotion of exchange rate stability, assistance in the establishment of a multilateral system of payments, and making resources available to members encountering balance of payments difficulties. In short, the IMF is responsible for ensuring the stability of the international financial system.

The IMF gets its resources from the quotas or capital subscriptions paid by its 190 members. The quotas are determined according to a member's relative size in the world economy. Accordingly, the US pays the largest quota (17.43 per cent at the end of March 2023) and Palau the smallest (0.001 per cent of the total quota). Unlike the UN General Assembly and some other international institutions, the IMF does not operate a one-member, one-vote system. It is the size of the quota that determines a country's voting power, and therefore, according to IMF policy, each member has 250 basic votes plus one extra vote for each SDR 100,000 of quota. This formula yields 831,401 votes for the US and 1,508 votes for Palau.

The IMF's main activities include

1. Lending: the IMF provides credits and loans to members in balance of payments difficulties and extends financial resources to its members via a range of facilities. The IMF's lending is conditional on countries following appropriate policies to correct balance of payments problems. It is the terms of this conditionality that have brought forward the most intense criticisms of the IMF. Some adjustments have been made to IMF conditionality to address some of the complaints, and the IMF is making greater attempts to tailor policies to individual country needs and to enable countries to retain ownership of their domestic policy programmes.

2. Technical assistance: the IMF offers technical assistance and training to help members strengthen their institutional capacity and design and implement effective macroeconomic and structural policies.

3. Surveillance: the IMF engages in a policy dialogue with each of its members and annually appraises the exchange rate policies of each of its members within the context of their overall economic policies. The IMF also conducts multilateral surveillance, the outcome of which is published twice a year in the World Economic Outlook and quarterly in the Financial Stability Report.

The formal role of the IMF has remained unchanged, but the institution has had to reform and adapt to major changes in the world's economic and monetary systems. Globalisation, particularly advances in technology and communication, has increased the international integration of financial markets and fostered more intense linkages between economies. Consequently, financial crises tend to be more contagious and spread their effects more rapidly among countries than previously, when borders were less porous.

Although primarily a monetary and not a development institution, the IMF has increasingly assumed a development role, requiring countries to adopt sound and stable macroeconomic policies. This has become a much greater imperative as its membership has expanded to include many of the world's poorest countries. Accordingly, there is some overlap between the roles of the IMF and the World Bank, as reflected in the joint IMF-World Bank *Initiative for the Heavily Indebted Poor Countries* (the HIPC Initiative). This development role was also evident during the COVID-19 pandemic when the IMF stepped in to offer support for states with emergency funding, grants, and other forms of liquidity, especially for developing states where there was the risk of a severe recession and/or long-term damage from the short-term curtailment of economic activity. This was evidenced by the actions of the IMF during the COVID-19 pandemic.

More recently, the IMF has come under pressure as debt levels among many sub-Saharan African states are rising, with much of this debt being owned by China. At the time of writing, many of the Chinese creditors were unwilling to take any write-downs on the loans offered, resulting in the IMF's limited ability to offer debt relief. The risk is that the money to support debt relief might simply go to the lenders rather than actually helping the state out of its difficulties. For China, the issue is that it has to shoulder too much of the risk in any write-down and that the IMF solely protects Western interests. This problem has been compounded by the absence of reform in those states to whom the IMF has already lent. The IMF is lending merely to preserve systemic stability rather than solving the source of the problem. These risks make the IMF irrelevant.

## The World Bank

Also set up at the Bretton Woods Conference in 1944, the World Bank's initial focus was on the reconstruction of post-war Europe. The official title of the institution, the International Bank for Reconstruction and Development (IBRD), which has 189 members, reflects the bank's role in reconstruction, an imperative that continues in terms of its work in areas like humanitarian emergencies, natural disaster relief, and post-conflict rehabilitation in developing and transition economies.

Since the early 1980s, the bank has become heavily involved in macroeconomic stabilisation and debt rescheduling in developing countries, a role that has led to some overlap with the work of the IMF. Social and environmental issues have also increasingly permeated the World Bank's work. All these issues are important for the World Bank, but its current overriding objective is to provide technical and financial assistance to reduce poverty and increase living standards in the developing world. The World Bank's approach to development issues has been the target of severe NGO criticism for applying market criteria indiscriminately across developing countries. The bank's approach, never quite as black and white as its critics asserted, has subsequently become more nuanced, with greater emphasis on the institutional and governance structures of the recipients of development assistance as well as the economic context.

These days, it is more accurate to refer to the World Bank Group rather than the World Bank. It consists of five institutions that specialise in different aspects of development. Technically speaking, the term 'World Bank' only refers to the IBRD and the IDA, whereas the IFC, the MIGA, and the ICSID are World Bank affiliates. The five institutions are:

- The International Bank for Reconstruction and Development (IBRD): the original World Bank institution, the IBRD's main role is the provision of loans and development assistance to middle-income countries and creditworthy poorer countries.

- The International Development Association (IDA): the IDA began its operations in 1960 and is the World Bank's concessional lending window, providing long-term loans at zero interest to the poorest developing countries.
- The International Finance Corporation (IFC): the IFC was established in 1956 to promote sustainable private sector development in developing countries and has become the largest multilateral source of loan and equity financing for private sector projects in the developing world.
- The Multilateral Investment Guarantee Agency (MIGA): MIGA was established in 1988 to promote FDI in emerging economies. It carries out this task mainly by offering political risk insurance (guarantees) to investors and lenders and by helping developing countries attract and retain private investment.
- The International Centre for the Settlement of Investment Disputes (ICSID): the ICSID was set up as an autonomous organisation (albeit with very close links to the Bank) in 1966 to provide facilities for the conciliation and arbitration of disputes between member countries and investors. Arbitration within the ICSID framework has become the main mechanism for the settlement of investment disputes under multilateral trade and investment treaties such as NAFTA, the Energy Charter Treaty, the Cartagena Free Trade Agreement, and the Colonia Investment Protocol of Mercosur.

## The World Trade Organisation (WTO)

Despite its transitory status, during the 47 years in which it operated as the main focus for the regulation of international trade, the GATT was extremely successful in its main task – the liberalisation of trade. As a result of the eight multilateral tariff-cutting rounds that have taken place, the weighted world average tariffs on manufactured goods have fallen from about 40 per cent in 1947 to 3–4 per cent following the Uruguay Round. Nevertheless, despite low average tariffs, tariffs remain substantial on a number of products, and tariff reductions remain an important aspect of the GATT agenda, which has been carried forward into the work of the WTO.

The basic objectives and principles of the GATT were also carried forward into the 1994 Marrakesh agreement setting up the WTO – that is, in search of … rising living standards and full use of the world's resources (substituted for by 'sustainable development' in the WTO), the WTO will seek 'the substantial reduction of tariffs and other barriers to trade and … the elimination of discriminatory treatment in international commerce'.

Notwithstanding this continuity, the role of the GATT/WTO has expanded and developed in the following important ways:

- Membership: membership has risen from the original 23 contracting parties in 1947 to 164 by 2023. Several new members have joined in recent years, including Afghanistan in 2016, Lao PDR in 2013, Liberia in 2016, and Russia in 2012. The most significant addition to WTO membership occurred in December 2001, when, after long and complex negotiations, China became a full WTO member, closely followed by Taiwan. As a result of expansion, WTO rules now cover over 98 per cent of world trade.

- Agenda expansion: as tariffs were reduced and market access became easier, other barriers to entry became more apparent, and negotiations to reduce these non-tariff barriers began. The Tokyo Round (1973–9) represented the first occasion when this happened in an extended way with agreements, among others, on anti-dumping, subsidies and countervailing measures, procurement, technical standards, and import licencing procedures. The Uruguay Round pushed an expanded agenda even further and included negotiations on previously excluded areas like trade in agricultural products and services. The expansion of GATT/WTO activity also marks a move towards deeper integration (see Chapter 1). In other words, as the removal of barriers existing at the border becomes more complete, the emphasis shifts to regulating away differences in domestic policies that may discriminate between domestic and foreign producers.

- Reduced plurilateralism: in the pre-Uruguay Round era, many GATT undertakings were plurilateral; that is, contracting parties would choose which of the agreements they would sign up to. As part of the obligations implicit in being a member of the WTO, member states have to commit themselves to complying with all the obligations of GATT, GATS, TRIPs, etc. This redresses the situation in which countries could pick and choose which regulations they wished to adhere to. This requirement is known as the 'single undertaking'. A parallel can be drawn between the single undertaking and the basic EU principle of the *acquis communautaire*, which states that to become a member of the EU, a country must accept all the existing policies of the EU.

- Strengthened dispute settlements: one of the most important developments of the Uruguay Round was the transformation of the GATT dispute settlement system from one that was weak and whose decisions could be vetoed by the contracting party against whom a decision had been taken to one in which decisions were enforceable.

The WTO continues to evolve in the same direction of wider membership and with a wider agenda but has encountered serious problems in carrying all its members with it during the current Doha Round, discussed in more depth below.

\* \* \*

The above constitute the major international institutions that regulate economic and finance matters that have an impact on business, but they are far from being the only organisations playing such a role, either on a regional or a global basis. For example, regional development banks such as the Asia Development Bank, the African Development Bank, and the Inter-American Development Bank complement the work of the World Bank. The main objective of the Bank for International Settlements (BIS), created in 1930 to deal with issues of war reparations, is to foster cooperation among central banks and other agencies in pursuit of market and financial stability. New institutions have also emerged in line with changing circumstances. The International Energy

Agency (IEA) itself is a case in point: it was established following the 1973 oil crisis for the purpose of coordinating the response of industrialised nations to the sudden tightening of crude oil supplies.

---

### Box 4.1: The Asian Infrastructure Investment Bank (AIIB)

The Asian Infrastructure Investment Bank (AIIB) was launched in 2016 with the aim of financing infrastructure that would enhance Asian interconnectivity across all the component sub-regions and so provide a platform for these states to connect more completely into trade routes to Europe. This tied the establishment of the AIIB to the development of the high-profile Belt and Road Initiative (BRI), which was launched by China to improve land and maritime trade routes between China and Europe. The AIIB has – as one of its major aims – the capacity to offer finance to states to upgrade national infrastructure systems so as to allow them to improve this international connectivity. In part, the AIIB was seen as a response to the failure of pre-existing international financial institutions (IFIs) to offer sufficient finance to allow many of these Asian states to modernise their infrastructure systems.

As of 2023, there are 106 members covering all continents, with the bank being given the highest credit rating by the leading rating agencies, which allows the bank to expand its lending capabilities. As of 2023, the AIIB had a capital base of $100 billion, which is around two-thirds of the Asian Development Bank and half that of the World Bank. However, the AIIB has a narrower focus than these other bodies.

The motivations for the development of the AIIB were – on behalf of China – both internal and external. The internal driver reflected that there was overcapacity in parts of the construction sector as the high infrastructure investment which characterised China over the formative decades of the 21st century started to tail off. Thus, these businesses were looking for new markets. The second was external, and this was based on a feeling that the existing IFI structure was not evolving fast enough to reflect the growing economic and political power of emerging economies and that being dominated by the US led to them being poorly focused on emerging economy needs and requirements. This resulted in a funding gap for key projects that were seen as central to the development of many emerging Asian economies. In particular, China was concerned that there was not enough emphasis within these bodies upon infrastructure investment and that the remit of bodies (notably the World Bank) was far too broad. There was also concern that these bodies were too slow in project preparation.

Opinions on the AIIB have been split. While many developing and emerging states have been in favour of the body, many developed states are suspicious of the intentions of the Chinese in developing the bank. Notably, there is a fear that China could use the lending to support its broad geostrategic goals over market-based investment. There is also fear that this is not as beneficial to other states as it might appear, especially if they are compelled to use Chinese inputs so as to absorb the aforementioned excess capacity within their construction industry. It is unlikely that the finance offered by the AIIB would be enough to absorb the excess capacity required. Moreover, this capacity forces this constraint on states, which depends on the integrity of local governance. Where it is strong, such approaches are unlikely to be successful, though they may work in states where there is weaker governance.

Ultimately, the BRI is bigger than the AIIB, so alone, the latter will be of limited influence. Also, the absorption of excess capacity will depend more upon internal reform than this export-driven strategy. The rise of the AIIB offers states another option to attain development financing, and one that is less dependent upon the US and the promotion of its narrow agenda. In short, this should be a welcome addition to the IFI system.

**QUESTION**

Did the global financial system need the AIIB?

## GLOBALISATION AND GOVERNANCE

The biggest and most challenging changes to global governance have occurred since the end of the Cold War and the collapse of many long-held assumptions about competing power blocs and ideologies. Within this context, Francis Fukuyama in 1989 spoke of the 'end of history', a reference to the ending of the struggle for supremacy between communism and capitalism with victory for the latter. In other words, the neo-liberal revolution that had begun in the early 1980s with Reaganomics and the Thatcherite Revolution in the UK (see Chapter 1) had spread to most corners of the globe. However, as the post-Cold War era unfolded, it became apparent that economic and political issues were as fiercely contested as ever but that the controversies were no longer couched in terms of competing political and economic systems and ideologies. For international institutions, this meant the expansion of membership as former Communist states adopted free market principles and focused their agenda on measures to help the market operate more efficiently.

In addition to these politically driven changes, other factors came to the forefront and challenged the agenda and workings of international institutions, including greater capital mobility, more flexible exchange rates, ongoing development issues, the growth of emerging economies, the spread of e-commerce, and the proliferation of regional trading arrangements. All these factors, many of which are discussed in more depth in other chapters, have come together to increase interdependence in the international economy and pose serious questions about how and to what extent these increased international transactions can and should be controlled and regulated. Although the rationale and motivations of participants in contemporary debates vary, many of the arguments are essentially about what is the most appropriate level for regulation in a more interdependent world in which commercial transactions are less and less contained within traditional political (i.e., state) boundaries. These debates are often expressed in terms of concerns about the undermining of national sovereignty and the alleged excessive power of multinational corporations.

In view of the economic, social, political, cultural, and technological pressures that have resulted in increased international interdependence, the key question becomes how to compensate for the restricted ability of member states to regulate economic and business activities on their own. Is it appropriate to try to reclaim some of the power of nation states, as parts of civil society would argue (see below), or is it preferable to seek international responses to regulation challenges, either through greater cooperation among countries or through multilateral arrangements?

The changing and increasing number and roles of international institutions are not accidental but a response to the manifold changes alluded to above. Robert Keohane (Keohane 1998) explains this enhanced role for international institutions in the following way:

> Institutions create the capability of states to co-operate in mutually beneficial ways by reducing the costs of making and enforcing agreements - what economists refer to as "transaction costs".

In other words, given the increased need for nations to make agreements about cross-border transactions, it is more efficient for them to do so within an established framework of agreed rules and understandings than for them to negotiate multiple (i.e., with many countries) agreements from scratch every time a new cross-border issue requires their attention. In this way, greater transparency and predictability within the international environment are achieved, both for governments and for MNEs working within the international system.

The pressure from increasing cross-border transactions to find new methods and forms of governance is felt in areas of labour market regulation, the environment, investment, intellectual property, finance, competition policy, etc. The optimal solution is not always a supranational one; in some circumstances, governance at a sub-state level (that is, at local, municipal, district, provincial, or the equivalent) may be the most appropriate. Indeed, many sub-state organisations and institutions have reacted to new cross-border realities by seeking direct contact with their equivalents in other states, bypassing their own governments, or by seeking direct contact themselves with supranational institutions. For example, many regions within EU countries and individual US states maintain an office in Brussels to facilitate contact with EU institutions. Furthermore, there has been a growing trend for the devolution of power from central state institutions to lower levels. Between the state and the international institution, there has also been the emergence of regional arrangements (see Chapter 3), many of which have devised new regulations and ways of dealing with increasing interdependence and integration. In some ways, regionalisation can be viewed as an alternative to globalisation, but in others, it is driven by similar forces of cross-border technological penetration and transactions and provides a less extensive platform for the reaping of scale economies in production, distribution, and marketing. In the latter sense, regional trading arrangements can be seen as a stepping stone to globalisation rather than a turning away from it.

In short, globalisation has profound effects on the governance of economic and commercial flows. However, it is too simplistic to view globalisation as merely implying a shift in governance from the national to the supranational level, although the latter is clearly becoming more important. Rather, governance is changing in two important ways. First, as discussed above, the location of governance is shifting to a multitude of different levels, both above and below the state level. Secondly, elements of governance are developing not in the public domain, as is traditionally the case, but are increasingly becoming the focus of private sector activity.

The privatisation of governance encourages a focus not on international institutions but on international regimes, that is, the norms, rules, and decision-making processes that have been created to govern international life within specific issue areas. The broadest definition of privatised governance regimes would include the activities of various NGOs as contributors to the work of international institutions and to the scrutiny of private sector schemes (see below). In a narrower sense, privatised governance is concerned with private or quasi-public sector involvement in regulating the international business environment. The International Organisation for Standardisation (ISO) is an example of a non-governmental international organisation that draws up and oversees international standards in a range of areas, including quality and environmental management, which affect business. In other areas, as well as NGOs, private sector accounting and consultancy firms are frequently used to carry out monitoring of corporate codes of conduct in relation to the treatment of the workforce and the environment. In the financial sector, the ratings given by private bond rating agencies such as Standard & Poor's have taken on a quasi-official status that impacts official policy at all levels. In collaboration with the UN, banks and insurance companies have adopted a Statement of Environment Commitment, and the high-profile 'Responsible Care' programme has been developed by chemical manufacturers to improve the environmental record of their industry. Inevitably, part of the motivation for this latter initiative is to forestall the implementation of more stringent or more inflexible mandatory regimes, but such initiatives only ultimately work if they are underpinned by substance.

## The failure of the Doha Round and its legacy

In 2015, the WTO formally ended the Doha round without formal agreement. The talks had meandered on for nearly 15 years, with very little progress made in the final decade of their operation. It was hoped at the outset that they would be concluded within three years. However, it was evident from the outset that the potential for a deal was oversold, with much of the low-hanging fruit having already been harvested. The labelling of this round as the 'development round' was wildly optimistic, with, as mentioned, a special focus on agriculture. Even at the outset, there were issues, not least the sheer diversity of developing states and their divergent priorities. Moreover, the period of negotiation saw rapid changes within the global trading system, notably with the rise of China as an economic superpower. Finally, there was little support in developed states to expose their domestic farming sectors to competition from developing state exports.

With the failure of this round, the response of states has been to pursue more limited market opening opportunities through regional and more limited preferential trading agreements. Notably among these has been the Trans-Pacific Partnership (which the US signed up for and then backed out of), which includes many leading developed states bordering the Pacific. These are seen as a poor replacement for WTO rounds as they tend to reflect the agenda of the most powerful signatory. On the plus side, there is the possibility that such limited agreements could act as a platform for the reignition of another round of global trade liberalisation.

This offers a way for global trade liberalisation to progress alongside the WTO. States can engage in plurilateral discussions, which could then be brought into the WTO system. This limits the problems with the WTO, where consensus is required before an agreement is reached. This clearly erodes the possibility of speedy decision-making. There is also the position that WTO rounds should be a lot less ambitious and focused upon. However, the efficacy of the WTO has been hampered by the erosion of its capability within dispute settlement (see case study). This is especially worrying as this is one area of the WTO's action where it was seen to be successful.

## CASE STUDY 4.2: THE NEUTERING OF THE WTO – THE US AND THE DISPUTE SETTLEMENT MECHANISM

The WTO's dispute settlement mechanism is at the core of the body's work. It offers a legal framework through which states – where bilateral negotiation has failed – can seek to resolve a trade dispute. This is done by requesting the formation of a panel, which eventually issues a report. States can appeal the conclusions of this report to the WTO's appellate body on questions of law. This appellate body offers a final decision upon the report, which it can uphold, modify, or reverse. Since 2019, this appellate body has been unable to deliver any final decisions as appointments to its seven-person panel have been blocked by the US. This has left many trade disputes in limbo.

The US has long expressed concern with regard to the appellate body, often feeling that there was a strong degree of judicial overreach in their decision-making and that this process was often too protracted. The concerns reached the stage of concrete action during the Obama administration when the US refused to appoint a US representative and objected to a Korean appointment. This disengagement by the US was accelerated during the Trump administration when it refused to approve the replacement of any members whose terms had expired. This led to a situation where there was no appellate body in place to hear any appeals. States could have accepted the panel decisions thereby rendering this issue irrelevant, but many – in practice – appealed, which left a series of disputes in stasis. Though the US and other parties have put forward an interim solution based on a multi-party arbitration arrangement, this is at best an interim solution and is still met with resistance from the US.

The danger of this stance by the US is that it becomes more difficult to enforce global trade rules. As long as disputes persist, the WTO will not be able to sanction retaliation. This creates the risk of a trade war. While the US can feel it has been unfairly treated by the body, it has still won more cases than it has lost within it. Indeed, its record against China was 21–5 in its favour. Moreover, the US seems to want to pursue a unilateralist approach that damages the multilateral order. This is a stance that has continued under the Biden administration. In addition, while the

US is the leading exponent of the multilateralist order, it needs to offer solutions to the problems that it sees with the system. To date (2023), it has yet to do so. The longer the impasse continues, the more the WTO – as a source of global cooperation in trade – is undermined.

**QUESTION**

Are the US' criticisms of the WTO valid? Or has the US damaged the multilateral system?

## THE CRITICS OF INTERNATIONAL INSTITUTIONS

The current role and policies of many international institutions are under attack. The most visible signs of this are the street protests that have dogged the most high-profile meetings of the IMF, World Bank, the WTO, and other forums in which international leaders get together. G-8 meetings for several years (especially the meeting in Genoa in 2001 when a protestor was killed), the annual meeting of the IMF in Prague in 2000, the 2000 World Economic Forum in Davos in 2000, and, most famously, the WTO Ministerial in Seattle in 1999, which helped delay the launch of the latest round of multilateral trade talks, are just some of the more prominent examples of campaigning against the current global governance system. Demonstrations at G-8 meetings have continued, with the latest occurring in Japan in 2008. The WTO continues to be a target for protests; many arrests of protestors, particularly South Korean farmers, occurred at the 2005 Hong Kong Ministerial. Other international events continue to attract protests, but, for the most part, not in such a high-profile way, with more demonstrations currently taking place in developing and emerging economies against rising food and energy prices.

The critics of international institutions are often referred to as 'global civil society'. The term 'civil society' has a long history, referring to the relationship between the individual and society in general and particularly to the responsibility of individuals to behave responsibly towards society and of society to take some responsibility for the individuals within it. Civil society, however, is not a call for a return to efforts to build collectivist societies; indeed, modern usage of the term stems from the emergence of the popular movements in Eastern Europe that were central in bringing down Communism. Rather, civil society in the contemporary context is a response to the absence of civil and social responsibility from the versions of unfettered markets and capitalism championed by arch-neo-liberalists. In short, the idea of civil society is a halfway house between excessive state control and no state control whatsoever and also implies a more active and responsible role for individuals, a role that is absent in both the communistic and extreme neo-liberal views of the world.

In more prosaic terms, global civil society refers to the broad range of NGOs that operate across borders. The global dimension is a response to the increased global interconnectedness and the complexity, uncertainty, and lack of control experienced by individuals and small groups within this environment. Global civil society is an attempt to regain some control. The methods that NGOs advocate to achieve this vary, ranging from efforts to reform the institutions and make them and the activities and organisations they regulate more accountable to the rejection of globalisation altogether and a re-assertion of individual autonomy and more local organisation.

In short, the protestors represent a diversity of views and interests that are only able to come together on the basis of their opposition to the policies of international institutions. There is no unity in terms of what they support or propose. This is unsurprising given the diversity of subject areas, organisational forms, and geographical locations from which civil society is drawn. Specific issues on which NGOs are campaigning include the environment, health, human rights, labour conditions, education, development, gender issues, food safety, animal welfare, etc. Groups belonging to civil society include trade unions, charitable organisations, humanitarian groups, church groups, business associations and organisations, and single-issue organisations. Bodies like Amnesty International, Oxfam, Greenpeace, the World Wildlife Fund, and Médecins Sans Frontières are high-profile examples of individual NGOs. Some NGOs are global in coverage, in large part thanks to the improved communications and organisational capacity offered by the Internet. Others are more strongly associated with a region; although they have an international dimension, trade unions, for example, are still organised nationally and represent the interests of their members, which can conflict with those of workers elsewhere in the world.

NGOs can be classified along a number of dimensions. The rejectionist-reformist dimension has already been alluded to; that is, rejectionists reject the current international system altogether, and reformists seek to work within the system to improve it. Green and Griffith (2002) take this further and break down the rejectionist group into 'statists' and 'alternatives'. The statists maintain that globalisation has been a disaster and seek to rebuild the role of the state in economic management. They are dominated by sections of the traditional left, parts of the labour movement, and a large group of southern activists. The alternatives tend to be small, decentralised, and anti-corporatist in nature. Although not anarchists in the strictest ideological sense, they reject globalisation, concentrate on developing small-scale alternatives, and resist the intrusion of the market and market power relations into their cultural and political spaces. The reformists account for the majority of formally structured groups and agitate for gradual and peaceful change within existing systems to offset injustice and inequalities. They accept a role in the market but want it to be better regulated and managed to ensure social justice and sustainability. This group includes some trade unions, faith groups, charities, development organisations, and most mainstream environmental groups.

Robertson (2000) draws a useful distinction between advocacy and operational NGOs. Advocacy NGOs are essentially political organisations that lobby to influence decisions taken by governments and international organisations. These groups tend to portray themselves as outlets for public participation when national governments are unwilling or unable to act; in other words, they see themselves as making good some of the democratic deficit that has arisen as a result of globalisation pressures. As such, they belong to the reformist NGO trend.

Operational NGOs are those NGOs that work with and for a variety of international institutions to deliver services, usually in the developing world. The utilisation of NGOs in this way by international institutions is an example of the privatisation of governance referred to above. These services include humanitarian relief, health care, education, and other development-related projects. Robertson (Robertson 2000) estimates that 15–20 per cent of total official development assistance is currently distributed by NGOs. Scholte (Scholte 2000) reported that more aid is now distributed by NGOs than by the recipient states themselves. Not only do NGOs provide assistance on the ground, but they also play an increasingly important role in terms of providing expertise and information to feed into the policy formation process. Indeed, many NGOs have long played a technical and operational role, but this has been in relation to projects financed by their own fund-raising, as is the case with development charities like Oxfam. It is this experience that gives them credibility when delivering programmes on behalf of international organisations such as the World Bank, the World Health Organisation (WHO), and the UN High Commission for Refugees.

The reliance of international institutions on the operational and technical expertise of NGOs reflects the underfunding and under-resourcing of many international institutions. UNEP, for example, is heavily reliant on environmental NGOs, who have played a central role in pushing forward a number of multilateral environmental agreements such as the Montreal and Kyoto Protocols and even have observer status in relation to their implementation.

## GENERIC CRITICISMS OF INTERNATIONAL INSTITUTIONS

The criticisms levelled by NGOs at international institutions are many and varied. Some are highly specific to issues and institutions. The WTO often gets criticised, for example, because its trade policies are deemed to be bad for labour or environmental standards (see Chapters 14 and 15, respectively). Others are more general and are aimed at some or all of the main international institutions, to varying degrees. These criticisms fall into three overlapping categories: sovereignty concerns, democratic concerns, and inclusiveness concerns.

### Sovereignty

In the traditional view of sovereignty, nation states exercise complete and exclusive authority over the territory within their borders. Globalisation has undermined this. Many issues now spread across borders, especially in view of the lowering of barriers to trade. Technology has reduced the importance of fixed locations and territory in the conduct of commercial transactions. Hence, US and European companies are, for example, increasingly utilising the back-office and call-centre facilities offered from within the Indian sub-continent. Financial flows, the use of credit cards, and pressures towards regional or global currencies have undermined the ability of countries to operate their own monetary and exchange rate policies.

In short, economic interdependence and the need to regulate it have changed the nature of sovereignty itself. Regaining exclusive authority for national governments over what happens within national borders would require a reversal of many of the current globalisation trends and a degree of isolation that has resulted in lower levels of economic growth in the past among more connected countries. The comparative experience of export-promoting countries from Asia compared to import-substituting developing countries and the contrast between the fortunes of Spain and Portugal before and after their accession to the EU (the pre-accession period was marked by high tariff walls and GDP per head significantly below that of other Western European countries, whereas integration into a much bigger market has stimulated growth and brought these countries up to European levels) indicates that a return to a less integrated world may not be desirable on a number of grounds. Moreover, it may not be feasible.

The response to sovereignty concerns may be to rethink sovereignty. That is, not to regret the passing of the all-powerful nation state but to reclaim control over events and trends that impact the lives of citizens. To some critics, the EU is a major cause of the loss of national sovereignty within Europe. To others, the EU is not a cause of the decline of national power but a response to it: through cooperation and joint decision and policy making, member states are pooling their sovereignty and regaining some of the lost control.

The above argument can also apply at the international level through the creation of effective international institutions that help states regain collective control over transnational issues. The 2020 financial crisis posed serious questions in this area. On the one hand, financial interdependence appeared to be exacerbating the weakening of financial institutions across an increasing number of countries. On the other hand, the resolution of the problem, or at least measures to prevent similar events, could lie in the emergence of a global banking or financial institution regulatory authority. This outcome is far from certain, but there is a possibility that the consequences of a collapse of the international financial system may concentrate the minds of key decision-makers.

## Democracy

A common criticism levelled at international institutions is that they are undemocratic and deny the individual citizen a voice in their proceedings. In many, albeit far from all, countries, dissatisfaction with a government's performance will result in their removal from office via the ballot box. No such accountability confronts international institutions. However, international institutions are largely supranational organisations made up of individual member states that collectively set the agenda and determine policy. In institutions like the UN, the principle is one nation, one vote, whereas in organisations like the IMF, voting weights are determined by relative financial contributions. Whatever the representative process, the institutions are ultimately responsible to the constituent member states that, in turn, are responsible to their electorate, where appropriate.

In the above sense, international institutions can be regarded as democratic, however imperfectly. However, the democracy in question is indirect, and the link between citizens and international institutions is so distant and remote that the anti-democratic complaints about international institutions are understandable. Many NGOs argue that this lack of direct representation can be overcome by greater engagement of civil society organisations in the activities of international institutions. On the positive side, this offers the possibility of natural coalitions forming across borders around key issues like the environment or human rights, creating communities of interest across national boundaries.

However, this suggestion raises a number of serious questions about the democratic nature of the proposed solution itself and the democratic deficit of international institutions. First, there are thousands of NGOs. How is it to be determined which NGOs should participate in the international institutions? Secondly, and most importantly, who do the international institutions themselves represent, and how are they held accountable? The governance structures of NGOs vary, but many of them contain no provision for the election of officers or a forum for scrutiny of their policies or finances. One potential partial solution to this problem is the development of codes of conduct for NGOs that would commit them to appropriate scrutiny and to respect relevant national laws. In practice, international institutions are becoming more open to NGO participation to varying degrees. However, the optimum solution to problems of democratic deficits within international organisations is to develop proper democratic forms that extend beyond the nation state and to ensure that these institutions are sufficiently powerful to regulate global markets.

## Inclusiveness

A key criticism of international institutions is that, in practice, their policies discriminate against the poor in favour of the rich. This argument reflects the arguments examined in Chapter One that globalisation is not really global but affects only a triad of countries. It also reflects concerns about over-reliance on neo-liberal policies as the driving force behind the international economy, as such policies rely on competition, which tends to favour the strongest. However, despite sharing the frustrations of NGOs regarding the domination of major international institutions by vested (that is, developed country) interests, developing countries also recognise the benefits of open markets and often choose not to align themselves with NGOs. Moreover, developing countries have asserted themselves more and played a greater role in the Doha Round of multilateral trade talks. However, so far, the outcome has been a deadlock and an inability to find common ground not only between developed and developing countries but among developing countries themselves.

## AN EVOLVING GLOBAL GOVERNANCE SYSTEM

The pushback against liberal internationalism, the shift of economic power to Asia, and most notably, the rise of China. With many controversies surrounding these global bodies, China has been stepping in to replace them, notably the IMF. Since the mid-2000s, China has been lending large amounts of money to many developing states. This finance is offered without the usual conditions – as set by the IMF – of undertaking often painful economic reform. A potential source of finance is both China's export banks (such as the China Export-Import Bank and the China Development Bank), but also the emergent Asian Infrastructure Investment Bank (AIIB; see Box 4.1).

This lending has frequently been to aid the development of these developing states by offering finance for infrastructure. While this may create 'policy space' for these governments, there is a fear that this finance could lead to a sharp rise in the debt of these developing states, leading to a resumption of the debt crises that these states have periodically endured. However, what is indisputable is that this finance offers these states an open alternative to the IMF, especially where these states want to avoid borrowing from this body and wish to avoid the attached reforms.

These loans could also have a more contiguous effect upon the global financial systems, not least through the manner in which they change China's relationship with the IMF. In this case, the finance offered to these states could increase its influence within this institution. This is a place where China has long contested that it has been underrepresented. Despite this train of thought, it is more credible to argue that these loans are more of a direct overlap with the work of the World Bank. These loans are really for the lender of last resort activities with which the IMF is more closely associated, though there are aspects where China supports states that are suffering balance of payments problems that are more evidently overlapping with this function of the IMF.

There are many debates as to whether this represents a direct challenge to the IMF. It can be argued that this challenge is overstated, as China is still motivated by return and is still very careful as to how and where it invests. Furthermore, it does not have the money to fully replace the IMF for all the states that might require support. China, having a broader set of interests than the IMF, may offer finance where it can get an alternative form of repayment, such as through preferential access to natural resources or through support for the geopolitical position China is taking. Thus, China will be careful as to what states it selects for reporting; if there is no prospect of pre-payment in any form, it will not lend. The conclusion, therefore, is that China operates as a limited alternative to the IMF. Indeed, in doing so, it is merely mimicking other powers, such as the US and Japan, who have also offered such finance to developing states.

---

**Box 4.2: IMF and COVID-19**

The COVID-19 pandemic, despite being first and foremost a public health crisis, was also very much a sharp economic shock to the global economic system. This sharp downturn in economic activity could have had a dramatic impact upon the financial well-being of countries, which would have seen tax revenues suppressed (as economic activity fell), debt servicing challenged, and existing public spending commitments challenged. On top of this, there was the anticipated sharp increase in public spending required by the pandemic, created by the need to fund vaccination programmes and by the need to enhance public health systems to cope with the anticipated surge in demand created by high infection rates. While many developed states would have coped with these short-term pressures, it was widely accepted that the exposure of many emerging and developing states to such a risk would create a contagious risk within the global financial system.

To mitigate against such risks, the IMF developed a short-term programme to support the most vulnerable states so that the public health crisis did not become a full-blown economic crisis. Thus, the IMF offered a series of actions to enable the most vulnerable states to cope with the short-term drop in revenues created by the COVID-19 pandemic. The main focus of this series of actions was to:

- Offer short-term emergency financing to enable the most vulnerable states to meet the immediate spending needs created by rising infection rates.
- Enable increased debt relief for the most exposed 29 states, allowing these states to channel more funding to public health.
- Suspend debt repayments for a short period – in agreement with the leading developed states – to facilitate increased fiscal space for the most vulnerable states.
- Increase financial safety nets available to the most exposed states.

Overall, the IMF provided short-term assistance to over 100 states, mainly to help these states cope with short-term balance of payments problems created by the pandemic. This help is likely to have to persist depending on how these states cope with the longer-term economic consequences of the COVID-19 pandemic (such as through erosion of a state's trading capacities and loss of labour force). These measures taken by the IMF were coupled with the large fiscal stimulus advanced by many of the leading states to maintain economic activity levels within their own territories. Inevitably, such actions spill over into the broader economic system, further militating against any long-term economic shock to the global system. These actions have to be supported by economic cooperation more generally, that allows for guaranteeing public health supplies in developing states and limiting any protectionist pressures in the post-pandemic recovery stage. This is needed to ensure that pre-existing interstate inequalities are not worsened as a long-term legacy of the pandemic. This underlines that recovery from the pandemic requires more than the IMF but a concerted long-term global cooperative effort.

**QUESTION**

Was IMF support during the COVID-19 pandemic necessary?

## CONCLUSIONS

The WTO, other international institutions, and their constituent members need to come to terms with the substantial changes that have occurred in the world economy during the final quarter of the 20th century and beyond. Globalisation implies a shift to larger and expanding markets that have moved beyond and no longer correspond to traditional state boundaries. Many anti-globalisation protestors argue that this places MNEs beyond the reach of national regulators and above the law. Their response falls into one of two categories: either to reject globalisation (an objective that would be difficult if not impossible to achieve) or to reform existing international institutions so that they catch up with the new market realities. Although international institutions have adapted their roles to changing circumstances over the years, their response to the implications of an increasingly borderless environment has been sluggish and lags behind market realities. This relative unresponsiveness is a function of the difficulties of reconciling the divergent interests of nation states and regions and the jealousy with which nation states guard their increasingly illusory sovereignty. The contemporary problem of global governance is that the globalisation process and the need for transnational regulation of this process are occurring at a quicker rate than the international institutions and their constituent national members can respond.

## KEY POINTS

- Globalisation has made it more difficult to regulate the activities of businesses and has created a regulatory gap.
- International institutions have been strongly criticised by NGOs; some NGOs seek to abolish international institutions and turn their back on globalisation, whereas others seek to reform them.
- The role of international institutions has evolved along with changing social, economic, political, and technological circumstances. Nevertheless, international institutions are reactive and lag behind economic and market realities.
- The imperative for increased global governance will strengthen as international economic integration intensifies.
- It is economically more efficient for states to engage in cross-border governance issues at a multilateral level. However, it may not always be politically expedient for them to do so.

## DISCUSSION QUESTIONS

1. From the perspective of international business, which is the most important level of regulation — the national, the regional, or the international?
2. Why is the WTO so controversial?
3. Discuss the contention that the NGOs represent no one but themselves and that they are no more democratic than the institutions they criticise.
4. Is the problem with international institutions that they are too powerful or that they are not powerful enough?
5. 'Global governance is just a euphemism for global government' – Jacques Attali. Critically assess this statement.

## SUGGESTED FURTHER READINGS

Brewster, R. (2018). The Trump administration and the future of the WTO. *Yale Journal of International Law Online (2018), Duke Law School Public Law & Legal Theory Series, (2019–2010)*.

Green, D., & Griffith, M. (2002). Globalization and its discontents. *International Affairs, 78*(1), 49–68.

Hufbauer, G. C., Schott, J. J., & Wong, W. F. (2010). *Figuring out the Doha Round*, Vol. 91, New York: Columbia University Press.

Keohane, R. O. (1998). International institutions: Can interdependence work? *Foreign Policy, 110*, 82–194.

Keohane, R. O. (2011). Global governance and legitimacy. *Review of International Political Economy, 18*(1), 99–109.

Lopez-Claros, A., Dahl, A. L., & Groff, M. (2020). *Global governance and the emergence of global institutions for the 21st century*, Cambridge UK: Cambridge University Press.

Park, S., & Vetterlein, A. (Eds.) (2010). *Owning development: Creating policy norms in the IMF and the world bank*, Cambridge UK: Cambridge University Press.

Robertson, R. (2000). The historical context and significance of globalization. *Development and Change, 35*(3), 557–565.

Tallberg, J., Bäckstrand, K., & Scholte, J. A. (Eds.). (2018). *Legitimacy in global governance: Sources, processes, and consequences*, Oxford, UK: Oxford University Press.

Van Grasstek, C., & Pascal, L. A. M. Y. (2013). *The history and future of the world trade organization*, p. 201, Geneva, Switzerland: World Trade Organization.

# CHAPTER 5

# REGIONAL INTEGRATION AND GLOBALISATION

## OBJECTIVES

By the end of this chapter, you should be able to understand:

- The nature and form of regional economic integration.
- The interface between the motives for regional economic integration and the process of globalisation.
- The diverse number and forms of regional economic groupings across the globe.
- The importance of regional economic integration for international business.
- The importance of new regionalism.

The process of international integration – as reflected in globalisation (see Chapter 1) – has bred a response from states both within and beyond the context of the regions within which they are located. Indeed, the trends which are stimulating integration on a global level are evidenced with greater intensity at the regional level. Even then, the degree of maturity between regions on the state of regional integration varies markedly among different parts of the global economy. These differences occur for both political and economic reasons. At its heart, regionalism is about preferential trading agreements among a limited group of states. In practice, formal economic integration very often, although not always, follows from such preferential trade agreements – the forms of which are highlighted in Box 5.1. All of these definitions highlight that the basis of regional economic integration is the removal of discrimination among economic actors in participating states. Despite this, regionalisation at its core implies discrimination between states that are members of the regional grouping and those that are not.

Initially, this chapter examines the motives for the push towards regional economic integration, highlighting the underpinning objectives of such actions. In assessing the role that these moves have had upon global trade, the chapter assesses the main regions where integration has risen upon the commercial and political agenda. The chapter then moves on to examine the development potential of preferential trading agreements

DOI: 10.4324/9781315184500-6

through the emergence of `new regionalism'. It then examines the implications of these developments for the internationalisation of business, before drawing conclusions.

---

**Box 5.1:** Levels of regional integration

Regional economic integration arrangements can take many different forms, including:

- *Preferential Trade Agreements:* this is the loosest type of arrangement and is based upon the granting of partial preferences to a set of trading partners. The concessions offered tend to be unidirectional, such as those extended by the EU to the African, Caribbean, and Pacific (ACP) states. If reciprocated, then the term preferential trade area is applied.
- *Free trade area*: when two or more states eliminate internal barriers to trade – such as tariffs and border restrictions – while sustaining their own independent tariffs vis-à-vis non-member states. Rules of origin are used to prevent trade deflection.
- *Customs union*: when two or more states not only eliminate internal barriers to trade but also introduce a common external tariff. This avoids trade deflection – where all goods and service imports from non-members enter the area through the state with the lowest tariffs – and implies a common trade policy.
- *Common market*: when member states agree to supplement free trade in goods and services with free movement in factors of production (notably labour, capital, and, increasingly, information). The removal of these barriers expands the size of the market available to most, if not all, enterprises, thereby allowing businesses to expand their operations to other member states.
- *Economic union*: this occurs when countries agree to coordinate core economic policies (such as interest rates and exchange rates). This implies a common stance on inflation and, ultimately, a single currency. As factors of production move freely between states, pressure grows for coordinated policies to manage these flows.
- *Political union*: when states agree to common policies in almost every sphere of activity (including foreign and defence policy). Deeper economic integration could stimulate political integration as governments increase interaction among them. Such interactions could legitimise moves towards political union.

---

## THE NATURE OF REGIONAL INTEGRATION

Regional economic integration is influencing an increasing number of states and is becoming ever more prominent in commercial decisions. The WTO has sanctioned an increasing number of preferential trade agreements over recent decades, covering all continents (see below). Current moves towards regional integration represent a departure from previous efforts, which have been neither as numerous nor as successful. The WTO identified four main trends in the formation of RTAs:

1.  Most states have placed RTAs at the centre of commercial policy, implying, in many cases, a shift of resources from multilateral trade objectives towards these preferential agreements.

2.  These RTAs are exhibiting a higher degree of sophistication, expanding to include trade in services and trade policy areas not regulated multilaterally, and their approach is becoming both innovative and not guided merely by physical proximity.

3.  There is a shift in the geopolitics of these zones as the number of north/south agreements increases, often replacing long-established non-reciprocal systems of preferences (see below).

4.  The expansion and consolidation of RTAs as different blocs are consolidating into single pan-continent-wide blocs.

In the last decade or so, there have been qualitative as well as quantitative changes in regional integration schemes. The first such change is a growing recognition that effective integration involves more than the reduction of tariffs and other conventional barriers to trade. Participants have come to recognise that new non-tariff barriers have worked to fragment markets. The second emerging facet is the shift from closed regionalism to a more open model. As mentioned, agreements have shifted from being based upon import substitution towards export-led models. A third development has been the emergence of trade agreements between developed and developing countries, such as the North American Free Trade Area. These have been compounded by the following factors:

1.  The replacement of national markets by global markets.

2.  The perceived success of existing agreements, most notably those in Europe.

3.  The decline of geographical determinants of financial location and the internationalisation of the division of labour.

4.  The continued strengthening of multinational and private policy-making structures relative to the authority of the state.

5.  A concern not to be left out of the growing web of preferential deals by both the US and developing states.

6.  A belief in the business community that as product cycles get shorter and multilateral negotiating cycles get longer, quicker results may be obtained regionally.

7.  The desire to use regional liberalisation as a catalyst for domestic reform.

8.  A concern by the government to use preferential trading deals for political or strategic purposes.

9.  Pursue non-trade concerns such as the environment or labour issues.

These factors stress how rationalisation and neo-liberalism are implicit in moves towards regional integration. The resulting exposure to international markets requires not only domestic policy adjustments but also an increased desire to solve common problems collectively. The result has caused a convergence between policymakers as to how exactly the challenges of globalisation should be met.

It is useful to make a distinction between the twin interrelated forces of regionalism and regionalisation. The former is policy-driven regional integration stimulated by formal economic cooperation agreements. The latter is market-driven integration spurred by regional growth dynamics, the emergence of international production networks, and related flows of FDI. Regionalism is often identified by preferential trading agreements among neighbouring states. These can take different forms, with the main difference being based on the extent of preference granted to members and the degree of policy coordination among states. Whether such agreements are beneficial or not is often seen as a trade-off between the benefits of liberalisation and the increased discrimination that arises as a result. Conventional economic theory dictates that economic welfare is maximised under conditions of global free trade. Thus, it is argued that, in the absence of the ideal scenario, regional integration represents a second-best option. A summary of research seeking to quantify the gains from regional trading blocs tends to be mixed. Indeed, many have reached the conclusion that, in the absence of clear-cut benefits, many have turned to rationales based on political economy.

It is difficult to quantify the rising importance of RTAs. Simply using a count of the number of RTAs signed as an indicator of regionalism is flawed, as many of those that are signed are of limited importance to the global economy. In particular, according to Pomfret (2007), many of these bilateral deals reflect the fallout from the transformation of Western Europe and the USSR. Using the share of world trade covered by Regional Trade Agreements (RTAs) as an indicator is an alternative measure. It is noted that RTAs cover 55–60 per cent of global trade and as much as 90 per cent of the total trade of members (2022). Many RTAs are predated by lower tariffs; thus, it cannot be argued that they necessarily caused increased trade, as the aforementioned political factors may be evidence. Furthermore, many of the new regional blocs reflect deeper integration as policy measures are included as a means of seeking to harmonise trade conditions. As RTAs extend beyond trade, measuring their importance in terms of trade can overstate their importance in terms of this transaction (as these were already taking place) but can understate their importance in terms of international political power.

The removal of discrimination between states – the raison d'être of the process – is a means of increasing the welfare of participating states. Such welfare increases are derived from the potential boost to competitiveness arising from the process of regional economic integration and greater efficiency in resource use. These welfare changes underline the core reasons as to why states form regional agreements, notably that:

- These agreements have the potential to raise economic growth through economies of scale.
- States can lower trade barriers to partners, increase discrimination against third parties, and increase the welfare of their citizens.
- Regional specialisation allows firms to derive tangible commercial benefits from 'learning by doing' and attract foreign direct investment.
- Domestic policy reforms can be sustained, thereby enhancing the credibility and sustainability of the chosen measures.

- There are evident opportunity costs from remaining outside a trading bloc.
- Regional economic integration can act as an effective platform for competing within global markets
- Such economic agreements can stimulate regional cohesion and security.

Many of the welfare effects of the creation of PTAs are derived from the relative effects of trade creation and trade diversion. This is based on the recognition that while governments will lose tariff revenue, they may gain through efficiencies in terms of the lower cost of alternative sources of supply and trade policy towards non-member states. The changes in the trade flows also alter the location of production, something that is determined by the comparative advantage of the respective member states. This will be influenced by cluster effects and by the possibility of technology transfer among member states. This process could lead to convergence of economic development between states as labour-intensive activities switch towards lower-wage states, although the opposite forces can also apply if activity focuses upon the wealthiest areas of the regional bloc. In addition to these benefits, there is a perception that the process of regional economic integration and the liberalisation that accompanies the process will aid in the channelling of resources from partner economies into activities where they are most likely to excel.

The notion of natural trading partners arising from physical proximity has often been called into question. Despite this, geographic proximity seems to be a feature of regional and/or preferential trading agreements. This reflects that there is an unavoidable spatial dimension to these processes. In part, this spatial dimension is created by savings in transaction costs, availability of specialised inputs and assorted spillovers. In addition, there are historical and geographical forces at play which can translate a home bias into a neighbourhood bias. Alongside these forces are those driven by politics. These are integral to regional integration, reflecting that political and economic forces are busy coevolving within any integration agreement. The most notable features of the new impetus towards regional integration are that:

- It reflects the move towards liberalisation.
- Most groupings tend to be outward-looking, looking at regional agreements as a reason for economic growth.
- It represents attempts by states to benefit from trade creation, economies of scale, product differentiation, and efficiency gains.
- The resulting agreements seek to encourage foreign direct investment between participants.
- Regional integration is a global phenomenon, with a rising number of agreements between the north and south becoming evident [e.g., North American Free Trade Area (NAFTA) and Asia Pacific Economic Cooperation (APEC)].
- Some states are members of a number of regional groupings (e.g., the US is a member of both APEC and NAFTA).

As Figure 5.1 shows, the majority of RTAs are FTAs, reflecting that this type of agreement best reflects the types of needs of the states in terms of speed, flexibility, and

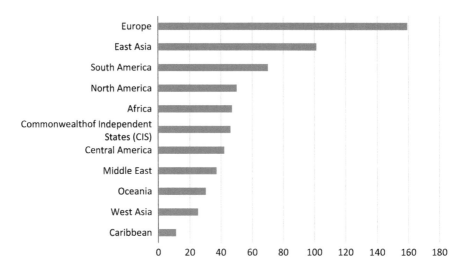

**FIGURE 5.1** RTAs in force: participation by region.
Source: WTO

selectivity. CUs appear to have become less popular and are perhaps out of tune with the current trading climate. Another key trend is the dominance of bilateral over pluri-lateral deals. Indeed, over 80 per cent of all RTAs are bilateral. This is caused by the fact that the opportunities for plurilateral deals are fewer and their technical complexity is simpler, though it should be noted that many of these bilateral deals are based around plurilateral agreements, pointing to the consolidation of established trading relation-ships. The erosion of proximity as a driver of RTAs is underlined by statistics which suggest that while almost 90 per cent of all RTAs in force are intra-regional, over 40 per cent of those that are signed and being negotiated are cross-regional. This figure is even higher for those that are proposed (as of December 2022), where over 50 per cent are cross-regional. These figures lead to a questioning of the rationale for RTA formation among natural trading partners and reflect the fact that states will look further into the field once regional opportunities have been exhausted.

It has been argued that the process of regionalisation exists in opposition to the pro-cess of globalisation. This viewpoint is based upon a perception that the latter is char-acterised by the openness of economies and an emerging global market for enterprises. Enterprises push for regional integration as an anti-competitive device to limit the nega-tive effects of competition. Others, such as Bhagwati (1992), see regional integration as a force that fragments the global economic system and removes the incentives for states to engage in global free trade. The result is that regionalism is at the direct expense of multilateralism. It is clear from basic economic analysis that the process of regional economic integration can be both negative and positive — negative in that it can lead to trade diversion and positive in that it can lead to trade creation (Robson 1980). Clearly, the relative benefits of trade creation and trade diversion determine the extent to which moves towards regional economic integration work to the advantage of integrating states.

It can be credibly argued that regionalisation is a logical response to globalisation. Traditional economic theory perceives regional integration as a second-best scenario compared to the ideal of global free trade. Thus, in a situation in which a truly globalised economy is not practical in either political or economic terms, regional integration is the next best thing. Regionalisation is also compatible with the process of globalisation, as the former can easily stimulate the latter, acting as a building block for deeper global integration. In a relatively closed environment, an island of free and preferential trade is likely to be detrimental to the efficient functioning of the global economy. However, if regional integration takes place against a background of liberalising global trade, then concerns are lessened as the benefits from more open markets can potentially offset losses from the absence of global free trade. In any case, increasingly few of these regional agreements emerge as solely protectionist measures.

Regionalism confronts states with a number of broad policy choices. First, they initially have to decide with whom to form an agreement. Broadly, states that are similar in terms of economic and political development as well as geographically close provide a greater case for regional integration. Secondly, they are faced with choices regarding the policy to be taken vis-à-vis non-members. States have to decide how discriminatory they will be towards non-members as well as how favourable they will be to key trading partners. Thirdly, they have to decide upon the degree of integration to be pursued. Different states have different motives for the integration process and differ on the salience of political sovereignty. Finally, states have to decide on the extent of the agreement. This depends on the policy areas covered as well as the number of states bound by the agreement.

The trend towards these agreements is not likely to come without political costs. In particular, there have been concerns expressed over the trade-off between a state's desire to preserve political sovereignty and the desire to enjoy the benefits of economic integration. This could become a salient issue if there is an internal dynamic within the process that moves states towards deeper political unification almost by default (Robson 1980). Broadly, according to Lawrence (1995), the political implications of the shift towards regional economic integration lie along a continuum of six options:

1. National autonomy: almost total freedom over decision-making by governments.
2. Mutual recognition: again, decentralised decision-making with market competition guiding moves towards common standards (notably the EU's guiding principle of mutual recognition).
3. Monitored decentralisation: limited restrictions on policy to secure international harmonisation. International bodies such as the IMF may monitor this.
4. Coordination: an open recognition of the need to converge policies with jointly agreed adjustments to policies.
5. Explicit harmonisation: this requires explicit agreement on regional-wide standards.
6. Federalist mutual governance: centrally enforced rules through supranational institutions.

The position of a state along this continuum would depend upon the extent and intensity of policy spillovers between separate states within the regional grouping. The more intense these spillovers, the greater the legitimacy of deeper levels of political integration.

There are evidently political motivations pushing states towards developing regional agreements. These are essentially threefold:

- Security: the participating states can use the regional economic agreement as security against non-members as well as enhancing security vis-à-vis other members of the grouping. The integration of states not only makes conflict more expensive, but the regular political contact involved also establishes trust and other forms of cross-border cooperation. However, this has to be counterbalanced by the potential for conflict through commercial tensions between participants, especially where the benefits of the moves towards regional integration are unevenly distributed.
- Bargaining power: this is based on the premise that when states combine their power, they can 'punch' more effectively within the global economy. These benefits, of course, depend on states being able to come to a common agreement on key issues.
- 'Lock in': the process of political and economic reform can be effectively locked in through membership in a regional integration body. Thus, the agreement acts as an effective commitment mechanism.

## GLOBAL TRADE AND REGIONAL INTEGRATION

Regional integration agreements are officially sanctioned (subject to conditions) for deviations from the GATT's rules on non-discrimination. Generally – under Article 25 of the GATT – three principal restrictions are imposed upon regional agreements.

- The agreement must not 'on the whole' raise protection against excluded states.
- They must reduce internal tariffs to zero and remove other restrictive regulations on commerce within the regional agreement area, other than those justified by other GATT articles.
- They must cover 'substantially all trade'.

These conditions seek to ensure that regional integration agreements do not undermine the access of other countries to the integrating area. The second and third conditions are designed to deter pressure to use tariffs to offer political favouritism towards either domestic industries or partner countries. The conditions imposed by the GATT/WTO can be imposed gradually, although greater leniency is generally extended to developing economies than developed economies. Article 5 of the GATS is tighter than Article 24 of the GATT and applies on a sector-by-sector basis rather than 'on the whole'. In addition, it gives businesses from third countries operating within the region before the agreement is signed the same rights as indigenous businesses. Again, developing states get greater flexibility over the rules. The conditions over the coverage of trade allow developing countries to reduce tariffs on mutual trade in any way they wish.

There is clear overlap between RTAs and the WTO in that both share the common objective of trade liberalisation, though the former is discriminatory, a facet not shared by the latter. While discrimination was meant to be outlawed by the GATT, the

MFN principle has been eroded by successive preferential trade arrangements. Some of these were introduced to account for differing levels of development, while others were introduced to allow likeminded members to pursue faster liberalisation of trade. Given the difficulties of multilateralism, it should come as no surprise that RTAs are proving increasingly attractive. This has implications for multilateralism, as the benefits of RTAs could be extended to a multilateral framework. Such open regionalism has no precedent, in fact. In addition, the lack of a framework for the dos and don'ts of the RTAs gives members significant flexibility in their design. As a result, these agreements rarely address sensitive sectors. Overall, international policy towards regionalism seeks to:

- Allow agreements to realise trade creation, avoid trade diversion, and ensure that the process does not unduly harm non-members.
- Permit deep integration among members.
- Preserve the effects of previous liberalisation and ensure that any liberalisation within the agreement has credibility.
- Support a liberalising dynamic throughout the global economy.

By 2016, all of the WTO's 164 members were parties to a regional trade agreement. Not all agreements notified to the WTO are still in force today, although, in practice, most of the discontinued agreements have been superseded by re-designed accords. Out of a total of 583 (2022) agreements that have been notified to the GATT/WTO, 355 are still in force. In the 1950s, there were very few notifications to the GATT. In the 1960s, notifications averaged two to three a year. In the 1970s, the number of notifications increased, reaching a peak of ten in 1973. During the 1980s and early 1990s, notifications dropped off considerably until 1992, when 11 new regional trade agreements were notified. Since then, an average of 11 regional trade arrangements have been notified annually to the GATT/WTO. In 2021, a new peak was met when 64 notifications of RTAs (across both goods and services) were submitted. The result of all these agreements is a complex set of interrelationships. In addition to those that have been notified to the GATT/WTO, the number of regional trade arrangements that have not been notified has also grown.

The number of trade agreements notified to GATT/WTO has increased from 20 in 1990 to 86 in 2000 to 355 in 2022. The agreements concluded over the past two decades have been mainly bilateral in nature and primarily between developed and developing economies. Furthermore, many of these have included provisions aimed at deepening integration through harmonising elements of national policies in line with agreements to free up market forces between partners. To some, the shift towards agreements between states from different geographical regions constitutes a 'new regionalism' (see below). Though most of these agreements are bilateral, the new regionalism represents a diversion from multilateralism as states grow frustrated with the protracted negotiations involved in multilateral trade negotiations. Overall, it can be seen that multilateralism affects RTAs on three levels:

1. Through WTO rules on RTAs.
2. Market access commitments.
3. Other trade-related rules and disciplines.

There are major difficulties with the rules provided by the GATT/WTO Treaty over regional integration agreements. There are uncertainties over what is actually meant by 'substantially all trade'. Does it refer to the proportion of trade or all sectors? Similarly, there is a lack of definition for rules of origin and no method of assessing the overall level of trade restrictions. Such uncertainties have resulted in weak enforcement of Article 24. This has resulted from the consensual nature of the enforcement bodies and from an inability to make an adverse comment without the agreement of the offending party. The rise in the number of RTAs created led to an administrative bottleneck, as according to GATT practice, a working committee has to be established to examine the agreement. As a result, the WTO established the Committee on Regional Trade Agreements (CRTA) to verify the compliance of notified RTAs with the WTO provisions and consider the systemic implications of such agreements for the multilateral trading system. However, failure to agree on the provision contained in Article XXIV became a major concern for the DDA.

The impact of regional integration arrangements on the multilateral system revolves around three sets of arguments.

- Multilateralism as a response to regionalisation: some states excluded from the regional integration process may respond by seeking to speed up multilateral liberalisation. Some saw the formation of the EEC as a catalyst for the Dillon and Kennedy rounds of GATT. This is simplistic: regional integration may not only be defensive but also offensive within the context of multilateral negotiations and therefore act as a powerful force driving the liberalisation process forward.
- Regionalisation and multilateral negotiation: if regional blocs aid and simplify the process of negotiation, it is feasible that freeing trade on a global basis would become easier. While this might appeal intuitively, it does assume that all blocs are able to present a uniform front – something that has often been lacking within trade negotiations. Indeed, the benefits of coordination may be outweighed by the costs of combining different interests. This issue is likely to be made more difficult as the WTO extends its capabilities into areas where the central bodies of regional agreements have little power. Thus, combining national and regional responsibilities further complicates matters. There is also a danger that regional integration may result in inward-looking blocs that may be less willing to negotiate multilaterally. The result would be harmful to the credibility and effectiveness of the WTO.
- Regional integration and the frontiers of liberalisation: it is claimed that regionalism makes it easier to handle difficult issues. Agreements between likeminded states can aid liberalisation, even if only on a limited geographical scale, in instances where multilateral progress is simply not possible. But in some areas (such as agriculture), there have still been problems with difficult issues. The impact of regional integration agreements depends on whether they are liberal and whether they are well suited to the needs of other countries.

The Doha Declaration recognised that RTAs could play an important role in promoting the liberalisation and expansion of trade and development. Indeed, while states have made a renewed commitment to multilateralism within Doha, they have also increased their commitment to regional groupings. This gives RTAs the green light, though Doha does seek to clarify and improve the disciplines applying to these agreements. Negotiations within the DDA have focused on two tracks: procedural and systemic/legal issues. There has been progress on the former, as member states have agreed to increase transparency in July 2006. The latter is proving more difficult due to the complexity of the issues involved. The improvement of transparency has set a procedure for early announcement, a timeframe for notification, the type of information to be submitted, and streamlined procedures for notifications and reporting. This should revitalise the CRTA, help overcome the problem related to the 'spaghetti bowl' (see below), and enable businesses to unravel the complexity associated with the multitude of agreements.

Some argue that all agreements should be open to outsiders if they meet the necessary requirements. However, this conflicts with the desire of some states to limit access to their grouping for political as well as commercial reasons. A more fundamental concern is the inadequate enforcement of existing rules. In part, this results from the prolonged period some states are given to implement GATT/WTO rules. The result is that all states lose out through trade diversion effects. Such poor enforcement is symptomatic of the lack of implementation of rules generally – something that potentially undermines the benefits states can gain from the internationalisation process.

There is a case to make for an economic system based upon regional groupings, especially in terms of the development of the progressive liberalisation of the global economy. In an increasingly complex system, any attempt to rationalise the number of parties around the table in trade agreements has the potential to make the liberalisation of the trading system easier. Also, as states exist in groups, they have the power to punch collectively above their weight and avoid any sidelining that may occur had they been negotiating alone. Thus, the development of a series of blocs could act as a system of countervailing powers, preventing any state from dominating the system. The WTO Report 'The Future of the WTO' criticised the proliferation of bilateral and regional trade agreements on the basis that they had made the MFN clause the exception rather than the rule. The consequence of this is that it has increased discrimination in world trade. Despite this, these agreements continue to progress, with the US being especially active, concluding many deals with developing states.

Research from the World Bank (Solaga and Winters 1997) reaches a negative conclusion on the argument that regional integration works to the benefit of the multilateral system. Indeed, the institution fears that regionalism could dilute the power of those bodies dedicated to multilateral trade liberalisation. Frankel (1998) suggests that if regional trading agreements are to work for and not against the global trading system, then they have to adhere to strict rules such as a proper enforcement of GATT rules, an insistence that barriers to exclude third parties are lowered, and an assurance that membership in these groups is open. By adhering to these principles, these blocs could lead the way in multilateral trade development.

To strengthen the rules governing regional integration agreements (particularly so that they do not reduce overall levels of welfare), many suggest that approval should be subject to a commitment to lower barriers vis-à-vis non-members. Such a commitment should reduce the potential for trade diversion as a result of the instigation of the regional trade agreement. Srinivasan (1998) suggests that regional trade agreements should be merely temporary and contain a commitment by participants to extend the benefits to other states within a given time frame. This would effectively ban regional agreements. Others suggest non-exclusive membership criteria, but this, due to geography, is often unrealistic. More feasible is to enforce existing rules more completely. A starting point would be to remove the legal uncertainty regarding key terminology (such as that surrounding 'substantially all trade'). In this sense, a benchmark figure needs to be established. The World Bank suggests 98 per cent within ten years of the initiation of the agreement.

Such changes need the political commitment of the member states and the WTO to take them forward. As of yet, the WTO seems unlikely to do this. It lacks credibility and legitimacy, as well as the resources to operate an effective scrutiny system for regional trade agreements. In short, the management of regional agreements and their compatibility with the global trading system cannot be ensured without credible regulation, scrutiny, and enforcement. Without this, the WTO relies on bilateral relations to ensure that these developments do not turn the mass of regional blocs in on themselves.

Baldwin (2008) argues that the global economy is characterised by a 'spaghetti bowl' of unilateral, bilateral, and multilateral deals, which no one agrees is the best way to organise trade. This can create too complex a system or a multilateral system to emerge. The spaghetti bowl is based on the following features:

1. Different rules of origin and/or exclusions of different lists of sensitive goods can mean that three bilateral agreements can procure trade that is less than free.
2. Bilateral cumulation (where inputs from one state are considered to originate in another) can distort the purchase pattern.

The result is a tangled web of uncoordinated and often conflicting rules of origin and bilateral cumulation. Among these trends, which could undermine multilateralism, the WTO, according to Baldwin, has remained largely passive. The spaghetti bowl creates a problem as it generates the following:

1. Economic inefficiency: multiple tariff rates introduce inefficiencies, especially within industries that have complex value networks.
2. Stumbling blocks: they can hinder progress towards multilateralism due to tariff differentials.
3. An absence of hegemony: the WTO rules tend to mitigate the power of the hegemons; this could be subverted by the complexity of the spaghetti bowl.

These problems could be overcome by setting all MFN tariffs to zero and switching to diagonal rules of culmination (a common set of rules of origin is agreed upon where once a product enters the market, the product is determined by common standards). Thus, the product will never lose its original status. The complexity of the spaghetti bowl reflects the complexity of the political and economic forces that evolved it. The result was a hub-and-spoke system that was highly selective over the form and nature of the deals. The power exists within the hubs, while the spokes will each face different rules with regard to access to the hub.

Baldwin (2017) argued for the existence of a domino effect within regionalism, believing that the forces of regionalism, initially working independently of each other, will at a certain point trigger a multiplier effect that would knock down trade barriers like a row of dominoes. This would open up a path to regional and potentially global liberalisation. This domino effect is generated by trade and investment diversion created by the process of regionalism, leading other states to join existing or establish their own RTAs. These effects are created through a new political economy in non-participating states, which pressures governments to join RTAs. Firms from excluded states see their performance undermined by exclusion and pressurise the government to act to ensure that export costs are not sacrificed for import-competing concerns. According to Baldwin, the key organising principle behind this process is reciprocity, which creates a juggernaut once export interest outweighs import competing ones.

The OECD (2003) highlights that many RTAs go beyond the WTO rules as they contain measures that are more far-reaching across a broader range of sectors. For services, many RTAs adopt a top-down or negative-list approach whereby everything is liberalised unless otherwise specified. This is in stark contrast to the positive list approach of the WTO, where liberalisation only applies to specified sectors. Furthermore, many RTAs eschew anti-dumping measures in favour of coordination in competition policy, allow limited labour mobility, allow freer FDI, and allow freer competition in public procurement. Overall, across many areas, the OECD highlights that RTAs go beyond the remit of the WTO. This can extend to issues such as the environment.

There is also a concern as to whether RTAs create convergence or divergence over multilateral standards. There is a concern that these agreements can create an a la carte approach in areas such as investment rules and competition that could result in confusion and inconsistency across the global economy. The OECD suggests the picture is mixed. The RTAs can promote harmonisation by applying WTO approaches, using other international agreements, or helping to forge future common standards. This can be complemented by RTAs facilitating cooperation and technical assistance. Alternatively, these RTAs can promote divergence, as convergence at the regional level does not always translate into harmonisation at the global level. This has already been evident in the treatment of IPR and approaches to anti-dumping, where approaches differ markedly across RTAs. This could raise transaction costs for MNEs and cause trade friction.

Similarly, the issue of whether RTAs are beneficial or harmful to outsiders has to be handled carefully. While these are clearly discriminatory, there is evidence to suggest that RTAs are willing to extend regional preferences to non-members on an MFN bias, especially under GATS. Similarly, there is scope for non-discrimination within the domain of competition policy as well as investment. However, there are clearly benign effects as they can alter investment patterns, making them vulnerable to capture by protectionist interests as well as other areas where politics may play a role.

## MOVES TOWARDS REGIONAL INTEGRATION IN THE GLOBAL ECONOMY

Although it is beyond the scope of this chapter to analyse all regional integration agreements, it is worth taking a brief look at their form and nature on a continental basis. It is evident that not only are these agreements – as noted above – becoming more widespread, but they are also becoming increasingly complex as states develop deeper relations with others at different levels of economic development. Thus, the regional trade agreements are not merely about the formally agreed groupings pursing integration plans but also regarding preferential trading agreements with more geographically dispersed states.

### Europe

Economic integration within Europe revolves around the EU, and to a lesser extent, the European Free Trade Area (EFTA). The EU was originally conceived as a political project that sought to promote economic cooperation among states as a strategy to ensure that war between these states became impossible. Membership in the group is open to all European states as long as they conform to basic principles, namely that they are European and are committed to democratic and market processes. The 1957 Treaty of Rome not only committed states to a customs union but also required deeper integration through the development of common policies in a number of areas. The management of such policies was aided by the establishment of a governance structure based on supranational institutions. The gradual enhancement of the power of these supranational bodies has been a salient factor pushing the integration process forward.

Europe has, for a long time, provided the model for economic integration. While the process was initially a political one, commercial forces have increasingly driven it. This has led to the deepening of integration as the EU has evolved from a customs union to a common market and, for the majority of states, into an economic and monetary union — a reflection of the acceptance by states that deeper integration was in their broad political and commercial interest. This gradual extension has resulted in states ceding sovereignty in an increasing number of areas. Successful deepening depends upon the continual commitment of member states to sustained micro-economic reform. A broadening process has accompanied this deepening as the membership has been extended from 6 to 27.

The cementing of political and economic reform is the primary reason for the ex-communist states of Central and Eastern Europe to apply to join the EU. On the whole, existing members are agreeable to such an extension. In practice, the deepening of European integration alongside the extension of membership is likely to result in the emergence of a multi-speed Europe or a Europe of 'variable geometry' given the variation in economic readiness and political enthusiasm for deeper integration among European states.

In 1992, the smaller EFTA grouping joined with the EU to form the European Economic Area. This effectively opened up the single European market to small northern European and Alpine states. In gaining access to the single market, the EFTA states had to implement the same competition laws as the EU. This agreement led the larger EFTA states to seek and obtain full membership in the EU. This highlights how important the Single European Market programme was to the integration process in Europe. The programme, in effect, kick-started an integration process, which had lain dormant for two decades.

With the accession of central and eastern European states into the EU and the likely accession of the remaining Balkan states, attention is turning to the limits of the defined European region. Of particular controversy is the proposed accession of Turkey to the EU. Many argue that Bosphorus is a natural physical barrier to Europe and that, as a result, most of Turkey is in Asia. Furthermore, there are cultural concerns and issues about whether the EU would be able to absorb a large state that is at a substantially lower level of economic development. However, political imperatives are pushing the EU towards integrating with Turkey as western economies seek to build commercial and cultural ties with Muslim economies.

However, formal economic integration between members seems to have reached some degree of impasse. Despite a growing list of states wanting to join, only one state has done so since 2008, namely Croatia in 2013. In part, this has been driven by enlargement fatigue by existing members who felt that the 2004 enlargement of many eastern European states created problems of absorption and integration, which has deterred many members from further rapid expansions. This has been coupled with rising degrees of Euro-scepticism across the EU, which has limited prospects for deeper integration within the bloc. This had its ultimate expression in the UK's decision to leave the bloc in 2016 and retreat to a very limited free trade agreement with the other 27 states (see case study). However, the difficulty of this process seems to have calmed down similar movements in other states.

The impact of the deeper integration initiatives upon outsiders is difficult to assess. However, two features are evident. First, deeper integration stimulated the expansion of the EU as applicants felt that the political and economic benefits of deeper integration outweighed any potential political and economic losses. Secondly, there is little indication that a deeper Europe resulted in a more protective Europe, as many feared, although the EU does remain, at best, a highly discriminatory trading partner. To this end, it has signed a number of preferential trading agreements with developing states.

Europe is the region that has signed the highest number of RTAs, accounting for over half of the RTAs notified to the WTO and in force. These are based around the EU, EFTA, and, to a lesser degree, south-eastern Europe. This latter sub-region has concluded the CEFTA agreement. The ties between this region and the EU are being formalised by the latter, as both Croatia and Turkey are under negotiation. In addition, the EU has signed a stability and association agreement (SAA) with Serbia and Montenegro. In the Mediterranean basin, the EU has signed an FTA that is gradually being deepened. Beyond its neighbourhood, the EU has signed RTAs with Mercosur, the GCC, and six economic partnership agreements with the ACP states. More recently, it has signalled its intent to develop new FTA arrangements with Korea, India, and state parties to ASEAN, CACM, and CAN. Parallel to the EU, EFTA has signed numerous agreements with Mediterranean states, the GCC, and some Southeast Asian states.

## CASE STUDY 5.1: BREXIT: THE UK'S DEPARTURE FROM THE EUROPEAN UNION

There is a long-standing belief that economic integration exhibits its own internal dynamism, where the development of the customs union creates the conditions for the development of a single market, which in turn creates the dynamics for economic union. The logic was that increased interactions promote interdependence, enabling fuller and more inevitable economic integration. This consensus on this seemingly unstoppable process was shattered with the decision of the UK to leave the EU in 2016, with the final departure secured at the end of January 2020. It was not so much that the UK left that was an issue, but the manner in which it left, with a bare-bones trade and cooperation agreement in effect decoupling itself from its largest market. For the UK, this was the necessary price to restore its sovereignty.

In practice, the UK had always sat uneasily within the EU (and its predecessor, the EEC). It did not join at the outset, but when it did join in 1973, it has always had a rather detached commitment to the process of economic integration. There are a number of explanations for this detached position, driven by a mix of physical separation from continental Europe, the legacy of the Empire, the fact that the UK has not been invaded since 1066, and differences in commercial culture, to name but a few. Nonetheless, Euro-scepticism was for much of its membership a niche political belief, and only then was it more about drawing limits to membership than withdrawing entirely from the group. The signing of the Maastricht Treaty in 1992 began to mainstream this otherwise minority view, believing that the EU was now stepping too far into state sovereignty. Symptomatic of this disenchantment was the rise of the UK Independence Party (UKIP), which started to eat away at the Conservative Party (in opposition in the late 1990s to 2010, but in government thereafter). This rise in its vote had less to do with strong feelings with regard to EU membership (which was low down the electorate's list of concerns) and more to do with the detachment of mainstream political parties from groups who felt they were excluded from mainstream political debate.

The rise of austerity in the UK in the aftermath of the global financial crisis and its impact on these excluded and 'left-behind' groups allowed UKIP to tie this to EU membership, especially in light of a sharp rise in the number of EU migrants allowed into the UK after the removal of barriers to mobility. The UK government expected 30,000 to arrive in practice, but more than a million did, and they moved into areas where they competed for public services (already under pressure from austerity) with these left-behind groups. Thus, what was a peripheral issue for the electorate was mainstreamed and linked into notions of how the UK's sovereignty (in this case, the control of its borders) was contravened by EU membership. This stoked the emergence of national populism across all major parties, though mainly the ruling Conservative Party.

In an attempt to finally settle an issue that had been a long-standing sore within the Conservative Party, then Prime Minister David Cameron called a referendum for the 23rd of June 2016. While the vote was a narrow win for leaving the EU, it heralded a sustained period of political uncertainty, largely because Brexit itself was largely undefined, especially with regards to the legacy trading rules. Would the UK leave the Single Market? Would it be part of a customs union? How would land borders with the EU in Ireland be managed? In the end, the UK opted for maximum sovereignty and a minimal trade agreement with the EU, leaving both the customs union and the single market. This was hugely disruptive for business but seen by the advocates of Brexit as a price worth paying for control to be restored.

It has often been said of the UK that it lost an empire and did not find a role. For many, being a European power within the EU was that role. With Brexit, that role is being redefined. For the advocates of Brexit, the new role is that of the UK as a global trader operating independently of any regional bloc. However, the longevity of such a strategy is questionable given the mutual geostrategic interests of both the EU and the UK. In truth, the UK is possibly the furthest point of its orbit away from the EU, and closer relations are inevitable over time. What has happened is that other movements in Europe that have advocated EU withdrawal have not shied away from it, having seen the difficult economic and political issues involved.

## QUESTION

Do you think the UK's experience of leaving the EU makes further departures more or less likely?

## The Americas

The economic turmoil that hit the Americas in the 1980s was a primary catalyst behind the moves towards economic integration in this part of the global economy. The debt crisis and deteriorating trade balances pushed a wave of reform, including privatisation and a sustained attack on traditional trade and investment barriers. Latin American states became especially vulnerable to US pressure to pursue reform. In the 1990s, virtually all Latin American states instigated reforms aimed at integrating their economies into the global economy. In short, there was a distinct policy shift from import substitution to export promotion.

For Mexico, the NAFTA agreement broke its traditional policy of intervention and was a means of securing access to the US market. The external impact of this agreement has yet to be seen. But the temptation of accessing the US market has led to other Latin American states seeking NAFTA membership, and NAFTA has come to be the focus of regional integration in the Americas. It is entirely possible that NAFTA could facilitate a restructuring of the hegemonic positioning of the US with regard to Latin America and ultimately eliminate the numerous Latin American regional trade agreements. The extension of the agreement concerns non-members, notably the newly industrialising states of Asia, as it could lead to a redirection of US investment away from them. The NAFTA agreement is much shallower in terms of integration than the EU. It seeks to remove all barriers to trade in goods as well as barriers to foreign investment and trade in services. Other states can join as long as all existing members assent, but unlike the EU, there are no explicit longer-term political objectives. NAFTA is unique as it represents an almost free trade agreement between two developed states (US and Canada) and a developing country (Mexico), though Canada and Mexico do little trade with each other as each uses it primarily as a platform for preferential access to the US market. The agreement has been criticised due to its rules of origin, which, according to many, will have large trade diversionary effects. However, evidence seems to suggest that these states are natural trading partners and that the current low tariff barriers will ensure that trade diversion will be limited.

In 1995, intra-group trade was 46 per cent of member states trade. By 2022, it was just over 49 per cent. This does not suggest that it was a great spur to intra-group trade, though trade in dollar terms (over this period) increased by almost a trillion dollars – an increase of over 250 per cent. While NAFTA was the direct stimulant for the creation of a proposed FTAA, such ambitions have been overtaken by events, notably the renegotiation of NAFTA on the insistence of the US to create a new agreement, the United States–Mexico–Canada Agreement (UMSCA; see case study), which came into force in July 2020. This is often called the 'new NAFTA' and reflects US concerns about the aforementioned rules of origin (see case study).

Efforts towards regional integration in Latin America had little success until their renewal in the 1980s. These new agreements were primarily export-driven and were part of a strategy of integrating with the rest of the global economy. For these reasons, these new efforts have proved more successful than previous attempts at integration. This export-led stance has led to the growth of manufacturing trade, intra-industry trade, and inter-regional specialisation in Latin America.

- The Central American Common Market (founded in 1960) sought to establish free and fair trade with a common external tariff as a means of fostering the economic development of these states. Internal frictions have left the ambitions of the group largely frustrated after an initial five-fold rise in intra-group trade. Since the 1980s, this project has waxed and waned with political instability. With emerging stability – both in economic and political terms – there has been a renewed push towards economic integration in Central America.

- The Andean Pact (established in 1969) was designed to increase the size of the market of the Andean states (Bolivia, Colombia, Ecuador, Peru, and Venezuela) through trade liberalisation and the coordination of common policies. Trade liberalisation and industrial planning were not really compatible and resulted in many exceptions to the trade liberalisation policies. Thus, its trade impact was severely curtailed, although intra-group manufacturing trade did rise sharply. In 1989, the process accelerated rapidly with the decision to create a common market by 1992. This decision resulted in the further liberalisation of trade and the dropping of the industrial policy coordination aspects of the agreement. These changes have had a profound impact upon the form and intensity of intra-group trade.

- The Latin American Integration Association (formerly the Latin American Free Trade Association) was formed in 1960 and covered the largest Latin American states. It sought to encourage the growth of members via the agreed removal of collective barriers to trade. This is a broader agreement than the above Latin American agreements, which are subsets of this larger group. Increases in intra-group trade result more from these smaller groups and their more liberal leanings than from this broader agreement. The conclusion, therefore, is that this agreement has had little impact upon intra-group trade.
- The Caribbean Community and Common Market (CARICOM) was established in 1973. It aims to foster economic cooperation and integrate economies through freer inter-group trade. As the states involved are small, the tangible gains have been slight, but there is evidence of growing inter-group trade in recent years. CARICOM launched the Association of Caribbean States in 1994 to increase the links of the group with Central America, but free trade concerns in this initiative are largely secondary to those of closer cooperation.
- The Common Market of the South (MERCOSUR) was founded in 1991 and emerged as a result of sectoral integration between Argentina and Brazil; other states (Paraguay and Uruguay) have joined, and more are still forming associate agreements with the group. MERCOSUR is a customs union, and since its formation, it has witnessed a surge in internal trade. Internal liberalisation was accompanied by external liberalisation, resulting in a cut in average tariffs from 56 per cent to 12 per cent.

The US has been active in developing RTAs, notably with Latin America, as well as agreements further afield in Africa and the Middle East. In Asia-Pacific, the US has opened discussions with Korea and Malaysia as a precursor to enhancing its ties with ASEAN states. This activism has also extended to the other NAFTA states as well as those in Latin America, where MERCOSUR is pursuing FTAs on an individual basis, though as a group it is aiming to sign agreements with the GCC and other states in the Middle East.

## Asia Pacific

Regional integration within Asia does not appear to have had any great impact upon the trade orientation of members. Indeed, most of the groupings that have emerged have been formed for reasons other than intra-group trade promotion. In terms of regional integration, this region differs from both Europe and the Americas in that inter-state relationships tend to be based more on bilateral relationships and are not grouped around common institutions or alliances. Historically, Asian states have been distrustful of regional agreements as follows:

- Asia has been successful without such arrangements.
- Smaller states risk domination by bigger states.
- The cost of exclusion from regional agreements is not prohibitive.
- It is perceived that trade-diversion effects would be greater than trade-creation effects at the moment.

However, rising economic pressures for greater integration are removing this initial hesitancy as formal moves to instil integration become common.

The progress of economic development and trade liberalisation has accelerated markedly on an inter-regional level. The result is that regionalisation is what Jilberto and Mommen (2002) call a *de facto* process, that is, the result of the complementarities (in terms of technological capabilities, factor endowments, and wage and income levels) of the constituent states. This underlines that the region's integration is driven by:

- A tradition of market-led growth.
- The large stake that these states have in the multilateral trading system.
- The inadequate incentives for states to engage in geographically exclusive regional agreements.
- The transfer of industries from early starters to latecomers.

Between 1980 and 2005, intra-regional trade as a share of East Asia's trade rose from 35 per cent to 52 per cent. This has been matched by a sharp increase in investment within this region. This has been driven by a more progressive attitude towards liberalisation among these states, the creation of production and supply networks across Europe, improved digital and physical connectivity, and the emergence of China. Thus, despite East Asia having been a relative latecomer to RTAs, the number of agreements has soared since the 1990s. This was driven by a combination of the deepening of market-driven integration, the perceived success of European and North American integration, and the fallout from the Asian financial crisis.

Generally, integration has taken place within two overlapping forums: the Association of Southeast Asian Nations (ASEAN) and APEC.

ASEAN was founded in 1967 and sought to foster the peaceful national development of member states through cooperation. The move towards establishing trade arrangements among members only started in 1977, when a limited PTA – the Asian Free Trade Area (AFTA) – was established. At the time of its instigation, this PTA only covered some 2 per cent of intra-ASEAN trade. By 1985, this figure had only risen to 5 per cent. The slow growth was due to the laborious nature of the negotiations (conducted on a product-by-product basis), the lack of credible offers of preferences, the high domestic content requirements, the long list of exclusions, and the limited nature of the preferences themselves. A free trade area was proposed in 1991. The aim was to reduce tariffs on intra-group trade to between 0 and 5 per cent during the 15 years from 1993. This process was speeded up in 1994 when certain products were fast-tracked towards liberalised markets by 2000. AFTA was a defensive move promoted by regional integration elsewhere across the globe. The ASEAN economic community is one of the three pillars of the ASEAN Community, and it was envisaged that the area would become a single market by 2020, though this target was missed. This requires new mechanisms and measures, which are expected to be introduced in areas such as labour mobility. ASEAN has been extended through the ASEAN +3 (Japan, China, and Korea) and ASEAN +6 (ASEAN +3 and Australia, New Zealand, and India) agreements, which have extended the scope of free trade arrangements throughout the region. Such agreements, especially the ASEAN+3, are likely to be the main vehicle for further integration.

There are a growing number of sub-regional agreements throughout the newly industrialising states in Asia. The ASEAN+3 grouping (essentially all the East Asian members of the APEC group) is becoming increasingly active in the development of regional integration. The agreement tends to happen much faster in terms of financial integration than in trade – an interesting contrast to the case of the EU. These groups have announced measures to closely integrate their financial systems to aid them in coping better with any repeat of the 1997 financial crises that hit the region. This is being complemented by a series of bilateral and multilateral trade agreements among these states. In turn, these will be complemented by agreements the area is forming with the free trade areas of Australia and New Zealand. The reason for this aggressive push towards integration is both positive and negative (the consequences of the 1997 financial crisis, the inspiration of the EU, disenchantment with the WTO, and disquiet at the attitude and behaviour of the US and the EU). However, the legacy of the 1997 financial crisis seems to be a paramount driver as states react against the perceived lack of support from the US and Europe. More latterly, these agreements have been consolidated into RECEP. This is an agreement between 15 Asian states which entered into force in January 2022. It includes all ASEAN states, China, Japan, and Korea, as well as Australia and New Zealand. This covers 30 per cent of the global GDP and population, with all expected to see a gradual reduction in tariffs between member states. The agreement brings the assorted agreements that ASEAN states have with other states into a single agreement.

- APEC, created in 1989, provides a useful contrast to the EU in the process of economic integration. APEC is not a formal trade agreement but a 'community' of diverse states from three continents. The agreement stresses its members' commitment to free and open trade. APEC was created under the framework of open regionalism. As such, members are committed to reducing barriers to non-members as they move towards freer trade within the region. Indeed, some members of APEC have conditionally agreed to extend APEC preference to non-members since the agreement has no intention of evolving into a customs union. APEC has established a degree of international division of labour, with Japan providing essential capital goods, Hong Kong, Taiwan, and Singapore finance, and Thailand, China, and Indonesian labour-intensive operations. Increased trade and investment links have increased these complementarities. APEC's antipathy to becoming an exclusionary block indicates that it can be a powerful force for the liberalisation of the global economy. Free trade among APEC states is only expected to be achieved by 2020 and will not be binding. This is further challenged by the fact that there is by no means a universal acceptance of the benefits of free trade between member states. As a result, tariff cuts are negotiated on a state-by-state basis. APEC is evolving into an inter-governmental body with a ministerial council and secretariat and is planning to extend liberalisation to functional cooperation. In 2005, an evaluation of APEC's achievements concluded that both tariffs and NTBs had been reduced to a great extent and that linkages between APEC members and the rest of the world had been strengthened. However, the benefits are not solely created by APEC, as they may also reflect the rise of China and of productivity gains in the US and Canada.

The overlapping nature of many of the RTAs within the Asia-Pacific region is putting consolidation on the agenda. Several individuals, such as ASEAN+3, are being pursued or suggested. Japan has been pursuing an agenda of enhancing its regional RTAs with cross-regional agreements. This pattern is also being followed by Korea. China is also following up on signing an RTA with Chile and Pakistan and has launched negotiations with the GCC, Pakistan, Singapore, Australia, and New Zealand. As a group, ASEAN is negotiating with India, Japan, and New Zealand, as well as considering an FTA with Korea. The reach of these formal integration blocs is being extended through a network of FTAs with other states. There is a concern that the proliferation of overlapping agreements is creating a 'noodle bowl' effect (the Eastern equivalent of Baldwin's 'spaghetti bowl'; see above), where the complexity works to counter multilateral objectives. The proliferation of agreements has created complexity through multiple rules of origin and the proliferation of standards, leading to increased business costs. Thus, to some, there needs to be a hub that can act as a focus of these RTAs to simplify these arrangements

Since its accession to the WTO in 2001, China has been active in concluding bilateral agreements, which it sees more as a tool for diplomacy than as a means of building commerce. This explains the lack of comprehensiveness in such agreements. They highlight a desire to play a leading role in East Asian integration, to promote a Northeast FTA with Japan and Korea and to secure the supply of natural resources (especially energy) from the Middle East and Australia. Initially, China dealt with culturally and geographically proximate states. This list has expanded as China has sought to increase its influence over world affairs. This pattern is being repeated in Japan, where the state has ditched the sole focus of external policy on multilateralism in favour of concluding a series of bilateral deals in reaction to the Asian financial crises and to deals being concluded elsewhere. Most of Japan's deals are within the ASEAN region.

---

**Box 5.2: The ASEAN way**

Aside from being the official anthem of the group of ten nations that comprises the Association of Southeast Asian Nations (ASEAN), the ASEAN way refers to the form and strategy of regional integration followed by these states. In contrast to the EU's commitment to an 'ever deeper union', the ASEAN way sets a limit on the degree of regional integration by explicitly committing to intergovernmental processes. This is a process of cooperation between states in areas where there is mutual interest between them and where states have retained discretion and supernationalism (i.e., dedicated decision-making bodies independent of states) is either non-existent or severely curtailed. This means that ASEAN as a regional group operates through a process of consensus where there is no regional cooperation agreement unless all states agree to the process. This means non-interference in each other's affairs, quiet diplomacy, and the non-use of force. This reflects that ASEAN emerged primarily as a tool of political security rather than for direct political and economic integration.

Introduced at its formation, the ASEAN way reflects that the group is voluntary and non-political and that every member state can preserve its own identity and sovereignty. In this way, the notion is that the group can find Asian solutions to Asian problems that are free from outside (often superpower) interference. There are a number of cited cases where this `ASEAN way' has been deployed, notably

- Myanmar, where ASEAN kept an open-door policy towards the state after a military coup rather than adopting the isolationist approach of the UN.
- Indonesia's haze crisis in 1997, where the burning of rainforests brought about pollution and public health problems in other states, led to a trans-boundary agreement.

However, the policy of non-interference has its limits, where there are direct spillovers between states but no real means of achieving reparation for any damage caused. In international environmental law. The offending state is meant to provide reparation for any damage caused, but non-intervention, as advanced under the ASEAN way, tends to preclude this. This highlights a weakness of the ASEAN way and its ability to solve the issues created by one state that impact the wellbeing of another. Moreover, the ASEAN way has not proved effective in promoting economic integration as it makes agreement very slow with modest gains offered. This is shaped by the fact that such agreements – under the ASEAN way – require consensus, which means that such agreements only proceed at the speed of the lowest common denominator. Thus, disagreements remain unstated and collective action underdeveloped. The next result is that, as much as the ASEAN way reflects the desire to respect state sovereignty, it also risks understating the interconnectivity and interdependence between states that require firmer action.

## The Middle East and Africa

For many years, regional economic integration in Africa was limited by political instability and economic decline. The lack of economic development meant that regional economic integration would not yield these states any significant influence or power over the global economic system. The reliance of African states upon bilateral trade and aid deals with developed states renders them subject to external scrutiny of their policy strategies. Increasingly, African leaders are coming round to the view that regional integration is necessary if they are to successfully address their marginal position within the global economy. This is despite the failure of past efforts to deliver much in the way of benefits to the states involved.

Across Africa, there are more than 200 regional groupings and agreements covering a wide variety of arrangements and issues. Some of these schemes have become quite mature, especially among West and Central African states. On the whole, the progress of economic integration has been very slow. Furthermore, the efforts that have been made have not been successful in terms of intra-regional trade, economic convergence, or policy harmonisation. In addition, Africa's share of intra-African trade has fallen continuously. The reasons for these problems highlight a number of potential deficiencies within regional integration schemes, especially when:

- The production structures of member states are not complementary.
- Tariff changes cause a loss of government revenue.
- The benefits of market integration are not assured to individual states.
- There is an unequal distribution of integration benefits.
- Long-term integration takes second place to short-term losses.
- There is an absence of central institutions at the national and regional levels.
- There is a lack of coordination and harmonisation of economic policies.
- Civil society is hardly involved in the integration process.

Some of the groupings within Africa date back to the colonial era and reflect a shared historical legacy among states with the same colonial power. This has created common institutions, a common language, and even a common currency. In others, regional groupings were based upon geographical proximity. Most of the African economic integration schemes came into existence during an era marked by inward-looking development mainly based upon import substitution. The goal of self-sufficiency was pursued through the creation of sub-regional markets, with the eventual aim of creating a pan-African community.

For the Maghreb states, difficulties in the 1980s pushed these states to work more closely together. The Arab Mahgreb Union, signed in 1989, was heavily shaped by its relations with the EU and its economic dependence upon Europe. The Mahgreb states and the Middle Eastern States (through the Gulf Cooperation Council) tend to be more developed than the sub-Saharan African states. The willingness of the EU to assist the Mahgreb states is limited by the dominance of Maghreb exports in products such as agriculture and textiles, in which the EU is very vulnerable to competition. EU aid is focused on helping these states promote intra-regional trade to make them more attractive to outside states and investors.

The Gulf Cooperation Council was established in 1981 and sought to create a customs union involving free trade among members and a common external tariff (CET). The initial phases of the plan were easy to implement (the removal of tariffs), but the establishment of a common external tariff proved more difficult. Generally, the desire for the development of such an agreement has ebbed and flowed with the price of oil. Overall, the agreement has had relatively little impact upon the relative share of mutual trade due to the similarity in the trade and production structures of member states and the fact that there is already a low level of protection vis-à-vis third countries. Indeed, in the first 20 years, the agreement only managed to marginally increase intra-regional trade. This is due to the low level of intra-industry trade, as many of these states rely heavily on oil. It is evident that Saudi Arabia, as the largest economy in the region, will not be a force for integrating these economies. Instead of operating as a leader, it has opted for trading outside the region.

The nature of these regional integration agreements is becoming increasingly diverse, and there has been an increasing number of trade agreements between states at different stages of economic development (see above). The World Bank suggests that developing states should seek regional trade agreements with developed states rather than with other developing states if they are to commercially benefit. Its research suggests that:

- Agreements among developing countries tend to create divergences between part-ners, with one state benefiting at the expense of others, as well as being more likely to lead to trade diversion.
- Developing-developed country agreements are more likely to aid technology trans-fer and provide lock-in mechanisms for political and economic reform.

For the middle-income states, the benefits of integration will only come with deeper integration, as this is more likely to realise scale and competition benefits. These meas-ures have been complemented by the Agadir agreement between Jordan, Egypt, Tunisia, and Morocco. This was signed in February 2004 and was seen as a precursor to the development of a pan-Arab free trade area. This will be aided by the gradual extension of the Agadir agreement to other members of the region.

Of all the regions in the world, sub-Saharan African integration conforms to the conventional concept of integration based on proximity. In many ways, these reflect the dominant role played by regional politics in the design of these RTAs. This also helps explain the ambitious agenda for these agreements despite the relatively low lev-els of trade between them. Extra-regional agreements have historically been based on non-reciprocal performances under schemes such as the GSP from the EU. Most states continue to benefit from such schemes, with the exception being states in north and southern Africa, which have tended to prefer reciprocal agreements. This shift towards reciprocal preferences will soon extend to other states as EPAs replace unilateral pref-erences. The EPAs are supposed to enhance regional integration, though this does not seem likely in central and eastern Africa, where asymmetries between members are leading to new configurations based around east and southern Africa. Such arrange-ments are likely to clash with existing agreements.

In 2018, the African Free Trade Area was introduced. It is pan-African, with 43 signatories, and was facilitated by the African Union. Under the agreement, all sig-natories are committed to reducing tariffs between members on goods over a flexible time frame of up to 13 years. This varies according to the product and the level of development in the state. This is seen as a precursor to the deepening of the process with a customs union and a common market foreseen over the longer term. This has also been reflected in

talk of the development of currency unions within Africa. This interest is generated by a desire to counteract the small size of their economies and by the successful launch of the euro. ECOWAS, COMESA, and SADC have all talked about creating a common currency between their members. In West Africa, this process is complicated by the fact that half of ECOWAS is already part of the West African Economic and Monetary Union (WAEMU). However, the non-WAEMU members of ECOWAS do not wish to join this club, which they see as largely a relic of French rule. Thus, these states have proposed establishing a monetary union of their own. As trade between these states is relatively low, it is hard to pinpoint the exact benefits of the creation of these monetary unions for these states, despite efforts by these states to increase trade through better investment in infrastructure, lowering political tensions, and lowering tariff and non-tariff barriers to trade.

## NEW REGIONALISM: A PARADIGM FOR ECONOMIC DEVELOPMENT

The fact that regionalism extends beyond those states that are geographically proximate opens up new forms of cooperation. These new agreements extend beyond trade into investment and other previously sensitive policy areas. What is also marked is that often these agreements can occur between states that would both not normally be considered partners due to differences in levels of economic development and performance. These two tenets (extension and penetration) are the two central planks of new regionalism, though the term can be misleading as they are often bilateral deals between states in different regions of the global economy. This trend has arisen out of frustration with multilateralism and a belief that such a framework can provide an alternative method of liberalisation and harmonisation.

Thus, in some ways, new regionalism can bypass multilateral institutions and arrangements while seeking to develop links between developed and developing states. Much of the rise in bilateral RTAs over the past decade or so is symptomatic of this new regionalism. Indeed, by 2007, 27 per cent of agreements in force were between developed and developing states, compared to 14 per cent in 1995. This rise can be accounted for by several factors, such as the fragmentation in central and eastern Europe and the desire of developed states (especially the US) to parallel multilateralism with bilateralism.

The incentive for developing states to accept such bilateral deals rests in the prospect of positive discrimination vis-à-vis other states. These have to be offset against potential problems where there is an inconsistency between the state's stance in multilateral negotiations and its obligations as part of the bilateral deal. This could be especially troublesome where the agreements enforce developing states to undertake liberalisation beyond what is expected under WTO commitments. Such commitments will limit the room to manoeuvre for these states. The benefits of these agreements are also undermined by the developed states agreeing to similar deals with other developing states. As a result, the size and durability of the benefits from such agreements can be highly uncertain. Another by-product of these bilateral deals is that they tend to weaken existing or evolving regional common markets that may offer long-term gains for these states. This may, in fact, lead to these agreements being unwound. Furthermore, such a network of deals may pose a new challenge to the coherence of the global trading system. For example, developing a number of diverse deals with a number of separate developed states may pose financial pressure on developing state customs authorities and firms. The former would have to deploy different treatments for the same products from different states, whereas the latter may have to adjust products to different markets. However, the EU and the US (who have both been active in developing such agreements) suggest that these deals are a stepping stone to a coherent multilateral framework.

NAFTA was perhaps the most high-profile example of new regionalism. Evidence provided by UNCTAD suggests mixed benefits for Mexico from such an agreement. It is evident that Mexico has enjoyed strong export and FDI growth. Its share of world-manufactured exports grew by over 150 per cent between 1994 and 2017. However, its value added in manufacturing has been low. This highlights that despite economic gains, its ability to translate these into tangible economic and social progress has been limited, as there is little evidence that the agreements have narrowed per capita income between Mexico and its partners. Thus, overall, these agreements have added little to the prospect of economic development. Indeed, in some areas, NAFTA has had negative consequences, notably in agriculture and banking. Indeed, perhaps the best indicator of the failure of NAFTA to live up to its expectations is that it has failed to stem the tide of migration from Mexico to the US. Such labour flows highlight that the pressure to migrate remains strong despite NAFTA.

Given the absence of any tangible benefits for economic development from such arrangements, an alternative may be intra-developing state agreements. These agreements have been growing the fastest of all forms of bilateral agreements. As intra-regional trade grows, the rationale for such agreements grows. In Southeast Asia, regional trade is 35 per cent of total trade and is increasing in other regions, albeit from a low base. For example, trans-regional trade in Africa has increased from 5 per cent in the mid-1980s to 10 per cent in 2022. The benefits of trade for development depend on:

- Links between the export sector and the rest of the economy.
- Amount of employment created.
- The extent of technological spillovers to the rest of the economy.
- The proportion of domestic value added in exports.
- The revenue generated.
- The share of revenue generated for domestic sectors.

Evidence offered by UNCTAD (2007) suggests that the composition of trade between developing states can often aid diversification and development more than trade in general. However, while regional agreements among developing states may promote trade and allow for efficiency gains through intra-industry trade, there is a tendency for these benefits to be unevenly spread. The more developed and larger states tend to benefit more than the smaller, less advanced states. Such differences reflect structural differences within the grouping. As a result, there may be a need to transfer funds between states to ensure the coherence of the group.

Overall, regional blocs enable developing states to find markets more easily than they would with bilateral deals with developed states. This suggests the possibility of a link between regionalism and industrialisation for these states. While not precluding multilateralism, these blocs can provide the basis for global competitiveness. This necessitates a strong commitment by states to deepen integration beyond trade liberalisation and may even involve regional policies.

## Box 5.3: The Regional Comprehensive Economic Partnership (RCEP)

On January 2022, the RCEP came into force. This is a free trade agreement with 15 East Asian and Pacific states. This includes the 10 ASEAN states, the three East Asia giants (China, South Korea, and Japan), and Australia and New Zealand. The block will be the largest single global trading block comprising 30 per cent of global GDP with the hope that the increased trade stimulated by the block (which is estimated to boost intra-regional exports by 2 per cent) will accelerate growth across the region. Trade within the region was worth $1.3 trillion in 2019; RCEP is expected to boost this by $42 billion as a result of trade-creating and diverting effects, though the latter is expected to exceed the former in terms of its contribution to intra-group trade flows. As of 2019, trade flows within the region are dominated by the big three states, which have 60 per cent of intra-group trade flows compared to states such as Cambodia, Laos, PDR and Brunei, which account for only 1 per cent of RCEP trade flows, even though they account for up to 70 per cent of their trade. For the big three East Asian states, the significance of intra-RCEP trade is less significant due to more diverse trading patterns.

Central to the RCEP is a series of tariff concessions offered by states. This is expected to remove tariffs on over 90 per cent of merchandise trade between members. In addition, states have agreed to limit the erosion of non-tariff barriers and trade facilitation measures in areas such as customs clearance and rules of origin. This is set to occur while allowing states a great deal of flexibility in terms of the pace at which these tariffs would be removed, with the RCEP being given an extended time frame of two decades for full implementation. There is also a need (arguably reflected in the ASEAN way of economic cooperation) for the agreement to reflect the sensitivities of states with regard to specific strategies for industries.

Despite RCEP, the region is a long way from being a regional trading bloc, as significant barriers remain. Indeed, in sectors such as agriculture and automotive, tariffs remain high, and some states are still highly protective of their nascent manufacturing capacity, which risks being inundated by cheap Chinese imports from elsewhere within the group. This reflects the flexibility of states to opt out of tariff commitments where they feel their strategic interests are at stake. This reflects that – as the tariff between RCEP states is already low – the main beneficiaries of the agreement to lower tariffs are the three East Asian giants. Thus, there is a need for these states to avoid being swamped by imports from these states within key sectors, especially for those states (namely Cambodia, Indonesia, the Philippines, and Vietnam) where RCEP tariff concessions result in lower exports due to rising imports from the big three states. However, these costs were small compared to what these states saw as the potential costs of exclusion from this agreement. The main losers in terms of the diversionary effects of RCEP are the EU and Taiwan, though these effects are insignificant. The same cannot be said for some impacted South Asian states, notably Bangladesh, which will see an estimated 12 per cent of its exports diverted to RCEP members.

## REGIONALISM AND THE MNE

The assessment of how industry responds to the strategic challenges posed by regionalisation has to be conducted on an ad hoc basis. Each industry differs in terms of its regionalisation drivers and the idiosyncrasies of its market segment. At a firm level, enterprises differ over the degree to which they need to have different regional strategies and the extent to which they should integrate operations. A starting point for analysis is to remember that the forces influencing strategy on the regional level also influence strategy on a global level. The core drivers pushing enterprises towards regional-wide strategies are:

- The convergence of customer needs and tastes.
- The existence of customers and channels that purchase on a multi-country basis. The most notable examples of this are multinational companies that buy on a regional basis and the emergence of regional-wide retailers.
- The rise of transferable marketing, whereby enterprises use the same marketing approaches in different states.

These pressures towards regionalisation of enterprise strategy are also driven by cost factors such as lower transportation costs, the wider availability of economies of scale, and the existence of cost-space and time-space convergence. As integration progresses, it is expected that variations in country costs will converge as industry locates to reflect intra-regional differences in cost. The extent of such cost differences within any regional grouping is a function of the degree of integration within the group. Conventional economic wisdom indicates that the cost advantages tend to increase with the higher degree of commercial freedom and greater degrees of transparency among states.

Furthermore, enterprise strategy is also strongly influenced by governmental actions, especially in areas such as trade policy, technical and related standards, and commercial regulations. Strategy can be as much reactive as it is proactive. The former implies that regional strategy could be a response to the actions of an enterprise's competitors. Enterprises may also respond through the development of shared services that increase the interdependence of states and lead to the creation of pan-regional networks. The result could lead to enterprises competing with each other through the framework provided by their respective networks. Within the context of these developing regional networks, there should be greater transferability of competitive advantage between states. For example, technology advantages have become more transferable in developed economies via the spread of high-technology enterprises responding to regional integration.

According to Yip (1998), within the context of regional integration, the strategic choices available to enterprises revolve around:

- The choice of markets in which to participate: the world economy is moving towards a hierarchical marketplace based on global, regional, and then smaller national or sub-national niches.
- The choice of products: this is especially pertinent when enterprises move towards standardised products – though marginally differentiated – on both a global and regional basis.
- The choice of location: in locating activities (including shared services), firms tend to centralise rather than develop on a national basis.
- The kinds of marketing to have: once again, standardisation is becoming increasingly evident.
- The kinds of competitive moves to take to secure new positions: such as cross-subsidies and linkages.

The nature of the chosen strategy will depend on the nature of the drivers noted above and how they directly impact upon the business concerned. Clearly, enterprises need to balance the regionalisation of their industry with the regionalisation of their strategy. However, 'going regional' could cause the firm to lose its position within indigenous markets to rivals who are more nationalistic in terms of strategy.

The strategic impact of this trend towards regionalism has impacted the strategy of the MNEs. Whether this impact is proactive or reactive is a moot point; however, the core focus of the above debate is that for the top MNEs, the notion of globality is a myth, as most tend to generate most of their sales within their home region (Rugman 2000, 2005). The regional focus of MNEs suggests that the global market is not becoming homogenised, and the psychic distance between regions still remains a significant barrier to trade. The majority of MNEs are mainly based in the triad of the US, East Asia, and Europe; it is these regions that are the focus of these enterprises' activities. Indeed, in 2020, 474 out of the top 500 MNEs (over 95 per cent) were from the triad.

Rugman's evidence suggests that there are no evident trends towards uniformity within the global economy. Firms neither desire to have a ubiquitous reach nor do they seek to deliver uniformity across the regions they operate in. In terms of branding, there are very few global brands, with Coke being a notable exception. There is also little evidence to suggest that value chains are being reconfigured and coordinated across regions. Indeed, most manufacturing tends to take place within the region served. This pattern is even more marked within the service sector. Further up the value chain, this regional pattern is also evident for R&D. Most R&D has tended to be undertaken by firms within their locality.

Rugman concedes that this regional focus of the 'front end' of the value chain may not be replicated at the 'back end'. There is evidence to suggest that while sales tend to be regional, production tends to be more global. This evidence should not be overstated – according to Rugman – as a significant amount of this production takes place within regionally based clusters. Indeed, it was only in electronics that there was evidence of a global production network. Often, the relative costs of distribution and assembly often inhibited the dispersion of the production process. The emphasis placed by Rugman on sales data is seen as a major weakness of his hypothesis. To many, such a narrow measure risks understating the extension of MNEs beyond their home region. For example, it is noticeable within the modern economy how firms have started to become active seekers of knowledge seeking to find pools of value-adding information. This might not show in sales, but it is nonetheless important to globalisation. A further criticism is that the definition of what is a 'region' has been fluid. Both formal and informal membership in regional groupings has been flexible, with many regions expanding over time.

This analysis supports conclusions made by Ohmae in 1985, who identified a geographic space based on the triad of Japan, the US, and the EU, which shared a number of common features (such as low macro-economic growth and mature technological infrastructure). To capture innovation costs, large MNEs need to achieve a deep penetration within each of these regions. MNEs face problems in seeking to enter these other regions, which can often only be overcome via the·use of networks. This may be often due to the inability of the MNE to transfer home-based advantage to other locations. However, Ohmae understated the degree of regionalism that would become apparent within the global economy.

The fact that MNEs are regionally focused reinforces the desire for governments to develop regional trading blocs. As a result, regional trading blocs should seek to support this activity through the development of the appropriate policy frameworks that enable regional sales and other value-added activities to find the most appropriate location within the specific regional theatre and enable these firms to resist external threats. This policy practice has been supported by Rugman and D'Cruz's (2003) advocacy of regional business networks. These networks create business systems around a 'flagship firm' which collaborates with partners for mutual advantage. The flagship leads the network with the intention of shaping the competitive position of the firms within it. Clearly, such cooperative frameworks need the agreement of the regulatory authorities.

## CASE STUDY 5.2: THE US–MEXICO–CANADA AGREEMENT (USMCA)

USCMA, which entered into force on the 1st of July, 2020, was a replacement for the NAFTA. The USCMA was in effect a renegotiation of NAFTA based upon the US' long-standing problems with the pre-existing agreement and how it undermined the US manufacturing industry. With the rise of populism within the US (with the election of Donald Trump), the US sought to address the grievance with trade relations, which he perceived as damaging to US interests. This was reflective of a more muscular trade policy pursued by the US in response to its disadvantages. Despite the agreement having bipartisan approval and being widely accepted to have been beneficial to all states, the US wanted to renegotiate to improve the competitive positioning of US firms from what it saw as unfair low-cost competition from Mexico.

Such was the hostility towards NAFTA that Trump was simply prepared to tear up the agreement if there was no re-negotiation. This threatened turmoil across the North American economic system, as both Canada and Mexico depend heavily on trade with the US. For Canada, this trade represents two-thirds of its exports and a third of its GDP; for Mexico, it is 78 per cent of exports and 30 per cent of GDP. Thus, the risk to these states of the agreement being avoided was substantial, and the stakes were very high, especially for the automotive sectors within their respective states, which depend heavily upon trade with the US. This renegotiation was reflective of an already hostile environment by the US towards its North American neighbours, where it had increased tariffs on Canadian steel and a host of other Mexican imports. These remain a real threat where the US is prepared to increase tariffs on the grounds of national security. The USMCA is subject to review every six years by the parties; thus, the threat of unilaterally ending the agreement is an ongoing threat. Furthermore, while this will encourage Canada and Mexico to diversify their trade away from the US, their grounds for doing so will be limited by the economies they can sign agreements with. Thus, agreements with China can be vetoed as incompatible with the USCMA, should the US so decide.

As suggested, the main changes have been in the automotive industry, where new rules of origin are being applied. This means that going forward, to qualify for preferential treatment, vehicles now have to have 75 per cent of their value North American sourced, with at least 40 per cent of the value created being undertaken by workers who are earning above $16 per hour. This latter point will mainly affect Mexico, and the rules in total will seek to exclude low-cost imports into the region from states such as China, though clearly the US wants to see itself as the main beneficiary of any import substitution that occurs as a result of these rule changes. Businesses seem uncertain about these changes, especially with regard to the discretion within them to allow states to diverge from them on security grounds. Many do not trust any free trade agreement made by a government with a protectionist instinct. The agreement also includes updates on issues like agricultural access and includes new issues such as digital products for the first time. However, unlike NAFTA, these rules are enforceable.

There are downsides to the new agreement. The most notable of which is that the rules of origin agreed upon will increase the costs of manufacturers, making it more difficult for USMCA-based automotive manufacturers to compete against Asian rivals. This will have a knock-on effect throughout the North American value chain, where sales could also be hit. There also seems to be little within the agreement for consumers who are likely to suffer high prices (especially for vehicles) as a result of the agreement. Indeed, arguably the only real benefit from the agreement is that it has removed uncertainty over trade relations, and this may only be temporary.

## QUESTION

Were the US' concerns regarding NAFTA justified?

## CASE 5.3: THE REGIONAL MNC

One of the facets of MNCs is that there are very few that are truly global in that they possess a presence in every recognised country and dependent territory. Those that do tend to be those that make a virtue of their extensive reach, such as logistics businesses, but even these countries tend to rely upon local alliances in the more remote and commercially challenged locations. Indeed, a core feature of MNCs is how – despite their title – constrained their multinationality is in terms of reach. This lack of globality is even more evident when the revenue of these businesses is considered. It has long been noted that, despite claims of globality, when it comes to how a MNC's revenue model is constructed, this globality is very asymmetric.

McDonald's has a presence in 119 countries, but the vast majority of its revenues comes from just five (UK, US, Germany, Japan, and Canada), with one state – the US – comprising 31 per cent of revenue on its own. Similarly, with Netflix, which has a presence in 191 countries, 45 per cent of its revenue comes from just two markets: the US and Canada. These two examples highlight a core trend, namely that not only are these businesses limited in the geography of their revenue model, but that this revenue is concentrated in a limited number of international regions.

This trend was noted by Rugman in the early 2000s, and while his approach does offer a limited snapshot, it does highlight the importance of regions to the MNC. In this context, Rugman defines the region not as those undergoing formal integration (as identified above), but as the broad megaregions of North America, Europe, and Asia (though in the case of the first two, there will be a strong overlap with formal processes within the EU and USMCA). Looking at the Fortune 500, it was noted that very few MNCs are global (i.e., operating across more than two regions) and that multinationalism means operating across multiple states within its home region. This reflects that the MNC sees a commercial advantage in operating beyond its home region. Moreover, when they do move beyond this home region, they face increased liability from foreignness with limited commercial benefits. This is compounded by barriers to mobility between blocks, which are absent when there are trade agreements between states within a region. In the case of McDonald's, it tends to be best when certain conditions are met with regard to its business model, namely a predilection for fast food and an ability to operate a franchise-based system. In the case of Netflix, it is not an accident that its core US-based products can be easily leveraged with minimal adaptation across markets. These trends reinforce the nature of regionalism within international strategy.

All this underscores that global strategy in a single global market is illusory. The fact that most trade takes place within regional blocks underlines this. This is also underlined by the fact that even within this structure, there are limits, notably that even within these regions, trade is concentrated, for example, in Europe, where there is greater integration between businesses within western Europe than in parts of the eastern side of the continent. Similarly, within Asia, the focus is on East Asia which then neglects other parts of the diverse continent. What is also evident is that parts of the global market seem largely of secondary interest to the largest MNCs, notably Africa. This reflects not only the realities of the market power of these developed and rapidly emerging states but also how the concentration of economic activity within developed and emerging economies is reflected within large MNC strategies.

## QUESTION

How do you account for the fact that MNCs tend to be regional rather than global?

## CONCLUSION

RTAs have become a common feature of the multilateral trading systems in recent years. It is unlikely that they are going to diminish in influence, notwithstanding the current impasse within the multilateral framework. Indeed, in response to the breakdown of the DDA, there has been a flurry of new agreements. These developments should not be overlooked or understood, as they will influence the form and nature of international trade relations. The World Bank (Solaga and Winters 1997) notes that moves towards regional economic integration have been more political than economic. The aim was to increase security, increase bargaining power, and spread cooperation. Inevitably, such benefits spread into the economic domain, especially if they lock states into a process of political and economic reform. It is clear that regional agreements can be economically harmful if they result in trade diversion or if they arrest progress towards liberal multilateral outcomes. Despite these dangers, states are committing themselves to regional integration agreements for all manner of reasons. It is probable that these agreements will develop further and prove to be significant landmarks in the international business landscape of the 21st century.

### KEY POINTS

- Regional integration agreements are becoming increasingly common within the global trading arena.
- Traditionally, agreements were seen as a second-best option in the absence of global free trade and are both offensive and defensive.
- The benefits of these agreements for the multilateral trading system are ambiguous.
- Regionalism is emerging as a channel for economic development.
- MNEs tend to focus on their home regions.

## ACTIVITES AND DISCUSSION QUESTIONS

1. To what extent is regional economic integration a logical response to the process of globalisation?

2. Examine a single developing state and assess how it is using preferential trade agreements for its economic development.

3. Using a single MNE, examine how its sales are broken down by region. Does this confirm or refute the notion of regionalism within MNEs?

## GROUP WORK

1.  Using a regional economic grouping of your choice, identify the motives, form, and method of integration.

## SUGGESTED FURTHER READINGS

Baldwin, R., Cohen, D., Sapir, A., & Venables, A. (Eds.). (2008). *Market integration, regionalism and the global economy*, Cambridge: Cambridge University Press.

Baldwin, R. E. (2008,). Managing the noodle bowl: The fragility of East Asian regionalism. *The Singapore Economic Review*, 53(03), 449–478.

Baldwin, R. E. (2017). Multilateralising regionalism: Spaghetti bowls as building blocs on the path to global free trade. In J. J. Kirton (Ed.), *Global trade* (pp. 469–536). London: Routledge.

Bhagwati, J. N. (2002). *The wind of the hundred days: How Washington mismanaged globalization*. Boston, MA: MIT Press.

De Lombaerde, P., & Langenhove, L. (2006). Multilateralism, regionalism, and bilateralism in trade and investment: World report on regional integration (United Nations university series on regionalism), Springer-Verlag New York Inc.

Frankel, J. A., & Wei, S. J. (1998). Regionalization of world trade and currencies: Economics and politics. In *The regionalization of the world economy* (pp. 189–226). Chicago, IL: University of Chicago Press.

Hoekmann, B., Schiff, M., & Winters, L. (1998). Regionalism and development, *World Bank Working Paper*, New York: World Bank.

Honninghausen, L. (2004). *Regionalism in the age of globalism: Concepts of regionalism*, Max Cade.

Jilberto, A. E. F., & Mommen, A. (2002). Globalization versus regionalization. In A. E. F. Jilberto & A. Mommen (Eds.), *Regionalization and globalization in the modern world economy* (pp. 1–26). London: Routledge.

Lawrence, R. Z. (1995). *Regionalism, multilateralism and deeper integration*. Washington, DC: The Brookings Institution.

Mattli, W. (1999). *The logic of regional integration: Europe and beyond*, Cambridge: Cambridge University Press.

OECD (2003). *Regionalism and the multilateral trading system*, Paris: OECD.

Ohmae, K. (1985). *Triad power*, Boston: Free Press.

Pomfret, R. (2007). Is regionalism an increasing feature of the world economy? *The World Economy*, 30(6), 923–947.

Robson, P. (1980). *The economics of international integration*. London: Allen & Unwin.

Rugman, A. (2005). *The regional multinationals*, Cambridge: Cambridge University Press.

Rugman, A., & D'Cruz, J. R. (2003). *Multinationals as flagship firms: Regional business networks*. Oxford: OUP.

Solaga, I., & Winters, L. A. (1997). Regionalism in the nineties: What effect on trade? *World Bank Working Paper*, New York: World Bank.

Srinivasan, T. N. (1998). Regionalism and the WTO: Is nondiscrimination passe? In A. Krueger (Ed.), *The WTO as an international organization* (pp. 329–350). Chicago, IL: University of Chicago Press.

UNCTAD (2022) World investment report 2022. www.unctad.org.

WTO (2005) The future of the WTO: Report by the consultative board to the WTO director general. www.wto.org.

## Websites

The WTO web site (www.wto.org) is an excellent first port of call for those seeking statistics of RTAs. The UNCTAD (www.unctad.org) website is also very good.

# PART II

# GLOBAL MARKET OPPORTUNITIES AND RISKS

The second part of the work underlines the importance of the state to the global system. As much as there is a narrative with regard to the erosion of the power of the state within a global system, there is little denying that they remain the core building blocks of the system. Trade, investment, and all other measures of the degree of globality are all assessed in terms of the state. Moreover, the attitude of states towards globalisation will have a heavy influence on the state and the form of its development. Thus, what goes on in these states is central to understanding the pattern of evolution of the global system as well as the risks and opportunities within it.

This section comprises three chapters, which are based on the analysis of states as per the broad degree of categorisation offered by the level of economic development. Developed states are the cornerstones of the global system, offering a platform for its stable and predictable operation. However, the states – who have been the main beneficiaries of globalisation – have begun to exhibit a higher degree of risk for global business, often borne of rising scepticism of globalisation. The following chapter looks at two states that are increasingly cornerstones of the global system: China and India. The chapter will explore their differing trajectories and how one has been more proactive in embracing globalisation than the other. The final section looks at economic development in a broader context and seeks to explore how economic development is an important prerequisite to effective engagement by states in the global economy.

DOI: 10.4324/9781315184500-7

CHAPTER 6

# DEVELOPED ECONOMIES

## The rising risks facing the world's most advanced economies

### OBJECTIVES

By the end of this chapter, the student will be able to:

- Understand the form and nature of developed economies.
- Comprehend the importance of advanced economies to the international business environment.
- Assess the nature of emergent economic, political, and social risks in developed incomes.
- Assess the strategies available to militate against these risks.

## INTRODUCTION

The global economy's developed economies are the cornerstone of the global international economic system. These are states that form the backbone of the global trading system and whose MNEs dominate FDI. In turn, these states are also the main forces shaping the governance of the system. As such, these states and their agendas (which, in practice, have been mainly US-led and determined) have been the most influential factors shaping the progressive moves towards globalisation over the past five or six decades. It is these states that have pushed the neo-liberal version of globalisation, which has come to dominate the international economic system. In securing this market-led governance framework, these states have also been both passive and active forces in the promotion of system stability. As long as these states – it was argued – had a consensus

DOI: 10.4324/9781315184500-8

as to the virtue of globalisation, the process would be sustained and enhanced. This stabilising force provided by these states has begun to be questioned as the system these states promoted has suffered repeated crises to the extent that the political consensus surrounding hyper-globalisation has become eroded. The legacy of this and how these once stabilising forces are now sources of systemic risk are the core themes of this chapter. Initially, this chapter will explore the core characteristics of developed states before moving on to examine emergent risks generated by the economic, political, and social systems of these states. The final section will examine how such risks might be mitigated.

## THE CHARACTERISTICS OF DEVELOPED ECONOMIES

There are various definitions as to what constitutes a developed state and what states should be included in such a list. Inevitably, economic factors have come to dominate such assessments. The World Bank uses a simple income measurement. This can include states (such as some in the Middle East) that have high incomes but, overall, relatively immature economic systems. Consequently, what is an advanced economy extends beyond simple income measures to include other criteria. These criteria would include the following characteristics:

- High level of industrialisation.
- Increased evidence of wealth generation from the service sector.
- Extensively developed economic infrastructure system.
- High generalised standard of living.

For the purposes of this chapter, the definition used will be that as offered by the IMF (2017), its definition of what it terms 'advanced economies'. Under these terms, the IMF differentiates between economies based upon per capita income level, export diversification, and degree of integration into the global financial system. The first criteria are straightforward, whereas the second is used so as to exclude those states that depend on a very narrow set of products to export (usually commodity products such as oil) and whose income would fluctuate with the price of that product. This includes states such as Saudi Arabia, for whom 70 per cent of its exports are a single product – oil. The choice of degree of integration into the global financial system is used as a proxy for the maturity of the system. According to these criteria, there are – as of 2017 – 39 advanced economies. These are indicated in Table 6.1.

What is evident when examining this list is that it comprises a lot of relatively small states. These are either states within the EU (or with close links to the EU) or ex-colonies that have been able to carve out strategic niches in specific regions (such as Singapore, Hong Kong, and Macao). What is also evident is that – in terms of EU states – some states (such as the Baltics and the Czech and Slovak Republics) have been classified as advanced, whereas others (notably Poland) have not. This is largely due to the legacy of the agrarian economy in some parts of Eastern Europe and the extent to which these states have advanced along the path of industrialisation. Finally, what also becomes

**TABLE 6.1** Advanced economies (figures in brackets are the placing in UN's Human Development Index)

- Australia (2)
- Austria (24)
- Belgium (22)
- Canada (10)
- Cyprus (33)
- Czech Republic (28)
- Denmark (5)
- Estonia(30
- Finland (23)
- France (21)
- Germany (4)
- Greece (29)
- Hong Kong (12)

- Iceland (9)
- Ireland (8)
- Israel (19)
- Italy (27)
- Japan (17)
- Latvia (44)
- Lithuania (37)
- Luxembourg (20)
- Macau (n/a)
- Malta (33)
- The Netherlands (7)
- New Zealand (13)
- Norway (1)

- Portugal (41)
- Puerto Rico (n/a)
- San Marino (n/a)
- Singapore (5)
- Slovakia (40)
- Slovenia (25)
- South Korea (18)
- Spain (26)
- Sweden (14)
- Switzerland (2)
- Taiwan (n/a)
- United Kingdom (16)
- United States (10)

Source: IMF (2020)

evident – with the large amount of small open economies on the list – is how the larger states and/or groupings will dominate. The larger advanced states (i.e., the US, Japan, Canada, France, Germany, the UK, Italy, and Spain) comprise 85 per cent of the collective GDP of these advanced economies, with nearly 60 per cent of the value of exports from this grouping (UNCTAD 2017).

It is worth noting at this juncture – though it is excluded from the criteria utilised by the IMF – that the advanced economies are also characterised by high levels of human development according to the UN's Human Development Index. The index reflects a composite measure of life expectancy, education, and per capita income. As to be expected, the higher each of the criteria, the higher a state is placed on the list. Table 6.1 indicates the placement of the 39 advanced economies in the UN's Human Development Index, and what becomes immediately apparent is the very close correlation between human development and economic development (UN 2017). While there are some Middle Eastern and Asian states that are high on the Human Development Index (such as Qatar and Bahrain) but low on the IMF's economic development list and some of the Eastern and Southern European states that tend to under-perform on the Human Development Index, the correlation seems almost perfect. The correlation grows stronger when those states [Andorra, Bermuda, the Faroe Islands, Guernsey, the Holy See (Vatican State), Jersey, Lichtenstein, and Monaco] are included in the CIA's list of advanced economies but excluded from the IMF's list are integrated into the analysis.

## THE IMPORTANCE OF DEVELOPED ECONOMIES TO THE GLOBAL ECONOMY

Not surprisingly, these states play a dominant role in the global economy. These 39 states (out of 195 globally) account for 42 per cent of global GDP. This is just 15 per cent of the global population. Of these 39 states, the leading seven (the US, the UK, France, Japan, Germany, Italy, and Canada) account for 31 per cent of global GDP. This dominance is also reflected in terms of exports, where these 39 states account for nearly 65 per cent of the global total, with the largest seven states accounting for nearly 35 per cent on their own. This pattern is also reflected in FDI trends, where, in 2016, these advanced economies accounted for 60 per cent of global FDI (though this is down from nearly three-quarters of FDI in the early 1970s). Of these, the leading seven states accounted for 52 per cent of global FDI (IMF 2020 *IMF Data* https://www.imf.org/en/Data).

This pattern of the dominance of the advanced economy is also evident in terms of the world's largest MNEs. 53 per cent are from five advanced economies (the US, the UK, Japan, France, and Germany). In terms of the top 10 states, only one state (China) is not an advanced economy, and when the other four advanced economies appearing on the top 10 list for MNEs (i.e., the Netherlands, Switzerland, Canada, and South Korea) are added, the number of advanced economy MNEs rises to nearly 65 per cent of the top 500 businesses. While the advanced states are dominant in terms of the amount of MNEs, there is evidently a long-term diminution of their power on this list as MNEs from emerging and developing states become ever more prominent. This has its most evident expression in the rise of the Chinese MNE, which by 2017 comprised 109 of the world's largest MNEs or some 22 per cent of the total (Forbes 2017).

This pattern is repeated in less objective measurements. The WEF Global Competitiveness Index for 2018–2019, which is based on observations by business executives of a number of criteria (see Chapter 3), also ranks the advanced economies as the most competitive. Of the 138 states ranked in the WEF index, 36 advanced states are ranked (Macao, Porto Rico, and San Marino are excluded). These advanced states dominate the top of the ranking, with all of the top 15 states having advanced economies. The top five globally were Switzerland, Singapore, the US, the Netherlands, and Germany. The highest non-advanced economy is the UAE (at 16th), with China being 28th on the list. Of these states, the Western European states tend to be the best performers, with the Southern and Eastern European states the worst. The outliers within this pattern are very much Greece (ranked 86th) and Cyprus (ranked), which reflect in no small part the legacy of austerity for these two states. The austerity agenda for these states has increased tax rates and policy instability, as well as highlighting the inefficiency of the institutions in these states. The political instability that emerged as a legacy of austerity (and the sovereign debt crisis) had a direct legacy on the performance of these states.

Interlinked into this ranking system is the World Bank's Ease of Doing Business Index. This index ranks global economies by the ease with which the local regulatory environment supports the development of business (both indigenous and overseas). Again, the rank is dominated by advanced economies (World Bank 2017). Of the 190 states ranked by the World Bank, the list – while dominated by the advanced economies – also shows a more diverse spread. Of the top 10 states (New Zealand is first, Singapore is second, and Denmark is third), only one state is non-advanced. Again, Southern and Eastern European states in the advanced economy list tend to do less well, with the lowest being Malta, ranked at 79th. This is largely due to problems obtaining finance, registering property, and the paperwork involved in starting a business.

A final index that also underlines the control these states exercise over the global system is the World Bank's logistic performance index, which measures the efficacy of national logistical systems. Out of a ranking of 160 states, the top 12 are all advanced economies, with Germany being first, Luxembourg second, and Sweden third. Indeed, of the 35 advanced states featured on the list, 26 of the top 30 have advanced economies. Again, it is the Southern and Eastern European states that rank lowest among advanced economies, with Cyprus ranking the lowest at 59th, largely due to the expense of international shipments and low logistical competence.

Overall, this summary of the statistics highlights three things. The first is that the advanced economies (despite the rise of the BRICs; see Chapter 6) continue to dominate the global economy. They are the largest in terms of major economic indicators such as income and trade. They are also home to the largest multinational companies. Second, the high level of development has largely enabled these states to create the conditions and platform through which their position can be sustained. These states have invested to create advanced technological infrastructure, effective education systems, and diverse economic bases. This suggests that – even though there are new markets emerging as alternative growth and development policies – these advanced economies will collectively retain their prominent position in the global economic system. However, these frameworks reflect embedded neo-liberal logic, and this has begun to be increasingly questioned over the past decade.

## CASE STUDY 6.1: WHAT HAPPENED TO JAPAN?

In the decades after the end of the Second World War, the Japanese economy expanded extremely rapidly, exhibiting average growth rates of 10 per cent per year between 1955 and 1970 and 5 per cent per year throughout the 1970s and 1980s. By the late 1980s, these high rates of growth had created large asset price bubbles in the property and stock markets. The beginning of this bubble lay in the Plaza Accord of 1985, which sought to strengthen the dollar. The consequences of this agreement for Japan were an appreciation of the yen, which hit Japanese exports, which were a core driver of GDP growth. As growth slowed, the Bank of Japan lowered interest rates by 2.5 per cent between January 1986 and February 1987. This monetary policy easing combined with tax reform stimulated the Japanese economy, causing growth to increase from 2.8 per cent in 1986 to 5.5 per cent between 1987 and 1990. The favourable economic conditions, combined with lax financial regulation, generated the aforementioned asset bubbles. The bubbles burst when interest rates were raised from 1989–1990, with both asset and property prices losing approximately half their value between 1989 and 1992.

Japan's so-called 'lost decade' between 1992 and 2002 was universally a period of economic stagnation, as growth was still 1 per cent per annum over the period. This was lower than the previous period, fuelled largely by the banking and corporate debt crises that emerged as a consequence of the bursting of the asset bubbles. In the banking sector - where there are large amounts of non-performing loans – the bank's strategy is to give borrowers more time in the hope that an economic recovery will eventually allow these debts to be serviced. Often, the banks continued to lend to bad debtors, which merely compounded the problem by creating 'zombie firms' (i.e., those firms only kept alive through more borrowing). This also constrained the ability of these banks to offer new loans. Despite fiscal expansion and low interest rates, the lost decade saw an erosion of the competitiveness of Japan's businesses.

Since 2002, the economy has begun to recover. This was helped by more aggressive measures by Japanese authorities to lower the level of bad loans across the sector. Indeed, between 2002 and 2005, these bad debts fell by over 70 per cent. This was aided by ultra-low interest rates and quantitative easing (i.e., printing money) to improve bank balance sheets and enable them to lend. The quantitative easing was also designed to counteract the trend towards deflation within the economy. This enabled a rise in business investment and lower corporate debt levels and allowed growth between 2003 and 2007 to expand to nearly 2 per cent a year. Moreover, the rising growth allowed government deficits to begin to fall (they fell from 8 per cent of GDP in 2003 to 2 per cent in 2007); these had been on the rise since the early 1990s.

This progress was brought to a halt by the global financial crisis, which pushed Japan into its deepest post-war recession. Between 2008 and 2009, Japan's GDP fell by 9 per cent though aggressive government measures meant that these output falls were largely regained by 2010. These aggressive measures saw a return to quantitative easing and ultra-low interest rates. However, this rate of progress was delayed by the 2011 earthquake, which contracted GDP by 2.6 per cent. The net result was that by the end of 2012, Japanese GDP was still 2.4 per cent below the levels seen prior to the global financial crisis.

Despite all of these measures, Japan has struggled since the collapse of the asset bubble, with growth being sluggish, though it does remain the world's third-biggest economy. Over the longer term Japan does face some major problems which could limit its ability to enjoy faster rates of growth, notably:

- An ageing population with an estimated 40 per cent decline in the working population by 2050.
- Historically protected sectors of the economy (e.g., energy, agriculture)
- Persistent deflation, which has subdued consumption.
- Weak public finances, with public debt at 238 per cent of GDP (up from 67 per cent in 1990).
- Segmentation of the workforce between regular and non-regular workers.

Since 2012, the Japanese government has renewed its effort to raise its growth rate with a growth strategy named 'Abenomics'. This is based on aggressive growth-centred monetary policy; a short-term fiscal boost and long-term structural reforms of these first two have proved largely successful. However, the third strand has been more controversial, with persistent resistance by many sectors to the opening up of the economy. This third arrow of the strategy has facilitated a greater number of trade deals, but widespread reform of labour and specific goods markets has been more elusive.

**QUESTION**

What do you believe is the likelihood that Japan will return to its pre-eminent position in the global economy?

## CRISES IN DEVELOPED ECONOMIES

Over the past decade, the advanced economies that had hitherto been beacons of stability within the global economic system have suffered a series of (interlinked) economic crises that have spread to political and social spheres, creating multiple risks for these states that have the potential, over the longer term, to erode the pre-eminent position that these states enjoy within the global economy. While it is not the purpose of this chapter to note the causes of each of the respective crises, it is worthwhile – at this juncture – to note the nature and form of each crisis before examining the broader impact of these crises upon the macro-environment of these states. Briefly, these crises were:

1. The global financial crisis: while this will be dealt with in more depth in Chapter 16, it is worth noting at this juncture that this had the effect of creating a 'credit crunch' causing the financial system to seize up and limit commercial access to finance.

2. The euro crisis: this is the result of the above banking crisis, morphing into a sovereign debt crisis provoking economic austerity and further challenging bank liquidity.

3. The commodity crisis: up to 2014, these states saw sharp rises in the prices of commodities, which (both directly and indirectly) squeezed household incomes as oil prices fell from 2014. The resultant price instability had a mixed effect of allowing disposable incomes to rise but also reshaping energy security strategies but also the negative investment sentiment that emerged from such volatile prices.

4. The immigrant crisis: political instability in the Middle East and in parts of central Asia, combined with high rates of youth unemployment (and the absence of economic opportunity) in sub-Saharan Africa and Central America, has hassled rinsing migrant flows into Europe and the US, to which states have been unable or unwilling to respond.

The legacy of these crises has been profound and has reshaped the risk environment for advanced economies. As argued in Chapter 1, this has shown the limits and downsides of hyper-globalisation and how it can negatively impact the advanced states that were previously seen to be the major beneficiaries of this process. This has not only created new risks within the political, economic, and social systems of some states; it has also exposed and brought to the surface longstanding fractures within these states that have radically reshaped their risk environment.

Moreover, with the rise of the BRICs (especially China), it is evident that the advanced economies are not as powerful as they once were. Much of the change has been stimulated by China's vast pool of savings, which have fuelled the power of Chinese capital, capital markets, and financial institutions. As a result, across a number of measures, advanced economies will be less influential. For example, according to the IMF (2017):

- Between 1990 and 2022, the share of world output in advanced economies will fall from 64 per cent to 39 per cent.
- Between 1950 and 2015, the share of the global population in advanced economies fell from 27 per cent to 15 per cent.
- The productivity of many advanced economies has slowed markedly due to under-investment in education, infrastructure, etc.
- As noted later, over 60 per cent of the population of advanced economies endured flat or falling real incomes between 2005 and 2014 (especially in Italy and the US).

Before moving on to briefly examine the causes and nature of these risks within advanced economies, it is worth stressing that, in practical terms, it is difficult to isolate economic, social, and political risks as there is self-evident overlap between them.

## ECONOMIC RISKS

While these economies are not the fastest-growing economies in the global economic system (that falls to the emerging economies; see Chapter 6), they nonetheless, as identified above, do constitute a powerful economic force within it to the extent that a rapid downturn in one of the major economies (i.e., the US, Japan, and large EU states) has the potential to fundamentally alter the growth trajectory of the global economy. In seeking to assess the major risks faced by the global economy, the WEF identified a number of risks, all of which are sourced from systemic risks created by advanced economies. Briefly, the main identified economic risks are:

- The emergence (or re-emergence) of asset bubbles (notably within property), which render such assets overpriced and subject to a sharp correction, has severe negative consequences for government, household, and private sector balance sheets.
- Persistent deflation within a major economy: Japan has been subject to this for almost two decades since the early 1990s when persistent falls in prices led to suppressed and/or deferred consumption. This matters as consumption – in the case of major advanced economies – is between 60 and 70 per cent of GDP, and falling or suppressed growth will limit growth or even lead to its decline.
- Failure of a major financial institution or mechanism: this will be addressed in Chapter 16, but such failures lead to a reduction in available credit within the economic system.
- The failure of critical infrastructure: this is to be addressed within Chapter 17. However, it is worth noting that the failure of energy or IT systems has the potential to undermine the ability of an economic system to function effectively.

- Fiscal crises: as will be examined below, the state plays an important stabilising role within an economic system. Any erosion of this capability can have profound implications for effective system functioning.
- Unemployment: this is not just a loss of resource capabilities but also constitutes a potentially destabilising social and political risk.
- Illicit trade and financial flows: these are measures outside of formal legal frameworks designed to bypass official controls and will include phenomena such as tax evasion, human trafficking, or other illegal activities. The danger of such processes is that they can erode international cooperation frameworks and lead to the fragmentation of the economic system.
- Energy price shocks (both increases and decreases): the impacts of large increases in energy prices can be widely understood as many of the advanced economies are energy importers, and such a price shift would have a net deflationary effect. However, sharp price shifts in the other direction can also be negative, as consumers may be tied into long-term contracts at high prices.
- Unmanageable Inflation: this induces uncertainty in the economic system, leading to delayed investment and increasingly volatile interest rates.

The majority of these risks have been shaped as a direct legacy of the nature of the global financial crisis but also of a number of succeeding events. While this is explored in depth in Chapter 17, it is worthwhile noting that its most immediate impact was in generating a 'balance sheet recession'. This balance sheet recession was caused by all main sources of demand in the advanced economies enduring a deteriorating financial position caused by the end of the property bubble, as banks had debt on their balance sheets backed by assets that were worth a fraction of what was paid for them, and consumers had overextended themselves to pay for these assets. Moreover, in some cases, states had to borrow heavily (Spain, Ireland, and Portugal) to bail out the financial system for fear that a failure to do so could possibly lead to a systemic banking crash and a full-blown economic crisis.

Consequently, debt lies at the core of the risks to the global system generated by advanced economies. By 2017, the combination of household, corporate, and government debt was 390 per cent of GDP for advanced economies. In advanced economies, most of this rise in debt up to 2017 has been generated by governments. Since the financial crisis, the corporate (especially the financial sector) and household sectors have been deleveraging (i.e., paying off debt), where debt has fallen by as much as 30 per cent in the decade after the global financial crisis (IMF 2017). However, government debt has continued to rise. In the UK and the US, government debt has more than doubled, with Japan and the Eurozone both showing a 50 per cent increase. This has led to increased debates about the need for public sector austerity. This 'austerity consensus' is based on the work of Rogoff and Reinhart (2009), who suggest that in the aftermath of a financial crisis, tax revenues collapse, causing government debt. However, they argue that once external debt (i.e., that owed to overseas creditors) rises above 60 per cent of GDP, annual growth is reduced by 2 per cent and once it rises above 90 per cent; growth is likely to be halved. To many, this justified public sector austerity as it was felt that large levels of government debt 'crowded out' private sector activity. These results have been widely disputed, not least by Blyth (2013), who claimed that 'it doesn't work' and moreover, that 'it has never worked', making bad situations worse. Moreover, these arguments aside, it is evident that austerity has had some unforeseen consequences through increasing political and social risks within the main advanced economies.

## POLITICAL RISKS

The main advanced economies are plural, democratic systems. That is, their governance is shaped by the political cycles where mass enfranchisement delivers a set of policies which are attained by popular consent. One of the benefits of such a system was that, despite the need for elections every four to five years, these systems were able to generate broadly stable political systems where decisions made by governments were – over the medium to long term – fairly predictable. For much of the post-war era, the advanced states had a broad consensus, first on the proactive welfare state and, more latterly, on the more passive needs of the competition state (see Chapter 3). However, in the aftermath of the global financial crisis (and the resultant policy measures), the stability of the political system and the consensus formed around the needs of the competition states have begun to be eroded. The effect has been to increase the level of political risk across the advanced economies.

In truth, the beginnings of this political uncertainty started in that state, which was arguably most affected by the extremes of economic austerity. During and in the aftermath of the euro zone crisis, the Greek electorate increasingly kicked back against the sharp austerity measures imposed upon it by other euro zone members and international financial institutions. To the Greeks, placing adjustment solely upon them to meet the onerous austerity conditions needed to meet the terms of a 'bail out' (i.e., emergency borrowing for the aforementioned financial institutions) was unfair. To them, the banks that lent the money to Greece (i.e., EU banks) needed to 'bail in' to the process (that is, write proportions of the debt owed by the Greek government). Failing to do so placed the burden of adjustment on the Greek population. The result was the fragmentation of the political system, with voters heading towards more extreme political parties on the left (Syriza) and right (Golden Dawn). While the former eventually acceded to power, they ultimately implemented the austerity agenda.

However, parallel to these processes reflecting the legacy of long-term economic decline and deindustrialisation across some parts of Western Europe and the US, the perception of the 'immigration crisis' (and subsequent issues of social-cultural integration), the disillusionment with globalisation, and the medium-term consequences of austerity (at least in western European states) was a fragmentation of political systems across larger states, most notably the US and the UK. While a full analysis of the reasons for the Brexit vote (i.e., the UK's decision to leave the EU) and the election of Donald Trump as US President is beyond the scope of this chapter, it is worthwhile to note how these have shaped the political risk environment. First, these reflect an anti-establishment trend in these political systems, where conventional discourses and policies failed to address the issue of long-term change. Second, economic, social, and political change has not just left some segments of society behind; it has left others detached from this process while others simply yearn for more traditional structures. Third, globalisation, and in the case of Brexit, its lesser cousin regionalism, has been sold as not delivering benefits to large segments of the population. The net effect was to tie the popular vote to a stronger sense of nationalism. The legacy of this is to formally reject hyper-globalisation and to move towards a global economic system that is more fragmented. For businesses, the risks of such moves are sourced from the potential disruption to markets and cross-border supply chains as populism morphs into a more malign economic nationalism.

In a more benign form, this rejection of existing political systems was evident in the election of Emmanuel Macron and his newly formed 'En Marche' party. This party brought outsiders into the political system and sought to reject the conventional centre-left/centre-right dichotomy by borrowing ideas from both. The rise of this party was set against the rise of the Far-Right National Front in France, which adopted a more isolationist and xenophobic stance. Indeed, across many EU states, there has been the rise of many anti-establishment parties and nationalist parties. In many states, the rise of the right has been more apparent than real, with many mainstream parties adapting policies to cope with this trend without fundamentally reshaping the political consensus. Thus, across the major states of Western Europe, the rise of more extreme parties (on both the left and right) seems, at least at the time of writing, to have been militated. Of course, the legacy of the populist revolt in the UK and the US remains, but both of these are surrounded by ambiguity at the time of writing, with the UK not really knowing what Brexit really amounts to and the populist US President also exhibiting ambiguity with regards to the implementation of this economic nationalist agenda.

## CASE STUDY 6.2: THE EURO CRISIS

The euro crisis emerged out of the global banking crisis as the contagion that infected the banks spread to the euro zone governments. The euro zone is the sub-group of nineteen EU states that share a common currency, the euro (though at the time of the crisis there were eleven states). Membership of this group was based on the pre-condition that all members were, if not demonstrating convergence in macro-economic performance (that is, in terms of government debt, public deficits, and monetary policy), then moving towards that objective. The euro system was comprised of a European Central Bank, with the participating central banks assuming responsibility for monetary policy. The introduction of the euro was driven by a mix of political and economic factors, which were expected to further integrate markets and promote system stability. The most immediate impact of the introduction of the euro was that interest rates between states began to converge at the lower levels exhibited by Germany.

The effect of this fall in interest rates (especially within southern euro states) was to promote credit growth as the risk premium on currencies fell and competition in the finance sector promoted innovation that enabled banks to borrow more easily abroad. This growth in credit was especially notable within the construction and financial services sectors. As property prices boomed, there was a corresponding increase in debt. This growth hid problems within the state's fiscal system as both public debt and government deficits worsened. This was compounded by the fact that rising growth for a number of states was accompanied by a worsening trade position as the current account worsened. These double deficits were financed by debt (especially in the case of Greece). Overall, it was felt that as long as growth was strong, the position could be sustained.

The global financial crisis was a trigger that led to the weaknesses within the euro system being exposed, especially as growth slowed. As this growth slowed, interest rates across the euro zone began to diverge, reflecting the risk attached to public debt. This created a problem for banks that had lent excessively to indebted governments. This created a liquidity crisis, which stimulated the EU to seek a rescue for those banks exposed to these states' debt. While these measures alleviated the banks' problems, they did make the debt position of states worse. Greece had to admit that its deficit was understated. This led to a crisis of confidence in the euro, with the debt problems being extended to Ireland, Portugal, and Spain.

In 2010, the EU and the IMF put together a rescue package linked to the implementation of severe austerity measures. This was later supported by the European Financial Stability Facility (EFSF) to offer financial assistance. This allowed the European Central Bank (ECB) to start buying debt. This was later supported – in 2011 – by measures to limit contagion. This was a commitment by the ECB to do whatever was necessary to defend the euro. To some degree, this reassured markets. To this extent, it offered further facilities to states in return for deep austerity measures.

The euro crisis highlighted weaknesses within the euro system, notably that it was a monetary union and not a fiscal union. As such, the ECB had no power to monetise deficits, which put pressure on states to follow the same fiscal trajectory without the means to enforce it. As such, states followed their own priorities. With no policy to transfer money to struggling states, states had to follow paths to which there was no incentive to adhere, and there was also precious little incentive to reform and remove the structural problems between eurozone economies. This state had vastly differing competitiveness differentials, mainly due to big differences in productivity between them. As such, peripheral states lost competitiveness vis-à-vis the core without the means to restore competitiveness via exchange rate devaluations. This placed pressure upon reform, which many states were loath to do.

The euro crisis is important for the global economy as the constituent states represent some 20 per cent of global GDP and have the potential to affect the rate of global economic growth. As such, the crisis has implications beyond the borders of the eurozone. This is especially so as the banks of non-euro states had exposure to the sovereign debt. This also extended to emerging market economies, for whom the eurozone was an important market. China took the opportunity to diversify its holdings by buying euro assets on the cheap. More importantly, the global banking system meant that the crisis could be transmitted throughout the system. The crisis also placed pressure on the reform of the eurozone, notably with regard to promoting a deeper fiscal union with a larger EU budget. At the time of writing, the plans for the reform of the eurozone have yet to be agreed upon.

## QUESTION

To what extent do you believe that a crisis in the eurozone was inevitable?

## SOCIAL RISKS

Inevitably, in democratic systems, the social upheaval will be felt not through revolution but through the ballot box, and as suggested above, the risky level of political risk experienced within advanced economies is a reflection of the rising social risks. These social risks – within advanced economies – are an increased reflection of the perceived and actual inequities within social systems. They reflect both long-term trends of industrial and social change and also more short-term processes. In the former, they are driven by the legacy of deindustrialisation across areas of northern Europe and the US 'rust belt'; in the latter, they reflect (at least, in part) the policy measures deployed to deal with the global financial crisis and an on-going immigration crisis and its legacy for social cohesion.

At the core of dissatisfaction must lie a perception that globalisation is not delivering the benefits anticipated across the socio-economic strata. The logic of globalisation was that its benefits would 'trickle-down' to all layers of society. This process stresses that while the immediate beneficiaries of globalisation will be high-earners, the higher spending by this segment leads to higher incomes for others due to the higher spending by those on higher incomes. Thus, so the argument goes, society as a whole benefits over the long term from this process of change stimulated by globalisation as inequalities are lowered over time. In global terms, investment by Western MNEs in developing/emerging economies would benefit advanced economies over the longer term as their higher incomes would be spent on Western economy goods and services. Moreover, advanced economy consumers would be expected to benefit from access to lower-cost products produced by these emerging and developing states.

There is increased scepticism with regard to the 'trickle-down effect'. It is evident that we are now thirty-plus years into an era of hyper-globalisation, and it is increasingly evident that this period has been accompanied by increased inequality. Anecdotally, it is evident that short-term adjustment costs suffered by many advanced economies industrial bases have turned into long-term economic decline. Either a misplaced faith in markets to promote adjustment or a failure to offer a sufficiently proactive regional policy has accentuated this economic stagnation that has led to the emergence of social 'underclasses' that are disengaged from the economic system. This has been formalised with growing evidence from the OECD as to the rising levels of inequality within advanced economies. Moreover, inequality of income tends to come through inequality of opportunity, which results in higher incomes having better access to healthcare, education, and wealth accumulation.

Picketty (2013) argues that inequality is integral to the global economic system. And if the rate of growth of capital (i.e., profits, dividends, interest, rents, and other income from capital) is greater than the rate of economic growth, then inequality results. This is because those who possess wealth are able to add to that wealth more than those whose income depends on the proceeds of growth. Globalisation, so he argues, has allowed that gap between return on capital and economic growth to grow as wealth has been able to move freely across borders to secure the best return even at the cost of economic growth. For Picketty, this represents a return to 'patrimonial capitalism' where the economy becomes dominated by inherited wealth, creating an oligarchic-plutocratic power structure. This is dangerous as it erodes plural power structures and risks delegitimising democratic systems, risking social upheaval and disorder. For Picketty, the solution to this problem is a progressive annual wealth tax, without which the global economy would be subject to rising inequality and low growth.

This trend towards inequality has also been highlighted by what has come to be known as the 'elephant curve'. This argues that trade liberalisation has shifted inequality from a global scale to a domestic scale. This is created by the tradability of low-skilled jobs. In this case, the loss of low-skilled workers in advanced economies (who see their incomes fall) find themselves substituted by low-skilled workers in developing states (who see their wages rise). Milanovic (2013) argues that the winners of the process of globalisation have been the top 1 per cent of wealth owners globally (whose income has risen by an estimated 60 per cent) and the emerging economy middle classes (whose income has risen by 70–80 per cent). However, the middle classes in advanced economies have seen their incomes stagnate. On top of this, these middle-class occupations have been impacted by the process of technological change, which has seen low-skilled manufacturing jobs replaced by automated technologies. However, these results have been criticised as indicating that the suppression of income growth in the advanced economy by the middle class is not simply due to globalisation, as domestic factors (such as population growth) were also likely to be large contributory factors to this pattern. In addition, the rise of middle-class incomes in emerging economies is largely seen as a Chinese phenomenon rather than a universal process across all these types of states.

The final element of social risk reflects the strategies to deal with the financial crisis, especially the austerity consensus. The advocacy of austerity to deal with the public sector consequences of the global financial crisis has led to the advocacy of austerity by many advanced economies as the states sought to repair their balance sheets. The focus of this adjustment has tended to fall on the expenditure side rather than the revenue-raising side. The neo-liberal logic of many states believes that increasing taxes in an era of global capital would merely erode the revenue base. However, in focusing on expenditure cuts, governments have targeted government welfare programmes and spending on other social goods. The net effect of such measures is to further increase inequality. Moreover, there is increased resentment by those affected by such measures that they are being made to bear the cost of the failures of a global financial system from which they are detached.

Addressing issues of inequality within advanced economies is not simply about securing and sustaining social order and militating risks to the economic and political systems from the social system; it is also good for the economy. The idea that rising growth and rising inequality are naturally linked has to be challenged. Growth has to be more evenly distributed between states. Lower inequality is good for an economy not just because of lower social and political risks but also because lower-income groups have higher rates of consumption, allowing for higher rates of economic growth. There is little evidence of the trickle-down effect, which suggests that new solutions need to be found, especially if strategies for removing inequality in one place do not simply create or embed inequalities elsewhere.

## TECHNOLOGICAL RISK

Overwhelmingly, theory has tended to view technological processes as a social and economic good. It is accepted that through this process, economic progress is created and sustained. This is borne out by the strong link between the technological sophistication of an economy and its level of economic development, growth and competitiveness through the process of invention, innovation and diffusion of new products and processes. The benefits of such processes are well understood in terms of how these lead to innovative products and processes that generate efficiencies, enhance the allocation of resources, improve productivity and allow economies to evolve. However, over recent decades, the process of technological change has accelerated, a process that has been a prime driver in globalisation, as highlighted in Chapter 1. However, as this change has become more widespread, the broader impact of these processes has become more widely understood and appreciated, especially with regard to their long-term impact on social, economic, and, ultimately, political risks within developed economies.

The inevitable consequence of technological change is that it generates both winners and losers. The issue is over the extent to which the losers from the process are absorbed into this process of change through proactive labour and industrial/regional policies. This process of technological change has many facets. The most evident is the spread of automation, notably through the rapid development of artificial intelligence and its impacts on the form and nature of automation. Convention dictates that the adoption of new technology has the greatest impact upon the lowest-skill occupations, with automation replacing labour for routine labour-intensive tasks. There is growing evidence that the combination of artificial intelligence and automation means that this process has the potential to be extended to more skilled forms of employment, such as accountancy, medicine, and other information workers. According to some estimates, nearly 50 per cent (Frey and Osborne 2013) of jobs in the US were at risk from automation, with jobs in transport and logistics, retailing, office support, and sales and services seen as especially vulnerable. In the UK, the percentage of jobs at risk was estimated at 35 per cent (this is lower as there is greater employment in more creative industries), and in Japan, it was 49 per cent. In short, the impact is most dependent on whether any given task is routine or not.

The social impact of such changes (other than the conventional immediate impact on employment) is that many expect to see this result in job polarisation where 'middle-skill jobs', which are routine, increase while low-skill and high-skill jobs increase. The result is that there is a split in the workforce between these two groups: one which is highly paid (for example, architects and other very skilled professionals with uncodified knowledge and skills) and the other that is low-paid and unskilled (such as cleaners and fast-food assistants). It is cited that the stagnation of median wages across leading developed economies is evidence that this process is already underway. However, isolating this effect from other processes such as offshoring (whereby routine tasks have been moved to low-wage economies) is difficult. However, the trend seems difficult to dispute. The danger, as advocated by authors such as Ford (2015), is that this is just the tin end of the wedge and that as more tasks can be broken down into their routine elements, the process will spread.

While such fears of mass unemployment generated by technology have been expressed before, there is a concern that the technologies of the 'fourth industrial revolution' mean that this time it could be different. With the rise of big data, companies have the option of developing and training new machine learning systems to do the jobs of an ever-expanding section of the workforce. As such, the conventional response to this process of changing flexible labour markets, allowing workers to move from routine jobs to routine jobs is diminished. The optimists argue that history tells us that as much as automation can eliminate jobs, it also has the potential to create new types of employment as a consequence. For example, the impact of the IT revolution thus far has been to create a demand for IT specialists. As such, technology can displace rather than destroy jobs. This still places an emphasis upon education, training, and HR systems to adjust to this process. Alongside these structural issues of technology, there are also broader societal impacts from the deepening of the use of technology systems. As identified within Chapter 18, the spread of these technologies creates an infrastructural risk generated by attacks on critical infrastructure and through the use and misuse of data. There is also the risk that widespread use of technologies can cause social fragmentation, as they have the potential to generate social unrest and provoke political division. As recent political events have shown, the widespread adoption of these technologies can have demonstrably disruptive political impacts.

Livesey (2016) takes a relatively contrarian view of this process, suggesting that technological change can work to the benefit of developed states and reverse the flow of employment to low-cost locations. Livesey (2016) argues that globalisation (notably the rise of disaggregated supply chains) has been stimulated by a process of 'labour cost arbitrage' (i.e., sourcing where labour costs are low) as well as the digitisation of production, for Livesey (2016), the fourth industrial revolution and the lowering cost of intelligent automation offers the potential to replace these overseas low-cost workers with 're-shored' or 'near-shored' activities, with them moving closer to the point of consumption. In effect, the world will globalise as a result of technology (which is contrary to the position argued in Chapter 1). However, trade in manufacturing is only one form of globalisation (data-driven globalisation is likely to act as a significant counter to this trend), and there is concern as to whether the type and volume of jobs created would be large enough to be significant.

## CASE STUDY 6.3: THE TURNAROUND AT FORD

Ford was an automotive business that was facing long-term structural problems. By 2006, when the new CEO, Alan Mulally, arrived, the company was anticipating a $17 billion loss. The new CEO initiated a turnaround that, in four years, saw the business make record profits. This turnaround started with the company beginning to recognise its faults and overcoming a culture of corporate complacency and executive rivalry. This growth is all the more impressive as it has been set against a background of sluggish growth within the core US market. Such a turnaround is not unique among the big three car makers (GM and Chrysler are the other two). The big difference is that while Chrysler and GM went bankrupt and into government hands, Ford avoided this scenario.

Its avoidance of state control reflected that Ford had already been sorting itself out prior to the GFC, which saw car sales tumble. At the root of its troubles was a desire by the firm from 1998 to move into more diverse segments of the automotive industry (it acquired Land Rover, Aston Martin, Jaguar, Volvo, and its Lincoln and Mercury brands into a single group: the Premier Automotive Group (PAG)). The role of this group was to help the group ride out variations in demand in the mass car market by diversifying its offering. The aim was for PAG to generate up to a third of its profits. However, this never happened, with PAG proving to be costly and distracting Ford from its core business. Though a change in management launched a 'back to basics' strategy, the company began to suffer from a declining reputation for quality and reliability. However, long-term change was delayed as the company was able to hide behind the high revenue growth from the sale of sports utility vehicles and pickup trucks (which were protected by trade restrictions). These segments became exposed as Asian companies moved in on this segment and set up US factories to get around duties. The effect was that Ford had to cut capacity. However, progress in this area was slow due to strong management and labour resistance.

By 2006, the company had hit a crisis point, having to take out emergency loans against the firm's assets to secure the business. Despite this, the plan lacked credibility with banks; to them, this was just another rescue plan. Alan Mulally began to turn the business around by selling off PAG and focusing solely on the Ford brand. This was aided by the decision to sell a narrower range of cars (from 97 to 36), which were of better quality, with the target of being best in class. Next, Ford sought to ensure that regionally successful products could be globally successful. This meant establishing global platforms (i.e., the basic floor plan and underpinning). Now, 80 per cent of platforms are global. From these global platforms, Ford can adapt the model to suit regional tastes and differences in regulations. Now, up to 80 parts in any single car are shared across models. Inevitably, on top of this came a rationalisation of the workforce, with numbers falling by around 60 per cent. The net effect was that by 2010, Ford had shed $14 billion in operating costs, and it's now able to compete with the Japanese transplant factors.

For Ford, the strategy is to only build what the company can sell. This new flexibility within strategy has been aided by the common platform strategy, as production can be shifted between models easily. Moreover, improvements in technology are speeding development times and leading to a seemingly perpetual refreshment of its product portfolio.

Thus, when the GFC occurred in 2008, Ford decided it could opt out of the Troubled Asset Relief Programme to which the other large car makers had succumbed. Indeed, the avoidance of the need for public support has given Ford some very positive public relations. Ford still has a way to go to fully adapt to the shifting environment as other car manufacturers continue to progress. To that end, Ford is making in-roads in growth markets. Ford did find itself at a disadvantage in the Chinese market, where the government chose GM as its early joint venture partner. Even if this does not come off, Ford is clearly planning to target other Asian markets. Europe has a long-term problem with chronic overcapacity; this is despite the market being one of its more successful. However, there is little denying that Asia and other emerging economies are the future of Ford sales growth. In 2016, 16 per cent of sales were in such regions, with 84 per cent being in Europe and North America.

### QUESTION

What do you believe to be the biggest strategic challenge facing Ford and other developed economy automobile manufacturers?

## COPING WITH GLOBALISATION: TOWARDS A UNIVERSAL BASIC INCOME

While there are assorted methods to deal with particular risks, one that is gaining currency that would impact all the risks identified above is the notion of the state providing a Universal Basic Income (UBI). The idea is to give every citizen a basic, no-strings-attached income. This is seen as a way of reducing inequality, sustaining growth, and militating emergent political risks without having to backtrack on the premise of an open global trading and investment system. The UBI could also work as a counterbalance to the resistance to automation within segments of the workforce. In addition, the UBI has an attraction in that it would offer workers more flexibility in terms of being able to train and also reward work that is either unrewarded or under-rewarded (such as housework). The policy is also seen as an alternative to a straightforward minimum wage that would tend to negatively impact employment after a certain threshold.

The UBI can be designed to phase out particular problems of current welfare provision, which is often selective and targeted. In particular, the UBI could be attractive as:

- There is tapering off as income rises, and therefore there is no cliff edge as welfare payments fall drastically beyond a certain level, making a worker with an incremental pay increase worse off.

- Universal benefits are less vulnerable to the government than targeted benefits, as more voters will be worse off if the former is cut than if the latter is cut, so the government is less likely to cut them.
- It would benefit people with no prospect of work.
- Replacing aspects of the pension with UBI could encourage more older people to stay in or return to work.

The usefulness of such UBI strategies has by no means reached a consensus. Aside from the cost of such strategies, there is the fear of the impact that breaking the link between work and income could have on economies, not least through productivity. However, the cost seems to be the major impediment, as it would clearly imply large tax rises, though some states could tap into sovereign wealth funds (though these are the states that would tend to need the UBI least). For the US, to offer a UBI of $10,000 a year would imply a 9 per cent tax rise (assuming the UBI placed rather than supported existing programmes). Inevitably, such strategies come with risks, as incentives could be swayed by them. The other downside is that it could fundamentally alter the incentive to work by, as mentioned above, breaking the link between income and employment. Work is more than just a means of income; it has other benefits too, in terms of offering structure and self-worth. There is also the fear that it could inhibit integration and lead to social alienation. Moreover, it could create tension within the system by eroding the premise of the welfare state (i.e., being a hand-up rather than a hand-out). This runs the risk of eroding the empathy between the supporter and the supported, which is key to legitimising the modern welfare state. A by-product of this is that it would legitimise tough immigration policies as UBI would be linked to citizenship, given the basis that the right to income would make a state attractive for migrants.

Ultimately, the UBI is not a no questions asked strategy. It is really an answer to the issue of how the welfare state can be reformed in an era of globalisation that has produced both winners and losers. In so doing, it does so without any obligation on the recipient to seek work. In some senses, the strategy can work in those areas where labour is immobile under conditions of long-term economic decline and welfare dependency is rife. If globalisation is about states adapting to change, then it is to be expected that welfare systems change to compensate for losers in this process of change. However, UBI should not preclude the right to work and the right of states to seek to upgrade the quality of human and non-human resources to become an attractive location for investment. In practice, UBI can only be one of a set of measures that militate against social risks within advanced economies.

## ADDRESSING THE RISE OF POPULISM

Arguably, a bigger challenge is to seek solutions to the rise of populism within these states. While it can be argued that the rejection of extremes of left and right by many Europeans has signalled that the populist wave may have reached its high water mark, this has often only been done by centrist parties moving to the left or right. Moreover, even if the watermark has been reached, there are still the longer-term consequences of the populist surge to be addressed, notably the four years of Trump's presidency and the process of the UK's disengagement from the EU. If we take the optimistic scenario that the Trump administration is a historical aberration and Brexit is a one-time expression of frustration, there is clearly still a need to prevent the conditions that stimulated the re-emergence of populism.

In commercial terms, the narrative of globalisation is opportunity. It is also evident that it also comes with risks sourced from an evidently complex global system, which means events and processes can have unpredictable events (Goldin and Mariathasan 2014). For example, the initial welcoming of the Arab Spring was later questioned when it led directly to the European immigration crisis. If systemic stability for advanced economies is going to be assured (with limited opportunities for populism to be regained), then inevitably changes have to be made to advanced economies' economic, political, and social systems. In periods of global instability and uncertainty, there is clearly historic precedent for states to close borders and limit international interactions in order to secure their prosperity; something goes against the consensual position of cooperation and collaboration. Emmott (2017) defined the idea that the Western values of openness and democracy work where they deliver both prosperity and fairness. Openness is also a vulnerability that – due to the nature of hyper-globalisation and the adaptation of states to it – has not been able to deliver the prosperity and/or fairness that was expected of it. For that reason, he believes advanced economies are characterised as decadent, demoralised, deflating, divided, declining, disintegrating, dysfunctional, and declining. For Emmott (2017), restoring the consensus on Western ideas means addressing the following:

1. Recognising that, while openness is a virtue, not everything has to be open all the time. This suggests that states can apply discretion to global flows (for example, immigration) without comprising a commitment to a global system.

2. Recognising that equality is vital to the system, and this is much about equality of opportunity and social progress as it is about income and wealth.

3. Building on point 2, identifying that education, at all levels and ages, is the single most vital support for equality as well as being a country's most vital economic and social resource.

4. Given the increase in demographic changes within many advanced economies (see Chapter 14), there is a need to ensure that there is equality between the young and old. There is evidently growing resentment between these groups, and harmony between them is vital.

5. The rule of law is a non-negotiable guarantor of equality and a source of confidence among citizens and between nations. Any derogation from this for powerful groups risks eroding the legitimacy of the system.

6. If the system is to work for all, then the right for all groups to be heard is vital. Freedom of speech is a vital bridge between openness and equality, not a trade-off between them.

7. There should be a boring consistency with regard to economic growth, as 'boom' and 'bust' are both short-term, destabilising, and, in the long term, harmful.

8. Fostering the international rule of law and international collaboration is essential to making the system work.

What Emmott (2017) is proposing is not less globalisation but a different form of globalisation. He recognises that those who have lost out on the process will continue to do so unless equality of opportunity is addressed and the rules of the games are applied fairly. This is made ever more important as many of the low-skilled jobs impacted by globalisation are likely to be further eroded as automation begins to spread across global value chains. Thus, the Western value of openness is not simply about the openness of national systems but also about an openness to change.

The WEF (2017) is also circumspect on how to reconcile globalisation with those populist forces that will resist its impact on inequality while imposing constraints on states to proactively do something about it. Again, the issue is to reconcile inequality without comprising globalisation, and its prognosis is to enhance human capital, spread the benefits of technological change, provide better public goods, and create more responsive governance systems. In short, it makes the state more competitive in the global economy. There is a degree of predictability in these measures, as they have been advanced as part of neo-liberal industrial policies for over four decades. In addition, adapting to a world where electorates are more nationalist is difficult, as there is a need to reconcile the desirability of selective immigration policies without entering into the dark domains of explicit discrimination. These attitudes were especially prevalent among older voters, who have a stronger attachment to traditional values and are less comfortable with a global system. However, low (and falling) turnout rates lead to a detachment between the political system and the electorate, with many being outside the system due to an absence of effective representation. In short, the WEF identifies that there are no short-term political measures to address populism other than to proactively engage with electorates that have been otherwise excluded and to seek to reconcile such divergences. Thus, over the longer term, there is evidently a need to promote inclusive growth, promote change within current institutional frameworks, and seek to reconcile multi-cultural societies with identity politics.

Overall, reconciling a sustained belief in an open global system with mass enfranchisement is a long-term project for advanced states. This is especially so when combined with austerity, where the means of enabling equality (especially education expenditure, etc.) are being curtailed. For many, the benefits of globalisation (i.e., lower prices, more choice, etc.) have come at a price of long-term decline and social exclusion. All this suggests that globalisation has to be reframed as an inclusive process — a process whose most intense and disruptive effects have to be managed or, in the very past, proactively adapted to. It is evident that simple laissez-faire strategies of adaptation have failed and have only generated longer-term economic, social, and political risks.

## CONCLUSIONS

The advanced economies are the cornerstone of the global system. These states in the era of globalisation have been a source of stability and risk ebbed and flowed across developing and emerging economies. However, over the past decade, risk within these advanced economies has been increasing. This has been largely due to the failure to deal (either in political or economic terms) with the long-term legacy of hyper-globalisation within many of these economies. The rise of populism and its actual and potentially disruptive effects upon the global economy has focused states upon this area of benign neglect as electorates have generated disruptive effects upon the global system. At the time of writing, there is little evidence to suggest either that this was a short-term phenomenon that would pass or a reflection of a long-term trend. However, there has been little by way of direct, concrete policy measures to address these problems.

## KEY POINTS

- Developed economies are pivotal to the state of international business.
- These states present the majority of economic activity within the global system.
- Developed states are facing increasing levels of political, economic, social, and environmental risk.

## QUESTIONS

1) How do you account for the rise of populism in advanced economies?
2) Is the 'trickle-down effect' a sufficient justification for globalisation?
3) Critically evaluate the case for a Universal Basic Income (UBI).

## ACTIVITIES

As a group, discuss the long-term implications and legacy of hyper-globalisation for advanced economies. What has been positive? What has been negative?

## REFERENCES

Blyth, M. (2013). *Austerity: The history of a dangerous idea*, Oxford: Oxford University Press.

Emmott, B. (2017). *The fate of the west: The battle to save the world's most successful political idea economist books*, London: The Economist.

Forbes (2017). Fortune 500. www.forbes.com.

Ford, M. (2015). *Rise of the robots*, London: Basic Books.

Frey, B., & Osborne, M. (2013). The future of employment: How susceptible are jobs to computerisation? http://www.oxfordmartin.ox.ac.uk/.

Goldin, I., & Mariathasan, M. (2014). *The butterfly defect: How globalization creates systemic risks, and what to do*, London: Wiley.

IMF (2017). World economic outlook 2017. www.imf.org.

Livesey, F. (2016). *From global to local: The making of things and the end of globalisation*, London: Pantheon.

Milanovic, B. (2013). *Worlds apart: Measuring international and global inequality*, Princeton: Princeton University Press.

Picketty, T. (2013). *Capital in the twenty-first century*, Boston: Harvard University Press.

Reinhart, C. M., & Rogoff, K. S. (2009). *This time is different: Eight centuries of financial folly*, Princeton: Princeton University Press.

UN (2017). Human development index 2017. www.un.org.

UNCTAD (2017). Unctadstat. www.unctad.org.

World Bank (2017). Ease of doing business report. http://www.doingbusiness.org/.

World Economic Forum (WEF) (2017). Global risk report. www.wef.org.

# CHAPTER 7

# EMERGING ECONOMIES

## The major beneficiaries of globalisation

## OBJECTIVES

This chapter will help you to:

- Describe what is meant by the terms 'emerging' and 'transition' economies;
- Identify key milestones in and characteristics of the transformation of China and India, including similarities and differences between them;
- Explain the importance of emerging economies for international business;
- Analyse the impact of the emerging economies, both regionally and globally.

During the formative decades of the 2000s, the emergence of new players in the world economy that could, and most probably would in the longer term, challenge the economic dominance of the developed economies became apparent. Suddenly, every commentator became aware of China, and to a lesser extent, India, and speculated about their impact on and the potential for change in the world economic order. Much of the debate has been tinged with fear – fear about job losses in developed countries resulting from production relocation and outsourcing and about the difficulties of competing with economic powerhouses with much lower costs.

Those of a more positive disposition have identified opportunities offered by the integration of these markets into the world economy and the potential to reconfigure value chains to enhance efficiency and competitiveness. In other words, the rapid development of emerging economies is seen as an extension and a validation of the globalisation process by incorporating a much greater proportion of the world's population and output into the global economy. Given that emerging economies, to a large extent, owe their success to the liberalisation of their domestic economies and to a greater opening to the outside world in the form of trade and investment (see below), this view has some justification.

DOI: 10.4324/9781315184500-9

Emerging economies are important because they bring new players into the global economy, opening up new markets and opportunities for businesses, as well as intensifying competition, which places a greater onus on businesses to adapt more rapidly to change. As a by-product, as has become clear since late 2007 in particular, their growing success and prosperity have also meant greater competition for resources, namely, food, energy, raw materials, and commodities in general. The large emerging economies – the BRIC economies of Brazil, Russia, India, and China – are important economic powerhouses in their own right, with sufficient economic weight in terms of markets and production to have a significant impact not only on neighbouring countries but also increasingly on the world economy. Their status as the world's fastest-growing economies and their increasingly prominent role in global economic relations also gives these countries a greater influence in international relations generally and could well lead, in the longer term, to a shift in the balance of power in international institutions and negotiations (see Chapter 4).

This chapter opens with an exploration of what is meant by the terms 'emerging' and 'transition' economies. Although many countries throughout the world can be described as emerging economies, the chapter focuses on the two largest: China and India. How they have reached their present status as two of the most rapidly growing and modernising economies in the world is described. In the process, similarities and differences in their development paths are highlighted. The chapter then discusses the emergence of these economies and their implications for business in terms of opportunities, risks, and challenges, both from the perspective of enterprises inside and outside the emerging economies. The chapter then discusses the growing contribution of emerging economies in the broader global context.

## WHO AND WHAT ARE EMERGING ECONOMIES?

The terms 'emerging' or 'transition' economies imply that some form of change is underway. This change involves the transformation of key aspects of the economy and also reflects an acceleration of the pace of change and development. Emerging economies are usually low- or middle-economies and can be big or small in size. They exist in Southeast Asia, eastern Europe, parts of Africa, the Middle East, and Latin America. The big emerging economies include Argentina, Brazil, Chile, China, Egypt, India, Indonesia, Mexico, Poland, Russia, South Africa, South Korea, and Turkey. Much of the discussion of emerging economies in the media, and in this chapter, focuses on two of the BRIC economies: India and China.

Each emerging economy sits within its own unique historical, social, cultural, political, legal, and economic context, but they have broad characteristics in common. In general, they are all experiencing the transition from developing to developed country status and/or from state-dominated to a freer, more liberal market economy. India and China, for example, can both be described as 'developing countries', but in certain regions/areas of economic activity, they are beginning to resemble more developed economies. Although state-owned enterprises remain important in China, their role is declining, and China is rapidly transforming itself from a command economy into a market economy. India has long been a mixed economy, but its recent past has seen, if not the elimination of, at least the scaling down and limiting of state intervention in the form of ownership and regulation.

These overarching characteristics have given rise to other trends. First, emerging economies are undertaking economic reform to varying degrees in the direction of freeing up the market. This can take various forms, from reducing restrictions on business, privatisation, and tax reform to developing the infrastructure of the market in the form of legislation (such as competition law or the establishment of private property rights) and institutions, such as ensuring that a viable and efficient financial system exists. Of particular interest to international business is the greater freedom accorded to inward investors, a reduction in trade barriers, and a greater orientation to the rest of the world. In short, emerging economies are engaged in opening up their economies, both internally and externally. In the case of China, this was exemplified by its accession to the WTO in 2001. Both countries have asserted themselves in international institutions, notably the WTO.

As a consequence of the above, and of the ongoing and incomplete nature of reform, emerging economies tend to exhibit common economic and structural performance characteristics. First, compared to developed countries, emerging economies retain relatively large agricultural sectors compared to developed countries (see Table 7.1). Indeed, agriculture in emerging economies accounts for a similar share of GDP as that prevailing in Europe in the mid-1950s. The share of agriculture in most European economies is currently no more than about 2 per cent of GDP – and is frequently less. Given the rapid growth of the industrial and service sectors in emerging economies, agriculture's role in emerging economies will see a relative decline. Many emerging economies are already experiencing significant migration from rural to urban areas in line with this trend.

Table 7.1 also throws up an important difference between India and China, which reflects differences in their development paths. Well over half of India's economy is composed of the services sector. Although this is not unusual for developed countries where services often account for three-quarters or more of GDP, it is unusual for a country at

**TABLE 7.1** The changing comparative economic structures of the US, EU, India, and China

| (% GDP) | US | | EU | | India | | China | |
|---|---|---|---|---|---|---|---|---|
| | 2008 | 2021 | 2008 | 2021 | 2008 | 2021 | 2008 | 2021 |
| Agriculture | 1 | 1 | 1 | 1 | 17 | 20 | 12 | 7 |
| Industry | 20 | 18 | 21 | 20 | 28 | 26 | 49 | 39 |
| Services | 79 | 81 | 78 | 79 | 55 | 54 | 39 | 54 |

Source: IMF (2021) *IMF Data* www.imf.org

India's stage of development and is a function of its strengths in IT, software, the outsourcing of backroom activities, and other service-related activities.

Secondly, as the constraints on business ease up, investors are seizing opportunities in emerging economies. Foreign investors in particular are taking advantage of the more business-friendly environment, especially in China (see Figure 7.1), where FDI inflows started to soar from the early 1990s. Increases of FDI inflows into India have grown steadily in recent years, but they remain a fraction of the funds being attracted to China. Such investment is a sign of confidence in emerging economies but is not without risks.

Thirdly, as a result of the reforms and greater investment, growth in emerging economies has been stronger and more buoyant than in most OECD countries since the 1990s (see Figure 7.2). In the case of China, growth has been at remarkably high levels since the onset of reform in 1978. India's growth has mostly been above 5 per cent since 1980 and has accelerated noticeably since 2000. The Russian economy, however, was declining through much of this period as it adjusted to the new post-Soviet political, economic, and social systems. However, Russia has benefitted from the increase in energy prices, which has resulted in a turnaround in its economic fortunes. Brazil's economic journey has been much more volatile and has been affected by financial crises and problems in commodity markets, but the fluctuation in its fortunes has been less marked in the 2000s. Growth in the world's largest developed economy, the US, has, since the downturn of the early 1990s, largely been within the 2–4 per cent range. It has been notable how China has not sustained its high growth rate, largely as it reached the limits on the flow of migrant labour into the major manufacturing hubs. More latterly, its growth trajectory was hit by the government's zero-COVID policy.

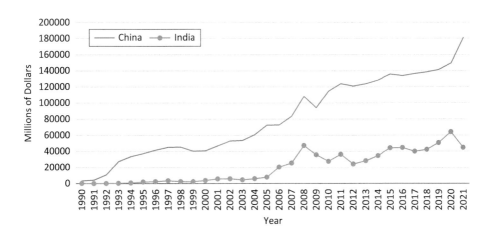

**FIGURE 7.1** Foreign direct investment flows in China and India 1990–2021

(Source IMF, 2021 *IMF Data* www.imf.org)

**TABLE 7.2** Comparison of China and India

|  | India | China |
|---|---|---|
| Political system | Democratic, weak coalitions. Emergence of 'strongman' government since 2014. | Authoritarian, one-party rule. Movement towards 'strongman' government since 2012. |
| Rule of law | 'Licence raj' toned down but still overly bureaucratic. Sporadic reform. | Many laws in place but weak and inconsistent enforcement of regulations and contracts. Government can be hostile to commercial sectors when challenges state. |
| Corruption | Widespread corruption in politics and business. Ranked 85th on Transparency International's Corruption Perception Index. | 'Red envelope' culture – corruption and bribery in public life – is rife. Ranked 65th on Transparency International's Corruption Perception Index. Seen as delegitimising communist rule. |
| Economic structure | Excellence in services – IT consulting, software, and call centres. Growing strength in financial analysis, industrial engineering, and drug research. | Manufacturing workshop of the world – increasingly sophisticated products. Strategy of Vision 2025 to move toward high technology. |
| Infrastructure | Poor infrastructure which is an obstacle to development: black-outs, much electricity obtained illegally, and inadequate transport. | Much investment has been made (more to be done): ten times more paved roads than India, power costs ten times lower, and phone penetration rates six times higher. |
| External trade | Gradual trade liberalisation but scope for more. FDI opened more recently but caps remain. | Well integrated into global economy and dependent on foreign firms (half exports by MNEs). Heavy use of FDI. |
| Public sector | Large and loss making – smaller in India. | Large and loss making. |
| Banking sector | Weak and underdeveloped but is being reformed. | Weak and under-developed but reforms are being undertaken to remove bad debts and shadow banking sector. |
| Income distribution | Some poverty reduction – but also potentially destabilising increases in inequality. | Many out of poverty – but impact of economic crisis is unknown, potentially destabilising increases in inequality. Increasing inequality: rural vs urban. Coastal vs Western provinces. |
| Environment | Deteriorating – could hinder growth. | Deteriorating – could hinder growth. |
| Education | Heavy investment in higher education – basic later. | Heavy investment in basic education – higher later. |
| R&D | Majority in public sector. | Majority in productive sector. |

Source: IMF

# THE EMERGENCE OF INDIA AND CHINA

In the formative decades of the 21st century, China and India are modernising, rapidly growing economies undergoing fundamental change. Although very different in many ways, in broad terms at least, they have key features in common. Both have their roots in ancient civilisations with their own rich culture and tradition of learning. Both have known great wealth, but by the 1960s and 1970s, had, for different reasons, become a byword for overpopulation, poverty, famine, and stagnation. Since then, their transformation, although far from complete, has been remarkable.

Key to their success has been a rejection of inward-looking policies intended to generate self-reliance and self-sufficiency in favour of liberalising domestic markets and opening up trade and investment to the rest of the world. The outcome has been the growth of around 10 per cent per annum for nearly three decades in the case of China, and for India, less consistent but nevertheless higher than average long-term growth levels in recent years (see Figure 7.2). As a result of reform, these growth levels have been achieved with the assistance of foreign capital and expertise, especially in the case of China, a development that would have been unthinkable in the pre-reform era. Both countries have benefitted from large diasporas: the early phases of inward FDI into China, for example, were bolstered considerably by capital inflows originating from the millions of individuals of Chinese origin located outside China, particularly but not only in Hong Kong and Taiwan.

Rapid growth has contributed to mass urbanisation, led to social and environmental pressure, and placed unprecedented demands on infrastructure, which China has been able to respond to more fully than India. Both countries have also experienced widening income disparities and the exacerbation of differences in regional development.

Although reform has been motivated by similar objectives and has created similar problems, the emergence of China and India as important players in world markets has taken place within very specific historical, political, economic, and social contexts, which have helped shape the progress of reform and its outcomes. China is traditionally a large, stable, centrally run state and, for the most part, has not experienced foreign rule. India has had the opposite experience: it has only been a nation since the middle of the nineteenth century; large parts, albeit not all, were under foreign control until independence in 1947, and its diversity has resulted in a federal system, albeit with a relatively strong centre.

The immediate post-World War II era brought crucial changes to both states: in China, the Communist Party came to power, where it remains, and began the systemic transformation of Chinese life, while India gained its independence. In both cases, there was a strong incentive to demonstrate that both countries could succeed independently and on their own terms. Both countries, for a period at least, were inspired by the perceived achievements of planning in the USSR and saw the state as the primary, if not the sole, driver of growth; they rejected foreign capital and sought self-sufficiency. Their initial instinct was to pursue industrialisation as their prime development objective, notably to focus on heavy industry such as steel and machinery, and to neglect consumer and light industrial sectors. China used its political monopoly to develop a central control and planning system which relied heavily on bringing industries under state ownership in the form of state-owned enterprises (SOEs). India had a lively democracy, but its first Prime Minister, Jawarhal Nehru, also operated a socialist economic planning system.

Neither approach brought long-term success. For ten years from 1966, after the failure of the Great Leap Forward, which was intended to modernise and revitalise the Chinese economy, Mao's China underwent the Cultural Revolution, which managed to paralyse Chinese society and the economy. India did not undergo such self-induced trauma, but its approach to development was far from successful, leading to low growth, increasing poverty, and, in some cases, starvation. In the late 1970s, after the death of Chairman Mao in 1976, Deng Xiaoping gradually asserted greater control over the reins of power and began the reform in China which continues today. India did not have a Deng Xiaoping, but it instituted desultory reform attempts in the 1980s before reform began in earnest in 1991.

The beginning of reform in China and India was motivated by the failure of the postwar approach. The speed, consistency, and extent of the reforms varied between the two, but in both cases, they have moved away from almost total reliance on the state, which retains an important but different role, and towards integrating into the world economy and markets rather than resisting them. To date, Chinese living standards have risen more quickly than those in India, but this should not undermine India's achievements in this respect.

## CASE STUDY 7.1: THE RISE OF CHINESE MNES

The most notable trend within the Fortune Global 500 (a list of the top 500 firms ranked by revenue) over the past decade has been the rise of Chinese MNEs. In 2001, there were only ten Chinese firms on the list; 20 years later, there were 145. Table 7.3 shows the top ten Chinese businesses as ranked by the global Fortune 500. Of the top 25 companies that are on the Fortune list, more than 80 per cent are state-owned. Those that are privately owned tend to be e-commerce companies. Of the rest, energy, construction/engineering, and financial sectors dominate the list.

The rise of these firms reflects the results of the long-term 'going out' strategy, whereby the Chinese government sought to encourage its firms to invest overseas largely to follow economic goals rather than any broader geostrategic gain. This 'going out' strategy has been reflected in the sharp rise of Chinese outward FDI, which was $145 billion in 2021, down from a peak of $196 billion in 2016. This represents a vast surge since 2001 when the total FDI outflow was just $6 billion.

An initial catalyst for this surge was not just its membership of the WTO, but in the aftermath of the GFC, these cash-rich businesses went on an acquisition spree globally, often in pursuit of a variety of resources both natural and human-generated (such as know-how and technology). While this was a global strategy, the main market focus was on Asia.

**TABLE 7.3** The top Chinese MNEs

| China rank | Company | Sector | Global ranking | Revenue ($ billion) |
|---|---|---|---|---|
| 1 | State Grid | Energy | 3 | 460.6 |
| 2 | China National Petroleum | Energy | 4 | 411.7 |
| 3 | Sinopec | Energy | 5 | 401.3 |
| 4 | China State Construction and Engineering | Construction and Engineering | 9 | 293.7 |
| 5 | Industrial and Commercial Bank of China | Banking | 22 | 209.8 |
| 6 | China Construction Bank | Banking | 24 | 200.4 |
| 7 | Ping An Insurance | Insurance | 25 | 199.6 |
| 8 | Agricultural Bank of China | Banking | 28 | 181.4 |
| 9 | SinoChem | Chemicals | 31 | 172.2 |
| 10 | China Railway Engineering Corporation | Construction and Engineering | 34 | 166.7 |

Inevitably, there are suspicions with regard to the motives of this FDI, notably with regard to the link between these businesses and the Chinese state. This brings concerns with regard to the geopolitical underpinnings of the 'going out' strategy. This was especially evident in the technology sector, where some investment by Chinese MNEs has been debarred. For many of these businesses, there seems to be little evidence of ulterior motives other than to counteract a mature or saturated domestic market and to seek new growth opportunities. There are evident motives with regard to facilitating China's technological catch-up with the West and also with regard to ensuring China can access the resources needed to sustain its level of growth and development trajectory. Moreover, some investment is made to use overseas knowledge and capabilities to secure a firm's position within its core domestic market.

It is argued that the rapidity of the process of internationalisation of Chinese MNEs reflects structural weaknesses within their domestic market. It is accepted that within their domestic market, Chinese firms face problems of poor transportation and logistics, a lack of branding, as well as inferior technologies and production processes. Indeed, some Chinese firms have to overcome the liability of foreignness created by the 'Made in China' brand. Thus, it was felt that to succeed at home, firms needed to go overseas to pick up the knowledge to mitigate their indigenous weaknesses. Thus, cheap labour and strong state support are used to leverage positions in overseas markets, which are then fed back to support a firm's domestic positioning.

Nonetheless, there has been increased resistance to increased Chinese FDI in many developed states. Moreover, with increased geopolitical tension and much talk with regard to decoupling, there is an increased potential for these flows (especially to developed states) to fall and the stock of FDI to decline. There has also been pushback in some developing states, where sometimes it was felt that the FDI came at the expense of local firms and control. Firms such as Huawei and ZTC (both in high technology) have found their routes for investment in developed Western economies curtailed and called into question, resulting in their having to radically change markets.

## CASE QUESTION

Why do so few Chinese MNEs become truly global?

## China

Following the Cultural Revolution (1966–1976), which was about ideological purification and the playing out of a power struggle in the upper echelons of the Communist Party, and the death of Mao in 1976, Deng Xiaoping became party leader. He recognised that existing economic policy was condemning China to economic backwardness and, from 1978 on, introduced a series of wide-ranging reforms to modernise China and transform it into a powerful, modern socialist economy. Initially, the reforms were stop-go, but by the end of the 1980s, they became more consistent as Deng consolidated his hold on power.

Deng's reforms were guided by the general principles of increasing the role of the market mechanism, reducing the direct control of the economy by the government, and centralised planning. The reforms were phased in gradually and were driven by pragmatism rather than ideology as in previous years. Nevertheless, they all pointed in the same direction: liberalisation of the domestic economy and greater integration with the economies of the rest of the world.

The key reforms in the late 1970s and 1980s were:

- Introduction of the household responsibility system in agriculture. Farmers were allowed to sell surplus crops on the open market. This gave them a strong incentive to reduce costs and increase productivity. As a result, food production increased quickly, and the people's communes were soon obsolete. By 1984, approximately 98 per cent of all farm households were on the responsibility system. This new system was important not only for the positive impact it had on farm production but also because it clearly demonstrated the potential power of market incentives.
- The beginning of trade and investment reform. China began to promote inward FDI as a means of acquiring technology and foreign exchange, and, as such, joint ventures were particularly encouraged by the government. Trade was also made easier. In pre-reform days, when self-sufficiency was one of the abiding principles of

economic management, the combined value of imports and exports rarely exceeded 10 per cent of GDP. As early as 1986, trade reached 35 per cent of GDP. The process of trade and investment liberalisation continues. China's 2001 entry into the WTO represents a major consolidation of trade reform and a commitment to further liberalisation.

- The creation in 1979 of four coastal special economic zones where foreign investors received special treatment and, in 1984, the creation of economic development zones in 14 of the largest coastal cities, including Dalian, Tianjin, Shanghai, and Gunagzhou. These latter zones were intended to create strong links between foreign firms with advanced technology and domestic producers. These initiatives represent an important reversal of decades of deliberate economic isolation from the rest of the world and a recognition that China could benefit from greater contact with the outside world.
- The reduction of the role of government in most sectors. Managers were given greater decision-making powers and autonomy, and less emphasis was placed on planned quotas. Enterprises were encouraged to produce outside the plan for profit and sale on the open market, a little like the household responsibility system in agriculture.
- Efforts were made to correct the imbalance between light and heavy industries, resulting in the rapid growth of the consumer and service sectors.

By the late 1980s, reform was well underway, but the state remained dominant, retaining control over the financial system, attempting to redistribute wealth, and organising grain rationing. Private ownership was in its infancy: agricultural land was farmed under lease, for example, but was formally owned by villages, towns, and townships, the collective units that replaced the communes. During the next period of reform in the early 1990s, the emphasis was on enhancing the price mechanism, creating market institutions, and reducing the role of the state in the allocation of resources. Accordingly, private entrepreneurship and free market activities were legalised and encouraged. A market-based system requires a robust banking system and capital markets to support it. It was during the 1990s that work on banking system reform began in earnest – work that continues in the 2000s, notably with regards to reforms of the shadow banking and the property sectors.

The move to the market mechanism exposed the deficiencies of the SOEs. Under the pre-reform system, SOEs were faced with fixed input and output prices, with the difference being used to fund social services. The introduction of the market mechanism and market prices meant that many SOEs were producing goods that no one wanted and chalking up impressive losses. By the late 1990s and early 2000s, many SOEs were restructured or closed, and an independent social security system was set up. By 2022, over 50 per cent of China's GDP was in the private sector. The remaining SOEs are located in industries that are regarded as strategically important, such as energy, utilities, and heavy industry.

For much of the period of economic change in China, growth has been driven by a high and rising level of investment. From a low of 32 per cent of GDP in 1983, its share rose to a high of 47 per cent of GDP in 2010. This was driven not only by investment in infrastructure but also by facilitating the technological catch-up with the developed economies and by building an extensive manufacturing base. By contrast, US investment as a share of GDP averages around half this figure. By contrast, consumption in China remains relatively subdued at around 50 per cent of GDP; in the US the figure is closer to 70 per cent. This reflects the high savings rate in China, which is around 45 per cent of GDP, compared to the US, where the figure is less than 3 per cent. Thus, the next phase of the reform is to promote consumption and lower the savings rate by lowering the need for higher savings through an enhanced provision of social and public services (such as education and health care).

After four decades of economic reform and change, China is an intriguing mix of old and new. The emergence of the private sector and the role played by foreign investors are attributable to the removal of barriers in many areas.

Nevertheless, despite the decline of the state's direct control over the economy, the state retains an important role in terms of the regulation and control of the private sector via the state bureaucracy. This was evident in the clampdown on Chinese technology and other private sector firms throughout the 2020s. As such, the Chinese economy is composed of a mixture of foreign-owned companies, and private Chinese companies, including former SOEs, foreign-Chinese joint ventures, and current state enterprises. The unique Chinese formula of a free market operating within the framework of a totalitarian state has led to questions about the long-term sustainability of the Chinese system, especially with its now declining population. Free market activity and the autonomy, personal choice, and freedom it confers upon economic operators, so the argument goes, are inconsistent with the continuing control of the Chinese Communist Party and a lack of political choice. It is also argued that, while the economy and living standards continue to flourish, any challenges to the political control of the Communist Party will be muted. However, a flashpoint became evident with China's long COVID policy when the high degree of control exerted through ongoing lockdowns started to restrict growth and led to rising unemployment, notably amongst the young. This eroded the social contract based upon strong control and high growth and prosperity and led to widespread protests, leading to a ditching of the policy.

## CASE STUDY 7.2: INDIAN CONGLOMERATES

In many Western business systems, the conglomerate (a multi-industry company) has become unfashionable. There is much talk within the business literature about a focus on the core business if any concern is to succeed. However, there is one state that seems to buck this trend: India. In India, there are 54 recognised conglomerates, of which the largest ones are:

1. Reliance Industries Ltd.
2. Tata Group.
3. Aditya Birla Group.

4. Mahindra Group.
5. Bajaj Group.
6. Adani Group.
7. L&T Group.

Part of the resistance to conglomerate capitalism is the close correlation between economic and political power. The rise of these businesses was linked to early reform processes and the powerful families that were able to take advantage of reform processes and develop businesses that were able to replace the state in key sectors of the economy. These businesses benefitted from low-cost finance, which they were able to use to build successful businesses that spilt over into other sectors. These businesses are important because they are the only real set of bodies (aside from the state, which is often poorly organised) with the financial clout to invest in India.

Nonetheless, political power was a key factor in their emergence. The connections that these firms were able to build were a key part of their development. In the era of the licence raj (where businesses could only operate with the permission of the government), these were businesses whose owners had good political connections and who could purchase and operate businesses under favourable conditions. These favoured entrepreneurs were able to establish monopolistic positions based on seemingly random opportunistic acts, which created diverse business groups without a core underpinning logic. In other cases, conglomerates emerged as a response to the limits to growth imposed by the licence raj, which meant that they expanded in any direction that was available. These conglomerates were and remain controlled by powerful families and clans. This is reflective of the salience of the family firm in India as a whole. In India, the complexity of these family-based conglomerates can also reflect intra-family disputes (such as Reliance), which often means rivals are given separate bits of the business to run.

These businesses remain very powerful in India, comprising 90 per cent of the top 50 companies and delivering revenue growth in excess of 20 per cent per year, due to their favourable positions. It is argued that conglomerates continue to thrive in India due to the nature of the local market, which is poorly organised. For example, there was no regulation that required high-quality accounts to be published or that let firms buy stakes in others without buying out minority shareholders. In the absence of institutional systems, the conglomerate steps into the void. Thus, where markets are underdeveloped, conglomerates seek to control the system via diverse ownership. As markets mature, the need for such internalisation of multiple businesses should be eroded. Indian businesses have bucked this trend and have sustained their influence largely due to political connections but also due to their ability to allow common businesses to operate across what may appear to be diverse businesses.

There are also cultural reasons to explain the salience of conglomerates, notably that of the main conglomerates in India, the majority come from the Marwari and Bania groups, which have a strong tradition of trading. These are often aligned with views on how to organise firms. Tax could also be a reason why family money would be reinvested in a new business rather than spirited abroad or earning low interest in bank accounts.

However, perhaps the most widely accepted reason for the emergence and sustenance of these family conglomerates was state failure. India is a state that has a history of state unreliability. Infrastructure can be poor; the legal system is time-consuming; and markets are unreliable. Thus, in the absence of an effective state, many enterprises feel that it is better to do these activities themselves. Thus, there has been the emergence of vertically integrated conglomerates that seek to internalise many, if not all, aspects of their activities. There are even cases where businesses generate their own energy and port facilities due to the failure of the state. Thus, conglomerates reflect a need to own and control in the absence of state support or other forms of effective governance. This absence of the state is reflected in the attitude of these businesses towards the state. Whereas, as in other countries, the state and conglomerates become entwined, in India, political connections tend to see the state relation as pragmatic, reflecting that the state is a barrier (see above) but also a useful partner on occasion.

With economic reform, the dominance of these businesses over India has come under increased pressure. Indeed – while Reliance and Tata remain India's biggest companies – there are constant changes as new family businesses emerge and older ones die off. This reflects that there is competition both within and between them. It also reflects a constant need to adapt to changing conditions. Although they persist and have a function to play in the development of India, they can be accused of being so dominant that they crowd out new entrants and limit entrepreneurship. History suggests that these businesses are just a phase of the development of a country that passes as capitalism and the state mature. This could well happen in India as the firms grow more complex and the clamour for outside influence on the firms grows, especially as investors will want to make sense of these complex businesses. Inevitably, the biggest problem is that businesses are sustained through effective succession, and whether the next generation will want to keep managing these complex businesses or if they are simply not up to such tasks.

## CASE QUESTION

How do you account for the persistence of Indian conglomerates?

## India

India's current development push began later than China's. There was some limited reform in the 1980s following the abandonment by Prime Minister Indira Gandhi of the ideology of self-sufficiency. During this period, India began to borrow from abroad, initially from the IMF, but Indian economic policy remained largely dirigiste, and India remained essentially a closed economy with high tariffs on imports and rigid controls on foreign investment. Indian businesses were subject to the 'licence raj' – that is, a regime that required a business to obtain a licence or permit before it could embark upon any type of activity. This highly bureaucratic system was time-consuming and susceptible to bribery and corruption.

This situation persisted until 1991 when a financial and balance of payments crisis made wholesale reform inevitable. The architect of the reforms was Manmohan Singh, who became Indian Prime Minister in 2004. The immediate response to the crisis was to take out a $1.8 billion loan from the IMF and to introduce macroeconomic stabilisation measures to reduce the budget deficit and devalue the rupee. It was apparent, however, that short-term measures were insufficient and that the Indian economy needed root-and-branch reform which would enable it to integrate with and ultimately compete with the rest of the world. The process has moved slowly and in a stop-go manner because of the need to build up coalitions and consensus in favour of reforms, which have been the subject of much political bargaining. The reversal of policies of regulation and government intervention continues, and much remains to be done, but growth has become more sustained and stronger, and Indian business has undergone major restructuring to help them reduce costs, improve quality, and meet foreign competition. Key reforms undertaken or in progress in India include:

- Trade reform: before 1991, Indian import tariffs were high and other trade barriers were commonplace. Imports of consumer goods were banned, and imports of raw materials, intermediate goods and capital goods, for which domestic substitutes were available were only possible following a complex licencing procedure. After 1991, India stepped up its commitment to free trade, even before its WTO entry in 1995. Tariffs were slashed on goods; trade in services and technology was liberalised; and import licences were eliminated. Scope exists for further reduction in import duties and in costly import and export procedures.
- Investment reform: prior to 1991, foreign ownership and investment were only permitted in some sectors, but even then, they were subject to many restrictions, including caps on investment. Many of these restrictions have subsequently been lifted, and 100 per cent foreign ownership is currently allowed in a majority of industries, excluding banks, insurance, telecommunications, airlines, and retail. The fear that inward investment will undermine domestic businesses means that some restrictions remain. The prime example is the retail sector, which is dominated by small, family businesses known as 'mom-and-pop' shops and which is closed to foreign retailers. There is a potential role for the latter, however, in distribution and wholesale, and mom-and-pop shops are beginning to feel pressure from Indian-owned retailers such as those set up by Reliance.
- Fiscal reform: individual and corporate taxes, excise, and customs duties have been lowered; the tax base has been broadened; and the system has been simplified to close loopholes and increase compliance. However, tax revenues are falling as a share of GDP, the budget deficit and public debt remain high, and spending cuts remain politically difficult. Tax evasion remains a problem, and greater coordination is needed among different levels of government.
- Financial sector reform: before 1991, lending was restricted to specific sectors, and all the funding activities of large manufacturers were controlled by the Controller of Capital Issues, a post which has since been abolished. Banks

were state-owned and subject to political forces. Subsequently, cautious efforts have been made to privatise and introduce competition among banks, but more could be done, especially in terms of access for foreign banks. The functioning of capital markets has been improved by the liberalisation of interest rates and the abolition of the complex approval system for financial transactions. Increases in the amount of venture capital and improvements and deepening of the debt markets are still needed.

- Privatisation and industrial reform: many government enterprises have been privatised and subject to competition, but many small-scale industries remain protected. For over a century, a handful of families dominated the large-scale industrial sector in India. This changed after 1947, when the government increased its role. However, following the retreat of the state, family conglomerates such as the Tata, Birla, Ambani, and Moda families (see Case study 7.2) once again dominate Indian business and wield enormous commercial power. India's success in the knowledge sector has been made possible by government policy and by the work of visionary entrepreneurial leaders such as Narayana Murthy of Infosys and Azim Premji of Wipro. Nevertheless, government-owned and controlled corporations are very significant in the airline, shipping, railway, post, steel, machine tools, mineral exploration, power, oil, and gas sectors.

- Dismantling of the licence raj: although bureaucracy and red tape remain a problem for domestic and foreign firms in India and are high by the standards of many other countries, the worst excesses of the licence raj have been abolished.

- Since the 1997 financial crisis, the process has been renewed, though it has been sporadic. The desire to allow 51 per cent FDI within the retail sector was only introduced after a great deal of protest from smaller shop owners. This has been coupled with reform of the coal sector, most notably, the Goods and Services Tax Act, which sought to remove intra-state disparities in sales taxes and replace them with a unified tax system. This has been further enhanced by corporate tax reform and proposals for reform in the labour and agricultural sectors.

## China and India: a comparison

China's reform began much earlier than India's and has been pursued consistently, whereas India's reform has been more stop-start as a result of weak coalitions and the complexity of India's politics. China's political stability has resulted in faster growth over a longer period. China's GDP and GDP per capita are both over twice that of India. China's strategy of developing through exporting is illustrated by the fact that its exports of goods were six times greater than those of India in 2022, though the value of these exports as a share of total GDP is roughly the same at 20 per cent. China also exports a greater value of commercial services than India, but these are converging, implying a relatively better performance for services in India given the difference in GDP between the two countries. This reflects the differing structure between the two countries: as Table 7.1 shows, China's development has been driven by manufacturing, whereas India's strengths lie in the services sector.

In terms of overall investment, China has generally outstripped India and has benefitted from high levels of domestic savings (noted above). Similar trends have existed in FDI, but since 1990, FDI inflows into India, although remaining far below Chinese levels, have tripled from $235 million to $64 billion in 2021. FDI inflows into China over the same period have grown significantly. As a result of years of stronger FDI inflows, inward FDI stocks in China were four times higher at $2 trillion. China's lead in these key indicators, however, should not mask India's progress.

The large Chinese and Indian diasporas have both been instrumental in boosting the economies of their countries of origin. The Chinese diaspora made a significant contribution to China's FDI in the 1980s and 1990s, when funds from Hong Kong, Singapore, and Taiwan, in particular, were directed to small-scale manufacturing investment and, according to some estimates, accounted for almost 60 per cent of Chinese FDI. Diaspora investment made use of the strong relationships and interconnected networks that are so central to the concept of guanxi (see Case study 13.1), the powerful and complex cultural dynamic that operates at the core of China's business environment. The Indian diaspora has played an important, but more modest, role in India's development. The size of India's diaspora is much smaller than that of China, and its influence has been mostly felt in facilitating the emergence of entrepreneurial activity in the IT and IT-enabled services sectors.

---

**Box 7.1:** Geopolitical rivals: China and India

There can be little doubt that India and China are two countries that will shape the future direction of the global economy. Beyond this, there lies deep-seated suspicion between these states that can often erupt into small-scale conflict both along the shared border and within shared spaces such as the Indian Ocean. There is evident increased competition between the states, and this erupted into a small-scale border conflict in 2022, but this is just one of many areas where these states are starting to compete, including military presence and infrastructure development in areas these states both claim as spheres of influence. On a broader scale, each country is both seeking to control the influence of the other, with each seeking to outcompete in areas of common interest in South and East Asia.

India and China are competing with each other for their strategic presence in South Asia. China wants to challenge India's naval hegemony in the Indian Ocean, and India sees China's role in neighbouring Pakistan as a direct threat to its position. The main areas of this geostrategic competition are South Asia and the Indian Ocean. These are key spheres of influence for India, and China wants to challenge this to ensure that key maritime routes between the Middle East, Europe, and China cannot be disrupted. To this end, China has engaged proactively through the Belt and Road Initiative to develop infrastructure throughout the region, which has – as an alternative aim – the erosion of Indian hegemony in the region. It has financed seaports in Pakistan, Sri Lanka, and elsewhere (the so-called String of Pearls) and improved overland connectivity to landlocked South Asian states.

This has rankled India, as it sees the Indian Ocean as 'India's Ocean' and has sought to counteract China's actions through a mix of policies. It has developed a 'Neighbourhood First' policy which seeks to support commercial activity in the region. This has been further enhanced by an 'Act East' policy which seeks to improve its relations with Southeast Asia and the Pacific beyond. This has been further supported by many Indian conglomerates becoming involved in overseas infrastructure projects in the region. It has also engaged in vaccine diplomacy (i.e., offering the COVID-19 vaccine in exchange for geopolitical favours) and offered direct finance for a series of infrastructure projects in the region. On a broader level, India has also engaged with Western powers to seek to contain the power of China within the region.

Ultimately, the rivalry between these states has the capacity to destabilise the region because, over the short term, it is offering benefits to smaller states in terms of investments. However, should tensions between the West and China continue to deteriorate, then India will be forced to choose sides. The more India sides with the West and the more China interferes in India's perceived interests, the greater the likelihood of this rivalry spilling over into evermore heated disputes with their consequences for the region and the global system as a whole.

## BUSINESS AND EMERGING ECONOMIES

The dynamism of emerging economies creates a multitude of opportunities, both for foreign and domestic businesses, and also carries certain risks. As discussed in Chapter 9, MNEs have several motivations for embarking upon FDI. One key reason, and one that is highly relevant for emerging markets, is market-seeking investment. The markets of the BRIC economies, in particular, are large and growing rapidly. Ownership of consumer goods that have reached a saturation point in developed markets is low in emerging economies, but growing prosperity means the demand for white goods, mobile phones, cars, etc. is extremely attractive for inward investors.

Although the large emerging economies and their domestic markets are developing rapidly, it is essential to recognise the diverse levels of development existing in the same economy. In China, the greatest levels of wealth are concentrated in the coastal regions, where there is well-developed infrastructure, a plentiful labour supply, and a good technological base. In the central and western parts of China, the country is less developed, more remote, and poorer, with a much bigger proportion of the population living in rural areas. India's development is also concentrated with software and business processing firms focused on cities like Bangalore and Pune. In both countries, the provinces and states have played an important role in development, with the more successful demonstrating a distinct entrepreneurial bent.

Moreover, although there is a growing, increasingly prosperous middle class in both countries, the general level of income is much lower than in developed countries, and mass marketing needs to recognise this. New entrants to emerging markets also need to take time to understand how consumer behaviour differs from that in known developed markets. Brand loyalty, for example, is unlikely to be as entrenched as in developed countries, and for many products, given the still relatively low living standards, the focus will be on value for money. However, for some market segments, there will be a demand for luxury items, and foreign brands may be prised over domestic brands. In Case study 6.2, for example, foreign-branded cars are dominant at the higher end of the market, whereas domestic producers are stronger at the lower-cost end of the market.

The impact of emerging economies on markets is also felt in other ways. The development process, as well as increasing consumer demand through rising prosperity, also increases demand for capital goods, plant and equipment, and raw materials associated with the creation and improvement of infrastructure and construction generally. Development also necessitates the need for deep and efficient capital markets. Accordingly, emerging markets are becoming increasingly open to foreign banks and other financial institutions.

A major attraction of China and India for foreign investors has been the low cost of production, particularly lower labour costs. Labour costs in Germany, for example, have been up to 40 or even 50 times higher than in China, depending on the sector. Manufacturing labour costs in India are even lower than those in China. In software and business processing operations, Indian costs remain considerably cheaper than in developed countries, but the gap has been narrowing. However, China's labour cost advantage, although substantial, is declining. In part, this is an inevitable response to development. It is also the result of labour supply problems, with a declining working population and increased labour shortages in some sectors. The resulting surge in labour turnover and wages has a number of potential effects. First, if wage cost increases are reflected by productivity increases, any potential impact on investment can be contained. Secondly, higher wage costs can be absorbed if the production of higher value-added goods can be increased. Significantly, China has gradually increased the technology content of its manufactures. Thirdly, higher wages in China create a larger consumer class and bigger markets for domestic and foreign investors. Fourthly, in sectors where, despite the above, China has lost its competitive advantage, production can be outsourced to cheaper locations. These could be in the interior of China, elsewhere in Asia, such as Vietnam, or even in Africa.

The potential rewards of doing business in emerging markets are high, and the opportunities for investment and trade in these markets are many, but this potential and these opportunities are also accompanied by a level of risk which is greater than in developed markets. This risk comes from many sources, including the rapid rate of transformation and growth. Emerging economies are beginning to resemble developed countries in parts but retain many of the characteristics traditionally used to define developing countries, such as large agricultural sectors, big disparities between rural and urban populations with significant migration from the former to the latter, a divide between traditional and modern sectors, low productivity, and underdeveloped infrastructure (more of a problem in India than China).

The bureaucratic and legal frameworks also need development in both countries. The degree of bureaucracy and red tape, although on the decline, is renowned in India. In China, the culture of guanxi emphasises relationships and downplays the notion of contracts – a factor which many foreign investors find confusing and which lacks transparency. This disregard for abiding by the written word also extends to laws and regulations. Although many market laws and regulations have been put in place in China, there are frequent reports of weak and inconsistent implementation and enforcement of these laws and regulations. In reality, what happens in practice is usually determined by local institutions and officials. This keeps the door open for corruption. Neither China nor India perform well on Transparency International's Corruption Perceptions Index. Bribery of officials is reportedly not unusual in both locations, despite, in the case of China, very severe punishments for officials caught engaged in corruption.

Both emerging markets therefore pose major challenges for foreign investors, but this has not deterred them. Market-seeking, efficiency-seeking, and strategy-seeking investments have all occurred in China and India. In the early years of reform, FDI was primarily about resources as firms sought to take advantage of low-cost factors of production, particularly but not only labour, as a prelude to export. Indeed, China's exports remain dominated by the output of foreign multinationals. The rising income of local populations has resulted in much more market-seeking behaviour. Major multinationals like Coca-Cola, Du Pont, General Motors, and Motorola, to name but a few are consumer goods companies active in China and India with an eye on the domestic market.

## EMERGING ECONOMIES IN A GLOBAL CONTEXT

Increasingly, MNEs can't afford to ignore the markets and production possibilities of China and India. In terms of population, they account for about 40 per cent of the world's population, significant both in terms of the number of consumers and the size of the labour force. More to the point, increasing living standards are making their markets more attractive.

China's and India's emergence is having a major impact on the rest of the world. China is challenging its neighbours in competitive terms, but it is also providing opportunities for them in terms of trade and investment. Indeed, FDI inflows into China from the rest of Asia have certainly been greater than those from Europe and have been of a similar magnitude to those from the US. Resource-rich countries like Australia have also benefitted from Chinese investment in natural resources.

The impact of China's development on developing countries has been mixed. On the one hand, they have benefitted from the increase in commodity prices that occurred in the face of escalating Chinese demand for crude oil, construction products, and agricultural products as a result of sustained high levels of growth. The hunt for commodities has resulted in substantial investment by Chinese companies in African oil, minerals, infrastructure, and simple manufacturing, a process helped by China's policy of extending concessional loans for such activities. India has followed suit to a lesser extent. However, the jury is out on whether the impact of such an investment is always positive.

On the other hand, developing countries have at times found it difficult to compete with Chinese light manufacturing. This has been the case with textiles and clothing, for example. After the end of the multi-fibre arrangement in 2005, many developing country textile producers were no longer able to hide behind the protection afforded to them by textile quotas and were subject to full competition from Chinese producers in their main overseas markets. Unable to compete, many textile producers from small, developing, and emerging countries began to struggle. It is not only in their export markets that developing country textile and clothing manufacturers have faced intense competition from Chinese products. Many, particularly in Africa, have been outcompeted in their domestic markets. Chinese labour costs are low (although not as low as those of many of their competitors), but Chinese manufacturers have the additional advantage of access to raw materials, economies of scale, and higher productivity stemming from advanced equipment supplied by Japanese, Taiwanese, Hong Kong, and South Korean investors.

Chinese manufacturing is no longer mostly about the production of lower-value products. Indeed, this has been the case for some time. Chinese manufacturing and exports have steadily been moving up the value-added ladder towards more sophisticated products with increasing high technology content. This process has been helped by technology-intensive investment from the US, Japan, and Southeast Asian NICs, supported by government policy, the growing number of graduate engineers and technologists, and the attention that has been paid to developing efficient infrastructure to support supply chains and logistics. The outcome of this will be even greater competition for developed countries, both internationally and in their domestic markets. This leads to the scenario of the US in particular running even bigger trade deficits with China, a prospect that raises the possibility of higher trade barriers at US borders.

**Box 7.2:** What went wrong with Brazil?

Brazil was a poster child for emerging economies. It was one of the high-growth economies that was supposed to drive global growth, along with China and India. However, unlike the other states, the growth it exhibited quickly tailed off and indeed entered a sustained recession by 2016. What went wrong?

The early 2000s boom was based upon the export of commodities (notably oil and iron ore) largely to China, which was also growing at a fast rate and was sucking in such products as it sought to sustain this growth rate. This export boom for Brazil coincided with the election of a new government led by Luiz Da Silva (Lula) in 2003. Lula launched a series of social programmes that allowed the benefits of this growth to spread throughout Brazil's social-economic structure, lifting 40 million people out of poverty. These social programmes were combined with economic reform that sought to make the business environment more conducive to growth. When he left office in 2011, he enjoyed a very high approval rating.

On Lula's departure, events quickly turned against his successor, Dilma Rousseff. The prices of its major commodities slumped. This left Brazil's consumption-led economic growth very vulnerable, for as economic growth declined and unemployment rose, the credit upon which a lot of goods had been purchased could no longer be repaid. This loss of export market was combined with the Petrobras (the state oil company) corruption scandal, where substantial quantities of the company's funds ended up in the accounts of leading politicians and well-connected businesspeople. The result was a social explosion in 2013 to protest about the state of the economy and poor public services. This also worked to erode the gains in equality that had been a hall-mark of the Lula government. In terms of economic performance, Brazil went from bad to worse, with inflation rising, rising unemployment, and a shrinking economy. Brazil faced its worst set of economic conditions for 80 years. The result was the removal of Rousseff in 2016 and his replacement with Michel Temer.

While the economy started to recover, the scars remained deep in 2019 as Brazil elected the far-right President Jair Bolsonaro. While initially promising economic reform and strong control, he quickly proved to be a divisive character, launching populist policies that did not help with his handling of the COVID-19 crisis, which he initially denied was an issue leading to a high death rate and increased levels of misinformation. This led to rising political instability as Bolsonaro's behaviour became increasingly erratic, especially with regard to threatening to ignore the results of the upcoming election. While he was narrowly defeated in the 2022 election, he was slow to admit defeat and help political divisions in Brazil, leading to the storming of Brazil's parliament, supreme court, and congress so as to restore Bolsonaro. This attempted coup failed, and Lula was restored.

It has often been said that Brazil is always the country for tomorrow. It is a resource-rich country but has suffered from persistently poor economic management and unstable governance. The hope is that the return of Lula will herald more stability. However, more has to go right, especially with regard to economic growth and the restoration of a credible strategy for the economy.

## CONCLUSION

Both China and India have undergone long periods of sustained growth. Both in 2008–2009 and 2020–2022, the world suffered a major economic crisis. Although sheltered from the first stages of the crisis by virtue of the limited integration of their financial sectors with the afflicted international financial sector, China and India could not avoid the second stage of the crisis, the more traditional economic downturn which resulted from the financial meltdown. China's growth in particular relied on exports, and the collapse of demand in several key markets has taken its toll with factory closures, growing unemployment, and the government encouraging workers that had migrated from the country to the town for work purposes to return to their rural roots. China's economic growth will inevitably slow, meaning other states will need to take up the slack, and one of these will be India. However, some commentators argue that China cannot lose too much growth momentum without facing negative social consequences and the resultant social unrest. In short, the world's two largest emerging companies continue to grow at rates significantly above those of most other countries, but they have a long way to go before they catch up with more developed countries and achieve their relative stability and sustainability.

## KEY POINTS

- Not so long ago, the economies of India and China were moribund and isolated from the rest of the world. Now they are the world's most rapidly growing economies.
- The recent economic and business success of India and China has come from the liberalisation of their domestic economies and an opening up of trade and investment to the rest of the world.
- The opportunities for foreign investors in India and China are significant, but not without risks.
- The growing economic strength of China and India is having an increasing impact on the rest of the world via increased competition, the emergence of Indian and Chinese multinationals, and the contest for resources.

## QUESTIONS FOR DISCUSSION

1. What are the major impediments to sustained growth in China?
2. Why has reform been so difficult in India?
3. The experiences of China and India demonstrate the superiority of the market over government intervention in the marketplace. Do you agree? Why?

## ACTIVITIES

1. Research how the COVID-19 crisis has affected China and India.
2. Choose an Indian or Chinese multinational. How has your chosen company internationalised, and what problems has it faced?
3. You are a consultant to a Western manufacturer or retailer considering a major investment in one of the BRIC economies (you chose the industry sector and location). Your role is to advise on whether this is a desirable objective. The CEO requires an analysis of the general business environment (in the widest sense) in which the investment will take place. He/she also needs advice on what form the investment should take (if you decide it should proceed) and on possible cultural or institutional obstacles to the investment. Also, feel free to include any other challenges or opportunities posed by the project.

Your findings can be presented in the form of an oral presentation, a report, or both.

## SUGGESTED FURTHER READINGS

Acharya, S., & Mohan, R. (2010). *India's economy: Performances and challenges*, Oxford: Oxford University Press.

Ahluwalia, I. J., & Little, I. M. D. (2012). *India's economic reforms and development: Essays for Manmohan Singh*, Oxford: Oxford University Press.

Enderwick, P. (2007). *Understanding emerging markets: China and India*, Routledge: London.

Keidel, A. (2022). *China's economic challenge: Unconventional success*, London: Routledge.

Panagariya, A. (2007). Why India lags behind China and how it can bridge the gap. *World Economy, 30*(2), 229–248.

Rajadhyaksha, N. (2007). *The rise of India: Is transformation from poverty to prosperity*, Singapore: John Wiley.

Tseng, W., & Cowen, D. (Eds.). (2007). *India's and China's recent experience with reform and growth*, Basingstoke: Palgrave Macmillan.

Weber, I. M. (2021). *How China escaped shock therapy: The market reform debate*, Routledge.

# CHAPTER 8

# DEVELOPMENT AND INTERNATIONAL PRODUCTION

## OBJECTIVES

This chapter will help you to:

- Describe and distinguish between major theories of development.
- Outline the major differences in development in different regions.
- Highlight how mainstream development thinking has changed.
- Explain commodity chain analysis and appreciate its relevance for business and development.
- Understand how progression through higher value-added export activities illustrates the interdependence of business and economic development.

The dominant trend in the international business environment in recent decades has been greater openness in trade, investment, finance, and technology, resulting in increased international integration and interdependence in business and between states. What is also apparent is that large swathes of the world's population are effectively marginalised or excluded from these trends (although there have been some improvements in the first decade of the 21st century; see Chapter 1). This exclusion has been a major factor in contemporary anti-globalisation campaigns and is frequently used to justify proposals to reform or even abolish international institutions and to reverse policies that have contributed to international integration.

Although aspects of globalisation and the policies of the IMF and the World Bank have not always been positive for developing countries, it is an oversimplification to place all or most of the blame for the marginalisation of developing countries on these factors. Development is a complex process, but some countries have managed it successfully. Significantly, it is those countries that have engaged most intensively with the outside world (that is, in East Asia) that have been most successful in their development endeavours. Equally significant has been the willingness of each state to take a central role in the development process, a role that varies from country to country depending on its culture and initial circumstances (see below).

DOI: 10.4324/9781315184500-10

Development is an important, and often neglected, issue for international business. Too often, international business and development are only discussed within the context of problems such as child labour or environmental degradation (see Chapters 15 and 16). Undoubtedly, these and similar issues pose serious challenges for MNEs and policymakers, but they are ultimately problems that, with sufficient political will, are amenable to solutions. Admittedly, the political will required is of a much greater magnitude than has hitherto been seen. Successful development, however, creates markets and improves the quality of labour forces and key aspects of infrastructure, thereby creating investment opportunities. Investment, in turn, is central to the development process.

This chapter explores the development challenge more thoroughly. It begins by tracing the development experiences of different groups of countries and tries to identify factors contributing to success and failure within individual countries and regions. It then explores different theoretical approaches and perspectives towards development, highlighting linkages where appropriate with the first section. It then discusses the evolution of production methodologies and how they have an impact on how developing countries engage with the external sector and how international business interfaces with developing countries.

## DIFFERENTIAL EXPERIENCES OF DEVELOPMENT

Developing countries are a heterogeneous group and are becoming more so. At the height of decolonisation in 1960, African, Asian, and Caribbean countries had similar development levels: the GNP per capita of South Korea was $217, and the equivalent figures for Haiti, the Central African Republic, Uganda, Togo, Egypt, Angola, and Nigeria all fell within 10 per cent of the Korean figure. By 2020, in terms of purchasing power parity, Korean GNP per head was 65 times greater than that of the Central African Republic, 35 times greater than Togo, 41 times greater than Uganda, 25 times greater than Haiti, and almost ten times greater than Egypt. Even in oil-rich countries like Nigeria and Angola, Korea's living standards in terms of GNP per head were 16 and 14 times greater, respectively, in 2020. Such widely differing experiences pose questions about why some countries have been able to transform their economic fortunes while others have not. These issues are addressed later in this chapter.

---

**Box 8.1:** Categorisation of countries according to their level of development

Countries are often categorised according to their level of development. Although inevitable, such categorisations are value-laden and often misleading, particularly as a country's circumstances can and do change over time. The following terms are in common usage:

The Third World: the term 'Third World' has outlived its usefulness. The term was a creature of the Cold War, essentially an ideological war between two economic systems: capitalism and communism, and two political systems: liberal democracy and the one-party state. The First World referred to the advanced Western industrialised economies. The Second World referred to the Soviet bloc and other communist countries such as China and North Korea. Countries outside these two systems, that is, countries in the process of development in Africa, Asia, the Middle East, Latin

America, and the Caribbean, belonged to the Third World. The 'Third World' was a useful unifying concept for the Non-Aligned Movement and for economically weak and underdeveloped countries, but given the end of the Cold War and the diversity of developing countries, the term 'Third World' has become inappropriate.

North-South: the 1980 Brandt Commission Report popularised this terminology. The 'North' includes all advanced economies, namely those of North America, Japan, Europe, and, from the southern hemisphere, Australia and New Zealand. The 'South' covers all developing countries. Superficially attractive, this categorisation is too broad, failing to recognise the different capitalist models in the North, such as Anglo-American capitalism, the Continental European welfare model of capitalism, and the more developmental Japanese model. More to the point, it treated the South as a homogenous group, whereas the reality is very different.

Developed, developing, less, or least developed: the terminology of developed and developing countries is adopted in this text, not out of a commitment to any particular development theory but because some words have to be chosen, and these are words used by the countries themselves and by international institutions such as the World Bank. Again, these words have their drawbacks. To describe an economy as 'developed' suggests it has reached the end of a long journey. This is clearly not the case. 'Developed' countries, such as those of North America, Western Europe, and increasingly East Asia, continue to evolve, as the emergence of the information economy (see Chapter 18) demonstrates. Their description as 'advanced industrialised economies' belies the fact that they are no longer as industrialised as many developing countries as possible and that the growth of the service sector means that industrialisation is no longer synonymous with the highest levels of development. Furthermore, at what point does a country move from the developing to the developed category? For some countries, particularly 'failed states' such as Afghanistan, the Democratic Republic of the Congo, and Somalia, to describe them as 'developing' seems overly ambitious.

Many of the world's poorest countries are located in Africa, although some Asian countries (Bangladesh, for example) and some island countries are also classified as least developed countries. From the 1960s to the 1990s, real GNP per head declined in many sub-Saharan African countries. However, in the first decade of the new century, the fortunes of some, at least, of these countries appeared to improve. This was, in many cases, created by the Chinese-driven commodity boom throughout this period as China sucked in copious quantities of commodities to build its manufacturing base. This created an export-driven boom for many commodities exporting to developing economies. This trend left many of these states very vulnerable to economic growth and development within the Chinese economy. This created issues for these states over the long term.

The experience of Latin American and Caribbean countries, which started from a higher base, has been more positive, although annual average per capita growth for the region as a whole from the mid-60s was not particularly high at 1.3 per cent. The most spectacular long-term performer is East Asia, where real GNP per head grew at an annual average rate of nearly 6 per cent between 1966 and 2021, a trend which continued into the new millennium with the result that living standards in Hong Kong and Singapore are on par with those in advanced industrialised economies.

**TABLE 8.1** LDCs real GDP growth rates per capita, 1992–2021 (annual average growth rates, %)

| | Real GDP growth | | | | | |
|---|---|---|---|---|---|---|
| | 1992–1995 | 1995–2000 | 2000–2005 | 2005–2010 | 2010–2015 | 2015–2021 |
| LDCs | -0.42 | 2.28 | 3.77 | 4.12 | 2.61 | 1.14 |
| African LDCs | -1.75 | 1.50 | 3.22 | 3.64 | 2.61 | 0.16 |
| Asian LDCs | 1.82 | 3.54 | 4.66 | 5.04 | 2.78 | 2.92 |
| Island LDCs | 0.84 | -0.55 | -2.81 | 2.24 | 2.06 | 1.97 |
| All developing countries | 3.25 | 2.73 | 4.15 | 4.97 | 3.86 | 2.15 |

Source: Derived from UNCTAD Stat (2023)

## Sub-Saharan Africa

Whichever measure is chosen: trade in goods, trade in services, or inward investment (see Chapter 1), Africa is the world's most marginalised continent. For the vast majority of Africans, poverty and subsistence are the order of the day. Apart from South Africa and the countries along the North African coast, the continent contains no emerging economies. Indeed, the economic reality for most countries has been a steady decline. According to UNCTAD and World Bank figures (see Table 8.2), GDP growth per capita in sub-Saharan Africa as a whole was low through the 1990s and into the new millennium; the rate picked up through the 2020s. This was largely a commodity-export driven growth created by the rise of China. However, as discussed below, the sustainability of such growth is questionable.

The reasons for the relatively poor performance of Africa in terms of development are varied and contested, and beyond the scope of this chapter, but some continuing problems and challenges can be identified. Many sub-Saharan countries, for example, face continuing structural dependency. During the colonial period, their role was defined as that of exporters of primary commodities to industrialised countries. Commodities still dominate the trade and economies of many sub-Saharan African countries. Commodity prices are notoriously volatile, subject as they are to the vagaries of harvest, stock levels, and supply and demand, but the movement of real primary commodity prices in most years has not favoured developing countries since the beginning of the 1960s.

Figure 8.1, for example, shows that the prices of non-energy commodities (which include agricultural products, fertilisers, metals, and minerals) have fluctuated within a narrow band during recent decades, after decades of stability prior to this. Moreover, with the rise of emerging economies, the price of all commodities has really risen over the first two decades of the new millennium. really soared during the first years of the 2000s, when demand was pushed up by the booming emerging economies. For these states, the problem illustrated in Figure 8.1 reflects a mixed blessing. First, prices for export commodities can fluctuate widely, making economic performance ambiguous. Second, this uncertainty extends to the commodities that these states have to import. These erratic prices, combined with poor relative purchasing power, leave these states very vulnerable to swings within commodity markets. African countries were not alone in their commodity dependence. However, other countries have been able to move away from it.

Overdependence on commodities is only a small part of sub-Saharan Africa's problems. In many cases, there is a big divergence between the traditional subsistence economy and the limited modern sector. This makes it difficult for the limited investment that does take place to start a virtuous circle of further development, i.e., there are few opportunities for backward linkages into the rest of the economy. Economic development is also hindered by inadequate and deteriorating infrastructure, a factor which deters inward investment and is concentrated in only a few countries in Africa, and indeed mostly in the oil and mineral sectors.

The geography of colonisation resulted in national boundaries that reflect convenient lines on maps rather than territories with common histories and cultures. This has resulted in post-colonial conflict and weak governance systems. The absence or

**TABLE 8.2** Growth in real GNP per capita in the main economic regions of Africa

| | Real GDP per capita (average annual % growth) | | | | | | |
|---|---|---|---|---|---|---|---|
| | 1992–1995 | 1995–2000 | 2000–2005 | 2005–2010 | 2010–2015 | 2015–2021 |
| World | 1.25 | 2.16 | 1.88 | 1.21 | 1.70 | 1.00 |
| Africa | -1.16 | 0.96 | 2.90 | 2.62 | 1.39 | -0.47 |
| Northern Africa | -0.15 | 2.20 | 3.00 | 2.62 | 1.00 | 0.52 |
| Sub-Saharan Africa | -1.62 | 0.40 | 3.04 | 2.81 | 2.05 | -0.81 |
| Eastern Africa | 0.38 | 0.59 | 1.50 | 4.06 | 3.34 | 1.66 |
| Middle Africa | 5.42 | 0.18 | 4.00 | 3.19 | 1.53 | -3.16 |
| Southern Africa | 0.82 | 1.27 | 2.86 | 1.84 | 0.94 | -1.32 |
| Western Africa | 2.59 | 0.57 | 4.60 | 3.59 | 3.13 | -0.47 |
| Asia | 2.96 | 2.25 | 3.85 | 4.26 | 4.05 | 2.77 |

Source: UNCTAD Stat

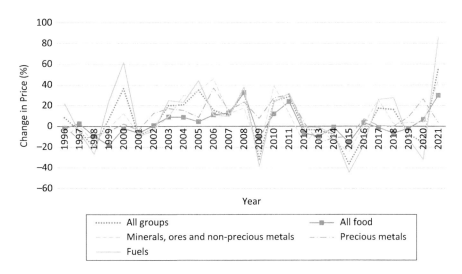

**FIGURE 8.1** Commodity price trends (UNCTAD Commodity Price Index (2015)
Source: UNCTAD

weakness of the traditional apparatus of statehood has also made it difficult for develop-ment plans to deliver their objectives, whether domestically or internationally inspired. The neo-liberal agenda and programmes of the IMF and World Bank have been heavily criticised as inappropriate for these countries, and many have been held up as failures. As discussed below, some of their shortcomings have been recognised, leading to greater adaptation to the specific circumstances of individual countries rather than the 'one size fits all' model that underpinned earlier programmes.

More than that, the stability of several countries has been precarious, and the state has, in cases like Somalia and the Democratic Republic of the Congo, virtually imploded. In less extreme cases, internal and civil strife have also deterred investors. In these cir-cumstances, it is hardly surprising that FDI has been limited in sub-Saharan Africa. There is much competition for capital from across the world, and the volatility and instability within Africa translate into too much risk for many potential investors.

Cutting themselves off individually or as small regional groups will almost certainly result in further deterioration of the political, economic, and social situations of sub-Saharan states. Yet these countries are not in a position to withstand the competitive pressure that immediate and full exposure to the external economic environment would produce. A more fruitful halfway house might be to nurture potentially viable sectors behind short-term protection, possibly within some form of regionally integrative frame-work to increase the size of the domestic market, and then launch the sector on the international stage in a more phased manner.

There is little evidence that many of the endemic problems that bedevil Africa, both Saharan and sub-Saharan, will be alleviated in the foreseeable future. Many North African states endured temporary political unrest associated with the Arab Spring. Any optimism that this would generate long-term change was quickly eroded, with many pre-existing elites re-establishing themselves, most notably in Egypt, where the Army has taken hold of vast swathes of the economy. In Libya, a long-lasting civil war has erupted between rival warlords, and in Tunisia, where progress looked possible, strongman rule has eventually been re-established. Elsewhere, states have sustained civil unrest, notably Sudan, which has now split into two. Ethiopia, a longstanding growth pole for the continent, has retreated into internecine strife, and the rise of Islamic extremism right across the Sahel has also created a more hostile business environment. Most notable here has been Nigeria. Thus, for many of these states, sustained poor economic conditions have created further outflows of people and capital. There are occasional bright spots across the continent, notably Kenya, Ghana (see case study 8.1), and Rwanda, but these do come with caveats. This unrest has also extended to southern Africa, where there are increased terrorist threats in states such as Mozambique. More worryingly is the decline of South Africa, where endemic corruption and underinvestment in infrastructure have knocked the growth trajectory of this once very promising outpost of sub-Saharan African growth.

## CASE STUDY 8.1: MARKETING GARDENING IN KENYA

Like many other developing states, a large share of Kenya's population lives in rural areas. Without large-scale rural-urban migration, which its cities are ill-equipped to cope with export-led growth therefore has to come (at least in part) from agricultural activity. In Kenya, this has fallen to horticultural exports, which comprise fruit and vegetables, fresh or processed, as well as cut flowers. As of 2022, agribusiness is the largest sector within the Kenyan economy; it comprises 29 per cent of Kenya's gross domestic product (GDP), provides nearly 60 per cent of employment, and accounts for 57 per cent of all exports. The EU is the biggest export market for these exports.

At the root of the success is the ability of Kenyan producers to integrate themselves into global value chains. This allowed these local producers to gain access to FDI to upgrade their farms to render them capable of export-driven production. Global MNEs offered key inputs into the process through the supply of seeds, fertilisers, agrochemicals (pesticides), farm equipment, and irrigation equipment. This export-led growth was also facilitated by a community of local entrepreneurs (often of foreign origin) with strong links to major export markets. These factors, in combination, enabled the scaling up of local production and also facilitated the development of supporting infrastructure to allow these (often perishable) goods to be rapidly processed and exported.

As these businesses matured and became more commercially savvy, so their souring strategies changed. There was a switch away from plantation production towards contract farming. These allowed for the development of a horticulture cluster to emerge within the sector, with these farmers supplying the major exporting businesses. The success of the sector in driving Kenyan export growth reflects both supply- and demand-side factors. On the former, there was a push by the global MNEs and other foreign investors to increase exports from the country in response to rising demand for largely developed economies.

The links between the local cluster of suppliers and the MNEs have been a powerful factor in shaping the competitiveness of this industry, with the latter being a major push factor in seeking to switch agriculture from a national or regional focus to more lucrative long-distance export markets. These firms were especially important in allowing producers to position themselves at the higher end of the price-value continuum and were central to these local firms establishing more sophisticated marketing strategies. These were also central in enabling local Kenyan firms to be adaptive to changing terms within their target markets, especially with regard to issues such as changing food standards, changing customer tastes, and the importance and management of just-in-time production systems to the nature of their value proposition.

These latter points stress the importance of the GVC operating to ensure that local suppliers are responsive to global buyers. In these cases, the latter are pivotal in organising the value chain and in supporting the evolution of local practices to ensure that they are best able to respond nimbly to shifting commercial contexts. These global buyers initiated the pre-programming of the supply chain and ensured the right standards were met throughout. In enabling this, global buyers were central to these businesses being incentivised to upgrade their facilities and were supported in these processes through the organised exchange of know-how, market information, inputs, and training. These upgrades have also been supported by public-private partnerships. This has been expanded to the development of GVCs elsewhere in East Africa.

This experience of market gardening in Kenya is important as it reflects how the establishment and management of GVCs can aid the process of economic development in developing states. It also highlights how such processes can have spillover effects on the broader economy. In Kenya, the experience of GVC engagement has been a platform that has facilitated the gradual transition away from agriculture towards an evolving manufacturing sector. It also shifted the agricultural sector to move beyond largely subsistence-based business models towards greater commercial sophistication and to establish a model for other parts of the sector. It also underscores the importance of an embedded entrepreneurial class and an openness to FDI and how – with some state support – this can be a platform for export-led growth.

## QUESTION

To what extent do you believe horticulture is a legitimate platform for development in Kenya?

## Latin America

Latin America is far more developed than sub-Saharan Africa, according to all main indicators, but it lags behind the East Asian NICs. Before the Second World War, Latin America was, like other underdeveloped regions, an exporter of primary commodities, most of which were produced on foreign-owned plantations and mines. After the war, most of the continent, under the influence of economist Raoul Prebisch, tried to escape from this traditional relationship by adopting an import substitution policy. This strategy required the state to take on a leading role in the development process through state ownership and high tariff walls to protect infant industries. It gradually became apparent that the restricted engagement of Latin American economies with the rest of the world failed to deliver sustainable, stable growth and that prosperity was confined to a small elite.

By the late 1970s, many Latin American governments were under military control and finding it difficult to escape from the heavy debt burden that resulted from extensive external borrowing from private banks. The absence of a significant export sector made it virtually impossible to meet debt-servicing requirements, and development was stymied. By the mid-1980s, several Latin American countries were taking large doses of IMF and World Bank medicine, and more were to follow suit. Initially, economic progress was stop-start, and some countries embraced the abandonment of import substitution with more enthusiasm than others. However, the policy change did herald a return to growth, but it has been less strong than that experienced in East Asia. Moreover, Latin America remains dogged by large income inequalities.

In broad terms, by 2000, or even before, it was possible to talk of a common set of policies within Latin America. However, there is great variation in how far countries have changed policy direction and in the effectiveness of the new policies. The majority of Latin American countries currently place their reliance on the market mechanism and the private sector, both in the domestic and external spheres, to deliver development. This has manifested itself in supply-side reforms focusing on trade liberalisation, privatisation, and regulatory changes such as more FDI-friendly policies. On the macro side, the emphasis has been on achieving stability, an objective that requires strict budgetary discipline, monetary restraint, and realistic exchange rates.

Compared to previous decades, Latin American economies have become much more open, competitive, and generally welcoming to international business. Although IMF and World Bank programmes have played their part in this turnaround, as time has progressed, it has been globalisation and the need to integrate with the rest of the world that have driven Latin American policy forward. In addition to the macro and micro policies referred to above, a number of countries have turned to regional integration schemes such as Mercosur (see Chapter 5) to deliver further growth. Tried previously as a way of extending the domestic market in a relatively closed world, the new regionalism in Latin America is an open regionalism intended to provide links for greater integration with the international economy.

Latin America remains a mixed bag of economic development trajectories over the past two decades. Some states, notably Chile, continue to make progress largely on the back of commodity exports. However, other states have regressed in the face of economic mismanagement and corruption. Brazil, which was a leading economy in the region, suffered repeated recessions as it failed to turn the commodity boom into a credible manufacturing exporter. This was also compounded by embedded corruption and a drift towards populism. These problems were also evident in other states, notably Venezuela, where nationalist populist governments misappropriated and misspent its substantial mineral wealth. These uncertainties were evident with the shift towards populism across many Latin American states throughout the early 2020s.

## East Asian NICs

By the 1990s, the four East Asian NICs of South Korea, Taiwan, Singapore, and Hong Kong were more properly described as developed than as developing countries. Behind them are Malaysia and Thailand; these second-generation NICs have also substantially transformed their economies, but not yet quite as fundamentally as the 'Big Four'. In all cases, though, the achievements are striking given that in 1960, these countries had more in common in terms of GDP per head and economic structure with many countries that were and remain among the world's poorest (see above). The big question relating to the East Asian economies is: why have they been able to develop, whereas the African story is one of stagnation and/or decline? This question is beyond the scope of this section, but it can identify some of the factors in the success of the East Asian NICs.

Whatever the reasons for East Asian success, it is inappropriate to attribute it to the full-blooded implementation of neo-liberal policies. Although East Asian countries have shown themselves prepared and able to take advantage of globalisation opportunities, particularly in relation to export-led growth, they have frequently followed a strategy of active state involvement in the developmental process, although the exact nature of this involvement varies (see below).

Like Latin American nations, the countries of East Asia also followed an import substitution policy during the 1950s. This allowed them to start the industrialisation process without being undermined by imports from developed countries. However, the restricted size of domestic markets and shortages of foreign exchange to pay for the machinery and equipment imports needed for industrialisation contributed to the shift to an export promotion strategy that occurred in the early 1960s.

South Korea and Taiwan had two further development advantages over other developing countries. First, they had a privileged role in the post-war foreign policy of the US, which poured substantial sums of money into them to reduce their vulnerability to Communist infiltration and/or takeover. The likely cessation of the US financial aid, worth about $100 million per annum to Taiwan alone, encouraged the shift to export promotion. Secondly, both South Korea and Taiwan began their post-war development with a more developed infrastructure and education system than other countries at a similar level of development.

Since 1960, East Asia has been the world's fastest-growing region. East Asian success has threatened to put obstacles to further development in their way. In the 1980s, access to the markets of developed countries was compromised by a wave of 'new protectionist' measures, including 'voluntary' export restraints, anti-dumping measures, and a focus on intellectual property rights. The 1986 US Trade Act identified a range of alleged unfair trading practices. Article 301 of the Act required the US Trade Representative to act against such practices. The East Asian trading position was also made more difficult by the high wage growth that eroded their original cheap labour advantage in labour-intensive sectors. On the other hand, their relatively skilled and educated workforces gave them advantages in the transition to post-Fordist production.

East Asian NICs partially overcame these potential obstacles in their traditionally strong sectors of electronics and textiles by engaging in the process of triangle manufacturing (see below). In other words, the more value-added, labour-intensive, and/or the final assembly phases of production are carried out in lower-wage countries, usually elsewhere in the region. Local producers, meanwhile, have moved up the production hierarchy to engage in more technology-intensive, higher value-added activities, bringing competition from the South Korean and Taiwanese electronics sectors, for example, to the erstwhile dominant US, European, and Japanese producers.

Despite these broad similarities, each of the East Asian NICs has followed its own distinctive development path, as discussed below.

## South Korea

The South Korean government has taken a decisive role in directing the economy to its current advanced state of development. During the key early days of development in the 1960s, a hybrid policy of import substitution and export promotion was followed. The government chose to do this through developing selected strategic industries such as automobiles, shipbuilding, and electronics. The chosen companies were granted subsidies and privileges, including protection from foreign competition, in return for establishing capital- and technology-intensive activities and export capacity. The favoured, largely family-owned companies evolved into giant industrial conglomerates (chaebol), several of which, like Samsung, Hyundai, and LG, are now among the world's top MNEs. In order to ensure efficiency and competitiveness, despite the isolation from foreign competition, the government encouraged competition among the chaebols.

This strategy met with some success; for example, South Korea dominated the world's shipbuilding industry by the 1980s. This strategy was not without its problems. It relied heavily on imports of capital goods and technology licencing against the background of a relatively small and, in the early days, a low-income domestic market. Much emphasis is currently placed on the need for developing countries to follow liberal FDI policies to promote development. However, South Korea's development was achieved by building up domestic capacity rather than by relying on foreign capital. In order to acquire the necessary technology, Korea relied initially on reverse engineering (i.e., the reproduction of another manufacturer's product following a detailed examination of its construction or composition) and increasingly on the development of its own research and development capacity; its research and development expenditure as a percentage of GDP is among the highest in the world. Educational spending and university enrollment are also among the highest in the developing world, reinforcing the importance of human capital in development.

## Taiwan

The Taiwanese government has also played a major role in economic development. Since 1960, Taiwan has moved away from import substitution towards a strong export promotion policy, including selective inducements to foreign investors and support for indigenous skill and technology development and acquisition. However, unlike South Korea, the Taiwanese government did not encourage the creation of giant private conglomerates or concentrate on the development of heavy industry. Rather, it has focused on developing the SMEs that dominate Taiwan's business sector.

SMEs can find it difficult to engage in the research and development needed for success in sectors like electronics, so the government has acted to ensure Taiwanese companies can compete. Government agencies undertake research that is too costly and risky for private companies in aerospace and advanced metal engineering, for example. Other measures include high levels of investment in education and training and the development of Taiwan's own Silicon Valley through the construction of the science town at Hsinchu, which brings together thousands of university researchers, several national laboratories, a huge technology institute, and over 400 high-technology companies involved in the integrated circuit, computing and peripherals, telecommunications, optoelectronics, precision machinery, and biotechnology sectors. Programmes to promote subcontracting, a strategy which strengthens the emergence of backward linkages into the rest of the economy, have also played a key part in Taiwan's development. Initially, such measures included minimum local content requirements for foreign affiliates based in Taiwan. Measures later became more indirect, such as offering incentives to local subcontractors.

## Hong Kong

Hong Kong has followed the most liberal economic policy of all the East Asian NICs and has not taken on the role of a developmental state like South Korea or Taiwan. During the final decades of British rule (which ended in 1997), official policy was described as 'positive non-interventionism'. In other words, Hong Kong's modernisation occurred under a system of 'laissez faire' – an approach which delivered significant economic success. However, Hong Kong's location, unique history and relationship with mainland China, and its traditional role as a trading entrepôt make it an unusual NIC and reduce its usefulness as a development role model. A combination of free trade and substantial inward FDI, together with its indigenous entrepreneurial population, the longstanding presence of large British companies, and associated trade and finance infrastructure, made it possible for Hong Kong to develop a dynamic, export-oriented, light manufacturing sector. However, Hong Kong's lack of government-driven or assisted research and development means that, although Hong Kong has seen some industrial deepening, it has not developed the same level of industrial complexity and technological sophistication as other East Asian NICs.

As Hong Kong's wages and other costs rose, much manufacturing activity relocated to mainland China. As the 1997 handover of Hong Kong to China approached, FDI activity became increasingly geared towards servicing the Chinese economy. Although losing a significant proportion of its manufacturing activity at home, Hong Kong has continued to thrive by moving into financial services, becoming the region's (and one of the world's) leading financial centres. The increased loss of faith in the 'one country, two systems' approach adopted since the handover has resulted in some degree of business uncertainty as the conventional business system – which underpinned Hong Kong's success – begins to be adapted.

## Singapore

Like Hong Kong, Singapore has a long history as a trading entrepôt. However, the similarity ends there. The Singaporean government has been much more interventionist. Import substitution was quickly abandoned in favour of selective industrial targeting and free trade. More than any other East Asian NIC, Singapore's development policy has been based on liberal FDI rules and attracting MNE investment.

Singapore's initial development occurred in the garment and semi-conductor industries, but the government intervened early and decisively to upgrade the industrial structure and encourage more higher value-added activity. Like South Korea and Taiwan, Singapore has recognised the importance of a skilled and educated workforce. As a small island with a population of only 4 million, Singapore has chosen not to spread itself too thinly, specialising in high-technology and guiding inward investors to higher value-added investment and technology provision. As a result, Singapore has developed a capacity for complex technologies without the existence of an extensive research and development base. However, the government encourages MNEs to establish laboratories in Singapore and is fostering indigenous research by targeting individual sectors like biotechnology. This process is not helped by a shortage of trained scientists, but investment in education is directed towards easing this problem in the long term. In short, as costs have risen, Singapore's response has been to systematically move up the high-technology production ladder and to identify and remove obstacles that might otherwise inhibit its strategy.

Overall, the East Asian economies have a propensity for export promotion and selective government intervention in common (with Hong Kong being the exception in the latter case). In other words, it is not liberal market economics but interventionist policies that underpin their success. Hong Kong, Taiwan, and Singapore (less so South Korea) have welcomed FDI, but their intervention strategies have varied. Their development has also been marked by less income inequality than in other regions.

Increasingly, as labour and other costs have risen, the East Asian NICs have engaged in outward investment in Southeast Asia and China, resulting in enhanced intra-regional trade and the emergence of a regional division of labour. This marks the reduced dependence of the region on Western capital and technology, the growing role of these NICs as the engine for growth in the wider region, and the emergence of regionally integrated trade and production networks. This integration, both formal and informal, reflects the emergence of greater intra-industry trade on a global level and represents the optimal path for future success, given the relatively limited domestic markets of the East Asian NICs and the potentially lucrative, albeit as yet underdeveloped, markets of the rest of the region.

## CASE STUDY 8.2: THE MAQUILADORA: EXPORT-DRIVEN MANUFACTURING IN MEXICO

Established in the 1960s, the Maquiladora is a Mexican manufacturing plant developed with the purpose of seeking to attract FDI into the economy as a precursor to solving longstanding economic problems, especially with regard to unemployment, though these factories can only be located in those areas that are deemed uncongested. As a result, these factories are largely foreign-owned. Due to the nature of the investment sought and the structure of Mexican exports, many of the manufacturing plants were established close to the US border. As an incentive to stimulate FDI in these regions, these plants were able to benefit from assorted benefits (see below) that enabled them to function as a low-cost manufacturing base that was able to service the US market. This has, in time, proved a source of controversy for this model of manufacturing development.

As the ultimate owners of the Maquiladora are often foreign-owned, these factors are essentially branch plants, with the ultimate owners largely being in the US. The designation of Maquiladora is not a given but is decided upon by the Mexican Economy Minister. This is important because being classified as a Maquiladora means that the plant is able to take advantage of a number of tax advantages (such as duty-free imports on specific inputs) as well as unlimited foreign investment. For US businesses, the attractiveness is largely driven by the fact that they can access a cheap labour force within easy reach of the US market. To date, many types of firms, from medical equipment to automotive, have taken advantage of the Maquiladora programme. Indeed, a major catalyst for this process was the North American Free Trade Agreement (NAFTA). Indeed, the success of the Maquiladora programme – and the consequent US resentment of the impact of US manufacturing – was a key driver in the reform of NAFTA.

From the above, the economic benefits of the Maquiladora are self-evident, but they include:

* Offering a source of employment in areas of low economic engagement and development in Mexico.
* Operating as a catalyst for broader economic growth within the FDI-receiving region.
* Costs and other financial incentives that are available to inward investors.
* A ready supply of cheap labour.
* Good proximity to major export markets with low logistics costs.

However, the Maquiladora is not without its problems, not least of which is that the programme is seen as essentially driven by the exploitation of cheap labour and that this undermines US manufacturing capability. Many of the wages offered within the Maquiladora are below the poverty line. In addition, there are issues surrounding the tightness of US migrant policies, with many migrants from Central America seeking work within these factories. This places further downward pressure on wages. This low-cost manufacturing can also impact the quality of working conditions. There is a degree of unionisation within the Maquiladora, but these tend to represent the government, not the workers.

Nonetheless, the benefits of the programme have seen the Mexican government extend the programme which offers further benefits and puts increased pressure on costs. This led to a surge in investment in these firms by US businesses. By the 2010s, these firms were comprising over 50 per cent of Mexican exports to the US, 17 per cent of employment, and 25 per cent of GDP. However, the success of the model has been copied by other states that have started to divert investment away from the Maquiladora programme. The Maquiladora were a key factor in the renegotiation of NAFTA within the succeeding USMCA (see Case study 5.2), seeking to militate many of the low-cost advantages offered by these firms, especially within the automotive sector. It also sought to get around the issue of Chinese investment in these branch plants to circumvent US controls.

## QUESTION

How do you think the Maquiladora will be impacted by the new USCMA trade agreement?

# THEORIES OF DEVELOPMENT

Consideration of development theory is important in that it influences the approach of developing countries and international institutions towards development and provides a context for the engagement of international business in developing countries. This section briefly outlines the two main competing development theories. It is far from an exhaustive discussion of all variants of development theory, nor does it purport to critique these theories, but it does outline two of the most influential strands of development policy that continue to shape thinking today.

## Dependency theory

At the heart of dependency theory is the contention that the problems of developing countries stem from their reliance on more developed economies for capital, markets, technology, etc. In colonial times, this dependence was perpetuated by the subordination of the interests of the colonised country to those of the colonising power, namely through the structuring of economic relations so that the colony's sole role was to supply primary commodities and raw materials to the industries of the colonial power (see above). Even after independence, so the theory goes, a dependency relationship persisted, not through political and administrative control as before but through continuing reliance on foreign capital in the form of MNEs. In other words, the negative effects of colonialism had been replaced by a new form of exploitation termed 'neo-colonialism'.

Ironically, given that most Latin American countries threw off their colonial bonds in the nineteenth century, dependency theory originated in Latin America during the 1950s and 1960s. However, Latin American economies were badly scarred by the 1930s Depression, which, within the space of four years, had slashed their export earnings by over two-thirds, creating severe problems in financing the import of manufactured goods from industrialised countries. This experience was interpreted as demonstrating the dangers of over-reliance on external economies. Given that the world's most successful economies had originally industrialised behind tariff walls, Latin American policymakers also concluded that the only way to develop was to do likewise. Thus, Latin America's post-war import substitution strategy was born.

Dependency theory quickly spread beyond Latin America and was important in attempts to generate developing world solidarity via the Group of 77 and the New International Economic Order in the 1970s. Such initiatives stressed the importance of self-reliance and the de-linking of developing economies from developed economies and were an unsuccessful attempt to shift the balance of power away from the dominant economic and political role of the developed countries and thus reduce the dependency of the developing countries on them.

Despite its attractiveness to Latin America and other developing countries in their early years of independence, dependency theory had fallen out of favour by the 1980s. Import substitution had not yielded the expected benefits. Indeed, import substitution did nothing to break the unequal relationship between developing and developed countries, as the former relied heavily on imports of capital goods and technology from the latter to promote their industrialisation. Furthermore, it had proved virtually impossible to forge a common identity for developing countries given their wide diversity of interests and experiences. Often, but not solely, used as a means of constructing an alternative model to capitalism, dependency theory became further neglected as the Cold War ended when the only choice available for developing countries appeared to be between competing forms of capitalism rather than between capitalism and something else. In short, the route out of poverty and underdevelopment increasingly appeared to be more, not less, engagement with the process of globalisation. Indeed, more and more countries started to shift their policies towards greater utilisation of market forces, both domestically and externally.

In addition, dependency theory has been criticised as too deterministic, too general, and lacking power to explain the divergent development experiences of countries in sub-Saharan Africa and East Asia. Nevertheless, dependency theory has left an important legacy: it emphasises the impact of and interaction of the international economic system with development. However, its analysis of the impact tends to run contrary to much contemporary thinking on the matter, and it underestimates domestic factors as an explanation of underdevelopment, a shortcoming addressed by modernisation theory.

## Modernisation theory

Modernisation theory is based on entirely different assumptions than dependency theory. Rather than attributing the failures of developing countries to their unequal relationships with developed countries or to their links, or lack of them, with the international economic system, modernisation theory focuses on shortcomings inherent in the developing countries themselves and proposes strategies to overcome them. In addition, dependency theory emerged from the developing countries themselves, supported by sympathetic left-leaning Western intellectuals, whereas modernisation theory originated within the developed countries and international institutions like the IMF and World Bank.

According to modernisation theory, lack of development stems from inadequate technology and cultural factors that inhibit economic growth and, more specifically, industrialisation, the process that delivered development to Europe, North America, and Japan. In other words, modernisation theory in its purest form requires universal application of the Western model of development. Walt W. Rostow, in his 1960 work *The Stages of Economic Growth: A Non-Communist Manifesto*, identified five stages of growth through which economies must pass in order to modernise (see Box 5.2). This highly prescriptive programme for development has been criticised for failing to take account of the political, economic, and cultural diversity of developing economies and for neglecting relationships between developing countries and the outside world.

---

**Box 8.2:** Rostow's five stages of growth

1. Traditional society: predominantly agricultural with a rigid, hierarchical social structure and little or no scientific endeavour.

2. Pre-conditions for take-off: often triggered by some external factor resulting in the economy becoming less localised, greater trade, improved communications, and the creation of an elite group.

3. Take-off: an increasing share of investment in national income and changes in social and political institutions to facilitate growth.

4. The drive to maturity: a period of continuing high levels of investment, political reform, and an expanding commitment to science and technology, enabling development to take a firm hold.

5. The age of mass consumption: consolidation of the above with the diffusion of economic benefits throughout the population.

In *Politics and the Stages of Growth* (1971), Rostow added a sixth stage: the search for a greater quality of life.

---

Given the underlying assumption that development is about convergence with the Western model, modernisation theory resulted in a highly technocratic, mechanistic, problem-solving approach to development, resulting in what Hoogvelt described as a 'how to develop manual for less developed countries' (Hoogvelt 2001). Given the geographical origins of modernisation theory, the measures proposed to achieve development are in line with the prevailing economic philosophy of the developed countries — that is, neo-liberalism, or reliance on freeing up the private sector and releasing the power of market forces to bring about this growth. This philosophy is reflected in IMF conditionality and in the World Bank's Structural Adjustment Programmes (SAP).

Modernisation theory has attracted much criticism. Particularly powerful are allegations of ethnocentricity — that is, the attempt to parachute inappropriate Western development models into developing countries and a failure to take into account the unique social, cultural, historical, and economic backgrounds of individual developing countries. Critics also argue that the success of the modernisation approach has been limited to parts of East Asia. Even in East Asia, it can be argued that development has not occurred as a result of convergence to the neo-liberal model but through adaptation and tailoring of development policies to the individual circumstances of South Korea, Taiwan, Singapore, and Hong Kong by the governments of those countries (see above). In other words, growth and development are more likely to occur when policies work with rather than against the culture and traditions of individuals.

## CHANGING APPROACHES TO DEVELOPMENT

Approaches to development have become more complex, more nuanced, and more sensitive to the specific conditions of individual developing countries. Consideration of the so-called 'Washington Consensus' is a useful starting point for understanding how development thinking changed in the 1980s and 1990s and how it has evolved since. The term entered common usage around 1990 following the publication of an article by economist John Williamson which referred to the common features of policy advice proffered by the Washington institutions (that is, the IMF, the World Bank, the US Treasury, and mainstream academic economists) about the development process. Box 8.3 lists the main features of the Washington Consensus, which essentially represents the neo-liberal SAPs to which developing countries had to adhere in return for financial assistance from international institutions like the World Bank.

---

**Box 8.3:** The Washington Consensus

The components of the Washington Consensus identified by John Williamson are:

1. *Fiscal discipline*: the restriction of budget deficits to avoid inflation and capital flight.

2. *Public expenditure*: the elimination of subsidies and the redirection of government spending towards education, health, and infrastructure.

3. *Tax reform*: development of a broad tax base with moderate marginal tax rates.

4. *Interest rates*: interest rates at a level to discourage capital flight and encourage saving.

5. *Exchange rates*: competitive exchange rates to promote exports.

6. *Trade liberalisation*: reduction of tariffs, especially on primary or intermediate inputs into export production.

7. *Foreign direct investment*: encouragement of FDI as a source of capital and skills transfer.

8. *Privatisation*: privatisation of state-owned enterprises as part of a drive to encourage the private sector.

9. *Deregulation*: deregulation of the economy to encourage the growth of private enterprise and to discourage bureaucratic corruption.

10. *Property rights*: the enforcement of property rights to encourage domestic capital accumulation and FDI.

Williamson himself expressed concern about the use of the term 'Washington Consensus'. His original intention was to identify 'which of the policy initiatives that had emanated from Washington during the years of conservative ideology had won inclusion in the intellectual mainstream rather than being cast aside once Ronald Reagan was no longer on the political scene' (Williamson 2000). However, the phrase soon took on a life of its own. In other words, the 'Washington Consensus' rapidly became shorthand for adherence to a set of policy prescriptions based on the primacy of the market and minimisation of the role of the state. In Williamson's view, the phrase 'intended to describe a technocratic policy agenda that survived the demise of Reaganomics came to be used to describe an ideology embracing the most extreme version of Reaganomics' (Williamson 2000).

Williamson is concerned that this gives the impression that much of the economic liberalisation in developing countries in the 1980s and 1990s was imposed by Washington-based institutions rather than resulting from a wider intellectual consensus he believed underpinned the reforms. Nevertheless, many would argue that the conditionalities attached to IMF loans and World Bank SAPs were imposed on reluctant developing countries. However, this view underestimates the extent to which developing countries themselves have taken on board elements of a less state-centric, more market-oriented approach to economic development. This process accelerated after the end of the Cold War when development ceased to be viewed as a competition between opposing political and economic systems and ideologies. The demise of communism and the bipolar world recast economic policy choices, but also for developing countries, into a question not of whether to accept the market but of how much and whether to accept the market at all.

Bringing a complex range of policies under the umbrella of a simple phrase froze debate at a certain point in time. In reality, the debate was always more complex than this phrase implies and was constantly evolving. Williamson himself later highlighted a number of areas where there were more policy disagreements than his original characterisation of the Washington Consensus implied. This was particularly true of interest rate and exchange rate policies.

More fundamentally, it was increasingly recognised that macroeconomic stabilisation and supply-side policies such as privatisation and liberalisation were not in themselves sufficient to deliver development and that the persistence of extremes of poverty and unequal income distribution impaired development and threatened stability and competitiveness. Consequently, poverty alleviation became the primary objective, not only of development NGOs but also of international institutions and development agencies. There was also growing awareness that even the most appropriate economic policy initiatives would fail without the existence of efficient and transparent governance systems. Consequently, much greater emphasis was placed on development thinking and policy on achieving impartial legal systems, incorrupt and incorruptible bureaucracies and political systems, transparent regulations, etc.

In short, development policy was more than a device to let market forces rip. Rather, it attempted to take onboard the implications of the end of the bipolar world and growing international integration and to reflect the growing concern for sustainable development. Although the operation of the market mechanism is integral to many contemporary development policies, it became more and more apparent that the Washington Consensus would not provide a miracle cure for development shortcomings. Policy proposals also increasingly recognised the importance of the development of health, education, and welfare policies for poverty alleviation and for the state more generally. These factors were reflected in the Sustainable Development Goals (see Box 8.4), launched in 2000 by the UN, which set out eight key development goals to be achieved by 2015. Moreover, greater emphasis has been placed on designing policies that address the structural and cultural realities of individual countries and on making public administration and service delivery more efficient and the legal systems more transparent and accountable.

## The flying geese theory of development

A more contemporary theory has emerged from the Asian experience and has proved influential in the development strategies of states in this region. Developed in the 1930s but gaining popular credence in the 1960s, this model refers to the pattern of development based upon the existence of a lead state (in this case, Japan), which operates as a lead for other developing states. The model stresses mutually supporting growth between these states based upon emulative learning.

The model stresses that, in this case, Asian states will catch up with the West via a regional hierarchical system of development where the production of commoditised components of value chains gradually moves along the hierarchy from more developed states to less developed states. This implies that as the lead state advances, it pushes labour-intensive activities down to other states. Then as these develop and lose their competitive advantage in cost-sensitive parts of the value chain, they are further shifted down to other less developed states. In Asia, the lead state is Japan, followed by the leading newly industrialised states, followed by the ASEAN states.

The driver of change within the model is the tendency of the lead state to instigate strategic change, which leads to the cascade effects mentioned. This is incentivised by rising labour costs and the technology transfer between these states that allows production capabilities to be transplanted across space. Thus, the model is very much a top-down model, though there is no presumption that these spillover effects amount to a trickle-down process between developed, emerging, and developing economies. In some sense, the model offers a restatement of old ideas through the logic of specialisation and differentiation, which is integral to the model.

## GLOBALISATION, PRODUCTION, AND DEVELOPMENT

Globalisation has changed the architecture of international production, with significant implications for developing countries. Pessimists argue that the opening of markets intensified competition, and the growing mobility of firms, lower wages and increase unemployment in developed countries while enabling the exploitation of developing world labour to continue. Optimists claim that globalisation is to be welcomed because it removes distortions in the world economy, enables firms to specialise, forces them to maximise efficiency, and, in the long term, facilitates improvements in the economies of developing countries.

Chapter 1 implies that the international economic integration that has taken place is not truly global in scope and that the intensification of trade flows and FDI affects a minority of developing countries only. However, the link between development and globalisation is about more than increases in trade and investment flows between developed and developing countries — as important as these are. It incorporates what Dicken describes as the 'functional integration of internationally dispersed activities'. In other words, international economic integration has facilitated the emergence of global manufacturing systems in which different parts of the production process are located in different parts of the world. These changes in production patterns have had a big influence on how developing countries interface with the rest of the world.

For many years, mass production, or 'Fordism', pioneered by Henry Ford in the automobile industry, was the most common form of production organisation. Mass production breaks down each part of the production process into basic tasks that are then performed repetitively by unskilled workers. In other words, Fordism relies on standardised assembly line techniques with clear demarcation of tasks. It is also a system that requires large amounts of capital, scale economies, and mass markets and is therefore not a viable industrialisation model for most developing countries.

Mass production methods have to some extent given way to more flexible production methods, which were also pioneered in the motor industry by Japanese car manufacturers and by Volvo in Sweden. The development of adaptable dies and tooling, for example, enabled the same equipment and machinery to be used to make a range of products rather than one product, resulting in batch and customised production. Flexibility was thus applied not only to manufacturing but also to marketing, as firms were able to tailor their production to specific niches or respond more quickly to changes in taste and fashion. This shift in production methodology also required changes in how the workforce was deployed. Rather than simply performing repetitive tasks on an assembly line, workers became members of teams responsible for all stages of the production process. This required multi-skilling and the empowerment of workers. Lean production and just-in-time management techniques also provided opportunities for cutting down on inventories and, hence, costs.

What does flexibility mean for developing countries? On the one hand, although flexible production does not require large-scale, homogenous production runs, the start-up costs of flexible production in terms of generic technology remain high, resulting in the need for large markets, although differentiated markets will do. On the other hand, flexibility has the potential to fragment production into smaller units, making it more suitable for smaller industries and workplaces.

The concept of global commodity chains, developed primarily by Gary Gereffi (Gereffi 1994 and Stallings 1995), draws on the mass production-flexibility dichotomy and also throws light on the development process. Global commodity chains refer to transnational production systems that link technological, organisational, and institutional networks for the development, production, and marketing of products. As such, they represent the emergence of global production systems or world factories, the practical manifestation of Dicken's view of functional integration across borders. In reality, these production systems do not cover the whole world but parts of it, resulting in the reservation by Hoogvelt (2001) of the term 'globalisation' for deepening rather than the widening of capitalist expansion, a process which corresponds to the intensification of the globalisation process in Chapter 2.

Each global commodity chain is unique, but, according to Gereffi, they have four main dimensions (Stallings 1995):

1.  A value-added chain linked across a range of relevant industries.

2.  Geographical dispersion of production and marketing networks of different sizes and types spanning national, regional, and global levels.

3.  Authority and power relationships between firms within the chain determine the allocation and flow of finance, materials, and human resources.

4.  An institutional framework that identifies how local, national, and international conditions and policies shape the globalisation process at each stage in the chain.

Gereffi then distinguishes between two main types of global commodity chains:

1.  *Producer-driven chains*: producer-driven chains are typical in capital- and technology-intensive industries such as automobiles, heavy machinery, computers, and aircraft. MNEs own most of the production system but not necessarily all of it; strategic alliances between rivals and the subcontracting of components are common. Indeed, most automobile producers maintain a complex and extensive network of component suppliers. In producer-driven chains, the MNE's headquarters exercise a large degree of control and coordination over all elements of the production process.

2.  *Buyer-driven chains*: buyer-driven chains are typically concerned with the production of consumer goods like footwear, clothing, toys, consumer electronics, and other household items — that is, industries that are labour, design, and marketing intensive. The companies concerned, which include large retailers and branded marketers such as Benetton, IKEA, Reebok, Nike, and The Gap, do not engage directly in production themselves but set up and manage decentralised networks across many, usually developing, countries. Entry barriers in these industries are not production-related but arise from product development, advertising, and marketing costs. Buyer-driven chains provide excellent examples of flexible production. By using electronic point of sale data, the retailer or branded company is in close touch with the consumer and

can closely monitor changes in consumer taste and fashion, thereby enabling production to respond rapidly to shifts in demand and keeping inventory, and therefore costs, down to a minimum.

The parent company in the buyer-driven model does not correspond to the traditional idea of a multinational, which owns and controls production through a network of subsidiaries and affiliates. Production in this model is almost entirely outsourced, enabling the parent company to avoid the risks of investment in production capacity. The parent company takes on the role of production broker; if part of the network becomes too costly, it can be replaced by other contractors relatively easily.

The competitive and cost pressures are intense for producers in buyer-driven chains. Production in early buyer-driven chains was frequently located in the NICs of Hong Kong, South Korea, and Taiwan, but as these countries developed (leading to higher wages) and became subject to import quotas in developed countries, a new form of managing the buyer-driven chains emerged: 'triangle manufacturing'. In this model, overseas buyers continue to place production orders with the manufacturer with whom they have a long-term outsourcing relationship. These manufacturers in turn outsource some or all of the production to affiliated production in low-wage countries like China, Indonesia, Vietnam, Guatemala, the Dominican Republic, etc. The NIC companies retain a foothold in manufacturing but in higher value-added production. As such, the role of NIC manufacturers in buyer-driven commodity chains has shifted from that of direct producers to that of production brokers for retailers and branded marketing companies. Higher costs have not cut them out of the network because the contractors have no production experience and rely on the NIC company to take responsibility for compliance with delivery schedules and quality requirements. However, as the countries and companies at the base of the triangle develop, it is probable that the 'middleman' role will disappear, and the contractors will again deal directly with the producers.

This analysis implies a hierarchy of activities within buyer-driven global commodity chains in which higher levels of development are associated with higher value-added activities. In the fashion industry, for example, exclusive designer products are produced in high-cost, developed countries like Italy and France, whereas inexpensive, high-volume garments like t-shirts are produced in low-cost countries like China, Sri Lanka, or Bangladesh. However, even this distinction is breaking down as high-end designers like Gucci and Armani source an increasing proportion of their products from China. Gereffi argues that the export role taken on by an individual country signifies their level of development and that development requires the ability to move towards more complex, higher value-added export functions. He identifies five rungs in the export development ladder:

- Primary commodity exports.
- Export-processing assembly operations.
- Component supply subcontracting.
- Original equipment manufacturing (OEM).
- Original brand manufacturing (OBM).

*Primary commodity exports:* the least developed countries depended overwhelmingly on the exports of one or two primary commodities, leaving them highly vulnerable to commodity price volatility. Indeed, over time, the terms of trade (the ratio of export prices to import prices – see above) have moved against these countries, requiring them to increase their commodity production to be able to buy the same quantity of imports (see above). The countries of sub-Saharan Africa, in particular, continue to be overly dependent on primary commodities and have barely moved beyond this stage of exporting.

*Export-processing assembly operations:* this form of exporting involves the assembly of manufactured products from imported components, often within export processing zones (EPZ), small areas with high-quality infrastructure allocated by governments for the development of export-oriented industries. Incentives are offered to companies to locate in the zone and to manufacture or assemble products from imported inputs and raw materials (often imported duty-free). EPZs sprang up in the 1960s in parts of Asia and Mexico. Most EPZs are currently located in Latin America, especially Mexico and Central America, the Caribbean, and Asia, and involve textiles, clothing, and electronic goods assembly. In Asia, the more advanced NICs have moved into higher-level manufacturing, but other Asian countries have taken up exporting processing assembly. EPZs are part of broader industrialisation strategies and offer a quick way to get started. However, their isolation from the rest of the economy renders linkages into the rest of the economy weak, thereby reducing their potential as motors of development.

*Component supply subcontracting:* component supply subcontracting involves the manufacture and export of components in middle-income developing countries, with final product assembly taking place in a developed country. This exporting role offers greater development potential than EPZs because it operates at a higher level of industrial sophistication, frequently entails technology transfer, and offers greater opportunities for generating links with local suppliers. This production role continues to be particularly important for Latin American countries, many of which produce parts for US and Japanese motor manufacturers. In East Asia, component supply subcontracting played an important role in the emergence of the electronics industry.

*Original equipment manufacturing (OEM):* OEM refers to the production of finished products by manufacturers in developing countries under contract to developed country retailers or branded marketers. In other words, OEM involves the production of products that are sold under another company's brand name. The OEM manufacturer must have the ability to interpret designs (hence the alternative name 'specification contracting') and source and manufacture the product in line with the client's price and quality requirements and according to tight delivery schedules. Given these heavy demands, OEM activity has involved only more advanced developing countries and has been central to the growth of East Asian economies. Constant demands by buyers for higher quality and new products have ensured that industrial and technical upgrading and the creation of a range of supportive industries have taken place, often with government assistance.

*Original brand manufacturing (OBM):* the drawbacks of OEM have encouraged a shift to original brand manufacturing. OEM producers face intense low-cost competition, but they do not have direct access to markets, the most profitable area of business. In order to overcome this, OBM companies establish and produce their own proprietary brand, and some companies engage in a mixture of OEM and OBM manufacturing. Garment manufacturers in Hong Kong, for example, continue to subcontract from developed-world retailers while establishing their own brand names and retail outlets. The most successful OBM companies manage the difficult task of establishing a brand beyond their region: Korea's Hyundai, for example, has become a respected brand in North American and European automobile markets, and Samsung and Goldstar have developed an international reputation in consumer electronics. Taiwanese companies have concentrated more on ICTs, with Acer, for example, selling their own brand of computer. Not all OBM producers are so successful, and some revert to OEM operations.

## CONCLUSION

The exclusion of developing countries from the globalisation process is frequently regarded as a testament to the iniquity of the globalisation process by many anti-globalisation NGOs and as justification for resisting and protesting against initiatives taken by international institutions to promote development. However, although developed countries criticise the dominance of the agenda of major institutions and strongly resist individual policy initiatives of international institutions, developing countries themselves tend not to join in the anti-globalisation rhetoric but rather strive to gain greater access to the globalisation process and engage more positively in it.

## KEY POINTS

- Development is often neglected in international business analysis, but successful development creates markets and business opportunities.
- Development policy now recognises the complexity of the development process and is moving away from a 'one model fit all approach' to one which takes account of good governance and the specific social, political, cultural, and economic circumstances of individual countries.
- The most successful countries in terms of development have tended to be those that have developed a positive approach to engagement with the rest of the world, initially in terms of trade promotion and latterly in terms of policy to encourage FDI.
- Commodity chain analysis, especially progression through higher value-added export activities, is a useful indicator of how business and economic development are interdependent and how far a country has developed.

## DISCUSSION QUESTIONS

1. Many developing countries have not prospered during the current globalisation era. Does this require a retreat from the globalisation process or greater engagement with it?

2. In your view, which of the major development theories has been the most useful in explaining the development process? Justify your answer.

3. Discuss the usefulness of commodity chain analysis in explaining the link between production and development.

4. Research the Millennium Development Goals with a view to assessing success in achieving them.

## ACTIVITIES

1. Research a company that maintains a buyer-driven commodity chain (e.g., Nike, Benetton, and The Gap) and assess whether and how it makes a contribution to development in the country in which it operates.

2. Research the experience of sub-Saharan Africa and identify the obstacles it faces regarding development. If this exercise is undertaken in preparation for a seminar, students can compare and pool their findings with research from different countries.

3. You are a consultant hired to prepare a report for an African country striving to develop. The government is anxious to attract foreign investment to help with its development strategy but is finding it difficult to do so. Your report should analyse why the government is encountering such problems and make recommendations as to how it can make itself more attractive to foreign investors. You may tackle this in a number of ways, including by identifying sectors on which the government may wish to focus or, conversely, by giving advice on the general attractiveness of the country for investors.

## SUGGESTED FURTHER READINGS

Brautigam, D. (2009). *The dragon's gift: The real story of China in Africa*, Oxford: Oxford University Press.

Broadman, H. (2008). China and India go to Africa: New deals in the developing world. *Foreign Affairs, 87*(2), 95–109.

Buckley, P. (2009). The impact of the global factory on economic development. *Journal of World Business, 44*(2), 131–143.

Chari, S., & Corbridge, S. (2008). *The development reader*, New York: Routledge.

Gereffi, G., & Korzeniewicz, M. (1994). *Commodity chains and global capitalism*, London and Westport: Praeger.

Haynes, J. (2008). *Development studies*, London: Routledge.

Henderson, J. (2009). *The political economy of East Asian development*, London: Routledge.

Hoogvelt, A. (2001). *Globalisation and the postcolonial world: The new political economy of development*, Basingstoke: Palgrave.

Luiz, J. (2009). Institutions and economic performance: Implications for African development. *Journal of International Development, 21*(1), 58–75.

Oetzel, J., & Doh, J. (2008). MNEs and development: A review and reconceptualization. *Journal of World Business, 44*(2), 108–120.

Padayachee, V. (Ed.). (2009). *The political economy of Africa*, London: Routledge.

Ross, A., Forsyth, D., & Huq, M. (2008). *Development economics*, London: McGraw Hill Education.

Special Issue (2008). Management in Africa in the global context. *Journal of African Business, 9*(1).

Stallings, B. (Ed.). (1995). *Global change, regional response: The new international context of development*, Cambridge: Cambridge University Press.

Stiglitz, J., & Charlton, A. (2005). *Fair trade for all: How trade can promote development*, Oxford: Oxford University Press.

Todaro, M. (2009). *Economic development*, 10th edn, Harlow: Addison Wesley/Pearson Education.

UNCTAD (2008). *Least developed countries, 2008 report*, Geneva: UNCTAD.

UNCTAD. (2023). UNCTADStat. https://unctadstat.unctad.org/

Williamson, J. (2000). What should the World Bank think about the Washington Consensus? *World Bank Research Observer, 15*(2), 251–264.

# PART III

# THE MULTINATIONAL FIRM

While states set the context for the development of international business, it is the firm that is at the centre of the everyday interaction that shapes the practicalities of international commercial interaction. In this case, the commercial entity seeks to plot a path for long-term commercial sustainability through market positioning within and across the domestic market where it seeks a presence. Conventionally, the focus of the analysis within this domain has been the MNC. While these continue to be of importance, there is a growing recognition of a process where internationalisation has become an important point for firms of all sizes. These themes are reflected throughout all of the chapters within this part of the text.

Initially, the chapter explores the issues of market selection and entry. This is the main issue of the micro-macro interface that has been addressed in previous sections. Thereafter, the book moves on to address the MNC itself and seeks to address the assorted issues involved in its evolution. In this case, the work will overlap with themes addressed within Chapter 2. The salience of globalisation for smaller businesses has been one of the more important innovations in international business over the past three decades, and this is addressed in Chapter 11. The final chapter of this section looks at how businesses have to adapt to the diversity of their marketplaces within their operations to reflect divergent cultures within the global system.

DOI: 10.4324/9781315184500-11

# CHAPTER 9

# MARKET SELECTION AND ENTRY

## OBJECTIVES

By the end of this chapter, the student should be able to:

- Understand the main issues involved in market selection.
- Comprehend that the selection decision is based on an assessment of firm-specific and environmental factors.
- Comprehend the major market entry modes.
- Differentiate between equity and non-equity modes of market entry.

## INTRODUCTION

The previous three chapters have highlighted core trends in the main groups of market within the global economy. With awareness of the main markets, firms face two core choices: what markets to enter and how to enter them. This involves, first, a process of market selection where the firm will choose to operate. As we demonstrate, this reflects an assessment of market risks relative to the rewards anticipated from such a decision. After this decision has been taken, the next step for the business is to choose how to enter the chosen market. Again, the mode of entry reflects the relative risk of entry and the desired degree of control and commitment by the firm to the chosen market. This chapter will explore these themes in international strategy. Initially, the chapter will explore the main forms of risks and opportunities attached to individual states, underlining that international strategy is a complex process of strategic change based on a degree of environmental scanning. Thereafter, the chapter will assess the relative merits of the alternative entry modes.

DOI: 10.4324/9781315184500-12

## INTERNATIONAL MARKET SELECTION

In a global economic system, the process of progressive liberalisation opens up new opportunities for businesses to tap into new markets and/or resources from which they were previously excluded. Alongside these emergent opportunities are emergent risks, reflecting that operational and/or marketing opportunities can also create new risks for the business. There is also the fact that opportunities and risks occur symmetrically across the system. Thus, the fact that a market becomes open does not always equate with an opportunity. The result is that the process of internationalisation has to be preceded by a scanning of the environment by the business to assess both the opportunities and the risks created by a more open commercial system.

The conventional understanding of market selection (the term market is used here not simply in a strict marketing sense but also in terms of operational issues where the firm will engage with resource markets) is in terms of geography. The economic map of the global economy is one where markets are territorialised and compartmentalised into what is largely a series of state-based markets. In this sense, market selection and entry are based on what part (or parts) of the global economic space to enter. Such territorial segmentation has become increasingly challenged as globalisation erodes the relevance of this compartmentalisation to allow firms to identify cross-state market segments. It is also the case – in the online world – that markets (i.e., customers) can seek suppliers, therefore turning the market selection process on its head (Gaston-Breton and Martín 2011). These are issues that will be dealt with in later chapters; this chapter will examine market selection in the conventional sense (i.e., the state-based method).

IMaS is based on the implied recognition of firm ignorance to the extent that the firm needs to undertake research to overcome such limited knowledge (Papadopoulos and Martín 2011). In theory, firms face multiple opportunities but have to access information regarding the market(s) as a means of filtering the relativity of opportunity or risk across these markets (Andersen and Buvik 2002). This implies two problems in International Market Selection (IMaS):

* Information scarcity: there is too little information available to allow rational IMaS to be undertaken.
* Information overload: there is too much information, which may be contradictory and inhibit rational decision-making with regard to IMaS.

These points also draw attention to the firm's capabilities and their ability to assimilate and understand the market information that is being generated and to fully comprehend which selection criteria are the most salient to their strategic orientation. This can vary by the firm's experience of the internationalisation process, by size, whether public or private, and by industry.

All of this suggests that the IMaS process is, in practical terms, difficult. This is due to:

* The need to understand cultures that are unfamiliar to the firm.
* The need to comprehend how to segment within a population given the sheer diversity of states and sub-nationalities and cultures within them.

- The number of states that could be considered commercially viable has ballooned over the past decades as communism has fallen, emerging economies have 'emerged' and developing states 'develop'.
- Information, especially within emerging or developing economies, can be very patchy and sometimes unreliable.
- Most firms do not use a formal, systematic method to assess market opportunities.

Nonetheless, in spite of these difficulties, IMaS is vital to international business as it seeks to militate against market diversity, the need to improve performance, enhance its position, and improve strategy implementation. In short, the need to grow to sustain the business model will drive the need to enter markets but to do so in a state of ignorance risks exposing the firms to unknown hazards.

## Firm factors in IMaS

While there can be little doubt that the core driver of the process of IMaS is the environmental scanning involved in country-based risk analysis, one cannot dismiss firm-based factors within this process (Malhotra and Papadopoulos 2007). These have to some degree been mentioned above, but it is worth more fully exploring these factors as a means of fully understanding the complexity of the process of IMaS (Papadopoulos and Martín Martín 2011). This reflects that environmental scanning alone cannot fully explain IMaS, as the process has to match country-specific firm capabilities, which will vary across firms. Generally, the main firm-based factors shaping IMaS are as follows:

## Degree of internationalisation and internationalisation experience

It has been widely recognised that firms are on an experience curve with regards to internationalisation and that much of the ease of moving into new markets is created by pre-existing experience. This can, to some degree, involve debates over psychic distance and the degree of cultural similarity between the home market, pre-existing markets, and the market targeted. There is also the fact that a firm with a large amount of experience will have embedded knowledge with regards to the challenges of managing the process, and in IMaS, which can be applied across multiple markets. These can help the firm overcome (to some degree) the information and operational problems involved in IMaS.

## Size and number of resources

In entering a new market, the firm is on a learning curve. Given the likelihood of incumbents and/or the high cost of establishing a presence, short-term operational losses are to be expected. The ability of the firm to select, enter, and stay in the market will be key to the IMaS decision, with large-scale enterprises being more able to absorb the financial implications of the process than SMEs.

## Type of industry/nature of business

Intuitively, the amount of risk attached to an IMaS is going to be directly linked to the cost of entry and the extent to which any costs incurred are retrievable or sunk. This will vary across markets. It is evident that some industries that require large economies of scale to establish a presence are likely to face higher risks in market entry. Thus, if an IMaS choice goes wrong, it could, in extreme cases, create an existential crisis for the business. For other firms (notably those online), where market servicing can be done virtually with minimal resource commitment beyond marketing spend, the risks will be considerably less.

## Internationalisation goals

The alignment between IMaS and what the firm wants from internationalisation is central to the process. A market might be selected not because of simple attractiveness but because the firm 'strategically' needs a presence in that market to be a credible competitor. Similarly, smaller firms may have very limited internationalisation goals and, as such, will not treat the process of IMaS as an existential one.

## Existing networks of relationships

To some extent, firms militate against the risks involved in international market entry by tapping into the knowledge of key partners who already have experience in the targeted market. These firms could be suppliers or customers, but the good relations between them can aid in the IMaS process.

## Country factors

There are a multitude of assessments that have been undertaken to assess the risks of market selection. The easiest and simplest has been the conventional PEST analysis, which assesses the political, economic, social-cultural, and technological factors of a country to assess the attractiveness or otherwise of the territory as a place for businesses to become engaged. Evidently, these themes are evident across many of the chapters within this book, and, as such, there is little need to revisit many of these themes in great depth at this juncture. As such, the country-based themes engendered within the IMaS process will be delimited into two broader categories: generic and specific characteristics (Andersen and Buvik 2002). The difference between these characteristics is their degree of measurability, with the former being easily measurable with ease of access to the data and knowledge which can easily be acted upon. The latter are considerably opaquer, with raw data upon them being much more difficult to access and therefore act upon (Sakarya et al. 2007). However, this does not downplay its significance, as these characteristics are highly relevant to the IMaS decision.

## Generic influences of IMaS

These generic factors include what many would consider the most obvious factors that would influence the market selection decision. The following list is not exhaustive but is suggestive of the main generic factors that will shape the IMaS process.

- Location: how close the target market is to the home market and geographic proximity shape transport costs and therefore influence desirability. Location could also be important, as geographically close states can also share other common traits such as climate and terrain that can also shape market attractiveness.
- Language: marketing and other business operations work through the medium of language, and the ease with which a company can operate in a location will be shaped by its adaptability to this feature. Fluency means not just ease of communication but also insights into the culture.
- Political systems: normally, it has been assumed that the more politically plural a system is, the better the state is to conduct business in, as this normally translates into a more open and fair commercial system. This has been evident in much of the literature on state competitiveness. The rise of China and the relative failure of India have tended to cast doubt on the robustness of this relationship. As such, there is an increased case that what matters most is political stability in the IMaS process rather than plurality.
- Demographic factors: the characteristics of the local population will tell the firm a great deal with regards to its potential. In short, the higher the degree of non-working population, the less attractive it is. However, in wealthy countries that are under demographic change (see Chapter 14), this link changes as fewer children and more pensioners will influence the market potential for specific types of products.
- Economic factors: the generic rule in this instance is that market attractiveness will be a function of the rate of economic growth and development. The faster these are occurring, the faster these states are moving towards economies based on mass consumption and production. A core benchmark in this case would be the rise of a middle class within an economy, as this will signify more complex consumption patterns.
- Industrial structure: the business population of the state is important as it indicates the maturity of the state's commercial system. Issues such as local entrepreneurship, the degree of monopoly control, the power of incumbents, the extent of subsistence agriculture, and the maturity of business networks all offer insights as to the local business structure and to the capability of the potential entrant to find a position within it.
- Technology: the technological sophistication of a state and the extent to which advanced technologies are embedded throughout its socio-economic systems is a core benchmark offering an indication of the extent to which customers will absorb information, accept new products, and adapt to new techniques. This is also related to a state's research and development spending and innovative potential.
- Social organisation: it is important for the business to understand how local social systems are organised. This is reflected in the relative importance of the nuclear and/or extended family. This can affect purchasing decisions as well as issues such as disposable income.
- Religion: the customs linked to the religious system within a state have the potential to influence both what type of products consumers will buy and when they will buy them. This can be linked to products that adhere to pre-established religious norms (such as Islamic finance) and holidays. Religion can also influence operations though workplace behaviour and practice.

- Education: this benchmark is important for what it tells the firm with regards to the skill set within a set. Issues such as level of literacy and a broad-based education system indicate that the workforce is adaptable to shift trends and has the ability to be re-skilled and/or easily trained. The higher the skills set, the more time the entrant has to spend on training its employees. Firms also need to understand the education system and how it compares across states.

## Specific factors

These are characteristics of a state that are more tactful and less readily understood at a distance, and which often can only really be fully appreciated by long-term engagement (Malhotra and Papadopoulos 2007). Getting information on these factors is difficult, and acting on this information can only be done with sensitivity. Despite this difficulty, this information is vital to the IMaS process as it reflects the intimacies of the local market with which the firm must engage. The main characteristics to be understood are as follows:

- Culture: while this has been dealt with extensively elsewhere within this book, it is important to stress that, in terms of IMaS, culture tells the firm a lot about the nature of the conditions and forms of production and consumption within a state.
- Lifestyles: this reflects localised consumption habits as well as practices that can have a direct bearing on production. This can reflect factors such as diet, attitude towards leisure, and/or work ethic.
- Attitudes and personality: these are both complex but reflect how business activities within a state can reflect local idiosyncrasies such as the tendency to bargain or the value of specific status symbols, which can shape the consumption decision.

Evidently, in a chapter of this length, a full examination of the nuances of IMaS is impossible. What is also evident is that this process is complex, which underscores that IMaS is undertaken under conditions of a certain degree of ignorance. It is also apparent that firms continue to proactively engage with international markets; the issue of what markets to enter grows increasingly important (Gaston-Breton and Martín Martín 2011). Of course, this is but one issue in the process of international strategy, for once a decision has been made about what markets to enter, the consequent decision is how to enter (Sakarya et al. 2007).

## FOREIGN MARKET ENTRY MODES

The nature of the mode in business terms is to define how something happens. In this case, mode refers to the method of engaging with international markets. The supposition is that mode is derived from a proactive approach to engagement in an international business environment. Figure 9.1 sets out two general categories of market entry that reflect different levels of engagement with foreign markets (Hill et al. 1990). Types of market entry are divided into equity- and non-equity-based modes. Each method has its

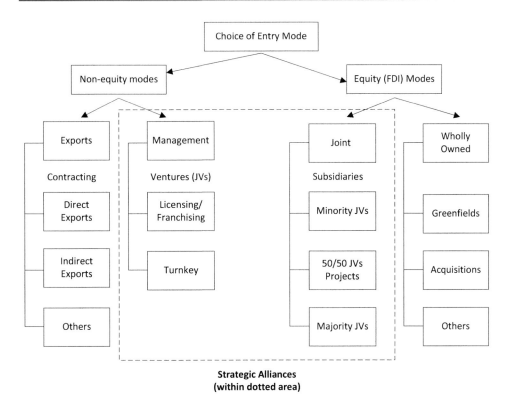

**FIGURE 9.1** Types of entry modes

own strengths and weaknesses (outlined below) and is a response to the specific circumstances of a company (Brouthers 1995). Contractual methods, for example, tend to be for specific periods of time, although these can be quite long. Equity-based methods, on the other hand, do not always entail no specific time restrictions, although equity stakes can be sold, and offer the company more control and a much more direct engagement in a foreign market than many contractual modes.

## Non-equity entry modes

Non-equity entry modes are based upon market involvement, with no direct physical or financial involvement within the target markets (Agarwal and Ramaswami 1992). These methods often involve entry from a distance (exporting) or via the use of intermediaries on either a contract or non-contract basis. The major forms of non-equity modes of entry are as below:

### Exporting

Foreign market entry via exporting is traditionally, and according to the Uppsala model, one of the first methods firms use to internationalise their activities. Exporting is relatively straightforward and less risky than other forms of internationalisation and offers a relatively cheap and simple exit strategy if required. Exporting is not entirely risk-free, however; exporters still have to contend with exchange rate volatility, for example, but exposure to political shocks and risks is less extensive than for firms that have physically invested in foreign countries.

Exporting is conventionally divided into two categories: indirect and direct exporting. In the former, responsibility for carrying out the export function, including the completion of export documentation and distribution, is delegated to third parties. The third parties, or intermediaries, take various forms, including

- Export houses: export houses buy products and sell them abroad on their own account, and the producer may not even be aware that its products have been sold abroad.
- Confirming and buying houses: confirming and buying houses are paid on a commission basis by foreign buyers to bring them into contact with sellers.
- Piggybacking: piggybacking occurs when the exporter (the rider) pays to export its product through a distribution system that has already been set up by an established firm (the carrier) in the chosen foreign market. It can be difficult for piggybackers to find appropriate partners; the ideal combination is complementary rather than competing products, as there is a danger that the carrier may not give the same priority to the rider's product as its own.

The advantages of indirect exporting are that the whole export process is handled by a third party. It requires no international experience or knowledge and avoids many of the costs of setting up an in-house direct exporting operation. On the downside, indirect exporting reduces the producer's control over the export process and yields little or no knowledge about local markets, a factor that is normally instrumental in increasing sales to particular markets in the long term. This is particularly true for exports conducted through export houses and holds to a lesser extent for other forms of indirect exporting. Indirect exporting also implies the absence of after-sales service, a factor that can have a negative effect on a firm's reputation or on future sales. In view of all these factors, indirect exporting is a technique most commonly used by smaller, inexperienced, or occasional exporters.

Direct exporting, as its name suggests, is more proactive and hands-on than indirect exporting and involves an enterprise distributing and selling its own products into a foreign market. This requires greater in-house expertise regarding markets and exporting technicalities. As with indirect exporting, direct exporting can be done in various ways. Direct selling involves sales representatives directly employed by the exporting company, either from the home country (typically used to sell high-value items such as ships or aeroplanes) or domestic representatives based in the target market. In the former case, representatives may lack local knowledge or language skills.

Direct exporters also use agents as direct representatives in foreign markets. Such agents are paid on commission and may be employed on an exclusive, semi-exclusive, or non-exclusive basis. This is frequently a successful strategy, but in the latter two cases, care needs to be taken that the freedom to sell the products of other companies does not result in a conflict of interest for the agent.

The most developed approach to direct exporting involves the establishment of a local sales office or affiliate in a particular market. This is the most expensive option and requires the greatest degree of local knowledge. Ideally, such affiliates are staffed by both home and host country personnel; the former bring knowledge of the company, and the latter contribute in terms of local and market knowledge. This exporting strategy marks a bigger and longer-term commitment to a specific market; it is able to accommodate growth and makes contact with the customer and the development of an effective after-sales service much easier.

## Licencing

Licencing involves the granting of permission in the form of a licence by the owner (the licensor) of a proprietary product or process to the licensee to exploit the licensor's intellectual property in a particular region and/or over a specific time period. The intellectual property in question includes patents, copyrights, trademarks, and increasingly management and technical assistance and product upgrades and improvements. In return, the licensor receives payment, usually an up-front payment and royalties, from the licensee.

Licencing is an attractive, albeit limited, form of market entry and is most common in high-technology and R&D-intensive sectors such as pharmaceuticals, chemicals, and industrial and defence equipment. It requires little or no commitment of resources by licensors while enabling them to exploit their research and development achievements through the generation of royalty income. Licencing also enables firms to avoid restrictive host country regulations regarding their entry into foreign markets. The licensor benefits from the licensee's local knowledge and gains a presence in a foreign market more quickly than through the establishment of subsidiaries or via equity joint ventures.

However, licencing does not provide a basis for further expansion into a market. Indeed, it is possible that licencing can create competitors for the licensor by handing over core competencies to potential competitors. Japanese companies, for example, became market leaders in the colour television field by licencing the technology when it was new in the 1960s. They were then able to adapt the technology and overtake its originators within a relatively short space of time. Also, the sale of a technology licence to a lower-cost producer creates the possibility that the licensee becomes a serious competitor in markets in which the licensor is currently strong.

## Franchising

Licencing and franchising are conceptually similar: in franchising, rather than buying access to patented technology, the franchisee buys the right to use the franchiser's name or trademark. Broadly speaking, there are two types of franchising. The first, often referred to as 'first generation franchising', is the more arm's length approach of the two and involves activities such as soft drink bottling and automobile and petrol retailing.

The second approach, known either as 'second generation franchising' or 'business format franchising', involves the purchase and transfer of a more comprehensive business package in which the franchisee not only gains access to brand names and trademarks but also receives extensive instructions on how to operate the franchise, management training, and, occasionally, financial support. Second-generation franchises are common in service industries like the hotel, fast food, and vehicle rental sectors. Well-known examples with international scope include Avis, Baskin Robbins, The Body Shop International, Burger King, Coca-Cola, Domino's Pizza, Hertz, Holiday Inn, Howard Johnson's, KFC, McDonald's, Pizza Hut, Pronuptia, TGI Friday's, Wendy's, and Wimpy's.

The establishment of franchises in foreign locations can pose significant challenges given the requirement that, as a result of the utilisation of the brand, the franchised product should be as indistinguishable as possible from the product sold in the home base. For example, when Pizza Hut established its first outlet in Moscow during Glasnost, it encountered severe problems sourcing the appropriate type and quality of cheese within Russia. In order to solve supply problems in Thailand, McDonald's itself engaged in potato production there.

Franchising is an attractive internationalisation option for service-based industries. It enables them to establish a presence in a new market quickly without significant direct investment, and it uses a standard marketing approach to help create a global image. Franchising also yields the usual benefits of market entry with a local partner – that is, local knowledge, especially in relation to dealing with local and national level public officials and authorities. Although the degree of control varies from operation to operation, the franchiser in business format franchises exerts much more control over its franchisees than in first-generation franchises; it must do so to protect and promote its global image. With over 70 per cent of its restaurants operated on a franchise basis, McDonald's has followed this strategy successfully for over forty years. A key component of its success has been the Hamburger University, which has its main campus in Illinois and branches in the UK, Germany, Japan, and Australia, and which trains its own employees and those of its franchisees in its philosophy and standards.

From the franchisee's perspective, franchising enables them to tap into the franchiser's goodwill, reputation, merchandising, centralised advertising, and promotion, and provides support in the actual operation of the franchise, including central purchasing. Above all, the franchisee avoids many of the risks of start-up businesses by buying into a proven business idea.

## CASE STUDY 9.1: MCDONALD'S GLOBAL EXPANSION

McDonald's is one of the world's leading fast food retail outlets. Founded in 1940 in the US, the business started with food based on the principles of the production line. On this basis, the company has engaged in a rapid process of internationalisation and serves over 70 million customers a day in around 120 countries. This rapid pace of international expansion was enabled through a mix of strategies where any restaurant can be run by a franchisee, an affiliate, or directly by the company. On that basis, the main revenue earner for the business comes from a mix of revenues generated by the franchise system (rents, fees, and royalties) and sales generated directly by the company. By 2017, the firm operated over 36,000 restaurants globally, of which 80 per cent were franchised. However – despite the predominance of franchises as a form of market entry – 60 per cent of all revenue comes from company-operated restaurants. Moreover, the company is still heavily dependent on developed markets, with the US accounting for over a quarter of all revenue and 50 per cent of all revenue from franchised operations. Thus, despite the headline figure of operating extensively – in practical terms – McDonald's depends on four of five major markets. As these markets are low-growth mature segments, the business recognises a need to expand into those locations of perceived potential.

The use of the franchise-based system for international business has allowed the business to undergo rapid internationalisation without the high degree of risk associated with such a process. The firm is able to attain rapid market presence without having to endure the high capital requirements normally associated with such a process. It has also allowed, where appropriate, the firm to tap into local knowledge to ensure that product offerings can be differentiated across states to reflect local tastes and preferences. In this sense, it does seek to put the local owner in charge and control of the business. Against this is the fact that over a third of all franchised restaurants are in the core US market, where there is likely to be minimal variation in product offerings and in the mature developed markets, where product differentials are also very slight. This does, however, offer the firm greater control over product and service quality. The franchises tend, as the figures above suggest, to be in less well-performing localities, suggesting that while the strategy enables reach, it is not central to revenue generation. This may not simply reflect a desire by the company to retain control of the more profitable locations but also that it may seek to use franchises in newer, riskier markets where – despite the less lucrative performance – the opportunities presented by the franchisee and the local entrepreneurial culture.

## QUESTION

What is the strategic value of the franchise-based form of market entry?

## Management contracting

Contractual agreements (or management contracting) are popular in the hotel sector, public utilities, health care, transportation, agriculture, and mining. In the international context, it entails the supply of management functions to a client in another country. A wide range of such functions, including general, financial, personnel, and production management, can be traded in this way. After the 1979 oil price shock, when oil revenues boosted economic development, management contracts were common in the Middle East, a region that at the time lacked indigenous management skills and capabilities to manage this development. A related category of foreign market entry concerns the provision of technical services across borders, a practice that has become increasingly popular in the maintenance and management of computer and telecommunication networks and has proved a fruitful vehicle for the development of India's call centre and software industries.

Management contracting maximises the value of the management skills of its service sector and increases the organisation's reputation and experience with limited risk and expenditure. The major benefit for the client comes not only from access to proven skills and expertise but also from the transfer of skills and learning resulting from the contract. Indeed, a central part of many contracts involves management training of the local workforce with a view to localisation of management at some future date and the avoidance of long-term reliance on third parties for key functions. The danger for contractors is that they are potentially training up their future rivals and competitors.

## Turnkey operations

A turnkey operation entails the construction of an operating facility under contract that is then transferred to the owner, who only has to 'turn the key' to enter the facility and begin operations when the facility is complete. Turnkey contracts are used in the construction of large infrastructure or industrial development projects such as power plants, dams, airports, oil refineries, roads, railways, seaports, telecommunication systems, etc. Given their size, only relatively few companies are able to undertake such projects: companies like Bechtel, Fluor, ABB, Brown, and Root and the Hyundai Group, for example, have signed many turnkey contracts, although smaller companies do get opportunities to participate as part of consortia or as sub-contractors.

Many turnkey projects are set up in developing economies that have urgent infrastructure and industrialisation needs. The client is usually the government or a government agency, and contracts are often awarded not only on a commercial but also on a political basis. French companies, for example, tend to do well in Francophone Africa. Increasingly, given their demands on the public purse, such large-scale projects are increasingly being built according to one of three variants of the turnkey model: BOOs (build-own-operate), BOTs (build-operate-transfer), and BOOTs (build-own-operate-transfer). The names of these models are self-explanatory. For example, in the case of BOTs, the contractor will build the facility, operate it for a period of time (usually 15–30 years), during which the contractor hopes to reap a return on the investment, before handing the facility over to the client. Such contracts frequently benefit from low-cost project finance from national or international agencies like the European Investment Bank, the Asian Development Bank, or the World Bank and from home government export credit agencies such as the US's Export-Import Bank.

BOOs, BOTs, and BOOTs have two major advantages for the host country:

1. A reduced burden on public finances: payment for a project comes in part from its revenues in the initial years of operation.

2. Access to high-quality engineering and management skills is a factor that contributes to the efficient operation of power stations, oil refineries, etc. However, there is a danger that, as the handover date approaches, incentives for the operator to maintain the facility are reduced.

These projects pose major challenges for the contractor, including

1. The type of project involved means they are often located in inhospitable or remote regions and are frequently subject to cost overruns.
2. BOOs, BOTs, and BOOTs are uncharted territory; these contracts only became commonplace in the 1990s, and as of yet, there are few examples of the transfer of BOTs and BOOTs back to the original client.
3. Given the notoriously difficult task of forecasting revenue on large-scale infrastructure projects over the long run, there is clearly a risk that returns will not live up to expectations.
4. There is a danger that participation in consortia or close cooperation with local companies will create future competitors for the contractor.

## EQUITY MODES

Compared to the above, these forms of market entry are based on the firm taking a direct equity or financial stake in the target market. The major forms of equity modes of market entry are as follows:

### Joint ventures

A joint venture is a long-term alliance in which each member has an equity stake and exercises control and influence over decision-making. Many joint ventures involve the establishment of a separate legal entity for a specific purpose, thereby creating a new identity. In other cases, joint ventures involve a degree of asset swapping. However, a joint venture falls short of a merger, as these involve the combination of all the assets of the partners involved. The organisational structure, membership, and control mechanisms within joint ventures vary according to the objectives and circumstances of each case. For example, joint venture partners can be private firms or public sector organisations. In some cases, the partnership may be equal in terms of equity participation and control, whereas in others, one party may have a majority share. What each party brings to the joint venture also varies; for example, some partners will be strong in technology, others in resources, and others in market knowledge.

In general, joint ventures enable partners to achieve objectives that are difficult to achieve independently. Joint ventures can offer more rapid and successful entry into a new location than trying to enter it alone. These benefits may spring from a partner's local knowledge, the presence of existing distribution channels, or the increased likelihood of a successful tender because of the presence of a local partner. In some instances, joint ventures have been formed because of restrictions on FDI. Although such instances are declining as restrictions on FDI are increasingly lifted, joint ventures remain popular. The involvement of a foreign partner or partners in joint ventures can bring access to proprietary technology or accelerate the process of management learning for the local partner.

Joint ventures also bring together different and complementary resources and skills; this may involve the marriage of one or two technologies or the coming together of an innovative technology with the appropriate capital or production facilities to exploit it. Joint ventures can also yield economies of scale and scope and enable partners to share costs and risks, an important factor in capital- and technology-intensive industries.

Joint ventures are more likely to be successful when there is agreement about long-term objectives and strategic direction. Within this framework, joint venture members must be clear about the type and quantity of resources each brings to the project, the organisation and breakdown of responsibilities, and the distribution of benefits. Many joint ventures fail because one or more of the above conditions are not met or because differences in management style and culture make the smooth running of the operation difficult or impossible.

## Mergers and acquisitions (M&As)

A merger with or the acquisition of a company located overseas provides a rapid way of fully engaging in a foreign market. Potential benefits of M&As include immediate access to plants, equipment, personnel, goodwill, brand names, distribution channels, and established networks of suppliers and customers – key assets that need to be painstakingly built up in the case of greenfield investment. In addition, unlike greenfield investment, M&As do not require the development of new capacity. Nor do they create new competition, an important factor for sectors already operating at or near full capacity.

On the less positive side, the success rate for M&As is not high. For example, equipment inherited in an acquisition may be obsolete, or at least in need of attention, whereas greenfield investment offers opportunities to begin operations with the latest technology. The industrial relations situation in an acquired firm may be troubled, a probable scenario given the uncertainty created within firms that are the subject of an acquisition. However, even if the acquired assets are in good condition, M&As still require major efforts to integrate both operations, including systems and personnel. The merger of two firms always involves the integration of two different corporate cultures, but the challenges are even greater in the case of international M&As that are also heavily influenced by divergent national cultures.

Two forces underpin the general trend towards more and bigger cross-border mergers and acquisitions:

1. Globalisation: the removal of barriers to trade and production encourages firms to reconfigure their patterns of production, marketing, and other functions to encourage greater efficiency. For example, why maintain five separate production sites when one bigger production unit could service all five markets?

2. Regional integration: regional integration (see Chapter 5) gives rise to similar considerations as globalisation but on a regional scale. Significantly, the EU, the world's most deeply integrated region, experienced a significant increase in cross-border mergers after the launch of the SEM programme.

## Greenfield investment

Along with mergers and acquisitions, greenfield investment represents the final link in the establishment chain. Greenfield investment, the construction of an overseas subsidiary or production facility from scratch, entails the greatest degree of commitment and involvement in a foreign location. The choice of greenfield investment over an acquisition in a particular location may be made because of the inherent benefits of the former (see below) or simply because there is no purchase candidate available. In the transition economies of Central and Eastern Europe, for example, privatisation provided opportunities for investment in a wide range of existing companies, but for some investors, there was no suitable candidate available. Motor manufacturers viewed the region, given its relatively cheap but skilled labour, as a potentially fruitful investment location. Although Volkswagen was able to link up with Skoda in the Czech Republic, General Motors, interested in Poland as an investment location, had no alternative but to engage in greenfield investment there because of the lack of domestic auto producers.

Unlike M&As, greenfield investment provides a clean slate with no inherited debts or other problems from the acquired partner and allows for the introduction of the most modern and up-to-date building, plants, equipment, and technology, as opposed to the obsolete or substandard equipment that a freshly acquired partner can bring. The workforce of an acquired company is often demoralised and has to be introduced to new working practices. Nissan's greenfield investment in its UK plant in Sunderland occurred in a region with a large labour surplus and an engineering tradition, albeit not in the motor industry. It was thus possible for Nissan to recruit suitable staff and introduce them to its own corporate culture. Greenfield investment also often attracts investment incentives from the host country's government, anxious to attract new jobs.

On the downside, building a new operation from scratch can be time-consuming and require extensive and, often, frustrating engagement with the local planning authorities. Indeed, the company needs to familiarise itself with many new laws and regulations, ranging from employment to taxation law and from the environment to import and export regulations. Even though a greenfield investor does not have to overcome resistance to changes in corporate culture (as can happen in an acquired firm), it can still encounter major national cultural hurdles. For example, when Disney established its theme park near Paris, it initially reportedly found it difficult to bridge the gap between its American culture and philosophy (in large part, what Disney was selling) and the local French culture of its employees and customers (see Tesco case study).

## Strategic Alliances

As highlighted in Figure 9.3, strategic alliances can cross the boundaries between equity and non-equity modes of market entry. Thus, alliances can be contractual (including comarketing, research, and development, etc.), which require relatively low levels of commitment and may be of limited scope and duration. Equity-based alliances involve a higher level of commitment and can include strategic investment (where one firm takes a stake in another firm) or a joint venture (where a new independent entity is formed whose equity is owned by a minimum of two partners). It is important to stress that not all strategic alliances are joint ventures, as alliances can involve two firms hitching up without creating a separate corporate entity.

A strategic alliance is an agreement between two or more independent firms to increase their level of interdependency via a cooperative agreement. The alliance is based on partners pooling part of their activities as a means of enhancing their market positioning while sustaining separate corporate identities. These alliances can be driven either by the desire for organisational learning or by skill substitutions. Thus, these act as a form of market entry where the alliance acts as a learning device for the entrant, especially where the partners have better skills or resources regarding operations within the target market. While strategic alliances should enhance knowledge, they are not a risk-free mode of market entry; partners have to be carefully chosen as their actions could simultaneously be both cooperative and competitive. Generally, for an alliance to be stable, the former needs to be stronger than the latter. This underlies the conclusion that gaining complementary knowledge is key to making an alliance work to the advantage of the firm.

Strategic alliances have been a common form of market entry within the network sectors, where a combination of institutional control, high entry costs, and a desire to exploit network externalities have facilitated such arrangements. Within telecommunications, a desire to offer uniform network coverage across all major places drove a sharp rise in telecommunication alliances throughout the early 1990s. Such alliances proved unstable, and their need was mitigated when markets were fully liberalised. The use of alliances within airlines was also driven by a desire to extend the reach of the network without having to directly enter a marketplace. The alliances were often marketing-based and allowed for the development of a seamless service across multiple networks. Such agreements were in lieu of consolidation among service providers.

Underpinning alliance formation is the anticipation that such agreements will create value for both partners. Value creation within an alliance can be derived from a number of sources, such as enhanced efficiency, risk reduction, access to assets and capabilities, and the aforementioned learning benefits. These issues have to be balanced against the possibility that these agreements can create problems through the possibility of choosing the incorrect partner, the transaction costs involved in alliance formation, the risk of partner opportunism, and opening up opportunities for competitors to emerge. Overall, the formation of alliances as a form of market entry will depend upon the underlying motives of partners. Thereafter, decisions made have to reflect whether to make the cooperation equity- or non-equity-based and how to position the relationship. Although alliances may be attractive in theory, they are prone to risks associated with trust and relationship management (Michalski 2015).

---

**Box 9.1:** Nation branding for competitive advantage

An increasingly prevalent feature of the international environment has been the attempt by states to seek to brand themselves in much the same ways as businesses. A leader within this process was the UK's 'Cool Britannia' strategy in the 1990s, which sought to position the UK as a global hub for media, design, music, and fashion. It was an attempt to press the UK's claim to be the most modern of states. This act has subsequently been followed by many states that have sought to use branding as a means of creating national success through the generation of a positive and competitive identity. This strategy further underscores the embedded logic of the competition state as addressed within Chapter 3. It can also reflect a desire by states to generate a positive image for the purposes of soft power strategies. Internally, such strategies can be used to facilitate and shift national identities by focussing on positive images to enhance competitiveness and attractiveness.

The focus on national branding, how national images can be a tool of national development, and the focus on geo-strategic practices in an increasingly globalised economy and — importantly, the trend towards nation branding — has gone beyond western states to involve all regions of the global economy. This highlights that nation branding has moved beyond the application of the logic of capitalism to the state to address more explicit geo-political issues. This has its expression within emerging geo-economic strategies, where the logic of the completion state seeks states to shift away from an emphasis on hard power to a focus on trade and the utilisation of cultural capital. This reflects the notion that a state's status, etc., is less a function of military power and capability and more a reflection of perceived attractiveness and ability to attract the attention of others. In short, nation branding is an expression of soft power.

The process of branding reflects a blurring of the boundaries between the state and the market, with national interest defined in economic terms as reflecting in narratives expressed by leaders in terms of 'UK Plc.' or 'Corporation Germany'. This pushes leaders to act like business leaders to push their states interests within international markets to attract global capital and promote overseas exports. It reflects a licence to trade to get the country known in international markets through enhancing its reputation. In these terms, the inability of the state to get attention can be seen as a cause of under-development. This has its most evident expression in Africa, where the absence of a strong brand or even negative branding leads to reputational problems that impact international positioning. This reflects that branding can also be a negative as well as a positive force on development and growth. The salience of such an issue is reflected in the fact that leading international benchmarks of competitiveness (notably the WEF Global Competitiveness Reports) include a measure of culture. This makes branding a key variable in discussions of competitiveness.

The push towards nation branding has not been without its critics, with many arguing that such narratives come with consequences, which can be problematic. The first is that the process assumes culture is static and can be commodotised. The result is that culture tends to be simplified, leading to stereotyping. Moreover, many states, in seeking to deploy cultural assets, tend to employ the same criteria, with the result that far from differentiating states end up copying each other. The second is that the process can be undemocratic and depolitical, especially when it is outsourced to foreign branders, which can shape what they feel is needed rather than offering a strong focus on actual identity. Finally, the notion of a national brand can work to influence the behaviour of citizens as they seek to 'live the brand'. Thus, branding only works if citizens behave in congruence with it; as such, it becomes a technique of governance.

# CONCLUSION

The heterogeneity of MNEs in terms of their motivations for internationalisation, their structures, and the variety of international entry modes adopted by them make it difficult to generalise about them. Indeed, the emergence of cooperative networks and alliances in recent decades has added to the complexity of multinational theory and has necessitated some reinterpretation and adaptation of the dominant thinking about multinational firms.

MNEs are major beneficiaries of globalisation. However, globalisation also threatens MNEs, especially those who are not so responsive to the competitive pressures in a more open, globalised world. Moreover, the shift towards a more globalised world has not necessarily resulted in global firms. Although many firms operate in a wide range of countries across the globe, their production and marketing approach in these countries is often national or regional rather than truly indifferent to national borders. Furthermore, many MNEs remain deeply influenced by and embedded in their home location.

## KEY POINTS

- The choice of market to enter reflects a systematic process of selection.
- The selection process takes place within the context of the business's limited knowledge.
- Entry modes can be equity- or non-equity-based.
- The choice of entry mode differs according to sensitivity to risk and desire for asset control.

## DISCUSSION QUESTIONS

1. What do you believe to be the major drivers of international market selection?
2. What types of risks are involved in the IMaS process?
3. Why might firms prefer a franchise form of market entry?

## ACTIVITIES

Using the example of an international firm with which you are familiar, assess their market strategy. You should consider why they entered particular markets and why they chose the mode of entry they did.

## SUGGESTED FURTHER READINGS

Agarwal, S., & Ramaswami, S. N. (1992). Choice of foreign market entry mode: Impact of ownership, location and internalization factors. *Journal of International Business Studies, 23*(1), 1–27.

Andersen, O., & Buvik, A. (2002). Firms' internationalization and alternative approaches to the international customer/market selection. *International Business Review, 11*(3), 347–363.

Brouthers, K. D. (1995). The influence of international risk on entry mode strategy in the computer software industry. *MIR: Management International Review, 35*(1), 7–28.

Gaston-Breton, C., & Martín Martín, O. (2011). International market selection and segmentation: A two-stage model. *International Marketing Review, 28*(3), 267–290.

Hill, C. W., Hwang, P., & Kim, W. C. (1990). An eclectic theory of the choice of international entry mode. *Strategic Management Journal, 11*(2), 117–128.

Michalski, E. (2015). Foreign market entry strategy. *Acta Scientiarum Polonorum. Oeconomia, 14*(2), 107–117.

Papadopoulos, N., & Malhotra, S. (2007). Export processing zones in development and international marketing: An integrative review and research agenda. *Journal of Macromarketing, 27*(2), 148–161.

Papadopoulos, N., & Martín Martín, O. (2011). International market selection and segmentation: Perspectives and challenges. *International Marketing Review, 28*(2), 132–149.

Sakarya, S., Eckman, M., & Hyllegard, K. H. (2007). Market selection for international expansion: Assessing opportunities in emerging markets. *International Marketing Review, 24*(2), 208–238.

# CHAPTER 10

# MULTINATIONAL ENTERPRISES

## OBJECTIVES

This chapter will help you to:

- Distinguish between different motives for engaging in foreign direct investment.
- Comprehend the risks associated with FDI.
- Understand the form and nature of the spread of MNEs.
- Demonstrate an understanding of network and alliance capitalism and why they are increasing in importance.
- Comprehend the knowledge-based view of the MNES.

Multinational enterprises (MNEs) lie at the heart of international economic integration and international production. MNEs are defined by the fact that they engage in foreign direct investment in more than one state as opposed to simply engaging with international markets through simple sales channels. While there are multiple definitions of what actually is an MNE (the definitions tend to differ by emphasis on control, ownership, strategy, or structure), it is evident that all have a common trait, namely the engagement with direct ownership and control of non-domestic assets. Currently, there are estimated to be over 60,000 MNEs operating nearly 700,000 affiliates. This suggests that there are many relatively small MNEs alongside the large organisations that tend to dominate narratives on MNEs: 69 of the world's 100 largest economies are MNEs. The purpose of this chapter is to explore the form and nature of the MNE as well as its impact on the international business system through FDI. It is this topic that the chapter will initially explore before moving on to assess how decisions over FDI reflect key strategic decisions for the MNE and address the theory of MNEs through comprehending the desire to undertake FDI.

## THE NATURE OF THE MNE

The conventional treatment of MNEs is one of size based on the presumption that the ability to engage in FDI requires a degree of scale. While, as Table 10.1 indicates, the

DOI: 10.4324/9781315184500-13

world's largest firms are MNEs, there are also many SMEs. What defines an MNE is that the firm exercises ownership or control in more than one country. The issue of control is key to understanding the nature of the MNE, as the blurring of the boundaries of the firm enables a wider range of business organisations to be regarded as multinational, including the buyer-driven commodity chains that make up the multinational organising strategy of firms like Nike and The Gap. Although these companies do not own all, or sometimes any part, of their production facilities, they nevertheless exercise a significant degree of control over the production chain and should be regarded as multinationals (see Birkinshaw 2016).

In 2016, as measured by foreign assets (which reflects the extensiveness of FDI by an MNE), the largest MNEs are indicated in Table 10.1. What is evident is that the 'old economy' industries dominate the list. The only representative of what can be termed 'new economy' industries is Apple. This can reflect the 'virtual' nature of these businesses, and other than facilities like data centres, etc., they tend to be relatively asset-light or see little need for large-scale FDI to enable their business model. Indeed, Alphabet (which is ranked fourth in market capitalisation) ranks only 100 in the ranking of foreign assets. What is also evident is the sustained importance of large-scale commodity producers on this list. Almost 20 per cent of the top 100 MNEs are involved in the extraction of commodities. The only sector that comes close is motor vehicles, with over 15 per cent of the top 100. With regard to the home states of the main MNEs, the US and the UK dominate the list with nearly 40 per cent of the total. Indeed, the states within the triad of the EU, Japan, and the US dominate the list, with five of the states within the triad (the US, UK, Germany, France, and Japan) accounting for 72 of the top 100 MNEs. Furthermore, of the top 100 firms, 58 belonged to six industries: motor vehicles (11), petroleum (10), electrical and electronic equipment (10), pharmaceuticals

**TABLE 10.1** Top 20 non-financial MNEs ranked by foreign assets

| | |
|---|---|
| 1. Royal Dutch Shell | 11. Enel |
| 2. Toyota | 12. Vodafone |
| 3. Total | 13. Chevron |
| 4. Volkswagen | 14. EDF |
| 5. Deutsche Telekom | 15. Honda |
| 6. Exxon | 16. C K Hutchinson |
| 7. Stellantis | 17. Mercedes |
| 8. BP | 18. Siemens |
| 9. Anheuser-Busch | 19. RWE |
| 10. British American Tobacco | 20. Hon Hai Precision |

Source: UNCTAD (2021)

(9), telecommunications (9), and electricity, gas, and water (9). Over the last decade, there has been little movement in the composition of this list.

## MULTINATIONAL ENTERPRISE AND FDI

While all firms are arguably subject to the international environment, MNEs are arguably more exposed than others, as they have directly engaged in the process of global engagement as a consequence of their direct ownership of value-adding activities outside their domestic market and, as a result, become directly subject to the risks of operating across more than one territory. For the MNE, FDI offers effective control of strategic assets within a host economy, with the choice of entry mode dependent upon the degree of control desired by the firm relative to the cost and risk of undertaking such a measure (Birkinshaw 2016). FDI may not always result in effective control, depending on the nature of the joint venture, strategic alliance, etc. Control is only total when the investment takes the form of an acquisition, a stand-alone, wholly owned subsidiary, or a greenfield project.

Furthermore, FDI can be categorised according to its motives. Horizontal FDI is where the firm invests in an overseas location to produce the same product it produces in other markets. This form of FDI is driven by a desire to serve the local market better and often involves the duplication of resources across multiple markets as a means of reducing the cost of market supply. This assumes the cost of horizontal FDI is lower than the cost of exporting as a market strategy. Thus, horizontal FDI is more common in larger markets where economies of scale are greater. Vertical FDI is where the firm invests in a foreign market to reconfigure its value chain as a means of injecting new inputs and greater efficiency into the production process. This form of FDI is normally export-oriented, often to the MNE's home market, and is often unresponsive to the size of the host market. Thus, where different parts of the value chain require inputs that vary in price across states, vertical FDI will be stimulated.

### The determinants of FDI

At the micro-economic level, many determinants of FDI are linked to process models of internationalisation. Alongside the Uppsala model (described in detail in Chapter 15), micro-economic explanations have centred on the product life cycle and industrial organisation-based theories. The former explains the shift in production in terms of the maturity of the product concerned. This assumes that FDI becomes more common when the product is at a mature stage of its life cycle and is in decline. This is symptomatic of domestic market saturation and of commoditisation of the product. Industrial organisation theories stress that FDI (notably horizontal FDI) is driven by the existence of firm-specific advantages. Vertical FDI is driven more by the avoidance of oligopolistic uncertainty.

At a macro-economic level, the following variables are seen as important in pushing a firm towards FDI:

- *Exchange rates*: there is assumed to be a negative relationship between FDI and the value of the exchange rate. Currency shifts reflect directly on the earning capacity of overseas assets. As the exchange rate of a host economy rises, the stock of FDI within that economy diminishes. Alongside the absolute value of the exchange rate, variability will also be an important determinant of FDI.

- *Economic growth*: the rate of growth within the host economy is also important and generally has a positive relationship with the level of FDI. Relative growth rates, rather than growth rates per se, are key when determining how resources are to be deployed globally.
- *Market size*: the size of the host economy has a generally positive effect on the level of FDI. Indeed, many studies have indicated that market size is the most influential factor in FDI. Market size influences the exploitation of scale economies and standard factor specialisation, allowing for cost minimisation and market growth.
- *Stage of economic development*: the more developed a state, the better the level of infrastructure, etc., and the more able the state will be to generate wider agglomeration effects.
- *Human capital*: for labour-intensive and export-oriented FDI, the quality and quantity of human capital are pivotal. Thus, as more capital is employed and more labour is trained, the attractiveness of FDI is sustained.
- *Agglomeration economies*: the presence of other firms, industries, and labour acts as an incentive to invest.
- *Governmental policies (see below)*: many governments consider FDI an important antidote to rising and high unemployment and introduce policies to encourage FDI. These can take the form of tax incentives, subsidies, regulation, and privatisation. Tax is especially important when subsidiary revenues are subject to both host and home country taxes. Linked to these concerns are the quality of the institutions (especially in developing states), which provide legal protection, transaction costs, and the supporting infrastructure.
- *Liberality of the trade regime*: there is assumed to be a positive relationship between FDI and a liberal trade regime. This is related to factors such as the liberalisation of foreign ownership, privatisation, and financial deregulation. The more open a market, the less the MNE has to use horizontal FDI to circumvent trade barriers.

In addition to the above, there are other FDI determinants such as the degree of openness, labour costs, privatisation, trade linkages and borders, risk and macro-economic stability, etc. Table 10.2 offers an extensive list of the major host country determinants across three major categories.

It is becoming increasingly evident that the major conventional determinant of FDI (the size of national markets) has decreased in importance as globalisation has matured. At the same time, cost differentials between locations, the quality of infrastructure, the ease of doing business, and the availability of skills have become increasingly important. Traditional economic determinants such as natural resources, low labour costs and the size of the market protected from export competition also remain important, but the relative importance of location determinants for competitiveness-enhancing FDI is shifting. Firms are seeking a competitive advantage based on a combination of wages, skills, and productivity when deciding the location of FDI. The emergence of regional markets is also important, and, in some cases, these are superseding national markets as

**TABLE 10.2** Host country determinants of FDI

| | |
|---|---|
| Economic conditions | • *Markets*: size, income, income distribution, and levels and growth prospects; access to regional markets; and distribution and demand patterns.<br>• *Resources*: natural resources and location.<br>• *Competitiveness*: labour availability, costs, skills, and trainability; managerial technical skills, access to inputs, and physical infrastructure; supplier base; and technology support. |
| Host country policies | • *Macro policies*: management of crucial macro variables, ease of remittance, and access to foreign exchange.<br>• *Private sector*: promotion of private ownership, clear and stable policies, easy entry/exit policies, efficient financial markets, and other support.<br>• *Trade and industry*: trade strategy, regional integration and access to markets, ownership controls, competition policies, and support for SMEs.<br>• *FDI policies*: ease of entry, ownership incentives, access to inputs, and transparent and stable policies. |
| MNE strategies | • *Risk perception*: perceptions of country risk based on political factors, macro management, labour markets, and policy stability.<br>• *Location sourcing, integration transfer*: company strategies on location, sourcing of products/inputs, integration of affiliates, strategic alliances, training, and technology. |

Source: Lall (1992)

important FDI determinants. This depends on how well the state is integrated into the regional bloc in terms of policy harmonisation and physical accessibility.

## Risks and FDI

Core to the FDI decision is an assessment of the risks faced by the MNE in entering a particular market. The market entry decision is a reflection of the trade-off between risk and control. The convention states that there is a negative relationship between these two variables. FDI as a form of market entry and of an ongoing commitment to a host economy represents a relatively high-control mode of operation. This suggests that FDI is characterised by a higher degree of risk than other modes of market entry and involvement. Consequently, FDI depends on effective country risk analysis to identify the imbalances that increase the risk of a shortfall in the expected return.

Cross-border risks typically emerge from national differences in economic structures, policies, socio-political institutions, geography, and currencies. The major categories of country risk are identified below.

1. Economic risk: this is the major shift in the economic circumstances of the structure or growth rate of a host that could generate a major change in the anticipated returns from FDI. These could arise from policy shifts or from the erosion of the host economy's comparative advantage (for example, major shifts in the price of natural resource endowments). Clearly, these risks overlap with the political system.

2. Transfer risk: this arises from a decision by the host government to restrict capital movements. This makes it difficult to repatriate profits, dividends, or capital. The degree of transfer risk is negatively related to the ability of the state to generate foreign exchange.

3. Exchange rate risk: this is driven by unexpected adverse movements in the exchange rate. This includes an unanticipated shift in the currency regime from a fixed to a float, for example.

4. Location or neighbourhood risk: this includes spillover effects created by problems in a region, a host country's major trading partner, or in countries with similar characteristics. The latter, for example, can make the host state subject to problems of contagion.

5. Sovereign risk: this is based on the ability and/or willingness of the host government to meet its loan obligations and the likelihood of it reneging on loans. This can occur when the state runs low on foreign exchange in a balance of payments crisis or when a government decides not to honour its commitments for political expediency.

6. Political risk: this involves the risk created by political changes stemming from changes in government control, social fabric, or some other non-economic factor. This form of risk includes the potential for internal and external conflicts, expropriation risk, and more conventional forms of political risk.

FDI involves the MNE considering the long-term time horizon and is at risk from a broader set of country characteristics (Lien and Filatotchev 2015). The nature of sunk costs involved in FDI opens the firm to higher degrees of risk: an MNE has to commit to the state and suffers a consequence from higher barriers to entry than other less substantive and more flexible investments (Meldrum 2000). These risks are assumed to be made in the local currency, and their perceived impact across these forms of foreign investment is subjective. Clearly, these risks would differ if the investments were held in reserve currency. However, the table does indicate the relatively high degree of risk faced by FDI compared to FII. Much of this is accounted for by the longer-term time horizon of FDI. Transfer risk is less of an issue for FDI as capital restrictions are unlikely to last for the entire period of the investment as they are often used as a temporary measure to counteract short-term difficulties.

## CASE STUDY 10.1: SIEMENS

Siemens is a German industrial conglomerate that has been at the forefront of a list of products, from traffic lights and gas turbines to domestic appliances. Overall, it employs over 370,000 people in more than 200 countries/regions. The company has extended value networks with production, manufacturing, warehouses, offices, warehouses, sales outlets, and R&D facilities in most of these states/regions. Over 60 per cent of its revenue is sourced from European, African, and Middle Eastern markets. This is based across a set of strategic business units in power and gas, energy management, building technologies, mobility, digital factories, process industries, health, and renewable industries. In terms of the global Fortune 500 list of multinationals,

Siemens ranks in a relatively low 66th position. This is down from a high of 21st place throughout the 2000s.

This fall in relative position reflects long-standing issues within the group, which often led it to be labelled the problem child of European heavy industry as it had large oscillations in profitability as large projects went wrong and spending went astray. This was compounded by the fact that even when profit was made, the margins were often very thin. This relatively poor financial performance is often blamed on the group's conglomerate structure, which many felt left the group unfocused. Indeed, it was felt that the group seemed to be spreading itself thin across multiple product groups; notably, the group seemed to be split between making things for the industrial economy or seeking to reposition itself for the emerging digital economy. This was compounded by the fact that for a long time up until the 2000s, Siemens – despite its global narrative – was heavily dependent upon its home market, which generated up to half of its sales. In this market, Siemens relied upon direct or indirect state contracts, which tended to lead to it being relatively isolated from the forces of international competition. Moreover, it was felt that as an industrial champion, it grew divorced from addressing shareholder concerns and was obsessed with engineering over profitability.

These structural issues were compounded by management problems, typified by the bribery scandal that engulfed the company between 2006 and 2008. This was indicative of a culture whereby managers routinely bribed local officials across the world to win contracts. After it was made illegal under German law in 1999, Siemens switched its bribery acts to front companies. The US estimates that between 2001 and 2007, the company paid over $800 million in bribes. However, over the longer term, this system seemed to do the company no favour as managers became increasingly unaccountable and the sales force signed up for profitable deals as they focused on winning contracts over cash generation. This was compounded by the fines incurred when caught, which cost the firm around $2.6 billion, with much of the firm's market value wiped out. The longer-term legacy was widespread corporate reform under a new chief executive, Peter Loscher.

The new chief executive set about reforming Siemens' culture to increase the accountability of senior managers and leaving businesses where the firm was not competitive, such as consumer electronics. The strategy was to reposition Siemens in core sectors linked to the provision of technically advanced infrastructure, such as energy and transport (which have high barriers to entry), or in sectors where it can bundle its products and services together (such as healthcare). Over the short term, this process worked as the company was able to tap into the switch to gas from coal via its turbine division, which has introduced a series of energy-efficient products. The company also successfully tapped into the renewable energy market, especially in the wind energy sub-segment. In this area, Siemens gains an advantage by focusing on offshore products, which are underserved by its competitors. This is aided by new products in electricity production that emphasise the company's green credentials, notably the rise of technology related to the so-called green power superhighways. Siemens also made progress in its rail division through advanced high-speed rail technology. In health care, there are more problems as competition is intense. Siemens has opted to focus on low-cost leadership rather than technological superiority. This reflects that Siemens' competitive advantage lies not just in its technological superiority but also in its scale.

Siemens' rivals (notably General Electric) are also not standing still. Many are also ramping up their R&D spending. Moreover, many shareholders are still unhappy with the conglomerate structure, with many believing that bundling does not offer big enough synergies to justify such a diverse set of businesses, with the company trading for less than the value of the sum of its parts. The reforms undertaken by Peter Loscher were clearly not enough, as they were removed in 2014. This was generated by a failure to reach profit targets driven by a series of cost overruns and operational problems, notably in a train contract with Deutsche Bahn. It also underestimated the difficulty of building offshore wind power and deployed faulty wind turbines. It also underestimated the cost of its cancer treatment centres, which led to them being abandoned. While Losher made early progress, the process seemed to run out of steam as the aforementioned problem emerged. It took on too many orders that it failed to meet on time or came in over budget. This again draws investor attention to the conglomerate structure of the company, which, despite being simplified to four divisions (energy, healthcare, industry, infrastructure, and cities), has too many weak sub-divisions, with the company making acquisitions that have failed (such as Solel, a solar power company, on which it lost over €600 million). The new boss, Joe Kaeser, sought to simplify the business further. However, the company faces constraints from its supervisory board (which includes unions and tends to be conservative), which, along with the German government, will seek to limit any loss of employment in Germany, where the firm employs over 130,000 people.

Joe Kaesner sought to focus the business on automation, electrification, and digitisation. To do this, he simplified the business into nine from 16 divisions and removed a layer of bureaucracy to merge these nine divisions into the four aforementioned sectors. While healthcare is the most profitable sector for the business, it offers little synergy with the mantra of electrification, digitisation, and automation. This raises the prospect of the business being spun off. Overall, almost 20 per cent of the group's revenues come from segments making no profit, such as train rolling stock and electricity transmission. Other segments that do not fit into the vision (such as airport logistics and hearing aids) are also expected to go. Siemens has work to do in project execution and operations, where it has incurred charges due to poor delivery and cost analysis. To some, this reflects a culture where managers are afraid to report difficulties to avoid accountability. This company also seeks to change. This reflects that, for many, the biggest issue lies in the company's culture and how this retards strategic change.

## QUESTION

Given the material in this case study, what do you believe to be the biggest challenge facing Siemens?

## MOTIVATING FACTORS FOR MNES' FDI

The major motivating factors for MNEs can be subdivided into the following broad categories. These groupings are not mutually exclusive, as FDI will often be influenced by a multitude of concerns, although one often tends to predominate.

### Resource-seeking investment

Resource seekers invest abroad to acquire resources that are either unobtainable or only available at a much higher cost in their home country. Typically, such investment involves primary products, especially agricultural goods, minerals, and raw materials. Usually, most of the output from these investments is exported. Oil production in developing countries, for example, frequently involves inward FDI (although the terms on which MNEs engage in hydrocarbon production depend on host country policies regarding the exploitation of natural resources by non-nationals). FDI enables oil companies to secure inputs for their downstream activities (refineries and ultimately retail outlets) located outside the country where the oil is extracted. From the perspective of the host country, multinational oil companies bring technical expertise that is particularly useful in exploration and production in difficult terrain or in enhancing recovery rates from existing fields.

Other resources sought by foreign investors include cheap unskilled, semi-skilled, and, increasingly with the development of software exports from developing countries, skilled labour. Such investors come from countries with high real labour costs; initially, they invested in the more advanced developing countries of East Asia or Latin America, but as wage costs have risen there, they are increasingly casting their net wider. Other location-bound resource-seeking investments (corresponding to Dunning's 'L' factor; see below) include tourism and construction – that is, investments that can only take place in a particular location because they utilise resources or attributes that are immobile.

Resource-seeking investment dominated FDI in the nineteenth century and into the twentieth century, representing the basis of the colonial relationship between Europe and Japan and their respective overseas possessions. It survived the end of the empire and remains significant, but has been overtaken in importance by other types of FDI.

### Market seeking investment

Market seekers invest in a country, not as an export platform but to supply goods and services to it. Advantages of locating production directly in a market rather than exporting to it include

- Greater proximity to the consumer: this facilitates the adaptation of products to local customs, tastes, and needs (polycentric firms).
- Market size: the presence of a sizeable emerging market in the Far East, China, India, Russia, or parts of Latin America.
- Continuation of existing relationships with major customers: for example, when Japanese car producers began to invest overseas, many of their suppliers followed them. The internationalisation of business services such as accounting, legal services,

and consulting is also a response to the movement of clients into an increasing number of markets.

- Government policy: government policy in the form of investment incentives can stimulate inward FDI. Government policy can also spark defensive FDI. For example, much of the FDI in Europe towards the end of the 1980s was driven by investors' fears that construction of the Single European Market (SEM) would lead to a 'fortress Europe' which would reduce, if not eliminate, their access to the EU market. In practice, these fears proved unfounded.
- The belief that it is necessary to maintain a physical presence in a foreign market because one's competitors do so.

## Efficiency-seeking investment

Efficiency seekers strive to rationalise their value chains. They focus and concentrate different parts of their value chain in diverse locations, seeking to maximise the benefits from each location by arbitraging costs and specialisations. On a global scale, efficiency seekers attempt to take advantage of traditional differences in factor endowments. This helps explain the concentration of labour-intensive activities in developing countries and of capital- and technology-intensive activities in developed countries.

Efficiency-seeking FDI is also prominent in regionally integrated markets; these markets are frequently similar in economic structure and income levels, enabling producers to exploit economies of scale and scope to serve a number of markets. Efficiency-seeking investment requires coordinated communication, production, inbound and outbound logistical networks, and a business environment in which there are few or no barriers to cross-border activity. The emergence of the SEM was intended to yield such efficiency gains for producers within Europe, and the introduction of the euro, which entered its final stage in 2002, is anticipated to extend these possibilities. Indeed, there has been significant rationalisation in several European sectors as a result of the SEM.

## Strategic asset investment

Strategic asset seekers engage in FDI to achieve long-term strategic objectives. These objectives vary. An acquisition may be motivated, for example, by a wish to make life more difficult for a rival in a specific market or to reduce competition in a particular market (provided the local competition authorities do not object). International conglomerates may collect acquisitions to spread risk across a wider range of markets and locations.

## CASE STUDY 10.2: THE INTERNATIONAL STRATEGY OF SAMSUNG

Founded in 1938, the South Korean MNE Samsung is the largest of that country's conglomerates (the so-called chaebol) and operates within a number of businesses, most of which are under its own brand. The company is a very powerful political and economic force in South Korea, comprising up to a fifth of its exports and 17 per cent of its GDP. Starting as a trading company, the group has spread into a number of other businesses, including food processing, textiles, insurance, construction, shipbuilding, securities, and retail. By 2016, it had over 80 affiliated businesses. The sector for which it is arguably best known globally, electronics, was entered in the 1960s. Since 1990, the firm has undertaken an aggressive internationalisation strategy (largely on the back of this electronics business), with mobile phones and semiconductors now representing the most significant sources of income for the group. Indeed, by 2015, its affiliate, Samsung Electronics (SE), was the world's second-biggest IT company (as measured by revenues). Siemens tends to be good at spotting small areas that are growing fast.

SE bases its international strategy on seeking synergistic advantages between the group's affiliates. This helps SE adapt products quickly to changing market needs, with its extensive geographic footprint enabling it to spread risks across markets. However, the growing interlinkages between markets suggest that this is less likely to be successful than it was in the past. Importantly, SE tends to base manufacturing activities in the major IT clusters globally (such as Silicon Valley in the US and the M4 Corridor in the UK, for example). For labour-intensive aspects of the process, it uses a location in Southeast Asia. These are areas where there is more labour flexibility and cost efficacy. The international strategy of SE does face a number of challenges, as it needs to balance standardisation and adaptation in its product lines and reconcile the cultural differences between home and host cultures in the business. South Korean culture is based on respect for seniority, whereas many of the new Western managers come from a more meritocratic culture. Moreover, many felt that SE was exposed to risk as it chose to retail its products through established dealers rather than establish its own network. The company tends to make small forays into a market to get familiar with it, then waits for the time to flood the market with the product, ramping up production and flooding the sector with cash. This enables the firm to gain a price advantage over rivals and helps it establish relationships with equipment makers, which allows it to stay ahead of rivals. As such, Samsung buys technology rather than developing it; thus, it assumes execution risk, not innovation risk. Samsung also positions itself to supply parts to its rivals, allowing it to drive down costs further. For example, nearly 20 per cent of the value of an iPhone is Samsung products.

The expansion of SE has been in three major phases. The first phase was in the 1980s when it made large investments in overseas manufacturing to account for explicit variations in national labour costs. This was later added to by a more extensive, higher-value investment in R&D facilities. The second phase was to establish, since 2000, a series of joint ventures and partnerships across a number of areas to extend its reach both in product and geographic terms. The final phase was to develop a coherent internal marketing strategy to reach high-end consumer electronic markets. This strategy has required Samsung to be quick to adapt to opportunities. SE is not the first to enter the market but tends to be a 'fast second' once an opportunity is noted. Its strategy is to enter a niche where the minimum efficient scale can be reached rapidly. Once this has been achieved, SE then invests heavily in R&D and marketing to overtake the first mover, supported by group resources (both financial and non-financial) to do so. This was evidently a strategy SE deployed in smartphones in 2010, where it waited for Apple's strategy to be evident before it entered with its Galaxy line of products. Within five years, Samsung had become the market leader. The use of joint ventures and partnerships is often based on the SE seeking to access the partner's technology that the firm requires to support its products and which it has neither the capability nor time to develop. This was evident with regard to the partnership with Google and its Android system for mobile phones. This was a good decision, given the dominance of the Android system over the smartphone market. The group has also used greenfield investment, notably in the tablet market.

Overall, SE has followed what would typically be called a global strategy of seeking a uniform value proposition across multiple markets, with product features and specifications basically being uniform across all markets. This has created both opportunities and challenges for the business. First, in allowing the business to enable economies on a location-by-location basis in each of the major regional markets (Asia, Europe, and North America), it chooses one location for R&D and another low-cost location for manufacturing. Second, it seeks to utilise its experience in a number of areas to support other businesses. Third, SE promotes standardised products as far as possible where adaptation is required; they are done so quickly and with minimum adaptation.

This international strategy has faced a number of problems. The first of which was that the group was accused of persistently infringing the IP of other companies. This hurt its image of being a successful follower and tainted the brand. Moreover, in Europe, it is seen not as a high-end brand but as mid-range. In addition, there is a long-held belief that the firm needs to change to adapt to new technologies as existing products become obsolete, especially as its market share in electronics is increasingly challenged by cheap Chinese manufacturers. To this end, it has moved into new areas that have synergy with existing product areas. This includes solar cells, LED products, and electric vehicle technology. The ability of Samsung to try the same strategies in these new markets as it has in others is called into question as it is not using the usual high-intensity strategy of flooding the market; it has rivals that are ready for it, and some segments are already subject to oversupply. There is also the long-term trend where the value of high technology is shifting away from hardware towards software. Samsung's response to this has been to acquire a set-off start-up. As the market evolves, data is becoming the core driver of the products Samsung offers. This will erode the dominance that Samsung has over smartphones.

## QUESTION

How do you account for the major challenges Samsung has incurred during its internationalisation strategy?

## Other motivations for investment

In some cases, FDI occurs because firms wish to escape restrictive legislation in the domestic market. Chapter 15 discusses the emergence of so-called pollution havens as firms seek to avoid expensive environmental legislation by locating in countries with less strict laws. Chapter 14 discusses a similar phenomenon in relation to labour laws. Some firms invest abroad, buoyed by success at home, to overcome limited growth prospects at home. Others invest because they feel that their competitors may gain an advantage over them by investing in a particular country or because they fear exclusion in the long run.

---

**Box 10.1: Perlmutter's classifications of MNEs**

MNEs can be categorised along dimensions other than those relating to their reasons for internationalisation. The value of these classifications lies in the way in which they highlight different characteristics of multinational firms. By distinguishing between ethnocentric, polycentric, regiocentric, and geocentric MNEs (Perlmutter 1969), Perlmutter, for example, draws attention to the extent to which MNEs are domestically or internationally oriented.

- Ethnocentric firms: the parent firm and the domestic market are the dominant factors in ethnocentric firms; the needs of domestic consumers determine product development, and the parent company headquarters, located in the home country, exercise significant control over foreign affiliates, either through highly centralised decision-making and/or the utilisation of expatriate senior management from the home country in the overseas operations. These firms are at stages one or two of Vernon's product life cycle.
- Polycentric firms: polycentric firms are more oriented to foreign markets. They are market seeking, closely attuned to the needs and cultures of the countries in which they operate, and act as a series of domestic firms, loosely linked to the parent company. Such firms are likely to operate in a less centralised and hierarchical way than ethnocentric firms, although some core decisions may be taken centrally.
- Regiocentric firms: regiocentric MNEs develop their strategy and organisation on regional lines. Regional offices are responsible for the parent company headquarters but have some autonomy. There is integration of links in the value chain within regions, but little integration across regions. This approach tailors the output to regional needs and is particularly suitable within the context of regional integration (see Chapter 3). Many Japanese and American firms, for example, adopted a regiocentric, or European, approach to the EU market as a result of the campaign to develop the SEM rather than separate strategies for each national market.

Geocentric firms: a geocentric firm views its value chain from a global perspective; it aims to integrate its activities across regions, and the most geocentric firms will develop global products while remaining sensitive to local or regional cultures and market peculiarities where necessary.

---

# THE EVOLUTION OF INTERNATIONAL PRODUCTION THEORY

A burgeoning literature on why and how firms decide to internationalise and engage in FDI only developed in the second half of the twentieth century, despite the fact that MNEs have existed in one form or another for centuries. It required the post-war increase in FDI among industrialised nations and the subsequent increase in the scale of international production to prompt a theoretical focus on the multinational firm. Until that point, explanations of the activities of firms outside their national boundaries relied heavily on neo-classical trade theory and the neo-classical theory of capital arbitrage. There were also contributions from writers like Edith Penrose, who, through her work on the theory of the growth of the firm, explored the idea that cross-border production represented not only an alternative to international cartels but was also a rational extension of the benefits of horizontal and vertical integration (Buckley and Casson 2016).

The real breakthrough in theorising about multinationals happened in 1960 with the work of Stephen Hymer. Hymer overturned the prevailing orthodoxy by focusing on the firm and on international production rather than on international trade and investment theory. His first step was to emphasise the distinction between portfolio investment and FDI (Forsgren 2017). Portfolio investment theory was based on assumptions of efficient, perfectly competitive markets, costless transactions, and perfect information and explained international capital flows in terms of firms taking advantage of differential interest rates. For Hymer, the key difference between portfolio investment and FDI was control. In the former case, the transaction involves the transfer of assets from the seller to the buyer via the market mechanism. In the case of FDI, the transfer of assets across borders is made within the investing company, and the control of the transferred resources remains with the investing company.

According to Hymer, the rationale for FDI is not to take advantage of higher interest rates but to finance international production through the transfer of resources, including equipment, technology, skills, and know-how. This option became feasible because of the existence of firm-specific advantages (FSAs). Hymer reasoned that domestic firms have a number of crucial advantages over foreign firms given their greater understanding of the local market, culture, and legislation (Forsgren 2017). Domestic firms may also have advantages in terms of preferential access to natural resources. In order for foreign firms to produce successfully in overseas locations, they need strong FSAs of their own to counteract the advantages of indigenous firms. These advantages could come from economies of scale, size, market power, brand ownership, know-how, or technological prowess, for example.

FSAs are notable in the evolution of thinking about international production for two reasons. First, they are central to the theoretical literature about the internationalisation of the firm, feeding into the 'O' factor of Dunning's eclectic paradigm (see below). Secondly, FSAs and their exploitation can only exist as a result of market failure – a distinctive move away from the assumptions of functioning markets in the cases of neo-classical trade and capital arbitrage theories. In other words, MNEs must have an advantage over competitors, including indigenous producers, to invest in another country. This implies the existence of an imperfectly competitive market structure and barriers to entry. FSAs, therefore, are tied up with oligopoly power. According to this view, the MNE is the result of market failure and exists to exploit market imperfections.

Although reliance on market imperfections remains a key dimension of multinational theory, another factor is emerging to challenge the oligopolistic-monopolistic view of the multinational firm. International economic integration and globalisation represent the reverse of market failure: they are essentially about the reduction or removal rather than the erection of entry barriers. As such, globalisation represents a move towards greater market perfection. This is not to say that the market imperfection view of the internationalisation of the firm is no longer relevant, but that some adaptation is required to accommodate globalisation and the implication that the multinationalisation of the firm can occur when no obvious FSAs are present. This development goes some way, perhaps, to explain the resurgence of interest in the work of Edith Penrose. While Stephen Hymer was interested in the expansion of firms as a means of exploiting or advancing monopoly power, Edith Penrose was interested in growth and expansion as a way of reducing costs.

## Internalisation

Internalisation theory implies that an MNE internalises its international transactions to overcome market imperfections. Work on internalisation and the firm generally derives from the writings of Ronald Coase and Oliver Williamson. The international dimension originated with the work of scholars like Peter Buckley, Mark Casson, Alan Rugman, and John Dunning. Although drawing heavily on Hymer, the international version of internalisation theory also evolved from a critique of Hymer in that his version of market failure emphasised the role of MNEs as monopolistic/oligopolistic profit maximisers and neglected efficiency considerations. The market failure concerning internalisation theorists arises not from market structure but from failure to carry out transactions in the marketplace at a lower cost than within a firm or hierarchy. Such market failure arises from imperfect information, giving rise to opportunism and bounded rationality, and is more likely to be present in the case of cross-border than purely domestic transactions. In other words, firms seek to overcome market imperfections by performing the functions of the market within its own boundaries – that is, by internalising economic activity to reduce transaction costs. The greater the market imperfections and general uncertainties, the greater the incentive to internalise transactions.

Internalisation potentially offers the international firm, indeed all firms, certain advantages. It provides opportunities for exploitation of internal economies of scope and scale, perhaps through vertical integration of production processes across borders with coordination and control exercised by the parent company. Such organisation of value-adding activities within the firm enables it to secure guaranteed and reliable sources of inputs for its production facilities and to secure outlets for primary products such as crude petroleum or metals.

Internalisation is also attractive to firms because of the control it offers them over their FSAs. This is especially appropriate when it comes to advantages arising from knowledge and technology. MNEs can exploit these advantages via franchising and licencing, for example (see below), but internalisation enables them to retain direct control of this asset and avoid a dilution of their property rights.

Internalisation theory is therefore primarily aimed at explaining why cross-border transactions of intermediate products are organised within the boundaries of firms rather than within markets. While the net cost of market transactions exceeds the net cost of internalisation, MNEs will continue to flourish.

## The eclectic paradigm

The dominant explanation for the growth of multinational activity since the 1980s has been Dunning's eclectic paradigm. The eclectic paradigm is not so much a theory of international production but a framework for investigation and analysis. It represents a synthesis and integration of different theories and draws upon various approaches such as the theory of the firm, organisation theory and trade and location theory. As such, the eclectic paradigm represents John Dunning's view that:

> it is not possible to formulate a single operationally testable theory that can explain all forms of foreign-owned production … At the same time … we believe that it is possible to formulate a general paradigm of MNE activity, which sets out a conceptual framework and seeks to identify clusters of variables relevant to an explanation of all kinds of foreign-owned output … Within this framework, we believe that most of the partial micro- and macro- theories of international production can be accommodated.
>
> *(Dunning, 1993, 68)*

In crude terms, the eclectic paradigm rejects an 'either/or' approach to international production and, as its name suggests, takes the most useful parts of apparently competing approaches to explain the internationalisation phenomenon.

The starting point of the eclectic paradigm is the Heckscher-Ohlin factor endowment explanation of international trade, according to which countries specialise in the production of goods that require inputs of resources in which they are well endowed and trade them for goods in which they are not. It was the limiting assumptions of Heckscher-Ohlin, such as factor immobility, identical production functions, and perfect competition, that stimulated the search for further explanation. These assumptions imply that all markets operate efficiently, that there are no economies of scale, and that there is perfect and costless information. Once these restrictive assumptions are relaxed, in addition to relative factor endowments, variables such as market structure, transaction costs, and corporate strategy become key factors in determining international economic activity, thereby opening up the debate about international production to a range of theoretical traditions.

The eclectic paradigm uses three sets of factors to explain the 'why', the 'where', and the 'how', respectively, of the internationalisation of production (see the case study on Guinness). These are:

1. Ownership factors: a firm needs ownership advantages over other firms in the markets in which it is located or in which it is considering locating. These advantages can include technology, general innovative capabilities, information, and managerial and

entrepreneurial skills. These factors link both to Hymer's FSAs and to the core competencies or resource-based school of corporate strategy.

2. Location factors: these advantages are specific to a particular country but are available to all firms and include the availability of natural resources, labour (either in terms of quantity or skills), and the general social, legal, and political environment.

3. Internalisation factors: internalisation relates to the extent of ownership and control. Transactions made through the market, such as exporting, are arm's length transactions. Internalised transactions take place within the boundaries of the firm and enable multinational firms to overcome examples of market failure or imperfection (see above).

According to Dunning, an MNE's degree of foreign value-added activities depends on the satisfaction of the four following conditions:

1. The degree to which a firm possesses ownership advantages over other firms in a particular market.

2. The degree to which an MNE believes it is in its best interests to exploit its ownership advantages rather than sell them to another firm, perhaps in the form of technology licencing or franchising (the internalisation factor).

3. The degree to which there are location-specific advantages in a particular country which raise the value of ownership advantages relative to elsewhere.

4. The degree to which foreign production is consistent with the long-term strategy of the firm.

## The evolution of network and alliance capitalism

Dunning's eclectic paradigm has become the dominant tool in the analysis of the internationalisation of production and allows for a number of theoretical approaches to nest within its framework. However, significant changes in the international business environment, brought about by globalisation and its main drivers, have necessitated a reassessment, or at least a modification, of thinking about international production.

The original eclectic paradigm is set within the framework of hierarchical capitalism; that is, given that market failures have become larger and more commonplace with the growing specialisation and complexity of economic activity and technological and political changes, large, hierarchical firms have developed to compensate for these failures. However, the nature of challenges to the firm is changing, and with it, their response to market failure. Rather than rein in their value-adding activities within the confines of a single hierarchical organisation, firms are increasingly acting to reduce the transaction and coordinating costs of arms-length market transactions by constructing complex networks of relationships and developing strategic and collaborative alliances (Buckley 2018).

Such networks and alliances take many forms and include cooperative and strategic alliances, various types of joint ventures, and the networks developed by clothing and sportswear companies in which most, if not all, production is outsourced. The role of the MNE therefore varies, depending on the rationale for and type of network involved. When extensive outsourcing takes place, the MNE acts as the coordinator of a complex network of interdependent, value-added activities across borders and long distances. When collaborating, perhaps over the development of complementary or joint technologies, cooperation and relationship building will be more important.

Cooperation and alliances have become commonplace for a number of reasons. The high cost of technological development has encouraged firms to collaborate to share both the costs and the risks of this activity. In other cases, collaboration may take the form of interaction between assemblers and component suppliers, a common situation in the automotive and electronic appliance sectors. Clustering and agglomeration of related activities is another development that, although not new, is intensifying. It also accentuates the role of networking and collaboration and reflects the growing international role of SMEs (see Chapter 11), which are steadily becoming embedded in many cross-border networks. Overall, alliances and collaborations enable companies to leverage the assets, skills, and experiences of their partners for the purpose of enhancing competitive advantage.

By blurring the boundaries between firms, cooperative and alliance capitalism challenge conventional thinking about the internationalisation of the firm. This is particularly apparent for the internalisation school of thinking and for the 'I' factor of the eclectic paradigm, which specifically claims that firms deal with the market failure represented by transaction costs by carrying out transactions within the firm rather than at arm's length. It is clearly possible to argue that alliance capitalism significantly weakens internalisation explanations of the internationalisation of the firm. However, Dunning (1995) argues that 'the internalisation paradigm still remains a powerful tool of analysis' provided it is widened and adapted to the new environment. He argues that external alliances and networks can be incorporated into internalisation if it is acknowledged that inter-firm agreements achieve the same objective as internalisation, albeit more effectively, and/or spread the capital and other risks among participating firms. In other words, Dunning recommends that an inter-firm alliance or network be either treated as an extension of intra-firm transactions or as a distinctive organisational mode in its own right – a mode that is complementary to rather than an alternative to a hierarchy.

Alliance capitalism also requires a broadening of both the 'O' and the 'L' factors of the eclectic paradigm. Indeed, the ability of firms to develop and manage networks, alliances, and other forms of inter-firm relationships to enhance product quality, integrate knowledge and learning, and externalise risk can be regarded as an ownership-specific advantage in its own right. Location factors, for their part, need to incorporate the concept of agglomeration and clustering; that is, there are certain geographical locations that have become centres of interaction and innovation within global networks. Such areas offer a concentration of contacts, knowledge, infrastructure, and institutions that attract economic activity. Examples include the City of London for financial services, Silicon Valley in California or Silicon Glen in Scotland for information technology, or general areas of concentrated economic activity like southern China or northwest Europe.

Although some would argue that the elasticity of the eclectic paradigm demonstrates that its generality enables it to fit all circumstances, others argue that its adaptability is its strength. The international business environment is evolving rapidly, and its organisational diversity is expanding along with it. The eclectic paradigm is not itself a theory of international production, but rather a framework to help analysts make sense of it. As such, its expansion to incorporate alliance capitalism does not appear unreasonable. In the early 21st century, the large-scale, single multinational firm remains the dominant player in the global marketplace and, as such, the focus of research on the internationalisation of the firm. However, this does not preclude a growing body of research and literature on networks, cooperation and alliances to complement and sit alongside such research and, in some respects, perhaps even replace it.

---

**Box 10.2:** The end of the global company

The MNE (that is, those businesses that earn over 30 per cent of their earnings from sales outside their home region) has always been a controversial aspect of the globalisation process. On the one hand, they are seen as key conduits through which technology and know-how are dispersed throughout the global economy. On the other, they are seen as exploitative, pushing labour standards and costs to a minimum by forcing states to compete for their investment. Despite this, the MNE through the late 20th and early 21st centuries continued to grow, notably as more states opened their economies to welcome this investment. For these economies, the notion of a global firm run by global managers controlled by global shareholders and offering global products was synonymous with modernity and with social, economic, and political progress.

The fact that MNEs have power is indisputable. They are powerful forces shaping business ecosystems at both the national and international levels and directing the flows of goods and services. Despite only accounting for 2 per cent of total global employment, these businesses – through their complex business models – account for over 50 per cent of trade and 40 per cent of the value of stock markets. On top of all of this, they control vast swathes of the world's intellectual property. Despite this pretext of control and power, the truth is that many of these businesses can be more fragile than they are supposed to be. Many are overextended and increasingly subject to the whims of state discretion seeking to influence their behaviour and shares of their profits. Part of this backlash is a reflection of the fact that as many of the top MNEs become technology services companies, they have had to face charges that they seek to evade the responsibilities of corporate citizenship in the territories in which they operate (for example, via proactive tax avoidance strategies).

The history of many MNEs was to run less as global companies and more as a loose federation of national businesses. In the era of hyper-globalisation, this shifted as firms sought to be truly global. In so doing, they sought to internationalise their customers, production, capital, and management. The message was less diversity and more uniformity. The legacy of these actions was that these firms began to engage in aggressive vertical (i.e., new sourcing and production strategies) and horizontal (i.e., new markets) expansion simultaneously. This was a rapid process, with over 80 per cent of the stock of MNEs being created after 1990. The logic was one of control and homogeneity across all territories. This trend has begun to be reversed as MNE investment since 2016 has begun to fall along with sales and the complexity of MNE value networks. Moreover, MNE profits are declining.

Explaining this trend lies in misplaced confidence in the benefits of scale that would be derived from globality. They saw the firm as being able to increase revenues and decrease costs from the operation of the MNE as a global system, thus generating higher growth rates and profits. However – over the longer term – such confidence was misplaced as profits fell by 18 per cent between 2007 and 2017. In part, this slump in profits has been driven by a sharp fall in commodity prices (which affects oil and mining firms, for example); it has also been driven by the poor performance of banks and specialised global service firms (such as logistics trading and supply chain firms). This low performance has also been evident within more multi-product firms such as Unilever, GE, and P&G, with only the technology giants bucking the trend.

While there were one-off factors that could impact individual performance, there is nonetheless a belief that the advantages of scale and international arbitrage have been severely eroded. As these firms grew, they became more difficult to run, and as low-cost locations, such as China, developed, wages rose, removing any advantages from locating in these economies. In addition, the ability to compete between tax regimes to minimise tax bills has been exhausted, as has the ability of rivals to catch up with any technology and know-how a firm may possess. The impact is that firms with a strong domestic focus are winning market share. This has been compounded by the increased negativity attached to MNEs post-GFC. These were not merely seen as not playing by the same rules but were also seen as agents of inequality. They created jobs overseas but not within their home states, with profits not being distributed to the mass population. This eroded any sense of political support for these businesses, with governments beginning to clamp down on support given to them.

However, a strategy of protection against these businesses is fruitless due to the sheer embeddedness of globalisation. This is typified by complex value chains, where any product can cross borders multiple times in its production. As such, clamping down on MNEs has to revolve around ensuring they are effective corporate citizens where they do operate. As such, many regulators are seeking to reduce the ability of MNEs to engage in aggressive tax avoidance. There is also rising political pressure – notably in the US – to curtail outsourcing. The likely outcome of such pressure is increasing costs and tax bills. While hosts will still welcome MNE investment, there is also growing evidence that this is not as unquestioning as it once was with China, for example, seeking measures by inward investors to enable 'indigenous innovation'. Many states are looking at how successful China is with such a strategy. In addition, as value shifts towards intangibles (such as IP-based activity), the need for a wider network of businesses is diminished. In fact, this trend may actively encourage reshoring.

It is evident that globality does not work for all businesses. Many industries work best as national or regional concerns, notably in areas like retail. Many other businesses have retreated to their home states or regions after failed foreign incursions. Indeed, for many firms, there is an increased focus on core markets as they retrench globality. There is also an evident political sentiment against large sprawling impersonal firms that don't belong 'anywhere', with their being reassured to reassert a stronger degree of national identity. The future MNEs are expected to either be a limited number of true (but more circumspect) MNEs who globalise production and markets, a set of technology firms with global reach but tend to (relatively) asset-light, or a set of SMEs using technology to establish a global presence. Overall, what is likely to happen is that capitalism increases in both its fragmentation and parochialism. This may be less efficient, but it may also be consensual.

## THE KNOWLEDGE-BASED VIEW OF THE MNE

The evolutionary view of the MNE (Kogut and Zander 1993) was seen by many as the end of the prevailing transaction-based perspective of the MNE. This novel perspective was informed by behavioural (Cyert and March 1963) and evolutionary (Nelson and Winter 1982) theories of the firm. The theory seeks to address three alleged weaknesses within internalisation theory:

- The focus on minimising transaction costs understates the potential value created by foreign entry.
- The internalisation perspective is overdetermined through neglecting the development of new firm-specific advantages.
- The internalisation perspective focuses on individual transactions and ignores (or at least underplays) the firm's past, future, and social context of these transactions.

Kogut and Zander conceptualise the MNE as a repository of knowledge. First, they suggest that the more tacit the knowledge, the more likely that knowledge transference will be internal. Secondly, they claim that the boundary of the firm is defined more by knowledge resources than internalisation. Consequently, they conceptualise the MNE as a social community that serves as an efficient mechanism for the creation and transformation of knowledge into products. Thus, the key criterion for whether a firm will transfer knowledge internally is its efficiency relative to third parties. Thus, market failure concerns are not required. As a result, MNEs exist because they are efficient means of creating and transmitting knowledge. Through repeated interaction, agents develop a common understanding of how to transfer knowledge from ideas into production and markets.

The central tenet is that firms grow by their ability to create new knowledge and replicate this knowledge so as to expand their market. Their competitive advantage rests on being able to understand and undertake this transfer more effectively than other firms and on the inability of rivals to duplicate and imitate this core resource. As a result, horizontal FDI is conceptualised as the transfer of knowledge within the firm and across borders. Such transfers are the primary expression of the growth of the firm. Thus, modal choice is a reflection of the likely revenues to be generated from that mode, given the experiential knowledge that would result. Thus, the lower the expectation of extra knowledge, the more devolved the mode will be (e.g., licencing, etc.). If the reverse applies, the firm will seek higher control modes.

This makes a break from market failure towards the efficiency of the firm in the transformation of knowledge relative to other firms as a key explanation of the development of MNEs. As a result, the firm boundary is determined by the difference between knowledge and the embedded capabilities between the creator and users. The more tacit the knowledge and the more experience agents have in sharing this tacit knowledge, the greater the incentive for the firm to internalise this knowledge. Thus, firms specialise in transferring knowledge that is difficult to understand and codify. MNEs are able to lower the cost of this transfer internally more than they would be able to do so via third parties. Furthermore, knowledge as a firm-specific advantage is something that will aid expansion.

Kogut and Zander also stress that the dynamic nature of this process underlines that these capabilities and knowledge do not stand still. MNEs seek to combine existing knowledge with new information to constantly evolve their stock of valuable knowledge. There is, thus, a key advantage in the combinative capability of the firm. This is also linked to the high absorptive capacity of the firm, that is, the ability to absorb, spread, utilise, and transform information into new knowledge stock.

The above is typical of an emerging research theme which stresses the knowledge component of the MNE. It seems logical that if the firm is a repository of knowledge, then central to this is the ability of knowledge to flow within the MNE between headquarters and subsidiaries as well as between subsidiary units themselves. This characterises the MNE as a differentiated network in which each subsidiary (as well as the headquarters) has access to different resources and the ability to generate their own valuable knowledge that can be valuable to other parts of the MNE network.

Gupta and Govindarajan (1991) offered a typology of the role of subsidiaries in the knowledge development process. This is part of a long line of literature that has sought to explore headquarter-subsidiary relations as a means of control and coordination. Gutpa and Govindarajan have examined knowledge flows within MNEs, which they see as the most important of all the flows between the constituent units of the network, and have identified two aspects of these flows:

- The magnitude of transactions (i.e., the extent to which subsidiaries engage in knowledge transfer).
- The direction of transfer (i.e., whether a subsidiary is a recipient or a provider of knowledge).

Using these two dimensions they have defined four generic subsidiary roles:

*Global innovator (high outflow, low inflow)*: as the firm moves towards a transnational model, the subsidiary becomes more important and acts as a centre of excellence for specific product lines.

*Integrated player (high outflow, high inflow)*: these engage in knowledge transfer but are also simultaneously receiving knowledge from other units. This makes it an important mode within the MNE network.

*Implementor (low outflow, high inflow)*: these do not engage in extensive knowledge creation and offer little to other units. Consequently, they are heavily dependent upon knowledge flows from either the headquarters or other subsidiaries.

*Local innovators (low outflow, low inflow)*: these are self-standing subsidiaries that engage in knowledge creation but do not seek to transfer this knowledge across the rest of the network. In addition, the firm also sees little value in knowledge being created elsewhere within the MNE network.

The above suggests that knowledge within the firm needs to be studied at the nodal (i.e., individual units), dyadic (i.e., focus on the behaviour of pairs), and systemic (i.e., focus on the network) levels. According to this model, the causes of knowledge flows in and out of a subsidiary are a function of the value of the source unit's knowledge stock, the motivational disposition of the source unit, the existence of a richness of transmission channels, the motivational disposition of target units, and the absorptive capacity of the target unit.

The value of a unit's knowledge stock to the MNE network is seen as directly related to the type of entry mode utilised. It is understood that acquired units tend to exhibit greater outflows to the rest of the group than greenfield operations, as acquisitions tend to be motivated by the unique resources within the acquired unit. Furthermore, the value of a unit is also positively linked to the size of the unit relative to other units and to the level of economic development relative to the home state.

These actions have to be supported by an open-minded attitude by managers within the units and may have to be linked to remuneration schemes. Units need to be open both as sources and as recipients of knowledge and rely on incentives within the firm to offer and accept knowledge, as well as similar economic levels that allow such information to be transmitted and understood between units. These strategies will be supported by the ability of transmission channels (both formal and informal) to aid the flow of knowledge. Formal mechanisms include direct interaction between personnel, etc. Informal channels include corporate socialisation mechanisms. Finally, absorptive capacity is key, as the unit has to be familiar with incoming knowledge and be able to diffuse and use the information for competitive advantage. Again, the entry mode is an important determinant, as acquired firms will be less obvious recipients of knowledge than greenfield operations.

## CASE STUDY 10.3: THE TURNAROUND AT FORD

Ford was an automotive business that was facing long-term structural problems. By 2006, when the new CEO, Alan Mulally, arrived, the company was predicted to have a $17 billion loss. The new CEO initiated a turnaround that, in four years, saw the business make record profits. This turnaround started with the company beginning to recognise its faults and overcoming a culture of corporate complacency and executive rivalry. This growth is all the more impressive as it has been set against a background of sluggish growth within the core US market. Such a turnaround is not unique among the big three car makers (GM and Chrysler are the other two). The big difference is that while Chrysler and GM went bankrupt and into government hands, Ford avoided this scenario.

Its avoidance of state control reflected that Ford had already been sorting itself out prior to the GFC, which saw car sales tumble. At the root of its troubles was a desire by the firm from 1998 to move into more diverse segments of the automotive industry (it acquired Land Rover, Aston Martin, Jaguar, Volvo, and its Lincoln and Mercury brands into a single group: the Premier Automotive Group (PAG). The role of this group was to help the group ride out variations in demand in the mass car market by diversifying its offering. The aim was for PAG to generate up to a third of its profits. However, this never happened with PAG, which proved to be costly and distracting from its core business. Though a change in management launched a 'back to basics' strategy, the company began to suffer from a declining reputation for quality and reliability. However, long-term change was delayed as the company was able to hide behind the high revenue growth from the sale of sports utility vehicles and pickup trucks (which were protected by trade restrictions). However, these segments became exposed as Asian companies moved in on this segment and set up US factories to get around duties. The effect was that Ford had to cut capacity. Despite this progress, this strategy was slow due to strong management and labour resistance.

By 2006, the company had hit a crisis point, having to take out emergency loans against the firm's assets to secure the business. However, the plan lacked credibility with banks, as this was just another rescue plan. Alan Mulally began to turn the business around by selling off PAG and focusing solely on the Ford brand. This was aided by the decision to sell a narrower range of cars (from 97 to 36), which were better quality, with the target of being best in class. Next, Ford sought to ensure that regionally successful products could be globally successful. This meant establishing global platforms (i.e., the basic floor plan and underpinning). Now, 80 per cent of platforms are global. From these global platforms, Ford can adapt the model to suit regional tastes and differences in regulations. Now, up to 80 parts in any single car are shared across models. Inevitably, on top of this came a rationalisation of the workforce, with numbers falling by around 60 per cent. The net effect was that by 2010, Ford had shed $14 billion in operating costs, and it's now able to compete with Japanese transplant factors.

For Ford, the strategy is to only build what the company can sell. This new flexibility within strategy has been aided by the common platform strategy, as production can be shifted between models easily. Moreover, improvements in technology are speeding development times and leading to a seemingly perpetual refreshment of its product portfolio.

Thus, when the GFC occurred in 2008, Ford decided it could opt out of the Troubled Asset Relief Programme to which the other large car makers had succumbed. Indeed, the avoidance of the need for public support has given Ford some very positive public relations. However, Ford still has a way to go to fully adapt to the shifting environment as other car manufacturers continue to progress. In the end, Ford is making inroads in growth markets. Ford did find itself at a disadvantage in the Chinese market, where the government chose GM as its early joint venture partner. Even if this does not come off, Ford is clearly planning to target other Asian markets. Europe has a long-term problem with chronic overcapacity; this is despite the market being one of its more successful. There is little denying that Asia and other emerging economies are the future of Ford sales growth. By 2020, only 16 per cent of sales would be in such regions, with 84 per cent being in Europe and North America.

## QUESTION

Given the case material, what do you believe are the major issues facing Ford in its turnaround strategy?

## CONCLUSIONS

MNEs are central to the process of globalisation. As in earlier chapters, they remain a controversial but important feature of the international business environment. However, it would be misleading to call them global in terms of reach, as many MNEs tend to limit their multinational endeavours. What is ap is that there has been a shift in the conceptualisation of the MNE. Increasingly, the MNE is seen as a differentiated network of subsidiaries where value is created by the knowledge flows within them.

### KEY POINTS

- MNEs are defined by the fact that they engage in FDI.
- FDI is driven by a desire to control overseas assets that are core to the firm's value proposition.
- The MNE is incentivised to engage in FDI for a number of reasons.
- A number of theories have been advanced to seek to explain why MNEs exist.

## QUESTIONS FOR DISCUSSION

1. How do you explain the existence of MNEs?
2. How do you believe the risks facing MNEs vary across space?
3. Using an MNE with which you are familiar, seek to identify the major components of its OLI configuration.

## ACTIVITIES

1. Using an MNE of your choice, explore and explain its pattern of FDI.
2. Compare and contrast the major theories explaining the MNEs.

## SUGGESTED FURTHER READINGS

Birkinshaw, J. (2016). *Multinational corporate evolution and subsidiary development*, Basingstoke, UK: Springer.
Buckley, P. J. (2018). *The global factory: Networked multinational enterprises in the modern global economy*, Cheltenham: Edward Elgar Publishing.

Buckley, P. J., & Casson, M. (2016). *The future of the multinational enterprise*, Basingstoke UK: Springer.

Cyert, R. M., & March, J. G. (1963). *A behavioral theory of the firm*, Englewood Cliffs: Prentice Hall.

Dunning, J. H. (1993). Multinational enterprises and the growth of services: Some conceptual and theoretical issues. In *Transnational Corporations in Service* (pp. 33–74). New York: Routledge.

Dunning, J. H. (1995). Reappraising the eclectic paradigm in an age of alliance capitalism. *Journal of International Business Studies, 26*(3), 461–491.

Dunning, J. H. (1997). *Alliance capitalism and global business*, London: Routledge.

Dunning, J. H., & Lundan, S. M. (2008). *Multinational enterprises and the global economy*, Cheltenham: Edward Elgar Publishing.

Forsgren, M. (2017). *Theories of the multinational firm: A multidimensional creature in the global economy*, Cheltenham: Edward Elgar Publishing.

Gupta, A. K., & Govindarajan, V. (1991). Knowledge flows and the structure of control within multinational firms. *Academy of Management Review, 16*, 768–792.

Kogut, B., & Zander, U. (1993). Knowledge of the firm and the evolutionary theory of the multinational corporation. *Journal of International Business Studies, 24*(4), 625–645.

Lall, S. (1992). Technological capabilities and industrialization. *World Development, 20*(2), 165–186.

Lall, S. (1997). *Attracting foreign investment: New trends, sources and policies*, Economic Paper 31, Commonwealth Secretariat.

Lien, Y. C., & Filatotchev, I. (2015). Ownership characteristics as determinants of FDI location decisions in emerging economies. *Journal of World Business, 50*(4), 637–650.

Meldrum, D. (2000). Country risk and *foreign direct investment. Business Economics, 35*(1), 33–40.

Nelson, R. R., & Winter, S. G. (1982). *An evolutionary theory of economic change*, Cambridge: Belknap Press of Harvard University Press.

Perlmutter, H. V. (1969). The tortuous evolution of the multinational corporation. *Columbia Journal of World Business, 4*(January/February), 9–18.

UNCTAD (2016). World investment report. www.unctad.org.

## Websites

www.unctad.org/wir/ – World Investment Report.

www.oecd.org/ – Survey Work on International Investment.

www.FDI.net – Foreign Direct Investment Information Portal of the World Bank Group.

# CHAPTER 11

# THE INTERNATIONALISATION OF SMALL AND MEDIUM-SIZED ENTERPRISES (SMEs)

## OBJECTIVES

This chapter will help you to:

- Identify the form and nature of small and medium-sized enterprises (SMEs).
- Assess the importance of SMEs to the global economy.
- Comprehend the impact of globalisation on SMEs.
- Understand the process of internationalising SMEs and the policy measures to support the trend.

SMEs, as defined by the OECD 2016, are those non-subsidiary, independent businesses that employ less than 250 people. As this definition covers around 95 per cent of businesses across the OECD, it also includes those businesses whose function is more subsistence than growth per se, where entrepreneurship is driven more by a desire to earn a living than expansion. The subject of SMEs within the international commercial system is nuanced, as their impact on it can be evidenced through a number of channels. This chapter will focus on two themes. The first is through the proactive approach to SME engagement with international markets through the internationalisation process. The second is that states seek to encourage SMEs and entrepreneurship as a means of enabling and sustaining competitive advantage.

## SME INTERNATIONALISATION: GRADUAL OR DISCONTINUOUS?

As suggested above, the importance of SME internationalisation as a policy area is generated by its strategic importance to modern economies. It is widely believed

DOI: 10.4324/9781315184500-14

that in order to sustain their growth trajectory, many growth-focused SMEs will at some point have to look beyond home markets into overseas markets. This has created widespread policy interest in the internationalisation of SMEs and how it can be enabled. The process is seen as especially important for economies, as these SMEs that engage proactively in international markets tend to be the most dynamic and innovative.

There are, when expressed in their simplest terms, two conflicting perspectives on what drives SME involvement in international markets. At one end are the traditional, gradual perspectives shaped by the conceptualisation of internationalisation as a risk-averse process characterised by ongoing learning by business. At the other end, and while not totally dismissing conventional perspectives, there is the argument that the internationalisation of the SME can be driven by less ordered processes where the geographic extension of business can occur unevenly over both space and time. These differing perspectives are addressed below.

There is no single perspective that explains SME internationalisation, simply due to the sheer heterogeneity of the businesses under consideration.

**TABLE 11.1** The distribution of SMEs

|  | Manufacturing | Trade | Services | Agriculture/other |
|---|---|---|---|---|
| Share of micro-enterprises |  |  |  |  |
| Developed | 8 | 35 | 6 | 1 |
| Developing | 11.5 | 44.3 | 38.9 | 5.3 |
| • G20 developing | 14 | 33 | 40 | 14 |
| • Other developing | 10 | 45 | 40 | 3 |
| • LDCs | 15 | 46 | 31 | 9 |
| Total | 11 | 43 | 42 | 5 |
| Share of small and medium-sized enterprises |  |  |  |  |
| Developed | 22 | 25 | 52 | 1 |
| Developing | 19.9 | 30.6 | 41 | 8.5 |
| • G20 developing | 21 | 31 | 44 | 3 |
| • Other developing | 18 | 32 | 41 | 8 |
| • LDCs | 24 | 23 | 37 | 16 |
| Total | 20 | 31 | 42 | 8 |

## SME internationalisation as a gradual process

A 1975 study (referred to as the Uppsala model) by Johanson and Weidersheim-Paul of how four Swedish firms had internationalised provides a framework that has proved useful on a wider stage. The authors argue that many firms begin the internationalisation process when they are relatively small and develop their overseas presence gradually. They establish themselves in their domestic market first and then start to move abroad via a series of incremental steps. This movement abroad tends to occur earlier in the case of companies established in small domestic markets, like the firms in the Uppsala model. Linked into process-based approaches (see below), the Uppsala model reflects observations of the operational activities of business as opposed to forming a theory per se.

The Uppsala model identifies four steps in the establishment and extension of a firm's operations, a process referred to by its authors as 'the establishment chain':

1. no regular export activities;
2. export via independent representatives or agents;
3. the establishment of sales subsidiaries;
4. foreign production and manufacturing.

Firms are expected to follow this pattern of internationalisation as they move from low- to high-commitment modes of operation (see below).

According to this model, initial movement abroad is carried out by independent exporting agents or representatives. This entails a limited resource commitment and a lesser risk than immediately setting up a wholly owned sales subsidiary (stage three) in a market of which the incumbent has little knowledge. Indeed, underpinning this model is the general assumption that moving through the different phases of development depends on the acquisition of the expertise and knowledge that enables the firm to move onto the next internationalisation stage. Firms only move to the final stage of the establishment chain (foreign production and manufacturing) when they have gained international expertise through other activities and specific knowledge of a particular location.

The authors do not claim that the model applies in all circumstances. They point out that there may be good reasons why firms do not follow the establishment chain exactly. For example, firms with extensive experience in other foreign markets may well jump stages in the establishment chain and invest in production facilities in a particular location without prior knowledge of it. However, the model is useful. First, it points out that firms are more likely to seek international opportunities when their founders or senior management already have international business experience or are internationally minded in some way. Secondly, and more importantly, it establishes the principle that firms engage in international activity in a way that gradually commits them to more intensive and extensive involvement. In a sense, the precise details of each of the four identified stages of the process do not matter, as they vary from case to case. What does distinguish each stage of the process, though, is the degree of involvement, as highlighted by the commitment offered to the host.

The theoretical underpinnings of the process models are the interrelated concepts of learning and experience. Process models regard experience as the main explanatory construct of the internationalisation process, reflecting the belief that the process is driven by 'learning by doing'. This ongoing experience removes uncertainties surrounding the process of internationalisation generated by a lack of knowledge. The role of experience is to lower the risk associated with the internationalisation process by increasing the firm's knowledge of operating in international markets.

Johanson and Weidersheim-Paul (1975) assume that the biggest obstacles to internationalisation are a lack of knowledge and resources. Incremental learning reduces the perceived risk of overseas investment, and continuing internationalisation is encouraged by a presence in a foreign market. This perspective is underpinned by the importance of psychic distance in the process of internationalisation. Linking to culture (see Chapter 12), the concept of psychic distance has been defined as both internal and external factors preventing or disturbing the flow of information between the firm and the market. The theory assumes that a firm's reach and depth are extended as the psychic distance is narrowed and the firm gets better at the process of internationalisation. Familiarity comes from language, culture, education levels, political systems, levels of industrial development, etc. Psychic distance will often be closely linked to physical distance (that is, internationalisation may start close to home), but that will not always be the case. The UK and Australia, for example, are physically far apart, but the psychic distance between them is much closer.

In terms of the internationalisation process, market knowledge is subdivided into objective and experiential knowledge. Whereas objective knowledge can be taught, experiential knowledge is unique and acquired through personal experience. Experiential knowledge is inversely related to uncertainty and derives from the size of the investment in resources and the degree of commitment offered to international markets. Variation in commitment implies that investments are idiosyncratic. Commitment decisions are made by managers to commit resources to target markets and are based on the knowledge that the MNE has of the market and the conditions within it. Thus, lack of knowledge is inversely related to commitment to the market. Missing knowledge can take the following forms:

- Internationalisation knowledge: this is knowledge of the firm's capability and resources for undertaking actions in international markets. This reflects historical actions, is firm-specific, and combines all past experiences of the process to inform current and future activities.
- Institutional knowledge: this is the knowledge of government and institutional frameworks, rules, norms, and values within the host markets.
- Business knowledge: this is the knowledge of the customers, suppliers, and market conditions within the host economies where the firm operates.

The above are interrelated and, over time, have the capability to inform objective knowledge as experience is taught to other parts of the organisation (see Figure 11.1). These will depend upon the depth and reach of the international activities followed by the operation.

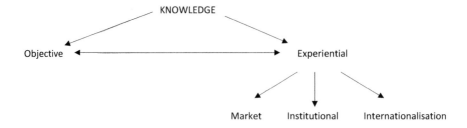

**FIGURE 11.1** Knowledge and the internationalisation process

Process models have attracted criticism, most notably for their simplicity. This reflects the fact that they understate the complexity of the internationalisation process. Clearly, the conception of the model is highly deterministic, suggesting that feedback loops exist that push the firm towards ever-increasing commitment. This may not be the case. Uni-directionality is not inevitable, as strategies do vary in their intensity of physical commitment over time. There is also a need to consider intangible commitment alongside tangible commitment, or else the degree of commitment offered to markets could be underestimated. In addition, the choice of market is likely to be determined by more than knowledge alone. The model ignores issues of market size, total resources, bandwagon effects, etc. that could determine the choice of market.

## SME INTERNATIONALISATION AS AN INTERMITTENT PROCESS

Contingency-based views of the internationalisation process initially grew out of rejection of the determinism and gradualism of the process views. The central tenet of this perspective is that firms have very uneven internationalisation trajectories and that incrementalism is no longer relevant for many firms. The shifts in the environment highlighted by the rise of international entrepreneurship (through Born Globals) mean firms can be international from their inception (Rialp et al. 2015). This is especially true where firms possess unique resources. This approach disputes the relevance of the stages model to increasingly service-intensive and high-technology-based economies. The main source of competitive advantage is a more sophisticated knowledge base that does not require the evolving features of process-based approaches. The evolution of this perspective has in part curtailed its ability to explore internationalisation beyond the formative period. Authors have attempted to move beyond this limitation by building network views into international entrepreneurship to offer a framework to explore how strategies evolve (Johanson and Vahlne 2003).

The network view of internationalisation emerged from reflection on the deficiencies of the process models. This perspective is based on empirical observations that networks are important to the internationalisation process through social exchange and resource dependency. Networks are defined as 'connections between firms and individuals in an industrial system built as relationships are established and maintained and linked through a variety of formal and informal mechanisms, resources and activities'.

Internationalisation occurs by using networks to extend reach, increase penetration, and connect and integrate different national networks. The network perspective identifies the difficulties in formulating and developing a market entry strategy. It highlights how social and cognitive ties between actors shape ongoing interactions that in turn shape the network structure. Network theory stresses how agents interact to influence the form and nature of the internationalisation process. Johanson and Mattsson (1988) argue that in the network view, internationalisation is based on the gradual learning and development of market knowledge through networks, which allows the firm to establish and develop positions in a foreign network. Thus, networks can be used to enhance strategic positioning through access to new resources, skills, and flexibility. This approach reflects that SMEs are often able to integrate themselves into global value chains.

Internationalisation through networks (defined as long-term relationships) occurs through one or more of the following methods:

- The establishment of relationships within country networks that are new to the firm.
- The development of relationships within these networks by increased penetration.
- Connecting existing networks.

These patterns of internationalisation suggest that networks are used to extend reach, enhance market penetration, and be mutually supportive. Unlike the process models, the network view focuses on the context of the business and the relationships that form the platform of the internationalisation process. Furthermore, the degree of internationalisation of the firm reflects the network, not the firm itself. As a result, a highly internationalised firm may have all its assets within its home market. The network perspective also has implications for the nature of commitment, where firms are committed to the internationalisation process through their participation in networks and not solely via host market presence.

Bell (1995) argues that network theory explains internationalisation better than process models, as they are more influential on market entry choices than conventional notions of psychic distance. More recent times have seen networks become a powerful framework for international entrepreneurship research. Andersen and Buvik (2002) suggest that relationships offer a more effective guide to international market selection than process models.

Conventional thinking states that, as economies of scale become ever more important determinants of competitiveness, larger, more global markets increase the dominance of LSEs and reduce the power of SMEs (Zander et al. 2015). Thus, over the long run, it is to be expected that the average firm size will increase. Despite this, the openness of economies has gone hand in hand with increased levels of SME activity. LSEs have been successful in the global economy through exploiting core competencies and ICTs – the ability to use and form alliances and the capacity to promote inter-firm collaboration. However, the synergy between LSEs and SMEs is important, including the role of SMEs in technological change, the strategic attachment of SMEs to local economies, as well as the contribution of SMEs to the growth and evolution of industries. The relationship between SMEs and LSEs in the internationalisation process is reinforced by the fact that, as global competition increases, LSEs pay increased attention to innovation. This places a greater compulsion upon them to develop stronger links with innovative SMEs.

As suggested by the 'steps models', the internationalisation of SMEs can be incremental and lengthy. The traditional focus of SMEs on local markets means that the change in emphasis towards international markets must be planned and based on a protracted learning process. There are important differences between conventional SMEs (such as newsagents, etc.) who see themselves as meeting primarily local needs and who will only undertake a protracted process of internationalisation and innovative SMEs who tend to be more global and focus upon narrow product/service segments within this context (Rugman et al. 2011).

Innovative SMEs highlight the importance of knowledge, of accessing and utilising networks effectively, and of accessing MNEs to support internationalisation. Much learning and knowledge is internally focused and based on trial and error. This implies that public policy needs to support this learning process. However, the pattern of internationalisation tends to vary depending on the type of firm (see Table 11.3)

The pressures of globalisation on SMEs are transmitted via a variety of mechanisms (see Table 11.3). The salience of each depends upon the socio-economic context, notably

- Imports and import competition.
- Competition from other more internationalised firms.
- Customer requirements.
- Large firm requirements.
- Alliances, joint ventures, etc.
- International conventions and standards.

As the push and pull issues (see below) highlight, SME internationalisation can often occur in a reactive and passive manner, underlining the fact that the process is not always a deliberate strategic choice by enterprises but occurs by default as more open economies expose their domestic markets to intense competition from external sources. Within international trade, SMEs have a variety of roles, including

**TABLE 11.2** Contributors to the internationalisation of SMEs

| Macro level | Micro level |
|---|---|
| • The emergence of common or open markets and the reduction of protectionist barriers<br>• The increased globalisation of large firms<br>• Increased levels of foreign investment and world trade<br>• Increased mobility of capital, technology, and management<br>• Increased currency movements that have changed the relative competitiveness of different states | • Changing technology, communications, and organisational forms<br>• Increased opportunities for SMEs to extend their value chains across borders as a result of cost differentials, etc.<br>• Changing attitudes and managerial skills |

**TABLE 11.3** Types of Internationalisation for SMEs

|  | Conventional SMEs | Knowledge-intensive SMEs |
|---|---|---|
| Motivations | Reactive | Proactive |
| Patterns | Incremental psychic markets | Concurrent lead markets |
| Pace | Gradual | Rapid |
| Method of distribution/entry | Use of agents/distributors and direct to customers | Use of agents/distributors, licencing, joint ventures, and overseas production. |
| Subsequent internationalisation | Ad hoc continued reactive behaviour and unrelated new customers | Structured/planned approach to international expansion and expansion of networks |

- Domestic suppliers of inputs to products exported by larger enterprises.
- Exporters of specialised niche products.
- Importers and distributors of goods from foreign SMEs.
- providers of support services for international trade transactions (for example, inland transport, freight forwarding, etc.).

In this context, the success of an SME in international markets is determined by an awareness of market imperfections that enable it to create a successful niche for itself. In practice, most actions by SMEs in international markets tend to be horizontally based as they strive to occupy the same position in different geographical markets and to develop a 'deep niche' strategy. This results in high market shares across a number of core markets within their chosen segment. Plietner et al. (1998) argue that finding a niche, and therefore achieving success in international markets, is heavily influenced by:

- Product quality.
- Reliability of delivery.
- Quality of management.
- Quality of sales staff.
- Ability to solve technical problems.
- Customer relations.

Welch and Luostarinen (1988) (quoted in Su and Poisson 1998) identify a number of factors that create a gradual approach to the internationalisation process, such as the level of acquaintance with foreign markets, the importance of communication networks, perceived risks and/or uncertainty, and the willingness of the manager to enter foreign markets. This implies that variations observed in relation to the internationalisation model could be the consequence of environmental changes. Etemad (2003) suggests that three forces are at play in the process of internationalising SMEs:

1.  Push forces: these are a set of drivers (usually internal to the firm) that impel the firm to move into international markets. These are entrepreneurial in nature, based on a desire to explore new opportunities. These could be the effects of managers, the maturity of the local market, etc.

2.  Pull forces: these are external to the firm and enhance the firm's competitiveness and signify the benefits of a move into international markets.

3.  Mediating forces: these are firm-specific factors that facilitate the acting of push and pull forces upon strategy and represent the internal dynamics of the firm. Within the firm, there are deterrents and enablers influencing its ability to develop international strategy.

Recent evidence suggests there is a group of (mainly small) firms that eschew this evolutionary approach by undertaking rapid and dedicated internationalisation. This has resulted in the emergence of international entrepreneurship. According to Zahra and George (2002), these are businesses that seek to derive a competitive advantage by operating across multiple locations from their inception. The issue of international entrepreneurs, though, has evolved from merely stressing new ventures to including corporate intrapreneurship (i.e., entrepreneurship within an LSE), though it is the former that will concern us within this chapter. These rapid internationalising firms are created by one or more of the following factors:

*   New market conditions in many sectors, especially the rise of niche markets for SMEs globally.
*   Technological developments in production, transportation, and communication.
*   The increased importance of global networks and alliances.
*   The more elaborate capabilities of people.

These trends can be expected to strengthen in the years to come. Research (see Rialp et al. 2015) has demonstrated that many SMEs are able to compete within their respective niches without any of the disadvantages that are assumed to arise from the absence of scale.

Oviatt and McDonald (1994) argued that there are three types of international new ventures:

1.  New international market makers: either through selling into new markets in which they previously had no presence or with minimal direct investment in target markets. These may be import/export startups (focusing on a few states with which the entrepreneur is familiar) or multinational traders (which focus on an array of states and are always scanning for new opportunities).

2.  Geographically focused startups: these service the well-specialised needs of a defined region through the use of foreign resources. Unlike multinational traders, these firms are geographically restricted to the location of need and involve more than just the coordination of inward and outward logistics.

3.  Global startups: these seek to coordinate offerings across multiple markets with an unlimited geographical reach. They both respond to and create new opportunities in globalising markets.

It is evident from past research (for a review, see Rialp et al. 2015) that many of these 'born globals' have emerged within high-technology sectors where the process of rapid change has allowed for the emergence of targeted niches. Further research indicates the evolution of early internationalisers beyond high-technology segments into other sectors. However, in developed states, born globals (BGs) tend to be in high-technology sectors, whereas elsewhere BGs are in other sectors. According to Bell et al. (2003), these firms tend to be in either knowledge- and/or service-intensive or knowledge-based sectors. The latter tend to rely on high-technology to create a niche in new technology markets. The former tend to base their internationalisation on applying knowledge to develop new value propositions but are not inherently knowledge-based firms. Thus, across both types of firms, knowledge is a pivotal factor shaping the process of internationalisation, confirming that BG firms tend to be knowledge-intensive or knowledge-based (Cavusgil and Knight 2015).

Internationalisation patterns are strategies in their own right. A comparison of patterns for BGs among regional and more traditional (yet global) firms shows that the BG path is characterised by rapid and extensive development of networks to facilitate simultaneous market entry (Hagen and Zucchella 2014). Such firms are found to be driven by an aggressive learning style that seeks experimentation, tolerates initial failure, and looks for solutions to problems as they arise.

Overall, Rialp et al. (2015) conclude that the following factors drive the emergence of BGs and early internationalisers:

1. A managerial global mindset from inception.
2. A high degree of previous experience in international markets by managers.
3. management commitment to international markets.
4. Strong use of personal and business networks.
5. Managers with a higher risk tolerance.
6. Market knowledge and market commitment.
7. Unique intangible assets based on knowledge management.
8. High-value creation through product differentiation, leading-edge technology products, and innovativeness.
9. A niche-focused, proactive strategy within geographically spread markets.
10. Narrowly defined user groups with strong customer relationships.
11. Flexibility to adapt to rapidly changing external conditions.

These factors imply that the firm must own valuable assets and use networks to create a sustainable advantage within its chosen niche.

Networks are seen as key to the internationalisation process. SMEs use these structures to gain access to resources, improve strategic positions, control transaction costs, learn new skills, gain legitimacy, and cope positively with rapid technological changes. They require trust within personal relationships with the network representing social capital that is intangible and idiosyncratic (see case study on immigrant entrepreneurship).

According to Oviatt and McDougall (1994), this implies that new internationalised ventures rely on alternative governance structures due to the lack of sufficient resources. Networks offer the resource-constrained firm a critical leverage opportunity to access resources without high capital costs. The learning process for small firms is also critical to achieving competitive advantage. The BG has to build knowledge stocks. In some cases, it can be argued that newness allows firms to learn more rapidly than older firms that develop barriers to learning. This runs counter to the idea that in knowledge development regarding international markets, there is a liability attached to newness.

Alongside 'born global' firms are the 'born again' globals. These are firms that, after a long period with a domestic focus, suddenly change to a strong international focus. This can be based on a sudden infusion of new human and/or financial resources, access to new networks, the acquisition of product knowledge, or some other event. These are reactive strategies as opposed to the proactive strategies followed by the BG. It is the shift in knowledge that creates scope for a rapid move into international markets after years of a sole home focus. Understanding and offering theoretical guidance to SMEs facing the internationalisation of their markets is important, as few of these businesses can afford to absorb the risk and costs of failure. SMEs in international markets face the double jeopardy of the risk of proactivism and the risk of reactivism from larger firms. Experience suggests therefore that SMEs cannot merely follow MNE strategies; their strategies must have their own drivers based on occupying their own niche using their own unique resources and competencies.

The importance of BGs is that they are seen as a set of firms that are key to state competitiveness (Rialp et al. 2015). These are seen as high-growth businesses that will counter structural change within developed economies. This reflects that many of these firms exist in industries that are by their nature global (such as IT). The BG is not a static phenomenon but one which co-evolves with its environment. Moreover, while the literature is phenomenological, there have been great efforts to really add more detail to flesh out the whys and hows of the process. However, entrepreneurship and growth are simply not driven by BG, as a major source of competitive advantage is entrepreneurship within established firms.

## CASE STUDY 11.1: CHINA'S INTERNET STARTUPS

For a state that seems to have had a problem with innovation. The last decade has seen a massive sea change in Chinese entrepreneurship in online environments. Alongside the Chinese Internet giants Baidu, Alibaba, and Tencent (BAT), there is an emerging set of startups, many of which echo their US-based equivalents, such as Didi Chuxing (a ride-hailing app) and Ofo (a bike-sharing app). These businesses (and ones like them) represent a change in innovation where, up to a decade ago, this meant copycats and counterfeiters. This new group of young entrepreneurs are reshaping this process, and these businesses are attracting international investors. Indeed, in 2016, China was leading the world in global technology investments and catching up with the US in other areas such as artificial intelligence, virtual reality, education technology, and autonomous driving.

By mid-2017, there were 89 'unicorns' in China (i.e., startups worth $1 billion or more), and they were approaching, in value terms, the combined valuation of their US equivalents. This rise is due in no small part to the ease of innovation within China (as promoted by the government as it seeks to move away from low-end manufacturing towards high-end products). This has also been aided by three other factors, namely:

- The size of the Chinese economy (the world's second-largest), which allows these businesses to gain scale without the need for rapid international expansion (even though this is occurring anyway). This is compounded by the relative homogeneity of this market (in terms of culture and language), especially when compared to Europe, and its excellent physical infrastructure. This latter aspect gives these businesses an advantage over their US equivalents.
- Chinese customers have proved open to innovation and change, which has proved an advantage to these businesses. They have also been keen adopters of new technology, have a high penetration of mobile phones and broadband, and were early and widespread adopters of cashless systems. This has allowed these Chinese technology startups to flourish very rapidly, especially in the financial technology sector.
- State-owned enterprises have proved notoriously hostile to customers, allowing newcomers to use their agile business models to create and define niches based on superior customer service and the deployment of the latest technologies.

However, as suggested above, the government is an active player in this strategy through its desire to support new businesses and in promoting these businesses to attain maturity. Indeed, it has played a very useful role as a market maker, notably in key areas such as electric vehicles. In this area, it has promoted new entry and created a directly enabling regulatory environment by not only increasing charging points for electric cars but also accelerating the demise of the petrol engine. This development has also been aided by the attitude of Chinese customers to try electronic cars, who, as a result of not being addicted to driving or car ownership, are more open to other forms of mobility such as ride-sharing. This has also opened up new opportunities for the sharing economy to emerge. Indeed, bike-sharing has proved to be an especially prominent area for businesses to emerge. China has dozens of bike-sharing startups, each using differentiated technology to create unique value propositions.

These businesses have also emerged in areas where there is evidence of state failure. Here, startups have emerged in niches that crowd out the state sector. This is already evident in the health sector, where startups have begun to reduce the notorious quest for care and access to drugs. These companies use online environments to dispense drugs and use better data facilities to enable better care systems. Such trends are also evident in logistics, where state-owned businesses are also being pushed aside. This allows for a more efficient logistics system, with fewer empty loads being carried based on the better use of data.

It is evident that even though these firms have a large indigenous market, they are keen to expand abroad. This global outlook is often in-built, reflecting that many of these entrepreneurs were educated abroad and often backed by overseas finance. In some sectors, especially those linked to the sharing economy, these businesses have already proved adept international operators. In other cases, the global market is the natural market, as the products developed are simply too innovative and/or expensive for domestic tastes. In many ways, the fast-growing and changing market of China is a better training ground for globality than the low-growth market of the developed world.

However, this process is not a one-way bet, as there are evidently still issues within the startup sector that could derail it. These businesses are exposed to economic downturns or a banking crisis that could see venture capital dry up. There are also remaining ambiguities with regard to the rule of law, with many firms in the sharing economy and online finance operating in grey areas and being vulnerable to sudden regulatory shifts. This was evident in 2020/2021 when the government began a clampdown on tech businesses as it sought to assert control over this segment, especially where it offered a platform that countered its desire for control of the media and to ensure that internal dissent was curtailed.

## QUESTION

What are the major issues faced by Internet startups in China?

## SME ENGAGEMENT IN INTERNATIONAL TRADE

There is a split between SMEs from developing and developed states in their engagement in international trade. In developed economies, SMEs account for over a third of all exports, with 9 per cent of micro-enterprises engaged in trade and 38 per cent of SMEs. This is compared to two-thirds of SMEs. This is much lower in developing states, where 2.4 per cent of SMEs are engaged in trade. This is compounded by lower levels of engagement in global value chains by businesses in these developing states. There can be little doubt that e-commerce has aided this process, where 97 per cent of SMEs with an internet presence export. This compares to an average of 2–28 per cent for other types of businesses.

These figures just tend to focus on direct trade via the export function. This is not the only means through which firms can engage in international trade, as they can also access markets through indirect trade (i.e., where a firm sells to a firm that then exports). This involves their participation in global value chains through two means. First, through backward linkages (where the SME imports goods for the enablement of the production of goods for either domestic consumption or re-export) or, secondly, via backward linkages (where the SME seeks to firm within the global value chain). Given the complexity of these processes, accurate figures on SME participation can be difficult to measure. Not surprisingly, these tend to be higher for developed-state SMEs than for developing-state equivalents.

The percentage of SMEs across the OECD engaged in international trade varies widely from state to state. This ranges from 10–40 per cent for exporters to 10–70 per cent for importers, though there tends to be an inverse relationship between the size of the state and the participation of its SMEs in international markets. This reflects the ability of these businesses to use large internal markets as the basis of their strategy, though there are some outliers in this relationship, most notably Germany. However, where SMEs did engage with international trade, it was more likely to be important than exports, a reflection of their increased participation in international value chains.

The advent of e-commerce trading platforms has been an especially important device in promoting SME internationalisation as they, first, lower the transaction costs associated with engaging in international trade. The use of this platform lowers distribution costs as well as information and search costs. Second, with the use of these technologies, SMEs are more able to reach remote customers. Third, it has allowed SMEs to participate in international production networks. This could also further enable their internationalisation process, both in terms of reach and velocity. These have, to some degree, been enabled by the development of SME-dedicated e-commerce platforms in both business-to-business and business-to-consumer segments of the marketplace.

The OECD indicates that international trade by SMEs tends to be highly concentrated, with the top 100 trading SMEs within each state tending to dominate the process. This can be up to 90 per cent in some states (such as Luxembourg). Moreover, a lot of the SME trade tends to be with a partner in a single state rather than engaging in multiple market participation. These single-state exporters tend to represent a relatively small percentage of the overall value of international trade for this class of business. Those businesses that export to more than ten states tend to dominate SME-based trade flows, representing 80–90 per cent of the total value of exports by this type of business. For SMEs, proximity is an important factor shaping their engagement with international markets. While only a relatively small number of SMEs tend to export to high-growth markets such as China and India, the value of such exports is disproportionately high.

In terms of sheer number of businesses and in terms of those exports by simple number (as opposed to value), most states see trade by SMEs dominated by micro-enterprises. SMEs tend to be especially prominent in low-intensity capital manufactures such as furniture, textiles, and clothing, where there is scope for specialised products and niche strategies where the firm is able to exploit branding and other knowledge-based assets. In addition, the barriers to SME internationalisation tend to be higher for exporters than importers.

## POLICY MEASURES TO SUPPORT THE INTERNATIONALISATION OF SMES

Since the oil crisis in the 1970s, policymakers have sought to enhance the impact of SMEs on economic growth. It became increasingly evident during this period that larger businesses were failing to adjust adequately to sudden changes in the economic environment (Gray and Farminer 2014). The flexibility and innovative nature of many SMEs were seen as important to the restoration of growth in and regeneration of industrialised economies, leading to the emergence of enterprise policy as an important strand of economic policy. Increasingly, those economies where SMEs account for a high share of economic activity (such as South Korea) have tended to be more successful since the 1970s.

The support for SMEs in the policy process is rationalised through their contribution to growth and competitiveness and their dynamism, especially with regard to access to international markets (Jones et al. 2011). Conventionally, SMEs were regarded as organisations that were less efficient, paid less to their employees, and offered lower innovative potential than LSEs (large-scale enterprises). Consequently, SMEs were widely seen as on the decline in all major states and as marginal businesses that were a luxury and a drag on efficiency. This view assumed that many factors in the global economy (such as access to capital, knowledge development, internationalisation, etc.) favoured LSEs. Traditional theory suggests that the more fragmented a country's economic base, the more growth will be retarded. Thus, post-war economic success was linked to scale, a factor that was reflected in policy. This view has been radically shifted over the past three decades.

SMEs are an important source of innovation, change, and rising productivity, driven, in part, by the perceived link between knowledge and flexibility and aggressive entrepreneurship and reflecting their risk-seeking, innovative, and opportunistic nature (Audretsch 2002). Indeed, a growing number of SMEs are emerging due to increased outsourcing and the micro-segmentation of markets, as well as a lowering of scale advantages, shifts in labour markets, and deregulation. Moreover, SMEs are an important driver of increased competition, rising variety, employment, facilitating change by acting as a seedbed for new ideas, and providing services to the community. Though it can be argued that such forces work to the detriment of SMEs, when knowledge starts to become increasingly valuable in its own right, individuals have the incentive to use it to their own advantage and establish their own businesses. This assumes the entrepreneur (through the business) has the ability to stimulate change through innovation and to offer a unique value proposition that differentiates the firm in the global market. These phenomena demonstrate that the impact of SMEs is not restricted to the SME sector, as their effects can be felt throughout the economy, including in larger businesses.

Despite this process, there is a lot of evidence to suggest that SMEs engage less in international markets. Evidence from the World Bank identifies that in developing states, sales from exports are half what they are for larger firms. SMEs face larger barriers to internationalisation than LSEs. The full list is reflected in Table 11.4. The main barriers are internal and external. Internal barriers reflect how internationalisation of the SME is constrained by inadequacies within the firm, including lack of information, lack of capital, and inadequate management skills. External barriers include technical trade restrictions, bureaucratic procedures, and marketing and distribution problems. Policy towards the internationalisation of SMEs should be based on enhancing internal strengths and external opportunities and mitigating internal weaknesses and external threats.

**TABLE 11.4** The main barriers to SME internationalisation

| Internal barriers (enterprise barriers associated with organisational resources/capabilities to export) | External barriers (barriers generated from the firm's home and host environments) |
|---|---|

### Informational barriers

- Limited information to locate/ analyse markets
- Unreliable data about the international market
- Identifying foreign business opportunities
- Inability to contact overseas customers

### Procedural barriers

- Unfamiliar exporting procedures/paperwork
- Difficulty in communicating with foreign customers
- Slow collection of payments from abroad
- Difficulty in enforcing contracts and resolving disputes

### Human resource barriers

- Lack of managerial time to deal with internationalisation
- Insufficient quantity of and/ or untrained personnel for internationalisation
- Difficulty in managing foreign employees

### Governmental barriers

- Lack of home government assistance/ incentives
- Unfavourable home rules and regulations
- Restrictions on foreign ownership
- Restrictions on the movement of people/ business persons
- Unfair treatment compared to domestic firms in tax or eligibility to affiliate
- Unfair treatment compared to domestic firms in public procurement
- Unfair treatment compared to domestic firms in competition regulation
- Laws and regulations are not transparent in the foreign country

### Financial barriers

- Shortage of funds to finance working capital for internationalisation
- Shortage of funds to finance investment for internationalisation
- Shortage of insurance for internationalisation

### Customer and foreign competitor barriers

- Different foreign customer habits/attitudes
- Keen competition in foreign markets
- Business environment barriers
- Poor/deteriorating economic conditions abroad
- Foreign currency exchange risks
- Unfamiliar foreign business practices
- Different socio-cultural traits
- Verbal/non-verbal language differences
- Inadequacy of infrastructure for e-commerce
- Political instability in foreign markets

(Continued)

**TABLE 11.4** Continued

#### Product and price barriers

- Difficulty in developing new products for foreign markets
- Difficulty in adapting product design/style
- Difficulty in meeting product quality/standards/specifications of foreign markets
- Difficulty in offering satisfactory prices to customers
- Difficulty in matching competitors' prices
- Difficulty in granting credit facilities to foreign customers
- Lack of excess production capacity for foreign markets

#### Distribution, logistics, and promotion barriers

- Difficulty in establishing/using distribution channels in foreign markets
- Difficulty in obtaining reliable foreign representation
- Difficulty in supplying inventory abroad
- Excessive transportation/insurance costs
- Difficulty in offering technical/after-sales service
- Difficulty in adjusting promotional activities to foreign markets

#### Tariff and non-tariff barriers

- High tariff barriers
- Inadequate property rights protection
- Restrictive health, safety, and technical standards
- Arbitrary tariff classification and reclassification
- Unfavourable quotas and/or embargoes
- High costs of customs administration
- Competitors with preferential tariffs through regional trade agreements

Source: OECD (2016)

The ability of SMEs to enter international markets is constrained by considerable barriers to entry arising from:

- The higher interest rates facing these firms because they are perceived as a bigger risk than LSEs.
- Imperfect information, especially regarding new entrants and access to new materials, labour, etc.
- Barriers created by incumbents.
- Barriers created by government actions.
- Intellectual property rights and innovation.

These barriers to entry are reinforced by the transaction costs of engaging in international trade as well as the costs of transforming an SME into an LSE. Government policy objectives should therefore revolve around lowering barriers to entry, reducing threats and weaknesses, and enhancing the strengths and opportunities facing these enterprises. SMEs, in internationalising, face the traditional problems of financing to expand their international presence. Over time, the expansion of private equity markets and enhanced access to venture capital for SMEs – though there are considerable differences across states – has improved the situation. Venture capitalists can also provide management support to these fledgling companies.

In seeking to assist entrepreneurship, policy has traditionally viewed SMEs as inefficient and therefore sought to protect them rather than expose them to competition. Exploiting the opportunities afforded by the internationalisation of markets requires that policy and governments facilitate a more entrepreneurial culture within states. In particular, entrepreneurship policy is needed in relation to three market failures:

- Network externalities: where the value of a firm's resources is dependent upon the existence of complementary firms. When firms are excluded from these clusters, they are at a disadvantage.
- Knowledge externalities: knowledge can spill over into the public domain, thereby eroding the uniqueness of a firm's resources.
- Learning externalities: when firms fail, other firms can learn from this experience. This lowers the incentive for a firm to be a first mover.

The role of public policy is to mitigate these market failures by encouraging interaction between firms. As a result, governments will help in the reduction of costs and risks and in the provision of information. The aim is to create networks and a greater openness to the risk-taking associated with entrepreneurship. To support the realisation of this aim, there is a shift towards enabling policy to be undertaken at the level closest to the enterprise. Consequently, many argue that in developing SME policy, direct stimulation through export promotion policies and the provision of general export market information are of limited use. The policy needs to be targeted at specific types of firms. For 'born globals', for example, there is likely to be a more evident resource constraint than for the 'born again global'. Support is best suited to helping these firms develop network relationships.

Programmes to aid SME internationalisation can be subdivided into internal and external policies. Export promotion programmes focus on financial support and assistance for knowledge development in SMEs. These are supported by external programmes that seek to aid SME internationalisation by removing trade barriers facing SMEs. Five types of intervention appear to be most effective in aiding SMEs:

1. Policy reforms to establish a stable, liberal, low-cost business environment. This is especially noticeable in terms of regulatory reform and the removal of obligations and bureaucracy from these enterprises that weaken their position internationally (see below).
2. Actions that lower the cost of loans for SMEs.
3. 'Light touch' technical and marketing support.
4. Policies that motivate and facilitate demand-driven access to training and technology. Training needs to be offered in a market-failure context to firms that otherwise cannot

afford to undertake such activities. Similarly, technology policy has to direct SMEs towards those technologies that are useful for their own circumstances and not for their own sake. These need to be supported through networks to share best practices and create a sound technological infrastructure.

5. Institutions and policies that enhance SME networks and clusters. These aid training, technology access, and skill development, as well as the organisation of finance. Public finance provides support services and helps connect SMEs.

These broad environmental measures need to be complemented by efforts to improve the access of SMEs to technical and managerial skills, to sources of information and knowledge, and to research and development. In many instances, a key constraint on SMEs is not always finance but access to and absorption of technology-related learning that allows these enterprises to produce specialised products of the quality demanded by modern markets. This is especially true in developing states.

Perhaps most important of all are policies directed towards stimulating entrepreneurship. These policies need to aid startups, not only through the above measures but also by developing innovative methods of finance such as access to venture capital and the development of secondary stock markets. Other policies include business angel networks, where public bodies seek to bring together financiers and SMEs. One of the best forms of public policy assistance is reducing the administrative burden on SMEs through concerted regulatory reform. Regulatory systems have often evolved to serve the needs of large enterprises, rewarding economies of scale and stability rather than flexibility. SMEs face high compliance costs, extensive and complicated paperwork, and economic regulations that prohibit certain activities. SMEs have a lower capacity to absorb unproductive expenditures because they have less capital as well as fewer managerial resources than LSEs, and they regard these burdens as directly inhibiting their competitiveness in international markets. Most states try to reduce this burden, not only through reform but also by offering assistance to address these regulatory issues. Alternatively, SMEs rely on regulation to secure their positions, as their weak bargaining position and their poor liquidity make them vulnerable. In short, these enterprises need a credible, but light, regulatory framework to secure their competitive position, notably with regard to their interactions with large businesses.

In line with the analysis offered above, many policymakers are working towards stimulating clusters. Policy bodies generally play a passive role by offering supporting infrastructure and freeing up resources, as well as by facilitating interactions. Thus, actions are based on developing an effective framework for clusters. This, as suggested above, is especially evident with reference to the globalisation process. The strategy of policymakers should underline a core principle of modern industrial strategy: working with markets, not against them.

For innovative SMEs, their attainment of commercial success can be assisted through the development of know-how agreements and effective partnerships. Thus, in many instances, innovation within an SME's strategy has to be viewed within the context of the cluster strategy mentioned above. The heterogeneous nature of SMEs also dictates the nature of policy. For example, for the more innovative SMEs, policy will need to enable them to access the finance needed to support their development. For others

– technology followers – policy strategy should revolve around offering advice, creating awareness, and improving collaboration.

As globalisation becomes more advanced and fewer SMEs are insulated from its effects, policymakers have to assess the nature and form of the support as well as the increasingly complex and varied forces acting upon an economy's SME base. In many instances, supporting the internationalisation of SMEs will seemingly achieve little beyond redefining the scope of existing policies to account for changes in the environment. Supply capability policies need to be geared to enable SMEs to access the information and knowledge needed to operate successfully within these markets.

## Policy to aid SME development in developing states

To capitalise on this shift, the G8 countries developed a strategy whereby remittances could be channelled through the financial systems of developing states to offer easier access to finance, to offer guidance in the creation of the necessary supporting business environment, and to expand access to micro-finance for local entrepreneurs. As a result, aid programmes are increasingly emphasising the support of entrepreneurship. Some are sceptical regarding the impact of such programmes. Those sceptics who believe that larger firms offer more advantages doubt whether SMEs are better at creating jobs in a developing country context and are generally dubious about their benefits. A decisive response to these concerns is hindered by the size of the informal sector, which makes policy effects difficult to measure as well as to predict and measure the impact of SMEs accurately.

The link between economic growth and entrepreneurship has become an increasingly prominent theme in the development agenda. To this end, policy initiatives have emerged from the international arena to use entrepreneurship as a tool to alleviate poverty. As such, the private sector has to be encouraged to support poverty reduction programmes. This requires the development of an interface between domestic and international policy actors that creates the right conditions for these businesses to emerge. This initially relies on the openness of developing country states to this path of development and the undertaking of the necessary domestic reforms. In many cases, entrepreneurs are situated in the poorest segments of the economy, recognising that the poor are consumers and also the partial solution to their problems.

In many developing economies, women are a majority of micro-entrepreneurs in both the formal and informal sectors, confirming that there is a will to undertake startups. However, three major challenges face SMEs in developing economies:

• The informal economy: many firms operate outside the legal system. This limits their ability to raise finances as well as limiting access to other aspects of the formal economy that could help their development. Similarly, formal businesses are hurt by the implicit subsidies received by informal firms. It can be costly to operate in the formal economy. Firms in this sector face taxes, registration costs, and complex government regulations. This is compounded by high compliance costs and issues related to bribery and corruption. Thus, there is often little incentive to go formal.

- SMEs face considerable (often financial) barriers to growth: despite their importance, many SMEs within developing states are marginal in the business ecosystem, with few growing to become larger businesses. They are often limited by the unevenness of the playing field against small firms, which reinforces the pressure to remain informal. This is compounded by low productivity and an absence of skills compounded by the use of outdated technologies, human and knowledge capital, and an inability to afford the business services to rectify such problems. However, the major constraining factor is a lack of access to capital. The high risks associated with these businesses and the absence of trustworthy information all raise interest rates for SMEs.
- The absence of competitive pressure upon larger firms: in many developing states, larger firms inhibit entrepreneurial activity by using weak institutional environments to stifle competitive pressure. This can inhibit the development of a mature financial system that offers cheaper finance to smaller firms. This is compounded by corruption and weak law enforcement.

As a result, the foundations for entrepreneurship are simply not in place in many developing states. There is an absence of a level playing field with entry, operating, and credit rules applied in an asymmetric fashion. Access to finance and skills and knowledge compound these difficulties.

In developing states, the policy issues differ as actions need to be based on developing the following pre-requisites for cultivating an entrepreneurial culture:

1. Enhancement of the rule of law, ensuring that it is transparent, open, and understood.
2. Enforcement of property rights with effective policing.
3. Creation of a level playing field through domestic reforms.
4. The reform of financial markets through enhancing competition within the sector and increasing the freedom of financing bodies.
5. The development of human skills and knowledge through building networks and public-private partnerships.

Clearly, giving small firms access to networks will be central to any policy measures. This can help alleviate many of the difficulties these businesses encounter when seeking to grow. To date, there has been limited use of networks beyond the Far East. Where networks do exist, they are often informal. Despite the obvious difficulties with such informality, these networks have proved powerful forces (for example, the example of Chinese entrepreneurs overseas).

## A FRAMEWORK FOR ENTREPRENEURSHIP

Based on frameworks advanced by the WEF, the annual Global Entrepreneurship Monitor offers a means of tracking the advance (or otherwise) of entrepreneurship across 65 economies. These economies cover two-thirds of the world's adult population and nearly 85 per cent of global GDP. The value of the approach lies in the offering of an awareness of the core characteristics of entrepreneurs and society's attitude towards them. The set of criteria is reflected in Table 11.5.

**TABLE 11.5** A framework for entrepreneurship

| Societal values and perceptions | Individual attributes of a potential entrepreneur | Entrepreneurial activity indicators | Perceived quality of entrepreneurial ecosystem |
|---|---|---|---|
| • High status to successful entrepreneurs<br>• Good career choice<br>• Media attention for entrepreneurship | • Perceived opportunities<br>• Perceived capabilities<br>• Entrepreneurial intention<br>• Fear of failure rate | • Total early-stage entrepreneurial activity (the section of the population in the process of setting up a business)<br>• Established business ownership rate (the section of the population who are established owners)<br>• Business discontinuation rate (the segment of the population that has discontinued a business) | Entrepreneurial finance<br>Government policy<br>Government entrepreneurship programmes<br>Entrepreneurship education<br>• R&D transfer<br>• Commercial and legal infrastructure<br>• Entry regulation<br>• Physical infrastructure<br>• Cultural and social norms |

Source: WEF (2013)

The GEM offers an excellent insight into the opportunities for developing entrepreneurship across the global economy. What is evident from the survey is that nearly two-thirds of the adult population sees entrepreneurship as positive for their economy, with those undertaking it enjoying high status in their societies. In many states, entrepreneurs do not enjoy high-profile media profiles. Interestingly, the GEM indicates that the positive attitude towards entrepreneurs tends to be strongest in states that are less developed (notably those in Africa). This stands in contrast to Europe, where just over half of adults see entrepreneurship as a progressive career choice.

Globally, just over 40 per cent of the adult population sees good opportunities for business within their respective territories. Many feel that they simply do not possess the skills to start a business (notably in African and Latin American states). This is reflected in the fact that just over a fifth of adults expressed an intention to start a business, with these figures again being the highest in Africa. Again, Europe is a laggard in the process, with many believing it possesses neither the skills nor the perception of opportunities to be effective entrepreneurs. All this supports the notion that early-stage entrepreneurship is highest among the less developed states. However, it also appears that many of these startups were driven less by the absence of any other option than by the identification of an opportunity. These are those economies that are factor-driven with a high reliance on unskilled, subsistence-based activity. The rate within these economies was almost double that of the more advanced economies. However, overall entrepreneurship tends to be higher in Latin America, Africa, and the Caribbean. When examining established business ownership, the rates are very narrow between developing, emerging, and developed states. Advanced economies tend to be very strong in employee entrepreneurship, which is between 400 and 600 per cent higher than in African states. These developed economies also have much lower business discontinuity rates than emerging or developing economies and also have greater innovation-driven entrepreneurship. This difference is driven by differences in spatial variances in business profitability.

The less developed states also have the highest levels of female entrepreneurship, with gender parity being most evident in Latin American and Caribbean states. Europe has a relatively low female entrepreneurship rate and also the lowest gender parity, as women in Europe are half as likely as men to be engaged in entrepreneurship, though the four states with higher entrepreneurship rates than men are Indonesia, Brazil, Malaysia, and Mexico. Globally, the highest rates of entrepreneurship tend to be in the 25–34 and 35–44 age groups. Youth entrepreneurship tends to be highest among the less developed states. In developing and emerging states, entrepreneurship tends to be especially strong in the wholesale and retail sectors. This is less true in developing economies where there is a stronger level of entrepreneurship in high-value sectors such as finance, IT, and other professional services.

With regard to the broader business ecosystem, infrastructure has the highest positive impact across all states surveyed. School-level entrepreneurship is strongest in developed economies, though overall, the broad-based ecosystem is strongest in developed economies. The less developed economies tended to lag in terms of R&D transfer as well as access to finance and market entry. Not surprisingly, the efficacy of government programmes varies widely across states, with more developed states having more effective supporting measures. Looking across the benchmarks of the business ecosystem, the small, developed states (notably Switzerland and the Netherlands) perform best.

These reflect that, at the core of a state, creating a sustainable entrepreneurial system depends upon what has been termed the enterprise ecosystem. These reflect the broad interaction between the entrepreneur and his/her context that shapes their ability to build and sustain businesses. The WEF (2013) identified the core components as highlighted in Table 11.6. While the state of the components of this ecosystem can vary across states, there is a consensus that three are of especially importance: accessible market, human capital/workforce, and finance/funding.

Looking across the regions, it is evident that certain specific aspects of the ecosystem matter more than others. For example, in the case of Silicon Valley, all these aspects of the ecosystem are in existence, and an average of 86 per cent of businesses felt all of

**TABLE 11.6** Components of infrastructural ecosystem

| Accessible markets | Human capital workforce |
|---|---|
| • Domestic market – large companies as customers<br>• Domestic market – small/medium companies as customers<br>• Domestic market – governments as customers<br>• Foreign market – large companies as customers<br>• Foreign market – small/medium companies as customers<br>• Foreign market – governments as customers | • Management talent<br>• Technical talent<br>• Entrepreneurial company experience<br>• Outsourcing availability<br>• Access to immigrant workforce |
| Funding and finance | Support system |
| • Friends and family<br>• Angel investors<br>• Private equity<br>• Venture capital<br>• Access to debt | • Mentors/advisors<br>• Professional services incubators/accelerators<br>• Network of entrepreneurial peers |
| Regulatory framework and infrastructure | Education and training |
| • Ease of starting a business<br>• Tax incentives and business-friendly legislation/policies<br>• Access to basic infrastructure (e.g., water and electricity)<br>• Access to telecommunications/broadband<br>• Access to transport | • Available workforce with pre-university education<br>• Available workforce with university education<br>• Entrepreneur-specific training |
| Major universities as catalysts | Cultural support |
| • Major universities promoting a culture of respect for entrepreneurship<br>• Major universities playing a key role in idea formation for new companies<br>• Major universities playing a key role in providing graduates for new companies | • Tolerance of risk and failure preference for self-employment<br>• Success stories/role models research culture<br>• Positive image of entrepreneurship and celebration of innovation |

Source: WEF (2013)

these were available. In South and Central America, only 41 per cent of businesses felt all these components were readily available. Indeed, these benchmarks are ideals, which are core characteristics of highly innovative clusters in developed states. As such, they are in less abundance in developing economies.

---

**Box 11.1:** Senior entrepreneurship

As the population of the world ages, with some 16 per cent being 55 years of age or older, there has been an increased focus on the entrepreneurial activity of this expanding age group. Indeed, it is estimated that entrepreneurial activity in the over-55s affects over 1.2 billion people globally. This entrepreneurial activity can take numerous forms, from startups to social entrepreneurs to acting as informal investors. Generally, the over-55s have been identified as having the lowest confidence in starting their own businesses, with this segment being the least entrepreneurial of all age groups, though risk willingness among this group – somewhat paradoxically – does tend to be higher. Despite this, entrepreneurial activity does tend to be lower in the over-50s. This is largely driven by household income, with entrepreneurial intent positively correlated to income. This tends not to be the case for other age groups. Overall, there is an evidently lower level of startup activity in the over-50s though entrepreneurial activity is higher in the workplace among this age group.

Generally, seniors are more likely to be social entrepreneurs than younger people. Thus, it suggests that there are retirees seeking to become engaged in activities with a social or community objective. Where entrepreneurship ceases, it is largely due to retirement rather than simply giving up due to profitability and/or difficulties in accessing finance. This latter point can be driven by the income issues noted above. Despite this (and the higher amount of self-finance), the sources of finance for seniors starting their own businesses are broadly similar, with many relying on family members and banks, and more and more turning to crowdfunding. On the flip side, there is a trend towards seniors operating as business angels, investing in new businesses being started by a friend or colleague.

Across the global economy, senior entrepreneurship is highest in sub-Saharan Africa, Latin America, and the Caribbean. In sub-Saharan Africa, nearly 20 per cent of seniors are engaged in such activity, which is largely driven by entrepreneurship in lower-skilled, lower-wage activities. The Middle East and North African regions show the biggest difference between intent and actual startup, though, as a whole, Europe shows the lowest level of entrepreneurial activity among seniors. In this region, this rate falls to as low as 5 per cent of the senior population, though this region also shows the highest rate of employee entrepreneurship activity by a large margin. The degree to which these patterns are driven by the extremes of necessity and/or opportunity varies markedly across the world. In the less developed parts of the world (notably Africa and South and East Asia), they are more often driven by necessity, whereas in the Middle East, Latin America, and Europe, they are very much driven by opportunity. This pattern is also reflected in trends towards social entrepreneurship across the global economy. However, discontinuity rates are highest in sub-Saharan Africa.

## CONCLUSION

The internationalisation of SMEs represents perhaps the most salient impact of the globalisation process underlining how far it has penetrated economic structures. SMEs were traditionally exempt from globalisation trends, concentrating as they did on local markets. Changes in the nature of the market and of SMEs have altered this conventional perspective. A new group of SMEs has emerged to deliberately exploit international markets, while others are being affected as their traditional markets are opened. This poses a number of policy challenges for authorities as they seek to be both reactive and proactive to these changes to ensure that the SMEs based within their territory are able to respond to the opportunities and challenges posed by globalisation.

### KEY POINTS

- Conventional SME internationalisation has been treated as a gradual, sequential process.
- There is an increased trend for SMEs to undertake a more rapid process of internationalisation.
- Many barriers to widespread SME internationalisation remain.
- The proactive promotion of SME internationalisation has become a major policy theme.

## DISCUSSION QUESTIONS

1) What is the value of entrepreneurship to states?
2) How do you believe the nature of entrepreneurship varies across states according to their level of development?
3) To what extent can the internationalisation of SMEs be seen as a sequential process?

## ACTIVITIES

Choosing a country at random, assess the extent to which it has or is seeking to create the conditions for entrepreneurship to flourish.

## SUGGESTED FURTHER READING

Andersen, O., & Buvik, A. (2002). Firms' internationalization and alternative approaches to the international customer/market selection. *International Business Review, 11*(3), 347–363.

Audretsch, D. B. (2002). The dynamic role of small firms: Evidence from the US. *Small Business Economics, 18*(1/3), 13–40.

Bell, J. (1995). The internationalization of small computer software firms: A further challenge to "stage" theories. *European Journal of Marketing, 29*(8), 60–75.

Bell, J., McNaughton, R., Young, S., & Crick, D. (2003). Towards an integrative model of small firm internationalisation. *Journal of International Entrepreneurship, 1*(4), 339–362.

Cavusgil, S. T., & Knight, G. (2015). The born global firm: An entrepreneurial and capabilities perspective on early and rapid internationalization. *Journal of International Business Studies, 46*(1), 3–16.

Gray, B., & Farminer, A. (2014). And no birds sing—Reviving the romance with international entrepreneurship. *Journal of International Entrepreneurship, 12*(2), 115–128.

Hagen, B., & Zucchella, A. (2014). Born global or born to run? The long-term growth of born global firms. *Management International Review, 54*(4), 497–525.

Johanson, J., & Vahlne, J. E. (2003). Business relationship learning and commitment in the internationalization process. *Journal of International Entrepreneurship, 1*(1), 83–101.

Jones, M., Coviello, N., & Tang, Y. (2011). International entrepreneurship research (1989–2009): A domain ontology and thematic analysis. *Journal of Business Venturing, 26*(6), 632–659.

McDougall, P. P., Shane, S., & Oviatt, B. M. (1994). Explaining the formation of international new ventures: The limits of theories from international business research. *Journal of Business Venturing, 9*(6), 469–487.

Pleitner, J., Brunner, J., & Habersaat, M. (1998). Forms and extent of success factors: The case of Switzerland. In A. Haahti, G. Hall, & R. Donckels (Eds.), *The internationalization of SMEs: The Interstratos project* (pp. 27–55). London: Routledge.

Rask, M., & Servais, P. (2015). Models of international entrepreneurship. In P. H. Andersen, J. Lauring, H. Kragh, & M. S. Linneberg (Eds.), *Preparing for the unexpected: Design of the future global enterprise*, 237–255, Copenhagen: DJØF Publishing.

Rasmussen, E. S., Madsen, T. K., & Servais, P. (2012). On the foundation and early development of domestic and international new ventures. *Journal of Management & Governance, 16*(4), 543–556.

Rialp, A., Rialp, J., & Knight, G. (2015). International entrepreneurship: A review and future directions. In S. Fernhaber & S. Prashantham (Eds.), *Routledge companion to international entrepreneurship*, 7–28, London: Routledge.

Rugman, A. M., Verbeke, A., & Nguyen, Q. T. (2011). Fifty years of international business theory and beyond. *Management International Review, 51*(6), 755–786.

Welch, L. S., & Luostarinen, R. (1988). Internationalization: Evolution of a concept. *Journal of General Management, 14*(2), 34–55.

Wiedersheim-Paul, F., & Johanson, J. (1975). The internationalization of the firm-four Swedish cases. *Journal of Management Studies, 12*(3), 306.

Zander, I., McDougall-Covin, P., & Rose, E. L. (2015). Born globals and international business: Evolution of a field of research. *Journal of International Business Studies, 46*(1), 27–35.

Zahra, S. A., & George, G. (2002). Absorptive capacity: A review, reconceptualization, and extension. *Academy of Management Review, 27*(2), 185–203.

# CHAPTER 12

# CULTURE AND INTERNATIONAL BUSINESS

## OBJECTIVES

This chapter will help you to:

- Define culture and explain its main characteristics.
- Identify and assess the main determinants of culture.
- Demonstrate how and why an understanding of culture is important to international business.
- Understand and assess the usefulness of theories of national cultural dimensions to international business.
- Begin to appreciate how firms can manage culture and use it to their advantage.

Globalisation and internationalisation increasingly bring firms from different cultures into contact with each other, thereby not only creating opportunities for cross-cultural contact that have potential for mutual benefit but also containing scope for serious cross-cultural misunderstandings. The increased cross-border reach of business requires an enhanced awareness of and sensitivity to differences in languages, values, and behavioural norms. The alternative is less effective or even failed negotiations, marketing drives, and investment plans. In a positive light, although it is far from easy, companies can attempt to manage culture to their advantage. This chapter begins by exploring the definition of culture and its key aspects. It then discusses some of the key determinants of culture and how they can have an impact on businesses. The chapter then examines individual business functions and tasks and how they are affected by culture in an international context. It concludes by considering the main theoretical approaches to culture, their implications for businesses, and criticisms of these approaches.

It is important to note the link between cultural and ethical issues. There is an absolutist dimension to some ethical issues, but many are perceived through a relativist lens; that is, the presumption of what is right or wrong can be greatly influenced by specific cultural contexts. In short, although some practices are clearly unacceptable in all

DOI: 10.4324/9781315184500-15

cultures, there are grey areas where practices that are commonplace in some countries are regarded as unethical in others. These issues are explored more fully in Chapter 13.

## WHAT IS CULTURE?

Culture is a complex concept, open to a variety of definitions and difficult to pin down precisely. Terpstra and David (1991) refer to 'a learned, shared, compelling, inter-related set of symbols whose meanings provide a set of orientations for members of a society', whereas Komin (1994) writes of 'total patterns of values, ideas, beliefs, customs, practices, techniques, institutions, objects and artefacts.' Hofstede (1994) brings this array of symbols, beliefs, values, ideas, etc., together and talks of 'a collective mental programming'. In other words, culture is the combination of acquired experience and values that feed into and influence the behaviour and responses of distinct groups.

Cultural analysis can take place at various levels and across various dimensions. There are two important distinctions to be made when talking about culture from a business perspective: national and organisational culture. National (or country) culture is external to the firm but provides the context in which the firm sits and influences the culture within the firm. The theoretical approaches discussed later in this chapter are examples of national culture.

Organisational (or corporate) culture is internal to the firm. Firms can try to shape their corporate culture to help them attain key objectives. The two concepts are linked. Clearly, national culture will help determine corporate culture. Several corporate cultures can exist within the same national culture; that is, the components of national culture can come together in a variety of ways, resulting in different outcomes. Moreover, corporate culture can be a useful way of unifying multinational firms with cross-cultural operations or operations in a number of different countries.

By definition, culture is a learned phenomenon, the outcome of shared experience over many years that is passed down the generations. In other words, individuals and their beliefs and behaviours are, to a large extent, conditioned by their history and passed on by families and institutions like schools. Some cultural influences can be traced back through the centuries: claims have been made, for example, that the roots of British individualism go back over one thousand years or that the more competitive and unfettered forms of capitalism and social organisation favoured by the US are a result of its early frontier and nation-building experiences.

An essential part of culture is a sense of belonging or identity. This can originate from several sources that may or may not correspond with national boundaries. Language, for example, is often an important symbol of belonging to a group and frequently coincides with national boundaries, but when it does not, it can be a divisive factor, as in Canada, Belgium, Switzerland, and several African countries where tribal allegiances coincide with language. Tribes, ethnic groups, and religions can thus be sources of cohesiveness or divisiveness, depending on the presence or absence of competition within a territory.

Nevertheless, despite the relative newness and fragility of the concept of the nation state in many locations and the surprising frequency of changes in national boundaries, a sense of belonging to a nation can be a key element of cultural identity and generate strong feelings. For example, a fear of those reluctant to engage in further integration within the EU is the potential erosion of national identity. Although not the only reason for opposition to the adoption of the euro in the UK and Denmark, the fear of identity loss is an important element in it, especially as currencies are often regarded as symbols of national identity and independence. The EU denies it is engaging in nation-building but is anxious to promote the use of key symbols such as the European flag and the European anthem to create a sense of European identity. European representatives are also anxious to point out that being European does not undermine or replace national cultural identities. An individual French or Italian citizen, for example, is still as French or Italian as before the launch of the euro. In short, individuals have multiple or layered cultural identities.

Culture is not static and non-adaptive; the cultural mix changes through experience, usually gradually, but it is occasionally subject to sudden change through traumatic events such as the collapse of the Soviet system in 1989 and 1990, which affected both the republics of the Soviet Union and its satellite states in central and eastern Europe. The sudden collapse of a whole political, economic, and social system put into question long-held views, values, and practices underpinning political, economic, and commercial life. In particular, the undermining of social safety nets and employment guarantees as a result of systemic change overturned expectations and destroyed value systems. The outcome has varied in different countries, depending on their previous experience of the workings of the market and the path chosen for reform by the authorities.

The Soviet experience is an example of a wholesale transformation of the social, political, and economic systems but cultural transformation can also occur as a result of significant change within a system. The utility privatisations that occurred in the UK towards the end of the 1980s demonstrate this. Prior to privatisation, the UK's gas and electricity utilities were dominated by engineers and operated as state monopolies. The emphasis was on production to meet the total demands of domestic, commercial, and industrial consumers. Privatisation and the subsequent opening of the markets changed all that, bringing with them new commercial risks and a greater emphasis on marketing. This shifted the demands on the managers in the industry, requiring the emergence of a culture that was much more responsive to market needs, innovative, and open to new opportunities.

The challenge for businesses when deciding upon modes of market entry is to read and correctly interpret the various cultural signs. Failure to do this can result in serious problems for specific initiatives or even the failure of joint ventures or mergers. In order to work with rather than against cultural factors, it is necessary to recognise that we all view the world through a cultural prism and that, although our cultural preconceptions may be shared by others within our organisation and to an extent by those with the same nationality, they may be alien to those to whom we are trying to export or with whom we are trying to set up a joint venture. Those who see the world solely in terms of their own culture have an ethnocentric disposition and can encounter serious problems when trying to carry out activities with an international dimension. On the other hand, those with a polycentric outlook are open to other cultures, attempting to see beyond their own cultural assumptions and develop an understanding of other cultures. This greater sensitivity to cultural divergence, while not guaranteeing the success of joint ventures, acquisitions, or other forms of involvement in non-domestic business ventures, does enhance the possibility of success.

## CASE STUDY 12.1: GUANXI: AN ESSENTIAL TOOL FOR DOING BUSINESS IN CHINA OR AN OUTDATED CONCEPT?

The acquisition of good 'guanxi' is often cited as a necessary condition for a foreign company attempting to enter the Chinese business community. At its most basic, 'guanxi' means relationships, and allied with the concept of 'xinyong' (or 'personal trust'), guanxi underpins business transactions in China. More in-depth analysis of guanxi reveals a much more complex, nuanced, and distinctive concept. However, relationships and the importance of relationships capture the essence of guanxi. At one level, relationships and trust are essential to business throughout the world and are not unique to China. The key questions therefore are: how does guanxi differ from business relationships elsewhere in the world, and what are the main implications of guanxi for investors in China?

Guanxi refers to an informal network of interpersonal relationships maintained by an individual. These relationships confer a status of mutual obligation upon those in the network and are maintained by a strong sense of reciprocity. Scholars have traced the roots of guanxi back to Confucius and, as such, placed guanxi firmly in the Chinese cultural context. A basic Confucian assumption is that individuals exist in relation to each other and that the five most important relationships are ruler-subject, father-son, husband-wife, elder-younger brother, and friend-friend. Over time, the salience of certain relationships has changed, but Chinese society continues to be highly relationship-oriented in all its dimensions, including business.

In order for guanxi to work, it needs to be based on trust, dependability, reliability, shared expectations, and reciprocity. In practical terms, guanxi in China is built on institutional bases, including family, a shared birthplace, a common school or university, and employment by the same organisation. None of these bases need to be contemporaneous. As China and its companies engage more and more with the outside world, the possibility of finding common guanxi bases for non-Chinese individuals with Chinese counterparts increases through shared alma mater or involvement with the same company, professional or trade association, etc.

A number of interpretations of guanxi are possible. On the one hand, some authors argue guanxi is unique to China, has grown out of, and is an essential part of Chinese culture, which has developed over centuries. On the other hand, some authors claim guanxi is merely a Chinese word for social capital and networks that exist in all economies. Although connections, relationships, and 'the old boy network' are clearly important in all cultures, the concept of guanxi does appear to be more complex and underwritten with more informal rules and expectations than many other relationship systems – a reflection, in part, of China as a high context culture. For example, much more time has to be spent establishing a relationship prior to conducting business in a Chinese context than in a Western context, and in maintaining the relationship once it has been established. This can seem frustrating to Western businesses, which tend to base their business dealings on contracts and legal agreements, whereas Chinese firms and individuals prefer to get to know and trust future customers or partners before working with them and are not so concerned with merely concluding deals.

There is also a view that guanxi is important because of deficiencies in the Chinese business environment. That is, informal networks are important given the inefficiencies and delays inherent in the Communist administrative system and the absence of a stable and predictable legal and regulatory environment, which itself is the outcome of ongoing and incomplete reform. The informal networks, so the argument goes, allow businesses to circumvent the problems inherent in the contemporary situation. In the long term, the implication is that as the market economy, institutions, and environment are fully implemented in China, the need for quanxi, which is incompatible with a modernised economy, will disappear. This interpretation, although having some appeal, ignores the deep-rootedness of guanxi in Chinese society, where individuals do not exist in isolation but in relation to each other. This cultural predisposition goes back centuries and is not merely a phenomenon of post-revolutionary China. Therefore, forecasts of the death of guanxi are probably premature.

Some authors regard guanxi as unethical. This stems from the view that guanxi is all about exchanging favours and gaining 'special treatment' from those in power and, as such, discriminates against those outside the guanxi network. At worst, guanxi networks, in this view, are seen as sources of bribery and corruption and at best stifle competition by allocating resources according to relationships rather than on market-led grounds. This latter interpretation is at odds with the above view that guanxi is necessary to compensate for institutional and regulatory inadequacies.

The practical benefits of guanxi for business are widespread. For foreign investors in China, being able to establish and link into established guanxi networks eases their entry into the Chinese business arena by providing good local knowledge about key players and regulations and by facilitating the development of markets and distribution networks. Such benefits potentially apply to a variety of entry modes (see Chapter 9). Indeed, it is good practice to tap into local knowledge and practices when entering any new market, especially when there may be significant differences in the business environment and expectations among those at home. This is inherently sensible and by no means corrupt. Problems can arise when relationships are utilised to gain an unfair advantage (for example, access to inside or confidential information or the granting of trading licences in exchange for favours or generally by-passing laws). Such transactions are clearly corrupt and occur to some degree in all economic systems. Undoubtedly, the potential for and actual examples of corruption exist in the guanxi system, but the effects emanating from the utilisation of guanxi can also be positive and, in effect, oil the wheels of business in China.

Another potential drawback of guanxi is that it is intensely personal and particularistic. In other words, guanxi exists between individuals and does not operate between organisations. This acts as a constraint. Once an individual leaves an organisation, guanxi is lost unless multiple guanxi points have been made. The latter can be time-consuming and costly to develop and maintain. Guanxi can therefore limit the scope of operations and is non-transferable. Therefore, a company entering China with pan-Chinese ambitions, or even ambitions beyond one province, will need to develop extensive guanxi. The regions are important in China in many aspects and help fragment the Chinese market. For example, although national laws are operational in China, their interpretation and implementation are often left to local and regional administrations. Local and regional guanxi are therefore important for companies aiming to extend their geographical scope within China.

## QUESTIONS

1. Identify and analyse the potential benefits and costs of guanxi.
2. Is guanxi doomed in view of China's continuing modernisation?

## WHERE DOES CULTURE COME FROM?

Hofstede (1994) speaks of the 'collective programming of the mind' but what is the source of the inputs into this programming? The common values, beliefs, customs, and norms of behaviour that constitute culture are acquired from social institutions like families and schools. These in turn are shaped by common or shared experiences, history, and religions, which determine factors like the relationship of the individual to the group (see below for the individualistic-collectivist cultural dimension), gender roles, communication rituals, and even details and norms associated with eating, drinking, and dressing. Figure 12.1 sets out the key determinants and expressions of culture. Although set out as separate items for the purposes of exposition, in practice these determinants interact with each other, and their unique combination produces the unique national and sub-national cultures that exist today.

Businesses are interested in culture to the extent to which it shapes behaviour and attitudes. A helpful distinction can be drawn between values and norms. Values are ideas and beliefs about what is good, morally correct, and desirable. Values are often shaped by religion, but there is also often an important input from social institutions such as the family and education (both of which may and may not themselves be influenced by religion). Some values, albeit relatively few, are universal (for example, murder is prohibited everywhere). Other values are uniquely shaped by individual cultures and can lead to difficult ambiguities for international business. The link between culture and ethics is picked up in more detail in Chapter 14.

Norms are the social rules, guidelines, and patterns of behaviour that predominate in a particular society. There is no value or moral content attached to norms, but transgressions of norms within a particular culture can lead to exclusion or difficulties in conducting a business relationship. For example, displaying the soles of one's feet is a serious breach of etiquette in Arab culture. In some cultures, nodding one's head

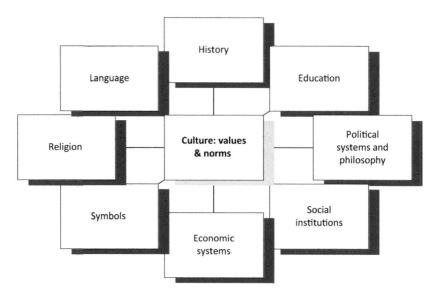

**FIGURE 12.1** Determinants of and expression of culture

signifies agreement, whereas in others it means 'no' – a phenomenon that can lead to confusion unless these differences are grasped. Attitudes to timekeeping and punctuality vary considerably: to be late in some cultures is impolite and shows a lack of respect for whom one is meeting, whereas in other cultures, being late is the norm. It is important to understand the degree of formality required in different cultures. Underestimation of the formality required (in how one addresses a potential customer or client or in the dress code followed) can also denote a lack of respect and cause offence. Such miscalculations can take place within a national culture but are even more likely to occur across national cultures.

## Religion

Religion is one of the most important factors shaping culture, both in terms of values and norms. At its core, religion lays down a set of fundamental principles and values that govern the behaviour and lives of its adherents. The influence of religion may be obvious in some nations or regions where the dominant religion has a strong presence. In states that appear more secular, the role of religion often remains strong, albeit in a less obvious manner. For example, in countries like the UK, this has manifested itself in the reduction of restrictions on Sunday trading. However, the country's Christian heritage means that Christian principles and values continue to underpin British laws and culture, even though the explicit role of Christianity in British life is less pervasive than it used to be. The persistence of religion has been demonstrated in countries like Russia, where religion was banned for many decades under communism. A striking feature of the post-communist era has been the revival, indeed thriving, of the Russian Orthodox Church.

From a business perspective, religion has to be taken into account in a number of ways. The most obvious are overt religious practices, laws, and traditions. These include the observance of religious holidays and the ban on alcohol and certain foods. These are explicit and difficult to misinterpret. More difficult to take into account are norms and practices that are rooted in religion and influence social behaviour. Different practices can abound under the same religion, and the impact of the same religion can vary as a result of national and other competing cultural factors. Catholics, for example, are subject to similar influences, whether they are Mexican, Italian, Irish, or Filipino, but the impact or expression of these factors varies. Similarly, the stereotypical view of Islam is that women are restricted in and, indeed, often excluded from the workplace. Although women may find themselves highly restricted in some Islamic societies, in others they have many more opportunities than those recognised by the stereotype.

## Language

Language is the main medium of communication, and a common language often defines a group within a society. It can therefore act as a great unifier or as a way of delineating groups when there are divisions within a nation. Language, at its most basic, is important to business as a way of conveying and collecting information, whether in negotiations, within a company, or in the interface with customers. In particular, language helps unlock local societies, giving an insight into local culture and mores in a way which is not possible when an interpreter is needed. The consequences of poor verbal communication can seriously undermine what a business is trying to achieve in its overseas investments or when seeking to enter foreign markets.

With globalisation and the growing internationalisation of business, the need to communicate in multiple languages increases. Ideally, international managers are bilingual or multilingual. In reality, particularly given the number of countries and languages with which contemporary MNEs come into contact, this is often not practically possible. Consequently, since the latter stages of the twentieth century, English has emerged as the international business *lingua franca* (that is, a language used for communication purposes among individuals with different mother tongues). The result is that when Japanese, German, and Spanish businesspeople meet, their common point of communication is likely to be English. The use of English has developed to the extent that numerous multinationals with headquarters in non-English-speaking countries but with operations across numerous countries have adopted English for all internal and external communications. Examples include Aventis, ABB, Alcatel, Novartis, Vivendi, Ericsson, and Volvo. This appears to give an advantage to native English speakers, and in one sense, it does. However, the lack of incentive to speak other languages can leave them at a disadvantage because even a rudimentary knowledge of a language (even if it is not the language in which communication is ultimately carried out) shows a willingness to try to understand the other party and can create a significant element of goodwill.

Even the use of a common language is not always sufficient for effective communication. The same words can be used in different ways in different regions and countries. The differences between British and American English are well documented. Indeed, the writer George Bernard Shaw allegedly said, 'England and America are two countries divided by a common language'. Similar differences also exist between Spanish, Portuguese, and French-speaking nations, for example. Differences arise not only because of different meanings attached to the same words (an inevitability given that languages are constantly evolving and that countries that use the same language can be situated thousands of miles away from each other), but also because of cultural differences that can shape the use of and interpretation of language. Communication in the US, for example, is usually very direct and literal (as befits a low context culture; see below) and positive, whereas in the UK, which is a low context culture compared to many Asian countries but less so than the US, communication is less direct and literal and often understated. These differences in language use reflect cultural differences between the two countries.

## History

As individuals, we are the product of our prior history and experience. The same is true of countries. History shapes national culture in a number of ways, including the development of the political and economic systems. Russia, for example, is evolving a form of capitalism which is rooted in the acquisition of wealth by a limited number of the elite and the denial of meaningful democracy. Although not inevitable, this outcome was always probable in a nation where large inequalities of wealth and the centralised concentration of power have been the norm for centuries. History also shapes attitudes towards other countries; long periods of distrust or violent conflict between nations can colour contemporary relations between countries.

A foreign investor must also respect the culture and heritage of the host country or encounter potentially severe problems. Following a successful Internet campaign led by Chinese TV personality Rui Chenggang, Starbucks, the Seattle-based coffee chain, closed its outlet in Beijing's Forbidden City in July 2007. The campaign claimed it had no objection to the presence of Starbucks in China, which has over 250 outlets there, but alleged that the firm's presence in the Forbidden City, the home to generations of Chinese emperors and the location of important events in Chinese history, was inappropriate. Similarly, when developing its northern Moscow store, Scandinavian furniture retailer IKEA encountered serious resistance to its plans. The company wanted to build a link road between the store and the ring road. This would have required the relocation of an important Second World War monument – a series of anti-tank spikes that mark the spot on the outskirts of Moscow where the Russians halted the German advance. Given the loss of life and the suffering endured by the Russians during this war, IKEA's original plans were rejected. The store was built, but with different access arrangements, and the monument remains a place for Russians to visit on Victory Day (May 9) and other important occasions.

## Education

Education is an important conduit for culture. Moreover, the culture of education is often an important consideration for foreign investors. Literacy levels and the percentage of populations educated to secondary or tertiary level can be important determinants of investment decisions. It was the existence of a large number of highly educated individuals with English language proficiency which facilitated the growth of the call centre and back-office outsourcing boom in India. Different education systems stress the acquisition of different skills. Germany, for example, has a long tradition of apprenticeships and vocational training which has provided generations of technicians, mechanics, and engineers, which have played an important role in Germany's manufacturing success. Other countries emphasise and perform well in mathematics and the sciences; Finland, Hong Kong, South Korea, and Japan, for example, consistently rank highly in OECD league tables of attainment in these key disciplines.

## Social systems and organisation

The way society is organised is important for business on a number of levels. The average size of families, for example, affects consumption patterns: the larger the family, the bigger the demand will be for grocery items sold in larger packs. There has been a trend in some developed countries for smaller households, including a big growth in one-person households. In societies where this is the case, products need to be sold in smaller quantities, and demand will be for smaller houses and apartments. Ageing populations, a situation facing many developed countries, boosts demand for health-related products and services and for leisure-related services and activities that appeal to older age groups. Moreover, family obligations sometimes need to be taken into account by HRM departments. In some countries, policies around parental leave are well-developed; in other countries, such policies are less developed or nonexistent.

The degree and type of social stratification can also have implications for business. If a society is highly stratified, then social mobility is likely to be limited, and certain groups will be favoured in recruitment, whereas other groups will find it much more difficult to develop their careers. India is well known for its rigid caste system, which traditionally fixed individuals into specific places in the social hierarchy and restricted their ability to move up the professional ladder. The caste still exists in Indian society but is reportedly diminishing in strength in urban areas while remaining strong in rural areas. In more stratified societies, the relationship within firms is generally going to be more hierarchical, with communication between managers and workers taking place on a formal basis (see below for power distance).

In societies with a very skewed income distribution system (for example, a few very rich people and many very poor, with a few in the middle), as is the case in some Latin American and African societies, the absence of a skilled, educated middle class could deter foreign investors. MNEs seeking to establish themselves in a new location frequently seek local managers to ensure that the company adjusts to their new business environment and culture and often to take over the management of the local operations of their enterprise in the long term. The shortage of such personnel and the absence of the entrepreneurial culture implied by this social structure make these objectives difficult to attain.

## Symbols

A symbol is something that represents something else by virtue of association, resemblance, or convention. The meanings attached to symbols vary across the world and are shaped by and help shape different cultures. An understanding of the different inter-pretations and meanings attached to objects, colours, numbers, gestures, etc., can be an important element of communication in international business.

The design of logos, websites, and advertisements can be undermined by the use of inappropriate colours. Black is the colour of mourning in Europe and the US. White plays this role in China and Japan, whereas in Western culture, white implies peace, purity, goodness, and brides. Mourning is signified by red in South Africa, by blue in Iran, by purple in Thailand, and by yellow in Egypt and Burma. In general terms, red implies good luck and prosperity in China, purity in India, and conjures up strong emo-tions like excitement, danger, passion, and anger in many Western cultures. Similarly, green is the colour of Islam. Green is regarded as a symbol for Ireland, also known as the 'Emerald Isle.' In many Western countries, green is also symbolic of nature, newness, and spring. In China, on the other hand, a green hat implies that the wife of the man wearing it has committed adultery.

Numbers, too, have their own symbolic meaning. In China, this has been taken quite far. The luck, good or bad, associated with a number in China comes for the most part from homonyms – words that sound the same as the number in question. Number four, for example, is one of the most inauspicious numbers in China because its pronunciation is similar to the word for 'death'. In East Asia, some buildings do not have a fourth floor, and in Hong Kong, some high-rise residential buildings miss out on all floor numbers with '4' in them. Therefore, a building with a 50th floor may, in reality, only have 36 floors as names for the 4th, 14th, 24th, and 34th, and all the floors from 40–49 have been missed out. In some regions of China, where dialects and accents lead to different pronunciations, four does not have such a bad reputation. Two of the luckiest numbers in China are six and eight. The homonyms for six are 'flowing' and 'smooth'. Whereas '666' is regarded as the sign of the devil in Western culture, in China, individuals seek to have the 666 combinations in their phone numbers and car registrations. Similarly, the homonyms for 8 are 'prosper' and 'wealth'. It is no coincidence that the opening date and time for the Beijing Olympics is at 8 o'clock on the 8th day of the 8th month of 2008. The Chinese culture was not the only culture that attached particular meaning to certain numbers. In Western culture, seven is generally regarded as lucky, whereas 13 is regarded as unlucky. The roots of the distrust of the number 13 lie in the Christian religion: there were 13 present at the Last Supper before Christ was arrested and cruci-fied, and one of those present at the table betrayed him.

## Economic systems

An economic system is the way a society organises the ownership and allocation of economic resources. In broad terms, economic systems differ from each other in terms of the degree to which there is government involvement in the economy. A pure mar-ket economy maximises the role of private enterprise, and public sector intervention is limited to the provision of public goods such as defence. The US represents the nearest approximation of this model, although, even there, the state plays more than the mini-mal role outlined above. At the other extreme, there are economic systems in which it is the state that takes on the role of resource allocator, deciding what and how much to produce. These state or command economies have become fewer and far between since the demise of the Soviet Union and the launch of Chinese economic reforms. In practice, most contemporary economies are mixed economies which strike a balance between the incorporation of aspects of the market system and a continuing role for the state.

In practice, the economic system is shaped by and helps shape the business culture. The more collective the economic system, for example, the more likely it is that group performance and teamwork are the predominant forms of work organisation (see below for Hofstede's collectivist/individualistic cultural dimension). Conversely, those economic systems that rely more on private enterprise are more likely to foster individualism. These are important considerations for foreign investors seeking to establish appropriate incentives for their employees in new overseas operations.

## Political systems

An understanding of political systems is invaluable for international business in identifying where key influences reside and getting to grips with the local culture.

Political systems refer to systems of politics and government, comprising sets of institutions, political organisations, interest groups, etc. As with economic systems, political systems are often hybrid: it is possible to have, for example, monarchies in which the monarch is essentially a figurehead and the system is overwhelmingly democratic or in which the monarch is an autocrat and democracy is underdeveloped.

Economic and political systems are often linked. Command economies and socialist/communist political systems go together, whereas a liberal economic system most naturally fits with a democratic political system. The current situation in China confounds this, however: the Chinese government has been freeing up the economy for several years while maintaining its strong control over the political system. Many commentators argue that this situation is unsustainable in the long run because private enterprise creates a new class of entrepreneurs and professionals who enjoy freedom in their economic lives and eventually will wish to see similar freedoms in other aspects of their lives. Parallels are drawn with other market-based economies in which the spread of economic prosperity ultimately resulted in greater democracy, though there is little evidence to date that increased economic freedom has fuelled an increased desire for political freedom in China, especially among the middle classes.

---

**Box 12.1:** Western state culture wars

For the past 30 years, there has been a steady emergence of a cultural conflict within some Western states (notably the US and the UK) based upon what is seen as irreconcilable differences between two opposing ideas: social conservatism and social liberalism. The former reflects a political philosophy that seeks to reassert traditional values based on fundamentalist, familialist, and moralist principles. Thus, there is an emphasis on traditional family values with opposition to feminism, abortion, and LGBT rights, among other forms of unconventional behaviours and attitudes. Social liberalism (as expected) stands in juxtaposition to such beliefs arguing for social justice and civil and political rights; this includes a progressive stance on LGBT rights, and family planning, for example. Too much of this social liberalism was generated by the expansion of higher education in the 1960s and how this shaped liberal attitudes.

While for two decades, these issues were bubbling under the fringes of political debate, these issues really began to be mainstreamed with the surge of populism within Western states in the mid-2010s. The attempt to redress long-standing injustices and prejudices led to a pushback from social conservatives and the mutual pursuit of power, which led to a zero-sum mentality within both groups. Social liberals clearly felt that an assent to power by social conservatives would lead to a retreat on freedoms won over the past 50 years (most notably on issues such as gay marriage and abortion). The pushback on such issues by social conservatives created a political cleavage within the US, especially as social issues became very salient political issues. The fear of a winner-takes-all all strategy and this politicisation of social issues have created a fear that culture wars lead to shooting wars. This was certainly a fear when Trump's supporters stormed Congress in 2021 and also when supporters of Brazil's outgoing president, Jair Bolsonaro, did the same a year later.

The big change and the mainstreaming of social issues as political issues emerged largely from the white middle class as well as the so-called 'left behinds'. These groups combined felt that these social pressures moved away from simply religion towards class and race issues, and they were an attack on their existence. A big catalyst was the GFC, which drove a wedge between classes where the notion was advanced that those who caused the crisis were exempt from its impact, whereas those who were impacted had little to do with its causes. This created a Wall Street versus Main Street mentality. This caused an understandable resentment that was fuelled by populist figures.

These fears were inflamed by populist rhetoric, which saw these developments as an existential threat to these marginalised groups. These pressures, along with the emergence of prominent social liberal groups (such as the defund the police movement and Black Lives Matter in the US), led to a broadening of the domain of culture war, with many seeing it as a perpetual conflict. There are broader concerns as to whether these cultural wars could lead to civil unrest.

There are beliefs that such fears have been overstated and that notions of culture war have been invented and inflated to suit a political agenda. It has been argued that these divisions have been created to create legitimacy for extreme views through a seek to artificially polarise systems. Moreover, these debates focus on what divides rather than the major issues where electorates are united and where consensus remains. Thus, the real division is between those who want a culture war and those who do not, and its emergence is a simple distraction from the real issues, such as economic inequality.

## WHY DOES CULTURE MATTER?

Culture, and more particularly the need to manage cultural diversity, is important in many stages of the internationalisation of business and in all forms of market entry. The following examples seek to demonstrate culture's general importance.

## Marketing

The use of inappropriate advertising language or images, for example, can completely undermine attempts to enter new markets. Entry into new markets also needs adaptation to specific consumer tastes. Even fast-food outlets like McDonald's, which attempts to deliver the same product throughout the world, must adapt their offerings in some countries. For religious reasons, beef is not a suitable ingredient for hamburgers sold in India, for example, and in order to enter the Indian market, McDonald's has had to localise its products. For reasons of taste and of reference to the local culture, MacDonald's has also developed products with a regional flavour in particular markets. These include the Teriyaki Burger (a chicken cutlet patty marinated in teriyaki sauce with sweet mayonnaise and lettuce on sesame buns) in Japan; the Kiwi Burger (a hamburger with a fried egg and pickled beet) in New Zealand; a McKielbasa in Poland (a Kielbasa – Polish sausage – patty with ketchup, mustard and onion on a sesame seed bun); and the Greek Mac, a pitta bread sandwich with two beef patties and yoghurt.

Cultural diversity can also require a radically different approach to all aspects of a new market. In March 2002, the giant US retailer Wal-Mart acquired a two-thirds share of Japan's fourth-largest supermarket chain. Wal-Mart cannot directly transfer its low-cost, high-bulk model, which was hugely successful in the US, to Japan. The Japanese retail sector is notoriously difficult for foreign companies to enter and thrive in as a result of the intricate distribution system and distinctive Japanese tastes and shopping culture. In the early 1990s, Wal-Mart had its first difficult experience of Japanese retailing: it found, for example, that its own-label biscuits did not sell well because they were too sweet for Japanese tastes. Furthermore, Japanese consumers place much greater value on presentation, with most products in Japan, including individual items of fruit such as oranges, individually wrapped in attractive packaging. As a result of a preference for fresh produce and smaller living spaces, which cuts down on the space for grocery storage, Japanese shoppers also still tend to visit the supermarket on a daily basis, whereas large weekly shopping expeditions are the norm in the US.

## Entry modes: international mergers, acquisitions, and joint ventures

Globalisation provides opportunities for firms to enter new markets and invest in new markets. As Chapter 9 shows, firms face a wide choice of how they go about this, but there is a cultural dimension to all entry modes in one way or another. Greenfield investment, which involves entering a new market without a partner from the host country, requires the acquisition of knowledge of the local culture and ways of doing things. Mergers, acquisitions, and joint ventures, however, bring together employees of at least two different enterprises, each of which has its own distinctive corporate culture. The way in which these various cultures are brought together can have a significant bearing on the success or otherwise of each initiative.

The 1998 Daimler-Chrysler merger (which quickly turned into a takeover by Daimler of Chrysler) is frequently cited as an uneasy match between two very different corporate cultures. The German partner's approach to resolution of the merged companies' problems was based on its traditional preference for engineering solutions and for seeking synergy via shared components and engines, whereas Chrysler's approach was deeply rooted in a tradition of using marketing promotions and price discounting. The former was more formal and dominated by managers with a background in engineering, and the latter by managers with a more informal approach and steeped in finance and marketing. The early years of the new company were rocky. Although the merged company's problems had several roots, the cultural dissonance between the two companies did not help, and the early years of the merged company were marked by large-scale departures of Chrysler's senior managers. Within ten years, the decision was taken to sell off the Chrysler arm of the company, a transaction that was completed in 2007.

## Human resource management (HRM)

HRM managers clearly have to consider the challenges posed by the integration of two or more companies involved in international mergers, acquisitions, alliances, and joint ventures, but they also have to become involved in decisions and strategies that are not relevant to purely domestic operations. In particular, decisions need to be taken regarding the extent to which foreign operations are managed by personnel from the home country or the host country and the type and range of opportunities to be given to host country personnel. Care also needs to be taken to manage the relationship between managers and staff from the home country and managers and staff from the host country in terms of working practices. For example, when Nissan in the early 1980s, later followed by Toyota and Honda, chose to locate their initial European manufacturing plants in the UK, there was widespread incredulity. The UK motor industry was notorious at that time for a poor industrial relations record, and there was scepticism about whether Japanese companies could successfully transfer their highly successful flexible working methods into an industrial culture that at that time was highly rigid and dogged by demarcation disputes. In the end, the Japanese investment was located in regions outside the traditional car-producing areas of the UK, and Japanese working practices were adapted, not exported wholesale, to the British environment. The UK business and working culture was itself changing as a result of the election of the Thatcher government, which reduced trade union powers and stepped back from granting heavy subsidies to failing industries. In fact, despite the reservations at the outset, the Japanese-owned car factories located in the UK proved to be the most productive in Europe – at least until the current concentration of automotive investment in Eastern Europe.

## CASE STUDY 12.2: THE US AS A CULTURAL SUPERPOWER

One of the imagined legacies of hyper-globalisation was that the freer exchange of ideas and cultural products would lead to a global convergence of cultures. This reflects an embedded logic of global competition where stronger, dominant cultures are reinforced by economic and political power. The export of this hard power was – it is argued – accompanied by the export of soft power. This would, over time, create a cultural convergence between states, rendering the US a hegemonic superpower with control over both soft and hard power systems of control. As with globalisation, this cultural power really started to emerge in the aftermath of World War II. The main channels through which this power has been exported throughout the global system have been the following:

1) The English language: English has become the main language of international business, mainly through the channel of American capitalism. This pattern was reinforced in the early days of the Internet, when the earliest versions of the system were overwhelmingly based on English-language websites. This pattern was also reinforced by the export of cultural products (see below).

2) Export of US cultural products: this includes a range of products, including the US dominance of syndicated media and TV programming as well as films, computer games, music, art, and sport. American values can also be absorbed through US control of the development and marketing of these products. The US has dominated mass TV production, and Hollywood is still the by-word for the global film industry. Important to this export is how innovative the US has been in the development of new channels for these exports to reach global audiences.

3) Global Sports: the US has also shaped global sports through its marketing and influence over the global port environment, where it played roles in developing rules and other forms of governance, and its businesses have also been major sponsors of many major sporting events. There is also the increased global export of US sports such as basketball and, to a more limited extent, American football, though the emergence of e-sports allows for US dominance in the gaming industry to entrench this process.

The use of US soft power is an important force in these processes. These cultural efforts to export soft power are also supported through US education and aid programmes, which further encourage non-US people to see the US in a positive light. However, this broad osmotic process of what has been termed the Americanisation of national cultures has also received significant pushback from states, especially those with established cultural markets of their own. For example, many states have enforced nationally produced quotas on television programming. There is a reality check with the extreme view reflected within the Americanisation process in that not all states were readily receptive to the osmotic pressures of the system and that such products would be readily absorbed into national cultures, especially where there was a significant divergence with US cultural products. Indeed, there is little evidence that national cultures are in decline. Indeed, the nature of global capitalism is that MNEs will adapt to national culture if that is what is lucrative, so there is little incentive to impose US culture on an unreceptive market.

National cultures must also reflect that the sheer movement of factors of production and cultural products, as well as data, will not leave national cultures unimpacted. Arguably a bigger threat is when these countries start to exhibit competing cultures within a single territory. Thus, the issue is less about globally competing cultures and more about different national cultures competing within a single space, especially where the differences between them are significant. For example, attempts to build a European identity alongside a national culture have proved elusive despite over five decades of attempts to create one.

**QUESTION**

How far do you believe the notion of cultural hegemony by the US is overplayed?

## CULTURAL THEORIES

Much of the work on trying to understand different cultures is concerned with the classification and categorisation of different cultural attributes and can be described as atheoretical in the sense that it attempts to describe rather than explain cultural determination and differences. This section deals with the major cultural distinctions drawn by commentators, beginning with Edward Hall's high and low context cultures and followed by the cultural dimensions of Geert Hofstede, Fons Trompenaars, and the more recent GLOBE project.

### Low and high context cultures

In his work on cultural differences, Edward Hall (1977) drew a useful distinction between 'low' and 'high' context cultures. In low context cultures, communication is explicit, clear, and unambiguous. Individuals from such cultures come directly to the point and say precisely what they mean. The US is a good example of a low context culture. In a high context culture, much important information is conveyed beyond and outside the words actually spoken. In order to fully understand what is going on in a high context cultural setting, an individual needs to be able to interpret body language, have a high degree of sensitivity to ambiguity, have the ability to read between the lines, and have knowledge of the unwritten or unspoken rules of communication. Many Asian countries count as high context cultures.

Problems can occur when individuals from low and high context cultures come into contact within a business setting or between individuals from different high context cultures with different unwritten rules. For example, what is regarded as directness and openness by individuals from low context cultures can be regarded as abruptness or even rudeness by individuals from high context cultures. Similarly, in certain high context cultures, it is virtually taboo to say 'no' to a request. In the course of negotiations, individuals from such cultures will adopt a variety of strategies to avoid a direct rebuttal of a request. Unless an individual's opposite number in the negotiation process understands the cultural incapability of saying 'no' and that a commitment to consider a request or consult further may not be a 'perhaps' but an outright negative response, the outcome for the individual in a low context culture will be confusion and frustration.

## Hofstede's cultural dimensions

The most widely discussed and influential work on business cultures is that of Geert Hofstede (1984). Following the administration of attitude surveys to over 100,000 IBM employees in more than 50 countries, Hofstede theorised that cultural and sociological differences between nations can be categorised and quantified, thereby allowing comparisons of national cultures to take place. Initially, he identified four cultural dimensions, to which he later added a fifth: short- versus long-term orientation. These dimensions are:

- **Power distance:** the power distance dimension refers to the extent to which power structures are hierarchical and reflect significant inequalities in power. Countries with large power distances exhibit wide inequalities in power — power that is often concentrated in relatively few hands in heavily centralised and hierarchical organisations. Individuals within such cultures view themselves as inherently unequal: subordinates are dependent on those higher up the hierarchy and accept the power of their superiors by virtue of their position in the hierarchy. All participants in the hierarchy expect their position within it to be clearly demarcated. Hofstede identified Latin American, Asian, African, and southern European countries as countries with large power distances.

In small power distance countries, individuals are more inclined to regard themselves as equals; rather than expecting to be told what to do, subordinates expect to be consulted and will argue a case with those higher up the organisation. Respect for individuals within the organisation comes from their proven capacity to perform a role rather than from the possession of a particular job title or their place in an organisation. Shorter, small power distance countries coincide with flatter organisation structures. Anglo-Saxon countries and countries of northern Europe were classified as small power distance countries.

Concluding a joint venture agreement or a merger or acquisition that brings together partners from large and small power distance countries poses important challenges for business. The imposition of a hierarchical structure on employees from a short power distance country could lead to a feeling of disempowerment and frustration, whereas individuals from a large power distanced culture could feel disoriented and unclear about their role in a flatter structure.

- **Uncertainty avoidance:** uncertainty avoidance measures the lack of tolerance for uncertainty and ambiguity. This manifests itself in high levels of anxiety and emotion. This in turn translates into a preference for highly structured formal rules and limited tolerance for groups and individuals demonstrating deviant ideas or behaviours. Hofstede identified the cultures of Latin America, Latin European, and Mediterranean cultures, plus Japan and South Korea, as exhibiting high anxiety and uncertainty avoidance. Low uncertainty avoidance countries include other Asian and other European countries. In these cultures, business is conducted in a less formal manner with fewer standardised rules, and individuals are expected to take greater risks and exert greater independence in the performance of their roles. Both large power distance and high uncertainty avoidance countries demonstrate a strong preference for structured hierarchies in which the individual's role is clearly defined and strong leadership is regarded as an antidote to anxiety and stress.

- **Individualism versus collectivism:** the individualist-collectivist dimension measures the degree to which the interests of individuals or of the group take priority. The social framework in an individualistic society is looser than that of a more collectivist society, and individuals take responsibility for themselves and their immediate families as opposed to extended families. Individualist societies demonstrate greater regard for individual rights and freedoms and tend to be characterised by assertiveness and competitiveness rather than by teamwork and cooperation. The most individualistic societies are to be found in Anglo-Saxon countries.

In more collectivist societies, it is the group (which could be the extended family, the employer, or society as a whole) that looks after the interests of individuals and gives them their sense of identity. In return for this protection, individuals offer the group loyalty and work towards the attainment of goals determined by and for the good of the group, organisation, tribe, or society. Hofstede categorises Japan, Latin America, and other Asian countries as being low on individualism. In such societies, group and teamwork are more common, and a greater store value is set by the cultivation of relationships than the completion of particular tasks.

An understanding of this dimension is useful when developing an incentive strategy for an organisation: instituting an individual reward system in a collectivist context is unlikely to be as effective as if it were introduced in an individualistic culture. However, such incentive schemes could be useful in trying to shift the culture of an organisation in a slightly different direction.

- **Masculinity and femininity**: societies that place a high premium on assertiveness, achievement, and the acquisition of material possessions are exhibiting aggressive or 'masculine' goal behaviour. Masculine environments also favour conflict and competition in the workplace. Cultures that place a high value on social relationships, quality of life, and sensitivity demonstrate passive or 'feminine' goal behaviour. Cultures and workplaces scoring high on the femininity dimension exhibit high degrees of cooperation, negotiation, and compromise.

There is some correlation between masculine and feminine scores and gender roles in individual societies. Japan, for example, scores high on masculinity and, among developed countries, has a low rate of women working outside the home and a dearth of women working in senior positions. Nordic countries and the Netherlands, on the other hand, with their well-developed welfare states, score very low on the masculine continuum. Care should be taken, however, not to regard the masculine-feminine dimension as a proxy for gender roles in specific societies, as there are too many counterexamples. Iran, for example, since the 1979 Revolution, has increased constraints on the activities of its female population but has a much lower masculinity score than many European countries, where women engage much more widely in employment and society in general.

- **Short vs. long-term orientation**: this cultural dimension was not included in Hofstede's original analysis but was added at a later stage. In countries with a short-term orientation, which is more characteristic of Western societies and of some Asian countries such as Pakistan and the Philippines, the emphasis is on the immediate gratification of needs, a focus on the present, and the attainment of short-term goals. In cultures with a more long-term orientation, which include the cultures of Japan, China, South Korea, and Taiwan, the satisfaction of needs is deferred for the sake of long-term benefits and growth. Associated characteristics include persistence and thrift.

## Trompenaars' cultural dimensions

Fons Trompenaars (1993) has also tried to identify key cultural dimensions. His research involved the administration of questionnaires to over 15,000 managers in 28 countries and identified the five key 'relationship' dimensions, plus two dealing with perceptions of time and engagement with nature, respectively:

- **Universalism vs. particularism**: this dimension measures the relative weight placed on rules versus relationships. In universal cultures, emphasis is placed on the use of formal rules to govern organisations and transactions, whereas in more particularistic cultures, there is a concentration on the cultivation of relationships, 'face', paternalism, and other types of social control and networks (see Case study 13.1). In negotiations or joint projects between parties based on universal and particularist tendencies, unless this fundamental difference is recognised, serious problems will arise. For example, representatives from a universal culture will focus immediately on the legal form of a contract or agreement, whereas representatives from a particularist culture will place a premium on developing trust and cultivating a relationship before determining the finer details of a contract. In these cases, the universalist emphasis on rules can seem rushed and rude to the particularist negotiators, whereas the particularist emphasis on relationship building can seem frustrating and a waste of time to individuals from a particularist culture. Western cultures like the US, UK, Australia, and Canada place emphasis on formal rules, whereas Middle Eastern countries and some Asian countries like China stress relationships more.
- **Individualism versus collectivism**: Trompenaars' definition of this dimension is similar to that of Hofstede, but there is some disparity in the classification of countries. For example, Trompenaars found Mexico and the Czech Republic to be more individualistic than Hofstede did. This possibly reflects the fact that the research of Trompenaars is more recent than that of Hofstede. Between the two surveys, Mexico moved towards a greater acceptance of market economics, with its implied greater individualism, a trend that has continued. Similarly, in relation to the Czech Republic, although the introduction of the market economy was only in its infancy when Trompenaars' research was conducted, the old collectivist systems had already been challenged and had effectively disintegrated, whereas Hofstede carried out his survey when the Cold War was at its height.

- **Neutral vs. affective or emotional culture**: in a neutral culture, individuals are reluctant to show their feelings, whereas in affective or emotional cultures, there is much greater openness about showing feelings and emotions. Japan is regarded as one of the most neutral cultures, whereas Mexico is among the most emotional. The conduct of negotiations or the implementation of projects involving parties from both neutral and affective cultures can be disconcerting for the participants, as both sides are unaccustomed to interpreting and dealing with the verbal signals and body language of their opposite number in an appropriate manner. Negotiators from an affective or emotional culture will have difficulty relating to the reactions, or lack of reaction, of their counterparts from a neutral background, whereas neutral-culture negotiators may well interpret an overtly emotional reaction as being much more significant than it actually is. In short, unless there is a great deal of cultural literacy between both parties, there is a danger of negotiations or projects going awry because of mutual misunderstandings.
- **Achievement vs. ascription-oriented culture**: in achievement-oriented cultures like the US and the UK, achievement is what matters, and the standing of an individual is related to that. In ascriptive cultures, more common in Asia, status is derived from the job title or general characteristics such as age or birth. Ascription-oriented cultures tend to correspond with Hofstede's high power distance dimension. Care needs to be taken regarding who represents an organisation in negotiations between achievement and ascriptive-oriented cultures. Representation of an organisation in negotiations by young, highfliers from an achievement-oriented culture is often regarded by an ascriptive organisation as an indication that the talks are not taken very seriously or even as a sign of disrespect. The size of the team can also be an issue: if the lead negotiator or company representative is not accompanied by a suitably large team of assistants, then an ascriptive-oriented organisation can reach similar conclusions about its counterparts.
- **Specific vs. diffuse culture**: in specific cultures, there is a clear distinction between work and private life, whereas in diffuse cultures, the distinction between work and private life is blurred. Similarly, in the development of business links and relationships, in a specific culture, it is the function or role that is the focus of negotiations, whereas, in a more diffuse culture, the successful conclusion of a deal depends not only on the precise details of the deal but also on the construction of a relationship between the parties. The US, UK, and Australia are cultures at the specific end of the specific-diffuse continuum, and China and Japan are at the diffuse end (see Case study 13.1).

## The GLOBE project

In the 2000s, publication began of the results of a major transnational research project, Global Leadership and Organisational Behaviour Effectiveness (GLOBE). GLOBE was established in 1992 and involved 150 researchers collecting data from 18,000 managers involved in the telecommunications services, food processing, and financial services industries in 62 countries. Hofstede's work served as the model and framework for GLOBE. Not only did GLOBE utilise the cultural dimensions approach, but it expanded the number of dimensions studied to nine. The study began with Hofstede's five dimensions. Hofstede's collectivism dimension was split into institutional collectivism (the active promotion of participation in social institutions) and in-group collectivism (an emphasis on family and friendship groups). His masculine-feminine dimension was split into an assertiveness (i.e., masculine) dimension and a gender egalitarianism dimension (that is, gender roles). Long-term orientation was relabelled 'future orientation', and two new dimensions – performance orientation (similar to achievement orientation) and humane orientation, which involves generosity, fairness, and altruism – were introduced.

The legacy of the GLOBE project was especially evident in understanding the nature of leadership within businesses operating across borders. It advocated the need for leaders to demonstrate leadership that was culturally endorsed. Thus, the GLOBE indicated that leadership needed to be charismatic/value-based, team-driven, participative, humane-oriented, autonomous, and self-protected. On top of this, across the cultural dimensions identified, researchers were able to score states to be able to identify how they generate and distribute wealth as well as their attitude towards welfare. It also enabled researchers to identify universally desirable and undesirable characteristics. In turn, the identified characteristics enabled the identification of the type of leadership deployed in different contexts.

## Critiques of cultural dimensions

Hofstede, Trompenaars, and latterly, the GLOBE project, have conducted the most extensive and commented-upon research in the field of business culture. However, their conclusions have been subject to intense scrutiny and criticism. Concerns about the work cluster around methodological issues and conceptual matters.

Hofstede's work in particular has been criticised on methodological grounds, particularly the fact that his survey was limited to IBM employees, a highly specific and self-selecting group of individuals within a country's population. These individuals tend to be white collar and middle class and have been socialised into IBM's strong organisational culture, which itself could override aspects of national culture. In addition, the fact that individuals are IBM employees probably means they intrinsically possess characteristics that are compatible with IBM's culture. However, it is also the case that since Hofstede first carried out his pioneering study, other work using a similar survey methodology using employees from a range of companies has been conducted, which confirms Hofstede's approach. The work of Trompenaars, for example, falls into this category.

The above criticisms have some validity, but the more serious concerns deal with the conceptual underpinning of the work. Culture is an enormously complex phenomenon, and it is overly simplistic to characterise it in terms of four to five dimensions that hide as many differences as they reveal, making it difficult, or even potentially dangerous, to draw conclusions about the appropriate management style from scores on a particular cultural dimension. High collectivist scores, for example, can reflect and act as a proxy for a range of different cultural characteristics: collectivism in the Japanese context can be different from collectivism in the Latin American context, with different organisational and management implications.

The unit of analysis in the work is the nation, itself an artificial and relatively recent construct that contains many subcultures. Large, industrialised countries like the US are a case in point: the US has a population of over 250 million, spanning the high-tech world of Silicon Valley in California to the farming hinterlands of the mid-West and from the oil-producing region of Texas to the more cosmopolitan world of the east coast. Smaller countries like Belgium and Canada are divided by cultural differences. In the case of Belgium, the Flemish speakers of the north probably have as much, if not more, in common with the Dutch population across the border as with the French-speaking Walloons in the south and east of the country. The divide in Canada is also highlighted by linguistic differences, in this case between English and French speakers. In other countries, the cultural differences within nations can be tribal and ethnic, as witnessed by several African countries such as Nigeria and Cameroon.

Similarly, national cultural differences do not necessarily coincide with other cultural signifiers, such as occupation. An Indian software engineer based in Bangalore, for example, although sharing many cultural experiences with his compatriots, will also find many common reference points with a software engineer based in the US, perhaps more so than with a hill farmer from Kashmir.

Large-scale studies like those of Hofstede and Trompenaars are also subject to the charge that they are static, reflecting a snapshot of a particular point in time. In reality, cultures are not set in stone; cultural shifts do occur, usually, although not always, over a lengthy period of time. Fixed-point studies like those of Hofstede and Trompenaars are unable to detect these cultural shifts.

Notwithstanding these critiques of the work of Hofstede and Trompenaars, their studies do contain valuable insights and emphasise the importance of sensitivity to cultural differences across nations and within businesses. The more recent GLOBE project uses more recent data and, in broad terms, develops and confirms their approach. There are, however, differences between Hofstede and GLOBE in terms of their methodology and conceptual approach (see Journal of International Business Studies 2006), and the resulting debate will help shape the future cultural research agenda.

## CONCLUSION

Globalisation adds an extra dimension to cultural issues within the firm. All organisations have their own culture based on common language and terminology, behavioural norms, dominant values, informality or formality, etc. This inevitably becomes more complex when an organisation has a presence in more than one country. Some companies believe a strong corporate culture is a means of overcoming diverse national cultures, whereas others evolve different cultures in different organisations and incorporate cultural diversity into their management strategies.

Culture also operates in markets as well as within organisations. The development of a global culture, although undesirable in many ways, would facilitate the development of global products, enabling companies to reap economies of scale at all stages of the value chain. Many organisations like Coca-Cola and McDonald's use core brands but still adapt their products for local markets, either out of necessity or to maximise returns.

Although it is fair to say there is a degree of cultural convergence, global culture is more ephemeral and less deeply embedded than national cultures, and localisation of output is likely to remain the norm for many years.

## KEY POINTS

- Globalisation brings divergent cultures into contact with each other, posing challenges to international managers and presenting them with opportunities.
- Cultural factors represent a complex interplay of values, ideas, beliefs, history, customs, practice, etc. and are powerful shapers of the business environment.
- Culture is an important dimension in most aspects of international business, including marketing, human resource management, entry modes, and negotiations.
- Hofstede pioneered cultural theory in international business. His approach to identifying key cultural dimensions that distinguish national cultures has continued to dominate work in this field.
- Cultural literacy is essential for the successful management of international business ventures.

## QUESTIONS FOR DISCUSSION

1. Discuss the main determinants of national culture. Is it possible to say which determinants have the biggest influence on international business, or does it vary between cultures?
2. Discuss the main implications for international business of differences in national cultures.
3. How useful are Hofstede's cultural dimensions?
4. Explain which of and how the theoretical cultural dimensions discussed above can be linked to the concept of 'guanxi' (see Case study 13.1).
5. Discuss ways in which companies can 'manage' differences in national culture.
6. Is cultural convergence taking place? If so, discuss whether it is taking the form of the 'Americanisation' of culture or if there is a merging of different cultures.

## ACTIVITIES

1. You work for a multinational cosmetics company seeking to sell your products to India for the first time. Prepare a short presentation for the board that alerts it to the cultural issues of which it needs to be aware.
2. Find examples of how businesses have successfully adapted to differences in national cultures.

## SUGGESTED FURTHER READINGS

Crane, D., Kawashima, N., & Kawasaki, K. I. (2016). *Global culture: Media, arts, policy, and globalization*, London, UK: Routledge.

Hofstede, G. (1980). *Culture's consequences: International differences in work-related values*. Beverly Hills, CA: Sage.

Hofstede, G. (2001). *Culture's consequences: Comparing values, behaviors, institutions and organizations across nations*. Thousand Oaks, CA: Sage.

Hult, G. T. M., Ketchen, D. J., Griffith, D. A., Finnegan, C. A., Gonzalez-Padron, T., Javidan, M., & Dastmalchian, A. (2009). Managerial implications of the GLOBE project: A study of 62 societies. *Asia Pacific Journal of Human Resources*, 47(1), 41–58.

Komin, S. (1994). *Psychology of the Thai people: Values and behavioral patterns*. Bangkok: Magenta.

Leung, K. (2008). Chinese culture, modernization, and international business. *International Business Review*, 17(2), 184–187.

Leung, K., Bhagat, S., Buchan, N., Erwz, M., & Gibson, C. (2005). Culture and international business: Recent advances and their implications for future research. *Journal of International Business Studies*, 36(4), 357–378.

Matviuk, S. (2007). Cross cultural leadership: Behaviour expectations: A comparison between United States managers and Mexican managers. *Journal of American Academy of Business*, 11(1), 253–260.

Sennett, R. (2006). *The culture of the new capitalism*, New Haven: Yale University Press.

So, Y. (2006). *Explaining Guanxi: The Chinese business network*, London: Routledge.

Stahl, G. K., & Tung, R. L. (2015). Towards a more balanced treatment of culture in international business studies: The need for positive cross-cultural scholarship. *Journal of International Business Studies*, 46(4), 391–414.

Terranova, C. (2007). Assessing culture during an acquisition. *Organization Development Journal*, 25(2), 43–48.

Terpstra, V., & David, K. (1991). *The cultural environment of international business*. Nashville, TN: South-Western Publishing Company.

Trompenaars, F., & Woolliams, P. (2004). *Marketing across cultures*, Chichester: Capstone.

### Websites

GLOBE website: http://www.thunderbird.edu/wwwfiles/ms/globe.

# PART IV

# INTERNATIONAL BUSINESS AND CIVIL SOCIETY ISSUES

As globalisation has progressed, it has gained importance and relevance to civil society. Very broadly, civil society is defined as those parts of the socio-economic system that are neither government nor business, such as charity, pressure groups, and the family. As globalisation has progressed, its impact has started to expand beyond the commercial and economic sphere into broader socio-environmental issues. The chapters within this part of the text seek to examine the main trends and processes impacting civil society through the globalisation process.

To address these concerns within the text, the section looks at a range of issues relevant to the broader range of stakeholders involved in international business. The first chapter examines the corporate and social responsibility issues emerging from engagement within the global commercial system. Congruent with these themes of social responsibility, the section then moves on to look at labour and environmental issues as they develop global value chains. It seeks to address how the firm will seek to balance efficiency with reputational concerns as it seeks to take advantage of the opportunities afforded by globalisation.

DOI: 10.4324/9781315184500-16

# CHAPTER 13

# CORPORATE SOCIAL RESPONSIBILITY AND ETHICS

## OBJECTIVES

This chapter will help you to:

- Understand the range and complexity of CSR and ethical issues facing MNEs.
- Explain why CSR and ethics have become mainstream issues for MNEs.
- Compare and contrast the view that the only responsibility that a business has is to its shareholders with stakeholder theory.
- Assess the usefulness of codes of conduct in shaping ethical and responsible behaviour.

Issues of corporate social responsibility (CSR) and business ethics are engaging businesses more and more, both domestically and internationally. This trend has been accentuated by high-profile breaches of accepted standards of ethical behaviour, such as the Purdue case, where inadequate checks and balances external to the firm enabled unethical behaviour to occur, a development made easier by the failure of the external regulator to fulfil its role properly. The quickening of the globalisation process has also highlighted CSR issues. For example, there is a time lag between rapid liberalisation and the development and implementation of the appropriate regulatory framework. Moreover, international governance in social and environmental areas, both key CSR issues, is underdeveloped and contested, and there is often inadequate or even a complete absence of governance in these areas facing MNEs in developing countries. These examples highlight how rapid globalisation can outpace the development of a legal framework to regulate the changing business environment. CSR initiatives can help fill this governance gap.

This chapter builds on Chapter 12, which deals with culture. Cultural and ethical issues are separate but related concerns. Business practices are the product of their own specific cultural environment. Although some practices are clearly unacceptable in all cultures, there are some grey areas where practices that are commonplace in some

DOI: 10.4324/9781315184500-17

countries are regarded as unethical in others, and it is these grey areas that present international businesses with some of their greatest dilemmas. This chapter also underpins subsequent chapters on labour and the environment (see Chapters 14 and 15), which have both an economic and CSR theme to them.

The chapter itself opens with a discussion of what constitutes business ethics and CSR and why these concepts matter. It then briefly discusses varying perspectives on business ethics. In practice, business ethics draw on a vast array of philosophical literature which ranges far beyond the boundaries of this chapter. The chapter then discusses the specific international dimensions of CSR and business ethics and some of the ethical challenges facing MNEs when confronted with different standards and practices and with defending the consequences of their actions in far-flung corners of the world. It concludes with attempts to provide ethical guidance to businesses.

## WHAT ARE CSR AND BUSINESS ETHICS?

It is relatively straightforward to define business ethics and corporate social responsibility. Business ethics refers to the moral principles and standards that guide business behaviour and highlight what is regarded as right, wrong, or otherwise unacceptable behaviour. CSR refers to the obligations of a business towards society. In particular, the firm should, as a minimum, limit the negative impact of its activities on society and ideally maximise the benefits. The motives for adopting a CSR policy can vary, but underpinning the idea of these obligations is a moral and philosophical perspective on the relationship between business and society.

The above definitions of business ethics and CSR are general and tell us nothing about what these moral principles and standards are or indeed should be. This is where problems begin to arise for international business. Although there are some very clear ethical principles which prevail in all societies (such as the prohibition of murder), there are other aspects of behaviour where it is not always clear which is the morally correct path to follow. These grey areas can also exist within societies. Once the complexities of international business (with the addition of different cultures, religions, and other traditions to the mix) are taken into account, the determination of appropriate behaviour can become even more problematic. These issues are teased out throughout this chapter and, to a certain extent, in subsequent chapters on labour and the environment, subjects which raise many ethical and CSR as well as economic issues.

### CASE STUDY 13.1: LAVA JATO (CAR WASH) SCANDAL BRAZIL

This scandal first emerged in 2014, arising from the activities of the state-owned oil company Petrobras. This was an extensive corruption scandal involving a wide network of politicians and high-profile businesspeople, where money was offered in exchange for the granting of contracts by this state-owned business. The scandal engulfed the administration of the then Brazilian President, Dilma Rousseff, eventually leading to her impeachment and removal from office. It also led to her predecessor, Lula da Silva, being incarcerated, though charges against him were eventually dropped. However, Lava Jato turned out to be Brazil's biggest-ever corruption scandal.

The defrauding of Petrobras started when concerns were raised with regard to the contract's issues for the exploration of offshore oil and gas reserves. Initially, the investigation started as a money laundering operation (it gained its name as investigations first focused on a car wash), but the investigation expanded as it became evident that these actions were a result of the embezzlement of funds from Petrobras. After initial investigations by several whistle-blowers, it became evident that there was an extended network of businesspeople, including Marcelo Odebrecht (then Brazil's richest man and owner of the eponymous construction company) and politicians who were involved in the process. This process lasted more than a decade, during which Petrobras managers and senior executives agreed to inflate contracts by as much as 3 per cent. So extensive was the fraud that it was estimated that a total of $2.1 billion was taken from the company, with the company suffering a significant write-down of over $17 billion due to overvalued assets and explicit graft. Petrobras had to cut capital expenditures and sell off assets to the value of nearly $14 billion to cover the fraud. This was coupled with a sharp reduction in the market value of the firm, compounded by the fact that the firm was now over $100 billion in debt. Overall, it was estimated that the fraud in the business depressed the Brazilian economy by nearly 1 per cent.

The problem of one firm's corruption became an institutional problem when it became clear how far this corruption had permeated and embedded itself within the political system. The money paid by businesses was used to fund re-election campaigns. The public's revulsion of this corruption focused on Dilma Rousseff, who appeared to be largely innocent of any illegal activity even though her party was clearly involved and Rousseff was chair of the board at the time when much of the fraud was started. However, the attempts to protect her predecessor, Lula da Silva, from prosecution undermined her legitimacy, and she was eventually impeached and removed from office in August 2016.

The affair demonstrated key flaws within the Brazilian system, not least of which was that Brazil suffers from institutionalised crime, where illegal activity occurs with the tacit sanction of the state's power structures and which has permeated deep into the political and commercial systems. Indeed, it is believed that this endemic corruption is rooted within the executive, legislature, and judiciary. This was not created by the Lava Jato system but long predates it, dating back to the 1960s. This has, for many, created an increasingly ineffective state that offers poor public services and where the exposed Lava Jato was only part of a network of corruption within the state. These findings are used for both personal enrichment and campaign finance. However, some feel that the process went too far and became a witch hunt through which political scores could be settled. As a result, public sentiment started to turn against the investigation, especially in terms of judicial overreach. However, arguably the greatest impact of the scandal was not simply the political unrest that engulfed their government but also the fact that Brazil has now implemented a reform that prohibits corporate donations. However, the deep reform needed and as suggested by the endemic corruption exposed by Lava Jato has yet to occur.

**QUESTION**

Why does the Lavo Jato case matter to those businesses operating in Brazil?

## Why do business ethics and CSR matter and why should firms behave ethically?

It has become the norm for companies to develop their own corporate codes of ethics (see below) and to commit themselves to behave in a social manner. Admittedly, firms have never declared their intentions to behave unethically or irresponsibly, but recognition of the requirement to behave responsibly has not always been high on the corporate agenda. What has changed? Apart from the fact that ethical behaviour is an appropriate end in itself (that is, firms should behave ethically because it is the right thing to do), why do corporations currently place a much greater emphasis on business ethics and CSR than in the past?

First, reputation is an important asset for a firm as an employer, as a supplier, as a purchaser, and in marketing terms. Nike, Gap, Nestlé, Monsanto, McDonald's, and Shell have famously been the subject of focused campaigns against various aspects of their activities. Such campaigns can take the form of publicity campaigns or can even extend as far as consumer boycotts. Popular issues for such boycotts throughout the formative decades of the 21st century include the environment, animal testing, the fur trade, the repression of trade union activity, sweatshop labour, and overtly political boycotts such as those against firms active in Burma or against Altria (formerly Philip Morris), Esso, Lucozade (owned by GlaxoSmithKline), MBNA, and Microsoft for making donations to the Republican Party.

There are mixed views on the efficacy of boycotts: some work and others do not. Some campaigners oppose boycotts on the grounds that they can harm the very people the boycott is designed to help. For example, boycotting a firm because of sweatshop conditions in a foreign supplier is as likely to lead to workers in those suppliers losing their jobs as to improvements in conditions. This is because MNEs are likely to end their contracts with suppliers, claiming that they, the MNE, knew nothing about the conditions. Nevertheless, bad publicity and boycotts can be damaging to a firm. Unless a proactive damage limitation exercise is undertaken, harm to a company's reputation from bad publicity can have a serious long-term effect on the bottom line. It is much better from a reputational point of view to behave responsibly in the first place and not incur the bad publicity resulting from exposure to bad practices.

Secondly, it has become a commonly held view that firms that behave ethically and responsibly tend to make bigger profits. In other words, as Anita Roddick, the founder of The Body Shop, once said, 'being good is good for businesses'. Although far from conclusive, research tends to confirm that there is a correlation between profitability and firms that have a strong commitment to CSR. However, it is unclear whether it is the CSR commitment that contributes to higher levels of profitability or whether it is the higher levels of profitability that yield the surplus that enables firms to adopt more responsible policies. Research into specific aspects of CSR is more conclusive. The Porter hypothesis, for example, posits a positive relationship between profitability and the adoption of green policies as a result of research into the printed circuit board industry.

Thirdly, the rise of the 'ethical consumer' and the 'ethical investor' who reward those firms regarded as 'good' by buying and investing in their products and punish those regarded as 'bad' through the withholding of custom. Positive buying is directed, for example, towards products that are cruelty-free, organic, recycled, do not exploit humans or animals, and do minimal damage to the environment.

In order to exercise ethical choices, consumers and investors need to have information about the companies themselves and about the impact of their activities. The latter can often be difficult to estimate as estimates of environmental impacts are often contested, and measures to improve a situation can often have unintended and negative consequences. Despite these problems, an expanding array of standards and labels has emerged to guide consumer choices in an ethical direction. These include Fairtrade, Social Accountability 8000, the Fair Labor Association, organic food, Co-op America, Product Red, Rainforest Alliance, etc.

Fairtrade is one of the fastest-growing such initiatives. Its aim is to ensure that producers get a guaranteed minimum price for their products. Products covered by the Fairtrade mark include bananas, cocoa, coffee, cotton, dried fruit, fresh fruit and vegetables, honey, juices, nuts, oils, seeds and purees, quinoa, rice, spices, sugar, tea, wine, cut flowers, ornamental plants, and sports balls. The Fairtrade minimum price is set at a level that ensures producers receive a price that covers the cost of sustainable production for their product. This is particularly valuable for farmers when prices for their commodities fall. Conversely, when market prices are above the Fairtrade minimum, the buyer must pay the market price. Products certified by Fairtrade must also meet a range of other standards relating to social, economic, and environmental criteria. As such, a consumer buying a Fairtrade-certified product should be able to do so safe in the knowledge that workers engaged in its production have enjoyed decent conditions, that the money he/she pays for a product is not swallowed up by the rest of the value chain, and that the producer receives a reasonable share of the final sales price.

Fairtrade itself was established in 1988 in the Netherlands under the Max Havelaar label. The initiative spread swiftly to other markets, including Belgium, Switzerland, Denmark, Norway, France, Germany, Austria, Luxembourg, Italy, the US, Canada, Japan, the UK, and Ireland. Fairtrade has subsequently spread to Mexico, Australia, and New Zealand. In 2021, the sale of Fairtrade products reached over €10 billion worldwide.

Figure 13.1 shows that the Fairtrade market has grown substantially in the decade to 2017, with the UK overtaking the US as the biggest overall market. This is a trend that is evident across all of the countries surveyed. Notably, Fairtrade sales are made in higher-income countries. As individual wealth increases, survival becomes less of an issue, and factors other than price enter the consumption decision.

Ethical investors increasingly have external assistance in determining which companies represent ethical investments. The Dow Jones and FTSE monitor the performance

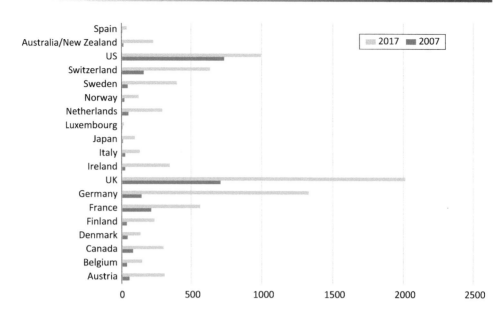

**FIGURE 13.1** Retail value of Fairtrade products by country 2007 and 2017 (source The Fairtrade Foundation)

of companies on the New York and London stock exchanges, in particular. Both organisations have launched their own index relating to the ethical behaviour of firms. The Dow Jones Sustainability Index is based on questionnaires and external assurance relating to economic, environmental, and social development criteria that determine eligibility for inclusion in the index. The FTSE4Good index excludes tobacco, arms, and nuclear power sectors and is intended to 'reflect the performance of socially responsible equities and facilitate investment in these companies'. Eligible companies are then selected for the index in accordance with social and environmental criteria in five categories: environmental sustainability, human rights, countering bribery, supply chain labour standards, and climate change.

Overall, the impact of the growth of ethical consumerism and investment is unclear. Firms are certainly paying more attention to ethical issues, and companies can lose a great deal of money if they encounter bad publicity about their activities. Shell claimed it had lost millions following the consumer boycott resulting from Green Peace's campaign against its plans for disposal of the Brent Spar oil platform in the 1990s. However, there is little evidence to suggest that firms reap much reward for 'good behaviour'.

Moreover, there is evidence to suggest that the growth of demand for these products tends to be cyclical, and any increases in the cost of living, especially with regard to core staples, could well challenge the commitment of consumers to ethical purchasing in even the richest countries, given that there is often a price premium entailed in purchasing 'ethical' products. Analysts frequently report a gap between consumers' views on ethical purchases and their actual propensity to purchase ethical goods. The behaviour of consumers during this difficult economic period will indicate how deeply rooted ethical consumption and investment have become.

**Box 13.1:** The problem of greenwashing

The fact that companies see strategic value in being seen as advocates of green and other social issues, along with a desire to militate some of the costs associated with such policies, has given rise to the phenomenon of `greenwashing'. This reflects a process where companies intentionally overrepresent to both the public and investors their green credentials for competitive benefit and to take commercial advantage of customer and investor sentiment for such activities. The company makes a greater effort seeking to convince stakeholders of its environmental credentials than it actually does in mitigating any impact that it might have. This process extends beyond the marketing perspective towards those actions that overemphasise its green credentials to cover those activities in which the firm is engaged which have a detrimental effect upon the environment. What is widely acknowledged is that many business leaders see it as a legitimate strategy to gain market share.

These strategies have been common within hospitality but also, more controversially, within the energy and utility sectors. In the energy sector, there have been attempts to oversell their commitment to the energy transition and investment in renewable energy technologies while still investing heavily in hydrocarbons. In the utility sector (such as water), providers have been known to oversell investment in environmental practices while at the same time engaging in activities that intentionally pollute (such as the spoiling of water sources). The process can also occur through misleading packaging and labelling where vague terminology is used and there is a strong power of suggestion. There is also the problem where companies selectively use data from research to stress green credentials while downplaying their harmful aspects.

The point is that greenwashing matters, as it is essentially a tool for misleading both consumers and investors. Often, green products can be sold at a premium, which also contravenes the ESG principles of investment funds, which target such priorities within their investment strategies. The legacy of such actions by the greenwasher is an erosion of trust between itself and other stakeholders and the consequent reputational damage that emerges as a result of such strategies. This could also introduce a degree of cynicism within the processes that undermines the green agenda across business generally. As a result, there have to be effective deterrents to the process and also to ensure external monitoring of the process. This can be achieved through sustainability ratings, kite marks, and other forms of external transparency in the process of green accreditation.

## THE INTERNATIONAL DIMENSION OF BUSINESS ETHICS AND CSR

Ethics and corporate responsibility are matters for all firms, whether they operate internationally or not. However, once the international dimension enters the equation, the complexity of ethical and CSR issues increases. A major concern for international business is the universal versus relativist debate. Universal values are those that have been adopted everywhere, or almost everywhere. There have been attempts to identify and codify such values in the UN-inspired Universal Declaration of Human Rights (UDHR) and in the Caux principles (see below), one of several attempts to develop a set of ethical principles which can be utilised by MNEs across the globe. The UDHR was adopted by the UN General Assembly and covered an array of political and civil rights and economic, social, and cultural rights that pertain to all UN members. The rights most directly concerning business include the right to equality before the law (that is, non-discrimination); the right to an adequate standard of living; the right to work in just and favourable conditions; the right to equal pay for equal work; the right to rest and leisure; and the right to paid holidays. In reality, despite its underpinning by the UN, it is not difficult to uncover many areas in which these principles are not respected.

Relativism reflects the extent to which different societies have different values and ethical standards to guide behaviour. These values are determined to a large extent by the many influences that have an impact on culture (see Chapter 12) and can lead to different principles of behaviour between societies. The problem for international business is which code of behaviour should be adopted when operating in another country. Should they adopt the 'when in Rome' principle that requires them to comply with host country values, or should they be guided by their own values? Both positions can create problems. The former case can create severe ethical dilemmas. For example, in South Africa during the days of apartheid, MNEs were required to comply with employment policies of racial segregation that the rest of the world considered abhorrent. Nevertheless, MNEs continued to invest in South Africa. Many argued that such behaviour was unethical and essentially propped up an immoral regime, whereas others argued that such investment represented a constructive engagement with the regime and that this, rather than isolation, would bring about change. On the other hand, if firms are guided by their own values, they can be accused of 'cultural imperialism' and of imposing their own values on other societies.

Two other concepts also need to be taken into account when studying business ethics: the difference between descriptive ethics and normative ethics. Descriptive ethics is about studying, describing, and characterising morality and ethical behaviour. It is this process that draws out the differences in belief systems between societies. A country like India, for example, contains a complex web of influences that have shaped values there. Hinduism is the main religion and influence in India, but Islam, Sikhism, Zoroastrianism, and Jainism also play their part. In the business field, the influence of Western management traditions can also be thrown into the mix. In reality, the values of many societies are subject to a wide range of influences and can be difficult to unravel for an outsider.

In practice, descriptive ethics are the starting point for an expatriate manager trying to come to terms with a new culture. For many purposes, differences in values and norms need not cause a problem for the international manager. However, understanding the ethical system of a society does not provide guidance on how to behave in a specific set of circumstances. This is where normative ethics – the determination not of 'what is' but of 'what should be' – takes on importance. Given the existence of different cultural and ethical traditions, the international manager has to decide the right thing to do when faced with conflicting values and complex issues.

## Varying perspectives on ethics

Perceptions of what is right and wrong are derived from a number of sources, including religion, family, society in general, etc. In democracies, the law reflects the values of the society in which it is located. Observance of the law may be necessary for an individual or a firm to behave ethically, but it may not be sufficient in itself as legal behaviour may only comply with the ethical minimum. Conversely, especially in non-democratic societies, legal obligations may be out of kilter with what is regarded as ethical in society at large and could require unethical behaviour by citizens and corporations.

In addition to religion, philosophical traditions also influence views of what is right and wrong. Business literature on ethics tends to be dominated by Western philosophical traditions such as Aristotelian philosophy, utilitarianism, Kantian philosophy, etc. The rise of Asian business will see greater attention paid to Eastern philosophical traditions. The influence of religion and philosophy on business ethics is beyond the scope of this chapter, but an awareness that business ethics is rooted in something that ranges far beyond and deeper is important.

In more practical terms, assumptions about ethics and business are inevitably influenced by fundamental beliefs about the role of business in society. On the one hand, there are those who believe that the sole social responsibility of business is to generate profit. The writings of Milton Friedman embody this view. For example, in 1962, in *Capitalism and Freedom*, he wrote:

> There is one and only one social responsibility of business – to use its resources and engage in activities designed to increase its profits so long as it … engages in open and free competition without deception or fraud.

For some proponents of this view, profit generation itself takes on a moral dimension, whereas others see profits as the key to wealth generation – the main way of addressing social issues.

On the other hand, others believe that the role of business is much broader than that of wealth generation and that all those who are affected by the way a company operates – shareholders, employees, customers, suppliers, the local community, and future generations (especially in relation to environmental issues) – have a legitimate interest and stake in the way a company conducts itself. Figure 13.2 highlights some of the typical stakeholders in a firm. Stakeholders may vary from firm to firm; in some circumstances, the impact of a firm on the local community may be greater than in others. In some cases, the relative impact of a firm on stakeholders may vary within a firm, depending on the activity or product in question.

Stakeholder theory acknowledges the responsibility of the firm towards its shareholders but also claims that the firm has obligations to others. In terms of employees, the firm must pay due regard to health and safety matters, pay a fair wage, and follow a policy of non-discrimination. The stake that customers have in a firm entitles them to expect that they should be dealt with fairly and honestly, that they should not be subject to misleading claims or advertising, and that the products they consume should be safe, healthy, and clearly labelled. Suppliers have a right to be fairly treated in terms of prices and the

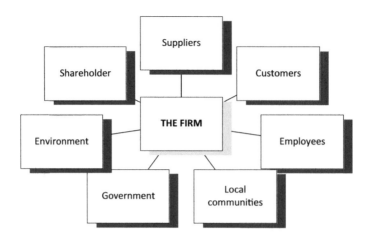

**FIGURE 13.2** Typical stakeholders in a firm

general conditions of their contracts. Late payment of bills, for example, can frequently undermine the day-to-day operations of small suppliers. The activities of a company can impact a community, both negatively and positively. The environmental impact of firms on local communities can often be a bone of contention, for example. On the other hand, MNEs also provide jobs for the local community. Moreover, it is often at the local level that firms engage in corporate philanthropy in the form of educational projects in the developing world or improvements to local amenities. Firms are also under an obligation to pay local and national taxes and to respect the laws and regulations passed by the government.

Stakeholder theory, developed most notably by Edward Freeman in the 1980s, holds that companies are under an obligation not to violate the rights of others and are responsible for the effects of their actions on others. As such, companies are seen as responsible members of the community, with all the accompanying obligations and privileges this entails. Operationalising the stakeholder concept can be complex; who exactly constitutes a stakeholder and what the existence of a stake entitles any individual or organisation to in any given situation is far from straightforward. It is possible that competing stakeholder claims can clash; how can and should these differences be reconciled?

## International ethical and CSR issues

The above concerns are relevant to business, whether it is domestic or international in nature. However, international business poses particular challenges and questions over and above those facing purely domestic business. The following, far from exhaustive, list includes some of the international ethical challenges facing MNEs:

- Human rights: it is a generally accepted principle that MNEs should not engage in direct infringement of human rights; the UN Universal Declaration of Human Rights (UDHR) is commonly taken as the appropriate benchmark. However, some people would go further, preferring companies to refrain from doing business in countries known to infringe on human rights on a systematic basis. Opponents of this view argue that if an MNE abstains from conducting business in a country with an ethically dubious regime, the only concrete result is to hand over business opportunities to companies without such reservations.

On coming to office in 1992, for example, President Clinton proposed to withdraw Most Favoured Nation status from China as a result of the Tiananmen Square massacre in 1989, in which many pro-democracy demonstrators were killed. Such action would have provoked retaliation against US companies operating in China, and US businesses lobbied hard to persuade the President to change his mind. They argued that US business interests would be irrevocably damaged in a rapidly growing market and that the outcome would not be an improvement in human rights in China but a boost to the business prospects of American business rivals in China. The lobbying campaign was successful: the link between trade and human rights was broken and replaced by the doctrine that the possibility of bringing about change is greater if business and other links and contacts are maintained. Although there is some support for this view, there are also those who believe it is a convoluted justification of 'business as usual'.

US politicians have found themselves caught between a desire to criticise China over its human rights record and the desire of US business to protect its high and increasing levels of investment in China. Donald Trump's sinophobic rhetoric and his and other administrations' desire to decouple from China always sat uneasily with business, which was looking to develop strategies that were exactly the opposite. Moreover, these businesses were also concerned that ratcheting up this rhetoric too far could see their existing investments jeopardised.

- Labour issues: international labour issues can be linked with human rights, especially regarding matters of forced labour and child labour (see Chapter 15). Ethical labour issues also occur outside the framework of the UDHR in circumstances where certain labour practices may be legal and commonplace in the host country but do not necessarily represent fair and equitable treatment of the workforce. The issue facing the MNE is: does it maximise its competitive advantage by locating in a low-cost, low-regulation country and adopting local practices, or does it refrain from reaping all the labour cost benefits by adopting higher standards and more ethical practices than strict compliance with local legal norms requires? A firm may choose to take the latter path and still experience significant competitiveness gains.
- Bribery/corruption: this is not as clear-cut an issue as might first appear; indeed, it can be rather a grey area. In some cultures, it is regarded as perfectly normal to give an official or host a gift. In others, only minimal-value token gifts or no gifts at all are allowed. A problem arises when it is the norm for a contract to be signed only after the payment of a 'commission' to a key official or officials. Such circumstances place MNEs in a difficult position: without payment of these commissions, the contract will not materialise, and if they do not make the payment, many other companies will (although that is not an ethical justification for going ahead with the commission). The position of the US is unequivocal about this: it regards all such payments as bribes, and, as such, they are both unethical and illegal. The Foreign

Corrupt Practices Act (FCPA), enacted in 1977, forbids US companies and companies linked to the US [perhaps through being quoted on the New York Stock Exchange (NYSE)] from making improper payments to foreign governments, politicians, or political parties to obtain or retain business.

By its very nature, the extent of corruption can be difficult to quantify. Transparency International, the world's most influential NGO concerned with combating corruption, has attempted to do this by surveying business perceptions about the degree of corruption in 180 countries. Table 13.1 sets out the outcome of the 2021 survey in the form of the Corruption Perceptions Index (CPI). The countries with the highest scores are perceived to be the freest from corruption. The world's most developed economies register the highest score.

The CPI does reveal that no region is free from corruption problems. As Table 13.1 shows, European countries dominate the top ten places in the CPI, indicating relative freedom from corruption. However, some eastern European states perform poorly on

**TABLE 13.1**  2022 corruption perceptions index for selected countries: top and bottom ten countries (out of 180 countries)

| Top ten | | | Bottom ten | | |
|---|---|---|---|---|---|
| Rank | Country | Score | Rank | Country | Score |
| 1 | Denmark | 90 | 180 | Somalia | 12 |
| 2 | Finland | 87 | 179 | Syria | 13 |
| 2 | New Zealand | 87 | 179 | South Sudan | 13 |
| 4 | Norway | 84 | 177 | Venezuela | 14 |
| 5 | Singapore | 83 | 176 | Yemen | 16 |
| 5 | Sweden | 83 | 171 | Libya | 17 |
| 7 | Switzerland | 82 | 171 | North Korea | 17 |
| 8 | The Netherlands | 80 | 171 | Haiti | 17 |
| 9 | Germany | 79 | 171 | Equatorial Guinea | 17 |
| 10 | Ireland | 77 | 171 | Burundi | 17 |
| 10 | Luxembourg | 77 | | | |

Source: Transparency International – www.transparency.org

Note: the scores are based on surveys of businesspeople and risk analysts regarding their perceptions of the degree of corruption among government officials. The lower the score, the greater the perception that officials are corrupt, and vice versa.

this measure, demonstrating that parts of Europe, at least, have endemic corruption problems. Many high-growth developed and emerging economies scored well, notably the Asian Tigers of South Korea, Hong Kong, Taiwan, and Singapore. Botswana stands out as a developing state with a comparatively low level of corruption. Of the large industrialising states, China performs best, notably as a result of ongoing anti-corruption purges by the current leadership. Other states, notably Russia and Brazil, seem to have endemic corruption problems. It is perhaps not surprising that these states have a corruption problem: they are in the process of major transformation, involving the construction of new institutions and governance systems. In a period of rapid change, it can take time for governance to catch up with the reality of what is actually happening in the marketplace. However, it is important for these emerging economies, if they are to sustain their rapid development in the long term and continue to attract foreign investors, that they pursue a strong anti-corruption line.

- Environmental protection: firms can encounter damaging publicity as a result of the environmental outcome of their activities (see Chapter 16), as pollution attracts more and more media attention. For many, environmental protection and corporate responsibility in this field have a clear ethical dimension. This debate is couched in terms of the 'global commons' in which all human beings have both a stake and a responsibility to ensure the well-being of the environment for future generations.
- Miscellaneous issues: international business frequently throws up issues that pose ethical issues in specific sectors. For example, the sale of formula milk in the developing world put Nestlé's activities under the microscope. The emergence of GM food has proved controversial on many fronts. Particularly concerning for some is the control it will give to firms like Monsanto over the range of seeds available to farmers in developing countries. The pharmaceutical industry is also under attack for pricing many of its products way beyond the reach of developing countries, thereby resulting in unnecessary loss of life.

## Initiatives to encourage ethical behaviour

Businesses have responded to the increased emphasis on CSR and ethics by drawing up their own codes of conduct and ethics, to the extent that they have become the norm in MNEs. Codes of ethics exist at a number of levels, including

- The organisational or corporate level: that is, relating to a single organisation.
- The professional level: for example, medicine, law, and accounting.
- The industry level: these are perhaps more commonplace in relation to specific CSR issues like the 'Responsible Care' initiative in the chemical industry or the Forest Stewardship Council.
- Programme or group codes: that is, a code to which companies sign up. These codes can be related to single initiatives, such as Fairtrade, or they can provide general guidance on ethical behaviour in business. One such example is the Caux principles (see below), drawn up by business leaders from Europe, the US, and Japan in an attempt to establish a global code of ethics for business.

Organisational and group codes of ethics are discussed in more detail below. Both corporate codes and group codes of conduct face the difficult task of developing policies that can be enacted across borders. That is, these codes have to grapple with the grey areas or relativist issues that have been alluded to throughout this chapter. Such issues include gifts, hospitality, and bribes; conflicts of interest; equal opportunities; discrimination; and environmental protection.

## CASE STUDY 13.2: RIO TINTO AND THE DESTRUCTION OF ABORIGINAL CAVES

Rio Tinto (hereafter Rio) is one of the world's leading mining companies. In 2013, the company received permission from the Western Australian government to expand its Brockman Mine within the main ore-producing region of the Pilbara. As part of the expansion of this mine, Rio decided to destroy two 46,000-year-old Aboriginal rock shelters. To gain access to $135 million worth of iron ore. The destruction of these culturally significant sites within Western Australia's Juukan Gorge while being legal was against the wishes of the local indigenous community, who claimed that they were misled by the company with regard to their intentions towards the site and the extent of their mitigating actions to limit any damage.

However, the decision to proceed and destroy the caves led to significant reputational damage to the business. The company faced considerable disquiet from many of its investors, who were extremely unhappy about the event and who felt that these acts undermined both the value of their investment and contravened their ESG-driven investment strategies. The company blamed miscommunication between itself and the local communities, who felt they had a shared understanding with regard to the site. The corporate damage was made worse by the admission that the company could have chosen three other sites to extract the ore from but instead chose a site that allowed access to a higher-grade ore. These other options were not relayed to the aboriginal groupings. This was compounded by the lack of initial remorse shown by the group over the destruction of these culturally significant assets. In part, this has been blamed on the scaling back by the business of a community and social performance division as part of corporate retrenchment taken in the aftermath of the decline in commodity prices in 2014.

For many, these cases show power differences between mining companies and Indigenous peoples, with the former being able to exercise significant power within local and national politics. The fact that the business at best miscommunicated and, at worst, misled these groups led to access to raw materials. It also arguably reflected a failure of governance at the state level to adequately protect significant cultural heritage. It led to the perception of the business as an environmental vandal as it rode roughshod over local issues in the pursuit of high-grade ore. The failure of this exercise has led to increased concerns from the industry that the longer-term legacy could be tougher legislation to cover such sites. This could lead to a slowdown in the development of new mining projects. Indeed, the future surrounding the destruction led to other miners reopening consultations with indigenous groups over other mining projects.

For Rio, the immediate legacy was that the investor backlash over the case led to the departure of the chief executive and two other senior managers. The reputational damage to the business has been extensive, and it has struggled to contain the damage. The resignation also reflected the importance of stakeholder power and activism in the business. The vow by the business to reflect indigenous population rights has faced a number of challenges, notably with the development of a copper mine in the US on Native American land. What was evident in this case was, first, the lack of trust between the business and local communities and, second, how cautious the business became in relation to the interface between Indigenous populations and its mining operations. In this case, Rio was subject to a high degree of scrutiny by investors and local communities, who all insisted on extensive reviews of the environmental and social impact of this investment. Further reflecting the reputational damage suffered by the business as a result of the events of Juukan Gorge.

## QUESTION

What can Rio and other miners learn from the experience of Juukan Gorge?

## Corporate codes

MNEs are increasingly developing codes of ethics to protect their reputation, not only in terms of their treatment of labour and the environment (see Chapters 14 and 15) but also in terms of the requirement of ethical conduct. The format of codes varies, but they tend to contain words like 'trust', 'integrity', and 'honesty' and deal with specific issues like the environment, bribery, treatment of employees, relationships with the community, health and safety, etc. Indeed, codes stand a better chance of being effective if they combine general principles to guide behaviour with specific guidance on how to behave in certain circumstances.

The Norwegian oil company Statoil, for example, has made a clear commitment to socially responsible and ethical behaviour. This includes a commitment to the values and principles of the UN Global Compact and the Global Sullivan Principles and to 'show respect for local cultures and traditions and cooperate with people affected by our operations.' The company has also made commitments to train its employees in commercial ethics and how to tackle ethical dilemmas, to carry out ethical audits of its own operations, to seek cooperation on best practices, and to support efforts by international organisations to fight corruption.

The UK's Co-operative Bank has taken its ethical commitment a stage further by polling its customers on a range of ethical issues such as genetic modification, animal welfare, the environment, human rights, factory farming, hunting, tobacco manufacture, currency speculation, and the arms trade. This practice began in the early 1990s, and the surveys are used to shape the bank's ethical investment policy, a policy that is unusually detailed and specific. On the one hand, this policy has the benefit of being responsive to what consumers actually want. On the other hand, the bank runs the danger that its investment decisions are based on what is ethically fashionable and that the policies emanating from such surveys do not take into account the ethical complexities and ambiguities of many situations.

In trying to act ethically, corporations need to ensure that their policy is real, that it has substance, and that it is not just a public relations exercise; otherwise, ethical initiatives can backfire. In other words, the adoption of a code of ethics alone is not sufficient to ensure ethical behaviour. Firms need to communicate the code to their employees, take great care in how their policies are implemented, and ensure the involvement, commitment, and training of all their employees. They need to ensure it is consistently applied and to demonstrate that breaches of the code can result in disciplinary procedures that are applied equally to those in both senior and junior positions within the organisation. One route followed by some companies is to regard NGOs not as 'the enemy' but as a potential ally in their search for a socially and environmentally responsible policy by engaging them to monitor and audit the observation of their codes.

---

**Box 13.2: The anti-ESG movement**

Within the investment industry, one of the key themes over recent years has been aligning investment industries with environmental, social, and governance (ESG) principles. The commercial logic of aligning these ESG themes is to avoid reputational damage to the business, where, alongside more normal financial considerations, the investor seeks to ensure that their investment strategies either make a positive contribution to social and economic cohesion or at the very least make no negative impact. These ESG themes cover a range of topics, from investing to mitigating climate change to corporate leadership and community action. Addressing these themes is supposed to reinforce corporate CSR and inhibit the investor from acting in a manner that is seen as unethical or risky.

Within the US, there is an emerging anti-ESG movement. These often reflect strong socially conservative beliefs held by some sections of the community, and ESG-shaped investment strategies run counter to such traditional belief systems. Resistance to ESG also comes from the other side of the political spectrum, claiming that such strategies are in effect greenwashing and are based on unreliable data. One of the main drivers of the anti-ESG movement was to reflect the dynamics of divergent stakeholders within the process of investment, especially within US state-level pension programmes. Where strategies are seen as not reflecting the sentiment of the state or its interests.

One of the core divergences is that ESG investing needs to account for the economic context in its investment strategies. In an area of economic uncertainty, investment strategies should focus on economic sustainability as opposed to environmental sustainability. Thus, commercial return should drive investment, not the pursuit of worthy long-term objectives embedded within ESG investing. In any case, such strategies may not be needed if regulation enforces these changing behaviours. There is also a concern that limiting investment to those firms that engage in certain types of behaviour could run counter to concerns with regard to competition law, especially if these external pressures lead to collusive behaviour or if non-ESG firms face overt or covert discrimination as a result of such strategies.

As noted above, there are also concerns with regard to whether these investment strategies are based on accurate data or that ESG merely represents a different form of greenwashing (see Box 13.1). This reflects the degree to which there is effective scrutiny of the investee and that their claims are truthful with regard to their ESG actions. This can reflect that there are different means of collecting data and a high degree of ambiguity with regard to the ESG actions within what are increasingly complex value networks. These issues are compounded by divergent local and national sentiments with regard to ESG issues. In US states with a strong energy sector, there has been a pushback against those funds that have an 'anti-energy agenda'. As a result, state governments have been divesting from those funds that pursue such agendas. This can also reflect a degree of climate change scepticism within such states. This trend has been especially evident in more right-wing Republican states in the US, where there has been an active pursuit of non-ESG investment strategies. These stress that the driving force of an investment strategy has to be the fund beneficiaries and not broader ESG aims.

In no small way, this trend towards anti-ESG investment is driven by local political concerns and the need to appeal to their socially conservative base and reflect the broader issues engaged in culture wars. In Florida, the governor has invoked 'woke' issues as part of his anti-ESG investment agenda. As of 2023, there are 16 states that have promoted an anti-ESG agenda insofar as it debars public assets from being invested in funds that are shaped by such considerations, though 32 states have initiated pro-ESG strategies.

## Group codes of conduct

The heightened concern about CSR has resulted in the adoption by many MNEs of their own codes of ethical behaviour. Accompanying this trend has been the emergence of a number of voluntary international sets of principles that provide a framework and foundation for the development of individual company codes. Three of the most prominent sets of international group codes of conduct are outlined below:

## The Sullivan principles

The original Sullivan principles were developed in 1977 by the Reverend Leon Sullivan, a director of General Motors, to provide guidelines for US companies operating in South

Africa under the apartheid regime. The principles required US firms adopting them to use US rather than South African workplace practices and to promote programmes that had a significant positive impact on the living conditions and quality of life of non-whites in South Africa.

At their peak, the Sullivan Principles involved 178 subsidiaries of signatory firms employing 62,400 workers. By 1986, the US Congress had passed a comprehensive anti-apartheid act that required US government agencies and US firms employing more than 25 people in South Africa to adhere to a code of conduct based on the Sullivan Principles. Penalties for non-compliance ranged from a $10,000 fine to ten years imprisonment for individuals or a $1 million fine in the case of companies. By 1987, Reverend Sullivan had himself withdrawn support for the principles bearing his name and recommended a policy of disinvestment and embargo.

In 1999, the global Sullivan principles were launched. Their purpose is to establish a set of ethical principles to which companies and organisations of all sizes, in all cultures, and in all sectors could adhere. The eight principles, primarily concerned with the advancement of human rights and social justice, are:

1. Support for the human rights of employees, suppliers, and the community in which the firm operates.
2. Promotion of equal opportunities in relation to colour, race, gender, age, ethnicity, and religion.
3. Respect for the freedom of association of their employees.
4. Provision of training opportunities and minimum basic remuneration.
5. Provision of a safe and healthy workplace and a commitment to environmental protection and sustainability.
6. Respect for fair competition, including intellectual and other property rights, and a commitment not to pay or accept bribes.
7. Commitment to work with governments and communities to improve the quality of life.
8. Promotion of these principles to business partners.

Companies endorsing these principles also make a commitment to the implementation of internal policies, procedures, training, and reporting structures to ensure the principles are applied. Companies endorsing the principles include the following MNEs: American Airlines, Avon Products, British Airways, Chevron Texaco, Coca-Cola, Colgate-Palmolive, Ford Motors, General Motors, Hershey Foods, Occidental Petroleum, Pepsi Co., Pfizer, Proctor & Gamble, Quaker Oats, Rio Tinto, Statoil, and the Tata Group.

## The Caux principles

The Caux Round Table is composed of business leaders from Europe, Japan, and the US. It was founded in 1986 by Frederik Philips, the former President of Philips Electronics, and Olivier Giscard d'Estaing, Vice Chairman of INSEAD, as a forum for reducing general trade tensions. However, the organisation quickly became focused on issues of corporate social responsibility. Its fundamental belief is that the world business community should play an important role in improving economic and social conditions and aims to establish a world benchmark against which to measure corporate behaviour. Contrary to the Friedmanite view referred to elsewhere, 'law and market forces are necessary but insufficient guides for conduct' (Preamble to Caux Principles).

The principles are in two parts. The first part established general principles based on *kyosei* and human dignity. *Kyosei* is a Japanese concept that means living and working together for the common good, enabling cooperation and prosperity to coexist with healthy and fair competition. Human dignity refers to the value of each individual as an end in themselves, not merely as a means to the fulfilment of another's goals. The general principles themselves state that:

1. The responsibilities of business go beyond the interests of shareholders; not only does business have a responsibility for wealth creation, but it is also responsible for respecting principles of honesty and integrity with customers, employers, suppliers, and competitors.

2. MNEs should contribute to social and economic progress, human rights, education, and welfare in the host country.

3. Compliance with the law is important, but not enough; companies should nurture the principles of honesty and integrity and develop a spirit of trust.

4. MNEs should respect domestic and international trade rules and be aware that, even if an action is legal, it can still have adverse consequences.

5. Businesses should support the WTO's multilateral trade system and similar agreements, cooperate to promote further trade liberalisation, and work to relax domestic measures that hinder global commerce.

6. Businesses should protect and, where possible, improve the environment, promote sustainability, and prevent the wasteful use of natural resources.

7. Businesses should not engage in bribery, money laundering, or other corrupt practices, nor trade in arms, materials used for terrorist activities, drug trafficking, or other organised crime.

## The UN Global Compact initiative

The Global Compact is a UN initiative intended to encourage businesses around the world to follow socially and environmentally responsible policies. First proposed by the then UN Secretary-General Kofi Annan at the World Economic Forum in Davos in 1999, the compact requires businesses to embrace ten principles (see Box 13.3 for further details) regarding human rights, labour, the environment, and corruption to help sustain the global economy and to spread the benefits of globalisation more widely.

---

**Box 13.3:** The ten principles of the Global Compact

**Human rights** – businesses should:

1. Support and respect the protection of human rights.
2. Ensure they are not complicit in human rights abuse.

**Labour** – businesses should uphold:

3. Freedom of association and recognise the right to collective bargaining.
4. The elimination of all forms of forced and compulsory labour.
5. The effective abolition of child labour.
6. The elimination of discrimination in employment.

**Environment** – businesses should:

7. Support a precautionary approach to the environment (see Chapter 15).
8. Promote greater environmental responsibility.
9. Encourage the development and diffusion of environmental technologies.

**Anti-corruption** – businesses should:

10. Work against all forms of corruption, including extortion and bribery.

---

Companies aspiring to membership must send a letter of their intent to the Secretary-General and submit annual details of efforts taken to implement the principles. They must also inform employees, shareholders, customers, and suppliers that they have done so and integrate the ten principles into the corporate development programme, the company's mission statement, and the annual report. By 2022, over 12,000 companies of all sizes across 160 countries had signed up to the Compact. NGOs, trade unions, business associations, UN agencies, and academic institutions take the membership to over 21,000.

Strictly speaking, the Global Compact is not a code of conduct, nor are there any penalties for failure to comply with the principles. Companies, however, do get classified as 'inactive' and are removed from membership if they fail to comply with the above obligations to report annually on progress in fulfilling the principles. This does not, however, prevent the Global Compact from encountering criticism about the lack of sanctions for non-compliance, the absence of a requirement to demonstrate progress, and the admission to membership of companies that have a dubious record on one or more of the ten principles.

## CONCLUSION

Globalisation adds an extra dimension to ethical issues for the firm. CSR and ethical issues inevitably become more complex when an organisation has a presence in more than one country, a factor that results from the link between culture and ethics. Senior managers in overseas subsidiaries can face ethical dilemmas when trying to determine the best course of action to follow. Should they, for example, follow local practices, which may be at odds with the values of the headquarters and home country? Should they act according to the principles of their home country and risk accusations of ethical imperialism? Are there universally applicable ethical principles to which they can appeal?

Corporate codes of conduct can help managers address these issues, but the process of drawing up the codes themselves is fraught with the issues raised by moral relativism. Moreover, while codes often set out general principles for employees to follow, they often require interpretation to fit particular circumstances, and employees are not necessarily any further forward.

## KEY POINTS

- In some cases, what constitutes ethical behaviour is clear-cut, but there are grey areas in which cultural factors influence ethical positions, thereby creating difficult areas of decision-making for managers of multinational firms.
- Corporate social responsibility is closely related to business ethics. Corporate social responsibility has traditionally incorporated human rights, labour, and the environment, but it is increasingly also concerned with issues of corporate governance and corruption.
- Companies increasingly consider themselves responsible not only to shareholders but to a much wider range of stakeholders.
- Ethical business behaviour is an appropriate end in itself, but it is also good for business. Unethical or irresponsible corporate behaviour can significantly damage a firm's reputation and, hence, profitability. MNEs also need to consider the ethical consumer and investor.

## QUESTIONS FOR DISCUSSION

1. What are the implications for international business of differences in dominant ethical values and religious beliefs? Choose two culturally diverse countries to illustrate your argument.

2. Is it ever appropriate for a company to engage in activities abroad that are regarded as unethical at home (for example, the payment of a 'commission' to a key official as the price of gaining a contract)?

3. Identify and assess the practical problems of putting stakeholder theory into practice.

## ACTIVITIES

1. Research a recent corporate scandal (there are plenty to choose from) and identify the main issues raised by it.

2. Research and compare and contrast the ethical codes of conduct of two MNEs. To what extent do the codes you have chosen provide a useful guide to ethical and responsible behaviour?

3. Write an ethical code of behaviour for students. Reflect on the difficulties of doing this and be prepared to justify all aspects of your code.

## SUGGESTED FURTHER READINGS

Blowfield, M., & Murray, A. (2008). *Corporate social responsibility: A critical introduction*, Oxford: Oxford University Press.

Burchell, J. (Ed.). (2007). *The corporate social responsibility reader: Context and perspectives*, London: Routledge.

Cramer, J. (2006). *Corporate social responsibility and globalisation: An action plan for business*, Sheffield: Greenleaf Publishing.

Crane, A., Matten, D., Glozer, S., & Spence, L. J. (2019). *Business ethics: Managing corporate citizenship and sustainability in the age of globalization*, Oxford: Oxford University Press.

Crane, A., Matten, D., & Spence, L. (Eds.). (2008). *Corporate social responsibility: Readings and cases in a global context*, London: Routledge.

Ferrell, O., Fraedrich, J., & Ferrell, L. (2007). *Business ethics: Ethical decision making and cases*, Boston: Houghton Mifflin.

Fisher, C., & Lovell, A. (2008). *Business ethics and values: Individual, corporate and international perspectives*, 3rd edn, Harlow: Prentice Hall.

Journal of Business Ethics – The Leading Journal on Business Ethics Which Looks at specific cases in some depth.

Keinert, C. (2008). *Corporate social responsibility as an international strategy*, Heidelberg: Physica Verlag.

Minus, P. M. (Ed.). (2013). *The ethics of business in a global economy*, Vol. 4, Basingstoke, UK: Springer Science & Business Media.

Trevino, L. (2007). *Managing business ethics: Straight talk about how to do it right*, Hoboken: Wiley.

Werhane, P. H. (2012). Globalization and its challenges for business and business ethics in the twenty-first century. *Business and Society Review, 117*(3), 383–405.

Werther, W., & Chandler, D. (2006). *Strategic corporate social responsibility: Stakeholders in a global environment*, Thousand Oaks: Sage.

# CHAPTER 14

# LABOUR ISSUES IN THE GLOBAL ECONOMY

## OBJECTIVES

This chapter will help you to:

- Demonstrate why and how labour market issues have become more controversial in a globally integrated market.
- Identify the potential impact of international migration on home and recipient countries.
- Describe contrasting approaches to labour markets and their differing implications for policy.
- Understand the concept of 'social dumping' and its implications.
- Distinguish between voluntary and compulsory methods for dealing with labour standards issues in a global marketplace and assess their respective advantages and disadvantages.

Issues affecting labour markets in both the developed and developing worlds are at the heart of the backlash against globalisation. Workers in developed countries and their union representatives allege that low-wage competition from developing countries reduces their real wages and pushes them out of jobs. There are two sources of this low-wage competition. First, globalisation, which is essentially about freer movement of the factors of production, should, in theory at least, increase the migration of labour, one of the main factors of production. An influx of labour in sufficient quantities will reduce or eliminate problems of labour and skill shortages and restrain wage increases. However, such arguments have increasingly faced a populist backlash, with many arguing that such flows undermine pre-existing socio-economic cohesion.

Secondly, if labour does not move to where the jobs are, then jobs can, and frequently do, move to where the labour is. In relation to the second scenario, concerns were initially expressed about competition for developed country businesses in lower value-added industries like textiles, but with the intensification of competition from the developing

DOI: 10.4324/9781315184500-18

world across a wider range of sectors, these concerns have spread across the economy. Workers' and human rights groups in developed countries have also become energised about 'unfair' developing country labour standards relating to health and safety, working hours, and other workplace rights such as non-discrimination and the right to form and join free trade unions. NGOs have also joined the debate as a result of the utilisation of child labour and forced labour in certain countries and sectors. Not only are such standards and practices portrayed as threatening job security and wages in developed countries, but they are also frequently presented as being ethically indefensible.

The addition of a potent moral dimension to what was already a lively economic debate and the growing clamour regarding corporate social responsibility (see Chapter 13) demand a response from companies that unwittingly or otherwise are seen to benefit from divergent labour standards. Developing countries themselves have responded vigorously to these complaints, accusing developed country interests of failing to understand the stark economic realities facing them and their population, of trying to impose values on them in a new form of imperialism, 'cultural imperialism' (that is, the process of disproportionate influence over social practices and ideologies by one socio-political group over a politically weaker and (frequently) less-wealthy group), and of trying to use concern about labour standards to impose restrictions on them in a form of 'disguised protectionism'.

This chapter highlights the interaction between globalisation and labour. It begins by examining the issue of international labour migration in terms of its extent and its impact on both the origin and the destination countries. The chapter then discusses some of the issues that arise when it is jobs rather than workers that move. The chapter concludes with a survey of how both the corporate sector and governments have responded to concerns about labour standards.

## MIGRATION OF LABOUR OR MIGRATION OF JOBS?

Globalisation is essentially about the removal of barriers to the free movement of the factors of production. In recent decades, barriers to the movement of goods, services, and capital have tumbled, and cross-border movements of these factors have risen accordingly. However, the same cannot be said of labour. In 2005, about three per cent of the world's population lived in a country other than the one they were born in. This does not exceed the migration rates of a century ago when immigration was positively encouraged by some receiving countries, nor is it particularly high.

The relative immobility of labour can be explained in part by cultural inertia (that is, the challenge of uprooting and relocating one's family great distances and to a location where the culture may seem alien or welcoming can act as an insurmountable barrier to migration) and/or by the restrictions imposed by recipient states reluctant to welcome large numbers of foreign workers who, in their view, may destabilise the social and labour market status quo.

Notwithstanding the above, there are some signs that labour mobility, helped by lower travel and ICT costs, is increasing. In 2019, it was estimated that there were 169 million international migrant workers, with two-thirds of these within the service sector. This represents some 62 per cent of the total migrant population, while the rest are migrants feeling forms of political persecution or are of non-working age. International migrant workers make up less than 5 per cent of the global working population. This group has a higher participation rate than non-migrants (69 per cent), compared to just over 60 per cent for non-migrant workers. The gender split of labour migrants is approximately 60:40 in favour of males. This reflects the conventional barriers that women have with regard to workforce participation. As indicated in Figure 14.1, these migrants are overwhelmingly within developed states.

However, it would be overstating it as yet to name this century 'the century of migration', as some have done. Figure 14.1 sets out the importance of migration in different world regions. Europe contains the most migrants in absolute terms; much of this migration is intra-European migration resulting from the process of European integration and, most recently, from the European Union's eastward enlargement, which, eventually, will result in free movement among its current 27 members, though this was a major factor in driving Euroscepticism and the UK's withdrawal from the block. Europe is also a destination for migrants from outside the EU. Member states maintain tight restrictions against third-party extra-EU restrictions, but the looming pressure on European labour markets from an ageing population could force a reconsideration of such policies and an easing of restrictions on both skilled and unskilled workers. These are reflected in Figures 14.1 and 14.2.

Figure 14.1 indicates that three regions (North America, North, South, and West Europe, and Asia) account for 60 per cent of the host states for migrant labour. As a share of the total working population, international migrant workers represent the highest share within the Arab states, where their share is over 40 per cent. However, nearly 70 per cent of migrant workers are in high-income states, with 20 per cent in upper-middle-income states. Thus, nearly 90 per cent of migrant workers are in higher-income states. Looking across high-income states, migrant workers constitute nearly 18 per cent of the total workforce. In developing states, it is less than 3 per cent. Despite these trends, the total share of migrant workers in high-income states has fallen from

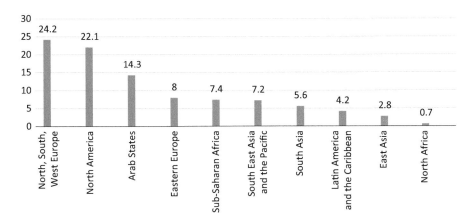

**FIGURE 14.1** Distribution of migrant workers by sub-region (2019) (source ILO)

three-quarters of the total to around two-thirds. This reflects the rise in opportunities within emerging middle-income states (such as China) that are attracting increased migrant workers (see Figure 14.2). However, it may also reflect more rigorous migration policies in many high-income states.

Asia is the second-largest area for migration in absolute terms, but the migrant share of that region's population is relatively low. However, there are signs that migration

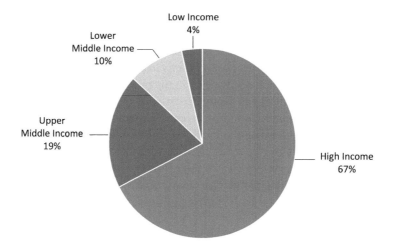

**FIGURE 14.2** Share of international migrants by income level, 2019 (source ILO)

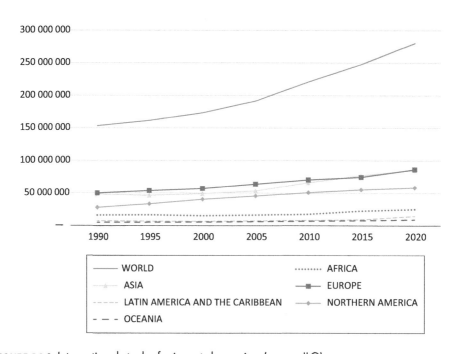

**FIGURE 14.3** International stock of migrants by region (source ILO)

to Asia is becoming more common. North America and Oceania (primarily Australia and New Zealand) are traditional migrant destinations, hence the relatively large share of migrants in their populations. Indeed, since the mid-2000s, Australia, after a long period of relatively tight migration limits by its standards, has actively been seeking to increase its number of migrants to fill gaps in its labour markets. Both Africa and Latin America have seen their already low share of international migration fall further in the new millennium.

In short, international migrants are concentrated in relatively few countries, and 60 per cent of them live in the developed world. In 2020, the top ten countries hosting international migrants were, in descending order, the US, Germany, Saudi Arabia, Russia, the UK, the UAE, France, Canada, Australia, and Spain. In most cases, the attraction of these destinations was the perception that the host offered opportunities for a better life. However, in the case of Russia, its relatively high position on the list is the result of the redefinition of borders. Traditional countries of migration like Australia, Canada, and the US continue to exercise an attraction for migrants, but new countries like Ireland, Italy, Norway, and Portugal have increased their attraction for migrants. Ireland is an interesting case in point. For many years, in view of the undynamic and depressed Irish economy, young Irish workers left their birthplace to seek their fortunes abroad. Given the transformation of Ireland into a fast-growing, prosperous economy, these labour flows have not only reversed, but many non-Irish workers also now see Ireland as a place of opportunity.

What are the effects of international migration in general and more specifically on the country of origin and the recipient country? Overall, freer labour markets should increase global efficiency as labour in surplus areas moves to regions where labour is in short supply. However, the global economy is a long way from the perfectly functioning market that this would suggest. The impact of international labour migration on individual countries varies and can have both positive and negative effects.

In countries of origin, there could well be improvements in labour markets for those remaining. For a start, the reduction in the size of the labour force could increase real wages, thereby raising living standards. Migrant workers tend to retain strong ties with their country of origin and often remit a significant part of their earnings to their families remaining at home. In 2020, migrant remittances worldwide totalled $702 billion, up from $128 billion in 2000. Nearly three-quarters of them were destined for developing countries, which since the mid-1990s have surpassed official development assistance. By 2022, there were 29 states which had a remittance-to-GDP ratio above 10 per cent. Tonga depends on remittances for over 37 per cent of its GDP, and Sudan for over 35 per cent. This has led to fears that it creates an over-reliance on remittances. It has been argued that the loss of skilled personnel can act as a brake on countries' development prospects by reducing growth, productivity, and tax revenue. Moreover, the quality of essential services can be hit as health service workers tend to figure largely in those migrating. The 'brain drain' effect can also make a country a less attractive destination for FDI. Some argue that international migration contributes to a 'brain gain' as well as a 'brain drain' (such as in sub-Saharan Africa). The former arises because the prospect of migration and the improved living standards it promises to provide an incentive for workers to improve their skills, thereby boosting the stock of human capital. Moreover, a proportion of migrants do return home, particularly if the conditions at home have improved, and in the process, they can further stimulate the economy by using knowledge, skills, technology, and capital acquired abroad. The example of Ireland has already been referred to above, but Ireland is not alone. Taiwan, for example, also benefited from returning nationals in the latter stages of the last century and the early stages of this process.

In destination countries, migrant workers fulfil multiple roles: they provide skills where there have been shortages. Examples of this include the migration of IT experts to the US and, to a lesser extent, Europe, and of doctors and nurses trained in developing countries to developed countries generally. Migrant workers also take on jobs in agriculture or in low-paid service industries, which citizens of the host country are reluctant to do. However, workers in destination countries are frequently suspicious of migrants; even if they retain their jobs, the fear is that the influx of new workers acts as a restraint on the growth of wages and salaries. A large influx of migrant workers can also place strain on the social infrastructure and increase social tensions resulting from cultural diversity. On the other hand, migrant workers generate additional wealth and tax revenue for their host country.

## GLOBALISATION AND LABOUR STANDARDS

Although, as the previous section shows, international labour migration is increasing its still relatively low levels mean that it is the movement of jobs more than the movement of people that so far has attracted the most attention from anti-globalisation protestors and has been a greater priority for MNEs. This has thrust the issue of differing national labour standards into the limelight. In a globalising world, it is argued that companies can gain an unfair advantage by locating in countries with no or very low labour standards. This is known as 'social dumping' (see below) and has been a major contributor to the endeavours of almost all MNEs to demonstrate their commitment to socially responsible behaviour (see Chapter 13).

Concern about the international dimension of labour standards is not new. Indeed, the International Labour Organisation (ILO) was set up in 1919 to deal with these issues. However, driven by globalisation and changing production patterns, the debate has become fiercer since the mid-1980s. Globalisation has intensified competition within the corporate sector by reducing national and/or regional barriers to trade and by 'shrinking' the world through more efficient and rapid communications. Consequently, those differences that remain, including differences in labour price (wages) and quality in terms of levels of education and skill, take on greater relative importance as a factor in competitiveness. Add the apparent ability of companies to relocate almost anywhere in the world, and it is not difficult to understand why developed-world workers feel vulnerable. However, the interpretation of what has been happening with respect to labour standards is controversial and reflects a fundamental theoretical divide regarding approaches to the labour market. These opposing theoretical views also result in different policy prescriptions regarding labour standards and the interaction between trade and labour standards (see below).

## Opposing views of labour markets

The neo-classical view of labour markets, given a boost by the resurgence of neo-liberal economic thinking (see Chapter 1), reflects a preference for highly deregulated labour markets in which competition is based on low wage costs and highly mobile global capital. Neo-classicists regard labour market regulation as an unjustifiable interference in the operation of the market, although they do tend to make exceptions regarding the prohibition of forced labour, the worst excesses of child labour, and basic health and safety regulation. Non-intervention, they argue, facilitates efficiency and enables employers to pay a market-clearing wage and to compete with low-cost suppliers, particularly from developing Asia, which are placing severe competitive pressures on developed world businesses. Neo-classicists also tend to argue for the rollback of the welfare state and social security benefits, which they claim raise the 'reservation wage' – that is, the wage below which the unemployed will not seek employment.

It is important to note that neo-classicists are not arguing necessarily for low standards and wages (although this is often the outcome of their approach), but for the market to regulate these issues. In times of labour surplus, wages will be low. However, if people are in jobs and generating wealth, surplus labour will be absorbed, and growth will deliver improvements in wages and living and working conditions. They point to the East Asian examples of Singapore, South Korea, and Taiwan, where this has occurred.

The neo-classical model gives employers a high degree of flexibility in terms of hiring, firing, and wages. It also tends to result in adversarial industrial relations in developed economies and a denial of rights to join unions in developing countries. The neo-classical approach also discourages internal organisational flexibility based on multi-skilling, goodwill, and higher levels of productivity resulting from greater investment in the workforce.

In contrast, neo-Keynesians and neo-institutionalists view labour standards as key devices in securing economic and social progress. This ties in with the 'flexible specialisation' view of the world. The phrase 'flexible specialisation' was coined by Piore and Sabel (1984) as a reaction to the shift away from 'Fordist' mass production methods and 'Taylorist' traditions of work organisation, which were too inflexible in the face of new demands for customised and high-quality products. The intensification of competition arising from globalisation also encouraged rapid changes in consumer tastes, necessitating more frequent product adaptations and shorter production runs, leading to leaner production and greater emphasis on teamwork, multi-skilling, flexible deployment of labour, and closer links between production and marketing. In other words, the new production techniques require a cooperative, skilled labour force that is both prepared and able to respond to rapidly changing consumer demands.

Failure to respect labour standards and a 'sweat shop mentality', according to this view, damages long-term competitiveness and economic efficiency prospects in developing countries. For example, child labour, employment discrimination, and exceedingly long working hours hold back productivity gains and have a long-term negative impact on the development of human capital – one of the key factors in contemporary economic success.

This view of the workplace implies a variant of labour market flexibility in which regulation does not inhibit adjustment to changing markets but provides opportunities to reconcile legitimate claims of labour with efficiency. Labour market regulation exists to protect the workforce in terms of health and safety, job security, and working conditions. Respect for workers' rights and welfare generates greater workplace flexibility by reducing the alienation frequently present in the neo-classical approach, encouraging worker identification with the long-term well-being of the firm, and generating trust between employer and employee. An emphasis on worker information and consultation and ongoing workplace training also accompanies this approach. Any rigidities in the model, it is claimed, are outweighed by long-term gains in terms of greater technical and organisational innovation. This approach has been criticised on the grounds that it is out of touch with the economic and social reality that persists in many developing countries.

## Social dumping

Central to the rise of labour market issues on the policy agenda is the issue of 'social dumping'. Social dumping occurs when companies relocate to regions with lower wage costs and less stringent labour regulations. This results in downward pressure on wages and standards in high-wage, high-standard countries as these countries strive to retain their businesses. Even the threat of the relocation of firms can lead to lower labour standards, so the argument goes. Furthermore, social security and welfare provision will also decline if it helps improve the ability of companies in higher-cost countries to compete. This process is commonly referred to as a 'race to the bottom' – an argument that finds parallels in the debate about the alleged flight of companies to countries with a lower level, and hence lower associated cost burden, of environmental regulation (see Chapter 15).

At the heart of the social dumping debate is the assumption that lower wages and standards are somehow 'unfair'. Although there are several compelling arguments against low wages and standards, it is fallacious to label all such differences as unfair. MNEs pay much lower wages in developing countries than they do in their home country. However, this is not an appropriate benchmark. In practice, in many cases, wages paid by MNEs in developing countries are frequently above average for the host region.

At a fundamental level, wage variations reflect a number of factors, including local labour market conditions and relative levels of productivity and development. Many developing countries, for example, have surpluses of unskilled labour and levels of labour productivity that lag far behind those in developed countries. Once productivity is taken into account, it can be the case that unit wage costs are higher than those in developed countries, making differences in wages perfectly tenable. In other words, actual wage levels (including fringe benefits) are only part of the story concerning labour costs. Higher wage levels are perfectly sustainable in a competitive environment, provided they are offset by similarly high levels of labour productivity. The way out of the low wage trap for workers in developing countries, therefore, is to achieve higher levels of productivity.

Furthermore, at one level, labour is only one factor of production, albeit an important one, among several. From the perspective of developing countries, low labour costs constitute a key and legitimate part of their comparative advantage. Any efforts to neutralise this advantage through trade sanctions or harmonisation of standards are in themselves unfair and a negation of the basic principles of free trade, principles promoted vigorously by the developed countries themselves.

Labour cost variations are only one of many reasons for relocation. The lower the share of labour costs in overall costs, for example, the less likely it is that social dumping will occur. In addition, as intimated above, wages and labour costs are only one part of the competitive equation. Among industrialised countries, those European countries with high levels of social protection and high labour standards, such as Germany and the Nordic states, are generally associated with high per capita income as a result of high productivity and other competitive advantages. These factors work among developed countries as well as between developed and developing countries.

## CASE STUDY 14.1: THE USE OF PENAL LABOUR IN THE US

Penal labour is the term used for forced labour compelled upon a prison population. While there has been a long history of penal labour within the contemporary global system, the utilisation of this source of labour has caused particular controversy within the US. Under the 13th Amendment to the US Constitution, penal labour is allowed, but the rate of usage accelerated after 1979 with the introduction of the Justice System Improvement Act. This act allows inmates to earn wages in private sector employment, which can be used for a variety of purposes, such as compensation and tax deductions as well as the cost of imprisonment. As a consequence, penal labour has become a fixture of the US production system, where in 2022, $11 billion worth of goods were produced using prison labour. Of this $11 billion, $2 billion is generated from the production of goods, and more than $9 billion is generated through prison maintenance services. Overall, nearly two-thirds of the US's 1.3 million prison population (some 800,000 prisoners) are engaged in such work for a wide range of industries, from technology to food. These industries are incentivised to utilise penal labour through assorted tax incentives, such as the Working Opportunity Tax Credit. For both the government and business, the utilisation of penal labour has been a useful course of indigenous labour operating as an alternative to the outsourcing or offshoring of such activities to low-cost locations overseas.

However, the extensive use of penal labour as a cheap input into domestic value chains and the consequent creation of a prison-industrial complex have become a core source of controversy. A report by the American Civil Liberties Union (ACLU) argues that the emergence of this arrangement is essentially exploitative, as these workers are essentially under the complete control of their employer and excluded from even the most basic workplace protections. Their research argues that penal labour is forced to work in often hazardous occupations and conditions with little training while earning a wage that is a fraction of the market level. Indeed, it was estimated that in 2021, compared to a federal minimum wage of $7.25, most penal labourers will earn between $0.23 and $1.15 per hour. Moreover, there are seven states where penal labourers are not paid at all for the vast majority of work that they undertake. These states use this labour for the upkeep and maintenance of public services and infrastructure. The pressure to work is compounded by the research, which indicates that prisoners are often punished if they refuse to undertake any work assignments. Furthermore, of those surveyed, more than two-thirds could not afford basic necessities from their prison earnings, did not receive the necessary training, and often felt insecure in the job they were undertaking.

In response to these concerns, there is a growing movement to reform the utilisation of penal labour. In many of the states where penal labour is not paid, there were referendums to abolish slavery without exception. In five of these states, these referendums were successful, though in one state, Louisiana, they failed. In other places, campaigners are seeking to improve conditions so that the prison-industrial complex removes its draconian facets and improves worker safety. The issue is not to end the practice but to seek to remove its exploitative features and also to offer an effective platform for the reintegration of ex-prisoners into society. This should mean offering workers some discretion over the type of work that is undertaken. While such reforms are a long distance in the future, there is nonetheless growing pressure to secure more rights and at least allow prisoners to redress if they have been harmed by the process of penal labour. For some, this remains the last bastion for the abolition of slavery within the US.

### QUESTION

To what extent do you believe that the use of penal labour by US businesses constitutes an infringement of CSR?

## Issues for developing countries

Campaigns for higher labour standards are ostensibly directed towards improving the number of workers in developing countries. Developing countries themselves have strongly opposed efforts by some developed countries and NGOs to link labour standards and trade through the introduction of a 'social clause' into trade agreements, that is, provisions within trade agreements requiring them to comply with some minimum level of standards.

Developing countries have marshalled various arguments to support their case. First, they argue that such initiatives are an unwarranted intrusion on their national sovereignty and that regulation of labour markets is purely a domestic issue. However, a key feature of globalisation is greater international coordination or harmonisation of traditionally domestic policies – that is, the shift from shallow to deep integration (see Chapter 1) – to keep pace with the realities of the marketplace. This does not necessarily imply total harmonisation of labour standards but does point towards some minimum agreement on labour standards. In reality, an international consensus has already been established in the form of the so-called 'core' ILO standards (see below) relating to freedom of association, the right to collective bargaining, the minimum age of employment, equality of treatment, and non-discrimination in the workplace. These standards have been signed, although not always ratified, by many developing countries.

Secondly, developing countries frequently argue that attempts by developed countries and NGOs to impose higher labour standards on them are inappropriate in terms of their level of development. In relation to child labour, for example, developing countries and their supporters often argue that child labour is not a response to low standards but to poverty and that depriving children of the right to work threatens the survival prospects of these children and their families. According to this view, child labour will gradually disappear as prosperity rises, and the most useful contribution of developed economies is keeping their markets open to goods from developing countries to enable this prosperity to occur. Opponents of this argument state that child labour perpetuates economic efficiency by standing in the way of the development of human capital and by depressing productivity and that the most successful countries in terms of economic development, which are the countries of East Asia, demonstrated a preference for sending their children to school rather than to work.

Thirdly, many of the arguments for higher labour standards are couched in moral terms. Developing countries argue that developed countries are attempting to impose their own cultural and ethical values on them. However, in reality, it is only around issues like slavery that there is universal recognition of the undesirability of a particular practice. Apart from this exception, there is a range of attitudes, opinions, and values regarding the economy and the workplace that make the attainment of universal attitudes difficult, if not impossible, to achieve. Some argue, however, that there is a consensus around core ILO standards that has existed for some time.

Fourthly, developing countries argue that the case for a social clause, although presented in high moral terms, is merely an attempt at 'disguised protectionism' by developed countries and their workers unable to compete in a more open marketplace. Differences in labour costs are not unfair and represent a perfectly legitimate trading advantage for developing countries. Attempts to deprive developing country producers of these advantages represent efforts to deprive them of their legitimate comparative advantage.

## Issues for business

Global commodity chain analysis provides a useful way of thinking about the relationship between multinational enterprises and production operations in developing countries. In producer-driven chains, production is controlled by the MNE itself. Some of the production outside the home country will take place through wholly-owned subsidiaries. The company will also be dependent on joint venture partners and component suppliers. Although these networks of suppliers are often complex, the relationship between the MNE and its partners and/or suppliers is usually close and subject to strict quality controls in view of the interdependence of the quality of components with the quality of the finished product, whether it be a computer, an aircraft, or an item of heavy machinery.

Producer-driven chains are not immune from criticism about labour standards in developing countries. However, it is primarily buyer-driven chains (located predominantly in the textiles, clothing, footwear, toys, and other relatively low-technology sectors) that have been the object of fierce criticism of the exploitation of the labour that is used to produce the final product. In this model, the production role of the multinational is limited (or non-existent), with production outsourced to sub-contractors, sub-sub-contractors, or even sub-sub-sub-contractors. This model, although not conforming to the stereotypical view of a multinational that owns and controls production through a cross-border network of subsidiaries and affiliates, does enhance the ability of such firms to exhibit footloose behaviour and change suppliers regularly and quickly, especially when price is the prime factor. Thus, according to their critics, such firms condone, indeed implicitly encourage, the continued exploitation of labour in terms of wages and working conditions by their suppliers.

The bad publicity arising from campaigns about their labour practices and the rise of the 'ethical consumer' with the threat of consumer boycotts have made it a priority for firms like Nike and The GAP, among many others, to make efforts to ensure that their outsourcing practices survive external scrutiny. The following section examines both voluntary responses to these concerns and more official efforts to ensure minimum standards and to make a link between labour standards and trade.

## RESPONSES TO LABOUR STANDARD CONCERNS

The arguments for and against international labour standards are complex and controversial. Various options, each with their own benefits and drawbacks, exist for introducing international labour standards. In broad terms, these policies fall into two categories:

- Unofficial/voluntary standards: that is, standards arising from corporate sector initiatives like product labelling and corporate codes of conduct.
- Official/compulsory standards: that is, laws and regulations introduced by nations, regional organisations, or international institutions that involve some form of sanction for non-compliance.

### Voluntary standards

Voluntary international labour standards are the result of corporate, industry, and occasionally NGO initiatives. The attraction of voluntary standards for companies is that, provided the standards have sufficient credibility, they can help forestall tougher legislative standards. Even without the immediate threat of compulsory standards, voluntary standards are attractive for businesses striving to overcome bad publicity from the exposure of unsafe working conditions, sub-subsistence wages, or the employment of child workers in their own overseas plants or the plants of their suppliers. Of course, there is a danger that measures taken to rectify the issues raised by such publicity will be widely disseminated as a cynical public relations attempt to convince the consumer that a particular company follows best practices without any change in substantive practice.

## Product or social labelling

Product labels indicate that the production of a particular product complies with a declared set of standards relating, for example, to the environment or employment. Entitlement to such a label may come from government-organised schemes, through schemes organised by a coalition of interests including NGOs and industry interests, or may be the result of self-labelling by MNEs. Social labelling is particularly appropriate for final products, where consumers have the practical option of engaging in ethical consumption, rather than for intermediate products. Industries using social labelling include carpets, textiles, apparel, sporting goods, and toys.

Schemes operate in a number of ways, but the most credible ones entail adherence to specific standards, often standards resulting from ILO Conventions, and require external verification of compliance with the declared standards to ensure claims about the product are not fraudulent. In this respect, product labelling has much in common with corporate codes of conduct.

Product labels are not problem-free. They are selective and rely on consumers' negative reactions to more emotive issues like child labour, but they are of less value in enforcing other core standards like freedom of association or collective bargaining. In practice, product labels also tend to apply only to conditions in export companies. This is unproblematic for those who support international labour standards on competitive grounds – that is, to ensure a more level playing field for companies. However, for proponents of international standards on ethical grounds, product labelling will do little for workers producing goods for domestic consumption. Indeed, product labels could indirectly result in a deterioration of the situation of affected groups, like children, who will be restricted to companies producing goods for the domestic market. In theory, if consumers in the domestic market oppose certain work practices, product labelling can be effective for non-export products. However, it is usually pressure from outside the producing country in question that results in the establishment of a product-labelling scheme. For the ethical supporter of product labels, the implementation of ILO Conventions is a better option, as they apply without discrimination both to exports and to goods sold domestically.

## CASE STUDY 14.2: GOODWEAVE

GoodWeave International (formerly known as RUGMARK) was established in 1994 by Indian NGOs and international aid organisations to eliminate the use of child labour in the hand-knotted carpet industry. At the time of GoodWeave International's foundation, an estimated one million children were employed in the industry worldwide, usually in poor conditions, for long hours, and sometimes under terms of bondage. In its first ten years, GoodWeave International claimed to have helped reduce child labour in the South Asian carpet industry by 80 per cent, an achievement helped by Nepal joining the scheme in 1996 and Pakistan in 1998. By 2021, it had over 400 participating companies across 20 countries. While it has a history within the rug and home textile sector, its reach has extended to the apparel, fashion jewellery, and brick sectors, as well as carrying out capacity-building projects in additional sectors. Overall, it is estimated that 160 million children are employed across these sectors.

Membership of the GoodWeave International scheme and the right to display the GoodWeave International label on their products are open to those producers and exporters in the targeted sectors who follow the following code:

- No child labour is allowed.
- No forced or bonded labour is allowed.
- Conditions of work are documented and verifiable.

The costs of inspection and labelling are covered by the payment of a levy of 0.25 per cent of the export value of the carpet. In addition, importers of GoodWeave International carpets pay at least one per cent of the import value of the carpets to GoodWeave International to finance education and welfare programmes for former child workers and their families. These programmes are intended to deal with the potential problems of removing children from the workplace and placing them in the education system without addressing the issues of need that pushed them into the labour market in the first place.

For producers, the GoodWeave International scheme and its independent verification of working conditions give them credibility with consumers about claims that their products were made without the use of child labour. GoodWeave International also lowers the cost of inspections: without a collective scheme, carpet manufacturers would have to engage their own inspectors to carry out inspections of looms – at a higher cost and with lower credibility in the eyes of consumers. In the importing countries, most of which are in North America and Europe, GoodWeave International's activities are directed towards raising public awareness of GoodWeave International and the meaning of the GoodWeave International label. From the perspective of consumers, GoodWeave International gives them the confidence that they can purchase carpets made without the exploitation of child labour.

Like most schemes, GoodWeave International is not without its critics. There are practical concerns that, even though GoodWeave International makes every effort to ensure the random nature of its inspections, the structure of the industry, which ranges from single looms in isolated rural villages to small to medium-scale factories, makes the process of inspection hit and miss. Indeed, critics claim that this makes it impossible to give child-free guarantees. Moreover, carpet manufacturers outside the GoodWeave International scheme who claim that they operate without child labour argue that GoodWeave International discriminates against them.

## QUESTIONS

1. Identify and evaluate the strong and weak points of GoodWeave International's approach.
2. Find other examples of product or social labelling and critically assess them.

## Corporate codes of conduct

Globalisation and the emergence of global supply chains have provided opportunities for MNEs to rationalise their production and raise their efficiency levels, but MNEs have also been left open to allegations of child labour, unsafe working conditions, and low wages. Firms that outsource much of their production to lower-cost locations in the developing world are particularly vulnerable to such allegations. The initial response to the controversy over labour standards was to establish corporate and supplier compliance with national laws and regulations. However, by the 1990s, in response to rising concerns about corporate social responsibility and socially responsible investment, almost all multinational enterprises had developed their own codes of conduct governing general corporate behaviour and the treatment of the workforce in particular. Some critics argue that corporate codes of conduct serve to prevent more thorough official intervention at a national, regional, or multinational level. Others suggest that, rather than bypassing the state, corporate codes of conduct offer the possibility of higher labour standards in developing countries, which may not have sufficient capacity themselves to enforce their own labour laws.

Corporate codes of conduct take many forms and have generated many heated debates about their function and effectiveness. Whatever the specific details of a code, they need to satisfy a number of conditions in order to be considered equitable and credible. Notably

- The contents of the code must be clearly worded and, at a minimum, comply with core ILO standards.
- The company adopting the code must be committed to it and provide the resources to ensure its implementation, including training, information systems for monitoring and compliance, and staff to implement the procedures.
- Knowledge of the code throughout the organisation is essential to its implementation; in particular, employees of the firm and its sub-contractors and suppliers must know the contents of the code, and a reporting system must be established that enables workers to report infringements without fear of reprisals.
- The code should ideally be subject to verification by independent assessors who have access to the site unannounced at any time; however, this has caused problems in some cases, notably in the case of Nike and its involvement with rogue suppliers.

The application of such codes can enhance internal governance and facilitate internal management across geographically dispersed sites. There is some evidence to show that real commercial benefits can be gained from the proper application of fair and equitable labour standards, although more widespread research needs to be done on this. Provided the code of conduct adopted by a firm has external credibility, it can both protect and enhance a firm's reputation. GAP withdrew a line of children's clothing following allegations of forced child labour by Indian sub-contractors. This follows GAP's policy of stopping working with 23 factories after its own monitoring efforts uncovered infringements of its child labour policy. Although embarrassing for GAP, the company's immediate response to the revelations and its own proactive stance towards monitoring child labour indicates that they serve to minimise the damage to its reputation.

Some industries have developed their own codes. An important example of such a code is the Electronic Industry Code of Conduct (EICC), which was launched in 2004. The code covers labour standards, health and safety, environmental issues, and business ethics and was heavily influenced by the Universal Declaration of Human Rights, Social Accountability International (see below), and the Ethical Trading Initiative. EICC membership includes some of the world's biggest electronics and related companies, such as Adobe, Apple, Cisco, Dell, Flextronics, Hewlett Packard, IBM, Intel, Lenovo, Kodak, Lexmark, Microsoft, Philips, Seagate, Sony, Sun Microsystems, and Xerox. The code itself is intended as a total supply chain initiative, and all participants must, as a minimum, require their next-tier suppliers to implement it. The code's key provisions are:

- No forced, bonded, or involuntary prison labour.
- No person is to be employed under the age of 15 (or 14 where the law of the country permits) or under the age of compulsory education, whichever is the greatest.
- Working hours must not exceed those in national law and should not exceed 60 hours a week, including overtime, unless emergency or unusual situations prevail.
- Workers are to receive at least one day off in seven.
- Wages are to comply with all laws relating to the minimum wage, overtime, and legally mandated benefits.
- No wage deductions on disciplinary grounds are permitted.
- No harsh and inhumane treatment or threat of such treatment.
- No discrimination on the grounds of race, colour, age, gender, sexual orientation, ethnicity, disability, pregnancy, religion, political affiliation, union membership, or marital status.
- Workers' rights to join unions and to communicate with management about working conditions are to be respected.

In addition, a range of health and safety standards are included in the code and were developed using OHSAS 18001 (an international occupational health and safety management system) and ILO Guidelines on Occupational Health and Safety as a reference point.

Framework codes have also been developed by NGOs and charitable organisations and applied by MNEs. For example, Social Accountability International, founded in New York in 1997, is a charitable human rights organisation with a mission to work for the improvement of workplace conditions by developing and implementing socially responsible standards. To this end, it has developed SA8000, a uniform auditable standard intended to ensure ethical conditions in the workplace throughout global supply chains. SA8000 employs a third-party verification system to provide clarity, consistency, and guidance to the multitude of individual corporate codes of conduct springing up. SA8000 is based on international norms defined in the ILO Conventions, the UN Convention on the Rights of the Child, and the Universal Declaration of Human Rights. It uses proven ISO auditing techniques, specifies corrective and preventive actions, and encourages continuous improvement by setting specific performance requirements with minimum requirements. It also contains a complaints and appeals mechanism to bring forward issues of non-compliance at certified facilities. By 2020, there were over 4,000 facilities certified as complying with SA8000, protecting over two million workers across 54 countries.

## Official/compulsory standards

Much of the debate about labour standards is focussed on the increasing practice of including 'social clauses' in trade agreements, that is, the provision within trade agreements for the withdrawal of trade preferences or the imposition of trade sanctions if specified labour standards are not respected. The most high-profile debate has been the controversy about the inclusion of a social clause within WTO agreements (see below). However, there are various examples of individual countries including social clauses within bilateral trade agreements or unilaterally.

Social clauses potentially satisfy both main sets of advocates of international trade standards. Social clauses provide those advocating their introduction on competitiveness grounds with a mechanism whereby they can offset what they perceive as 'unfair' competitive advantages. However, as indicated above, what constitutes a legitimate competitive advantage and what is an unfair advantage is open to interpretation. Social clauses also enable those favouring their introduction on moral grounds to impose a specific set of ethical values. Debate also rages about whether there are moral values around which a consensus can develop to form the basis of social clauses within international trade agreements. Some of these controversies are aired above. However, practical outcomes in terms of bilateral, regional, and multilateral agreements are discussed below.

## Regional standards

Regional economic integration is well underway in many parts of the world (see Chapter 5). Regional integration, as with globalisation, is essentially about reducing barriers to trade and unifying markets. Inevitably, remaining barriers take on much greater relative importance in the eyes of group members, giving rise to fears and charges of social dumping from members with higher labour market standards. Given the more ambitious and advanced stage of integration within the EU, it is not surprising that the issue of differential labour standards arose early within the EU and that it has developed its own solutions. Other regional integration initiatives like NAFTA (see below), Mercosur, and the South African Development Community (SADC) have adopted their own social provisions that incorporate the ILO's core labour standards.

The labour standards issue in the EU manifested itself around competitiveness and social dumping concerns. These concerns were voiced most loudly at the end of the 1980s, at the height of the construction of the Single European Market (SEM). In order to implement the SEM, the EU amended its treaties by means of the Single European Act (SEA). Article 118A of the SEA required member states to pay particular attention to the harmonisation of workplace health and safety standards while maintaining improvements already made. In other words, Article 118A, reinforced by 100A, tried to ensure that the SEM would not result in a choice between the general lowering of workplace health and safety standards (the race to the bottom) and the loss of jobs.

Nevertheless, the SEA did not dispel fears of social dumping. The European Commission chose to combat these fears via the community charter of the Fundamental Social Rights of Workers, signed by 11 out of the then 12 member states (the exception being the UK, which adopted it in 1997 but relinquished it upon its departure) in December 1989. The social charter rights included freedom of movement, employment, and remuneration; improvement of living and working conditions; social protection; freedom of association and collective bargaining; training; equal treatment for men and women; worker participation, information, and consultation; workplace health and safety; protection of children and adolescents; and the elderly and the disabled. The charter was not a legally binding document but a 'solemn declaration' that established basic minimum rights in the workplace. These minimum rights served both as a defence against alleged social dumping and as a response to concerns about an over-preoccupation within the SEM programme with the priorities of business.

The debate over the social charter generated a lot of hot air over very little. It has resulted in relatively little change in labour market standards within Europe, even within the UK, where several labour standards were lower than in other member states. In practice, differences in labour standards among EU states were not great compared to differences in standards between EU members and non-members, and there was no systematic evidence of sustained social dumping occurring within Europe.

Given the much wider differences in labour standards among Canada, Mexico, and the US than in the EU, the North American Free Trade Area (NAFTA), although much less ambitious than the EU in terms of its integration objectives, posed greater labour standards challenges. US and Canadian workers were concerned that companies would migrate to Mexico to take advantage of cheaper labour whose basic rights were not respected. This fear was succinctly expressed by one-time US presidential candidate Ross Perot when he declared, 'that sucking sound you hear is the sound of US jobs going to Mexico'. Freedom of movement of firms (not mirrored by freedom of movement of workers) in combination with the maquiladora system, in which multinational firms are given additional investment incentives, would, it was feared, destroy US and Canadian jobs, depress wages, perpetuate sub-standard employment conditions, and deny basic rights to Mexican workers.

NAFTA came into force on 1 January 1993. Labour issues were not originally included, but after President Clinton succeeded President Bush, the US negotiated the North American Agreement on Labour Co-operation (NAALC), often referred to as NAFTA's 'labour side agreement.' The NAALC does not propose any specific labour standards or harmonisation of standards; each signatory retains the right to establish its own domestic labour standards and is obliged to comply with and enforce them. There is an obligation to 'provide for high labour standards consistent with high quality and high productivity workplaces' but there is no definition of what constitutes these high standards.

Under the terms of the NAALC, the US, Mexico, and Canada have committed themselves to promoting the following 11 labour principles:

1. Freedom of association and the right to organise.
2. The right to collective bargaining.
3. The right to strike.

4. Prohibition of forced labour.
5. Workplace protection for children and young people.
6. Minimum employment standards.
7. Elimination of employment discrimination.
8. Equal pay for men and women.
9. Prevention of occupational injuries.
10. Compensation in the event of occupational injuries and illnesses.
11. Protection of migrant workers.

At first sight, the NAALC holds substantial promise for upholding basic labour principles and standards within a diverse trading area. However, the agreement's operation has left many hopes for improvements unfulfilled, not only in Mexico but also in Canada and the US, where there are alleged infringements of the basic right to organise. The major problems with NAALC are:

- A lack of agreement or compulsion regarding core labour standards. The NAALC talks of the provision of high standards but does not define them.
- The weak response to non-compliance with NAALC principles. For most infringements, recourse to ministerial consultation is the only course of action available. It is only violations of child labour, minimum employment standards, and health and safety principles that can lead to arbitration and sanctions.
- The complexity, cost, and protractedness of the submission of a complaint. Critics contrast the NAALC process with the speedier processes, which also offer redress for violations and are available to investors and defenders of intellectual property rights within NAFTA's dispute settlement procedure.

The renegotiated agreement (known in the US as the USCMA) sought to tighten up labour rights in trade between these states. It includes a labour chapter that is fully enforceable, which is in contrast to NAFTA, which has labour as a side issue. The agreement includes a Rapid Response Labour Mechanism, which can take action against facilities if they fail to adopt policies on union recognition and other labour rights. The agreement also seeks to remove any competitive disadvantage felt by US factories by including provisions on wages, ensuring that any worker in the automotive industry has to earn about $16 an hour if the product is to gain tariff relief. If a firm is breached, these tariff benefits are removed and extra ones are applied. Enforcement is supported by a large budget to ensure it is effectively policed. These provisions were a response to the US's long-standing complaints with regard to the costs of production in Mexico and to create a more level playing field.

## Bilateral standards

Since their first tentative use in the 1980s, social clauses have become the norm in many regional and trade agreements. The European Union and the US currently routinely include social clauses in their bilateral trade agreements. In part, the popularity of these clauses is a response to the failure to include such provisions in multilateral negotiations (see below). Social clauses in bilateral agreements subject developing countries to the type of external pressure on labour standards that they have consistently resisted at a multilateral level. Indeed, it has proved more difficult for them to resist this pressure bilaterally than multilaterally.

As far back as 1984, the US incorporated a social clause in its Generalised System of Preferences (GSP), a scheme run by many developed countries whereby developing countries are granted trade preferences. This clause made compliance with certain criteria mandatory before developing countries were granted eligibility for GSP membership. For example, the US administration had to determine whether a country 'has taken or is taking steps to afford workers in that country (including in the free trade zones) internationally recognised worker rights. The 1988 Trade Act, for example, defined the denial of internationally recognised workers' rights as an unreasonable trade practice and therefore potentially subject to trade sanctions, thereby giving the US government a generic right to act against alleged infringements of basic labour rights by any of its trading partners. The US, for example, excluded Swaziland from benefits under the African Growth and Opportunities Act (AGOA) and threatened to exclude it from the GSP unless it removed labour regulations that the US regarded as oppressive, which Swaziland duly did.

Since 1993, a period in which US involvement in bilateral trade agreements increased in scope, social clauses have been included in all bilateral and regional trade agreements negotiated by the US. Completed agreements include NAFTA (see above), Chile, Jordan, Morocco, Singapore, and Bahrain. The 2000 US Trade and Development Act encompassed AGOA and the US-Caribbean Trade Partnership Act (CBTPA), both of which contained clauses not only requiring the agreement's beneficiaries to respect core ILO standards regarding rights to organise and collective bargaining but also to establish minimum wage and maximum working hours and to ban the use of forced labour. This Act developed the provisions of the earlier Caribbean Basin Initiative that contained eligibility criteria relating to working conditions. The troubled multilateral WTO talks have also encouraged the US to look more towards bilateral trade agreements. After the relatively unsuccessful Cancun Ministerial in 2003, US Trade Representative Robert Zoellick reportedly said, 'as WTO members ponder the future, the US will not wait; we will move towards free trade with can-do countries. As such, the US is exploring possible agreements with Australia, South Korea, countries in Central America, and Latin American countries within the context of the Free Trade Area of the Americas.

The EU has also embraced social clauses in its trade agreements. Unlike the US, whose approach is based more on sanctions or the threat of sanctions, the EU's approach is to give incentives to partner countries to respect internationally recognised standards. Since 1998, the EU's GSP scheme has granted additional preferences to countries applying the ILO's core labour standards (see Box 14.1). In 2004, for example, the European Commission granted additional benefits to Sri Lanka under its GSP scheme on the grounds that it was making good progress towards full compliance with ILO core standards. However, on two occasions, the EU has withdrawn trade preferences because of violations of these standards. In 1997, it removed Myanmar's access to its GSP schemes because of the persistence of forced labour practices, and in

June 2007, the EU suspended GSP preferences that had been extended to Belarus on the basis that Belarus flouted core standards on freedom of association. In both cases in which the EU has taken sanctions against a trading partner for infringement of core labour standards, the EU has been embroiled in broader debates with the countries in question – Myanmar and Belarus – about democracy, the rule of law, fair elections, and other related issues.

In 2001, the European Commission adopted a strategy proposing action at European and international levels to support the effective application of core labour standards globally. The strategy requires that the EU integrate core labour standards into its development policy and include them in its bilateral agreements with third countries. Since then, the EU has systematically included a social clause in its bilateral agreements. Indeed, the EU's 1999 Agreement with South Africa included a commitment to ILO core standards and predated the systematic policy change. Subsequently, the Cotonou partnership agreements with the African, Pacific, and Caribbean and the Association Agreement with Chile have incorporated a social clause. The EU has also signalled its intent to make social clauses an integral part of ongoing and future bilateral or regional negotiations.

## Multilateral standards

The prospect of developing a multilateral framework to protect labour standards within the context of international trade goes back many years and has always been controversial. The 1948 Havana charter (see Chapter 3) contained an explicit link between labour and trade, requiring members to take measures against 'unfair labour conditions. This was too much for the US, which refused to ratify the Charter, leaving the transition measure, the GATT, as the main regulator of international trade for almost 50 years. GATT was much weaker on this issue, but Article XX, the general exception clause, did allow for the introduction of restrictions relating to the products of prison labour.

The issue has not made much progress at the multilateral level, a factor that helps explain the enthusiasm for 'social clauses' in bilateral trade agreements. Given its enhanced enforcement mechanisms, the WTO has become a preferred institution for many countries and NGOs lobbying to develop the trade-labour standards link. Accordingly, at the 1996 Singapore WTO Ministerial, the US, France, and a number of other developed countries were keen to push the link, but the inclusion of labour standards within the WTO's mandate was opposed by the developing countries and other developed countries, including the UK. The Singapore Declaration therefore supported the continuation of the status quo:

> We renew our commitment to the observance of internationally recognised core labour standards. The International Labour Organisation (ILO) is the competent body to set and deal with these standards, and we affirm our support for its work in promoting them… We reject the use of labour standards for protectionist purposes, and agree that the comparative advantages of countries, particularly low wage developing countries, must in no way be put into question. In this regard, we note that the WTO and ILO Secretariat will continue their existing collaboration.

Nevertheless, the issue of trade and labour continued to dog the WTO. Indeed, it was President Clinton's championing of the trade-labour standard link immediately prior to the 1999 Seattle Ministerial that had been intended to launch the next round of multilateral talks that made a major contribution to the failure of the Ministerial. However, in the two years between the failure at Seattle and the Doha Ministerial, which belatedly did what Seattle had intended to do, the heat appeared to have been taken out of the labour standards debate from the WTO viewpoint, and the Doha Declaration took no new initiatives in this area, merely reaffirming the above declaration made on this issue at Singapore.

The lack of any push to place labour rights on the agenda is partially a function of the more business-friendly orientation of the Bush administration, which came to power between the two Singapore and Doha ministers, and partially a reflection of a negotiating strategy that wishes to give more weight to the concerns of developing countries. Developing countries generally oppose the introduction of labour issues into the WTO, a move that they regard as 'disguised protectionism' and delays improvements in economic growth, which they argue increases labour standards in the longer term. In the absence of the WTO taking on a bigger role in labour matters, the ILO remains the main focus for multilateral action on labour standards (see Box 14.1).

---

**Box 14.1: The International Labour Organisation (ILO)**

The ILO was created as long ago as 1919. As such, it is one of the world's oldest international organisations and the only surviving major creation of the First World War peace settlement and the associated League of Nations machinery. Motivations underpinning the founding of the ILO continue to be relevant, including

- Humanitarian: The Preamble to the ILO's Constitution notes that 'conditions of labour exist involving ... injustice, hardship and privation to large numbers of people' and speaks of 'sentiments of justice and humanity' as part of the rationale behind the foundation of the organisation. Given contemporary reports of sub-standard health, safety, and general working conditions and the widespread existence of child labour and forced labour, this reason for the foundation of the ILO remains current.
- Political: The Preamble notes that injustice produces 'unrest so great that the peace and harmony of the world are imperilled' implying that without improvement in working conditions, serious social unrest would result. Although at the beginning of the 21st century, there were no upheavals like the 1917 Russian Revolution, which gave rise to the above fears of social unrest, persistent social injustice is commonly regarded as a source of political instability with the potential to spill over into regional instability.
- Economic: the ILO preamble notes that 'the failure of any nation to adopt humane conditions is an obstacle in the way of other nations which desire to improve the conditions in their countries'. In other words, low labour standards elsewhere place countries adopting social reform at a competitive disadvantage because of the effects on their cost of production. In short, the concepts of the 'race to the bottom' and 'social dumping' were not unknown in 1919.

- Development: this motivation reflects the view that the retention of low labour standards locks a country into reliance on low costs and productivity and hence into a cycle of poverty. A country's development needs are best served, according to this view, by upgrading the quality of labour input through higher standards rather than suppressing it through lower standards.

In 1944, 41 countries met in Philadelphia and agreed to the Philadelphia Declaration, which still comprises the organisation's main aims and objectives. The Declaration confirms the ILO's original general principles while both spelling them out in more detail and broadening the standard setting to cover more general but related social policy and human and civil rights issues. In 1946, the ILO became the first specialised agency of the UN, and by 2022, it had 186 members.

## The role of the ILO

The ILO has three main roles:

1. The formulation of minimum standards of basic labour rights: these cover freedom of association, the right to organise, collective bargaining, the abolition of forced labour, equality of opportunity, non-discrimination at the workplace, health and safety, and basic working conditions, etc.
2. Technical assistance for vocational training and rehabilitation, employment policy, labour administration, labour law and industrial relations, working conditions, management development, cooperatives, social security, labour statistics, and occupational health and safety.
3. Promotion of the development of independent employers' and workers' organisations and the provision of training and advisory services to these organisations.

## Core ILO standards

Corporate codes of conduct, codes of conduct developed by NGOs, trade agreements, etc. often include the requirement to comply with core ILO standards, of which there are four:

1. Freedom of association and the effective recognition of the right to collective bargaining.
2. Elimination of all forms of forced or compulsory labour.
3. Effective abolition of child labour.
4. Elimination of discrimination in employment.

In order to operationalise these core standards, the following eight ILO Conventions have been declared fundamental to the rights of human beings at work and should be implemented and ratified by all ILO members:

1. Freedom of Association and Protection of the Right to Organise Convention, 1948 (No. 87) – gives workers the absolute right to form and join independent trade unions.
2. The Right to Organise and Collective Bargaining Convention, 1949 (No. 98) – allows workers to organise union activities without threat of dismissal or action short of dismissal and protects their right to promote their interests via collective bargaining.
3. The Forced Labour Convention, 1930 (No. 29) – not allowed under any circumstances.
4. Abolition of the Forced Labour Convention, 1957 (No. 105).
5. The Discrimination (Employment and Occupation) Convention, 1958 (No. 111) – requires states to introduce policies to eliminate workplace discrimination on the grounds of race, colour, sex, religion, political opinion, nationality, or social origin.
6. The Equal Remuneration Convention, 1951 (No. 100) – establishes the principle of equal pay for men and women for work of equal value.
7. Minimum Age Convention, 1973 (No. 138) – the minimum age for employment must not be below the age for compulsory schooling and should not be below the age of 15.

Worst Forms of Child Labour Convention, 1999 (No. 182) – designed to eliminate bonded and other forms of slavery; the recruitment of children for armed conflict, prostitution, illicit activities, and any other activity that could harm the health, safety, or morals of a child.

## CONCLUSION

Globalisation and labour are closely linked. In an increasingly interdependent world with reducing barriers to cross-border transactions, labour migration, although showing signs of increase, is relatively limited. Indeed, it is often easier for firms to move production to workers in new locations rather than to seek to attract workers to their existing operations. This has created its own controversies and challenges, with allegations of 'unfair' competition and sweatshop labour being levelled at many multinationals operating in developing countries.

There is no lobby for low labour standards worldwide, but low labour standards are frequently the outcome of the current business environment. However, there is a great deal of controversy about what, if anything, should be done about them. Supporters of higher standards argue that even the threat of investment in a country with lower standards gives rise to lower standards in higher-standard countries. Developing countries argue that they are not in favour of child labour and other examples of low labour standards, but that economic reality means that preventing children from working can condemn them and their families to starvation. The best way to end these poor stand-ards is, so the argument goes, through higher growth levels.

In the interim, corporations are developing codes of conduct for themselves and their suppliers and participating in product and social labelling schemes. Social clauses are being introduced in bilateral trade agreements in an attempt to ensure a minimum level of standards, but their inclusion in multilateral trade negotiations has so far failed to materialise.

## KEY POINTS

- Normally, globalisation should boost the movement of labour, but although international migration is increasing, labour is considerably less mobile than other factors of production.
- Work moves to labour more than workers move to work. This creates concerns over employment in developed countries and social dumping in developing countries.
- Efforts to develop minimum labour standards fall into voluntary (product/social labelling and corporate codes of conduct) and compulsory measures ('social clauses').
- Developing countries often oppose efforts to introduce international labour standards, claiming that they damage those they are intended to protect and that they represent 'disguised protectionism'.
- Virtually all MNEs have developed their own codes of conduct, which cover, among other issues, minimum conditions in their operations and those of their suppliers.
- 'Social clauses' are becoming the norm in regional and bilateral trade agreements, but efforts to give the WTO greater responsibility in this field have stalled.

## QUESTIONS FOR DISCUSSION

1. Workers can move to jobs, or jobs can move to workers. What are the arguments for and against each alternative?
2. Discuss the implications of social dumping for workers in developed countries and for workers in developing countries.
3. Discuss the opposing views that corporate codes of conduct:
   a. Are intended to reduce the calls for more stringent and widespread labour stand-ards measures by states, regional organisations, and/or international institutions.

   **b.** Serve to increase labour standards in developing countries where the government may have limited capacity to enforce labour laws.

4. What are the costs and benefits to key stakeholders of including social clauses in bilateral trade agreements?

5. Should the trade-labour standards link become an item on the WTO agenda?

## ACTIVITIES

1. Compare and contrast the corporate codes of conduct of two multinational companies and assess whether they will meet the objective of attaining a minimum level of labour standards.

2. Find examples of firms relocating to take advantage of lower labour costs.

3. Make the case for and against including labour issues within the WTO. This can be used as the basis for a class debate.

4. You are an adviser to the Labour Minister of a developing country. Write a brief for the Minister that can be used as the basis of a speech on child labour to be given at an international forum.

5. You are an adviser to the CEO of a multinational enterprise that has been exposed as tolerating very poor conditions in the overseas factories of its main suppliers. What strategy would you advise to enable the company to counter its critics?

## SUGGESTED FURTHER READINGS

Athukorala, P. (2006). International labour migration in East Asia: Trends, patterns and policy issues. *Asian-Pacific Economic Literature, 20*(1), 18–39.

Auer, P. (2006). Perspectives: The internationalisation of employment: A challenge to fair globalisation. *International Labour Review, 145*(1–2), 119–134.

Bhagwati, J. (1997). Trade liberalisation and "fair trade" demands: Addressing the environmental and labour standards issues. In Bhagwati (ed) *Writings on international economics*, 35–56, Oxford: Oxford University Press.

Brewster, C., Sparrow, P., & Vernon, G. (2007). *International human resource management*, 2nd edn, London: Chartered Institute of Personnel and Development.

Cohen, R. (2006). *Migration and its enemies: Global capital, migrant labour and the nation state*, Aldershot: Ashgate.

Craig, J., & Lynk, S. (Eds.). (2006). *Globalization and the future of labour law*, Cambridge: Cambridge University Press.

Cranger, C., & Siroen, J. (2006). Core labour standards in trade agreements: From multilateralism to bilateralism. *Journal of World Trade, 40*(5), 813–836.

DeTienne, K., & Lewis, L. (2005). The practical and ethical barriers to corporate social responsibility disclosure: The Nike case. *Journal of Business Ethics, 60*(4), 359–376.

Dine, J. (2005). *Companies, international trade and human rights*, Cambridge: Cambridge University Press.

Doumbia-Henry, C., & Gravel, E. (2006). Free trade agreements and labour rights: Recent developments. *International Labour Review, 145*(3), 185–206.

Edwards, T., & Reece, C. (2006). *International human resource management: Globalization, national systems and multinational companies*, Harlow: FT Prentice Hall.

Granger, C., & Siroen, J.-M. (2006). Core labour standards in trade agreements: From multilateralism to bilateralism. *Journal of World Trade Law, 40*(5), 813–826.

Grynberg, R., & Qalo, V. (2006). Labour standards in US and EU preferential trading arrangements. *Journal of World Trade, 40*(4), 619–653.

Hatton, T., & Williamson, J. (2006). *Global migration and the world economy: Two centuries of policy and performance*, Cambridge: MIT Press.

Hepple, B. (Ed.). (2002). *Social and labour rights in a global context: International and competitive perspectives*, Cambridge: Cambridge University Press.

Hepple, B. (2005). *Labour laws and global trade*, Oxford: Hart.

Lee, E., & Vivarelli, M. (2006). The social impact of globalization in the developing countries. *International Labour Review, 145*(3), 167–184.

Locke, R., Kochan, T., Romis, M., & Qin, F. (2007). Beyond corporate codes of conduct: Work organisation and labour standards at Nike's suppliers. *International Labour Review, 46*(1–2), 21–37.

Massey, D., & Taylor, E. (Eds.). (2004). *International migration: Prospects and policies in a global market*, Oxford: Oxford University Press.

Moses, J. (2006). *International migration: Globalization's last frontier*, London: Zed Books.

Muchlinski, P. T. (2001). Human rights and multinationals: Is there a problem? *International Affairs, 77*(1), 31–48.

Piore, M. J., & Sabel, C. F. (1984). *The second industrial divide*, New York: Basic Books.

Trebilcock, M. J., & Howse, R. (2004). *The regulation of international trade*, 3rd ed, Chapter 17, London: Routledge.

Zimmermann, K. (2005). European labour mobility: Challenges and potentials. *De Economist, 153*(4), 425–450.

# CHAPTER 15

# THE ENVIRONMENT

## Greening international business

**OBJECTIVES**

This chapter will help you to:

- Explain the principles of ecological modernisation.
- Outline the link between globalisation and the environment.
- Describe and critique the 'pollution havens' and 'race to the bottom' hypotheses.
- Demonstrate an understanding of the key principles of contemporary environmental policy.
- Describe the role of Multilateral Environmental Agreements (MEAs) and the WTO in the development of international environmental policy.
- Assess the response of international business to environmental issues.

By the 1990s, environmental factors had become an issue for governments, businesses, and society in a way that was unheard of only a few years previously. The common perception is that the environment has been deteriorating for many years, that it continues to do so, and that human beings bear the primary responsibility for this. The reasons for this view are not difficult to understand. The world's population has expanded from an estimated 2.5 billion in 1950 to 8 billion in 2022, with forecasts of a global population of 9.7 billion by 2050 and 11 billion by 2100 as the norm. The increase in economic activity that has accompanied this population growth places additional demands and strains on the world's resources. World energy demand, for example, has risen inexorably, promoting additional emissions of greenhouse gases such as carbon dioxide. Pressure on water resources is also increasing (see Chapter 19); deforestation continues; world fish stocks are under pressure; and biodiversity is generally threatened as a result of the threat to habitats and pollution.

The challenge of combatting environmental degradation and reconciling the views and interests of a multitude of stakeholders occupies increasing amounts of time for

DOI: 10.4324/9781315184500-19

businesses, politicians, international institutions, NGOs, and civil society generally. Unsurprisingly, given the relative lateness with which environmental concerns became the subject of mainstream scientific endeavour, the complex issues involved are frequently fiercely contested. There is, for example, a general consensus that climate change is occurring. However, the causes of climate change are not universally accepted; the majority view at present is that much of climate change is anthropogenic (that is, man-made). However, there is a significant minority view that climate change has always occurred and that human input is relatively unimportant. The outcome of this debate has major implications for policy: if the minority are correct, for example, then policy initiatives to reduce greenhouse gases are not only irrelevant but represent a serious diversion of resources away from other pressing issues. If the majority view is correct, then initiatives to reduce greenhouse gas emissions are urgent. However, this is by no means a consensus, with some arguing (see, for example, Lomborg 2001) that the conventional portrayal of a constantly deteriorating environment is not supported by hard evidence. Though it has to be said that such views are becoming more marginalised in public debate as extreme weather as a consequence of climate change becomes more evident, many climate sceptics remain critical of the policy prescriptions offered.

This chapter begins by discussing the evolution of thinking about the environment before focussing on the increasingly dominant ecological modernisation paradigm that reverses the traditional view that economic growth and environmental activity are incompatible. This is followed by an exploration of the interface between globalisation and the environment, particularly in relation to 'race to the bottom' and 'pollution haven' arguments. The chapter then discusses international policy responses to environmental problems, especially the proliferation of multilateral environmental agreements (MEAs) and the emerging, but still limited, environmental role of the WTO. The chapter concludes with a discussion of corporate options and responses to environmental challenges.

## EVOLVING VIEWS OF THE ENVIRONMENT: THE EMERGENCE OF ECOLOGICAL MODERNISATION

Contemporary environmental concerns have their roots in the 1960s. In those days, many proponents of greater environmental protection were on the margins of politics and society and proposed radical action, arguing that only a profound transformation of the political, social, and economic systems would protect the planet. By the early 1970s, environmental issues had become more mainstream and were being debated by international think tanks and conferences. At that time, two environmental battle lines were drawn that remain important to this day.

The first relates to the view that economic growth and environmental protection are incompatible. The title of the Club of Rome's noted report, 'Limits to Growth', published in 1972, sums up this assumption. Another 1972 publication, 'Blueprint for Survival' reinforced this view, arguing that continuation of existing trends of production and consumption would lead to 'the breakdown of society and the irreversible disruption of life-support systems on this planet.'

The second relates to the divergent environmental interests of developed and developing countries. This became apparent at the landmark UN Conference on the Human Environment in Stockholm in 1972. The developed countries argued for collective action to address environmental issues, thereby avoiding the unilateral action they believed would disadvantage their own industries. The developing countries, on the other hand, regarded development as their priority and were unwilling to sacrifice it to correct pollution problems caused by developed nations. They also argued that developed countries had developed without environmental constraints and that it was only fair that they should be allowed to do the same.

Significant polarisation between developed and developing countries on environmental issues continues to this day.

However, a rethink of the supposed incompatibility between growth and environmental protection has occurred. The change began in the early 1980s and initially took root most strongly in Europe, where countries with a strong commitment to environmental protection, like the Netherlands and Germany, were able to exercise a strong influence on EC policy. By the 1990s, the perceived positive correlation between economic growth and environmental protection had become the dominant strand in environmental thinking, requiring a reconsideration of attitudes towards environmental policy.

This new mode of thinking is termed 'ecological modernisation'. Initially, ecological modernisation ideas were merely implicit in policy debates; explicit articulation was rare. Indeed, in 1992, Albert Weale wrote, 'there is no one canonical statement of the ideology of ecological modernisation'. However, since the mid-1990s, ecological modernisation, which was already having a significant influence on policy and stakeholders, has also figured centrally in academic discourse. The implications of ecological modernisation for business can be narrowed down to the following:

- *The reconciliation of environmental and economic objectives*: in other words, economic growth and environmental protection are mutually beneficial. Economic growth is qualitatively different from the past, given the incorporation of environmental features into technology. This integration of growth and environmental objectives results in a 'win-win-win' situation for the environment, the economy, and business.
- *Technocentricism*: that is, the emphasis on innovation and technology (modernism) to deliver both growth and environmental benefits. This is reflected in the so-called 'Porter hypothesis', which states that not only are growth and environmentalism compatible but also that competitiveness depends on this link. Accordingly, stricter environmental regulations and policies act not as a cost burden for industry but as an incentive to innovate and compete. In other words, profitability and the observance of high environmental standards go together. Moreover, there is potential for environmental activity to go hand-in-hand with job creation.
- *The primacy of the market* (albeit a market modified by state intervention to correct for market failures). This is marked by a movement away from the command-and-control regulations and standards used to regulate and constrain business activities in the early days of environmental policy activism. Such instruments proved to be inflexible and relatively ineffective. Instead, policymakers are increasingly seeking to use policy instruments that tap into market dynamics, such as taxation,

eco-labelling, and emission trading schemes. This reliance on the market makes eco-logical modernisation entirely compatible with the dominant neo-liberal economic philosophy (see Chapter 2) that has driven globalisation and is the complete antith-esis of the radical ecologist view that environmental protection requires systemic transformation. Indeed, 'ecological modernisation can best be understood as a late twentieth century strategy to adapt capitalism to the environmental challenge, thus strengthening it'.

These characteristics of ecological modernisation make it attractive to several stakehold-ers. In the political sphere, ecological modernisation has transformed the environmental debate from one of confrontation to one of consensus and cooperation and has been captured by, or adapted to, the market economy and capitalism. Ecological modernisa-tion thus holds out the possibility of resolving environmental problems within existing social, political, and economic systems. As such, it has marginalised the more extreme critics of the status quo and coopted its more moderate critics, who see opportunities to bring pragmatic, technical solutions to bear on environmental problems and to bring environmental issues into the political mainstream. Ecological modernisation has not only made environmental protection much less threatening to businesses, but it has also encouraged companies to regard the search for greater environmental protection as a positive factor in competitiveness.

Ecological modernisation not only promises greater competitiveness but also job crea-tion, whereas pollution haven concerns (see below) point to job losses in higher-standard countries (however, the total number of jobs worldwide may well increase if firms relocate to areas of lower labour productivity). The biggest environmentally induced positive impact on the job market originates from the creation of 'green jobs' in waste management, noise abatement, recycling, the rehabilitation of soil and groundwater, resource management, renewable energy, renovation of urban areas, nature and landscape protection, and conser-vation, etc. The growth of these eco-industries has been rapid in recent years. Demand for environmental equipment and services has traditionally been limited to the advanced indus-trialised countries of the US, Japan, and Europe, but greater interest is anticipated from the rapidly developing countries of South and East Asia and Latin America.

Despite the benefits claimed for it, ecological modernisation is not accepted whole-sale – far from it. Many ecologists continue to regard reductions in consumption and the cultivation of self-sufficiency as the only long-term sustainable option. These and other less radical critics argue that ecological modernisation is effectively a 'business as usual' ploy used to head off legitimate environmental concerns and to ignore demands for a fundamental reassessment of approaches to environmental degradation. Many busi-nesses also continue to lobby against environmental measures on cost grounds.

Developing countries are also suspicious of ecological modernisation. They continue to argue that development remains their overriding priority, that they cannot afford to embrace costly environmental measures, and that, given the responsibility of the devel-oped countries for much of the world's environmental degradation, it is the developed world that should take and pay for the necessary corrective measures.

However, a concept closely related to ecological modernisation, the Environmental Kuznets Curve (EKC) (see Figure 15.1), would appear to support the view that growth

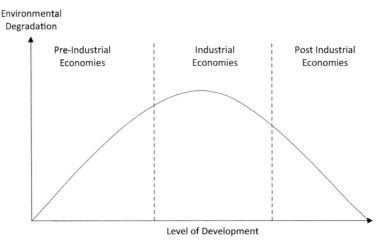

**FIGURE 15.1** Environmental Kuznets Curve

will ultimately also contribute to the solution for environmental problems in the developing world. The EKC derives its name from the original Kuznets U-shaped curve that posited that as growth increases, income distribution becomes more uneven, stabilises at middle-income levels, and then starts to even out again. In the case of the EKC, as growth gets underway, environmental degradation and pollution grow. It then stabilises at middle-income levels and starts to decline with prosperity. Once basic needs are met, so the explanation goes, priorities shift towards improving the quality of life. If this hypothesis is correct, the emphasis of developing countries on attaining growth is compatible with environmental protection and in line with the philosophy of ecological modernisation.

The, albeit limited, available evidence suggests that the EKC applies more to local pollution issues like urban air quality and freshwater pollutants than to degradation resulting from global phenomena like greenhouse gases. It is also conceivable that the EKC effect may not be attainable for the least developed countries, especially if the EKC effect already experienced by developed countries occurred as a result of the migration of polluting industries to developing countries (see below). For the least developed countries, there will not necessarily be any countries to which they can pass on their own polluting industries. However, the evidence supporting the pollution haven hypothesis is not strong. On the other hand, the EKC effect may occur if developing countries can utilise technologies that were not available to developed countries when they were at a similar stage of development. In short, it is likely that economic growth is a necessary but not sufficient condition for pollution to decline with higher levels of growth. The downward turn of the U-shaped curve also requires the implementation of appropriate policies and has occurred more readily in democratic countries, according to the WTO (Vaughan 1999), which has claimed that in countries with similar income levels, environmental degradation tends to be worse where greater income inequity is greatest, literacy levels are lower, and there are few political and civil liberties.

# GLOBALISATION AND THE ENVIRONMENT

Through its elimination of economic borders and the subsequent emergence of MNEs as networks of globally integrated production, globalisation clearly alters the context in which environmental regulation occurs. Deregulation and liberalisation, major globalisation drivers that favour competition imperatives, are widely held to increase pressure to lower environmental standards. In addition to the transborder nature of much pollution, globalisation critics point to the diminished ability of local and national regulators to implement environmental regulations given the mobility of MNEs and the alleged priority given to economic and trade matters over environmental concerns by policymakers generally. As such, globalisation raises issues related to links between trade and the environment, technology, corporate competitiveness, governance, and institutions.

Some, albeit not all, environmental NGOs have demonised globalisation, blaming it for many of the world's ecological ills. To the extent that globalisation increases production, consumption, and trade flows, it is held responsible for an accelerated rundown of the earth's natural resources and a general increase in environmental degradation. Trade flows, for example, involve more journeys over longer distances, thereby increasing fuel consumption and the greenhouse gas problem. The primacy of market forces fostered by globalisation, it is argued, has also intensified competition. The resulting competitiveness concerns make attention to environmental issues an unaffordable luxury. This potential stepping back from environmental responsibility applies to all levels of government and to MNEs themselves. In reality, notwithstanding the dictates of globalisation and competition, large and small companies and rule-making bodies at the local, regional, national, and international levels pay much more attention to environmental concerns than previously.

## CASE STUDY 15.1: CLIMATE CHANGE AND TRADE

The process of globalisation itself directly contributes to the process of climate change through a multitude of channels, not simply through states seeking to invest in pollution havens mentioned within the text but also through the very process of international exchange itself. The fact that trade flows have been a contributor to greenhouse gas emissions has long been acknowledged, with an estimated contribution of around 20–30 per greenhouse gas if the production of traded goods is included as well as those emitted during the transportation phase. The actual number of emissions within any given state's international trading activities is difficult to truly ascertain as it is driven by a mix of factors such as:

- The size of the economy.
- The sectoral composition of its foreign trade.
- Its level of participation in global value chains (GVCs).
- The modes of transportation used for its imports and exports.
- The energy efficiency of its production system.

However, of these figures, nearly three-quarters of the emissions from the globally traded sector stem from trade in energy and the transportation process. International transportation is arguably the most obvious manifestation of globality's greenhouse gas emissions, and the international logistics sector contributes around 12 per cent of the greenhouse gas emissions. This is just one of a few sectors where the greenhouse gas emissions from the transmission process are greater than those generated by the production process. Overall, developed economies tend to be net importers of greenhouse gases, while developing states are net exporters. The process of trade can only lower greenhouse gas emissions when overseas activity, which is less emitting, replaces domestic sources that are heavy emitters, even when the emissions from transportation are included.

While trade can be a contributor to greenhouse gas emissions, it can also be directly impacted as a legacy of climate change. While these impacts on trade flows are expected to be uneven across space and time, there is nonetheless a recognition that extreme weather investments can lead to global supply chain disruption and increase the cost of trade. These costs are often driven by any damage that extreme weather events have on the infrastructure (ports, roads, rail, etc.) that enables trade flows in and out of a country. These facilities are especially vulnerable in developing countries, where such systems tend to be less resilient to extreme weather events. In terms of product categories, it is agriculture that is the most exposed and where extreme weather can impact directly upon production and trade flows. The tourism sector is also exposed, and small island developing states are especially reliant upon this sector for foreign exchange but are often especially exposed to extreme weather events. There can also be damage to manufacturing plants and production, especially where these activities are clustered within a tight locality and where extreme weather can cause physical damage to production facilities.

Thus, overall, the impact of climate change can be considered complex in that the processes of international trade directly contribute to the process of global warming. This can be done directly through the fossil fuels burned during the transmission and distribution of completed and semi-completed goods within global value chains. This is on top of the environmental impact of the production of the exported goods. Trade is also impacted by climatic events, where extreme weather can disrupt trade flows.

**QUESTION**

Given the material offered within the case, does climate change strengthen the case for the localisation of production?

## The pollution haven hypothesis and the race to the bottom

The pollution haven hypothesis and the so-called 'race to the bottom' constitute two of the alleged environmental negatives of globalisation. Both are concerned with the impact of differential environmental standards in a world of globalisation-driven free-factor mobility. These arguments find parallels in social dumping, the argument that globalisation lowers labour standards as a result of the enhanced potential for firms to move to countries where lower standards prevail (see Chapter 14).

More specifically, the pollution havens hypothesis states that in order to avoid the costs of complying with high environmental standards, firms will relocate to countries (pollution havens) where standards and hence costs are lower, resulting in the loss of jobs and investment in the higher-standard country. In this scenario, higher standards, ironically, lead to greater environmental damage as firms liberate themselves from environmental constraints in their new location. Pollution havens also trigger a 'race to the bottom' by increasing pressure to lower standards to prevent such migrations from occurring. In essence, so the argument goes, open markets undermine national environmental policies and create intense pressure to weaken regulations in order to retain investment, maintain competitiveness, and remove the incentive to relocate to countries with lower standards. The outcome is a downward spiral of environmental standards.

The pollution haven hypothesis ignores the increasing tendency of MNEs to standardise their technology across all plants; this strategy increases compatibility between different parts of the production chain, yielding cost benefits in the process. According to the US International Trade Commission, 'much research indicates that multinational firms tend to replicate the technologies employed in their home markets when operating in developing countries. Indeed, the ability to duplicate technology in a number of countries is deemed central to the competitive strategy of most multinationals' (Vaughan 1999). Furthermore, if the home market has stricter environmental regulations than the host country, thereby requiring the integration of pollution control into its technology, FDI will be less polluting than domestic plants in the host country.

Both the pollution haven and the race to the bottom hypotheses depend on the assumption that environmental regulations impose compliance costs that are sufficiently high to become a determining factor in business location. The limited evidence that exists indicates that environmental compliance costs are no more than two per cent of total costs, even for the most polluting industries. US Bureau of Census data published in 1996 indicates that, on average, US industry spent no more than 0.6 per cent of its revenue on pollution abatement. For the vast majority of sectors, the figures were lower than this, as the average was pulled up by higher figures for the most polluting industries (petroleum and coal products, chemicals, primary metal industries, and paper and pulp products). This phenomenon has also been noted by the OECD, the WTO, and the US NGO, the Worldwatch Institute.

However, the additional costs incurred as a result of environmental regulation can be a determining factor in relocation, especially when profit margins are tight and the economic environment is generally unfavourable. Furthermore, it is possible that it is not actual increased costs or job losses that result in governments backing off from higher standards or lowering standards, but the threat or fear of such effects. Again, there is some, albeit limited, evidence that fears of job losses arising from environmental regulations are much bigger than actual job losses and that the cost burden imposed by regulation turns out to be less onerous than originally envisaged. Nevertheless, it can be difficult to gather support for new regulations if the general perception is that the cost

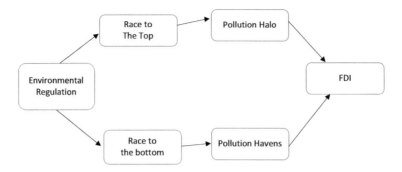

**FIGURE 15.2** Pollution havens and halo effects

of proposed regulations will bear heavily on domestic industry. It is certainly the case that business often appeals to competitiveness concerns in its lobbying efforts against proposed new regulations.

## The pollution halo hypothesis and the race to the top

An alternative to the pollution haven hypothesis is the pollution halo hypothesis. This holds that inward investment into developing economies from firms that are normally subject to higher environmental standards in their pre-existing markets has the effect of raising the level of environmental protection within the host economy. These firms arrive with new and cleaner technologies and deploy them as the norm wherever they seek to operate. These technological benefits from FDI are further enhanced by better management practices and know-how. This hypothesis is viewed as especially relevant where local, incumbent businesses are seen as particularly polluting. These effects are especially noticeable where the investment is in higher-technology products.

The effect of this process is to create an opposite process to the conventional notion of a race to the bottom by creating a 'race to the top'. This reflects reputational and commercial benefits from advancing environmental technology (notably that related to green energy) and know-how in contexts where their advancement would otherwise be protracted. For the incoming MNE, the logic of this does not merely lie in the promotion of uniform processes and technology across the network of businesses but also in working to counter any suspicion that the FDI is driven by a desire to exploit lax environmental standards in the host economy.

The attractiveness of the pollution halo effect and of a race to the top by states, especially those at lower levels of economic development, can be seen as an important facet in enabling these states to meet their international obligations with regard to climate change. It can also enable these states to comply with any trade obligations related to the environmental effects of production within that country. Thus, there is a virtue to the country of being seen as environmentally virtuous, allowing inward investment that won't mean the MNE endures reputational damage.

## Trade and the environment

Trade and the environment are frequently portrayed as being in conflict with each other. The main thrust of international trade policy in past decades has been liberal and non-interventionist, whereas environmental policy intervention is needed precisely because, without full internalisation of external costs, the market fails to deliver the optimum outcome. The result is an intervention to correct for market failure.

Although examples of companies moving to 'benefit' from lower environmental compliance costs exist, there is scant evidence that this occurs in any systematic and sustained way. Analysis of trade and FDI patterns does not reveal a relative shift of 'dirty' industries from developed to developing industries. Indeed, such a move would go against the Heckscher-Ohlin principle that it is differences in factor endowments, namely capital and labour, which determine trade patterns. Accordingly, capital-intensive industries should be attracted to developed countries and labour-intensive industries to developing countries. Trade encourages specialisation, implying an increase rather than a decrease in pollution in developed countries, given their specialisation in more polluting, capital-intensive industries. This effect has been offset to some extent by the introduction of new technology and the relative increase in the role of services in developed economies.

Free traders anticipate environmental benefits from trade and the growth flowing from it (see earlier section on ecological modernisation). For example, liberalised trade facilitates the spread of environmental services and clean technology. Indeed, one of the objectives of the Doha Development Agenda is the elimination of tariffs and other trade barriers on environmental goods and services. If the EKC effect holds, the increased income generated by trade will foster demands for cleaner environments. Trade encourages specialisation and restructuring according to comparative advantage, resulting in greater efficiency and economies of scale. This will reduce global environmental problems if improved efficiency entails the use of cleaner technology, which is plausible, although by no means certain. The impact on the local environment will depend on the net environmental impact of sectors that are expanding and contracting as a result of trade.

The interaction of trade and the environment in a policy context is far from straightforward. Given the cross-border nature of many environmental problems, increasing convergence and harmonisation of environmental policy would appear to be the most promising environmental approach to tackling these problems. However, given differences in environmental conditions between, and even within, countries, it is perfectly plausible that in order to achieve a common objective, it is appropriate for different jurisdictions to adopt different policies or for international environmental regimes to adopt common but differentiated responsibilities.

Furthermore, what seems like a sensible policy can have unforeseen and undesired effects. For example, in order to halt the process of deforestation, a ban on trade in forestry products might appear to be a good idea. However, by depressing returns from forestry activity, such an initiative can accelerate rather than halt deforestation by increasing incentives to look for other sources of income from the land. This has already happened in Latin America, where forests were destroyed so that more land could be used for biofuel production. Trade restrictions are also often proposed as ways of dealing with environmental problems but are often suspect in the eyes of free traders who believe (often, albeit not always, with good cause) that such measures are trade rather than environmental protectionists.

The most appropriate relationship between trade and environmental policy is one of trade liberalisation carried out against a background of environmental policy that provides for full internalisation of external costs. This is in line with the current trend towards greater use of market-based instruments such as eco-taxes. A market-based environment and trade policy working together could make a positive contribution to both the economy and the environment by bringing about a more efficient allocation of resources.

---

**Box 15.1:** The Paris Agreement

In 2015, parties to the United Nations Framework Convention on Climate Change (UNFCCC) agreed to a new treaty to combat climate change and shift the global economic system towards a low-carbon future. Building upon the UNFCCC, the agreement commits all signatories to a common cause to combat climate change processes and to offer increased support to developing states to facilitate this change. The ultimate aim is to limit any increase in global temperature to 2 degrees Celsius above pre-industrial levels. On top of this, there are measures to seek to limit this change even further to 1.5 degrees Celsius. These goals are to be supported through enhanced finance and an increasingly transparent framework for monitoring progress.

All signatories to the agreement (there were 55 signatories in the immediate aftermath covering 55 per cent of emissions; currently there are 194 out of 198 possible signatories) have set national targets with regards to decarbonisation that are expected to be improved upon in successive revisions. The agreement is subject to a five-yearly review to assess the combined progress towards the stated goals. The key components of the agreements are noted below.

**Long-term temperature goal** – as mentioned, the agreement seeks to limit the global temperature increase to below 2 degrees Celsius while also seeking to limit the increase to 1.5 degrees.

**Global peaking and 'climate neutrality'** – this seeks to attain the peak of carbon emissions as soon as possible. This will be achieved by levels of state economic development.

**Mitigation** – in establishing binding commitments on states, there is pressure upon states to enact domestic legislation to attain and progressively improve on set targets.

**Sinks and reservoirs** – this agreement seeks to facilitate action by signatories to improve and conserve key carbon sinks and reservoirs (such as tropical forests and permafrost).

**Voluntary cooperation/market- and non-market-based approaches** – voluntary cooperation is allowed so as to enable the spread of best practice in managing the decarbonisation process.

**Adaptation** – this agreement seeks to enable the development of resilient systems that can readily adapt to climatic events and also to the measures to combat their impact. This requires plans for transitory adaptation by states.

**Loss and damage** – this agreement seeks to get signatories to recognise the threat of accounting for the losses caused by and the damage created by climate change (notably extreme weather events). This requires more action on planning and support for and by impacted parties.

**Finance, technology, and capacity-building support** – this is a renewed commitment by developed countries to support climate change efforts in developing economies where the resources should both enable adaptation and mitigation. This is set at $100 billion per year.

**Climate change education, training, public awareness, public participation, and public access to information** – this agreement seeks for this to also be enhanced.

**Transparency, implementation, and compliance** – this requires that all actions taken by parties towards these objectives are transparent and flexible in implementation to reflect the differing capacities of signatories. It also seeks to ensure that pressure can be exerted on states to meet these commitments.

**Global stocktake** - every five years, combined progress by signatories will be assessed.

Nonetheless, despite these ambitious goals, state actions still fall way short, with many states' actions being more in line with a 3-degree Celsius increase than the one proposed within the agreement. To keep to the 2-degrees Celsius target means that carbon emissions will peak well before 2030 and be totally eliminated by 2050. This is a long way from being met, and states have a lot of flexibility to diverge from set targets. This reflects the need to account for a shifting context throughout the life of the agreement. It was notable how the Ukraine conflict has made some states backtrack on commitments due to a need to find quick replacements for Russian gas, while for others it has sped up the replacement of renewable technologies in their energy mix. Nonetheless, the Paris Agreement is an important point in climate change action, with all states agreeing that the issue needs to be addressed and that cooperation and mutual support are the way to progress.

## INTERNATIONAL ENVIRONMENTAL POLICY

Globalisation has played an important role in the appearance of environmental policy on the international agenda, but given the lack of respect for pollution on national borders, the incentive to formulate international environmental policy would exist even in the absence of globalisation. The development of multilateral trade policy preceded the emergence of environmental issues and policies on the international stage, but environmental issues in turn got their first international airing ahead of other globalisation-driven issues such as competition policy and labour market regulation.

The crucial event in the evolution of contemporary international environmental policy was the 1972 Stockholm Conference on the Human Environment. The conference was held to consider 'problems of the human environment … and also to identify those aspects of it that can only or best be solved through international co-operation' and was attended by delegations from 114 countries. Stockholm's long-term importance lies in its hitherto unique focus on environmental issues, which both aroused public interest and stirred national governments to become involved. More specifically, the Stockholm Conference resulted in the creation of the UN Environment Programme (UNEP), an organisation which, in addition to organising environmental information and monitoring networks, has been instrumental in providing support for key MEAs. Although UNEP is the most important, it is not the only international organisation involved in the creation of MEAs. Other UN bodies like the International Maritime Organisation (IMO), the Food and Agriculture Organisation (FAO), and non-UN institutions like the OECD and the International Atomic Energy Authority (IAEA) also play a key role in their development and operation.

Up to 2012, over 700 multilateral agreements were concluded relating to the environment. These cover over 3,000 separate instruments. Of these, the majority are regional. Furthermore, there are believed to be over 1,000 bilateral environmental agreements in existence. Although the first MEAs were negotiated in the nineteenth century, the biggest increase in the incidence of MEAs has occurred since the Stockholm Conference. They can be approximately classified into the following areas:

- **Biodiversity** – e.g., the Convention on Biological Diversity (CBD) and the Convention on International Trade in Endangered Species (CITES).
- **Atmosphere** – e.g., UNFCCC and the Montreal Protocol.
- **Land** – e.g., the UN Convention to Combat Desertification (UNCCD).
- **Chemical and hazardous waste** – e.g., the Basel Convention on the Control of the Transboundary Movements of Hazardous Wastes and their Disposal and the draft Stockholm Conventions on Persistent Organic Pollutants.
- **Regional seas and related matters** – e.g., the Protection of the Arctic Marine Environment (PAME) and other regional marine initiatives.

Many MEAs effectively limit the way businesses carry out their activities and use trade as an instrument in environmental protection – a development that potentially brings them into conflict with the WTO. Indeed, the main objective of the Convention on International Trade in Endangered Species (CITES) is to control trade in endangered species of animals, plants, and products made from them. The Montreal Protocol, for example, banned the production and use of several categories of industrial chemicals known to contribute to the depletion of the stratospheric ozone layer and imposed restrictions on others.

The action businesses had to take as a result of the Montreal Protocol was immediately clear, but the requirements emanating from the UNFCCC and subsequent related initiatives like the 1997 Kyoto Protocol are more extensive but less homogenous. The UNFCCC and Kyoto (and more latterly, the Paris Agreement) attempt to deal with the complex issue of climate change via a range of strategies, most of which are designed to restructure economic development so that it is less dependent on greenhouse gases. It is left up to signatories to develop strategies to determine how they develop strategies to meet their emissions targets under Kyoto and its successors.

In addition, although MEAs have often thrown up deep differences between developed and developing countries (the Basel Convention, for example, was essentially a response to divergent interests over the disposal of hazardous wastes), they have not attracted the same negative publicity from NGOs as other multilateral instruments, such as the failed Multilateral Agreement on Investment. This can be partly explained by the tendency to involve rather than exclude NGOs and other aspects of civil society, either as observers, advisers, or sometimes as full participants, in the deliberations of MEAs. This is certainly true of CITES and the Basel Convention, among others.

---

**Box 15.2:** Key principles of contemporary environmental policy

A degree of consensus has merged around the need to encompass the following underlying principles in environmental policy enacted at local, national, regional, and international levels:

**The 'polluter pays' principle (PPP):** stipulates that polluters should pay the full cost of the environmental damage they cause. Environmental costs are often referred to as 'externalities' (for example, damage to health, rivers, the air, etc. arising from economic activity) that are not incorporated into the costs of a product but are borne by society as a whole. By making the polluter pay the full cost of its activities, including externalities, the PPP provides an incentive to make products less polluting and/or to reduce the consumption of polluting goods. This internalisation of external costs can be met through the use of market-based policy instruments.

**The prevention principle:** involves changes to products and processes to prevent environmental damage from occurring, rather than relying on remedial action to repair damage after it has taken place. This implies the development of 'clean technologies'; minimal use of natural resources; minimal releases into the atmosphere, water, and soil; and maximisation of the recyclability and lifespan of products.

**The precautionary principle:** acknowledges that our understanding of ecology and environmental processes is, at best, incomplete. Policy is therefore formulated against a background of uncertainty. However, lack of scientific knowledge should not be used to justify failure to introduce environmental policy. Indeed, even without conclusive scientific evidence about outcomes, precautionary action should be taken if the potential consequences of inaction are particularly serious or if the cost of action is not high.

**Subsidiarity:** environmental policy is formulated at a number of different levels – local, national, regional, and international. The subsidiarity principle requires action to be taken at the lowest possible level of government at which it can be effectively taken. This poses interesting challenges for environmental policy given the lack of respect for pollution at borders. In many instances, regional or international action will therefore be suitable, but in some cases of cross-border pollution, a more local policy approach may be appropriate given differences in environmental conditions.

**Common but differentiated responsibility:** environmental regimes that deal with environmental problems with international implications often distinguish between countries when formulating policy. For example, all countries have a responsibility for global warming, but the contribution of richer countries to the problem has been greater, and the poorer countries have greater calls on their resources in terms of basic development needs. Therefore, international regimes, while acknowledging common responsibility for the global environment, will allocate differential policies for dealing with the problem.

**Openness:** the representation of all stakeholders in the formulation of environmental policy is important for good environmental management. Many MEAs are noteworthy for their openness and transparency, encouraging participation from business and environmental NGOs, and utilising modern technology to communicate their activities to the public. A recurring criticism of the WTO, on the other hand, is its lack of openness and transparency when dealing with environmental, and indeed other, matters.

## The WTO and the environment

The WTO has attracted more than its fair share of NGO opposition (see Chapter 4), and no more so than in relation to its environmental approach. Given the heterogeneity of anti-globalisation groups and environmental NGOs, it is easiest to characterise them as existing along a continuum: at one end sit groups that regard trade and sustainability as incompatible and lobby for the latter. In their eyes, trade liberalisation and the WTO are the environment's main enemies. At the other end of the continuum sit groups that believe the best way of tipping the trade-environment balance towards the environment side of the scales is by working to influence and to 'green' organisations. Indeed, an increasing number of NGOs are working with companies, governments, and international institutions to do just that.

The most common criticisms levelled at the WTO on environmental matters are that business interests always override those of the environment and that the WTO is essentially undemocratic in nature, failing to take into account arguments that originate from non-business interests or smaller member states. In its defence, the WTO and its predecessor organisation, the GATT, were established to uphold a rule-based trading system, not to protect the environment.

In 1947, when the GATT came into existence, environmental considerations were not regarded as important. However, it did incorporate an exception clause, Article XX, which allows countries, under strict guidelines, to set aside normal trading rules if it is deemed necessary to protect human, animal, or plant life or health or to conserve exhaustible natural resources. Such departures from the rules were allowed provided they did not discriminate between imports or act as a 'disguised restriction on international trade'. In other words, environmental claims should not be used as a pretext for protectionism.

Environmental issues hardly troubled GATT during the first three decades of its existence. This gradually began to change in the 1970s. In 1971, the GATT Council established a Group on Environmental Measures and International Trade (EMIT) 'to examine, upon request, any specific measures relevant to the trade policy aspects of measures to control pollution and protect the human environment'. The group was to be activated upon the request of a contracting party, something that did not occur until 1991.

Even though environmentalism had become more prominent by the mid-1980s, the environment was not explicitly included in the Uruguay Round of multilateral talks. However, the 1995 Marrakesh Agreement that ended the Uruguay Round and established the WTO firmly secured the importance of the environment to the work of the WTO by:

1. Including a reference to the objective of sustainable development and the need 'to protect and preserve the environment' in the preamble of the WTO Treaty. In other words, the traditional economic objectives of the WTO must be balanced against environmental considerations.

2. Requiring the WTO's General Council to establish a successor to EMIT, the Committee on Trade and the Environment (CTE). CTE has a broad mandate, requiring it to identify the link between trade and environmental measures and to recommend modifications to the multilateral trading system to bring it in line with sustainability.

The Doha WTO Ministerial Declaration of November 2001, which launched the next round of multilateral trade talks, expressed the conviction 'that the aims of upholding and safeguarding an open and non-discriminatory multilateral trading system and acting for the protection of the environment and sustainable development can and must be mutually supportive.' In particular, the declaration registered a continuing commitment to avoid the use of environmental measures as a form of disguised protection and welcomed cooperation with UNEP and other inter-governmental environmental organisations. The declaration also contained a commitment to the presentation of a report on technical assistance and – lding in developing countries issues for the Fifth Ministerial Session in 2005. Such declarations were intended to calm developing countries' fears that environmental concerns could be given higher priority over trade issues and that 'green' conditionality could become attached to conditions of market access.

With the failure of the Doha Round, the WTO has sought to develop a new set of basics with regard to the trade effects of environmental policy. The key focus post-Doha is threefold:

1. Greater openness in trade in environmental products: the aim is to promote global change through the spread of environmental technologies, first through lower tariffs on these products (this is in areas such as waste treatment, which have an indirect impact). Also, the focus is on lowering NTBs, which inhibit the spread of technology. To this end, 46 states are seeking an agreement to remove tariffs on specific environmental goods such as such as generating clean and renewable energy, improving energy and resource efficiency, controlling air pollution, managing waste, treating wastewater, monitoring the quality of the environment, and combatting noise pollution.

2. Greater coherence between trade and environmental rules: this depends both on greater transparency with regard to the measures deployed but also, by implication, on greater coordination between states.

3. Better cooperation: this feeds on the themes above, where there is a need for states to better align policies to remove ambiguities in policy.

4. Fishing subsidies: these are an explicit problem leading to the loss of biodiversity and overfishing. These measures also discriminate against developing states.

---

**Box 15.3:** The environmental dimension of WTO instruments

In general, WTO rules allow members to adopt their own environmental protection policies provided they observe key WTO principles: that is, there is no discrimination between imports and domestically produced products (national treatment) or between like products imported from different trading partners (the most favoured nation principle). In addition to general WTO principles, the preamble to the WTO agreement, Article XX, and the work of the CTE, environmental protection is also a factor in the following WTO instruments:

The Agreement on Technical Barriers to Trade (TBT): the TBT Agreement concerns the preparation, adoption, and application of product technical requirements and compliance procedures for industrial and agricultural products. While recognising the right of countries to take measures to protect health and the environment at levels they deem appropriate, the agreement attempts to prevent the misuse of standards for protectionist purposes, a practice that is both subtle and widespread. For example, standards can be written in such a way to match the characteristics of domestic products, effectively excluding imports.

The TBT Agreement encourages countries to use international standards to limit standard proliferation but does allow digression from them if there are specific fundamental climatic, geographical, or technological factors that make an international standard inappropriate.

Agreement on Sanitary and Phytosanitary Measures (SPS): The SPS Agreement was negotiated during the Uruguay Round to guard against risks from additives, contaminants, toxins, or disease in food. Food safety has become a contentious issue following the controversies over BSE, beef hormones, and the resistance to genetically modified (GM) food.

The principles and provisions of the SPS Agreement parallel those of the TBT Agreement in that governments have a legitimate right to maintain their preferred level of health protection, provided they respect non-discriminatory principles and notification obligations. In addition, countries intending to impose more stringent standards than international norms must do so on the basis of scientific evidence and/or an assessment of the risks to human, animal, or plant life and health. The Agreement allows governments the right to take precautionary provisional measures (see Box 16.2) in the absence of scientific evidence while seeking further information.

General Agreement on Trade in Services (GATS): Article XIV of the GATS parallels GATT Article XX by listing general exceptions to its provisions. In short, measures can be exempt from GATS regulations provided they are deemed necessary, among other things, 'to protect human, animal or plant life or health.' As with the GATT, GATS exemptions should not be discriminatory or operate as disguised forms of protectionism.

The environmental services sector within GATS includes sewage services, refuse disposal services, sanitation, and other services (i.e., noise abatement, nature and landscape protection, etc.), many of which face obstacles to market access such as discriminatory taxes, subsidies, non-recognition of foreign qualifications, inadequate intellectual property protection, and restrictions on investment. Removal of these obstacles is on the Doha agenda and will reduce the costs faced by companies when attempting to operate in a sustainable manner.

Trade-related Aspects of Intellectual Property Rights (TRIPS): Article 27 stresses that countries can make certain IP ineligible for patenting where the inventions seek to protect human, animal, or plant life or health, to avoid serious harm to the environment and plants and animals where the invention protects specified processes. This reflects that the agreement allows countries to refuse to patent those inventions that may harm the environment, as well as for moral and ethical reasons.

The Agreement on Subsidies and Countervailing Measures (SCM): this allows the use of subsidies to promote the adaptation of facilities to evolving environmental conditions.

The Agreement on Agriculture (AoA): this allows exemptions to this rule where support is offered that protects the environment. Such support is covered in the preamble of the agreement. Allowed are those policies that do not impact trade but facilitate adaptation to best environmental practices.

## THE WTO AND THE SHIFT TO A LOW-CARBON ECONOMY

As countries seek to make the transition to a low-carbon economy, the interface with trade law is becoming evident, especially where there may be increased constraints on the form and nature of the type of environmental policy followed and how these impact trade. Precedents within trade regimes have shown that states are prone to using the virtues of environmentalism as a cover for discriminatory practices. These issues are also already proving evident in the shift to a low-carbon economy, notably with regard to the transition to renewable energy technologies. While there is a consensus between countries on the endpoint, the timing and nature of the transition are less so. As a result, there are emerging trade issues where environmental policies are asymmetric, causing divergent cost structures for businesses, and where these divergences occur, states may introduce counteracting parallel policies.

For the WTO, trade is integral to the shift to a low-carbon economy. It argues that it is the freer exchange of environmental technology, know-how, and enabling services that will be central to the smooth and speedy transition to a low-carbon economy. There is a belief that the energy transition will also allow new types of trade to occur or for those areas where trade is currently at a low level to expand. This is notable in areas such as the aforementioned environmental technology (such as solar panels, batteries, etc.), electricity, and trade in renewable fuels and other raw materials core to the transition, such as rare earths. Looking across the notifications to the WTO within the broad area of environment, just 18 per cent reflect themes of climate change. These reflect methods of support offered to deal with adapting to climatic events rather than a shift to a low-carbon economy. Thus, to date, much of the work has been dealing with climate mitigation, notably within agriculture, rather than adaptation.

One area where the transition to a low-carbon economy has generated increased trade is solar power. Photovoltaic cells have seen a marked increase in the globalisation of their value chains in the decade to 2020. Trade in these products has tripled, notably as China has become a solar power powerhouse in the past decade. This has happened as tariffs on these products have been falling. Though the ability to turn this into a truly global market is mitigated by non-tariff barriers, standards have to adapt to the different operating conditions across the different global regions. Moreover, while tariffs on photovoltaic cells are low, many states do deploy trade remedies to protect domestic industry to prevent unfair trade practices such as dumping. Of the trade remedy cases on renewable energy, more than half deal with solar power. Trade has also been skewed by support measures at the national level to link the introduction of solar power technology with high local content rules.

However, the shift towards a low-carbon economy also raises issues with regard to the shifting competitive advantage of states. This is compounded by issues of energy security becoming increasingly entwined with renewable technologies. There is increased competition between states to seek to secure a competitive advantage in the supply of these technologies. This is compounded in the case of many Western countries by the fact that the transition could create a dependence on potentially hostile states (i.e., China). This has led to more and more offers of financial inducements to ramp up domestic production of renewable energy technology. This has led to some disputes and tit-for-tat measures between Western trading partners, notably the US and the EU.

The US has long complained about the subsidies it offers to its renewable energy sector, which it believes are contrary to WTO rules. Nonetheless, in 2022, the US launched its Inflation Reduction Act, which included $369 billion worth of subsidies and tax breaks for businesses investing in green energy technology production within the US. For example, the purchase of electric vehicles produced within the US gains a $7,500 subsidy. The fear of the EU and other trading partners is that this will lead to a race to the bottom as countries compete to attract this investment. These measures directly contravene WTO rules as they discriminate against non-US renewable technologies. The EU fears that these measures will redirect investment away from the EU towards the US and lead to a series of retaliatory measures and, potentially, a trade war. Indeed, many larger European countries are already calling for retaliatory measures, especially as some European businesses are already making moves to shift production.

The EU's options would be to first take the US to the WTO. However, this is expected to be a protracted process which can often generate ambiguous results. In any case, this process has been slowed down even further with the US's resistance to appointing judges to the dispute resolution panel. This is why the US is arguing that the EU should follow a similar route to itself. This would level the playing field with the US but at the cost of disrupting the Single European Market as subsidies would be skewed towards the biggest states. Thus, there would be a need for the EU to undertake the measures rather than member states. However, at the time of writing, this dispute is still evolving against the background of geopolitical uncertainty created by the Russia-Ukraine conflict and how this is speeding up the transition.

## THE CORPORATE SECTOR AND ENVIRONMENTAL POLICY

The pressure for companies to abide by principles of corporate responsibility, which include respect for the environment, has increased, and businesses must and do take environmental issues into account in their planning. It is now the norm for both large and small companies to integrate environmental planning into their strategic planning and to appoint a senior manager or board member to take responsibility for the environment. This is regarded as essential for a host of reasons, not least because a bad environmental record or bad environmental publicity can inflict serious damage on a company.

Moreover, and most importantly, companies have to be aware of and respect the myriad of environmental regulations that are being established at a number of levels, ranging from the local, municipal, state, and provincial levels to the national, regional, and international levels. The Montreal Protocol, for example, stopped the production of certain chemicals, forcing companies to look for alternatives. The implementation of the Kyoto Agreement will fall on the shoulders of companies as governments pass down framework strategies to enable their countries to reach individual targets.

In addition to compliance with regulation, businesses are also pressing for greater use of voluntary environmental measures, which they argue give them more flexibility in achieving environmental objectives than more rigid traditional approaches and, they hope, reduce the likelihood of the introduction of more restrictive mandatory schemes at a later stage. These voluntary methods can take a number of forms. For example, the provisions of ISO 14000, a voluntary international standard for environmental management that has been accepted remarkably quickly since its introduction in 1996. Industrial sectors, usually through trade associations, are also developing schemes to promote the environmental credentials of their members. The 'Responsible Care' initiative by the US chemical industry, which is also becoming increasingly adopted in Europe, is a good example of this. Eco-labelling schemes, both voluntary and mandatory, are also becoming more commonplace.

Traditionally, businesses have complained about the costs and other burdens placed upon them by environmental regulation. Although the cost argument is still heard and indeed can be justified in some cases, the business response has become more complex and responsive to environmental pressures and much less prone to resistance, almost as a matter of principle. This change has occurred as companies realise the damage that a bad environmental reputation can do to them and the benefits that can accrue from a positive environmental reputation and green marketing. Shrewd firms also realise that their green claims must have substance behind them.

More positively, increasing numbers of companies are recognising the benefits to their bottom line by incorporating environmental considerations into their planning — that is,

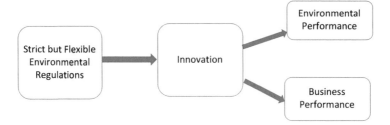

**FIGURE 15.3** The Porter hypothesis

there is growing acceptance of ecological modernisation ideas and of the Porter hypothesis that environmentalism stimulates innovation generally, which in turn has a positive impact on competitiveness, an essential ingredient in globalised marketplaces (see Figure 15.3). Porter and Linde's 1995 study (Porter 1995) found that of the major process changes at ten manufacturers of printed circuit boards, environmental staff were behind 13 out of 33 major changes. Of these 13 changes, 12 contributed to cost reduction, eight to improvements in quality, and five to extended product capabilities. This in turn helps reduce costs and promotes innovation, both crucial elements of competitiveness. Matsushita also applies its environmental targets and strategy throughout its domestic and overseas operations, although some differences are necessary as a result of diverse local and national regulations. However, it is rational for companies that have invested in environmental innovation to try to seek the benefits of this throughout the company, thereby weakening the pollution haven hypothesis.

Furthermore, the limited evidence that is available suggests that firms that take sustainability more seriously also tend to perform well in terms of profitability. This may simply be because better-managed companies also take environmental issues more seriously. It is also sometimes claimed that attention paid to environmental matters conveys first-mover advantages to a firm; that is, firms adopting an aggressive environmental approach ahead of regulation will have significant advantages once regulation is introduced.

## CONCLUSION

Environmental issues have a strong international dimension with significant implications for business, both domestic and international. Pollution is no respecter of borders; many anthropogenic environmental problems, such as stratospheric ozone depletion and the movement of hazardous waste and chemicals, are just some of the cross-border environmental issues demanding the attention of policymakers at local, national, regional, and international levels. Even apparently purely domestic environmental concerns that spawn purely domestic regulations have international implications if the regulations operate as trade barriers. Business must respond to and take into account in its planning the host of environmental regulations to which it is now subject, and increasingly, it is voluntarily undertaking environmental initiatives.

## KEY POINTS

1. Many environmental issues have a cross-border or even global dimension. However, a differentiated response may be the best way to deal with them.
2. Although companies still resist environmental regulations on the grounds that they increase costs, good environmental practice is increasingly seen as boosting competitiveness.
3. Trade-environmental disputes and the potential clash between multilateral environmental agreements (MEAs) and multilateral trade rules have thrust the WTO under the environmentalist spotlight.
4. New disputes are likely as the transition to a low-carbon economy evolves.

## QUESTIONS FOR DISCUSSION

1. Is the claim that attention to environmental issues by businesses has a positive impact on the bottom line and competitiveness justified according to the principles of ecological modernisation? Please discuss.
2. 'The criticism of the WTO on environmental matters is totally unjustified'. What are the arguments for and against this statement?
3. Choose a multinational company and research its environmental claims and records. Does the evidence indicate that the company's claims are genuine, or are they merely a public relations exercise? Justify your conclusions.
4. 'Concern for the environment and globalisation are incompatible'. Discuss this statement.

## ACTIVITIES

Research the approach to environmental matters in an emerging economy of your choice. Do your findings support or undermine the assumptions of the Environmental Kuznets Curve?

## SUGGESTED FURTHER READINGS

Calomiris, C. (2007). Food for fuel? Debating the trade-offs of corn-based ethanol. *Foreign Affairs*, 86(5), 157.
Goudie, A. (2006). *The human impact on the natural environment: Past, present and future*, Malden: Blackwell Publishers.

Harvard Business Review (2007, November). *On green business strategy*, Cambridge: Harvard Business Press.

Hussein, A. (2008). *Principles of environmental economics*, Rev. ed, London: Routledge.

Kolk, A., & Pinkse, J. (2008). *International business and global climate change*, London: Routledge.

Lomborg, B. (2001). *The skeptical environmentalist: Measuring the real state of the world.* Cambridge: Cambridge University Press.

OECD (2007). *Biofuels: Is the cure worse than the disease?* Report for the Roundtable on Sustainable Development held on September 11, 2007, SG/SD/RT (2007)4.

Porter, M., & Van der Linde, C. (1995). Green and competitive – Ending the stalemate. *Harvard Business Review*, 73(5), 120–134.

Runge, C. F., & Senauer, B. (2007). How biofuels could starve the poor. *Foreign Affairs*, 86(3), 41.

Trebilcock, M., & Howse, R. (2005). *The regulation of international trade*, 3rd ed, Chapter 16, London: Routledge.

Vaughan, S., & Nordström, H. (1999). *Trade and environment*, WTO Special Studies 4, Geneva: WTO.

# PART V

# INTERNATIONAL BUSINESS RESOURCE ISSUES

The final section of the book looks at the resource issues that emerge either as a legacy of the globalisation process or as a direct facilitator of the process. As such, there is a concern with both natural and human-generated resources within this section of the work. These reflect that the global system needs to be underpinned by a set of assets to allow the global system to evolve and support the international activity of business. There are also resources involved in globalisation that emerge as direct causes of the process, namely the international exchange of energy.

The first chapter of this section examines the rapidly evolving and dynamic international monetary system that has been a perennial source of instability within the global system. This monetary system has been a major cause of global systemic instability. Thereafter, the section moves onto the related themes of infrastructure and the global cyber system. The former looks at the importance of the physical systems that channel flows and enable cross-border connectivity. Linked to this is the increasingly important global data system, which channels the increasingly valuable flows of data across borders. The final section examines natural resources through the lens of the food-water-energy nexus. In so doing, it examines how globalisation is shaped by the desire for security across each of these domains.

DOI: 10.4324/9781315184500-20

# CHAPTER 16

# THE INTERNATIONAL MONETARY SYSTEM AND GLOBAL FINANCIAL INTEGRATION

## OBJECTIVES

This chapter will help you to:

- Identify the form, nature, and evolution of the international monetary system (IMS).
- Appreciate the role and function of the IMS in international business.
- Understand the emergence of global financial capitalism.
- Identify the causes of the global financial crisis.
- Understand the challenges of reforming the IMS.

The integration of national finance systems into a single integrated global financial system is, perhaps, the ultimate expression of the global process of economic integration. In no other market has the process towards a global resource base been so evident. Yet throughout its history, this increasingly integrated system has proved to be a source of instability for the global economic (and increasingly political) system. Through an assorted period of exchange rate instability through various developing and emerging (and more latterly developed) economic debt crises through the more recent 2008/2009 Global Financial Crisis, the IMS has perpetually demonstrated a capability to directly challenge the hegemony of the neo-liberal consensus that underpins the international business environment. Inevitably, a good proportion of this chapter will deal with the global financial crisis and its aftermath, as much of the process of global integration is shaped by its legacy. However, before addressing this issue, the chapter will initially offer a brief overview of the global financial system, including its evolution, form, and function. These are core to understanding why the global financial crisis had such a profound legacy for international business.

DOI: 10.4324/9781315184500-21

## THE IMS AND GLOBAL FLOWS

There is no single definition of the IMS, but Eichengreen (2008) offers arguably as close a definition as any by defining it as

> the glue that binds national economies together. Its role is to lend order and stability to foreign exchange markets, to encourage the elimination of balance-of-payments problems, and to provide access to international credits in the event of disruptive shocks.

This highlights that the IMS is the set of rules, connections, and practices that guides the interfaces between the global economy and the enabling international financial system. This is done through exchange rates and rules on trade balances/imbalances as a means of enabling international investment (both direct and indirect) and the allocation of finance between states. Implied within the agreements between states on the existence of the rules of the IMS is that states have confidence in them, that such rules are accepted and credible, that they offer liquidity to the system, and that rules for the elimination of potentially destabilising imbalances can be agreed upon. At the core of the IMS (and of the rules outlined above) is the existence of financial flows moving across borders in search of the most effective use based on the relative risk and reward that occur across different financial and economic systems.

The goal of the IMS, as a set of rules, is to create the conditions for the global financial system that allow for its orderly functioning and, in so doing, enable the exchange of goods, services, and capital and sustain economic growth. As such, the system should enable:

- The attainment of internal balance to allow for non-inflationary growth through the correct macro-economic policies.
- Enable efficient allocation of capital.
- Generate financial stability by seeking to identify, isolate, and counter risk to the system.

This depends on balancing the needs of states with those of the system as a whole, as well as accounting for and adapting to change within the system. As defined by the IMF, the core characteristics of a well-functioning IMS are:

1) A set of universally agreed rules (or conventions), mechanisms, and supporting institutions that define and enforce the core agreed rules of operation. This will include facets such as exchange rates, means for balance of payments adjustments, capital movements, and the holding of international reserves.

2) The absence of a large buildup of imbalances in either stocks or flows of capital. The system should allow for efficient allocation of resources, and its smooth operation should prevent imbalances both emerging and being sustained. This also involves preventing exchange rates from becoming misaligned or unstable.

3) The facilitation of global economic and financial stability through the effective governance of its monetary system to sustain and enable a stable and predictable system.

4) The ability to demonstrate effective system surveillance of both states and the system as a whole to forewarn of any potential instability and to mitigate systemic risks as soon as they become evident. The system also has to offer sufficient liquidity to support the alleviation of imbalances and to provide a framework for dispute resolution based on clear and understood rules.

Central to the ability of the IMS to be a credible set of beneficial rules is that it has to be shown to be adaptive to change. In that sense, it has to adapt its rules to reflect shifts in economic power and tensions within it caused by imbalances and divergent state strategies.

## GLOBAL BUSINESS AND THE IMS

The commercial salience of the IMS has grown with the shift towards global financial integration in both developed and developing states. The resulting global capital market is a core asset, enabling businesses to achieve their strategic ambitions. In a truly global capital market, the market for savings and wealth is driven by the highest bidder or the outlet that offers the highest returns, irrespective of the location of the investment. A global capital market also means that a wide range of assets carry the same risk-adjusted return. The development of a genuine global capital market is still some way off because of factors such as currency risk, the threat of government intermediation, and the resistance of actors to utilise foreign facilities.

The importance of the IMS to the global business environment derives from the rules established to enable states to value and exchange currencies. The system also provides a mechanism for correcting imbalances between a state's international payments and its receipts. A further aspect of the IMS is the determination of the cost of converting currency. Importantly, the framework provides a system for managing the internal and external aspects of economic policy. Within this framework, governments should seek to rationalise domestic policy objectives and stabilise the external value of their currencies. These policy objectives have increasingly been shaped by the globalisation process, notably the moves towards free capital mobility and global financial market integration. Domestic economic policies have often been guided by the need to manage these flows through the sustenance of a stable exchange rate. This underlines the importance of commitment and credibility to the rules of economic policy.

Inevitably, the business environment is shaped by access to and the availability of capital. The point of the system is to ensure that the emerging global capital market can allocate resources to maximise returns for the pool of available investment funds. To enable businesses to access this pool of funds, the system needs a degree of stability to overcome market impediments to their efficient allocation. There have been concerted efforts by policy bodies to secure an enhanced degree of stability within the system through measures to offer effective and coordinated management of economic policy through inter-governmental bodies such as the IMF and the World Bank or through measures via organisations such as the G20.

The most evident impact of the IMS upon business and its performance is through the exchange rate. Exporting businesses need to operate in foreign currencies, and the rate of conversion directly influences pricing strategies and feeds into non-price competition. The rate of conversion has a direct bearing upon the ability of businesses to compete effectively within both domestic and international markets. Issues related to the costs of converting currencies compound the issue of overvalued and undervalued currencies. For multinational businesses and SMEs alike, these costs can be substantial. Thus, minimising such impacts can be an important factor in shaping the form and location of an enterprise's activities. The exchange rate can affect the business environment, inducing uncertainty and increasing the risks associated with globalisation and trade. Exchange rate effects can also transmit themselves into the broader economic environment, causing further uncertainty and risk within businesses by stimulating inflation, altering the nature of growth, and creating unemployment with consequent effects upon fiscal and monetary policy.

Issues surrounding the exchange rate also highlight another key issue for business: economic stability. Economic stability is measured in broad macro-economic terms by low and stable inflation, a sustainable balance of payments position, low and mildly positive real interest rates, and a sustainable fiscal position. These conditions are key factors influencing investment decisions by enterprises. These broadly defined macro-criteria are increasingly related to the state of micro-economic reform, especially in terms of the regulation of factor and commodity markets. They are further related to another powerful factor, namely, the degree of political stability within a state or within the IMS as a whole. Political commitment and the credibility of political systems to deliver a favourable set of economic circumstances are powerful factors promoting the stability of the economic system.

These issues, in combination, influence the behaviour of investors, and their effects have their most evident short-term expression via changes in the value of the exchange rate. These issues also hint at the nature of the interface between business and the IMS, which stems from the need for foreign currencies to:

- Underpin trade, including export credit.
- Realise foreign direct investment (i.e., investment in physical capital, etc.).
- support portfolio investment (for the purchase of financial assets for long-term holding).
- Finance speculation (a demand based upon attempts by speculators to exploit differentials in asset prices, etc., purely for short-term gain).
- Underpin arbitrage (that is, the exploitation of price or rate of return differentials between states).

These cross-border flows highlight differences between investments made for short-term gain and those made for the long term. Each form of capital movement has a different motive and desired outcome and can expose the enterprise to risks from instability in local political and financial systems that can either reduce the value of the investment or render the funds irrecoverable. These are the financial risks faced by any business involved in the process of globalising. Changes in financial conditions also have the capability to undermine the profitability of investments. Avoiding this risk has been a primary motive behind the development of the single currency within the EU, where it was felt that the elimination of the exchange rate risk would stimulate trade among member states.

While there is an absence of any clear evidence to suggest that exchange rate risk deters globalisation, most internationalising businesses develop strategies to counter such risks. Companies can deal with exchange rate risk because:

- The hedging of risk on specific transactions is easy; the advent of advanced ICTs allows businesses to manage multi-currency cash flows to minimise the effects of currency fluctuations.
- A global financing policy provides a natural hedge, as funding foreign assets in local currency will offset currency movements and protect the value of the company.
- Not all currencies collapse at once, allowing companies to offset changes in one currency.
- Currency movements also affect competitors, meaning that a company may not be adversely affected vis-à-vis their competitors.

## THE EVOLUTION OF THE IMS

The evolution of the IMS has been shaped by market forces and by changes in policy design as priorities alter. These changes are most evident in terms of how policymakers have sought to reconcile exchange rate stability and domestic policy objectives in an environment marked by increased capital mobility.

The contemporary history of the IMS starts in the post-World War II era. Prior to this period, there were more informal regimes. For example, throughout much of the 19th century, sterling was the main international reserve currency of the gold standard era. Indeed, 60–90 per cent of trade was invoiced in sterling throughout the 19th century. In the gold standard era, each currency was denominated in a set amount of gold. For much of the pre-World War I period, this was sufficient to allow for financial system stability (see below). Over time, as the value of the gold standard was eroded, it was replaced by 'paper money', where the value was guaranteed by the strongest political and economic power. Formerly the UK, but more latterly the US. This was done by currencies seeking to maintain a fixed value vis-à-vis this currency. However, eventually, this proved difficult with states moving towards floating systems of exchange rates and eventually to the managed flotation of currencies that prevails today.

The gold standard appeared to manage free capital mobility with exchange stability, as it was underpinned by the commitment of the participants to the maintenance of gold convertibility, and domestic policy actions were subordinate to this objective. This was coupled with a lack of political pressure to re-orient policy towards other, more politically expedient objectives. The stability of the system was also assisted by the smooth interaction of the gold standard with private markets. Adherence to the gold standard was treated by investors as a seal of approval and allowed states greater access to foreign capital. This was aided by other stability-promoting factors such as freer, more flexible markets that facilitated internal adjustments to shocks without the need to resort to a change in the exchange rate.

This period of stability ended with the outbreak of the First World War. The legacy of the war in terms of its massive political and economic upheavals meant that the gold standard could not be restored as it had after previous conflicts. It was resurrected in the mid-1920s but had lost its robustness and was unable to cope with the 1930s depression and the reversal of globalisation that accompanied it. This fragility was driven by the emergence of competing policy objectives that undermined the credibility of the system. Further strains were created by the legacy of war reparations and debt, increased market inflexibility, and less frequent central bank cooperation. In 1931, the international system collapsed, capital flows diminished rapidly, states developed beggar-thy-neighbour policies, and there was a general shift away from the view that internationalisation was beneficial. The result was that protectionism increased and the global economy disintegrated.

No firm rules emerged for the IMS until towards the end of the Second World War, when the Bretton Woods agreements were signed (see Chapters 2 and 4). The new system allowed for fixed yet adjustable exchange rates and the use of exchange controls to avoid destabilising speculation. It also created the IMF as a means of facilitating monetary cooperation. Because of this flexibility, realignments were rare within the Bretton Woods system. Policymakers were unconvinced of the desirability of floating exchange rates and thus tried to keep rates as stable as possible. For many states, the exchange rate became the cornerstone of an economic policy in which the stability of the real economy and the exchange rate reinforced each other. With robust growth within the global economy, there was generally an absence of pressure to devalue or to revert to the beggar-thy-neighbour policies of previous eras. This was aided by the fact that states kept a tight rein on any potentially destabilising capital flows. This was not to last: business attempts to circumvent capital controls, diverging domestic policy objectives, and the inadequacy of international reserves helped bring the system to an end. The inflation of the 1970s was a primary cause of the collapse as states sought to delink themselves from the dollar as a means of preventing the spread of inflation to other developed states from the US.

The move to flexible exchange rates was a seemingly spontaneous reaction to changing economic circumstances. States could no longer offer the same policy solutions to solve their problems. Over time, this created a policy shift towards open markets, economic reform, and policy priorities shaped by a low inflation goal. This was the era when the removal of global capital controls began. The increased flow of capital across borders, combined with domestic policy imbalances and volatile exchange rates, created a number of crises within the IMS (see below), leading to calls for further reform of the system.

It is clear that a pegged exchange rate, free capital movements, and an independent monetary policy cannot be achieved concurrently. Much of the development within the IMS has revolved around shifting priorities among these criteria. For example, pre-1914, domestic policy was subordinate to the exchange rate. Bretton Woods used capital controls to give a greater degree of discretion in domestic economic policy. Policy priorities have been slow to evolve, possibly due to the strong grip of the ideologies that have shaped these arrangements, vested interests in favour of the status quo, a desire not to break ranks with other states for fear of upsetting markets, and the failure of policymakers to promote a coherent strategy for change.

By the turn of the millennium, over 100 states had declared a policy of allowing their currencies to float against others. This was a marked increase – around 37 per cent – over the previous decade. Despite this move towards flexibility, other states were trying to induce greater stability through the development of currency boards, dollarisation, or other semi-fixed exchange rates. This supports the view that the choice of exchange rate objective is perhaps the most important macro-economic policy issue to be addressed by states.

In its current phase of evolution, the IMS is characterised by a set of 'non-rules'. That is, there are no hard and fast rules regarding the exchange rate regime states must adopt, and consequently, most states have an independent monetary policy. However, the notion of freedom implied by such a framework is severely limited, and states are constrained by market-generated rules over the form and nature of economic policy. These stress the growing interdependence and integration to which domestic economic policies have to adjust. Thus, there is a culture of best practice that states hold as a means of ensuring stability within the context of the IMS. There is, however, a growing dissatisfaction with this framework as it has failed to solve instability within the system (see below). Such instability has the potential to undermine the benefits of the shift towards globalisation.

The Plaza Accord was to prove the cornerstone of the current rules of the IMS, namely that states would manage exchange rates as part of a broader strategy of inflation targeting. This was to be done via coordination between states. In this system, exchange rates are nominally floating but are subject to intervention by banks to maintain their value with reference to the desire to maintain price stability (most banks seek to maintain an inflation target of, at the most, 2 per cent per year). This can also be shaped by the need to adhere to the rules of localised currency areas where states (with a high degree of interdependence) seek to link currencies together on a regional basis. Such arrangements seek to reinforce price and monetary stability. Thus, there is no single set of rules, with states free to choose the type of exchange rate regime that best fits their monetary strategy. Thus, there are states within the IMS with fixed exchange rates, floating exchange rates, or hybrid managed floats. In short, states have discretion over which exchange rate regime they choose to follow. However, the practicalities are that free floats are really only followed by developed states. Most states will seek to manage the value of their currency to some degree.

Despite this discretion, there are also clear asymmetries within the system, of which the most important is that the dollar is still the dominant currency in international transactions and that the IMF has evolved to become increasingly important as a 'watchdog' over the IMS. This influence has risen to such an extent that the body has become an increasingly controversial component of the IMS, where it still sticks to neo-liberal logic, as embedded within the Washington Consensus, in the process of alleviating balance of payment problems.

## GLOBAL ECONOMIC CHANGE AND THE IMS

As mentioned, one of the core functions of the IMS is to adapt to change within the global financial and economic system. It is evident that there are major shifts happening within the global economy as the global centre of gravity shifts and as emerging economies become an ever more pivotal part of it. It is also apparent that financial interdependencies are becoming ever more obvious and intense, with the result that shifts in global financial cycles are becoming increasingly extreme in amplitude and duration. These changes – and as well as others – will have a big impact on system functioning and governance.

One of the most evident changes is that the global economic system is increasingly multi-polar, with emerging economies (especially the BRICS) becoming increasingly prominent economies and political forces within it. However, many of these states have not developed as effective governance and regulatory systems as those evident in advanced economies. Moreover, many of these states have built up large cross-border liabilities (notably China and its investment in US Treasury bonds). To the IMF, these factors can potentially raise a future risk within the system.

Another change has been driven by the characteristics of global financial integration and cycles within the system. Over the past three to four decades, global capital flows have increased tenfold. The flows have not only increased in volume and intensity; they have also become more geographically extensive, notably with regard to emerging economies. Alongside this, there has been a sharp rise in global external liabilities, which have grown from 30 per cent of global GDP in 1980 to around 256 per cent of global GDP in 2020. These flows of capital have also fuelled asset price booms across a number of states (as evident in US housing, a key driver of the GFC). This has driven an increased synchronisation of financial cycles between states, many of which are now closely related to the US cycle.

Fahri et al. (2011) identify that the IMS has to adapt to four key trends: two on the demand side and two on the supply side. On the demand side, the first is the 'great convergence' as emerging economies converge on the development of advanced economies. The legacy of the IMS is that the resultant growth in incomes runs ahead of the development of the local financial system to offer risk-free means of absorbing these funds, with the result that there is an increased demand for dollar-based assets. Second, the financial crisis in some emerging economies has increased the demand for lower-risk assets, notably those denominated in dollars. On the supply side, first, there is the emergence of new reserve currencies, though these seem far off from rivalling the dollar. Secondly, fiscal and demographic trends in the US suggest that consolidation is necessary and that the supply of assets will not be unlimited.

---

**Box 16.1: The emergent Beijing Consensus**

The idiom 'Washington Consensus' emerged in the late 1980s (see Box 8.3) as a collective term to describe the set of policy measures that Latin American states had to undertake as a means of avoiding their seemingly perennial debt crises. While the measures were developed by John Williamson in 1989, they were adopted by

Washington-based organisations such as the IMF, the World Bank, and the US Treasury as the preconditions under which support would be forthcoming. Very broadly, the term has become synonymous with the push towards market-based reforms within economies that needed support.

With the rise of China, there was increased reference within the policy narrative to a new consensus based on the form of capitalism adopted and promoted by this emerging power. This was in part a reflection of the disillusionment with the Washington Consensus but also that, in the aftermath of the Global Financial Crisis, new ideas had to be sought. The Beijing Consensus seeks to offer a more pragmatic and less prescriptive solution for development. This would involve a commitment to innovation, a concern with broader measures of economic success other than GDP (such as income distribution and sustainability), and a focus on self-determination. The main themes within this alternative perspective are:

1. Incremental over 'big bang' reform.
2. Innovation and experimentation.
3. Export-led growth based on a commitment to an open economy.
4. Macro-economic stability.
5. State capitalism to guide, control, and shape the liberalisation and deregulation process.
6. Authoritarianism, as there is no need for economic freedom to equate with political freedom.

These are based on the Chinese experience, and not all will be applicable to all. Indeed, many exclude authoritarianism in their definition of the Beijing Consensus. However, they do represent a step away from the neo-liberalism of the Washington Consensus. What these represent are competing conditions to generate growth. Importantly, the attention given to the Beijing Consensus not only represents a rejection of the Washington Consensus (though in practice China adopted many of the measures advocated by Williamson) but also of states seeking to approach globalisation on their own terms.

The rise of the Beijing Consensus reflects two important trends within the global economy. The first is the rise of China and how it is asserting its power within it, largely to the detriment of the US. China's hard power is creating increased influence through soft power channels, to the extent that many states are looking to China's example in their engagement with the global economy. Second, the Beijing Consensus reflects a decline in the core values that have underpinned the global economy, notably that growth requires democracy. In addition, there are economic implications, especially where enabling Chinese growth is an issue of global concern. Moreover, given the economic difficulties of the leading industrialised states, many emerging economies are looking at China as an alternative role model for economic development. The result is that they are abandoning the Washington Consensus as a set of guiding principles, with China looking to proactively change the rules of the game (notably with regard to trade distortive mechanisms). For some states, these latter actions indicate that it pays to undermine international rules or to apply them selectively.

# FINANCIAL STABILITY AND CRISES IN THE GLOBAL ECONOMY

The history of 20th- and 21st-century international finance is characterised by bouts of stability and instability. Investors of all shapes and sizes crave stability within the IMS to facilitate the making of investment plans, but involvement within the international financial system inevitably involves investors undertaking some degree of risk. While some investors seek out riskier investments in the hope that they generate an above-average return, others seek to avoid risk at all costs (the main forms and types of risk are highlighted in Table 16.1). However, when investors take excessive risks and returns from that risky investment are threatened, then the system tends to lurch towards a crisis: investment capital moves quickly out of specific economies or types of investment, causing instability within the financial system if the flows are of sufficient magnitude. Since the mid-1990s, the IMS has witnessed periods of stability and instability as the system continues to adjust to the legacy of a more open global financial system.

**TABLE 16.1** The risks of neo-liberal financial integration

| Risk | Definition | Drivers |
|---|---|---|
| Currency risk | Risk of a sharp decline in the value of the currency | • Absence of foreign reserves<br>• Inability to orchestrate multilateral currency rescues |
| Flight risk | Risk that holders of liquid financial assets will sell their holdings en masse in the face of perceived difficulty | • Investor herding<br>• Interaction with currency risk<br>• Rise in political uncertainty<br>• Absence of mechanisms to manage capital flows |
| Fragility risk | Vulnerability of an economy's internal and external borrowers to internal or external shocks that inhibit their ability to meet obligations | • Borrowers finance long-term obligations with short-term credit, creating vulnerability to changes in credit conditions<br>• Borrowers finance debt in overseas currency, making them vulnerable to currency shifts<br>• Finance of debt with capital that is subject to flight risk |
| Contagion risk | The risk that a state will fall victim to financial and macro-economic instability that is sourced elsewhere | • Financial openness<br>• Extent of capital flight and fragility risk |
| Sovereignty risk | A risk that a government will face constraints on its ability to pursue independent socio-economic policies | • Pursuit of contractionary policies to limit capital flight<br>• Contractionary policy to attract capital to the state<br>• Consequence of external assistance |

Source: Grabel (2000)

In general, the following types of crises can be identified:

- Currency crises: these are generated by a sustained speculative attack on the exchange value of a currency with the result that, to avoid rapid depreciation, the authorities are forced to act by using foreign exchange to defend the currency or by devaluing sharply (see, for example, the Argentinian crisis of the early 21st century).
- Banking crises: runs on banks or banking failures induce banks to suspend the internal convertibility of their liabilities. This compels the authorities to act to prevent the failure from causing a damaging loss of confidence in the banking system, as highlighted below. This was the type of crisis that was pervasive in 2007/2008.
- Systemic financial crises: these are severe disruptions to financial markets that curtail their ability to act effectively, with consequent damaging effects on the real economy. Again, this type of crisis was evident in the events of 2007/2008.
- Foreign debt crises: a situation in which a state cannot meet or service its foreign debt (see, for example, Mexico in the mid-1980s).

These different forms of crisis often have common origins (all of which can exist simultaneously), notably the accumulation of unsustainable economic imbalances and misalignments in asset prices or exchange rates. A crisis will be triggered by a sudden loss of confidence that exposes fundamental weaknesses in the economy in terms of the sudden correction of overvalued assets or the failure of key institutions. The vulnerability of states to such crises depends on the credibility of economic policy, the robustness of the financial system, and, of course, the size of the imbalance itself.

The factors that underlie the emergence of the imbalances that render an economy vulnerable to a financial crisis include

- Unsustainable macro-economic policies (such as a growing budget deficit).
- Large foreign debt.
- Large amount of short-term borrowing (which can result in a liquidity crisis).
- The size of the current account deficit.
- Weakness in financial structures.
- Global financial conditions.
- Exchange rate misalignment.
- Political instability.

These trends can also be accentuated by shifts in the trade cycle. These underlying causes of crises need to be differentiated from 'proximate' causes such as news and events. Assessing the vulnerability of states to such crises is difficult. However, indicators such as sharp changes in interest rates and the indebtedness of the banking system can be used as broad indicators. The presence of key features that render a state vulnerable to contagion (such as slow growth, an appreciating real exchange rate, and domestic macro-economic imbalances) compounds these issues. The herd-like behaviour of contagion is difficult to explain in any other terms than the fact that the cost of collecting information is increasingly at a premium in global markets.

The phenomenon of contagion challenges the conventional wisdom that currency crises are caused by undisciplined fiscal and monetary policy. Currencies are increasingly coming under attack despite underlying policy consistency. Currencies are increasingly attacked simply as a result of a shift in market expectations about the viability of a fixed exchange rate – a position that can become self-fulfilling as authorities raise interest rates to defend the currency's value. These changes in expectations are not formed in a vacuum but are usually the result of weakness in some aspect of an economy's fundamentals. Moreover, it is not evident that globalisation is to blame for these developments because, as the IMF has pointed out:

- Capital mobility was greater between 1870 to 1914.
- Foreign financing was more important during the period of the gold standard.
- Portfolio investment was more important during the gold standard.

In terms of preventing contagion, several approaches are possible. The first option is to make certain that banking regulation is adequate to ensure that the financial system is sufficiently constrained to limit the potential for a crisis to start, especially in terms of ensuring banks do not overexpose themselves to risky investments. Second, it is important that a credible exchange rate policy is backed by complementary domestic policies. The third option is for the economy to exhibit sound fundamentals in areas such as public finance and macro-economic performance.

Ensuring stability through market discipline is the solution chosen by many states. Indeed, support from the IMF is dependent on such measures. Some states have looked at the possibility of returning to capital controls or taxes to limit the flows of 'hot money' across borders. Such measures are unlikely to be promoted, as they are seen as a backward step in the globalisation process. In this context, pressure falls upon the relevant authorities to ensure the proper regulation of the banking sector and macro-economic stability.

According to Mishkin (2006), the major lessons for policymakers from financial crises are:

- To establish a sufficiently strong banking regulatory and supervisory system to ensure that banks do not take excessive risks.
- While it is beneficial in the long term, there are dangers to financial liberalisation without sufficient regulation.
- If the banking system of a state is fragile, a pegged or fixed exchange rate becomes increasingly risky.
- That there is an argument for the state to act as a lender of last resort to ensure financial stability.
- Price stability is important to solving financial problems, as inflation is a key economic risk.

According to Rose (2007), the common cause of most previous financial crises was monetary policy geared towards sustaining a fixed exchange rate. The problem with these exchange rate systems is that they require the subordination of domestic interests.

Ultimately, history has shown that when domestic needs conflict with the fixed link, the latter will be broken. However, the traditional policy of going for at best a managed float has been gradually replaced with a monetary strategy based upon inflation targeting. Under this regime, the central bank has a transparent pre-set inflation goal for which it is accountable. While less than half of the 30 OECD states follow such a policy, it is influential as many states (including the US) operate implicit targets. In addition, some developing states follow such a policy.

The attractiveness of inflation targeting is based on the belief that it delivers financial stability. The objective of low inflation is to reduce risk and add transparency to the financial system. Financial stability depends on reducing inflation as a means of restoring macro-economic stability. It also limits the ability of governments to use monetary policy to support the political cycle (that is, to engineer mini-economic booms in the run-up to elections). The policy means letting the exchange rate float relatively freely based on liberalised capital movements. Rose (2007) claims that the system would spread through Darwinian principles and that inflation targeting would reduce the role of the IMF and the US in the global economy.

## CASE STUDY 16.1: CHINESE SHADOW BANKING

An emergent force within the Chinese economic system (especially since 2010) is China's shadow banking system. This system is comprised of financial firms that operate in a similar manner to banks, offering the same services and assuming the same risks. However, they exist outside the formal banking sector, which means they do not have the same level of state-backed deposit insurance, access to lenders of last resort facilities from the central bank, or lower regulatory oversight. In combination, these increase the risk to the financial system due to these lower safety margins. Despite these risks, these banks are seen as important to the growth process by increasing access to financial services as well as lowering their price and availability, though these have to be set against the aforementioned risks.

The rise of shadow banking in China is best understood within the context of a system that is dominated by large (frequently state-owned) banks. In this formal system, the state offers a big steer to the banks through the regulatory system as well as more formal and informal guidance. However, since 2010, these constraints have been so tight that they have pushed customers towards the shadow system. This shift has also been compounded by:

- Caps imposed on lending by the central bank.
- Limits on loans to deposits of 75 per cent which is seen as constraining.
- The discouragement by the state of lending to certain sectors.
- Shadow banks have lower capital and liquidity requirements.
- Shadow banks are not bound by limits on loan or deposit rates nor by the central bank's requirements for reserves.

As a result, it is estimated that over 60 per cent of the business of shadow banks is disguised bank loans, where a bank uses the non-bank to sidestep regulatory constraints. As a result, the bank gets most of the rewards, burdens most of the risks, and pays the non-bank to operate as a front for its actions. The rest of the business of the non-banks results from the activity generated by the lower level of constraints on these businesses and in serving those users who are not generally well served by the conventional banking system. In serving these underserved customers, these shadow banks tend to use one or more of the following methods/instruments:

- Loans and leases by trust companies: these are financial companies that have an adaptable charter, which allows them to combine aspects of banking and asset management.
- Entrusted loans: made by large companies, these loans use banks and other financial bodies as intermediaries, often to companies within the same group or to customers or suppliers.
- Bankers' acceptances: these are issued by banks on the promise that a fixed sum will be paid in the near future (usually a couple of months) and are often used for non-financial transactions such as goods.
- Microfinance companies: there are firms (separately regulated from banks) that are allowed to lend small quantities of finance to support access to finance by small and rural borrowers.
- Financial leasing: this includes all types of leasing that are currently not on bank or trust balance sheets.
- Guarantees: these companies offer financial guarantees (such as enabling shadow banking transactions) and even extend to loans (even though this can be in contravention of their licences).
- Pawn shops and various unofficial lenders: these can be important lenders to households and small businesses. Their activities are also enhanced by other informal or even illegal lenders.
- Trust Beneficiary Rights (TBRs): these are, in effect, a basic type of derivative transaction where the TBR acquirer gains either all or a large portion of returns from a trust. These are often used by banks to mask loans on their balance sheets by moving them to a different investment category.
- Wealth management products: these are products (offered by banks or trusts) that generate a return based on the performance of a range of assets, such as a large loan or pool of loans. These are part of the shadow banking system, as they are seen as a ready substitute for bank deposits.
- Interbank market activities: these are also a substitute for deposits and are often used by the financing arms of large businesses that lend to banks as a means of avoiding regulations.

There is no direct consensus as to the size of the Chinese shadow banking sector. Estimates vary from 8 to 80 per cent of GDP, depending on the definitions deployed. Even then, this constitutes between RMB 5 trillion and RMB 46 billion. The Chinese government (via the Central Bank) estimates the sector to be 20 per cent of GDP. However, by 2017, it was estimated to be 25 per cent of GDP, though again, this figure is heavily disputed by Western financiers. Such ambiguity is clearly part of the problem, as there is no real consensus as to how big the risk to the system is from this source of finance. Evidently, the Chinese authorities are concerned, as they have begun to clamp down more completely on the shadow banking sector. This is compounded by the fact that of the two broad types of shadow banking activity (small lenders to small borrowers and Chinese banks transferring credit from their own balance sheets into the shadows), the latter is the dominant form and can often be used to hide bad loans or those that are illegal. Banks can either transfer assets internally via the creation of wealth management products sold to investors or externally via non-banks, who then channel these assets back into the system via asset management products. The important point is that this hides the health of the banking system. By the end of 2016, $3.7 trillion was invested through internal channels and $1.6 trillion into external channels. Of the former, there are about 44,000 wealth management products outstanding by the end of 2016. These are seen as especially problematic as they have short maturities, and they are almost six times the number of mortgage-backed securities that led to the GFC. Thus, for many, these represent a ticking bomb under the global financial system.

## QUESTION

Why is the rise of Chinese shadow banking such a concern for the global economy?

# THE GLOBAL FINANCIAL CRISIS (GFC)

While occurring – at the time of writing – over a decade ago, the GFC is nonetheless worth reflecting upon in terms of the development of international business. The GFC was a watershed moment in the development of the global economy. It was the moment when the global consensus on the benefits of globalisation began to break down. It is no exaggeration to say that the GFC has had a long-lasting impact on the global political economy. Not simply because it was a precursor to extreme austerity, it also fed populism and a clear erosion of the narrative that globalisation was always a good thing. It highlighted how emergent global complexity can allow singular events to penetrate deep into any state's socio-economic and political structures.

The GFC emerged after a period of relative stability within the IMS. This period of stability within the IMS led to the emergence of a number of illusions with regard to the state of the global system. The first of these was the 'great moderation' in the leading developed economies, which led to complacency as policymakers felt that growth was achievable without inflation by taming the business cycle through inflation targeting. This led many states to feel they could cope with financial innovation. Second, there was a perception that developed and developing states were decoupled, which led to the latter believing that they did not depend on the former. The result was that developing states did not invest or initiate reform. Third, there was a belief that growth was good for the poor, which led governments to ignore rising inequality. It was evident – but ignored – that the so-called 'trickle down' effects of global growth were not that evident for many citizens (especially in the US).

However, of the crises that have hit the IMS in the post-war era, there is little doubt that this was the most severe both in terms of impact and reach. It was not just a crisis within the global banking system that spread to the IMS; it was a process that led many to begin to fundamentally challenge the neo-liberal system and challenge the very basis of globalisation. Indeed, at the time of writing (nearly a decade since the GFC), it is evident that the crisis is still resonating throughout the global economic and political systems.

Prior to the GFC, there was a strong narrative regarding the rise of global financial capitalism, which created large volumes of transnational flows driven by deregulation, benign inflation, changes in financial economics, and technology, which led to an explosion of finance (as the ratio of global financial assets to annual world output rose from 109 per cent in 1980 to 316 per cent in 2007). This was also reflected in the emergence of new complex, innovative financial products (such as derivatives), transforming financial risk. These innovations were often driven by new players (such as hedge funds and private equity funds) and also a global glut of savings. These drove the emergence of an ever more polycentric global system based not just on big banks but also on smaller hedge funds and private equity investors.

Perhaps the major impact of this trend was to democratise global capital markets. Households can hold a more diverse array of assets and borrow more easily, thereby allowing them to smooth out consumption over their lifetime. At the corporate level, it has become increasingly easier for companies to merge or be acquired by other companies. This has caused controversy, especially with regard to the activities of private equity funds. However, the global market for corporate control has greatly increased the power of owners over management. Indeed, the move to this global financial capitalism had a number of arguments in its favour:

- Active financial investors can identify and attack inefficiency.
- It improves the global efficiency of capital.
- It imposes disciplines on management.
- It facilitates the financing of new activities.
- It can put old activities in the hands of people who can run them better.
- It is better able to cope with global risk.
- Investors can put capital where it will work best.
- It enables ordinary people to manage their finances more successfully.

However, from its outset, many were wary as to the risks created by this system, notably as it created new socio-economic divisions, was dependent on benign conditions, encouraged players to take big risks that were simply not sustainable (as was borne out by later events; see below), was untested by crises, and enabled tax avoidance. There was also a fear that the need for ever higher returns makes financiers take greater and greater risks that could undermine confidence in the system, something borne out by the events of 2007/2008 (see below). These risks were evident as rapid product innovation outstripped the capacity of users and regulators to understand these products, and the global nature of these products and organisations made their regulation problematic. In effect, the rise of global financial capitalism reflected the high point (as highlighted below) of the long process of deregulation that began in the 1970s. The incremental deregulation unleashed high rates of innovation within financial markets. This rate of innovation made global financial markets considerably more difficult to regulate.

In the post-financial crisis era, global financial flows have fallen substantially. From 1980, flows grew from 0.5 trillion (about 4 per cent of global GDP) to almost $12 trillion in 2007 (over a fifth of global GDP). However, since then, these flows have fallen back to around $5 trillion (in 2014), with them being about 7 per cent of global GDP. By 2020, the level of flows had still not reached the levels (as a share of global GDP) seen in the pre-GFC era. This fall in the level of cross-border flows has been created mainly by a fall in cross-border lending, though this may simply reflect a return to long-term trends in this international process. However, this has also been compounded by declines in both FII and FDI. McKinsey (2016) suggests that the share of global GDP represented by financial flows has remained broadly stable at 2 per cent of GDP. Moreover, when looking at inter-regional flows, the flows between North America and Western Europe are the most evident, but these only comprise between 0.5 and 1 per cent of global GDP. The only other financial flow of significance is between Western Europe and Latin America, which, in 2014, was between 0.1 and 0.25 per cent of global GDP, and China and Latin America, which was between 0.05 and 0.1 per cent of GDP. The other flows between regions were all between 0.02 and 0.05 per cent of global GDP. These figures suggest that despite all the rhetoric surrounding the size of global financial flows, they are of secondary importance to other flows such as merchandise trade (around 25 per cent of global GDP) and services (just over 6 per cent of global GDP). Moreover, between 2002 and 2014, McKinsey estimates that these flows only grew by 230 per cent compared to over 1,000 per cent for merchandise trade.

The decline in cross-border lending has been caused by new restrictions on capital and liquidity. This has been compounded by pressure on assorted stakeholders to lower the level of risk that financial institutions have in their investment portfolios. This has been exhibited by the trend of banks for the leading economies to lower their geographic reach with a renewed focus on home markets. This led to a short divestment of assets (many of which were overseas assets) with a value of over $¾ trillion in the five years since the financial crisis. In addition to this fall in lending, there has also been a reduction in investment in other assets, with cross-border flows for bonds, equities, and FDI being either down or, at the very best, stable. Indeed, cross-border FDI flows have both fallen by between 30 and 40 per cent over the seven years to 2014. This pattern for developed economies has also been mirrored in developing states. The only flows that sustained an upward trajectory over this period were international remittances for overseas workers back to their home economies, though these are relatively small proportions of total financial flows.

McQuade and Schmitz (2016) refer to the current post-crash period as the great moderation, as the intensity of hyper-globalisation in global financial flows has been replaced by an era of lower volatility and smaller volumes of international transactions as cross-border capital flows have returned to a long-term trend level. This has been fed by an almost permanent lower level of cross-border banking, with a trend in finance that is moving across borders, tending to flow 'downhill' to states with lower incomes and development where such flows have gained in importance. This great moderation has been driven by a number of factors, such as many of the factors that drove the hyper-globalisation of financial markets having run their course, financial integration in the euro zone, financial deepening in advanced economies, and portfolio diversification. These have been compounded by tighter regulatory oversight.

Since the onset of the GFC, international capital flows have fallen by almost 65 per cent. Banks are staying closer to home, with those flows that are occurring tending to be more long-term than short-term speculative. This reflects that liquidity has declined markedly since 2007, with European banks being the main cause of this decline.

The GFC highlighted the centrality of the US to the global system. It was in the US that the GFC started, and it was a process that was rapidly transmitted across the global economy. The effect of the GFC spread from the financial system to the trading system as economic activity fell, trade flows fell back, and unemployment rose. The direct impact on any given state was driven by the extent to which it was integrated into the global economy. However, even those states that are largely peripheral to the global economy (such as sub-Saharan Africa) were still indirectly affected as commodity prices fell.

While the catalyst for the GFC was the collapse of Lehman Brothers in September 2008, it was a result of a number of problems within the global financial system, but it can be synthesised as follows:

- Global financiers: there was a growing belief in the banking sector that risk could be banished when, in fact, all that happened was that it was lost sight of. High-risk mortgages that were offered to 'sub-prime' borrowers (i.e., those with poor credit) were turned into low-risk securities by being pooled with other loans. However, there were too many high-risk loans within these pools, which were tightly correlated. A surplus of funds led investors to seek out these risky products. However, when the housing market turned, these mortgage-backed securities slumped in value, which eroded trust within the system and led to a curtailment of short-term interbank funding. This led to the bank being light on capital, with balance sheets exposed to these risky assets.
- Regulators and central banks: these made a number of mistakes, including allowing the Lehman Brothers to go bankrupt, which panicked the markets. The result was that for non-financial firms, there was a lack of available credit to cover short-term financing concerns. This led to the crisis spreading from the financial to the non-financial sector, with governments having to bail out more firms than they would otherwise have had to. However, there were also longer-term issues where regulators allowed housing bubbles and current account deficits to rise. Moreover, central banks were too light on regulation, allowing banks to lower capital ratios (i.e., that proportion of their assets has to be in relatively liquid form). Thus, their cash flow was left exposed when the value of these assets turned down.

- Macro-economic backdrop: a period of low inflation and stable growth created an environment of complacency and risk-taking. This was compounded by an Asian savings glut, which pushed down global interest rates. The global saving glut led to a rise in demand for these risky mortgage-based securities. This was compounded by house price bubbles in locations like Spain and Ireland, which were fuelled by credit from northern eurozone states. This exposed European banks to a house price bubble, and credit surged into the peripheral states of the eurozone.

The GFC highlights the complexity of the IMS and how seemingly random events can have consequences far beyond what would normally be expected. This was evident through the process of contagion as a banking crisis turned into a sovereign debt crisis. Moreover, the spread was also aided by a 'credit crunch' as the desire by banks to repair their balance sheets led to them reining in funding other parts of the economy. For example, banks (both US and European) reined in international loans, leading to severe problems for those states and businesses that depended on these flows, and international trade credit was also reduced, meaning that exports and imports came to a standstill in many sectors and countries. This led to a deep recession. This, combined with the need for governments to shore up their banking systems with cash injections, led to a sharp rise in government debt. This led to the aforementioned sovereign debt crisis, as the funding of government debt began to raise questions as to whether governments could pay these funds back. Thus, at the core of the crisis was a triple dose of debt problems: households, corporations (especially financial businesses), and governments. With all the main players in the economy having debt issues, there was little scope for fiscal expansion to militate against the effects of the GFC.

The desire of consumers, businesses, and governments to deleverage and pay down debts at the same time created a big problem of contagion, enabling the crisis to spread from the financial sector to the rest of the economy and have a lasting impact. This created a balance sheet recession as cutting spending was better than other options, namely deflating debt or selling off assets against which that debt was raised. To militate against these governments and central banks in the crisis was to slash interest rates. However, this did not deliver growth, as the real economy was proving unresponsive to monetary stimulus. These bodies also engaged in 'quantitative easing' (by effectively printing money by buying financial assets) in the hope that this deposited cash would get them lending again and lowering long-term interest rates. However, these did not prove effective, as banks often used the cash to repair their balance sheets rather than lend. Moreover, monetary policy is being asked to do too much.

The unresponsiveness of the global economy to ultra-low interest rates led some states (notably the US) to undertake fiscal expansion. However, for many states, this was simply not possible, as many states saw debt rise as a result of the crisis. This was not due to expansionary fiscal policies but to lower tax receipts (about 60 per cent of the increase in debt) and a need to offer financial bailouts to secure the banking systems. As growth returned, many states sought to pare down debt with aggressive austerity policies to restore confidence in the system. This reflected an increasingly consensual view offered by Reinhart and Rogoff (2010) that if governments allowed debt to rise above 90 per cent of GDP, then growth would become more inhibited. Moreover, there was a belief that austerity could create growth by 'crowding in' the private sector, as they compete less with governments for funds. However, it does seem to suggest that austerity was more of a detriment to growth than a stimulant. This was borne out largely by the experience in the US.

While the most immediate causes of the collapse have been identified, it has been argued that these are actually driven by deeper-seated problems within economic systems. The first of these is that rising inequality set the platform for rising housing prices, as there was an emergent gap between expectation (rising) and income (flat or falling in real terms) that was to be filled by increased borrowing. This was to be done by allowing easier credit for home borrowing, thus enabling lower incomes to become more asset-rich. This, it was argued, offered a platform to begin to reduce inequalities. However, this strategy backfired, as the aftermath of the GFC was to actually increase inequality and its consequent social and political risks. The second is that banks grew too big to the extent that they became too big to fail. This systemic importance led to them taking excessive risks and creating a mortal hazard problem. Third, management performance-based pay systems facilitated excessive risk-taking. Managers who pay in stock have an incentive to drive stock valuations higher by taking on higher risk and higher return activity, which ultimately failed. Fourth is regulatory capture, where lobbying by firms led to regulators being compliant with industry demands rather than seeking to offer a check upon them. This facilitated deeper deregulation and allowed for higher risk-taking.

There are also questions to be asked as to whether economic liberalisation of capital is in every state's interest. It was pushed as part of the neo-liberal Washington Consensus, but there is little evidence that the benefits have been obtained by all. Indeed, it can credibly be argued that it actually made the GFC worse. This was compounded by the absence of global coordination between states, as the opening of markets has meant that credit and capital can no longer be managed under the jurisdiction of national bodies. This loops the argument back to the regulatory capture arguments and failure position noted above. This stresses that regulatory failure was structural due to the liberalisation of capital accounts.

## PROBLEMS IN THE IMS

The GFC also highlights a number of problems with the configuration of the current IMS.

The current system, more than any other system that preceded it, has been characterised by instability. The IMS does not seem to be particularly adept at enabling states to maintain internal stability while allowing for mechanisms to correct imbalances. It has been characterised by an ever more severe financial crisis. The Bank of England suggested that the current system has four main failures:

1. Missing markets: many emerging markets did not have sufficient mature financial markets, which led to surplus savings being attracted to advanced economies, fuelling asset price bubbles within them.

2.  International institutional frictions: in particular, the role played by WTO rules in encouraging some countries to undervalue their exchange rates. This was especially true for those states that were pursuing export-led strategies, which led to current account surpluses, which led to capital inflows into advanced economies.

3.  Imperfect information (particularly in financial markets): this includes asymmetric information, legal uncertainties, and differences in accounting practices; these do not allow investors to properly assess risk and generate moral hazard.

4.  Nominal rigidities: the ability of states to adapt to imbalances reflects the flexibility of prices (wages, prices, exchange rates). If these don't adjust, then imbalances are sustained. In general, these prices tend to be inflexible downwards.

Fahri et al. (2011) argue that the 'non-system' can be heavily criticised on a number of grounds, namely: generating exchange rate volatility; causing sudden switches of private capital flows; persistent external imbalances caused by net capital flows moving from emerging to advanced countries; unevenness in the adjustment process between borrowing and lending countries, as well as the asymmetry between the US, whose currency lies at the centre of the current arrangement, and every other state; and too large an accumulation of foreign reserves by emerging countries.

First, while the need to solve systemic imbalances in a manner that does not harm growth is still core to the IMS, the means of doing it through collective action is not. The result is that the focus of adjustment is on defect states. This means forcing them to adjust by undertaking measures to reduce imports, with the result that output will be lower. This problem has been evident in the eurozones as surplus northern states placed pressure on the deficit southern states to adapt, which resulted in tensions within the system. The other problem is that adaptation by deficit states can result in competitive devaluations, again creating tension within the IMS. This suggests that there are very limited policy options for states, some of which may exacerbate imbalances.

Second, the sheer volume of money floating around the system means that simply correcting this shortfall by the necessary volume of inflows (if in deficit) or outflows (if in surplus( of capital is not so straightforward. A state adjusting interest rates to attract capital to attract enough capital to cover its deficits is likely to attract capital flows way in excess of what is needed, creating vast speculative flows that can create chaotic capital markets.

The third problem is a reflection of the central role of the dollar (which is still the dominant reserve currency) and of the US. Those states following the dollar account for around 60 per cent of their GDP and population. This includes states that float in parallel to the dollar and those that peg their currency to the US currency. However, the Federal Reserve set dollar policy to suit US needs alone, meaning that currency moves follow US sentiment alone.

However, at the heart of the problem – which is magnified by these issues above – is the so-called 'trilemma' that states can only have two of three things: a stable exchange rate, openness to global trade, and discretion over interest rates. These problems have been highlighted in recent crises (such as the Asian crises), to which states have responded by placing the process of adjustment upon exchange rates. This meant de facto constraints on economic policy to limit the risk of disruptive speculation. However, even when making the trade-off, the system still has the ability to create turbulence as capital flows become increasingly widespread, for every time the US begins to signal a shift in policy, capital sloshes around the system, creating instability somewhere. For example, the US tightening of monetary policy has hindered capital flow out of emerging economies. Elsewhere, such action by the US leaves those states with dollar pegs having to endure rising exchange rates.

The core point is that the IMS remains subject to instability and ongoing crises. There seems to be little means by which imbalances are going to be rectified. In some cases, these imbalances reflect a glut of savings in Asian economies (where there is high precautionary savings due to an absence of welfare provision), which are looking for safe havens. In addition, governments have a strong incentive to run imbalances (especially trade surpluses) and to build up big reserves to militate against any economic instability. It is also noticeable that the US relationship with emerging economies (which often shadow the dollar) has become disruptive.

## REFORMING THE IMS AFTER THE GFC

Initially, the main regulatory response to the crisis was to revise the main international banking regulation that was agreed upon in 1989. The new agreement, the so-called Basel III, is a tightening up of the rules. It has sought to lower exposure to risk throughout the system via three main means:

1) Requiring banks to hold more equity and liquid assets.
2) Requiring banks to hold less debt.
3) Requiring banks to rely less on short-term funding.

Where states were especially exposed to the banking crisis and where bailouts were needed, many regulators sought to go further. Many have sought to reduce the scale of the so-called 'too big to fail' banks, which will split them into smaller entities with simpler business models. This, it is hoped, will prevent contagion throughout the rest of the economy. Other measures seek to limit the ability of banks to engage in too much risky activity that would leave depositors exposed. In the EU, there has been the pursuit of 'ring-fencing' where retail and investment banking are separated, though inevitably this will not eliminate risk entirely as retail banks will still offer mortgages. However, banks are resistant to activities that limit aspects of risk-taking and are concerned that too high requirements for equity or capital will limit growth as it will reduce their ability to lend. In the US (the source of the GFC), the Dodds-Frank Act was introduced, which sought to limit reckless lending, make risk assessment less opaque, and rein in the activities of the 'too big to fail' banks. The extent to which it has sought to inhibit bank activities across a range of activities has brought some resentment from the sector, which the Trump administration is looking to pare back.

At the level of the IMS, there were evident pressures emerging as a result of the GFC. The main problem was the failure of the system to prevent conflicts between domestic priorities and global stability. Moreover, the institutions of the IMS could be seen as negligent through their inability to really foresee the crisis. In reflection on the crisis, the IMF (2016) identified that in the pre-crisis era, the IMS was characterised by four weaknesses:

(i)   Inadequate global adjustment mechanisms.
(ii)  No global oversight framework for cross-border capital flows.
(iii) Lack of systematic liquidity provision mechanisms.
(iv)  A number of structural challenges in the supply of safe assets.

The net effect of these was to allow for the persistence of trade imbalances, exchange rate misalignment, large fluctuations in capital movements, and an excessive buildup of international reserves. Based on these issues, the IMF believed that any reform of the system had to focus on remedying these problems, namely improving policy coordination, improved surveillance of capital flow, improving safety nets, and improving the resilience of the system through lowering the risk profiles of those operating within it.

At the core of what the IMF tried to do to reform the IMS after the GFC was to more accurately reflect the complexity of the system through its governance. In practical terms, that has meant better surveillance of the system with more robust risk warning systems, enhanced liquidity, and improved mechanisms for cooperation. This latter goal was to be achieved through the creation of the Financial Stability Board as a means for covering means to improve coordination.

The Bank of England (2011) suggested a multi-level process of reform. At the level of the states, it suggests that there needs to be a reform of financial, labour, and product markets to allow for greater flexibility in prices but also – in terms of finance – to allow greater opportunities for finance to stay at home. At the global level, there is a sense that there could first be external pressure for states to adopt global norms to overcome imperfect information but also to undertake the reform desired due to market rigidities. However, the main thrust is to establish the correct mechanism through which more effective coordination can take place. This requires cooperation to ensure more consistent policy frameworks, and where such inconsistencies generate negative externalities between states. However, the limit to the effectiveness of such strategies is that they do effectively rely upon peer pressure for implantation. If peer pressure does not work, then the other option is to move to a formal rule-based system.

The 2008 crisis led many states to re-examine their regulations and to update and review constraints in light of events. Indeed, the severity of the crisis led many states to seek direct control via nationalisation of or (at the very least) increased state intervention in key financial institutions. The return of direct state intervention has led many to claim that this vindicates criticisms of a lightly regulated financial system. In addition, some states have taken unilateral actions to outlaw (albeit often temporarily) those products (such as derivatives) and practices (such as short selling) that contributed to the crisis and to limit or even ban investment by sovereign wealth funds.

However, the crisis within the global financial system – despite these nationalistic rules – reinforced the mutual dependence between national systems. This was reflected in a common global agreement among the leading industrial nations to coordinate efforts to address the problems. To some degree, this action superseded the initiatives of multilateral institutions that had not been involved in the formative stages of the crisis. These bodies only began to get involved when the crisis spread from banks to states (see above). As it evolved, the 2007/2008 crisis witnessed a sea change: as countries entered more difficult phases, they did not turn first to the IMF for support but to other states, most notably the high-performing emerging economies. These states not only had the necessary resources but also did not insist on the onerous conditions linked to the IMF. For example, Iceland initially turned to Russia for help. Ultimately, however, the slow pace of these talks led Iceland to approach the IMF. It is possible that this new approach could lead to the pragmatic emergence of a successor to the IMF. However, aid from these states can come with political rather than economic conditions attached.

The above reflects the credibility gap facing the IMF. The conditions attached to its loans proved unpopular with many recipients, although many states often ignored the requests of the fund to pursue their own interests. In some cases, states bypassed the fund, as highlighted by the creation of the Financial Stability Forum (an association of developed state policymakers and regulators) in the aftermath of the 1997/1998 financial crisis, which allowed many states to bypass the IMF. Others accused the US of undermining the IMF by bullying it into forcing exchange rate realignments as part of its strategy to force China into a revaluation. The increased reluctance of states to go to the IMF reflects its obsession – so claim its critics – with conditionality. This suggests the IMF needs to be more flexible in terms of funding (something it was already doing as, in recent times, it has gradually loosened its terms and conditions for funding). Indeed, the IMF has moved towards offering policy prescriptions only when absolutely necessary. This suggests that the Washington Consensus (see Chapter 5) is being reined in by stealth. However, there are also concerns as to whether the IMF's instruments offered are quick and flexible enough for the full range of crises.

The impact of the financial crisis of the early 21st century was so pervasive that the IMF started to regain some of its lost popularity. Massive extensions in its lending capacity were offered to enable developing states to gain access to the finance that dried up in the credit crunch. Between 2007 and 2009, financial flows into developing economies fell by almost 80 per cent. The fear that developing states could be shut out of an increasingly nationalistic financial system has led many to return to the IMF for finance. However, the extra funding from the IMF is unlikely to be enough. It is estimated that up to $1 trillion is needed, more than double what is currently on offer.

Over the longer term, many believe re-regulation of the banking and finance sectors is needed to avoid future crises. However, it is naïve to assume that re-regulation will solve the problems within global financial capitalism. Many of the innovations that created the problems in the first place emerged as a direct consequence of the desire of the financial industry to get around regulation. Thus, new regulations may only create new products to circumvent such rules. The problem was also created by the actions of politicians keen to spread access to cheap finance in support of their visions of home-owning democracies. To blame the financial crash solely on markets (see above) is simplistic: governments themselves played a key role in feeding the crash, notably by keeping interest rates too low for too long and by placing too much confidence in the ability of markets to regulate themselves. Past experience suggests that re-regulation needs to proceed slowly to control for unintended consequences.

## CASE STUDY 16.2: THE TOBIN TAX

In the aftermath of the GFC, there were many calls to seek to negate some of the more disruptive elements of the international financial system. One such proposal – and it is a longstanding one – is the Tobin tax. A Tobin Tax proposes to tax international financial transactions as a means of limiting the disruptive effects of speculation. The so-called Tobin Tax was proposed as far back as 1972 as a means of increasing the efficacy of macro-economic policy. The use of the tax is problematic because most bankers and economists dislike the very idea of taxing transactions and see it as unworkable. However, every time there is a financial crisis, the finger points at the destabilising effects of international transactions. This increases debates on the use of such taxes as a deterrent for such flows. However, these come against arguments about what exactly to tax and how to limit the avoidance of such taxes. Moreover, there is mixed evidence as to whether the tax would actually decrease volatility as intended. Indeed, some evidence suggests it might actually increase volatility.

In the aftermath of the GFC, the tax was not only seen as a means to deter the aforementioned speculation but also to enable the state to reclaim some of the money it had spent supporting domestic financial systems. Moreover, many states saw it as a means to build up a fund to cushion the system against further challenges from financial system instability. However, it was widely accepted that such measures would not ultimately prevent a financial crisis and that any tax could easily be passed on to consumers in terms of higher costs or lower interest rates. In addition, there is a fear that such a tax may push investment into less secure channels. Furthermore, there is a concern that the Tobin tax could be problematic as the volume of transactions may be a poor proxy for the benefits and costs of such flows, and the tax does not address the fundamental causes of financial instability – institution size, interconnectedness, and substitutability – that generate risk within the global finance system.

Some governments began to introduce independent measures to discourage banks from engaging in potentially destabilising activities. The UK, for example, introduced a levy on banks' balance sheets and on their overseas operations. These were alongside measures developed by the French and German governments. However, there is a consensus that the means of seeking a tax transaction won't work unless there is consensus. To that end, there have been discussions among the leading industrialised nations under the forum provided by the G20. However, agreement between these states has proved elusive. While they all accept that banks should contribute to securing the system, exactly how remains up for discussion. This reflects a largely zero-sum mentality among states with regard to its introduction.

The EU has been more proactive in the introduction of a financial transactions tax. This was an ambitious proposal, though yet again, the 27 states of the EU failed to agree on a common position. Many of those states with a sizeable finance sector were aggressively opposed, believing that the policy would lead to a reduction in EU GDP. Eventually, the application of the tax was on a more limited level, with just eleven EU states agreeing to implement the tax. This was allowed under the EU's 'enhanced cooperation mechanism' that allows such variances. On that basis, the measure was agreed upon in 2013. Though the UK challenged the proposal in the EU courts, fearing that it would disadvantage UK financial services businesses, this complaint was dismissed. However, with postponements (and despite its popularity with the EU electorate), the final decision to draft the tax was only completed in late 2016 – eight years after the GFC.

Overall, despite a lot of rhetoric with regard to the desirability of taxes to operate as a constraint on what is seen as the destabilising impact of speculative global finance, there has been little progress towards a global strategy. Where it has occurred, such as in Sweden and, to a limited extent, in the UK, the effects have been varied. When it was introduced in Sweden in 1984, there was a fall in trading but also no large increase in tax revenues. The measure was abolished in 1991. In the UK, the exemptions from the tax made their effect largely illusory.

## QUESTION

To what extent is the use of a Tobin tax justified?

## CONCLUSION

The integration of capital markets is only half complete, and full integration will only be achieved, if at all, within several decades. Restrictions persist on the ownership of international financial resources, especially pension funds. Thus, international portfolio diversification is very much in its infancy. Despite these limitations, this chapter has indicated that the IMS is a powerful force shaping the global economy. The power of international finance is an increasingly dominant issue on the domestic policy agenda as highlighted by persistent crises within the system. Despite the crises, any large-scale overhaul of the system seems distant.

## KEY POINTS

- The financial system has become increasingly globalised over the past three decades.
- This process has integrated national financial systems into a global system.
- The global financial system is subject to occasional crises due to imbalances within the system.
- The 2007/2008 Global Financial Crisis has led to a reconsideration of the benefits of global financial integration.

## DISCUSSION QUESTIONS

1) What is the rationale for the creation of a global financial system?
2) What are the major costs and benefits of the creation of a global financial system?
3) To what extent does the 2007/2008 global financial crisis erode the case for global financial integration?

## ACTIVITY

As a group, discuss the proposition that the 2007/2008 Global Financial Crisis demonstrates the limits of globalisation.

## SUGGESTED FURTHER READINGS

Bank of England Financial Stability Paper No. 13 – December 2011.

Eichengreen, B. (2008). Ten questions about the subprime crisis. *Financial Stability Review, 11,* 19–28.

Farhi, E., Gourinchas, P.-O., & Rey, H. (2011). *Reforming the international monetary system,* London: CEPR.

Grabel, I. (2000). The political economy of policy credibility: The new-classical macroeconomics and the remaking of emerging economies. *Cambridge Journal of Economics, 24*(1), 1–19.

King, M. (2016). *The end of alchemy: Money, banking and the future of the global economy,* Boston MA: Little Brown.

Mishkin, F. S. (2006). How big a problem is too big to fail? A review of Gary Stern and Ron Feldman's too big to fail: The hazards of bank bailouts. *Journal of Economic Literature, 44*(4), 988–1004.

Schmitz, M., & McQuade, P. (2016). *The great moderation in international capital flows: A global phenomenon?* (No. 1952). European Central Bank.

Reform of the International Monetary and Financial System.

Reinhart, C. M., & Rogoff, K. S. (2010). Growth in a time of debt. *American Economic Review, American Economic Association, 100*(2), 573–578.

Rose, A. (2007). Economic resilience to natural and man-made disasters: Multidisciplinary origins and contextual dimensions. *Environmental Hazards, 7*(4), 383–398.

Wolf, M. (2014). *The shifts and the shocks: What we've learned – and have still to learn – from the financial crisis*, London: Penguin.

## Key websites

Bank of International Settlements – www.bis.org/.
International Monetary Fund – www.imf.org/.

# CHAPTER 17

# GLOBAL INFRASTRUCTURE

**OBJECTIVES**

At the end of this chapter, the student will be able to:

- Identify the role that infrastructure plays in the global economy.
- Understand how global transportation shapes global interaction.
- Identify the core physical features of the global energy system.
- Comprehend the challenges posed by global information infrastructure.

## INTRODUCTION

Infrastructure has evolved into a rather amorphous concept, but as defined here, it is the physical facilities that enable the transmission, distribution, processing, and storage of tangible and intangible materials across space. Commonly, these physical systems are developed on a national basis to support national needs. However, with growing interaction between states, there is a need to reflect upon how these systems facilitate international flows between states. In this context, this chapter will focus on those aspects of the global infrastructure system that enable global interaction. In so doing, the chapter will focus on the three major physical infrastructures that have distinct global and international dimensions, namely transport, energy, and information. While recognising the interlinkages between these sectors, the respective sections within this chapter will address the salience of each to the maintenance and development of the global system. These will be addressed in turn, though at first, the chapter will turn to the form and nature of the global infrastructure system.

## THE NATURE OF GLOBAL INFRASTRUCTURE

Infrastructure supports the core basic functions of society and can include a wide range of facilities, including social (e.g., hospitals and schools) and soft (i.e., institutional

DOI: 10.4324/9781315184500-22

systems) infrastructure. However, it is economic infrastructure that concerns this chapter. These are the infrastructures that enable and support economic interaction within and between economies. Nonetheless, there is a strong interdependence between these soft and hard infrastructures, as they remain central to economic and social development at the state level. This deems them critical to state system functioning, meaning that should they be damaged or fail in some way, then economic, social, political, technological, and political systems would be deeply impacted, and normal functioning would be impossible. For these reasons, these critical infrastructures are developed, controlled, and frequently owned by the state to ensure universal access for all users and to ensure their ability to support economic and social activity within a state. This means that new infrastructure systems have to exhibit the following characteristics:

- Sufficient capacity to cope with the demands placed upon it by users. In the case of economic infrastructure, this is represented by anticipated traffic flows.
- Users can be secure in the process of utilisation, notably that the system is safe to use and free from threats that could impede safe passage.
- The system is reliable in that once traffic enters the system, it can expect to reach its destination free from any known disruption. This implies that systems need to be maintained and adapted to the forces (such as climate change) acting upon them.
- That the system is accessible to all. Thus, while users can expect to pay a fee for usage, they are not actively excluded from using such systems due to the wide penetration of infrastructure systems across a territory.

These facets underline why the provision of infrastructure is central to the effective economic functioning of a country and to its competitive positioning (and of those businesses located within it) within the global economy. It is widely accepted that infrastructure does not merely allow a state to control the space under its jurisdiction but also offers significant economic benefits, notably in terms of increasing labour productivity, lowering transaction costs, and lowering the cost of core inputs (transport energy, etc.) into a business. Businesses also benefit and have an incentive to locate within a state if they know that a country's infrastructure system exhibits the aforementioned characteristics (i.e., capacity, reliability, and security). Of course, this does depend on a state building an infrastructure system that responds to user needs and not vanity projects.

Of course, the notion that infrastructure exists as a separate global entity is a misnomer. The global infrastructure system is the totality of national systems, and the globality of a feature of such nature exists insofar as flows between these national systems are the ease with which international flows move between these systems. In these terms, two issues with regard to national systems become important:

1) Border infrastructure: those are the points at which flows move between national systems and the impediments to such flows. The nature of state borders is that flows seeking to cross borders are concentrated in a limited number of places to ensure effective management and filtering. Clearly, such impediments are likely to be higher for tangible products, but intangibles will also be subject to filtering and examination when entering or exiting a territory. The longer these checks take, the higher the transaction costs

involved in engaging in international interaction. This suggests that to aid international flows, these border systems need to have sufficient capacity to cope with anticipated traffic and effective administration to ensure speedy filtering.

2) Hinterland infrastructure: these are those infrastructures within a territory beyond the point of entry or exit to ensure that traffic flows are readily dispersed across a country they have entered. This depends on high-capacity backbone networks (e.g., motorways, high-speed rail, fibre-optic information infrastructure, etc.). This underscores that all major arteries within global systems have to ensure that flows can be readily dispersed from points of concentration.

In combination, these border and hinterland infrastructures operate as gateways for the development of a global infrastructure system based upon the development of a global network of national systems. While such gateways have been a perennial feature of national infrastructure systems, there has been increased pressure upon these structures due to the nature of globalisation in particular the increased intensity, extensity, velocity, and impact of global flows. It also reflects an increased interdependency between national systems where there is a high degree of interaction between states. These place an adaptive tension upon national systems to adapt to enable the benefits of such flows without increasing the risk to national security. This creates the risk of a potential conflict between a country's political and economic needs and suggests a need for increased international coordination and cooperation to mitigate the risks created by such a conflict so as to ensure the confidence and security of cross-border flows.

However, despite such concerns, it does have to be remembered that cross-border flows, or those flows that are internationally sourced or have a non-domestic final destination, are only a small fraction of the total flows that move across a country's infrastructure. Overwhelmingly, the flows that move across a country's infrastructure systems are internal, meaning they are between users located within the same state. Most trade (81 per cent) is within the borders of a country, 93 per cent of telephony, and over 90 per cent of human mobility. Thus, the main purpose of a national infrastructure system is to support internal movement, not mobility between states. In many states, this interstate movement is largely peripheral to the operation of national infrastructure. Where such international flows are salient to a state is in the case where a country operates as a small open economy and where it operates as an important conduit for global flows (such as Singapore and the UAE). Nonetheless, however secondary these flows may be to the flows within a country, they are often important and underline the complexity embedded within such systems.

Being based on national systems, the global infrastructure system has a number of discrete dimensions. These all, singularly or in combination, reflect the embedded nature of globality to varying degrees within national systems. The main components of the global system are noted below.

• Inter-state connectivity: this is the conventional dimension of globality noted above. This is where products move into a country via border crossing. These can be across locations where states have physical borders or where goods being traded across long distances enter the jurisdiction of the end user.

- Global commons: while this is not considered infrastructure in a conventional sense as it often has no physical structure (notably in transport), the global commons are those areas of the earth's surface over which global flows pass through and over which there is no direct territorial control. Included within the definition of the global commons are the high seas, airspace, outer space, and cyberspace. The management of these global commons is often done via international treaties.
- Transit connectivity: this is where international flows move over the territory of a third state, where that state is neither the source nor the destination of the flow. This issue is especially important for landlocked states that either have no direct access to the main global logistics channels or where energy pipelines have to pass through a third state. This vulnerability is also evident for small island developing states where inadequate domestic infrastructure leaves them dependent on other states.

These three basic facets reflect an embedded dependence within the global system. It is evident that this dependence is higher for certain types of states than it is for others. These states need intense interaction with other states' systems in order to function effectively. However, looking across the global economy as a whole, it can be argued that a global network of interconnected national networks aids the development of global economic systems through the following channels:

- Control: cross-border flows are channelled through a limited number of entry and exit points (see above) at a country's borders. This enables the country to monitor, manage, and, where required, tax the cross-border flows. The government of any given state seeks to monitor cross-border traffic for a multitude of reasons, not the least of which is the desire to inhibit the entry into the indigenous economy of illicit products and other restricted flows. It also seeks to prevent the export of products the country has banned or limited in terms of transnational flows. This is important so as to allow states to maintain trust in the global system and to ensure that transnational movements are effectively policed.
- Security: the link to security is in part linked to the notions of control noted above, especially with regard to the security threats posed by illicit entry into the system. Therefore, border infrastructure is key to filtering out those movements that contravene domestic security. Infrastructure is also linked to broader security themes, notably with regard to the extent to which the country depends upon international markets for core necessities such as food and energy. In this case, infrastructure is intimately linked into food and energy security.
- Cohesion: when looking between countries, interconnecting infrastructure systems promote a time-space and cost-space convergence that lowers the transaction cost of engaging in international interaction. Thus, the ease of flow between separate national systems will be a core driver of the globalisation process.
- Growth and development: as mentioned above, the development and maintenance of a mature infrastructure system is central to a state's economic development and growth. When viewed in an international context, the development of such systems

will be a foundation stone for a country's international competitiveness. Moreover, the development of such mature systems globally should allow for the growth and more extensive development of international trading systems.

The above analysis operates as a core building block through which the separate global systems can be contextualised. These broad facets are evident across all of these separate, but interconnecting, infrastructures that are at the core of facilitating global interconnectivity.

---

**Box 17.1:** The vulnerability of the global infrastructure system: the case of Iceland's Eyjafjallajökull volcano

There is arguably no better expression of the vulnerability of the global infrastructure system than the impact of the 2010 eruption of the Icelandic Eyjafjallajökull volcano and its disruption to the air traffic system. The ash plume from the eruption threw ash up 3 km into the air, with the resultant concerns regarding energy safety causing the largest disruption to global air traffic since 2001. The closure of a large section of European airspace not merely disrupted the global travel business; it also had extensive knock-on effects on exporters as well as general production and productivity. This underlines the central role that air transportation plays in the basic functioning of society and commerce.

The most immediate impact of the eruption was a sharp decline in air traffic across Europe, which fell by over a quarter on the first day of the eruption (it lasted six days) and then fell steadily as the risk was assessed, with the level of disruption peaking at 80 per cent of flights cancelled on the third day of the disruption, with flights falling from 25,000 a day to 5,000. Over the entire six days of the eruption, some 100,000 flights were cancelled (a 53 per cent reduction from the previous week), with the UK, Ireland, and Finland being especially affected. This affected nearly 2 million passengers internationally (i.e., outside Europe), as many of the affected airports were major hubs for international traffic. These are dwarfed by affected European passengers, of whom up to 7 million were affected. This highlighted that the impacts were global, as they disrupted the entire aviation system, especially the key trans-Atlantic and Europe-Asia routes. It is estimated that the cost to the aviation sector was US$2.2 billion. However, these were direct costs for the airlines themselves. In addition, there was an impact upon destinations where there was an impact upon hotels, restaurants, taxis, shopping, and entertainment. Here, the loss was estimated to be US$1.6 billion in lost revenues, primarily to the hospitality sector. To some extent, these impacts were mitigated by the spending undertaken by stranded passengers in hotels and restaurants.

Looking beyond the effects on the hospitality sector, there was also an impact on other sectors, notably those that relied upon air transportation. This was especially evident in the supply of fast-perishing goods (such as flowers, fresh fruit, etc.) from locations such as Kenya, Zambia, and Ghana and in those value systems that rely heavily on just-in-time production methods. This disrupts the movement of high-value items, which are often low-weight (e.g., electronic components). This highlights how the eruption had a broader impact on international trade, especially within the two segments noted. In addition, there was the economic impact of stranded passengers, which represented a net loss of 2.8 million working days. This was estimated to be US$490 million.

## Box 17.2: China's Belt and Road Initiative (BRI) strategy

Launched in 2013, the BRI is an overarching term to cover two separate initiatives. The first is the Silk Road Economic Belt (SREB), which seeks to improve overland infrastructure between China (especially western China) and Europe. The second is the Maritime Silk Route (MSR), which seeks to improve ports and other maritime infrastructure as a means of improving maritime connectivity between China and European markets. In combination, within the BRI, the aim of these programmes is to increase connectivity between Asia, Europe, and Africa to enhance trade and promote growth. The ultimate endpoint of both the SREB and the MSR is Venice, where it will connect to national and regional systems. To support the realisation of this project, the Chinese government has set up the Asian Infrastructure Investment Bank to run a Silk Road Fund (estimated to be worth some $40 billion).

The five routes included in the BRI will involve (both directly and indirectly) some 65 states stretching from the Western Pacific to the Baltic Sea. These states account for only 65 per cent of the global population, nearly 40 per cent of its GDP, and just over 30 per cent of its consumption. The links between these states will not merely focus on the physical connectivity offered by infrastructure but also those linked to policy, trade, finance, and people. These are seen as central to creating the common economic zone that is at the core of the BRI. However, trade and investment between China and other states are not the only drivers of the BRI. It is also planned to be a means through which China can increase the demand for Chinese infrastructure products and services, such as construction and engineering. There are also less tangible and indirect objectives, such as increasing Chinese diplomatic goodwill and helping to internationalise the renminbi.

In many cases, the BRI is a repackaging of existing programmes, especially those in western China and Eurasia. Increasingly, these otherwise disparate initiatives are bundled together into sub-programmes of the BRI, such as the China-Pakistan Economic Corridor. The priorities within the programme will be linked to two domestic objectives. The first is to promote the development of Western China through the promotion of external trade links. In China, 16 of its 27 regions are covered by the BRI, with more seeking to participate; the undoubted aim is to stabilise the more restive provinces. The second is to improve Chinese connectivity with Southeast Asia due to its importance for trade. The MSR is seen as a longer-term objective due to the geopolitics of the South China Sea and China's limited advantages in this domain. This reflects that BRI is mainly a domestic strategy to secure China's long-term strategic objectives, which are reflected within its 'going global' action plan. These positions BRI as very much an export-driven strategy linked to offering finance for the development of partner states infrastructure systems. Indeed, it is estimated that China will offer up to $1 trillion over the decade from 2016 to support the BRI. This finance is not aid but more often preferential debt funding to states (though equity will also be part of the plan), but it is merely 20 per cent of the amount needed to fulfil the programme. Overall, the timeframe for the BRI is at least 30–40 years, with 2049 seen as a key date as it coincides with the centenary of the foundation of the Chinese Communist state.

Evidently, BRI is a key development strategy for China, and it's in part a reaction to a slowing rate of economic growth and falling exports, as well as a need to transform its economy towards service-driven growth. Moreover, BRI is also a reaction to its overcapacity in specific sectors (such as construction and steel), which need to find new markets to avoid painful restructuring. Thus, BRI will in part seek to export excess capacity while also stimulating demand for its goods and services. However, as mentioned, BRI is not simply about trade, as there is an aspect where China is seeking to use the programme as a means to attain a regional leadership role. This underlines that the BRI is not an aid programme but one where China seeks a 'win-win' scenario.

As China seeks to only cover around a fifth of the amount needed for BRI, it will rely upon other sources of finance to ensure its realisation. These parties will include other states and private finance. To realise this finance from the latter, BRI has to offer a clear demonstration that it offers benefits to international businesses beyond China. This can be done directly through the construction process (either solely or in partnership with Chinese firms). They can also be key suppliers of technology and know-how for these projects. There may also be indirect benefits from improved trade relationships. There could also be opportunities for finance to get involved in projects that have a low-risk profile, as they are deemed 'too big to fail' by the Chinese state.

The BRI is not without its critics. Many see that the programme is strong on vision but often weak on the practicalities of implementation. For example, infrastructure will be developed through debt, not through largesse, with no clear idea as to how that debt is to be repaid or what would result if it did not. Moreover, there is concern that the BRI is more about transit than development. As such, for many states that may come to rely upon the BRI, there will be little long-term benefit. This is compounded by the fact that in the construction phase, there is a strong preference for builders to use Chinese over indigenous suppliers. This means that local economic impacts could also be minimised during the construction phase. Finally, China's recording of the development of foreign infrastructure is not unblemished. There are many projects funded by China that have not lived up to the developmental potential promised.

# THE GLOBAL TRANSPORT SYSTEM

While transportation infrastructure can cover a multitude of modes, for the purposes of the analysis within this section, the focus is on those infrastructures that underpin the global mobility of goods and people, namely the global network of maritime and aviation ports. These are the modes that dominate the global logistics and international passenger sectors, respectively. Inevitably, in a book of this length these issues cannot be explored in the depth they deserve.

## The global maritime network

This network consists of a network of logistics hubs (often based around port infrastructure but with strong links to other modes) and links that connect these major hubs together. These create a network of hub and spoke systems that enable global transmissions of goods. The trade in goods is dominated by maritime traffic (including rivers and oceans), with over 90 per cent of goods traffic by volume. This underlines the centrality of port-based infrastructure to the global trading systems and to the global value chains that support this process of economic interaction. The dominance of maritime trade over global trade flows is driven by a number of factors, namely

- Divergences between places of production and places of consumption (such as energy), and the fact that maritime transport is the most effective means of moving these materials over long distances.
- The emergence of global value chains is based upon the international division of labour and a need to ensure that partially completed goods can be moved in volume across this global value chain.
- Technical improvements that allow for the rapid loading and unloading of containers and other forms of maritime traffic.
- The availability of economies of scale as the size of ships has grown.
- The ability to offer high-capacity continuous services that are able to operate on a global scale even if they are at comparatively slow speeds.

The core components of maritime transportation are the dedicated routes that traffic goods across the globe. These routes operate along dedicated sea lanes (often only a few kilometres wide), often traversing the global commons to interconnect seaports, though most maritime traffic tends to occur along coastlines. The services are based on regular services between these ports that keep a constant flow of traffic between the major economic centres of the global system, namely East Asia, Europe, and North America. Thus, at the core of the global system are regular circuitous east-west routes between these major economic centres (which cover 40 per cent of container traffic on their own). On this route are major hub ports such as Singapore, Dubai, and Rotterdam, which then feed the short-sea shipping networks that serve locations with lesser volumes of trade as well as connecting to other modes of transport such as road and air.

For much of the 20th century, maritime traffic was dominated by the transmission of liquid bulk (i.e., oil, etc.). This has shifted towards dry bulk and containerisation. The rise of containerisation (an inter-modal form of freight transfer that allows goods to be placed in standardised containers) has not only allowed for rapid movement between moves but also allows for easier movement over longer distances. This is more efficient when compared to other modes, such as dry bulk shipping, and now comprises nearly 90 per cent of non-bulk cargo flows. Over the 20 years since 2000, this traffic has grown

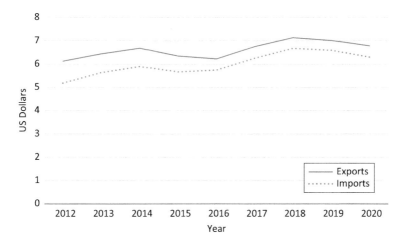

**FIGURE 17.1** Trends in ocean trade (Source UNCTAD

nearly threefold, fuelled largely by the rise of Chinese manufacturing and the use of containers to transport these products to major markets. China, on its own, represents some 30 per cent of global container traffic. This reflects a broader domination of container traffic in Asia, which represents nearly 60 per cent of total flows. This represents a long-term shift of maritime traffic away from the US and Europe.

## CASE STUDY 17.1: GEOSTRATEGIC SIGNIFICANCE OF THE GWADAR PORT

The port of Gwadar lies at the end of the China-Pakistan economic corridor (CPEC) on Pakistan's Indian Ocean coastline. Not only is it one of Pakistan's major ports, but it has become increasingly important as a key conduit and project for China's Belt and Road Initiative (BRI). One of Pakistan's major seaports occupies critical points on sea routes from the Middle East to China, notably with regard to its proximity to a number of major choke points. This proximity is important not simply for the importance of maintaining the openness of these sea lanes (notably with regard to the flows of oil that move through these channels to China), but also in providing a gateway to Africa and also in being at the end of the CPEC. In an area where piracy has been common, there is also the potential for the port to be used as a base for counter-piracy operations. The CPEC is important to both China and Pakistan, not simply through the fostering of economic development in the latter, but also by offering maritime access to the landlocked (and often remote) provinces of China (notably Xinjiang). These benefits for the regions are also expected to extend to other states, notably those that are landlocked (such as Afghanistan), which are also offered better access to maritime channels. To support this role, China is investing heavily in the port to expand its capacity. Over time, the plan is to expand the capacity of the port from being able to berth two or three large ships (above 50,000 tonnes) to 150 by 2045, with the capacity to hold up to 400 million tonnes of cargo. The port is central to Pakistan's export strategy, as the other major ports will not be able to match this increase in capacity.

For Pakistan, the development of Gwadar is important to allow the state to diversify trade away from the current dominant maritime hub of Karachi. This port accounts for 60 per cent of Pakistan's maritime trade. Pakistan is mindful that Karachi's proximity to India creates a strategic vulnerability should relations between these South Asian states deteriorate. There are similar security concerns with regard to China and its relations with India. China's dependence upon Middle Eastern energy means that it has a strategic vulnerability in the sea lanes within proximity of India, as well as addressing China's ongoing Malacca Dilemma created by the bottleneck in this region, which could work to restrict flows through these channels. Thus, one of the functions of the CPEC is to develop energy pipelines to bypass these potential bottlenecks and transport oil through Pakistan into the western provinces of China. It is envisaged that Gwadar port will be a major terminus for this evolving energy system.

In time, it is expected, as suggested above, that Gwadar port will evolve from being a purely commercial infrastructure to becoming a dual-use military-commercial facility. The view is that this allows China to project hard power across the region, notably with regard to ensuring the sustenance of flows through the major transit channels. This clearly ties the port to Chinese security concerns. However, the capacity of Gwadar and the CPEC more generally to support these interests is directly impacted by the relatively poor level of security within Pakistan, where projects linked to the CPEC (as well as Chinese citizens employed on such projects) have been attacked. This problem is especially acute within the Baluchistan province in which the port is located. This will limit traffic flows into the port and its ability to act as a catalyst for further investment. This declining internal security position within Pakistan is compounded by the deteriorating economic performance of the state.

However, China has only increased its commitment to the port. It has turned loans into grants to support the port and broader infrastructure development around the port and has also taken over the day-to-day operations of the port. Overall, under the agreement, 90 per cent of the port's revenues go to the Chinese operators. Despite this, there is a feeling that the port is something of a 'white elephant', not simply due to the underdevelopment of the CPEC it was designed to enable but also due to the sustained dominance of Karachi in terms of export flows. By 2023, the port had yet to generate the anticipated traffic flows, nor had its development trickled down to improve the lives of the region's citizens. Part of the problem is that the supporting infrastructure to facilitate the development of the port has yet to be developed. This poor connectivity exists both within the port and its immediate environment but also beyond into the region, state, and as a whole. In short, traffic struggles to reach and depart from the port. This applies not just to transportation but also to an unreliable energy supply to the port. Indeed, two power stations designed to support the port have been subject to substantial delays.

## QUESTION

Is the development of the Gwadar port more in China's interests than Pakistan's?

Of the top 50 container ports (in 2020), the trends noted above are evident, with East Asia making up 31 of the totals and Europe and the US comprising just 11. Overall, Asia has 36 of the top 50 ports. This dominance by East Asian economies of containerised port infrastructure is also reflected in the fact that of the top ten container ports, nine are in East Asia (with seven in China), and Rotterdam is the only non-Asian port on the list. This dominance of East Asian ports over global maritime trade has highlighted what can be seen as a key vulnerability within the global system of maritime trade. The more flows are concentrated on these East Asian ports, the more global traffic is at risk of being disrupted. This was evidenced during the COVID-19 pandemic, where the Chinese zero-COVID policy led to periodic sharp reductions in Chinese port capacity, this was a major contributor. There was a backlog at the main container ports, with travel restrictions limiting access to truck drivers, and this was compounded by shipping companies cancelling sailings as activity within the main manufacturing hubs was constrained. COVID-19 and the policies to counteract it highlighted a further danger of concentrating activity within a few locations, as it led to the global logistics systems being severely restricted in terms of growth. As the Chinese ports had limited capacity, this fed into lower port volumes and large backlogs in ports. This in turn led to a sharp rise in container prices as logistics capacity was mothballed. While it is only a single event, it does highlight one of the major challenges within the global logistics systems, namely that of choke points. The major global logistics choke points are mentioned in Table 17.1. These choke points do not merely impact the transportation of goods from the manufacturing hub of East Asia but also reflect that substantial amounts of oil and gas are also transported through maritime channels and are also subject to these potential constraints.

## The global aviation network

Prior to the formative decades of the 20th century, the majority of international passenger traffic was through maritime channels, notably the global liner system. This has now been replaced by the aviation industry. Figure 17.4 highlights that since the 1970s, there has been a rapid rise in the volume of international air passenger traffic, though the sector remains marginal in the freight sector, where its role is limited to high-value or perishable products. Like the maritime sector, the global aviation sector is built around a hub and spoke network of major international airports that enables passengers to access

**TABLE 17.1** Maritime bottlenecks in global logistics

| Choke Point | Impact |
| --- | --- |
| Panama Canal | Connecting the Atlantic and Pacific Oceans, this suffers from being both narrow and shallow in parts and is vital for all forms of maritime traffic. |
| Dover Strait | Connecting the North Sea and the Atlantic Ocean, it is a major strait to access key global hub ports for entry into European marketplaces and is 33 km at its narrowest point. |
| Danish Straits | Key for Russian-based oil exports connecting the Baltic and North Seas through three narrow channels |
| Strait of Gibraltar | Connecting the Mediterranean Sea and the Atlantic Ocean. It is 13 km at its narrowest between the European and African land masses. |
| Suez Canal | An artificial waterway connecting the Mediterranean and Red Seas, avoiding a long detour around the southern tip of Africa. The canal is narrow and shallow in parts. Key to food, oil, and gas trade. |
| Strait of Bad-al-Mandab | Between the Red Sea and the Arabian Sea, this is 18 miles wide and is vital for both food and hydrocarbons towards Europe and Asia. |
| Strait of Hormuz | 30 per cent of global oil and 30 per cent of LNG flow through a narrow waterway between Iran and Oman in the Persian Gulf. There is no alternative maritime route. |
| Turkish Straits | This comprises both the Bosporus and Dardanelles Straits. The former connects the Black and Mediterranean Seas but is very narrow and has difficult geography. 80 per cent of Eurasian exported grain passes through these straits. |
| Malacca Strait | Connecting the Indian and Pacific Oceans via the South China Sea, while being long (800 km), it is at its narrowest at 2.3 km and is also shallow. Vital for not just hydrocarbons but also for broader freight flows |

a wider variety of destinations via an airline feeding traffic into these hubs to allow for economies of scale in flights. This has enabled the progressive liberalisation of the sector. For an airport to act as a hub, it needs to be attractive to airlines offering a high degree of interconnectivity with a high capacity and utilisation and good supporting services with a quick flow of traffic.

By concentrating passenger traffic into global and international hubs, a number of benefits are offered, namely:

- Creates network effects.
- Expands the range of destinations.

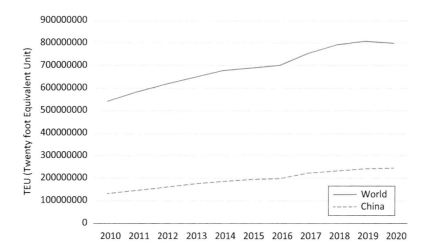

**FIGURE 17.2** Container port throughput, annual

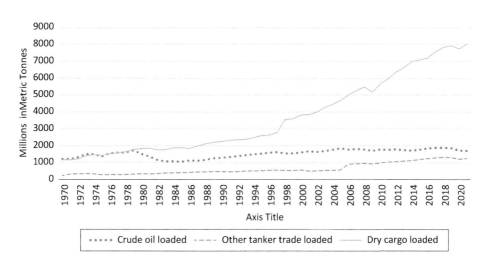

**FIGURE 17.3** World seaborne trade by types of cargo and by group of economies, annual (Source UNCTAD)

- Enables speedier transfer of passengers between flights to and from different parts of the network.
- Consolidates traffic from a number of locations to render flights to low-volume destinations commercially viable.
- Increases attractiveness to passengers and airlines.
- Aids the financial sustainability of flights to a wide range of destinations with a higher frequency of service.
- Increases competition between airlines.

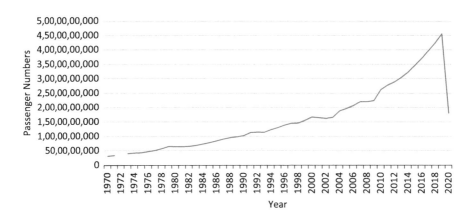

**FIGURE 17.4** International aviation air passenger numbers

This has benefits beyond simple tourism, as the concentration of passenger flows into single points of departure can render low-demand and/or remote destinations more accessible and financially sustainable and can be integrated into global aviation networks. This is especially relevant for small islands and developing states that could find themselves peripheral to global networks and/or be cut off should maritime infrastructure be damaged. While there has been an increased trend towards 'point-to-point' systems (between two locations with a high volume of traffic) for charter and low-cost airlines, the hub and spoke system remains the cornerstone of the aviation industry, especially for scheduled flights.

There are recognised to be a number of types of hub airports, namely

- Long-haul transfer hubs: these serve long-haul destinations and consolidate traffic from a series of short-haul locations towards these more distant locations. Other than feeding these long-haul flights, there is very little short- and medium-haul traffic.
- Mature hub airports: these serve a mix of long and short-haul flights.
- Cargo hubs: these are used by freight companies as the focal point within their logistics hub and spoke system. For example, Memphis for FedEx. The flights out of these hubs are overwhelmingly freight-focused.
- Focus city: these are hubs that serve point-to-point networks where the hub operates as a focal point for the local market with limited interconnectivity.
- Fortress hub: this is where a single airline controls the majority of flights out of a hub, which gives them an advantage. This strategy has often been used by the main state-flag carrier airlines.
- Primary and secondary hubs: this is a capacity-driven arrangement where the airline has a core hub, but once it reaches capacity, a second hub is opened to which traffic is diverted. These are also linked to reliever hubs, where the airline has excess capacity in another hub should its main hub become congested.

As enablers of inter-state connectivity, these hubs are seen as a key platform for economic growth and development. They not only facilitate trade, but they are also effective for high-value, time-bound trade. Thus, while it has a tiny share of global trade by volume, aviation carries 35 per cent of global trade by value. It is often used by manufacturers for high-value components and by producers of fresh produce where there is a need to reach the end user quickly. Aviation is especially valuable in tourism, where 54 per cent of all tourists travel by air, and this has broader spillover benefits for local economies. This was also true for business, where the high degree of rapid connectivity enabled by the hub and spoke system facilitated business operations globally. However, how this continues in an environment where online meetings have proved effective is, at the time of writing, a matter of conjecture. This reflects how aviation connectivity took a sharp fall during the COVID-19 pandemic (it fell on average by 70 per cent).

Of the top 50 global aviation hubs measured by the number of connections, 18 are in the US, with nearly half of the total being in North America. This reflects the maturity of the US system and the large number of airports in this country. It has over 20,000, compared to the next largest state, Brazil, which has nearly 4,000. When measured by passenger numbers again, the US dominates, with 18 of the top 40 being American, reflecting the intensively developed hub and spoke system. Chinese airports were traditionally very busy, especially with regard to internal mobility, but the COVID lockdown suppressed passenger numbers for 2021 when these figures were gathered.

**TABLE 17.2** The top global hubs (by seats – both domestic and international) (2023) (Source IATA)

| Ranking | Airport | Number of seats |
| --- | --- | --- |
| 1 | Atlanta Hartsfield-Jackson Intl. | 5,058,763 |
| 2 | Dubai Intl. | 4,649,381 |
| 3 | Tokyo Intl. (Haneda) | 4,255,951 |
| 4 | London Heathrow | 4,031,394 |
| 5 | Dallas Dallas/Fort Worth Intl. | 3,882,625 |
| 6 | Denver Intl. Airport | 3,794,789 |
| 7 | Istanbul Airport | 3,682,380 |
| 8 | Guangzhou (CN) | 3,664,820 |
| 9 | Chicago O'Hare Intl. | 3,609,423 |
| 10 | Delhi | 3,561,511 |

# THE GLOBAL ENERGY SYSTEM

The themes with regard to energy are revisited within Chapter 18, notably with regard to the energy transition and the commercial implications of this process. What this section will focus on is the infrastructure component of the current system. This is based on the international transmission of hydrocarbons between the points of consumption and production. This spatial disparity for oil and gas production and consumption is reflected in Table 17.3. These reflect the international asymmetry between hydrocarbon production and consumption. In oil, it is notable with regard to the variations in OCED and OPEC production and consumption. This stimulates flows between the main oil producers and consumers (i.e., industrialised states). Of the main consumers, the US imports 13 per cent of the global import total, the EU 20 per cent, and China 19 per cent. Of global oil exports, the Middle East accounts for a third and Russia for 13 per cent. This pattern is also evident in gas, where there is also, though less stark, a spatial disparity, notably again for the developed economies of the OECD. Gas moves through pipelines and maritime channels as liquid natural gas (LNG) (see below); these are roughly equal in terms of their contribution to international trade in gas. In summing these up, the major states with major gas deficits are Europe (both pipeline but increasingly LNG) and China (mainly LNG). The major exporting states for gas are Russia (mainly popped gas to Europe but also LNG) and the Middle East (mainly LNG).

This process reflects how the global energy system has, over the past century, become globalised. For much of human existence, energy systems were mainly localised, though with the advent of industrialisation, the energy systems were scaled up to the national level in those states that had strong domestic supplies of energy, leading to industrialisation. However, as industrialisation deepened and widened, the disparity between what an industrialised state produced and what it needed to consume widened. This was compounded by the revolution in transportation systems that promoted oil and derivative products as a major source of energy. By 2022, energy would comprise around a quarter

**TABLE 17.3** Spatial disparity of hydrocarbon production and consumption

| Oil | | Gas | |
|---|---|---|---|
| Production (000s barrels a day) | Consumption (000s barrels a day) | Production (production in billion cubic metres) | Consumption (production in billion cubic metres) |
| Total global production world – 89,877 -OECD – 28,405 -non-OECD – 61,471 (OPEC is 31,745 of non-OECD total) | Total global consumption world – 94,088 -OECD – 42,941 -non-OECD – 51,147 (OPEC is 8,160 of non-OECD total) | Total global production world – 4,037 -OECD – 1,503 -non-OECD – 2,534 | Total global consumption world – 4,037 -OECD – 1,795 -non-OECD – 2,243 |

Source: BP Annual Energy Review (2023)

of the total volume of global trade, with its major companies comprising some of the largest MNEs. In terms of infrastructure, this global system requires an international transmission system in both the oil and gas sectors. This international transmission lies in the increasingly external dependence that lies at the core of many countries' energy security.

## Oil infrastructure

These are the infrastructures that operate across the oil industry value chain. These physical facilities are used to explore, extract, process, transmit, distribute, and store oil and oil-derived products. Evidently, this encapsulates a wide range of facilities, and as such, the main focus of this section is on those infrastructures used for the international transmission of oil. This focuses on two main sets of infrastructure: maritime and pipeline. A small amount is moved by road, but this is largely peripheral to the global energy system, so it will be bypassed in this section.

It is estimated that around 60 per cent of all crude oil and refined petroleum products are moved through maritime channels. As noted above, before the rise of containerisation, oil was the single largest form of maritime transport. While the volume of crude and derived oil products moved through maritime channels has remained broadly static in volume terms, their share of total flows has fallen from 32 per cent in 1970 to 15 per cent in 2021. This dependence upon the maritime system for trade exposes the oil sector to the same chokepoints identified in Table 17.1. In this context, the Strait of Hormuz is seen as being particularly vulnerable (for both Europe and China, especially) not simply due to its narrowness but also due to the hostile relations between Iran and the other states whose coasts border this narrow strait. The UAE and Saudi Arabia are seeking to overcome this potential problem by using pipelines that cross the Arabian Gulf from the main oil export terminals on the Persian Gulf to loading facilities on the Red Sea.

Alongside these maritime transmission channels are the main export-focused terrestrial infrastructure, namely the oil terminals that export and import the oil flows moving through the maritime channels. These terminals are mainly storage facilities for crude and refined oil from inland oil fields that are filled off-load by oil tankers when imported. The largest dedicated terminals tended to be in oil-importing countries, where flows from a number of states coalesce. Of the top ten oil terminals by volume, three are Chinese, five are American, and two are European. In China, this pattern reflects that, while it imports a lot of crude oil, it also exports a lot of refined oil products. This is the same for the US, where oil terminals are used for both importing and exporting, especially in the Gulf of Mexico, reflecting the variance in crude quality and also the fact that these also refine and export both US and Mexican oil. In the Middle East, these oil terminals are closely integrated into large-scale oil refineries. Saudi Arabia has seven major ports, most of which are oil terminals, especially Jeddah and Ros Turana.

Pipeline infrastructure is used less frequently for the export of oil. These are used for short to medium distances. They are used to reach the end customer, notably in Europe, or to transport oil from inland fields to the main oil export terminals, where they are loaded onto tankers. This latter point reflects that, in most cases, oil pipelines are mainly used for intra-state transfer of oil. The highest number of bilateral pipeline systems are between the US and Canada, where five pipelines cross the border between these states. The major locations of international oil pipelines are in the states of the former Soviet Union, where oil is often inland, away from major tanker loading locations, or even in landlocked states. Thus, there is a network of oil pipelines across the former Soviet Union leading to the major markets in China, though more frequently in Europe, though the Ukraine-Russia conflict has inhibited flows between Russia and the states of the EU.

## Gas infrastructure

As with oil, gas is distributed through the maritime system and pipelines between the point of production and the point of consumption. Gas has become a key fuel in the energy transition due to its lower environmental impact and the fact that it is cheap to use. However, this comes up against the problem that it is expensive to transport. Historically, gas was consumed close to where it was produced. However, more recently, the trade in gas through both pipelines and LNG has increased (see Figure 17.5). As noted in Figure 17.5, international transmission of gas by maritime channels, such as LNG, has now become the single largest form of trade in gas. This is expected to increase as the main channels for international pipeline trade for gas (between Russia and the EU) have been severed since the start of the Ukraine-Russia war, with no likelihood of them ever being restored. Thus, both Russia and the EU are building LNG facilities. The former is for export (liquefaction plants) and the latter for import (regasification plants).

The major transmission channels by mode are mainly Russia to the EU, where this link comprises up to 40 per cent of inter-regional pipeline gas trade. As noted, this is likely to diminish due to major geopolitical issues. Most of the rest is made up of intra-American trade between the US and Canada and within Latin America. The major exporters of LNG are the Middle East (notably Qatar), which comprises around a quarter of total LNG exports, and the US, which provides around 17 per cent. Thus, when looking at the infrastructure required for international trade in gas, there is a transition underway as the system switches towards LNG and away from pipelines. The trend towards LNG also reflects that when transported by pipeline, the gas is transported to a

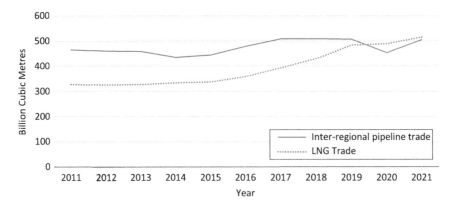

**FIGURE 17.5** International trade in gas by pipeline and LNG 2011–2021

specific point (often the end user) rather than a more generic distribution point. LNG is not constrained by such demands. Furthermore, pipelines are also only economical over short distances.

This LNG infrastructure comprises three core elements:

- Liquefaction plants: these transform gas into liquid gas by cooling it and then loading it abroad on specially constructed ships.
- Gasification plants: this transforms the liquid gas back into gaseous form.
- Floating LNG facilities: where there are only small gas reserves or there is a need for rapid access to LNG imports, then these can be used. These can be used in both the liquefaction and gasification processes and can be moved to alternative locations once their usefulness has expired.

Globally, there are now 188 LNG import terminals in existence, with another 179 planned and another 300 either being constructed or in the proposal phase. Of the currently operating LNG facilities, 87 are in two states: Japan and China. Many of those that are proposed are in East Asia and Europe. This has been coupled with a marked increase in export capacity in the major exporting states, namely Qatar, the US, and Australia. Overall, there are now 50 states with LNG terminals. This is expected to expand again, both in those states with existing capacity and as others build their first LNG capacity.

***

The legacy of the energy transition will be to change the nature of the energy infrastructure. Oil and gas infrastructure will become legacy (and even stranded) assets as they are replaced with renewable energy technologies. This will also impact the structure of the global energy system, as there will be a shift away from the global transmission of hydrocarbons. At this junction, a mixture of two trends is foreseen. The first is that the energy system deglobalises as more of the energy supplied as a result of the shift towards renewables is produced locally. This leads to the descaling of the infrastructure system, where electricity production through solar and wind power can be disaggregated to the level of the community or even the household. This reflects the multi-scalar nature of the energy transition. The second trend could be a move towards increased trade in electricity based on the internationalisation of electricity grids. This reflects that demand and supply of energy for renewables (as with hydrocarbons) are uneven in both space and time. There are evidently some places (such as in the Arab states) where solar power potential is greater and also places (such as the North Atlantic) where wind power potential is more evident. To reflect the unevenness of this capacity, a set of interconnected grids will need to be established, at least on a regional basis. This is already evident in East Asia, Europe, North America, and Africa. This will also need to be coupled with increased battery storage facilities so as to iron out temporal differences between supply and demand. However, the latter technology is still embryonic, and the long-distance transmission of electricity remains problematic as the power declines as it is transmitted.

## CASE STUDY 17.2: THE EAST AFRICAN ENERGY PIPELINE

While it is not on the scale of West Africa, East Africa has, over the past three decades, witnessed an extensive development of its oil and gas resources. With the sharp rise in oil prices between 2004 and 2014, there was a sharp increase in the rate of exploration, with new onshore oil fields being found in Uganda (2006) and Kenya (2012). This was on top of the pre-existing (though declining) oil fields in South Sudan and Tanzania. In addition, Ethiopia is also in the process of exploring its oil potential. Despite initial optimism, it did not take long for the difficulties and risks of resource extraction in this area of Africa to become apparent. On top of long-standing regional and domestic political and security conditions (see below), many of these new investments faced long regulatory hurdles (in the case of Uganda) as well as the outbreak of civil war in South Sudan. This was compounded by the sharp fall in oil prices in 2014. Typical of the risks and uncertainties faced by the investors in this region are the difficulties faced by these states in seeking to build a regional pipeline, something that is central to unlocking the potential of oil in this region. This pipeline underscores how important regional relations are to the realisation of the extraction of East Africa's energy resources. This was evidenced by the fact that with South Sudan's secession in 2011 from Sudan, the former's dependence on the latter represented a key strategic vulnerability.

Given the high cost of extracting the oil, it was felt that the best way for oil to enter international markets was through shared infrastructure, which would start from Uganda's field and go via Kenya's field to Lamu. In so doing, it would include conduits for pipes from elsewhere in the region. The pipeline would run from Lamu (a port in Kenya) to various destinations. However, states cannot agree on a joint plan, with many focusing on refining over transporting. Indeed, South Sudan is building two refineries. This refining-based strategy has little logic as some fields will run dry quickly, and this asset will have little economies of scale, with refining in Asia making more sense. There are three potential routes: the north (the planned), the central (via central Kenya), and the southern (via Tanzania). Overall, many states are prioritising national over regional needs. Some states choose pipelines to avoid overdependence on another region. The divergent interest suggests that these states will erode the benefit from the oil by duplicating infrastructure.

It is widely acknowledged that of all the political risks facing the extraction of oil in East Africa, the geopolitics of the pipeline infrastructure are the greatest. For landlocked states with oil reserves, there is a self-evident need for regional pipelines to enable the monetisation of these resources. This is also true for littoral states, where much of the oil lies inland. In theory, the solution to oil development strategies for Uganda and Kenya lies in the development of a joint pipeline to the Indian Ocean. However, Uganda has baulked at this due to political uncertainties in Kenya and has sought a new route via Tanzania. Meaning that Kenya had to find its own solution. This change of position from Uganda came shortly after an agreement with Kenya was struck. However, Uganda remained unconvinced with regard to the security assurances offered by Kenya over its segment of the pipeline. This was created by the fact that the pipeline would pass through the restive Kenyan western region of Turkana (where the major oil finds are located), where Islamic militants were particularly active.

For Kenya, the development of the pipeline was central to the development of a wider economic development strategy for its marginalised areas. In so doing, it believes that raising living standards will improve security, making allegiance to terrorist groups less attractive. Others see this strategy as simply an expression of the ruling Kenyan government rewarding tribal loyalties, and this may actually stoke dissent and worsen security. Moreover, the necessary supporting infrastructure (roads, etc.) needed to make the pipeline work is also lacking in these regions. While an alternative route through the centre of Kenya was also looked at to keep the Ugandans involved in the project, this was also demised due to technical difficulties as well as the aforementioned political priorities. While Kenya may look to develop the northern route (through Turkana), its ability to do so against a background of uncertain oil prices looks doubtful.

As the northern route looked suspect, Total of France, as a shareholder, looked to the southern route through Tanzania. This upset investors in Kenya's oil field. The southern route was attractive as it was cheaper, offered lower security concerns, easier terrain, and more straightforward land acquisition, as well as possessing pre-existing necessary support infrastructure. For example, there is an existing port that can be upgraded. Moreover, Tanzania is offering lower transit fees. Thus, the southern route offered many advantages over the northern route. However, the pipeline continues to face long-standing financing issues.

As of 2020, there has been little progress in the development of these pipelines. There has been little reduction in regional risk. It is now hoped that these pipelines will be realised by the 2020s. There continue to be unhealthy relationships between local and national politicians. While the southern route looks notionally attractive, regional politics continue to play a big role, with many states wary of becoming too dependent upon another state. For example, Uganda already relies extensively on Kenya for its access to international markets and does not want to increase this via oil infrastructure. For Kenya and Uganda, the central route is the most cost-effective, but local politics mean Kenya refuses to consider it seriously. This does suggest that maybe the region needs to consider a multiple pipeline situation. However, this will prove costly.

## QUESTION

Given the material offered within the case, what do the major difficulties seem to be in developing an international energy pipeline?

# THE GLOBAL INFORMATION SYSTEM

The global information system (GIS) is based on a network of interconnected information networks. This is arguably the only sector where there is a direct physical global network. While – like other networks – the basis of the network remains the interconnections between national systems, the focus of this section is on the creation of a global information system that allows for rapid and secure transmission of global data between multiple points within the global information network. This has become ever more important as the quantity of data created and traded has expanded rapidly. It is difficult to get exact figures on the extent to which data is traded, but the data created has grown from two zettabytes (a zettabyte is $10^{21}$ bytes) in 2010 to an estimated 18 zettabytes in 2025. Therefore, this chapter will focus on two distinct elements of the global information system, namely the trans-oceanic cable system and the network of cloud server farms.

## Oceanic cables

The trans-oceanic cable system is a network of submarine telecommunication cables laid on the seabed to convey communications between two land stations. These networks have a long precedent in the global system, with many 19th-century colonial powers using them to manage their overseas territories. This capacity has expanded throughout the 20th and 21st centuries, with 552 active and planned submarine cables as of 2023. These cables remain an important feature of the global economic system and carry around 95 per cent of global traffic (the rest is mainly via satellite systems). This can rise to as much as 99 per cent for some states (such as Australia). There is currently over 1.5 million km of cable laid on the ocean floor. These are of varying length and can vary from as little as 121 km (the CeltixConnect between the UK and Ireland) to over 20,000 km (the Asia-America cable between the US and East Asia) in length.

The major thrust of these networks was to cover the main trans-Atlantic routes. However, over time, Asian routes have become ever more important in terms of global traffic. These cables were traditionally developed by public telecommunications operators. More recently, many of the tech giants (notably Facebook, Microsoft, and Alphabet) have become involved and have been developing their own fibre-optic cable systems. These underpin their own commercial offerings, connect their servers, and facilitate not simply high-speed communication in finance, for example, but also the wireless network and smartphone communications that underpin the information economy. Given the uneven development of the global information economy, the major traffic routes for trans-oceanic cable traffic remain the trans-Atlantic, trans-Pacific, and Asia-to-Europe routes. This pattern reflects the nature of the dominance of Europe, Asia, and the US in the global economic system.

However, the development of these cables and the dependence of the global economic system upon them do highlight a strategic vulnerability. Any disruption to these cables can lead to interruptions to the flow of data throughout the global system, and there have been a number of incidents that have had this effect. There can be disruptions due to accidental or malicious activity. In the case of the former, there are a number of incidents where these cables have been snagged by fishing boats. In the case of the latter, these submarine cables are a key target for hostile agents and states if they want to disrupt the global economic and political system. These were frequent targets during the Second World War. These systems can also be impacted by natural events such as extreme weather and volcanic activity. There are also concerns with regard to the impact these systems can have on maritime ecosystems.

## Cloud farms

These cloud farms are data server centres that operate as shared facilities for a business's data operations. These centres operate either as a backup facility should a business's own systems go down or could simply represent an outsourced function for the firm and its data collection and management facility. These centres have increased in importance with the evolution of the global information economy. As the use of data increases within more functions of the socio-economic system and also due to changing socio-economic operations (such as remote working), there is an increased need to store the data that these changes are creating. This data flow is only expected to increase as more data is created through the evolution of the information economy into the Internet of Things. As of 2023, there are around 8,000 data centres globally, of which over a third are in the US alone, which also represents 40 per cent of the global market. The other major locations for these data centres are Germany, the UK, and China. However, the largest single data centre is in China.

With the COVID-19 pandemic and its legacy of remote working and online video calls, the pressure on and demand for these centres have increased. Indeed, the 2020–2022 period saw a 10 per cent increase in infrastructure spending as a response to the pressures created. This pressure is only expected to increase as remote working becomes normalised and as new data-rich technologies become embedded within social-economic systems. However, this trend is not without its costs. This cost is not simply in terms of the development of infrastructure but also in terms of energy consumption. Overall, it is estimated that these data centres will consume 20 per cent of all energy by 2025. There are also strategic risks created by the use of these centres, where they could become vulnerable to natural, malicious, or accidental human activity. These centres could become subject to terrorist attacks so as to disrupt an economic system. In the US, many centres are located within earthquake zones. These centres are also vulnerable to cyberattacks to access the data within them.

## CONCLUSION

The global flows between national infrastructure systems underpin the global economic system. These are physical structures that enable international flows. However, these infrastructures also reflect a key strategic vulnerability to the global system, as each of these systems, when operating across the globe, can be subject to disruption created by a mix of human and naturally occurring events. These reflect a key risk for both businesses and states as they operate across borders.

## KEY POINTS

- Infrastructure underpins the global economic systems.
- These are national systems that interact to create a de facto global system.
- The global transport system underpins the global logistics systems.
- The global energy system is based on the global exchange of hydrocarbons.
- The explosion of data has increased the importance of the global information infrastructure system.

## DISCUSSION QUESTIONS

1) Why does infrastructure matter to the operation of the global system?
2) What impact will the energy transition have on the global logistics sector?
3) How do you account for the surge in LNG infrastructure?
4) What do you believe are the main drivers causing the fragmentation of the internet? Were such trends inevitable?

## GROUP ACTIVITY

Look at one of the renewable energy technologies (wind, solar, or hydro) and examine the infrastructural requirements of the widespread adoption of this technology. Consider what it means on all scales, from the household to the international exchange of energy.

## BIBLIOGRAPHY

BP (2023). Annual energy review. www.bp.com.

IATA (2023). Annual review. www.iata.org.

Rodrigue, J. P. (2020). *The geography of transport systems*, London: Routledge.

Turner, C. (2020). *The infrastructured state: Territoriality and the national infrastructure system*, Cheltenham: Edward Elgar Publishing.

Turner, C., & Johnson, D. (2017). *Global infrastructure networks*, Cheltenham: Edward Elgar Publishing.

Yergin, D. (2020). *The new map: Energy, climate, and the clash of nations*. London: Penguin UK.

# CHAPTER 18

# THE GLOBAL INFORMATION ECONOMY AND DIGITAL GLOBALISATION

## OBJECTIVES

This chapter will help you to:

- Understand the emergence of the information economy.
- Assess how the rise of the information economy impacts international business.
- Comprehend the challenge of the global information economy created by big data.
- Understand how the Internet is being de-globalised.

There has been a great deal of focus over the past two decades on the long-term influence of the emergence of information-based technologies (especially their networking) on the development and implementation of international business. This has given rise to debates around digital globalisation, whereby there is the near-free global movement of data across borders. This process reflects a maturing of this process, with the focus within the development of the information economy shifting away from simply dealing with access to technologies towards dealing with the implications of this process, especially as narratives regarding the information economy have given way to an increased focus upon the rise of 'big data' and how this is transforming international business. This chapter will explore the rise of international data flows and how data and information are changing the operation and efficacy of international business. It will also reflect on how public policy is adapting to the rising power of big data.

## THE EMERGENCE OF DIGITAL GLOBALISATION

While there has been growing disillusionment (as identified within other chapters) about the process, progress, and legacy of globalisation, the trends in the globalisation of data

DOI: 10.4324/9781315184500-23

seem to be on an inexorable rise. Over the period 2005–2020, there has been a 45-fold increase in global data flows. This has been driven by the fact that businesses and individuals are using digital technologies to find new markets, re-order existing processes, and engage more easily in international interactions. In many senses, if 20th-century globalisation was characterised by rising trade and investment flows, then 21st-century globalisation is increasingly characterised by the sheer veracity of data flows. Indeed, digitisation is seen as enabling globalisation through:

- Lowering the cost of international communications.
- Allowing wider commercial networks to be established and embedded.
- Allowing wider participation in the process through shared digital platforms.
- Through supporting and enhancing the pre-existing flows.
- Reducing the minimum scale necessary to engage in globalisation, allowing the rise of the micro-national (see Chapter 10).

However, of course, for incumbent businesses, these new data flows also pose a core challenge to their established position.

Digital globalisation represents a different form of globalisation as the emphasis shifts to the international transmission of information, ideas, and innovation. It is, as such, a more intangible form of globalisation. The forms of data transmission are based on information generated by users (both corporate and non-corporate), which offers both value in their own right and is also increasingly central to the management of physical cross-border flows (for example, tracking the global movement of logistical flows). Indeed, by 2019, 12 per cent of business-to-consumer transactions were enabled by online systems such as eBay. This is only expected to grow as the connectivity related to the emergence of the 'Internet of Things' matures. By the end of 2019, nearly half of the world's 7 billion people were online.

Interestingly, this process of digital globalisation is a more economically plural process. The processes driven less by governments and larger businesses and more by smaller businesses as well as individuals, the digital platforms offer businesses of all sizes a 'plug and play' process of internationalisation. More interestingly, through social media platforms, the process of globalisation has been extending right throughout the socio-economic strata to the level of the individual. For these effects to have a true global effect, the network should possess spatial ubiquity with the areas that were newly connected, demonstrating the greatest gains from the emergence of data globalisation.

The most digitally connected states (i.e., those with the highest level of cross-border data flows per capita) are usually developed states with a high level of service activity, such as the Netherlands, the US, Singapore, and the US. Moreover, like globalisation generally, data mobility tends to be focused on the region rather than on the global economy per se, with more than two-thirds of all data flows occurring between states within the same region. There is also a split by level of development, with over three-quarters of all flows generated by developed states (though this is down from nearly 90 per cent in 2005). This, in truth, reflects its role in supporting the mobility of tangibles and intangibles.

# THE NATURE OF THE INFORMATION ECONOMY

The most important development associated with the rise of the information economy is the pervasive use of knowledge and information as both an input and an output throughout the economy. Knowledge workers (that is, those workers for whom embedded knowledge rather than physical capability is the source of their value) account for over 80 per cent of jobs within modern developed economies, according to the OECD. This process has been aided by the shift towards the 'weightless economy' as production becomes increasingly dependent upon intangibles (notably the exploitation of ideas) rather than physical inputs. This has made it harder to measure economic activity and the size of economies, especially as knowledge and information can be codified into digital bits that can be endlessly replicated, adding value every time they are duplicated.

Increasingly, every business is an information business, especially in activities (such as software and media) where content is a core source of value. In addition, more traditional companies are becoming more information- and knowledge-intensive. A good example of this trend is the automobile industry, where an increasing percentage of the value associated with these companies is directly related to the value of information and knowledge embedded within their products. In short, the salience of information and knowledge across industries is becoming increasingly evident. There are, however, differences between industries where information is the product and those where it is a core component of the final product or service. For example, within the automobile industry, a high percentage of the value of the output is reflected in the knowledge of engineering and technology.

Reflecting the above trends, the information economy has given rise to the creation of virtual value chains, where the emergence of important information at all stages of physical value chains needs to be captured and utilised to sustain competitive advantage. This information not only improves processes and operations within a business but also improves the performance of an enterprise by creating greater coordination across it. This increasingly applies not only within enterprises but also between them, as witnessed by the growing use of extranets, which provide communications links between enterprises and trusted buyers and suppliers.

There are both internal and external challenges for business with the emergence of the information economy. Employees and customers need to be able to deal with increasing quantities of information and decide what information is most valuable. Information overload has the potential to undermine many of the benefits of the information economy by making decision-making more difficult and reducing the efficiency of businesses. Enterprises therefore face a challenge, not only to make themselves 'heard' over the vast quantity of information available but also to ensure that internal processes are able to handle the large quantities of information generated in the modern economy.

The more extensive deployment of ICTs is having a major effect on the nature of the global economy by creating the potential for cost-space and time-space convergence. High-capacity fibre optic cables are a symptom of the latest logistical revolution and constitute an infrastructure that creates instantaneous communication and (in the case of digital goods) trade. Such developments are closely linked to the development of the Internet as a global phenomenon. The wider deployment and usage of this core technology have fundamentally altered the costs of conducting business where these capabilities are more developed. In addition, through the expansion of human processing power and the collection and dissemination of information, some of the most pervasive effects of the advent of electronic commerce are felt through the provision of services.

The impact of the Internet upon commerce, trade, and society depends upon the adoption of the technology by all aspects of the socio-economic spectrum. This is influenced by the following factors:

- Culture: notably, the openness of society to new ideas and processes.
- Convenience: the extent to which these technologies meet a defined need.
- Cost: this includes the hardware and software to access networks and process data.

If these factors can be reconciled, these technologies can have a profound effect on consumers, commerce, the structure of companies, politics, government, and the nature of the economy as a whole.

The changes in the business environment wrought by ICTs are different from the logistical and commercial revolutions that preceded them. An important facet of the development of the information economy is its sheer pervasiveness. Not only does the information economy apply to all sectors of the economy, but it also affects every function within an enterprise. As such, the information economy changes the functioning and structure of industries and also leads to the development of new products in its own right. This process has been aided by the sharp decline in the price of processing power – indeed, an unprecedented fall in the price of a key input. These factors have facilitated the realisation of the following commercial advantages:

- Cheaper transaction costs.
- The rapid codification and diffusion of the increased range of knowledge.
- Fewer claims are made on resources by IT than by preceding technologies.

Figure 18.1 highlights the three main channels through which the extension of ICT usage can deliver advantages and competitive benefits for businesses. The first channel is through capital productivity growth, where rising ICT usage improves the efficiency with which capital contributes to output. The second channel is labour productivity growth, where rising ICT usage leads to capital deepening, in which the amount of ICT capital per employee increases to assist production across all sectors. Finally, ICT usage

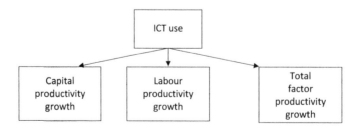

**FIGURE 18.1** Channels through which ICT contributes to productivity growth

improves total factor productivity growth by enhancing managerial and organisational effectiveness through cost savings and improved communication.

The information economy also has an impact on the economy as a whole. As with other 'revolutions', the information economy both destroys and creates jobs, in this case by reducing the demand for manual workers and increasing the demand for information and knowledge workers. Thus, the demand for teachers, computer programmers, etc. increases as a result of the emergence of the information economy. This places greater pressure upon enterprises to engage in effective training and upon education systems to produce individuals capable of becoming value-adding knowledge and information workers. There is a fear that such developments could create a new underclass relying on low-skilled service sector employment, resulting in widening income differentials between low- and high-skilled workers.

Within the information economy, not only is knowledge a key resource, but it is also a scarce one. Effectively, knowledge workers own the means of production. The largest group of knowledge workers are what Drucker (1969) terms 'knowledge technologists', who work with their hands but whose pay is determined by their embedded knowledge. This includes computer programmers, dentists, etc. These workers require two things if they are to succeed. The first is formal education to accumulate knowledge, and the second is continuing education throughout their working lives to sustain their 'valuable' knowledge. This latter point acknowledges the rapid obsolescence of knowledge and that lifelong learning is a key feature of the information economy.

The development of the information economy has raised fears of a net loss of jobs in developed states as large companies no longer need to sacrifice contact with head office in return for locating production in the more remote states of the global economy. With low wages and a rudimentary IT infrastructure, developing economies could become super-competitive. However, such arguments are simplistic: they ignore productivity differences and misunderstand the difference between absolute and comparative advantage. There is, however, a fear that ICTs allow previously untradeable services to be traded globally and that any service undertaken online can be transferred anywhere. There has been a trend, for example, for firms to outsource an array of commercial services, from ticketing to computer programming to developing states.

What is more likely is that ICTs will allow firms to decentralise production and specialise by country. ICTs enable enterprises to exploit national comparative advantages more widely and efficiently. The comparative advantage between states will depend upon how well workers apply knowledge and information resources. This means that the better-educated states should be able to sustain their competitive advantage within the information economy.

## INTERNATIONAL BUSINESS AND THE INFORMATION ECONOMY

The previous section highlighted how the development of the information economy is shaping the competitive environment in which international businesses will operate in the coming decades. These changes have a further and more direct effect on the international business environment through their influence on international trade and investment. This will be most noticeable, over the short term at least, in trade in ICTs and in the development of electronic commerce.

It is logical that as the information economy matures, trade in its raw materials increases. The late 20th and early 21st centuries have seen a sharp increase in trade in ICTs. However, the effect of ICTs on trade amounts to more than the sum of ICT trade. The all-pervasiveness of ICTs across the economy has had a broader impact on the trade of goods and services. The application and dissemination of these technologies enable traditional businesses to expand into new markets, both nationally and internationally. This is especially evident in the domain of electronic commerce (see below). ICT effects are also substantial in the generation of further investment in areas such as training, research, and technological development. By helping to disseminate the latest technologies, trade in ICTs also plays a role in the innovation process. ICTs are also important in terms of trade facilitation (that is, the use of ICTs to aid the process of communication and the simplification of the transaction process). However, capturing and measuring these effects is difficult.

In the aftermath of the WTO's (signed in 1996) Information Technology Agreement (ITA), trade in ICTS grew strongly. A key by-product has been the emergence of Eastern European and non-OECD developing states as key producers and growth markets of ICT products. Thus, the information economy is not merely about users but also about the producers of supporting products. As ICT-related technologies have undergone commoditisation, their production has shifted towards low-cost locations. The trade and spread of ICTs have been central to facilitating trade in specific types of services that do not require face-to-face contact. The WTO ITA Agreement was renewed in 2015, expanding the scope of the agreement to cover, by 2023, 10 per cent of global merchandise exports, with the 82 signatories accounting for nearly 97 per cent of trade in ICTS.

Anecdotally, there is an assumption that higher spending on ICTs is closely linked to increased growth and trade. However, this effect has not been universal: some states with high ICT spending do not exhibit such growth (e.g., Greece), while others exhibit the opposite characteristics (e.g., Spain and Mexico). However, given all the other factors that can influence trade, isolating ICT effects can be difficult. Indeed, it is possible that it may take a decade or more for the effects of investment in ICTs to be reflected in trade figures. The impact of ICTs takes a long time to feed through into the broader economy; for example, a prolonged period is needed for workforce training and for labour markets to reflect the structural changes stimulated by the increased investment in ICTs. Thus, there is expected to be a prolonged lag before investments in ICTs are reflected in improved competitiveness.

As the information economy matures, the effect on trade will increase as transaction costs decline further, telecommunication costs will fall, and the cost of adopting these technologies will also decline. As costs fall, most sectors will utilise these technologies, and more sectors will become exposed to international competition. Trade will thus become an option for an increased array of businesses. These changes will also create a demand for a new set of goods and services, notably those that can easily be digitised. For such products, the above issues are especially pertinent given that the marginal production cost is minimal or even zero. Consequently, it will become immediately profitable to export these products, therefore bypassing the need for economies of scale or market testing. The same will also be true of those services that can be easily adapted for delivery online, such as financial services. A more indirect impact of electronic commerce upon international trade will come through trade facilitation, enabling firms to fulfil customs requirements more quickly and easily – a potentially significant impact given that trading costs can represent around ten per cent of the value of international trade. The submission of documents through electronic media, for example, has the potential to cut the time and costs associated with undertaking international trade.

The expansion of trade related to the development of the information economy is also related to network effects. Improved access to ICTs will spread the benefits, but as more people access these technologies, there is an increased incentive for others to utilise them. Thus, as new economy trade expands, it creates (eventually) its own virtuous cycle of development. This trend depends on the improved spread of ICTs throughout the global economy. In turn, the process of dissemination also depends on the progressive liberalisation of the telecommunications and IT sectors. These processes are essential to the price effects that stimulate access to these technologies. As it is accessed by more people, the information economy will mature, and its relevance will spread throughout the socio-economic spectrum.

Aside from the increased trade in information and communication technologies, the more general impact of the emergence of the information economy on international trade has been through the rise of electronic commerce. Very broadly, electronic commerce involves the use of electronic channels (most notably telecommunications) for the purpose of stimulating or undertaking transactions. With improved customer information and better knowledge of marketplaces, the Internet has the potential to create a virtual global marketplace for goods and services by overcoming the problems of distance and costs that inhibit trade for many agents. Analysed through the framework of the five forces, electronic commerce can alter industry dynamics by:

* Eroding the power of suppliers.
* Increasing competitive rivalry.
* Increasing the power of buyers.
* Increasing the range of substitutes.
* Increasing the threat of new entrants.

Through these pressures, the emergence of this new channel will impact international strategy in the following ways:

* In customer needs and tastes: this is especially true if brands are global and product offerings are common between states.
* The Internet creates global customers: MNEs act as global customers by coordinating or centralising their purchases.
* The Internet facilitates global channels: channels of distribution that have emerged on a global or regional basis.
* The Internet makes global marketing more possible: the Internet potentially has global reach, enabling global marketing to occur. In addition, the Internet increasingly demands globally standard brand names.
* The Internet highlights lead countries: the Internet offers greater openness in identifying industry leaders and monitoring their offerings.

The Internet has also contributed to globalisation through assorted cost factors. First, the Internet has enabled global economies of scale and scope by allowing smaller firms to benefit from such efficiencies. Secondly, it enhances global sourcing efficiency and speeds up global logistics, as well as exploiting differences in costs between states. Thirdly, the Internet can reduce product development costs. Furthermore, the Internet also reduces barriers to globalisation by sidestepping trade policies, spurring the development of global technical standards, and confronting diverse marketing regulations. In terms of the competitive environment, the Internet accelerates the needed speed of competitive action and reaction, makes competitor comparison easier, aids the transferability of competitive advantages, and creates global rivalry.

The impact of the Internet on the pace and form of internationalisation varies from limited to rapid. Ultimately, its impact is a derivative of the form and nature of the firm as well as the usage of the Internet. The most immediate impact of rising Internet usage on the internationalisation process is felt through lower levels of uncertainty as the channel allows better access to host market information and knowledge. Furthermore, the Internet enables the firm to access, absorb, and utilise host market information more readily and therefore assists experiential learning. Overall, the Internet speeds up internationalisation if it aids transaction efficiency, facilitates experiential learning, and lowers sunk costs linked to market entry. On a more negative note, rising internet usage can also create information overload and spread misinformation within the firm. Consequently, Petersen et al. argue that the firm may place false trust in the ability of the Internet to solve its problems and overcommit to markets.

Alongside learning aspects, the spread of the Internet can impact internationalisation in the following ways:

Pace: some firms have experienced demand-driven effects where high profiles have pulled them into overseas markets. In other words, the pace of the process has been sped up by the Internet. However, these effects depend on the interface between culture and the increased interactions that result. These effects could just as well be negative as positive, where the ability to enter a market runs ahead of the firm's knowledge about international operations.

Product/value chain activity: the Internet should lessen the need for localisation of marketing and other sales activities, although elements of the firm's value-adding activities (such as R&D) are often less amenable to the digitisation process that allows this to occur.

Foreign operation mode effects: it is accepted that the Internet offers the opportunity for externalisation as contracts and partners are easier to monitor and transaction costs are reduced. This favours the use of the market mechanism rather than the internalisation of functions. However, these effects may be offset by the need for global coordination. In addition, this effect may also be felt through disintermediation, which allows firms to drop their role as intermediaries and sell directly to customers.

Geographic spread: global exposure can increase the reach of the business. This demand-driven process increases the number of markets available to the business, although this will be limited by the spread of Internet usage and the ability of the website (the basic unit of business on the Internet) and customers to deal with many languages. This could be a problem for smaller businesses. Thus, despite the espoused benefits of uniformity generated by the Internet, the issue of languages means that localisation remains an important factor for these businesses.

On the demand side, the impact of ICTs on international business is self-evident as firms seek new markets. On the supply side, the effects are less unidirectional. Producers of digital products seek to serve as many customers as possible to mitigate the high up-front costs involved in their production. This encourages the firm to go global. In contrast, producers of physical products have less incentive to internationalise if they are able to use ICTs to create more flexible production.

If we look at economies of scope (instead of scale), the Internet allows for the possibility of finding a partner or partners for the firm. This can be especially important to smaller firms and improves their internationalisation capacity, as better information and knowledge allow them to understand markets better than incremental approaches to internationalisation suggest (see Chapter 11). However, the symmetry of such effects may limit the ability to use these technologies for advantage.

In its formative period, the Internet was regarded as providing strategies for low-cost leaders whereby customers could find what they wanted at a cheaper price. Indeed, initial actions involving the disintermediation of retailers allowed customers to buy wholesale and benefit from lower costs. However, strategies in global cyberspace have matured as there are only so many low-cost leaders that the Internet can support. Indeed, the dot-com crash of the late 1990s highlighted the limits of intense cost competition. More recent phases of business model development within electronic commerce have been characterised by a higher degree of commercial maturity as many smaller businesses in particular move into more differentiated strategies and away from low-cost positions.

Overall, electronic commerce affects international trade at many levels. Electronic commerce increases the intensity of competition between states as consumers have access to more information, requiring businesses to be more responsive. Thus, consumers are empowered at the expense of the producer. However, this can be curtailed by too much information clouding market signals. Competition can also benefit companies themselves, especially where business-to-business transactions deliver cost and efficiency benefits. Furthermore, electronic commerce can enhance price flexibility and increase the efficiency of markets. This is especially evident on auction sites. Further benefits to business can be derived from new media for advertising, commercial transactions, after-sales service, and the dematerialisation of goods and services with accompanying savings in distribution. While these effects are difficult to measure, the rise in electronic commerce does not always mean that international trade will increase. There can be a substitution effect as existing offline trade goes online and as a result, the rapid growth in electronic commerce may not necessarily be reflected in increased trade flows.

As of 2022, there is only really anecdotal evidence to highlight the impact of conventional MNE. This tends to be done through two main channels.

## Digital supply chains

Many MNEs are centralising global and back-office functions and increasingly using the cloud to share information within MNE networks. These are streamlining processes and have been generated by new digital startups offering new technologies to streamline existing processes.

## International production

The impact on conventional MNEs tends to be more anecdotal, with evident usages of digital technology right across the process, allowing, for example, the emergence of distributed production, which is closer to end users and is utilised through technologies such as 3D printing. It also allows for accelerated servicification of the value chain, allowing it to be more clearly disaggregated and devolved. It also facilitates further disintermediation of the value chain and flexible production.

## THE RISE OF BIG DATA

Paradoxically, as the global information economy has evolved, key debates within the information value chain are focusing less on the downstream elements of the information economy (i.e., knowledge acquisition, etc.) and more on the collection and utilisation of the raw material of the information economy: data. It is the power that data has to give its holders that has been driving many developments in the information economy. It is eroding the pluralist ideals that stimulate the process and is operating as a catalyst that is legitimising many of the forces that are fragmenting what was once a single system.

The nature of 'big data' is created by the fact that the modern economy is characterised by the sheer volume, veracity, variety, and velocity speed with which it is generated of information that is being generated and collected, as well as the uses to which it is being put. This process is distinct from the notion of the Internet as a physical system, as this is merely about communication. Big data is about learning more about phenomena that were simply not possible when lesser amounts of data were available. In 2000, only 25 per cent of data was digital; by 2017, the non-digital component of data storage was less than 2 per cent with digital data doubling every three years. Alongside this vast increase in the quantity of data generated is the process of 'datafication', whereby many things that were not previously codified as data are now being datafied. Moreover, as this data is being created, new methods are being found to harness this data to form new value-enhancing products and processes.

Daily, it is estimated that 2.5 quintillion bytes of data are created, with 90 per cent of the world's data being created in the last two years alone. By 2020, there will be an estimated 20–100 billion connected devices, all of which will generate data. By 2025, there will be an estimated 180 zettabytes (1,080 followed by 321 zeros) of data. At the corporate level, 53 per cent of the data generated in customer centric, 40 per cent was operationally focused, and 7 per cent was utilised to manage financial issues. Of this, it is estimated that only 0.5 per cent of the data is ever analysed.

The phenomenon of big data for the global economy tends to be limited to those states with more advanced levels of IT literacy, infrastructure, and education systems. This means that big data tends to be focused on developed economies. In theory, its impact on international business should be to reinforce the trend towards hyper-global systems as more activities and processes are more easily moved across borders as data flows between states. Moreover, the quality of the information generated about ever more groups of users in multiple jurisdictions has the potential to be a truly globalising force. This is not just in terms of creating more exact marketing strategies but also in terms of improving supply chain operations. In short, big data should reinforce trends towards cost-space and time-space convergence within the global economy as firms know more about more users from more locations. This is created in part by the fact that this process allows more activities to be undertaken by distance than were otherwise possible. All this suggests a smoother path to more intense globalisation through protracted trade and investment negotiations.

## THE RISE OF TECH MNES

These firms are the main catalysts behind the development and spread of the global information economy. In rankings compiled by UNCTAD in 2005, these businesses (which are responsible for the hardware and/or software underpinning the global information economy) barely featured in the list of the top 100 businesses. Fast forward over ten years, and there are now over ten tech MNEs on the list. This number expands to nearly a fifth of the list if telecom companies are included in the list. Sixty per cent of the tech MNEs (Apple, Alphabet (Google), Oracle, HP, IBM, and Microsoft) are user-based, with the others being a mix of German (SAP), Japanese (Sony), Korean (Samsung), and Taiwanese (Hon Hai). Many of these companies have relied upon the accelerated spread of the Internet to realise their strategy, while others are direct catalysts in this process. What is common across all of these is their rate of growth, which has significantly outpaced that of old-economy MNEs.

This relatively high rate of growth has been fuelled by many factors, such as a high rate of change in technology markets, strong revenue flows, high capital expenditures, and a corporate culture focused on innovation. The result has been an increased dominance by these businesses over their respective segments (see below) and also a seemingly endless expansion into new product areas. These businesses are, in short, emerging as digital conglomerates. What is evident is that, unlike old-economy MNEs, these firms are not big employers. While they have increased employment by about 5 per cent per annum in the ten years to 2020, this has been lower than the growth in total assets, suggesting that tech MNEs have more value in capital (especially intangibles such as knowledge, brand, and IP) than in labour. These firms also tend to hold higher volumes of cash, as they see liquidity as key to growth through their ability to easily acquire new businesses to add to their information portfolio.

In some senses, the rise and global impact of these tech MNEs can have a mixed impact on international business. In some sense, the removal of the need for a physical presence to support activities in a marketplace may actually cause FDI to fall, though this seems to be conjectural at this point in time. Alternatively, these firms may also be key enablers in facilitating internationalisation through the creation of online marketplaces and digital value chains. However, as much as market-seeking and efficiency-seeking FDI may be challenged by digitisation, it can actually encourage other forms of FDI, especially those that are driven by knowledge-seeking or for the purposes of tax efficiency, though these tend to have a more limited impact on firms.

In terms of their global strategies, these tech firms exhibit different kinds of characteristics when compared to conventional MNEs. One of the facets of these firms is that they tend to be comparatively light on foreign assets relative to sales. This shows these firms can gain a global footprint without high levels of FDI. Telecom MNEs eschew this model as these businesses tend to rely considerably more on overseas assets to generate revenue flows. This does reflect a tendency by the largely US tech sector to keep its assets at home, with the subsidiaries of these companies also tending to be home-based. This also represents a sharp digression from the conventional MNE, which tends to have a higher number of foreign subsidiaries (80 per cent compared to 40 per cent for tech MNEs). This reflects a desire by these largely US-based tech MNEs to keep their productive investments in their home economies. The most valuable assets these companies keep overseas are their cash holdings. Thus, the tech MNE presents a new type of business model.

## THE RISE OF THE FANGS

The impact of this sharp rise in big data has increased concern over the increased power that this ability to collect and harness data gives to those companies that are at the forefront of its collection. Collectively known by the acronym 'FANGs', these companies (Alphabet (Google's parent company), Amazon, Apple, Facebook, Microsoft, and Netflix) comprise the most valuable global companies and are beginning to raise concerns as to their potential power in the evolving information economy. Excluding Netflix, these businesses are exhibiting surging profits based on their ability to harness this data to capture online spending and corner the market in digital advertising. This power is only expected to increase as they evolve their product offerings into more innovative products, such as those linked to the spread of artificial intelligence. This process reflects that the absence of data markets is increasingly creating a competition problem as these companies are controlling a vast amount of data. This vast amount of data allows these firms to quickly detect competitive threats and use their cash to buy rivals. These firms can also tailor the software to suit their own interests over those of their rivals.

The scale of these businesses is impressive. This is demonstrated by a few basic facts:

- Of the 3 billion people using the Internet, over half were or are Facebook users, and this is despite it being banned in China and disrupted elsewhere. Moreover, these figures exclude its WhatsApp messaging service, which has nearly a billion users.
- Nearly 1.5 billion people regularly use Google to search for information, conducting over 3 billion searches a day and 100 billion a month.

- YouTube (Alphabet's video channel) has over 1 billion users every month, with Alphabet's mobile operating system (Android) having a global user base of over 1 billion users.
- Apple's iTunes store has nearly 900 million accounts, with the company selling over 500 smartphones per minute (in 2020).
- Amazon has a regular customer base of over 30 million a year.
- There are over half a billion tweets sent by Twitter's over 300 million active users daily.

Not surprisingly, there are increased calls for these businesses to be broken up. There can be little doubt that these businesses are exerting tremendous influence over the systems where Google has extended to not just control search (it has 90 per cent of the general search market) and advertising, for example, but also has control – via its Android system – of over 80 per cent of all smartphones sold globally. When combined with Apple's share, these two businesses have over 97 per cent of the mobile operating system market. In the desktop video market, YouTube and Facebook have a combined market share of nearly 90 per cent. Moreover, Amazon exerts dominance over the main e-markets for many retail segments. In eBooks, it has over a 90 per cent market share. In addition, it has also begun to exert considerable power over the cloud computing sector. The fear is that left unchecked, these businesses can limit competition and prevent the emergence of new businesses that might undermine their power. In social media, Facebook had a nearly two-thirds share of users. One of the main drivers of these companies' growth is their ability to spot and absorb new businesses that might add to their portfolio and so underpin their preeminent position. It is also helpful that many of the services provided by these businesses are free at the point of use.

The concerns over the rise of these companies are focused on three issues:

1. The rise of 'winner-takes-all' markets in online environments. The legacy of network effects is that once a firm has market share, it becomes difficult to challenge it. Microsoft may have invested vast amounts into its own search engine (Bing), but it is still largely peripheral to the 90 per cent share enjoyed by Google. This is also evident in social networking, where Facebook enjoys a near-monopoly position.

2. The desire of these firms to generate 'stickiness' to their own platforms that are frequently not compatible with rival systems. This stickiness is created by tying in multiple online services and applications that run on appropriate hardware (such as tablets or smart phones). Such bundles are attractive to consumers as a single device can offer an entry point for digital life. However, the fact that these are often 'walled gardens' (where services cannot be moved across platforms) can limit interoperability.

3. These firms have a tendency to acquire emerging firms before they become a threat. All of these businesses have made acquisitions to support and enhance their platforms. In so doing, they remove potential threats to their position and limit the path for creative destruction.

By 2012, Google was already under the gaze of regulators, notably in Europe and the US, due to its perception of excessive power over the search industry. It was alleged that

Google was skewing search results to favour its own products. It was also accused of using patents to limit competition in the smart phone market. This clearly raises parallels to the fight that Microsoft had over a decade ago, where regulators were concerned over its power over desktops and Internet browsing. These attempts at curtailing the power of these businesses have been targeted at specific sections of their activity rather than to challenge the core underpinnings of their business model with the aim of attaining a swift resolution that curtails anti-competitive behaviour. Some want these bodies to go further, potentially breaking these businesses up so that competition can be promoted. For example, it has been suggested that the search business of Google should be separated from its other activities. In short, there is a belief that these businesses should be made to focus on either being a provider of digital content, a producer of hardware, or information distributors. To counter such a position, many of these tech giants argue that they don't actually charge for the use of the service and, thus, there can be no abuse of a dominant position. Moreover, while network effects work to give these companies power, there is also the possibility that the process could work in reverse, as switching costs are low and the industry is subject to disruptors. The more they acquire startups, the less likely this is to occur.

However, there is little evidence to suggest that breaking up these problems would ultimately solve them. If, for example, Google was broken up into separate businesses, there is no guarantee that the network effects that led to its dominance in the first place would not simply re-emerge in one of the companies that were split off. A possible compromise to this situation could be that regulators could become more aware of data in their decisions and not simply focus on scale or market share. For example, regulatory action could seek to open up data sources to all businesses to allow new challengers to emerge. They might also consider how mergers between firms affect or alter data assets and the consequent power that such consolidations might generate.

Moore (2016) raised broader issues created by the power of these tech giants via their impact on civil power. As suggested, these giants have had, in some senses, a positive impact on civil society through allowing and facilitating civil power. In this sense, these businesses have not merely acquired economic power; they have also acquired civil power. Moore identifies six channels through which they can influence power structures that emerge through their position as intermediaries in the digital economy:

1. The power to command attention through their sheer number of users and targeted use of messages.

2. The power to communicate news, which these businesses can filter and personalise.

3. The power to enable collective action, which is an unintentional side effect of their reach, has to be used judiciously, or it could lead to clamping down on these businesses.

4. The power to give people a voice and sustain plurality is also a feature of these business civic powers, but they also have the ability to remove such facilities.

5. The power to influence people's vote occurs through three channels: by affecting voter turnout, influencing the information people are exposed to about an individual candidate or party, or by enabling the targeting of specific individuals with particular views in precise locations.

6. The power to hold power to account, which can be a public good, but also raises the question of who holds these firms to account.

Given such power, there are clearly issues of trust between civic society and governments that these businesses will use such powers responsibly and not seek to influence processes in their own interests. The immediate set of actions by the government to seek to limit such contraventions of trust are linked to regulatory concerns over security, data usage, and user privacy. There have also been questions over the degree of trust where the tax strategies of these businesses often seem to contravene such positions.

While there are evident concerns with regard to the emerging market power of these companies, there is also considerable evidence that their emergence has been of direct benefit to their users (both consumers and businesses). Among the benefits of these companies are that they have offered a wider choice, improved logistics, and lowered the cost of consumption. There is also the belief that the more data the firm collects, the better its products will be. This creates positive feedback loops as better products create more data, leading to even better products, and so on. They have also offered fewer commercial benefits in terms of their impacts on free speech and democracy. In addition, too-strong pre-emptive moves by regulators may do long-term harm where these benefits are understated. It is evident that bundling platforms work for consumers, who are willing to trade a limited choice for convenience and ease of use. Moreover, any switch is relatively easy, either via a click on a new browser, a new music provider, or simply by buying a new smartphone. In addition, these actions understate the extent to which these firms are actually competing, with no firm being dominant (as was the case with Microsoft a decade or so ago). For example, Android has emerged to rival the iPhone, and the Kindle Fire rivals the iPad, and these are just a couple of the examples where these businesses are competing. The point is that these markets are very fluid and can change relatively rapidly.

## CASE STUDY 18.1: THE INTERNATIONAL EXPANSION OF SPOTIFY

Spotify is a music, podcast, and video streaming service that was initially launched in Sweden in 2008. Its model is to offer an IP-secured service that allows record companies to monetise their content through a mix of an advertising-based free service and a subscription-based (advertisement-free) premium service. As of 2016, the company has half a billion users (of which over 100 million are regular users). Of these, 40 million pay for the subscription service. Since almost its inception, Spotify has sought to expand internationally. However, it has tended to approach the issue differently from other companies, which move rapidly into as many overseas markets as they can as quickly as possible. Spotify has a more considered strategy, largely due to the need to handle the localisation of content and its need to engage with local record labels and rules and regulations. This means the process is more protracted than it is for the other technology companies.

There is little evidence that this slower approach has any negative impact on the success of its international strategy. Spotify has a localisation strategy and a presence in more than 60 states. Localisation is key to Spotify and its international strategy. This reflects that while the music industry is global, tastes diverge markedly. In each of these localities, Spotify seeks to be the streaming channel of choice, which it can only do by recognising the diversity of tastes. Finally, the core notion of Spotify is not to pay for ownership but access to music. This requires a disruption of the model but needs considerable network effects to work.

While Spotify has a few rivals in the market (such as Deezer), its approach has been to focus on large markets rather than reach per se. While Deezer has a presence in over 180 states, it largely ignores its big, difficult markets, such as the US. Spotify took this market head-on, even though it took ten years to get results. In entering the US market, Spotify made sure to understand how music was consumed, notably with regard to a more passive listening culture. To enter the US, Spotify sought to build this into its product offering. Spotify is seeking to utilise universal features to allow an effective market presence. For example, Spotify uses a 'running feature' to adapt playlists to running speed. This reflects that, over time, Spotify has altered its value proposition to offer a more personalised listing experience. Importantly, Spotify adapts to local buyer behaviours and payment systems. This means pricing according to local conditions and understanding how and why they buy. In Brazil, that has meant adapting to income disparity and diverse musical tastes. In Europe, payment systems have adapted to the ubiquity of mobile phone payment systems.

With its strategy of taking on big markets, Spotify has also entered the potentially lucrative Asian market. Spotify entered Asia in 2013, focusing on Singapore, Hong Kong, and Malaysia. This was later followed by Taiwan and the Philippines in 2014, and Japan in 2016. The latter is seen as especially difficult to break into but is also potentially the most lucrative. Asia is a diverse market but also very different from those markets where the firm already has a presence. For example, in India, the diversity is such that it is akin to 28 different markets. Again, the strategy is knowing to whom users listen and how. That has meant promoting Spotify via mobiles initially, as the content has a high mobile penetration rate with high local content, and then utilising social media to give the firm traction. In addition, Spotify has been proactive with offline users via concerts, etc. Moreover, as credit cards are rare in some markets, the firm has learned to take cash payments and other easily accessible channels, such as convenience stores. Japan has proved a difficult market to enter, with many streaming firms (such as Apple, Google, and Amazon) all entering with little success as CD sales remain strong. To counter this, Spotify used a completely free approach based on local content (85 per cent of music listened to in Japan is local). At the time of writing, it is still too soon to see if the localisation strategy has worked.

## QUESTION

What do you believe are the major benefits of Spotify's localisation strategy?

# THE FRAGMENTATION OF THE INTERNET AND THE CHALLENGE TO DIGITAL GLOBALISATION

The problem posed by the Fangs is one faced by the global nature of the information economy. When the process of expanding the Internet began, many states were willing to embrace what was seen as the inherent globality of the system. This position is changing as states have caught up and become more fully aware of the implications of the information economy. Over the past two decades, there has been a big shift in states' desire and capabilities to regulate the emergent and evolving data economy. This has been driven by a mix of factors, such as

- Better technological capabilities make it easier for states to enforce borders in cyberspace.
- A pushback against the 'Americanisation' of local cultures driven by the increased pervasiveness of the Internet.
- Incumbents in many sectors have grown increasingly threatened by the reach of Internet-based businesses.
- Popular resistance to tech firms' tax policies and strategies.
- A large amount of highly skilled immigrant labour is used by tech firms.

It is not only states that have been seeking to apply real-world borders to the virtual environment, as tech firms have also been engaged in such activities through walled gardens. These walled gardens are commercial systems whereby users are kept within limits as to what they can access within a given domain.

Despite the narrative on the process of digital globalisation, it is evident that, like in the offline world, the process tends to be regional rather than global. This may reflect that digital globalisation is, in fact, mirroring the physical world, which also tends to be regionally focused, as much of the movement of data reflects that these flows are often generated in support of physical flows. This is compounded by the fact that content production tends to be concentrated in a few economies and the unevenness of access to the core enabling technologies.

Core debates within the global Internet community are increasingly focused on the fragmentation of the Internet into what can best be called loosely coupled islands of interconnection. These forces have been happening due to a mix of changing technology, shifting government sentiment, and the adaptation of commercial practices. These have been felt right across the Internet systems, from the underpinning physical infrastructures (see also Chapter 17) into the broader-based user communities through applications, content, and transactions. While such trends do not entail the full fragmentation of the Internet into separate territorial or propriety systems, they can impede its development as a tool of global business. This is despite the more widespread development of a global Internet system, based on the widely hyped 'Internet of Things' (IoT).

As suggested by Drake et al. (2016), the process of fragmentation occurs along a number of dimensions. This is where the process of fragmentation leads the system to depart for an openness that facilitates global reach, universal accessibility, mutually agreed governance, and broadly open innovation.

## Technical fragmentation

This is where the operation of the core physical infrastructure begins to or is actually impeded to the extent that full interoperation, interconnection, and interaction within the system cannot operate seamlessly and consistently for all users. This process seems to violate a core underpinning principle of the core initial vision of the Internet as a universal communication method allowing every device to connect with any other. However, universal connectivity is being challenged as the Internet has evolved into a more complex system. In particular, there are issues with regard to Internet addressing, interconnection, naming, and security. Across these broad categories, the authors identify up to a dozen forms of fragmentation, including the use of firewalls, the rise of private networking, segmented Wi-Fi in private domains, blocking, and private naming servers.

## Governmental fragmentation

These are state-driven strategies that seek to limit or actively constrain certain forms of Internet usage, thereby limiting the ability of the system to freely create and distribute and for users to access all available resources. The fear is that increased government action could fragment the global system along territorial lines as states seek to define national interests within cyberspace and seek to impose borders within this domain. In an extreme case, this process could impede the technical and commercial interoperability of the Internet and lead to impositions overflows across borders. These concerns tend to be especially evident in six areas: content and censorship; e-commerce and trade; national security; privacy and data protection; data localisation; and fragmentation as an overarching national strategy. Across these divisions, Drake et al. identified ten types of fragmentation, such as the use by the government of filtering and blocking of websites, attacking undesirable content, limiting e-commerce in specific areas, controlling international interconnections, local content requirements, localising flows, and limiting flows of data where it challenges cyber-sovereignty.

## Commercial fragmentation

These are commercially driven actions that seek to limit universal access to specific uses and/or information resources. These have led to fears that commercial actions can lead to the systemic fragmentation of the Internet. As the Internet has matured, many commercial enterprises have evolved business models to fragment systems behind paywalls and other such devices to limit access to specific types of data. This process fragments the system through the creation of such unique digital spaces as firms seek to target specific markets. This enables differentiation of service between users but also has the potential to impact the underlying physical infrastructure and broader operational environments of the system. In the context, the main areas of concern were peering and standardisation; network neutrality; walled gardens; geo-localisation and geo-blocking; and infrastructure-related intellectual property protection. Across this area, a number of fragmentations were evident, such as the use of proprietorial standards to limit inter-operability, discriminating between users according to the service used, walled gardens, blocking content according to the geography of the user, and using naming and number-ing to block access to content so as to protect intellectual property.

Overall, there is no particular set of challenges that represents the greatest driver of what has been termed the 'splinternet'. The authors believe that six issues are deemed to have especially pressing significance in the maintenance of a coherent network of networks. These are:

- Fragmentation as a strategy.
- Data localisation.
- Digital protectionism.
- Access via mutual legal assistance treaties.
- Walled gardens.
- Information sharing.

There can be little doubt that states are becoming increasingly involved in the governance of the Internet as control continues to shift away from non-governmental bodies towards states. Many of the states that are leading the drive towards a more controlled system are those that have tighter constraints on personal freedoms within their territory. This has had its most evident expression in states like China with its highly published 'Great Firewall of China'. However, this trend – as suggested above – is not solely the preserve of what might be conventionally termed authoritarian states, as many Western liberal democracies are also getting involved in seeking to control what flows in and out of their respective national information infrastructure systems. This not only reflects an emer-gent cyber risk for these states based on security concerns generated by not only the free flow of data across borders but also the vulnerability of these systems to cyberattacks that could undermine critical infrastructure. Indeed, by 2016, only 31 per cent of users were totally free to access material.

As much as governments seek to control the Internet and seek to impose some degree of control upon it, they increasingly find themselves bypassed by technological change. As such, blunter weapons become increasingly attractive when those they seek to regu-late are technologically inferior to those they are seeking to regulate. It is evident that the means to asset sovereignty in cyberspace are different from those strategies that would be deployed in physical domains.

## THE INFORMATION ECONOMY AND DEVELOPING STATES

Evidently, much of the debate surrounding the evolution of the information economy has been shaped by events that have been driven by activities within developed economies. However, if the global information economy is to be truly global, then its impact has to be extended to developing states. The rhetoric that accompanies the potential of the information economy is inevitably attractive to developing states. It offers the potential for relatively rapid economic development, to allow for the better provision of public services, and to offer deeper economic integration. Separating the rhetoric from the reality means that many developing states are simply not ready for the information economy, as they possess neither the hard infrastructure nor the skills to take advantage of such developments.

The narrowing of the digital divide has been a long-term goal of many international bodies, seeing a close link between this process and economic growth and development. This has also been evident at the state level, with many developing states seeking to roll out broadband, upgrade skills, etc. This has been through a mix of public and private sector action, with the latter lining up the process of closing the digital divide with the process of sector liberalisation. Interestingly, an increased level of investment in national broadband infrastructure is coming from tech MNEs, though this is largely incidental to the levels that are desired by these developing states.

Across many developing states, the spread of mobile Internet has been a key driver, with access outpacing adoption in many places. However, even with mobile, this does not solve access to broadband in areas with low population densities. Moreover, where there is mobile coverage, the upgrade to broadband has not happened as there is insufficient demand to justify the investment. Even where there is access, adoption can be low due to low levels of market-creating activities by states and high prices. These gaps for mobile broadband are highlighted in Figure 18.2.

Framed within this deployment of mobile infrastructure, the adoption gap within many developing states is defined by the need to upgrade systems to more advanced infrastructure systems. This adoption process is driven not only by the market potential of the system (with the extent of pre-existing upgrades being a major factor) but also by factors such as geography and topography and the need for electrification. It is estimated that the cost of universal access for developing states is $100 billion, with most of this

**TABLE 18.1** Development differentials in the information economy (by region)

| | Share of population using the Internet | Share of businesses using the Internet |
|---|---|---|
| Developed economies | 83 | 81 |
| Developing economies | 39 | 58 |
| - Africa | 20 | 45 |
| - Asia | 49 | 69 |
| - Latin America/Caribbean | 55 | 75 |
| - Transition economies | 55 | 71 |
| - LDCs | 14 | 40 |
| - Total | 49 | 61 |

Source: UNCTAD (2020)

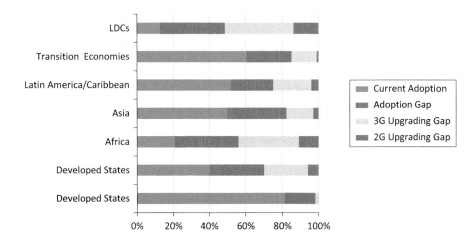

**FIGURE 18.2** Internet connectivity and adoption gaps (by region) (Percentage of population using or connected to mobile broadband)

needing to be spent on upgrading; this is only a fraction of the cost of new deployment (about 10 per cent). This suggests that, through mobile technology, the cost of universal access might not be exorbitant. These do not include the running costs of such systems, which can be very high and, when combined with low adoption, can render these investments uneconomic. This is compounded by other factors such as the cost of devices, communications costs, awareness and skills, and issues surrounding local content.

Given that demand-side factors are largely beyond the capability of national bodies, the focus on seeking to close these gaps rests on the supply side. This means generating an environment in which the desired level of investment would be forthcoming. This, according to UNCTAD, depends upon the maturity of liberalisation and the unbiasedness of the regulatory framework. These also have to be enabled by demand-side measures to create a mature information culture. This is also linked to stimulating the development of local information firms. It also requires that existing firms also become more widespread users of ICTs within their value chains. This at the moment is quite low, with only 36 per cent of businesses in LDCs using any form of ICT in their interactions with buyers, sellers, or partners within their respective value chains.

## CONCLUSION

The information economy has, over the past two decades, become embedded within debates around international business. Indeed, it is a factor that has enabled many smaller businesses to reach international markets. However, as the information economy evolves, not only does it create new competitive and strategic pressures, but it has also attracted the attention of states, which have increasingly sought to apply offline conventions and policies to an online environment. In part, this has been driven by the growing power of big data but also by more basic challenges such as security.

**KEY POINTS**

- The information economy is increasingly core to the operation of international business.
- The rise of the information economy poses new challenges and opportunities for the operation of international business.
- Pressure points are emerging within the information economy as it begins to fragment under a mix of technical, state, and commercial pressures.

## DISCUSSION QUESTIONS

1. How do you believe the information economy changes the competitive dynamics of international business?
2. How do you account for the rise in big data?
3. Is the rise of the FANGs something to be worried about?

## ACTIVITY

Using one of the FANGs as an example, research how the business collects and utilises consumer data for competitive advantage.

## SUGGESTED FURTHER READINGS

Deibert, R. J., & Crete-Nishihata, M. (2012). Global governance and the spread of cyberspace controls. *Global Governance: A Review of Multilateralism and International Organizations, 18*(3), 339–361.

Drake, W., Cerf, V., & Kleinwächter, W. (2016). Internet fragmentation: An overview. *Future of the Internet Initiative White Paper, World Economic Forum.*

Drucker, P. F. (1969). The knowledge society. *New Society, 13*(343), 629–631.

Moore, M. (2016). *Tech giants and civic power' centre of media, communications and power,* London: Kings College London.

UNCTAD (2016). World investment report. www.unctad.org.

# CHAPTER 19

# NATURAL RESOURCES AND INTERNATIONAL BUSINESS: THE FOOD-WATER-ENERGY NEXUS

## OBJECTIVES

This chapter will help you to:

- Understand the nature of the food-water-energy nexus.
- Comprehend the challenges posed by food security.
- Assess the nature of water risk and its impact on business.
- Identify the nature of the energy transition and its link to energy security.

Secure and reliable economic activity depends on sustained access to a range of natural resources. Without these resources, economic activity would effectively cease. While there is a plethora of natural resources that are involved in economic activity, there are three interrelated groups of resources that are universal across all activities, namely those that supply food, water, and energy. As the global economy and population grow, the pressure on the resources supplying these requirements grows. This has given rise to increased concern with regard to the security of supply of each of the resources that enable these requirements to be met. Moreover, these three natural resources are mutually supportive and enabling, as reflected within the food-water energy (FWE) nexus (see below), so the diminution of one will impact the efficacy of the others. Increasingly, the resources that underpin the supply of these requirements are enabled by a global system. Both food and energy have very well-developed global trading systems where countries attain supply security through engagement with other states. In water, while its physical supply is local and possibly regional, there is a well-established virtual trade. However, it is becoming evident that concerns over security over the global supply of natural resources are leading to an increased risk of conflict between states. This chapter

DOI: 10.4324/9781315184500-24

initially explores the nature of the food-water-energy nexus and why it matters to business. The chapter then moves on to examine challenges within each of the global systems of supply for each of the core themes within the nexus. In so doing, the chapter will examine change within each of these natural resource-based systems and its impact on business.

## THE FOOD-WATER-ENERGY NEXUS

The FWE nexus reflects the interdependencies between these core resources that are central to economic and human development. It also implies that no part of this resource base can be managed in isolation from another resource. The links between these assets can often be implicit but are nonetheless vital to the operation of the global system. These are reflected in Figure 19.1, but the links between these resources are:

1.  Energy-water links: these interconnections are based on the fact that water is used extensively for energy generation through hydropower and for cooling systems within thermal electricity generation. Energy is also extensively used within water systems, where it is widely used for the processing, transportation, and treatment of water.
2.  Energy-food links: these links are born of the well-understood links where energy is used extensively in the production of food, notably through the mechanisation of the food production process. The two-way links between these resources are also evident in the increased use of biofuels, where food is directly used as a source of energy.
3.  Food-water links: the link between these resources is established throughout pre-history, where water has been extensively used for irrigation purposes. The contribution of food to water is opaque and emerges as a virtual act in the transmission of food (see below).

The fact that these resources are mutually enabled and that the existence of each is an existential activity for human activity has forced economic agents to look at the stresses on each and how the operation and sustainability of one resource impact the efficacy of another. The centrality of these resources to human activity has tied them intimately into notions of security, notably that all economic and non-economic actors need access to a secure supply of these resources. Conventionally, these have been provided locally, but over time, they have been scaled up to be increasingly attained through the operation of global systems (see below). This creates two levels of pressure within the nexus:

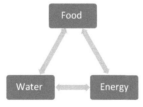

**FIGURE 19.1** The food-water-energy nexus

1) Pressure on any single component that can damage the efficacy of any other on a global level, either through direct or indirect channels.

2) States that are abundant in any one of these resources can disrupt the nexus by limiting the supply of the resource.

The increased attention given to the nexus does not merely reflect a growing awareness of the interconnectivity between these systems but, more importantly, how the process of climate change and the regulatory response to this process are placing pressure on this nexus. This, as suggested above, can impact issues of state security and lead to an increasingly fractured and unstable global system. This latter point reflects how the globalisation of trade has led to a more complex interaction of this nexus. In a global system, food, water, and energy are constantly crossing borders, not just in their own right but also in a 'virtual' manner, as a result of their contribution to the production of completed and/or semi-completed products. This international transmission has also been evident in the large-scale land acquisitions (see below) made by some developed states within developing states as a means of securing food, energy, and/or water. What has been concerning is that such land acquisitions to support a state's FWE nexuses are often at the expense of denying local resources to the indigenous population.

As mentioned, the FWE nexuses and their state are linked to conditions of social well-being. This reflects not simply the human need for these resources but that constraints in one or more of these resources will act as a break upon economic growth. This applies not simply to states but also to businesses, which are highly involved in the provision and management of these resources. For these reasons, many argue that the nexus has to include livelihoods because the nexus has limited value without being contextualised within this broader objective. Thus, notions of sustainability implicit within the FWE nexus reflect not merely issues of resource availability but also the ability of that system to drive growth and development in a manner that does not deplete the nexus.

## THE GLOBAL FOOD SYSTEM

Food is not simply about addressing simple calorific needs. It is also about social interaction, how we interact with the environment, and cultural identity. Over time, this system has changed from being localised and small-scale to becoming a global entity that is, as a sector, the world's single largest employer, with up to 2 billion people employed both directly and indirectly, from agricultural production to retailing. Treating food production as a system underpins that its operation depends upon sectors whose primary purpose is not agricultural output but transportation, processing, etc. The underpinning rationale for this configuration is that it reflects an effective method of delivering food security on a global basis, where food security is defined by the World Bank as a situation when all people, at all times, have physical and economic access to sufficient safe and nutritious food that meets their dietary needs and food preferences for an active and healthy life.

Figure 19.2 highlights the steady rise in food trade over the past three decades. This trade in foodstuff has risen along with the global population as more states depend on external (i.e., non-domestic) sources for food supply. This increase in demand has also been driven by increased use of fuels for biofuels and by dietary changes, notably as rising levels of development in emerging economies (notably China) have led to a higher protein-rich diet. Alongside that, there are still some sections of the global population (at all stages of development) that suffer from food poverty or insecurity. Moreover, these increases in demand for food are placing increased pressure on competition for water and energy.

As globalisation progressed, a global food system (which is defined as the spatial expansion of the production, transmission, and consumption of foodstuffs) emerged, with states using these processes to diversify both the quality and quantity of food items as well as the type of food consumers. The food system comprises the totality of human and institutional activity, processes, and infrastructure required to produce and consume food. This includes a range of activities, including growing, harvesting, processing, packaging, transporting, marketing, selling, cooking, consumption, and disposal of food and any food-related items. The food system has a number of interconnected actors, including states and their agrarian policies, MNEs, global trading businesses, etc. As of 2022, around 30 crops account for 95 per cent of total production, and around a third of the global total of agricultural land (around 1.5 billion hectares) is used for food crops. The rest is mainly used for cattle feed. Indeed, only around 20 per cent of agricultural land is used for crops for direct human consumption. Moreover, international trade in foodstuffs is only about 14 per cent of total production and less than 9 per cent of total merchandise trade.

Integral to the global food system are global value chains built around a seamless flow of agricultural products across political borders, where the different stages and components of the system are dispersed spatially. Importantly, these global value chains place a great deal of emphasis on services. These services are essential to the flow of food as they depend on logistics, trade, financial, and other business services. These GVCs are based around large agricultural states (such as China and the US). However, these GVCs

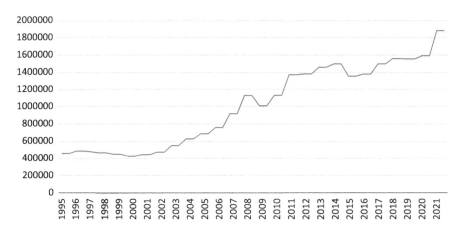

**FIGURE 19.2** Global trade in all foods (1995–2001) (Source: UNCTAD)

tend to be a feature of larger, more developed states. They tend not to exist in developing states where trade remains local.

The global food system became entwined with issues of food security, as the rationale behind the food system is that it allows more food to be produced more efficiently and at a lower cost. Global trade has created a disconnect between the security of supply and indigenous production. This has been facilitated not simply by lower tariffs (though agricultural production remains controversial in the trade arena) but also by advances in technology and transportation that allow food to be transported quickly while maintaining its freshness. This trade tends to be concentrated in the largest states with the most accommodating climates. Thus, the four largest food producers are China, the US, India, and Brazil. These have a mix of climates, available land, and large populations.

Change within the food system is driven by six identified drivers:

- Biophysical and environmental drivers such as available land resources, pollution, and climate.
- Demographic drivers such as changes in the structure and size of populations as well as issues such as rural to urban migration.
- Innovation, technology, and infrastructure, including issues such as the transmission of products as well as changes in inputs that can impact the form and nature of output.
- Economic factors such as income, trade, prices, and financial systems.
- Socio-cultural drivers, notably those aspects of culture, religions, and rituals.
- Social traditions, education, health, values, and identity, which impact diets and dietary requirements.
- Political factors, which include governance, public policies, conflicts, and humanitarian crises, can impact the operation of the food system at both local, national, and global levels.

There are clearly interrelationships between these drivers, but these, in turn, are impacted by factors that are internal to the food system that can drive change within it. These can be the result of decisions such as what crops to grow and what animals to breed, or energy intensity, for example. It is the interactions between these factors that are shaping the broad set of issues noted below with regard to the main issues of change in the food system and its capacity to drive food security.

## Issues in the global food system

### Climate change

The change in climate impacts the food system through a multitude of channels. The first impact is the increase in extreme weather events, which can lead to increased disruption in agricultural production. This includes not just flooding of irrigation channels but also droughts, which limit the efficacy of rain-fed agriculture. This can increase the risk of famine within affected states and underscores the need for a global system to mitigate this localised risk. However, climate change can also impact those states that are big food suppliers, and this is a greater risk. The US and China are both big food producers and have been suffering ongoing droughts for decades. This has been coupled with the extreme weather events that have become widespread as a result of the La Nina weather system throughout 2020–2021, which produced droughts in some areas and flooding in others. There is also the fact that food systems are direct contributors to greenhouse gas emissions. Indeed, it is estimated that food production contributes up to a third of the overall emissions of these gases. These emissions are expected to grow by over 90 per cent as food systems expand to increase production to cope with an expanding global population.

## Food poverty

Despite decades of improvement since the 1980s, there has been a marked increase in food poverty since 2019. This reflects both the sharp rise in the price of foodstuffs and the unevenness with which many states have emerged from the COVID-19 pandemic. As Case study 19.1 notes, this had a big impact on food prices as many aspects of the food system had their functioning impaired. This reflects how the pandemic exacerbated pre-existing inequalities, especially within the lower-skilled parts of the labour market, which were most vulnerable to unemployment and food insecurity. Between 2019 and 2020, the share of malnourished people rose to around 10 per cent of the global population – some 700–800 million people. This rose by 150 million during the COVID-19 pandemic. By 2030, some 9 per cent of the global population is expected to be undernourished. With regard to less severe but still very serious forms of food insecurity, around 2.3 billion people faced moderate or severe food insecurity in 2021 – about 12 per cent of the global population. On top of this, 3.1 billion people could not afford a healthy diet.

## Geopolitics

The notion of geopolitics feeds into food security and the operation of the global food system through its ability to fragment and disrupt flows between states. Extended GVCs within the sector can be subject to this geopolitical disruption if a state is a major supplier of foodstuffs or if it is a major transit point in the process (see below on global chokepoints). The geopolitical risk to the global food system was highlighted most evidently during stages of the Russia-Ukraine conflict, where the former sought to limit exports of Ukrainian foodstuffs and fertiliser into the global system as a means of inhibiting its ability to defend itself. The impact of this restriction was to cause a sharp rise in food and fertiliser prices. This created an impact beyond Eurasia into North Africa and the Middle East and deepened geopolitical risk globally, as there was a widespread impact on food security globally. This geopolitical issue also extends to other food suppliers, where the process of supplying that food can involve significant environmental degradation. This was evident in the geopolitical pressure applied to Brazil and its destruction of the Amazon rainforest for agricultural purposes.

## Chokepoints

In the global trading systems, there are points where there is the potential for the transmission of foodstuffs to be disrupted. This reflects the fact that the global food system depends on international logistics systems for its effective operation. At points in the global logistics networks, there are a number of points where large volumes of foodstuffs pass. There can be maritime channels (such as the Suez Canal), coastal infrastructure (such as ports), and inland infrastructure (this moves the produce from the point of production to the point of export). The fear is that disruptions (whether natural or as a result of human activity) could lead to severe supply disruptions, or at the very least, they could lead to increased waste, delays, or other issues linked to the smooth supply of food throughout the global economy. The most common choke points include the Turkish Straits, which connect the global system to the Black Sea ports, US rail and inland waterways systems, and Brazilian ports. These chokepoints are impacted by the main types of risk: climatic, geopolitical, and institutional (such as erratic governance). The risk posed by these bottlenecks is increasing due to their increased use, the threat of climate change, and the poor maintenance of many of these facilities. This can leave all food-importing states (especially those in the developing world) especially vulnerable to food security issues.

## Protectionism

The evolution of a global food system has linked food security to broader notions of globalisation. It argues that the expansion of trade in foodstuffs has allowed for enhanced food security by diversifying sources as well as increasing the quantity and diversity of options available. It is also believed that those states that have a comparative advantage in food production are able to exploit that advantage leading to a net gain for the global economic system. However, for many countries, agriculture remains a key strategic industry deserving of protection. This reflects a fear that excessive dependence on imports of food at the expense of indigenous production could leave the state vulnerable. This can often give farmers a great deal of political power, which they can use to stymie freer trade in agricultural goods, especially where they are small-scale farmers who would struggle to compete against large-scale concerns. Thus, the globalisation of food systems has often been coupled with flanking policies that limit the social impact of any trade opening. On the whole, tariffs are higher on agricultural goods than they are on non-agricultural goods in 90 per cent of states.

## Governance issues

These concerns are shaped not by the fact that the system is global but by how that system is controlled and how this arguably leads to exploitation by powerful food multinationals over small-scale producers. It is estimated that the earth's population of 7 billion is fed by 1.5 billion producers, with 70 per cent of this output being controlled by 700 MNEs. It has been argued that the control of agricultural GVCs has allowed these businesses to exploit and push aside farmers (especially small-scale subsistence producers) and to offer food at a low cost that is of limited nutritional value. The sensitivity of the issue has been sharpened not only by the aforementioned issues related to climate change and water resources (see below) but also by increased levels of obesity within countries at all levels of economic development. These have been facilitated by their control of a global food system, which gives them access – so some NGOs argue

– to cheap land and labour. In part, these governance issues are created by a global food system that has grown so complex that not all of the largest food producers are always aware of the ongoing activities within their respective supply chains.

---

**Box 19.1: Global pandemics and food security**

Food security is based upon the resilience of the global food system and its ability to maintain flows between those states that are net producers of food and those that are net importers. The vulnerability of such a global system was exposed in the COVID-19 pandemic when there was a sharp rise in food insecurity globally. The sharp restrictions placed on economic activity as a means to contain the spread of the virus had a direct impact on food production. The system was also impacted by changes to the food system created by the closure of food outlets (such as supermarkets) and the reliance on alternative forms of access, as well as the impact on the food hospitality sector. This was compounded by the limits on exports of foodstuffs imposed by some states as a consequence of the pandemic. All four pillars of food security were impacted by the pandemic through:

1) Constraints on food accessibility.
2) Limits on food availability.
3) Uncertainty over food utilisation where there are limits on the form and types of protein to be consumed.
4) Limits on the stability of supply.

In terms of access, the immediate impact was that restrictions on food supply led to a sharp rise in prices that led to issues of affordability and increased levels of food poverty. This issue of food poverty was compounded by a loss of income for the lowest-income households as economic activity slowed. This was an issue across both developing and developed states. The net effect of these processes, without state support, would be an increase in undernourishment in lower-income segments of the population. Importantly, this could have a long-term legacy for the well-being of populations where poor diets become embedded and where, especially in young children, there is a legacy with regard to their physical and cognitive development.

With regard to food availability and stability, the impact of agricultural production will be mixed. Where there is a high degree of mechanisation of the agricultural system, the impact on food production is expected to be slight. The impact will be significant where the system is more labour-intensive and where labour shortages will directly impact agricultural productivity. Nonetheless, there are vulnerabilities created by pandemics beyond simply production, notably with regard to supply chain disruption. Again, where there is a high degree of mechanisation and where social distancing can be observed, the impact will be mitigated, though where the transmission requires a high degree of labour input (e.g., in marketplaces and low-mechanised ports), the disruption will also be highest. The greater impact is expected to be downstream in food processing and the distribution of public food (such as school meals).

In these cases, close human interaction is necessary, and as a result, there could be significant disruption. These processes could lead to increased domestic concerns with regard to food security, leading to restrictions on food exports. In the COVID-19 pandemic, these measures were temporary as countries sought to make sense of how global food systems would adapt. In many cases, these measures were quickly removed as food systems proved more robust than initially expected, and these measures actually made food security worse. Pandemics can also shape food choices with regard to the nutrition of the food purchased. It was evident that as food prices rose, lower-income facilities purchased poor nutritional food and cut back on those foods with a higher nutritional value. There was an increase in the consumption of processed foods and a decline in fresh foods.

Pandemics – as witnessed by the COVID-19 episode – pose challenges for food security. In many cases, food poverty increases, so social safety nets need to be in place to counter the impact of the slowdown in economic activity that occurs as a result of an attempt to limit the impact on public health of the spread of any virus. It is also needed to ensure that the global food system remains resilient throughout. This means increased mechanisation to allow the system to continue to process through these episodes, as well as the prioritisation of food industry workers during any processes where economic interaction has to be subdued to limit the spread of any virus.

## THE CHALLENGE OF GLOBAL WATER

This is arguably the least global of the triumvirate of resources within the FWE nexus framework, though it has no less global significance. Much as the earth is covered in water, it is the supply of freshwater that is of concern. Freshwater is suitable for consumption due to the absence of dissolved salts. This is only three per cent of the water available on this planet. This three per cent is in lakes, streams, and glaciers, and while it is a renewable resource, an expanding population means that per capita water availability is falling. Every year, humanity draws 4.5 trillion cubic metres of water from its freshwater sources, and its usage has increased sixfold over the past century. Thus, there is a need for states to have an effective water system to ensure that water is accessible, usable, disposable, and reusable. This water system, defined on a national level, comprises those facilities and processes that supply water for human use, whether for drinking, irrigation, or industry, and treat wastewater to protect public and ecological health. Pipes, home faucets, water towers, treatment plants, watersheds, and estuaries are key parts of the water system. It is through this system that water security is defined as the availability of the required quantity and quality of water for health, livelihoods, and production, coupled with an acceptable level of water-related risks. The latter point underscores that water security is not simply about conditions of water shortage but also about conditions of water excess created by random inundations. Thus, the water system needs to be expanded to include those facilities (such as flood protection systems) that protect human well-being under such conditions, which are key components of water systems. Overall, water security encapsulates a number of themes, namely

- Access to safe drinking water;
- Protection of socio-economic and cultural well-being;
- Preservation and protection of ecological systems;
- Support economic development and those commercial activities that depend directly on water;
- Protection from the dangers of polluted water;
- Cooperation in the preservation and utilisation of international water resources;
- Resilience and sustainability in the face of extreme oscillations of water flows and other water-related hazards.

The main usage of water is agriculture, which comprises, on average, 70 per cent of use; industry, 19 per cent, and households, 11 per cent. However, this can vary according to the level of economic development, with developed states using more water for industrial purposes. These usages highlight the core issues for the water system, namely increased demands on a resource that, while recyclable, is ultimately fixed. While water is recyclable, this does depend on there being sufficient water infrastructure and sanitation systems to allow water to be purified and released back into freshwater sources.

The global nature of the water system is reflected in its nature as a common, universally required resource that occurs (at least in freshwater form) unevenly across the globe. Thus, there has to be a transmission of water from places of abundance to places of shortage. This occurs not through the direct export of water but through a virtual water system. This is created when arid countries rely on the water resources of other countries to supply them with goods that utilise large amounts of water. This means that as goods are traded globally, their water footprint (i.e., the volume of freshwater used) follows them. This helps those countries that are exhibiting water stress preserve

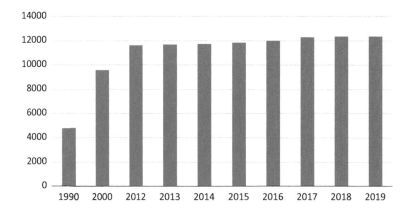

**FIGURE 19.3** Levels of water stress: freshwater withdrawal as a proportion of freshwater resources

(Source: World Bank)

domestic sources. Such strategies are common in states such as Mexico, Saudi Arabia, and the Mediterranean. Interestingly, northern states are also large importers of virtual water, though this is driven less and more by the use of hydropower from water-rich states. As agriculture is the largest user of water (about 80 per cent) the largest food producers are also the largest exporters of virtual water. Similarly, the major food importers are also the major virtual water importers. The impact on water security of such trade depends on the efficiency of water usage in the exporting state.

The global dimension of water is also underscored by the fact that water stress (when the demand for water exceeds the available amount during a certain period or when poor quality restricts its use) is a global, not a local, problem. Localised water issues can easily spill over across borders not simply through limits on flows of trade (see above) but also through increased migratory flows and other potentially disruptive processes. This threat is getting worse by 2050. It is estimated that 5 billion people will live in areas that are water-stressed, notably the Middle East, the US, Eurasia, and North Africa. For businesses, water stress can translate into lower growth due to the intensity of water use in many forms of production, as well as its role in energy production. Water shortages undermine the economic viability of an area.

## Issues in global water

The issues below reflect the main challenges that are facing the global water system.

## Climate change

The impact of climate change on water systems can be manifold, notably potentially resulting in extremes where, compared to normally or expected weather patterns, there can be scenarios where there is too much or too little precipitation, both of which can be equally destructive to both human and natural systems. This absence of predictability in water resources places further pressure on notions of water security. In many states, there are natural variations in rainfall. Climate change threatens to erode this degree of predictability over such variations. This is also compounded by the belief that climate change will also lead to more extreme weather events, be they droughts, severe storms, or flooding. This increases levels of water insecurity across the globe because there is both too much and too little water. The quality of water is also impacted by climate change, where warmer water has lower self-purifying capacity as well and impurities within water flows being increased as concentrations increase in drought conditions. These expectations are likely to be especially severe within tropical and sub-tropical zones (where 60 per cent of the global population lives), notably in many small island developing states. The fact that these extreme events are expected to become increasingly common means that there will be a direct need for human and natural systems to adapt. Where climate changes faster than these systems, there is likely to be a substantial impact. Thus, there is expected to be an impact on agricultural systems as well as urban areas due to the physical impact of extreme variation in weather. This can mean that freshwater supplies can either not be replenished at the necessary rate or that the natural storage systems for this resource are damaged by regular inundations.

## Inter-state conflict

The notion of water stress has an undercurrent between states of increased competition for water resources. As populations expand within states that share a common water resource, there is an increased risk of tension between states as they compete for this shared resource. While there has been substantial cooperation between states on water resources, there is nonetheless a fear that this could be eroded when set against the context of water stress. The risk for conflict between states only increases where there is a go-it-alone strategy being followed by states with the result that it creates a zero-sum situation in water management. Globally, there are 276 transboundary water systems (with a further 300 international aquifers being identified), and 148 states share at least part of their freshwater resources with another country, with 39 of these states having over 90 per cent of their reserves in such shared resources and 21 of these having the entirety of their reserves within such transboundary systems.

## Industrialisation and growth

The demands on global water resources can only be expected to grow. This is not just due to the expected increase in the global population, which, by definition, lowers the per capita water supply and increases the demand for food, but also to the rapid processes of industrialisation in many parts of the world that are currently emerging or underdeveloped. This places pressure on the global water system not simply through increased demands for industry but also through the inevitable increases in the use of water that accompany such trends, most notably as a result of changing diets. The impact is also felt through the use of water for transportation as well as in many processing industries. The rising urbanisation and economic development require more food to be produced, as well as being more diverse. Moreover, precedent tells us that this increasingly affluent population wants food that is more water-intensive to produce, notably products such as beef, which is notoriously water-intensive in its production. Thus, overall, it can be anticipated that the growth in water usage will outstrip the rise in population growth. Moreover, the reusing levels of development will also increase the demand for energy, which will also cause the demand for water to increase further. The result could be a 40 per cent shortfall in water by 2030, with many states already extracting more freshwater groundwater quicker than it is being replenished. Thus, concerns over water security can likely lead to lower levels of economic growth for states.

## Governance issues

Integral to the notions of water security are those related to the governance of water resources. There is a long-standing perception that water is often priced incorrectly and that the absence of market-based systems leads to an undervaluation of these resources and thus leads to waste and overuse. These also have to align with the broad interests involved in the process of water security. Thus, it is not simply how much it is used but also how it is used to support broader (often environmentally led) objectives. This governance system has to exist to allow for the effective management of water resources. There is a clear correlation between good governance and secure water systems. Governance of water systems is often problematised by the fact that there is a sharp divergence between assorted stakeholders over the value attached to water. These can diverge for a diverse number of reasons, from culture to economic pressures. There also seems to be a special undervaluation of water hydraulic infrastructure (flood protection, water pipes, etc.) that has suffered from years of neglect and is declining in capacity, with leaking across the pipeline system being common amongst developed economies, for example. There are also measures needed to promote the efficiency of usage within the main uses of water, notably agriculture and industry.

---

### Box 19.2: China's water security issues

Water – along with energy – is often seen as China's Achilles heel with regard to the sustainability of its economic growth and development. As the economy has grown throughout the late 20th and early 21st centuries, the pressure on China's already fragile water resources has grown. This is compounded by the fact that China's water supply is unevenly distributed across the state, both spatially and temporally, and that, like other countries, water usage is very inefficient. In the case of the former, this distribution is a problem because there is a disparity between water demand and supply across China's provinces, with the driest being at the centre of China's economic development. For example, north China has 19 per cent of total water supplies but 65 per cent of total arable land and 45 per cent of China's population. Moreover, the usage patterns in northern China reflect a high degree of inefficient usage compared to southern China. This relative aridity of northern China stands in contrast to southern China, which has 400 per cent higher per capita water availability. Moreover, 70 per cent of China's precipitation (the main supply of freshwater) occurs in just four months. This issue of water quantity is compounded by issues of water quality, where wastewater treatment has not kept up with increased water demand, leading to increased levels of pollution within major waterways. Thus, while there has been progress in the development of water infrastructure, it has not been nearly fast enough to keep up with the pressures within the system.

These issues are compounded by a complex water management system that is, historically, more focused on technology and big projects than measures that support water management and conservation. Thus, when water issues emerge, the trend is to seek an engineering solution (e.g., a new dam, etc.) rather than other socio-economic solutions such as efficiency of usage. This process is based on simply meeting increased demand with increased supply without considering supply constraints or how that water is used. Moreover, this engineering-based solution has tended to give little thought to the ecological consequences of increased water extraction or the health of the main river systems. This does not just raise issues for the sustainability of such ecological systems but also increases concerns with regard to water pollution and public health and well-being, especially with the contamination of drinking water. There have also been increased incidences of cancer due to contaminated water supplies.

These structural and governance issues are compounded by long-term trends in the water supply within China, which are placing further pressure on the system.

Arguably, the major challenge is climate change and the risk that it makes the precipitation that drives China's water supply increasingly erratic and leads to uneven flows in the major water sources. Indeed, it is estimated that as a result of climate change, the more arid regions of northern China will become even drier, thus compounding existing problems of spatial aridity. In contrast, the southern regions of China are expected to get wetter. The climatic issues are compounded by China's sustained path of economic development with increased urbanisation and industrialisation. These processes place pressure on the FWE nexus, whereas water quantity and quality begin to be erratic, so the pressure is placed on agricultural systems, especially as China has around 20 per cent of the global population, 10 per cent of global water, and around 6 per cent of global arable land (much of which is located within the arid north). The pressure on this nexus is only expected to increase as rising prosperity increases protein-rich diets, which are water-intensive and will cause further pressure on water systems. This pressure is also evident due to the high use of water in energy production.

The Chinese government has begun to develop more holistic strategies with regard to water security. It has placed an increased emphasis on water conservation. The cornerstone of its strategy is the South-to-North Water Diversion Project, which shifts large volumes of water from the wet south to the arid north. However, overwhelmingly, the focus is still on increasing supply rather than aggressive conservation measures, which still seems like a secondary issue.

## THE GLOBAL ENERGY SYSTEM

The provision of energy within the global economy seems to be turning full circle. For much of human history, energy was sourced and provided locally (either through local biomass or by locating close to another known energy source). However, the late 19th and early 20th centuries saw this local link eroded, largely due to the rise of oil and gas as major sources of energy (the former driven by the rise of petrol-driven internal combustion engines), which created a global energy system based on the trade in these hydrocarbons from areas such as the Middle East into developed countries. With the onset of the global energy transition (which most of this section will deal with), there is a trend towards the localising or, at the very least, the regionalising of the global energy system. In truth, as reflected in Figure 19.4, the energy system has been in a state of ongoing transition within the modern industrial age as coal replaced traditional biomass, which was in turn replaced by oil and gas, which is now being replaced by renewables. It is the last of these transitions that will be the focus of this section.

The shift towards renewables involves a wholesale change within the global energy systems, notably with regard to how energy is generated and distributed, and an international commitment to limit carbon emissions so as to keep the anticipated global rise in temperatures to an agreed limit (1.5 per cent). This requires a large-scale investment in renewable energy technologies and the decarbonisation of our economic activity. At the

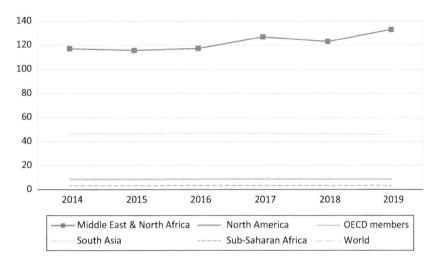

**FIGURE 19.4** Annual freshwater withdrawals (per cent of internal resources)

core of the transition is energy security, namely that any economic system has sufficient energy supply to ensure the uninterrupted supply of energy at a level that is necessary to sustain and enhance this activity. In the current era, security is understood to mean access to hydrocarbons, notably oil and gas. In an era of global energy systems, security became an increased concern where energy could be used as a geopolitical tool and where prices could be highly variable. Thus, notions of security are not simply defined by the quantity of energy available but by a range of factors. These have been encapsulated within the four A's of energy security, namely

1) Availability: the physical existence of sources of energy or elements relating to geological existence.
2) Accessibility: that the energy resources are physically available to the user due to the geopolitical willingness of the energy user and supplier to engage in a transaction.
3) Affordability: the costs of extraction, processing, and distribution allow end users to access this fuel in a manner that does place undue strain on corporate and/or household finances.
4) Acceptability: that the source of energy used is acceptable in terms of its legacy for environmental and societal processes.

There is intuitive potential for inconsistencies between these facets of energy security, most notably between the notions of affordability and acceptability. There is also potential conflict between issues of energy poverty and the desire for energy companies to return on their investments that involve high sunk costs. Also, alongside these issues, other themes come into play such as the diversity of geographic sources and fuel types and import dependency. These reflect that energy security is subject to a number of risks, such as

- Geopolitical uncertainty disrupts the global supply chain;
- The risk of resource nationalism (see Case study 19.1);
- Infrastructure failures created by power surges and human activity, for example.

All of these can worsen the supply conditions for energy systems and hinder the sustainability of flows. Conventionally, the globality of systems was seen as a core theme within energy security. This allowed for diversity in both supplies and types of energy. Indeed, the global market for fuels and trade in these materials is seen by many leading countries as depending upon robust trading links supported by strategic reverses (storage) of key fuels. However, as we shall see, there has been some pushback on globality within energy systems. These conflicts and contradictions within the global energy systems and the four A's approach outlined above have been captured by the World Energy Council's Energy Trilemma (see Figure 19.5)

This identified the three challenges facing investment in energy and the trade-offs that have to be faced within the process. That all three cannot be thought of in isolation indicates that energy faces dilemmas. For example, the shift towards renewables (see below) requires new investment, which will impact affordability. The notion of security relies on renewables that can be intermittent in their output. There are also evident issues with regard to security, where a choice has to be made between short-term access to polluting hydrocarbons and longer-term investment in renewables. Moreover, security might mean using indigenous sources that are highly polluting. The trade-offs within the

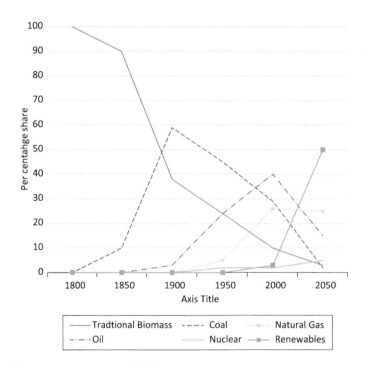

**FIGURE 19.5** Energy transitions since 1800

energy system are therefore multitudinous and are at the core of the energy transition towards renewable energy.

As suggested in Figure 19.4, the current energy transition is based upon the replacement of hydrocarbons as the mainstay of the global energy system with renewable sources of energy. This will lead to electricity being the main source of energy within the global system. This is driven by the increased use of electricity in buildings and transport. The goals are set within the context of the legacy of carbon-based energy for the natural and human environment, largely as a result of changes in climatic conditions caused by the burning of these fossil fuels. Instead of a shift generated by technological change and market dynamics, much of the transition is being driven by shifting government priorities that seek to limit future global warming. The most high-profile impact of these processes is the deployment of renewable technologies (i.e., solar, wind, hydro, and geothermal energy) (see Figure 19.7). This process of deploying renewable has been facilitated by the rapid price declines of these technologies. Indeed, over the past decade, the price of photovoltaic cells has fallen by 85 per cent; concentrated solar power projects by 68 per cent; onshore wind by 56 per cent; and offshore wind by 48 per cent. By 2050, the aim of the transition is that renewables will account for 50 per cent of total energy generation, 90 per cent of electricity generation, and 79 per cent of total energy consumption. This is up from 12 per cent in 2020. Table 19.6 shows the share of the respective forms of renewable generation (including conventional hydropower). This shows that hydropower accounts for nearly half of renewable energy generation, and while the capacity of the other forms is increasing, they still lag far behind this conventional form of renewable energy generation (BP, 2022).

However, the shift to decarbonisation of business does not occur simply through the increased deployment of renewable energy. Indeed, by 2050, it is estimated that just 25 per cent of targeted decarbonisation energy efficiency will come from the electrification of end-use sectors (e.g., electric vehicles and heat pumps); clean hydrogen and its derivatives; bioenergy combined with carbon capture and storage; and last-mile use of carbon capture and storage. This suggests that the transition is not a simple process of replacing one type of energy with another but of radically altering the form and structure of the global energy system. The challenge of the transition is that the energy system is still able to meet the core requirements of energy as well as reconcile the tension identified within the trilemma. The transition also throws up a number of other issues. These are addressed below.

**FIGURE 19.6** The energy trilemma

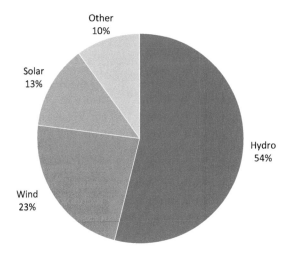

**FIGURE 19.7** Share of renewable energy generation

## Issues in the energy transition

### Geopolitics

One of the core facets of the global energy system based on hydrocarbons was the emergent role of geopolitics within the system, especially in the mid-1970s, where the supply was used as an overt political weapon to influence the actions of other (oil-importing) states. Logically, the shift towards renewable energy generation should diminish the power of these states. It is feasible to argue that, with the potential deglobalisation of energy production (see below), geopolitics will be less of an issue for the future development of the system. However, renewable generating capacity is spread unevenly across the global system. Moreover, the 'rare earths' that are central to the scaling up of electronic vehicles are also unevenly produced across the planet. This is compounded by a rush by leading states to develop competence in renewable energy technologies. This can be expected from a new set of energy superpowers based on their ability to control global electricity generation. This will be compounded by the proposed development of international electricity grids to move this power from states generating surpluses to those where deficits exist. Thus, the geopolitical dimension of the global energy system will not be eroded by the renewable energy transition; it will simply be transformed as power shifts from oil- and gas-producing states to those with high renewable energy technology and generating competence.

### Global versus local

On the flip side of this emergent geopolitical pattern is the belief that the latest energy transition will militate against the perceived vulnerabilities of the global system by creating a more localised generation of energy. While such a system will rely on global energy value chains for its components, the rise of distributed generation allows for a higher degree of independence from the global energy system. The falling cost of renewable energy technologies is allowing for the development of small-scale (mainly firm-level) off-grid electricity systems. These have been combined with small-scale generation (often at household levels), which is on-grid. This disaggregates and descales generation away from the conventional hub and spoke system based on large-scale infrastructure systems. This is seen as a path for promoting the development of electricity systems without the need for large upfront investment but also to increase the role of renewable technology at the local scale. This could be a key part of the rollout of these technologies and the promotion of energy systems in developing countries. Moreover, it loosens these countries' dependence on the global energy system and shows how oscillations in energy prices impede the development of these states. However, there are downsides related to the loss of diversity of fuels, the cost of installation, and the loss of economies of scale in production.

## Stranded assets

A problem for energy businesses with the transition is that it could render existing assets linked to the utilisation of hydrocarbons worthless. The belief that an asset may become worthless due to the progression of the renewable energy transition may lead to a short-term underinvestment in energy assets that could leave the system vulnerable to disruption. This is also already evident where oil companies mothball oil fields before they are fully exhausted or simply limit further exploration for such resources. The legacy of this could be to cause supply disruptions within the transition period where there are insufficient hydrocarbon resources coming forward to replace those exhausted and/or retired, or where there is simply a disruption to supply channels. This, combined with the fact that renewable capacity is not scaled up sufficiently, could create an energy 'crunch' where demand exceeds supply, creating a sharp rise in prices. This stranded asset issue could also create a problem where the lifespan of a key energy asset is sufficiently shortened that it is insufficiently maintained, creating further stresses within the energy system.

## Uneven and disruptive transition

One of the core risks is the uneven nature within which the transition takes place, with the result that there is a negligible impact on carbon emissions. However, the fact that different states are on divergent trajectories and that many leading countries are competing with each other to lead this transition suggests that this process of change will be disorderly with limited cooperation between states. This could result in some states seeking an advantage over other states by limiting the deployment of renewable technologies and seeking the cost benefits over delaying their introduction. There is also a need within the transition to ensure that the process has minimal economic and social disruption, as many industries remain carbon-intensive and the introduction of these technologies runs the risk of increased levels of unemployment and the social disruption that results from such a process. Moreover, there is a risk that if change is too slow, it will occur at too limited a pace to make a meaningful impact, or that deep and severe emissions cuts will take place further down the line as 2050 approaches. This raises the prospect that the transition can be impactful because it is going too fast, too slow, or in a spatially uneven manner.

## CASE STUDY 19.1: RESOURCE NATIONALISM

Resource nationalism is a process whereby states seek to take control of activity within natural resource sectors and has, over the past decade, become an increasingly common feature of the international business environment. This process normally involves producer states seeking to control the flow of certain natural resources into the global marketplace. There is also a tendency for this process to occur within consumerist states that seek to enhance their access to resources that are located in other countries. There is also a third type emerging where investments by sovereign wealth funds which are based on resources, seek to invest in assets in other states. This has also led to pushback from some states, especially if the purpose of such investments is to control another state's natural resources.

While a state has the right to determine the control of any resource within its territorial domain when it does so for geostrategic reasons, it is referred to as resource nationalism. Often, these events are temporally specific and are driven by the belief that the overseas investor is getting too good a deal on these territorial assets when these assets are directly impacted by rising prices for the commodity concerned. This process often reflects that the concessions awarded to foreign investors to extract these raw materials are long-term and involve an ongoing royalty and tax rate. Often, these agreements are not well designed, so they may not reflect shifts in the prices of commodities extracted. This can lead to states challenging the initial contracts awarded. This has been done on a number of occasions, such as the deployment of windfall taxes on North Sea oil producers during the energy crisis of 2022–2023. This latter point underlines that such strategies can be a feature of the investment climate of all states, not simply those in developing or emerging economies with weak and/or corrupt governance.

The classic means of resource nationalism is expropriation, where the state takes direct ownership (through nationalisation via government decree or legislation) of the asset. This process can take, as suggested above, more indirect forms where the state seeks to take an increased share of the economic rents earned by the foreign investor. This can occur through:

- Increasing the tax, royalty, or any other payments the investor has to make to the government.
- Altering, suspending, or even terminating the licence the operator needs from the state in order to operate.
- Developing and implementing new regulations for the business to make its operating environment more hostile.

As noted above, there is a long precedent with regard to the use of resource nationalism as a policy tool by states. Its use tends to reflect that what was once a friendly environment for FDI in given assets has turned hostile. With the trend towards liberalism within the global economic system, the process became less frequent during the late 20th century. The formative decades of the 21st century have seen a renewed trend towards this broad set of policy measures. The surge in cases of resource nationalism reflects a multitude of overlapping causes as well as the traditional socio-political ones that have driven previous surges. Generally, the rise in resource nationalism has been driven by one or more of the following:

- Resurgent political nationalism within resource-exporting states.
- To generate resources to diversify an economy away from an overdependence on natural resources.
- To address the needs of fast-growing populations and the aligned need for increased investment in public services and infrastructure.
- The need to address high and rising levels of unemployment within the indigenous working population.
- A desire to reflect outdated laws and practices that can often be a legacy of colonialism or other asymmetric power relations.
- That the original tender was subject to processes that were corrupt or not transparent.
- To renegotiate contracts that, in reflection, were exploitative as overseas investors took advantage of poor governance, financial problems, or some other issue to gain terms that were unfavourable to the state.
- A sharp rise in commodity prices and increased competition for resources allow the investor to make supernormal profits.

All of these pressures (either singularly or in combination) place pressure on the state to seek to increase the return it gains from the exploration of its natural resources. This strategy faces the problem that the expertise needed to develop and extract resources might not be available locally and that such actions might scare off future investors in both this and other sectors. Thus, strategies that pursue resource nationalism might actually do more long-term harm to the country.

### QUESTION

Under what circumstances do you believe resource nationalism is justified?

## CONCLUSIONS

The FWE nexus highlights a core series of interlinked resource constraints that impact business as it adapts to ongoing themes raised by climate change. Nexus, while not a flawless framework, does nonetheless focus on core issues that will shape interface business and its interaction with the natural environment. It is evident that food systems have a high degree of vulnerability, as do water systems, from the ongoing human utilisation and exploitation of their natural environment. The energy transition reflects actions by countries and businesses to seek to rebalance this nexus so that the pressure on food and water is not as intense. However, it is evident that the pressure on these core resources is unlikely to relent in the foreseeable future.

## KEY POINTS

- Food, water, and energy are interlinked in a mutually supportive nexus.
- Food supply is under pressure from a range of issues, from climate change to issues of geopolitics.
- Water resources are increasingly under threat from excessive usage and from climate change.
- The transition to renewable energy represents an attempt to decarbonise the FWE nexus, though this process is subject to a number of issues.

## DISCUSSION QUESTIONS

1) How valuable do you think the food-water-energy nexus is for understanding business resource issues?
2) To what extent do you believe global obesity is a problem for business?
3) Is desalination a credible long-term solution to rising levels of water risk?
4) How do you account for populist resistance to the energy transition?

## ACTIVITY

Choosing either Unilever or Coca-Cola, prepare a report as to how these businesses are both being impacted by and adapting to rising levels of water risk.

The following material will support themes addressed within this chapter:

## KEY READINGS

BP (2022) Statistical Review of World Energy 2022 www.bp.com

Cherp, A., & Jewell, J. (2014). The concept of energy security: Beyond the four as. *Energy Policy*, 75, 415–421.

Endo, A., Tsurita, I., Burnett, K., & Orencio, P. M. (2017). A review of the current state of research on the water, energy, and food nexus. *Journal of Hydrology: Regional Studies*, 11, 20–30.

Magill, G., & Benedict, J. (Eds.). (2019). *Cascading challenges in the global water crisis*, Cambridge: Cambridge Scholars Publishing.

McDonald, B. L. (2010). *Food security*, London: Polity.

Muller-Kraenner, S. (2018). *Energy security*, London: Routledge.

Prosekov, A. Y., & Ivanova, S. A. (2018). Food security: The challenge of the present. *Geoforum, 91*, 73–77.

Yergin, D. (2020). *The new map: Energy, climate, and the clash of nations*, London: Penguin UK.

Zeitoun, M. (2011). The global web of national water security. *Global Policy, 2*(3), 286–296.

## Useful websites

The World Energy Council – https://www.worldenergy.org/ – a global forum for thought-leadership in the energy sector.

Waterfootprint Network – https://waterfootprint.org/en/ – a body monitoring water usage.

The International Energy Agency – https://www.iea.org/ – provides policy recommendations, analysis, and data on the entire global energy.

The International Renewable Energy Agency – https://www.irena.org/ – mandated to facilitate co-operation, advance knowledge, and promote the adoption and sustainable use of renewable energy.

# CHAPTER 20

# THE EVOLVING INTERNATIONAL ENVIRONMENT

During the writing of this book, we have, as both authors and observers of international business, witnessed the seemingly 'inevitable' and irreversible process of globalisation not only lose momentum but (in some cases) go into decline. Naturally, such developments do not erode the value of the preceding analysis but should encourage students to develop a critical approach to the process and to understand the historical forces that have shaped the ebb and flow of globalisation throughout the history of humanity's commercial activities. Thus, the fact that globalisation reached a high point in the early 21st century should, in historical terms, come as little surprise.

Despite these trends, it is far from evident that globalisation will be unwound. Our confidence in this assertion again relates to the historical context of the process. It was apparent that, at times in the late 20th and early 21st centuries, conflict and economic turmoil did turn states away from moves towards a global economy. It is evident that the economic and financial turmoil created by the global financial crisis has created a higher degree of scepticism with regard to the globalist consensus, notably with regard to the rise of national populism. However, the current disruption of globalisation appears different from previous interruptions in the sense that globalisation has penetrated deeper into political, social, and economic structures than previously. Indeed, it is fair to argue that this phase has permeated directly down to the individual and has not been restricted to political and economic elites.

The themes within this text typify the deep roots that globalisation and its associated processes have established within the modern business system. While this process has been uneven over time and space, it has made a tangible impact on the nation-state, the conventional building block of the economic system. Indeed, it is noticeable how attempts by nation-states to regain some control over key aspects of their economies have either been frustrated or have met with limited success. Thus, in spite of the prevailing turmoil, one must not expect the environment analysed within this text to alter radically in its aftermath.

## GLOBALISATION AND THE CONTEXT OF INTERNATIONAL BUSINESS

The nature of international strategy is an adaptive response by businesses to their evolving commercial environment. Conventionally, the response of firms to this environment

DOI: 10.4324/9781315184500-25

has been defined by the integration and responsiveness framework and the typology that it has generated. While such a typology is useful, the student of international business should treat its conclusions with caution, as it risks chronically understating the degree of complexity of strategies deployed by the modern MNE. As the complexity of the modern MNE grows, so does the nature of the strategies it follows. As such, the firm can employ multiple strategies across multiple locations. This process is reinforced by the increased complexity of the modern business environment.

While the core drivers behind this increased complexity have been widely acknowledged, what they mean for environmental change is less certain. The very term 'globalisation' is suggestive of a process that has a recognisable beginning and end. However, history has shown that environmental conditions can alter markedly over time and that, as a consequence, so does globalisation. Thus, globalisation is a matter of degree, and the conditions and drivers that shape it evolve unevenly over time. What is perhaps more accurate is that globalisation historically has both low and high watermarks. Such cycles are driven by the state of the drivers and national sentiment towards them, underlining that globalisation is anything but a historical certainty.

A more controversial suggestion is that the logical end point of the 'globalisation' process is a global economy. That is an economy in which the mobility of goods, services, labour, and capital is entirely without hindrance. Political sentiment has highlighted how unlikely this is, further underlining that globalisation is a process without a beginning or end that waxes and wanes over time. This underlines a paradox within the modern international economy, namely that while there is an appetite for globalisation, the desire to see this process through to its seemingly logical conclusion is notable by its absence.

In the absence of any appetite for the creation of a truly global economy, the push for regional integration seems like a logical compromise. In a globalising international economy, overcoming the disadvantages of fragmentation through regionalism makes sense. However, to use the emergence of such agreements as a barometer of the appetite for liberalism would be wholly inaccurate, as the underlying motives behind group formation are not uniform across either space or time. Indeed, sentiment in some groups suggests using these agreements as a deterrent and not as a compromise to globalisation. The ability to accentuate the positive and mitigate the negative effects of such processes depends in no small part on measures deployed at the meta-level of the global economy. In other words, the emergence of an effective system of global governance will mitigate these pressures.

The role of the main international economic institutions has evolved over the years in parallel with the changing business environment. The World Bank, for example, slipped into a development role as the original reconstruction part of its portfolio, which related to postwar reconstruction in Europe, was fulfilled and superseded by the challenge of development in the rest of the world. As import tariffs fell in successive rounds of trade negotiations and barriers between states generally fell, the agenda of GATT and its successor organisation, the WTO, expanded. Indeed, a strong case could be made that issues that had long been considered matters for domestic policy (for example, aspects of competition policy, standards, labour regulation, etc.) should increasingly be determined at a higher level by regional groupings or international economic institutions. Some issues have been increasingly accepted as a matter of supranational governance of some sort, whereas states hold on tightly to others. In general, international institutions have developed slowly and are not noted for their rapid and appropriate response to a swiftly changing business environment.

The major institutions are also the subject of much criticism, both by those opposing and those supporting globalisation. For the former, international institutions have too much power and undermine national sovereignty. For the latter, global governance does not go far enough and urges further development of these institutions to help nations regain some of the control and sovereignty they have lost in the globalisation process. Despite the controversies surrounding global governance, nation-states have been lining up to join key institutions, and the membership of the WTO in particular has expanded significantly in recent years.

The institutions are particularly challenged by the legacy of growing global scepticism. Questions of how they should respond to the new situation have dogged the institutions since the GFC and have continued in the years since its onset. It remains unclear at the time of writing whether the institutions will emerge from the legitimacy crisis in globality with their powers or roles enhanced or diminished, though the curtailment on the power of the WTO suggests the latter. However, it is certainly true that major changes only tend to occur in such institutions in response to crises. Moreover, although there are signs of growing protection and of states wishing to take matters into their own hands, there are also strong countervailing indicators of countries searching for a way out of the crisis through greater cooperation and policy coordination. What is clear in the current situation is that, unlike previous crises, the way out of the problem is not overwhelmingly seen as pulling back to national boundaries. As stated above, this is almost certainly a function of the deeper penetration into aspects of contemporary economic, business, and social life of the most recent wave of globalisation.

A major criticism levelled at globalisation and international institutions stems from the alleged exclusion of large parts of the world – particularly developing countries – from the global economy. In a real sense, this criticism of globalisation is an argument in favour of it; that is, if developing countries are marginalised by globalisation and unable to escape their grinding poverty, then the way out of this mess should, logically, be to make it easier for these countries to engage in the globalisation process. It is certainly true that large parts of the developing world appear to be trapped in a vicious cycle of underdevelopment, but some countries have escaped. The Asian NICs were the first to do so, but increasingly large emerging economies like China and India are transforming their fortunes.

What unites the success stories is a willingness to embrace both the domestic and international markets by moving away from protected markets and isolation. It is too simplistic to attribute all their success to their embrace of the market and globalisation: each country has its own unique history, social context, culture, specific advantages, etc. that have helped shape its fortunes. Parts of sub-Saharan Africa, the world's most problematic region in terms of development, have seen some improvements in the last decade as a result of more open, market-driven policies and have benefited to some extent from higher commodity export prices (although many suffered as a result of higher oil and food import prices). Steering their way through the financial and economic crisis is a major challenge for these countries, whose integration into the world economy remains limited and vulnerable.

# ENTERPRISE ISSUES IN THE GLOBAL ECONOMY

The above issues establish the terms of engagement for enterprises in the international economy. Inevitably, the meta-level concerns engendered by these themes have a limited direct impact on business strategy but trickle down into changes into opportunities and threats in the enterprise's commercial environment. Consequently, translating these issues into a set of adaptive strategies relies on a set of supporting or intermediate conditions. These are the conditions for trade, internationalisation, and other forms of policy and commercial measures that facilitate a managerial response.

International trade is perhaps global business's greatest success and its greatest failure. Since the Second World War, there have undoubtedly been a great number of successes in this domain of the evolving international economy. Sharp reductions in tariffs, the agreement on services, and the commitment of states to non-discrimination all stand as testaments to progress in promoting international trade. However, the failure of states to agree on agriculture, the emergence of non-tariff barriers, and the penchant of states to resort to protectionism when expedient have to some degree mitigated many of the benefits delivered by global agreements on trade. Agriculture is an especially salient issue given the asymmetry between its economic importance and its political influence, which demonstrates the delicate political economy that drives the trade debate.

How such issues will be affected by growing global scepticism – at the time of writing – is a moot point. In the aftermath of the GFC, there was a decline in global trade and investment, but this has recovered. But states, against a more hostile geopolitical environment, are introducing more active industrial policies, which go against the liberal consensus embedded within the globalisation process. While these are far from the 'beggar thy neighbour' policies of the 1930s, the desire of national policymakers to ensure that the macroeconomic stimuli do not 'leak' into other states and maximise the domestic impact is a setback for system globality and risk. These processes risk fragmenting the global system into a number of subsystems. Others are more optimistic, suggesting that the international complexity of value chains is so embedded that any attempt to discriminate would be self-defeating.

A sea change can also be expected in international investment over the forthcoming period. During the past few decades, international investment has increased manyfold as markets opened, funds increased, and the associated risk fell. This was driven in no small part by the aforementioned freeing up of international trade. This phase of globalisation was characterised by an increased dispersal of investments as many 'emerging economies' not only attracted funds from developed economies but also began to act as overseas investors in their own right. Throughout this text, it is noticeable how emerging economies have become increasingly aggressive in international markets as they emerge as economic powerhouses in the global economy. However, it is likely that the major sources of FDI for the forthcoming period will remain the larger developed states, though China is becoming an increasingly prominent player, notably through its Belt and Road Initiative.

One would expect that international investment would be substantially affected by any pushback in the process of globalisation. Increased political-economic risks as well as emerging sentiment stressing economic nationalism are working against the mainte-nance of high investment flows in the short term. While the flow of funds has taken a downturn, it is unlikely that this will persist in the long term, notably with regard to FDI driven by the decarbonisation process.

At the core of these trade and investment trends have been MNEs. MNEs are perhaps the most controversial feature of the current globalisation phase. In an era of US-led global capitalism, many of these controversies are driven by the legacy of shareholder capitalism and its implications for the management of MNEs. However, for every MNE that acts in a fashion that is detrimental to host economies, there are many more that engage positively with their host for mutual benefit. Furthermore, the majority of MNEs are not the leviathans they are commonly characterised as but are often relatively small concerns. No matter their size, MNEs are bound by the fact that they are profit-seeking entities.

The past decade has seen the emergence of MNEs from China. These have tended to pursue broader geopolitical aims within the investment process. Notably, there has been a desire to use this investment to secure the desire of the Chinese state to access the necessary resources and competencies that are central to its meeting its aggressive growth targets and to gaining access to the resources that will enhance its rapid move up the global value chain. The alignment between the Chinese MNC strategy and the requirements of the Chinese state has led to growing security concerns in Western states that have pushed back against this investment and debarred investment from China in key critical infrastructure. This again creates the risk of fragmentation in global systems, especially if it leads to two competing technological systems.

The process of becoming multi-national has been formalised within models of internationalisation. In the past decade or so, the main explanations of interna-tionalisation have converged around the network-based perspective. The growing hegemony of a network-based perspective reflects the growing complexity of the modern economy, in which the decision to internationalise and the process of market penetration and reach cannot be divorced from the broader context of the interna-tionalising firm.

The emergence of these contextual-based perspectives as the dominant view of the process of internationalisation has impacted modal choice. Conventionally, internation-alisation has been conceptualised as sequential, as issues of risk are mitigated through experience. With the maturity of globalisation, firms are moving to relatively high-commitment market entry modes. Again, this reflects the complexity of the modern economy and the relationships that contextualise the decision and mitigate the risks involved. Thus, as internationalisation matures, its complexity increases. With matu-rity, it becomes increasingly inappropriate to talk of a single trajectory or modal choice. Across all locations in which an MNE has a presence, modal choice and the internation-alisation path vary according to the set of environmental conditions encountered by the firm.

As mentioned, the major differentiating factor between this phase of globalisation and those that have preceded it is its sheer pervasiveness. One of the more demonstrable symptoms of this is the emergence of globalisation involving small and medium-sized businesses, which are normally expected to be exempt from such developments. The impact of this trend has been both passive and active. The focus of this text is on the latter and highlights how the growing complexity of the international economy has allowed small entrepreneurial concerns to inhabit small, identifiable niches. This process has been supported by business networks, which have shaped the context, pace, and path of the process. Given such trends and complementary technological developments, this process is likely to continue over the coming decades.

Supporting the rise of the 'born global' has been the globalisation of the value chain. The trend towards globalisation has allowed more firms to disperse both primary and supporting activities across the global economy in order to maximise the value derived from each of these functions. In some cases, this has resulted in the outsourcing and/or offshoring of specific functions as the firm focuses on core competencies. In addition, the potential for the dispersion of activities has been supported by the globalisation of existing operations as they seek to cope with and adjust to shifting environmental conditions. Thus, as the firm enters new international markets, issues of international human resources management and the diversity of marketing strategies become ever more salient.

Matters of culture, corporate social responsibility, and business ethics also add to the complexity of managing international businesses, both large and small. Internationalisation poses cross-cultural challenges for MNEs across their major functions. The most successful are able to adapt to new ways of doing business and treat cultural differences as part of their competitive advantage. Closely tied to culture are business ethics. Although some practices are regarded as ethically wrong throughout the world, many more are subject to different interpretations that are shaped by culture, frequently creating dilemmas for expatriate managers. This is on top of the additional attention paid to corporate social responsibility in recent years and the external scrutiny to which the international activities of firms are increasingly subject.

## CHALLENGES FOR THE GLOBAL RESOURCE BASE

Corporate social responsibility is at the heart of many international labour and environmental issues facing the MNE. However, international labour and environmental issues are not merely about CSR, important though that is. Labour, together with finance, knowledge and information, energy, and raw materials, are crucial inputs and resources for the firm. The environmental challenge for international business is also about managing the use of resources.

Globalisation has created challenges for the use of resources. As part of the globalisation process, barriers to the free movement of the factors of production have been lifted, a process that has transformed finance and the role of knowledge and information. However, labour mobility is more limited, partly for cultural reasons and partly because nation-states continue to exercise control over the movement of people across their borders. Moreover, the continuing fragmentation of labour markets means that significant differences in labour standards and practices persist. This leads to accusations of social dumping. In the current crisis-ridden climate, it would not take much, in an effort to protect local jobs, for countries to use differences in standards and costs to raise trade barriers or restrict the labour mobility that does exist. In 2016–2018, the rise of national populism was in no small part driven by fears over immigration.

In contrast to labour, there is perhaps no other market that represents a higher water-mark of globalisation than finance. By the end of the 20th century, it was fair to say that global market finance had been created. This created many benefits and ushered in an era of global financial capitalism. However, as the GFC noted, this created a higher degree of complexity within the global system that was poorly understood, and when those risks were exposed, they created cascade effects throughout the global system. This highlighted the emergence of the so-called 'butterfly defect', which stressed how within complex global systems seemingly small effects can have widespread negative effects. It also reflected the limited power states had to influence these processes once they had started. This was something that was further illustrated by the COVID-19 pandemic. Governments have attempted to mitigate their relative powerlessness by aiming to ensure that national measures benefit the national economy. This should not be read as a lack of appetite for globalisation, merely that the form of globalisation based on the hegemony of Anglo-Saxon capitalism is no longer seen as the best or the only way to manage the global economy. As such, a more regulated global system based on state-based capitalism is emerging.

The emergence and establishment of the global economy as an information economy give confidence that the attitude towards globalisation is not a matter of 'if' but 'how'. The emergence of new technologies has created a time-space and cost-space convergence that has played no small part in the process. Save for the prospect of the disinvention or outlawing of these technologies, we can assume that these are permanent features of the global commercial landscape. This implies that the information and knowledge resources that drive the economy will be sourced from interaction between economic agents over a dispersed spatial domain. This underlines the sheer pervasiveness of the globalisation process and how such interactions are now considered the norm for a large majority of the economically active population.

Natural resources, notably energy, water, and raw materials, are more tangible inputs for MNEs. Access to supplies of these products is essential for the smooth running of the international economy. Given that the markets for most natural resources (with the exception of water) are international, the impact of any disruptions to the nor-mal supply-demand balance for these heavily commoditised products spreads rapidly throughout the world. There are a number of instances where oil price hikes disrupted economies everywhere and, although not the only cause of the international recessions that followed, were certainly major contributors to them. It did not take long for oil and commodity prices to take their toll in many areas of business. This was a trend evident as many countries sought to cope with the sharp rise in commodity prices created as a result of the Russia-Ukraine conflict.

## CONCLUSION

As the first decades of the 21st century progressed, globalisation (if not at a crossroads, as that could imply a change of direction) faced a change in the nature of its journey. Throughout history, the balance between the local and the international has shifted, depending on a host of historical and environmental factors. The current international financial crisis provides the potential for another such shift. It is too early to say what form that shift might take. It is possible to conceive of scenarios in which some reversal of globalisation might occur. Equally, the process could either decelerate or accelerate. That is, the process of globalisation would continue, but the pace of the process would change.

It is our contention, supported by evidence throughout this volume, that one of the two latter scenarios will prevail, and globalisation will not be reversed but will simply be more managed. This view is based on the argument that many facets of globalisation have become so entrenched and embedded in so many aspects of business, economics, and social life that it will be both difficult and undesirable to reverse them. That is not to say that there will not be instances in which deglobalisation appears to be happening, but the overall momentum of globalisation will continue, perhaps at a slower pace. We may, of course, be wrong, but in our view, it is the dynamic, rapidly changing rich, international business environment that makes international business such an exciting subject.

# Index

*Note*: Page numbers in *italics* indicate figures, and page numbers in **bold** indicate tables in the text.

state 69; communism and 192; competitive in US 5; demands created by FDI for goods 26; footloose 67; in globalisation 8–10, 213; human 243, 286, **289**, 347, 349, 353; IMF resources acquired through subscriptions 89; inflow by FDI in China 173; international flows 412; in market-based system 177; mobile 68; national branding 237; neo-classical theory of arbitrage 253; rate of growth of 158; resistance faced in conglomerate 179; social 297; South Korea domination in shipbuilding industry by imports of capital goods 202; state-based in China 87; supremacy between communism and 94; trade reform 181; transfer risk in movement of 245

*Capitalism and Freedom* (Friedman) 329

Caribbean 192–3, 215; distribution of FDI inflows **25**; export processing zones (EPZ) 215; FDI **25**; GDP, exports of goods and services, and population **19**; Internet connectivity and adoption gaps *467*; preferential trade agreements 108; RTAs in *112*

Caribbean Basin Initiative 362

Caribbean Community and Common Market (CARICOM) 125

Caribbean Trade Partnership Act (CBTPA) 362

CARICOM *see* Caribbean Community and Common Market

Cartagena Free Trade Agreement 91

case study(ies): Asian Infrastructure Investment Bank (AIIB) 93–4; Brexit 122–3; chocolatiers in Switzerland 41–3; climate change and trade 375–6; conglomerates in India 178–80; dispute settlement mechanism and US 97–8; Djibouti 80–1; DP World 65–6; economy of Japan 149–51; energy pipeline in East Africa 442–3; euro crisis 155–7; Eyjafjallajökull volcano, Iceland 427–8; floods in Thailand, 2011 32–4; Foxconn manufacturing strategy 48–50; geostrategic significance of the Gwadar Port 431–3; GoodWeave International 355–6; guanxi in China 297–9; Inflation Reduction Act (IRA) 29–30; international expansion of Spotify 461–2; international strategy of Samsung Electronics (SE) 249–51; internet startups in China 276–8; Lava Jato (car wash) scandal in Brazil 322–4; manufacturing strategy of Apple Inc. 49–50; Maquiladora (manufacturing

plant) in Mexico 205–6; market economy and China 86–7; marketing of gardening in Kenya 198–9; McDonald's global expansion 230–1; MNCs 138–9; MNEs in China 174–6, **175**; penal labour in US 351–2; resource nationalism 488–9; Saudi Vision 2030 71–3; shadow banking in China 407–9; strategic business of Siemens 245–7; Tobin Tax 419–20; turnaround at Ford 161–2, 262–3; US as cultural superpower 308–10; US–Mexico–Canada Agreement (USMCA) 137–8; water security issues in China 481–2

Casson, M. 254

Caucuses **19**

Caux principles 328, 334, 338–9

CBD *see* Convention on Biological Diversity

CBTPA *see* Caribbean Trade Partnership Act

Central Africa, FDI in **25**

Central African Republic 192

Central America 22, 215; FDI **25**; merchandise trade exports **21**

Central American Common Market (1960) 124

Central Asia **19**

CET *see* common external tariff

Chile 128, 169

China 6, 18, **19**, 20, 23, 29, 32, 48–9, 54, 75, 80, 102, 103, 127, 169; Belt and Road Initiative (BRI) 93, 183, 428–9, 431, 495; coastal special economic zones 177; Communist Party 173; comparative economic structure of **170**; compared with India **172**, 182–4; Cultural Revolution 174, 176; efforts to reduce imbalance between light and heavy industries 177; emerging economy of 176–8; GDP of 177–8, 182; geopolitical rivals 183–4; guanxi in 297–9; household responsibility system in agriculture 176; internet startups in 276–8; merchandise trade exports **21**; Most Favoured Nation 331; reasons for foreign investors attraction in 185; reduction of government role in sectors 177; shadow banking in 407–9; trade and investment reform 176–7; water security issues 481–2

China-Pakistan economic corridor (CPEC) 431–2

chokepoints, in global food system 474–5

CITES *see* Convention on International Trade in Endangered Species

civil society 98–9, 371, 383, 460

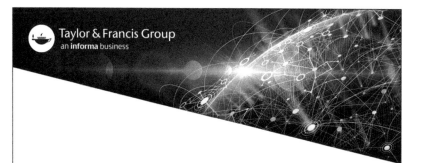